Pro Crystal Enterprise/Business Objects XI Programming

Carl Ganz, Jr.

Apress®

Pro Crystal Enterprise/Business Objects XI Programming

Copyright © 2006 by Carl Ganz, Jr.

ISBN-13: 978-1-59059-759-0

ISBN-13 (electronic): 978-1-4302-0277-6

Printed and bound in the United States of America (POD)

Lead Editor: Matthew Moodie
Technical Reviewer: Ryan Follmer
Editorial Board: Steve Anglin, Ewan Buckingham, Gary Cornell, Jason Gilmore, Jonathan Gennick,
    Jonathan Hassell, James Huddleston, Chris Mills, Matthew Moodie, Dominic Shakeshaft, Jim Sumser,
    Keir Thomas, Matt Wade
Project Manager: Sofia Marchant
Copy Edit Manager: Nicole LeClerc
Copy Editor: Ami Knox
Assistant Production Director: Kari Brooks-Copony
Production Editor: Ellie Fountain
Compositor/Artist: Kinetic Publishing Services, LLC
Proofreader: Linda Seifert
Indexer: Kevin Broccoli
Cover Designer: Kurt Krames
Manufacturing Director: Tom Debolski

Distributed to the book trade worldwide by Springer-Verlag New York, Inc., 233 Spring Street, 6th Floor, New York, NY 10013. Phone 1-800-SPRINGER, fax 201-348-4505, e-mail orders-ny@springer-sbm.com, or visit http://www.springeronline.com.

For information on translations, please contact Apress directly at 2855 Telegraph Avenue, Suite 600, Berkeley, CA 94705. Phone 510-549-5930, fax 510-549-5939, e-mail info@apress.com, or visit http://www.apress.com.

The source code for this book is available to readers at http://www.apress.com in the Source Code/Download section. You will need to answer questions pertaining to this book in order to successfully download the code.

To Wendy, my beloved wife and inspiration, without whose patience, support, effort, and friendship this book would not be possible.

Contents at a Glance

Foreword xv

About the Author xvii

About the Technical Reviewer xix

Acknowledgments xxi

Introduction xxiii

■CHAPTER 1   Welcome to BusinessObjects XI 1

■CHAPTER 2   BusinessObjects XI Server Architecture 13

■CHAPTER 3   Administration Tools 47

■CHAPTER 4   Using the Central Management Console 73

■CHAPTER 5   BusinessObjects XI SDK Programming I 103

■CHAPTER 6   BusinessObjects XI SDK Programming II 149

■CHAPTER 7   Crystal Reports and BusinessObjects XI 199

■CHAPTER 8   Programming the Report Application Server 229

■CHAPTER 9   Enterprise Solutions Using the BusinessObjects XI SDK 281

■CHAPTER 10   Security 337

■CHAPTER 11   BusinessObjects Unified Web Services SDK 367

■CHAPTER 12   Third-Party Solutions 395

■INDEX 437

Contents

Foreword xv

About the Author xvii

About the Technical Reviewer xix

Acknowledgments xxi

Introduction xxiii

■CHAPTER 1   **Welcome to BusinessObjects XI** 1

History 1
From Report Writing to Business Intelligence 2
BusinessObjects XI Release 2 3
Licensing 4
Service-Oriented Architecture 5
Reporting Considerations 6
Preprinted Forms 7
High-Volume Printing 7
Legal Issues 8
Availability and Distribution 8
BusinessObjects XI vs. SQL Server Reporting Services 9
Market Considerations 9
Feature Differences 11
Summary 12

■CHAPTER 2   **BusinessObjects XI Server Architecture** 13

InfoStore 13
FileStore 14
Servers 16
Programmatic Access 19
Central Management Server 22
File Repository Servers 24
Event Server 26
Page Server 29
Job Servers 32

Cache Server 34
Report Application Server. 37
Server Groups 39
Creating a Server Group. 41
Adding Servers to a Server Group. 41
Extracting the Servers in a Group 42
The Auditing Database 42
Scalability 43
Backups and Disaster Recovery 44
Summary 45

■CHAPTER 3   **Administration Tools** 47

Central Configuration Manager. 47
Properties Tab. 48
Dependency Tab. 49
Connection Tab. 50
Configuration Tab. 50
Protocol Tab 53
Import Wizard. 53
Publishing Wizard 57
Administration Launchpad. 61
Central Management Console 61
InfoView. 62
Administration Tool Console. 62
Business Views Manager 68
Crystal Reports Explorer. 69
Summary 72

■CHAPTER 4   **Using the Central Management Console** 73

Folders and Reports 73
Folders. 74
Reports 75
Objects 96
Calendars 97
Events 98
File and Schedule Events 99
Custom Events 101
Summary 102

▓CHAPTER 5   BusinessObjects XI SDK Programming I 103

Connecting to BusinessObjects XI 103
    Connecting with User IDs 104
    Connecting with Tokens 106
    Connecting with Trusted Connections 108
    Examining the Connection Objects 109
Querying the InfoStore 112
    The InfoStore SQL Language 113
Working with the InfoStore 125
    Extracting Folder Information 126
    Creating Folders 129
    Deleting Folders 130
Report Refresh Options 131
Scheduling Reports 131
    Report History in the CMC 132
    Building Your Own Report History 133
    Adding New Reports 138
    Run Now 139
    Retrieving and Saving Schedules 140
    Adding Executable Code 144
    Handling Report Parameters Generically 145
Summary 148

▓CHAPTER 6   BusinessObjects XI SDK Programming II 149

Scheduling 149
    Notifications 149
    Alerts 152
Report Format Options 156
    TextFormatTabSeparated 159
    TextFormatPaginated 159
    TextFormatCharacterSeparated 160
    RichTextFormat 162
    RichTextEditableFormat 163
    PlainTextFormat 163
    PDFFormat 163
    ExcelFormat 164
    ExcelDataOnlyFormat 165
Destination Options 166
Printer Options 170

Programming Categories 171
Programming Events. 173
Programming Calendars. 175
Data Access Techniques. 177
BO XI Web Controls 179
     Getting Started 179
     Web Controls 187
.NET Providers 192
     Membership Provider 193
     Using the .NET Providers 194
Summary 197

▨CHAPTER 7   **Crystal Reports and BusinessObjects XI** 199

Crystal Reports Viewer Control 199
     Setting Up the Control. 199
     Communicating with the BusinessObjects XI Server. 204
     Running a Report on Disk. 205
     Passing Parameters. 207
     Passing an Entire SQL Statement to Crystal Reports. 208
Embedded vs. Nonembedded Reports. 209
     Exporting Reports 213
     Filtering 215
     Field Structure 216
     Sections. 217
     Database Connectivity 220
     Printer Options 220
     Summary Information 220
Unmanaged RAS 221
Passing Data Sources. 222
Crystal Reports Web Services 224
Summary 227

▨CHAPTER 8   **Programming the Report Application Server**. 229

Introduction to RAS Programming 229
Working with Reports 230
     Connecting to the Data Source 231
     Building the Body of the Report. 236
     Exporting Reports 265
     Setting Parameters 267

Filtering Reports 268
Sorting 269
Charts 272
Report Options 274
Summary Information 276
Printing Reports 277
Saving Reports 279
Summary 280

■CHAPTER 9   **Enterprise Solutions Using the**
BusinessObjects XI SDK 281

On-Demand Web Service 281
On-Demand Web Service Internals 282
Scheduling Assemblies 289
Creating Criteria Screens 294
Building the WinForms Interface 295
Web Interface 308
BO XI Windows Service Monitor 313
Reporting Against the InfoStore 318
GetReportTree Web Service 319
Reporting Against the XML Output 325
Building Dynamic Menus 327
Storing Custom Metadata 330
Using Your RDBMS 330
Custom Properties 331
The Limits of Crystal 334
Summary 335

■CHAPTER 10   **Security** 337

Security Considerations 337
Managing Security Through the CMC 338
Creating Users 339
Creating Groups 341
Adding Users to Groups 342
Extracting the Users in a Group 343
Subgroups 345
Access Levels and Security Rights 347
Roles 348
Rights 349

Limits. 355
Non-Enterprise Security Management. 359
    Validating NT Group Users 360
License Keys 362
Summary 366

▓CHAPTER 11   **BusinessObjects Unified Web Services SDK** 367

Configuring the Unified Web Services SDK. 367
    Why Use the Web Services SDK? 370
Programming Web Services 370
    Services. 370
    Creating a Connection. 371
    Queries 373
    Extracting Data. 376
    Working with Reports 380
    Working with Folders. 389
    Managing Servers 390
    Managing Security. 392
Summary 393

▓CHAPTER 12   **Third-Party Solutions** 395

APOS Systems Inc. 395
    AddressBook Gateway 395
    Archive Manager 396
    Bursting Manager 398
    InfoScheduler 400
    Instance Manager 402
    Instance Monitor 404
    Key Performance Indicator 404
    Object Manager 406
    RealTime Monitor. 408
    Report Package Booster 412
    RunTime Manager 413
    Solutions Kit for ESRI GIS 413
    View Time Security 416
Software Forces. 418
    .rpt Inspector Enterprise Suite. 418

Teleran Technologies 421

    iGuard 421

    iSight 422

CRD 424

Excel Solutions 425

    Syncfusion's Essential XlsIO 427

    SoftArtisans's OfficeWriter 431

Word Solutions 434

Summary 435

INDEX 437

Foreword

Data. More data. Still more data.

Think application complexity and Internet systems are driving the torrential increase in data volume? Think again. Life's only going to get more interesting with Service-Oriented Architectures (SOAs), which will expose richer data sources less siloed than ever before. This means that the limitations related to what vendors control and choose to expose about an application's inner workings will become less restrictive over time (whether by design or as a side effect of the SOA movement)—leading to easier data access for a wide variety of systems.

Now, more than ever, tools make IT possible.

The previous statements are not nearly as daunting as they might seem. Products like Crystal only continue to get easier (depth of designers), richer (presentation delivery mechanisms), and more complete (flexible data-access layers and programmatic object models). Indeed, Crystal's very reason for existing is to simplify and enable the formatting of complex data into more usable forms—from simple banded reports to sophisticated drillable context-sensitive dashboards and exception-based push reports that do more than present a situation—it enables interaction with them. The line between operational and analytic reporting continues to blur—and the application end user only stands to benefit, and by extension, the savvy developer who understands reporting as more than a thankless boring task stands to win also.

But maintaining the appropriate depth of understanding to utilize these advanced reporting toolsets to their best advantage, requiring knowledge of SDKs, APIs, and, in their most evolved state, object models, is more important than ever. Virtually all products now incorporate object models to influence the behavior of all aspects of report development, deployment, security, and usage analysis. This is more than a trend: it's now a requirement to compete for virtually all reporting tools.

While the GUI designers embedded in products such as Crystal continue to evolve, it's inevitable that you'll need to exploit the inner workings of a toolset to create custom behaviors—the alternative is to build them yourself. Building your own wrappers seems like a good idea at first, until you begin to understand the breadth and depth already included with the product. Why build a narrow situational façade when it (probably) already exists, and ships with the product anyway? A great deal more value is generated by using what's already there—whether you define value as speed of development, flexibility of evolution and use, or replicable standardized deployment.

Or, put another way, this stuff can make you look pretty darn smart.

Crystal's SDK has a remarkable amount of depth, but it has been hard to make sense of the various layers in the object model—this book makes this task simpler.

Understanding the division of power between Crystal's various layers is a critical IT skill: this book will make that easier, parsing the important from the inconsequential—and perhaps most importantly, making a broad subject accessible in targeted bite-size chunks.

Fred Seyffert

President, VeriPoint LLC

About the Author

CARL GANZ, JR., is president of Seton Software Development, Inc., a provider of software design and development services located in Raritan, New Jersey. He has an MBA in finance from Seton Hall University and is the author of three other books on software development as well as dozens of articles on Visual Basic, C#, and Microsoft .NET technology. Carl has created numerous solutions over the years using the Crystal Enterprise and BusinessObjects XI .NET and RAS SDKs. He is the president and founder of the New Jersey Visual Basic User Group and has been a featured speaker at software development conferences in both the U.S. and Germany. Carl and his wife, Wendy, live in Raritan, New Jersey, with their son, Carl III, their dog, Elke, and their cats, Jack and Jake. Contact Carl at seton.software@verizon.net.

About the Technical Reviewer

RYAN FOLLMER is a technical lead for Ciber, Inc., an international system integration consultancy. He specializes in user interface development using the Microsoft .NET Framework. As a consultant for nearly 10 years, Ryan has developed multiplatform applications for the financial, life science, and service industry markets. Ryan lives in Pittsburgh, Pennsylvania, with his dog, Toby, and can be reached at ryanfollmer@gmail.com.

Acknowledgments

There are several people whom I would like to thank for making this book possible.

Ryan Follmer, who performed a thorough technical review of the entire book to make sure that everything within is complete and accurate. His work was outstanding, and he caught some truly subtle issues. After working in varying capacities on about a half-dozen book projects over the years, I can honestly say that Ryan has been the best technical reviewer I've ever had the pleasure to work with.

The technical support staff at Business Objects, especially everyone at Elite Team B and developer support, who patiently answered so many of my rather esoteric questions.

The management and editorial staff at Apress—specifically Ewan Buckingham, Sofia Marchant, Matt Moodie, and Ami Knox—for their professional guidance and overall kindness in steering this project through to completion.

My clients, whose many challenges over the years have provided the foundation of literally all that is contained within these pages.

My wife, Wendy, and son, Carl III, for providing me with the love, affection, and support that makes all these efforts worthwhile.

Most importantly, thanks be to God for the ability to do this kind of intellectually demanding work.

Introduction

BusinessObjects XI is a powerful middleware server product that allows you to distribute your Crystal Reports and BusinessObjects reports to the enterprise. Out of the box it offers an intuitive, feature-rich front end that allows system administrators to load reports to the repository as well as schedule them to run, track report histories, send notifications, monitor events, and many other features as well. It also offers a powerful object model that allows you to create custom solutions for your enterprise applications. It is this object model that is the topic of this book.

Though the interface is quite intuitive, the object model definitely is not. While the documentation and sample code have improved dramatically since the first release, it's still not at the quality level worthy of a product in this price range. My hope is that this book fills in that gap. BO XI does not offer the solutions out of the box that SQL Server Reporting Services offers. Currently, it's the Catch-22 of the reporting world. BusinessObjects offers a slick, mature interface with a clumsy server object model (with no canned service-oriented programming solutions) and a poorly documented programming interface. SQL Server Reporting Services offers an ever-improving-but-still-not-close-to-a-Crystal-Reports-replacement interface with a well-documented and easy-to-use object model with server solutions provided right out of the box.

Crystal Reports was first released in 1991 and has been bundled with Visual Basic starting with the 3.0 release in 1993. This relationship has continued through the 2.0 release of Visual Studio .NET in 2006. Of course, since Microsoft released SQL Server Reporting Services in 2002, where the Microsoft/Crystal relationship is ultimately going still remains to be seen. In 2002, Crystal Decisions released the first version of its enterprise server known as Crystal Enterprise 8. This was really version 1 of the enterprise product as the number 8 was used to keep the version numbering in sync with the incarnation of Crystal Reports on the market at the time. In 2003, Business Objects purchased Crystal Decisions and began the rebranding effort toward the BusinessObjects name. The current incarnation of the server product, BusinessObjects XI Release 2, is a synthesis of server technologies that supports both Crystal Reports XI and Business Objects 6.5. The Crystal Reports product has even been enhanced to access BusinessObjects universes.

Crystal's technology is superior to that of the BusinessObjects product, which is one of the reasons Business Objects bought the company. The good new for Crystal developers is that rather than "BOizing" the Crystal product, Business Objects is "Crystalizing" their original product. Therefore the structure of the Crystal Enterprise object model will continue to be expanded to support BusinessObjects reports and will be with us for many years to come.

I started using Crystal Enterprise with the 9.0 version, and at this writing have been working with the product for over three years. Each release has offered major improvements over the last one without revolutionizing the object model to such a degree that a code rewrite was needed. The BusinessObjects XI release is no exception. The goal of this book is to explain the product from a developer's perspective. The BusinessObjects XI Management Console is an administrator's tool that is not intended to be offered to every user of the system, and the InfoView end user interface may not suit all your needs. Therefore, I'll explain how to build solutions to handle on-demand reporting, scheduling, notifications, server management, report histories, security and user management, and many other tasks. In essence, you'll learn how to build all the features offered by the Central Management Console and InfoView. I'll accomplish this by examining production code adapted from real-word applications that are in use at several of my clients. We'll look at the thinking process behind the architectural decisions for the code samples as well as attempts that failed as I learned by trial and error. My hope is that you can use this code, with little or no modification, in your own production applications.

This book focuses mainly on the programming aspects of BusinessObjects XI, approaching the product from the perspective of a Crystal developer. Therefore, BusinessObjects-specific technologies such as Web Intelligence, Desktop Intelligence, and universes are not covered. Chapter 1 introduces BusinessObjects XI, reviews licensing issues, and compares its features with SQL Server Reporting Services. Chapter 2 discusses the server technology. Chapter 3 explains the tools that ship with the product, such as Import Wizard and Publishing Wizard. Chapter 4 covers the entire Central Management Console from a user's point of view. Chapters 5 and 6 introduce the object model of the .NET SDK. If you're already familiar with BusinessObjects XI as a system administrator, you may wish to stop here first. Chapters 7 and 8 cover the programming extensibility of Crystal Reports and the Report Appliction Server (RAS), respectively. Chapter 9 explains how to develop enterprise solutions using BO XI and is illustrated with a number of real-world production applications. Chapter 10 covers security, and Chapter 11 explains the new Unified Web Services SDK. Finally, Chapter 12 discusses some of the third-party products available for BusinessObjects XI.

Carl Ganz, Jr.
Seton Software Development Inc.
Raritan, New Jersey
seton.software@verizon.net

CHAPTER 1

■ ■ ■

Welcome to BusinessObjects XI

*B*usinessObjects Enterprise XI is a server-based, middleware product that allows you to distribute your Crystal and BusinessObjects reports throughout your organization. In addition to reports, you can also register compiled EXEs that can run customized business logic. You can upload static documents—Excel, Acrobat, Word, and text files, and so on—so as to publish them to the enterprise. BO XI is a scalable tool that can be deployed across multiple servers so as to handle high-volume report access. With its FTP functionality, you can even use BO XI as a conduit to other computer systems. It offers scheduling, report history, notifications, events, a security model, server management, and much more. Most of the features offered by BusinessObjects XI are exposed through APIs contained in a set of SDKs. Regardless of how you use BO XI, you'll likely take advantage of this object model to develop some kind of a customized front end. These object models and how to develop enterprise solutions with them is the subject of this book.

History

Crystal Reports was first released in 1991 and achieved market share quickly, rapidly overtaking R&R Report Writer as the dominant report-writing tool on the market. In 1993, Crystal was bundled in Visual Basic 3.0, the first version of Microsoft's flagship development language that had any real database capabilities. Its inclusion in what became the most popular Windows development language ever launched Crystal Reports into its position as a de facto standard.

As good a product as Crystal Reports is, for the first decade of its existence it didn't have a server product behind it as did other competing business intelligence tools such as Cognos, Actuate, or BusinessObjects. To fill this gap, Crystal Decisions in 2002 released its *Crystal Enterprise* product, which allowed you to make reports available from a server with a zero-client footprint. Anyone who has ever developed applications across multiple pre-.NET versions of Crystal Reports knows that installing an application using one version of the Crystal runtime on the same machine as an application using another version of the Crystal runtime routinely resulted in unpleasant DLL conflicts. In many cases they simply wouldn't work together, as Crystal's technical support would often reluctantly admit.

In 2003 one of my clients paid $150,000 for a two-processor license for Crystal Enterprise 9. They had been using Crystal Reports since it was first released and had legacy applications going back to VB 3.0 and every version of Crystal shipped subsequent to it scattered throughout the enterprise, each using different versions of the runtime. This client maintains a matrix of which applications use which versions of Crystal Reports and therefore would or would not be compatible on the same machine. All these troubles disappeared when we brought Crystal Enterprise and its zero-client footprint online. The elimination of the headaches caused by the DLL conflicts alone was worth the price of the Crystal Enterprise 9 license.

Crystal Decisions was originally part of Seagate Technology, a manufacturer of disk drives. It was spun off in 2000 when Seagate was acquired and had been a privately held concern ever since. The company was intending to go public in May 2003, and its IPO registration listed revenues of $271 million and net income of $27 million. That year, Business Objects purchased Crystal Decisions for $820 million.

The technology offered by Crystal Decisions complements that of Business Objects very well. Crystal Reports is first and foremost a report-writing tool. Such a tool is used by developers and very sharp end users who understand their relational data models, understand SQL, and can pull together a report. Business Objects is first and foremost a business intelligence firm whose flagship tool reports from universes. A *universe* is a metadata layer created by a database professional that shields end users from the intricacies of their RDBMS. Therefore, it is much easier for a nontechnical end user to create a report from a universe than directly from an RDBMS.

With this acquisition, Business Objects plans to keep both reporting technologies, as they each fill very specific niche markets. The server product, BusinessObjects XI Enterprise, will support distribution of both sets of reports—Crystal and the Web Intelligence and Desktop Intelligence reports offered by BO—to the enterprise. Moreover, both products will begin to share some of their core technology with one another. Not only will BusinessObjects XI host traditional BO reports, Crystal reports will be able to access data in universes.

In a July 2004 interview with *Computerworld*, Bernard Liautaud, the current chairman and then CEO of Business Objects, said

> *Crystal will use the semantic layer of Business Objects and use the Business Objects [data] universe. Business Objects has built its success in query technology at the semantic layer and Crystal Decisions has built it on reporting. . . . Now the two things will be together in one product. We've got a unified portal and dashboard for both Crystal Decisions and the Business Objects products for the user to log in with a single user name and password and see all Crystal reports or do a document search and link reports. It's a true common user experience between the two products.*

In November 2005, BusinessObjects XI Enterprise was released, and the product is currently in its second release, known as R2. The tool allows both Crystal developers and BusinessObjects users to approach the server tool from their own technology base.

From Report Writing to Business Intelligence

The terms *report writing* and *business intelligence* are often used interchangeably. Though both terms are related, they are not synonyms. Crystal Reports is primarily a report-writing tool. Its purpose is to allow developers to build reports against RDBMSs and other data sources and output their contents to the user. Though it can be used by nonprogrammers, it is aimed at the developer market. Crystal is known as a *banded report writer*. This means that a report operates on a band hierarchy where one band can represent subtotal information, another band holds the total level, and another band displays the grand total level. Other bands represent page and report headers and footers. At runtime, the placeholders in each of these bands are replaced with the data they are linked to in a data source to produce a report. The basic hierarchy of a banded report writer is shown in Figure 1-1.

| Report Header |
| Page Header |
| Details |
| Page Footer |
| Report Footer |

Figure 1-1. *Banded report writer*

Over the years, Crystal's reporting tools have evolved with the addition of Crystal Analysis. *Crystal Analysis* is an On Line Analytical Processing (OLAP) tool that allows you to connect to the dimensions and cubes of your OLAP back ends to perform analysis and drilling into the data.

Business intelligence, commonly known by its initials BI, is an industry term that refers collectively to the processes and technologies involved in the collection and analysis of business information so that the organization can use it to make informed decisions. Often, BI systems are referred to as *decision support systems* or to a lesser degree, *executive support systems*.

One of the principal buzzwords in the BI world is *key performance indicators*, also known as KPIs. KPIs allow an organization to measure and monitor, in as real time as possible, the performance of the enterprise. KPIs will vary across industries, but they may include such metrics as week-by-week sales trends, current headcount, percent of sales goals achieved to date, or number of phone calls to technical support. These are the types of summary numbers that would likely appear on an executive dashboard.

As you can see, BI is far more comprehensive than simple report writing, if only because nontechnical business professionals are intended to accomplish it. These professionals are then free to focus on the metadata that abstracts their information rather than the technical details of using a complex report-writing tool and navigating often labyrinthine database structures while optimizing SQL statements.

BusinessObjects XI Release 2

The key word in the name BusinessObjects Enterprise XI is *Enterprise*, and as this word implies in any product name, it is not cheap. Since the product is intended as a centralized reporting middleware solution that services the entire organization, large companies can focus on assigning software professionals skilled in the tool and its SDKs to service the product full time and so eliminate the need for every department and workgroup from developing and maintaining their own solutions.

Licensing

Licenses can be acquired either by named user or by processor. Named user licenses cost about $2,000 per seat. I have a client who prefers the user approach because the client has multiple departments that use BO XI, and each department has the product installed on its own servers. Since the load on any given server isn't sufficient to justify an entire server license, user licenses make more sense for that client.

Business Objects prefers not to publicize the cost of its enterprise server licenses. Each customer configuration is unique, and there are a number of variables that come into play when computing a license cost. Here is the company's official policy:

> *BusinessObjects Enterprise is available in two editions, Professional and Premium with two flexible licensing options: Named User and Processor-based. For specific pricing information, please contact Business Objects, or a certified Business Objects partner directly.*

I do know from past purchasing experience that a two-processor license of BO XI costs in the neighborhood of $150,000. The nonproduction versions of these licenses are usually offered at 50 percent of the full price. Note also that multicore processors require licenses for each core. There are a number of technical support options as well, and you can find the details on them here: http://support.businessobjects.com/programs/enterprise_bi_products.asp.

Because BusinessObjects Enterprise XI is a rather expensive product, it may not be financially viable for all organizations. As its name states, it is enterprise software, and even a large organization may not even need something that may well only be used by a single department or workgroup. Fortunately, there is a version of the tool, called *Crystal Reports Server*, that is scaled and priced for smaller organizations.

The base Crystal Reports Server product comes with a five-concurrent-access license. With a license cost of $7,500, most small to medium-sized organizations can afford it. You can scale the number of concurrent users up to a maximum of 20 concurrent access licenses, with each block of 5 licenses up to this limit costing an additional $7,500 for a maximum cost of $30,000. When one more than the maximum number of users attempts to log on, they will be denied access until an existing user session either logs off or expires.

You can only use Crystal Reports Server to run Crystal reports, and it cannot be scaled across multiple servers. The single Windows or Linux server you can run it on is restricted to a maximum of four processors. There is no Unix edition. Other than these restrictions, Crystal Reports Server has most of the same features as the Enterprise version.

Business Objects changed the licensing model once it purchased Crystal Decisions, which, starting with Crystal Reports 8, allowed much more flexibility than was available before. Previously, the licensing model prevented you from installing Crystal Reports on a machine and building software that instantiated its objects so as to act as a report server or, in effect, a replacement for Crystal Enterprise should you choose to add enough features. If you wanted to do this, you needed a broadcast license. Broadcast licenses were not cheap. A license for 500 users would cost you $10,000 per year, 1,500 users would cost you $25,000 per year, and more than 1,500 users would cost you $50,000 per year (a user being any individual who during the course of the year utilizes the report server at least once). The main goal of Crystal Decisions' licensing structure was to prohibit you from making your 8.x+ reports available to the enterprise without purchasing the rather expensive BO XI Enterprise license. I've read various posts to Internet newsgroups that refer to this licensing scheme as "extortionate" and "gouging."

Business Objects has removed these restrictive licensing requirements. If you wish to do so, you may install Crystal Reports on a server machine and develop your own report server as a few third-party companies have. By storing report schedules and on-demand requests in a database, you can create a Windows service that continually queries the report server data tables and, based on the attributes, creates a thread that instantiates the Crystal Reports API to run a report. This change in licensing is what allowed the CRD product from ChristianSteven Software, Ltd. (www.christiansteven.com) to be significantly cheaper to deploy, as a broadcast license is no longer necessary. This tool replaces much of Business Objects XI by sitting on top of your Crystal Reports DLLs, as well as implementing its own unique functionality, and is discussed in greater detail in Chapter 12.

The Crystal Reports Developer Edition offers a license for unlimited deployment of the reporting engine components within the enterprise. There are no additional licensing fees involved should you wish to build an application that uses these components and make that application available to the enterprise. Should you develop a product for distribution to other organizations, you'll need to purchase a license for each organization that uses your tool.

Service-Oriented Architecture

One of the leading buzzwords in the IT field today is *service-oriented architecture* (SOA). As a middleware application, BusinessObjects XI certainly lends itself to an SOA implementation. Given the rise of web services since the release of .NET in 2002, the SOA approach has taken off and gained acceptance in the industry. BO XI is essentially a service, specifically one that provides reporting services to the enterprise. This functionality is exposed through the user interface of its management console and through its object model SDKs. By creating a web service wrapper to this object model, you can expose BO XI's power to the enterprise as illustrated in Figure 1-2. Creating web service wrappers for the BO XI SDK is explained in greater detail in Chapter 5.

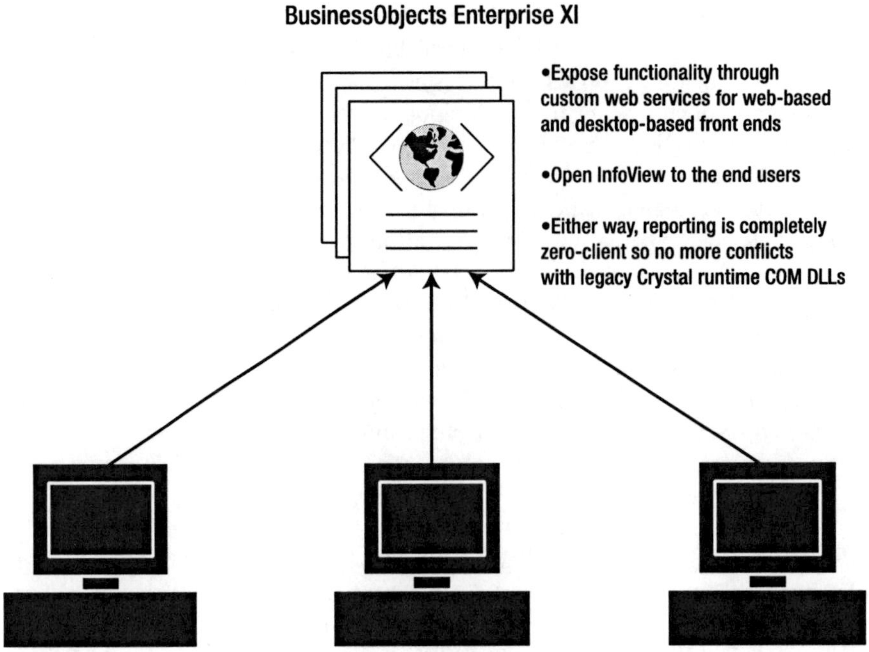

BusinessObjects Enterprise XI

•Expose functionality through custom web services for web-based and desktop-based front ends

•Open InfoView to the end users

•Either way, reporting is completely zero-client so no more conflicts with legacy Crystal runtime COM DLLs

Figure 1-2. *SOA architecture for BusinessObjects XI*

SOA is a service-based approach to application interoperability. It shares data using ASCII-based XML that is completely platform independent, enabling a common way for components to communicate with each other, and in doing so expose their functionality to the larger service ecosystem. Using a web service paradigm, you get a self-descriptive component (WSDL), a common invocation mechanism (SOAP), and a common data-exchange format (XML), all communicating across common communication layers (HTTP, among others). SOA allows you to build reporting functions that aren't an architectural afterthought, but rather grounded in a reliable methodology for integrating reporting functionality with every application in the enterprise.

Business Objects recently released their Web Services SDK, which implements this service-oriented architecture. The web services object model differs in varying degrees to the one offered in the .NET SDK. Chapter 12 is dedicated to the Web Services SDK.

Reporting Considerations

Before embarking on any reporting project, there are some practical considerations to keep in mind. A very broad definition of reporting would be "anything that comes out of a printer." If this is your mindset, then there are a few issues to consider when handling certain types of reporting projects.

Report distribution has made huge leaps since the introduction of the Internet and corporate intranets. Since many reports are built in to applications (compiled EXEs), users would normally need a copy of that application installed on their desktops in order to access the report. Now, the reporting functionality can be completely Web-based. Using Web-based technology, the comparatively finite number of desktop applications can still have access to report functionality via web services, while the often much larger number of web users can access a Web-based application that will provide them with report criteria screens allowing them to filter, run, and export reports.

Preprinted Forms

Oftentimes you may need to print a report on a preprinted form, such as an IRS 1040 or a W-2. If this is the case, you should examine whether the application really needs to print specific pieces of data at specific locations on the preprinted page, or simply reprint the entire form itself on blank paper. I have a client who was once spending $7,000 per year on preprinted forms. When I showed him that the same result could be achieved if he performed a mail merge with a document composed in Microsoft Word, he was naturally elated at the annual savings. Moreover, he now has the flexibility of being able to change the document at will without coordinating the forms printer with the software developer.

High-Volume Printing

High-volume printing raises issues that must be examined for cost efficiency. It's very easy to create a mail-merge application; quite another thing to manage it hands on. One of my clients is an elected official who printed his constituent reports on an ink-jet printer. Ink-jet printers are relatively cheap, and a decent one can be purchased for about $100. The hidden costs here are the ink cartridges. With cartridges costing about $40 each, you don't want to do high-volume printing on an ink-jet printer. In fact, ink-jet printers are loss leaders for the printer industry, as the real profits are in the replacement ink cartridges. Since they are used up at a much faster rate than laser toner cartridges costing twice as much, you'll end up spending more on ink-jet replacements than you will on toner. There are companies that also sell recycled toner cartridges at a sizable discount compared to new cartridges. In addition to this, ink-jet printers operate at only a fraction of the speed of laser printers. When my client indicated he wanted to print an annual newsletter to send to his 5,000 constituents, I recommended a laser printer. He now prints the text of the newsletter and merges the addresses as well.

Mass mailing can be a science unto itself. If your client needs do customized high-volume mailing pieces—for example, a monthly telephone bill as opposed to a supermarket circular where every recipient receives the same one—you may wish to examine an automated mailing solution. I have a long distance reseller client who sends thousands of telephone bills every month. The billing software creates print images of the bills and sends them to a Pitney Bowes machine that prints the bill, folds it, places it into a postage-paid window envelope, and seals it. Machines such as those sold by Pitney Bowes are designed specifically for this type of high-volume mailing, and the staff are experts on how to sort and organize the letters to achieve the maximum bulk-rate postage. If you have a requirement for customized high-volume mailing, examine the product solutions at www.pb.com.

If your volume of mail is so great that it cannot be realistically done in-house, consider the services of a bulk mailing company. These firms have the computers and printing equipment to print millions of documents and mail them within a few days. Mailing firms are large, high-volume facilities, some of which print and mail several hundred million documents per year. You can use your software to produce print images according to specifications given to you by the mailing company and then e-mail the data to their facility. Optionally, you could simply give them the raw data, and they will create the print routines for you. Depending on cost, you can work out with them where your work will leave off and theirs will begin. Because it doesn't matter where the mailing company is located, you can contract with virtually any in the country to obtain the most reasonable rates. Be open to the idea of a mass mailing company—you could very easily become overwhelmed with printing and mailing tasks in a high-volume environment.

Legal Issues

One often-overlooked area of report design is the legal implications of system output. Usually, data that is intended for internal corporate use is not an issue. Output that is intended for use external to the organization can often bring with it significant legal liability. As a rule, every report, certificate, fax, statement, or letter that is intended for use outside the organization should be passed by legal counsel for approval. Seemingly innocuous documents may have enormous legal ramifications, and these ramifications may differ from industry to industry. For example, one of the first systems I ever built was a target market mailing system for the sales agents of a leading insurance company. A sales agent would buy a list of names, and my system would merge these names with a marketing letter. As I made the system more flexible, I allowed the users to create their own letters. They gladly did so without ever consulting with in-house legal counsel. There were no safeguards in place preventing an agent from sending out a letter promising, say, a guaranteed 20 percent return on a particular product. In the past, courts have ruled that such statements are contractually binding on the company who issued them.

Documents as simple as account statements or even invoices can be potential traps for legal liability. Alert counsel to the format of these documents and exactly what information they contain. Counsel may create a disclaimer that accompanies the text of the document as a safeguard. Even these disclaimers have potential pitfalls as some states do not recognize this proverbial "fine print" if the print is, literally, too fine. This means by law that if the font is too small, the courts will disregard the existence of the text as having been too small for someone to reasonably read.

Copyright is also a property right that must be guarded. The summarization of even publicly available data has long been held to be copyrightable. Therefore, the database of a company like Dun and Bradstreet, which compiles credit information on millions of business entities worldwide, has an intellectual property interest in the data it has collected and in the unique way it presents it. Therefore it is necessary for any reports that may present this data to individuals outside the organization to affix a copyright notice declaring the information in the report to be proprietary. Absence of a copyright notice can make prosecuting a case for infringement difficult to impossible, as it is incumbent on the copyright owner to make a clear and visible declaration of ownership.

A good rule of thumb is to contact corporate counsel before distributing any information to the outside. The attorneys (and your client) will be impressed by your foresight on these legal issues and will appreciate the fact that you consulted them.

Availability and Distribution

The final design issue is to determine who needs to run the reports. Traditionally there is a Report option on the main menu of desktop applications from which criteria screens are launched and reports printed, displayed, and exported. While there may be only 20 users of your application, there may be 100 users of the reports. This is where hybrid application development comes into play. Therefore, it may make sense to select some or all of the reports that are needed by users who are not users of the application itself and create them as web reports.

The Web is no longer the only way to make reports available to the masses. As PDAs (Personal Data Assistants) become more prevalent, more users will want to access their data remotely via a wireless connection to the server. Due to the current state of PDA and wireless technology, there are a number of limitations you'll need to deal with when allowing reports to be transmitted to a PDA. Because of the slow connection speed, you'll need to limit the amount of data you can transmit between the server and the PDA. Note that this speed problem occurs with wireless modems. People using PDAs with wireless LAN cards enjoy speeds above 10 mbps. This will affect the way you design your reports, especially the HTML exports that the PDA device often uses. Another problem is how to handle the ergonomics of a small screen that may or may not have a color display.

In many instances, users are more interested in receiving reports on a regular basis than they are in running them individually. This is known as the *"push" versus "pull"* approach. BO XI offers this in its scheduling feature. You can set a report to run at a certain time and with a certain frequency and then deliver the results in a desired format (Excel, PDF, etc.) to a printer/fax, e-mail address, or FTP server—the "push" method. Or, you can run reports on demand and download them to the client—the "pull" method.

BusinessObjects XI vs. SQL Server Reporting Services

BusinessObjects/Crystal Enterprise and Crystal Reports have long competed with other report-writing and business intelligence solutions in the form of Actuate, Cognos, and Hyperion, among other competitors, and have always dominated market share. For years, Microsoft never entered the report-writing market, and with the exception of the reporting tools in MSAccess, never released a report writer. In 2002, that all changed when Microsoft released the first version of its SQL Server Reporting Services (SSRS). The second version was released three years later along with the premier of SQL Server 2005.

Market Considerations

SSRS is Microsoft's first stab at a report-writing and business intelligence tool. Like BO XI, there are two main parts to the tool: a user interface to write reports and server software to schedule and distribute these reports. Currently, SSRS is offered as a "free" add-on to a SQL Server license. Since the recommended Microsoft configuration calls for a dedicated server to host SSRS, you need to purchase a SQL Server license for that server in order to obtain your free reporting software. Since SSRS and SQL Server are both resource-consuming applications, you don't want them battling one another for the memory and CPU of the same machine. Therefore, you'll want to install them on separate machines since it's not possible to allocate memory between the two products.

If you have a large centralized reporting application, you'll likely want to scale it across multiple servers to perform load balancing and implement redundancy. You need to purchase a SQL Server license for each of these servers as well in order to install your free copy of SSRS. Depending on your reporting needs, your free copy of SSRS could cost you up to $100,000.

When Visual Studio 2005 was first announced, there was much concern among the developer community as to whether Microsoft would continue its relationship with Business Objects and bundle Crystal Reports with the .NET development suite. Microsoft promised to do so from the beginning and has kept that promise so far. Will Microsoft eventually drop the Crystal bundling and start offering only SSRS? Only time will tell. There may be some antitrust implications from doing this and offering only its own tool, as was the case in its battles with Netscape in the late 1990s. History, however, is not on the side of Business Objects. Lotus once dominated a spreadsheet market that is now controlled by Excel. WordPerfect once dominated a word processing market that is now owned by Word. dBase once reigned supreme in a desktop database market that it long ago surrendered to Access. Novell once overwhelming controlled the local area networking market but has been marginalized by Windows NT. Remember when IBM's OS/2 was once considered a "Windows killer"? I've read one respected Microsoft authority (nonemployee) who referred to SSRS as a "Crystal killer."

I'm not at all suggesting that BusinessObjects/Crystal Reports is dying and you should run to SSRS before it's too late. Quite the contrary, Business Objects is a thriving company and BO XI is a thriving product. With over 15 million registered copies of Crystal Reports throughout the world and a decade-and-a-half of developer experience, this tool isn't going anywhere anytime soon. SQL Server has been on the market for ten years now and has not managed to unseat or even marginalize Oracle. Reporting tools are one of the more difficult IT items to replace, though not quite as difficult as replacing a database. I'm merely stating that SSRS is now a player in the reporting market, it's not going away, and it needs to be carefully considered and respected as it grows to become a stronger rival. Watch this product closely and carefully.

Should you wish to move to SSRS from Crystal, the transition won't be an easy one. If you have a large base of Crystal reports, converting them to the Report Definition Language (RDL) format used by SSRS will not be a simple task. Hitachi Consulting (www.hitachiconsulting.com/downloadPdf.cfm?ID=251) offers a tool call RDL Generator that will convert the majority of each report to RDL, and Jeff-Net (www.rpttosql.com/faq.htm) offers a service that does the same thing. Both companies can only perform a partial (60 percent or better) conversion. These products can convert page headers and footers, field position and formatting, special fields, formulas, groups, and parameters. Other features will not convert and need to be handled manually. The report formats are too different to allow the creation of a single tool that can take any Crystal report and output it to the RDL format without further modification required. It's not as simple as opening a Lotus spreadsheet in Excel.

At this writing (September 2006) the market has not overwhelmingly taken to SSRS. The best way to cut through the hype on any product is to see what companies are hiring for and are therefore willing to immediately spend money on. After checking with several IT recruiter contacts, they have all told me that Crystal Reports and CE/BO XI are still far more in demand than any other report development skill. SSRS appears to be still very much in the margin. A search of the Dice (www.dice.com) and Monster (www.monster.com) sites shows the number of job openings for Crystal Reports and Crystal Enterprise/BusinessObjects XI developers is dramatically larger than the demand for developers with SSRS expertise. The third-party book market has responded well to SSRS, as there have been as many titles published about it in the past 4 years as Crystal Reports has had published about it in 15 years, excluding multiple releases of the same title for different versions of the product.

Feature Differences

SSRS reports use an XML format for the report definitions called RDL. Microsoft publishes the specification for RDL, as third-party developers are encouraged to develop technologies to complement SSRS. It had been hoped over the 4 years since the release of SSRS that someone would develop a user interface that would stand superior to the rather anemic one offered by Microsoft. So far, no one has stepped up to the plate. Crystal's interface has been refined over 15 years of use and 11 releases. SSRS's interface has been around for 4 years and 2 releases. Understandably, Crystal offers a far superior report designer interface to that of SSRS.

Crystal Reports and BusinessObjects XI both offer many features over SSRS. One of these advantages is the fact that the report-writing product and the server product are not married to one another. You need Crystal Reports to create reports, but you don't need the server middleware to run or distribute them. If you have an application that needs to be distributed to a large number of users, you can include the Crystal Viewer control and the necessary Crystal runtime DLLs with the installation set and you have a self-contained application. SSRS does not work this way. The reports can only run on the server middleware, and there are no runtime DLLs that will allow an RDL file to execute independent of the server software. Thus, SSRS would not work for applications distributed to the general public.

SSRS has fewer export options than BO XI—Excel, PDF, MHTML, TIFF, XML, and ASCII only. BO XI does not support TIFF, XML, or MHTML but offers many others that SSRS does not support. MHTML is a self-contained web file that embeds images within the report. It is the default rendering format for Internet Explorer 6.0. Both products allow you to create report schedules and distribution lists. SSRS calls these schedules *subscriptions*. You can create data-driven subscriptions whereby a list of users in an external data source are set to subscribe to a series of scheduled reports and can receive them via e-mail or disk file.

The concept of servers also exists in SSRS, only here they're called *processors*. When scheduling reports, for example, SSRS uses the SQL Server Agent service. Scheduled reports exist as jobs in SQL Server Agent. When a job executes, SQL Server Agent adds an event to the queue maintained in the report server database. The Scheduling and Delivery processor polls the queue periodically to determine what jobs are in the hopper. When the time comes to execute them, SSRS processes them accordingly.

Where BO XI has the Report Application Server (RAS) for programmatic report creation (see Chapter 8), SSRS offers a documented object model for the RDL format only. Each element of a report can be output to an RDL file via an `XmlWriter` object. This is a long way from the power of the RAS.

Another point to keep in mind when comparing the two products is that SSRS is primarily a developer's tool, not an end-user tool, though in SSRS 2005 Microsoft did introduce a designer that allows end users to create ad hoc reports. Crystal Reports is aimed at both developers and end users. There are Standard, Professional, and Developer editions to choose from, each with its own feature set tailored for the specific type of user.

One area where SSRS is superior to Crystal is in its documentation and Knowledgebase. Microsoft has traditionally offered excellent documentation, and SSRS is no exception. The Knowledgebase for SSRS also has a substantial amount of material that explains the different features of the product in more detail. Business Objects documentation is complete for the user interface of the product but rather weak for the .NET SDK, and even weaker for the RAS SDK. Its Knowledgebase does have some useful articles and technical papers but nowhere near the quality level of MSDN.

Though SQL Server Reporting Services is not nearly the mature product Crystal Reports/ BusinessObjects XI is, it does offer one distinct advantage in the web services it exposes. BO XI offers a powerful, if not completely intuitive, object model. From this object model you can build enterprise solutions that provide all the reporting features you can imagine. The problem is that you need to build these solutions yourself.

SSRS on the other hand exposes a collection of web services that offer you access to the features of SSRS. Probably the most commonly used web method is the Render() method of the ReportExecutionService web service that allows you to run reports with specified parameters and return the output to the proxy application. Other web service methods allow you to read and set report parameters, retrieve report histories, set limits on the report history instances, and create schedules that determine which users will receive which reports when and in what format. Should you desire a custom interface to any of these features in BO XI, you'll need to create, deploy, and maintain your own web service application and write the code yourself.

Summary

Business Objects can get you into the enterprise reporting world relatively cheaply with Crystal Reports Server. When your organization grows beyond the bounds of this tool, you have the unlimited resources of BusinessObjects XI awaiting you. Though Business Objects is firmly rooted in the reporting world, you still need to keep a careful eye on SQL Server Reporting Services as it gradually continues to gain market share.

Now that you know what BusinessObjects XI is, what it can do for you, and where it stands in relation to other reporting tools on the market, we'll start taking a look as to how it works. In the next chapter we'll discuss the collection of servers that together comprise BusinessObjects XI.

CHAPTER 2

∎∎∎

BusinessObjects XI Server Architecture

BusinessObjects XI is a multitier, server-based product that comprises a number of logical servers. These servers run as Windows services, and they can all be installed on one machine or distributed across multiple machines, each running multiple processors as your needs demand. In this chapter, we'll examine how to manage those servers, command them programmatically, and extract information about them. We'll look at programming examples of how to work with servers and server groups. If you are unfamiliar with the basics of programming with the SDK, see Chapter 5 for an introduction.

InfoStore

When you first install BusinessObjects XI, the product creates a series of tables in your designated database back end. This database is known as the *InfoStore*. The default RDBMS is SQL Server, but you can use almost any database on the market. The InfoStore tables hold the information about all your reports, folders, users, and object packages. In short, any data that you see in the Central Management Console (CMC)—except for the actual report and image files themselves—is stored in the InfoStore.

BO XI provides an `InfoStore` class in its SDK to act as an abstraction layer to these database tables. We'll examine this `InfoStore` class in much greater detail in Chapter 5 as it is the sine qua non of the entire object model. There is no reason for you to ever access the InfoStore RDBMS tables directly. Altering the database directly in any way will likely cause damage to your installation, and BusinessObjects can no longer be held accountable for technical support. The four RDBMS tables are `CMS_InfoObjects5`, `CMS_Aliases5`, `CMS_IDNumbers5`, and `CMS_Relations5`. The main table is `CMS_InfoObjects5`. This table stores all the data about your reports either indexed in named columns or unindexed in binary columns. A partial data display from this table is shown in Figure 2-1.

ObjectID	ParentID	TypeID	OwnerID	LastModifyTime	ObjFlags	UserFlags	ScheduleStatus	NextRunTime	Aliases	CRC	Properties	SI_GUID	SI_CUID	SI_RUID	SI_INSTANCE_OBJ
9826	6122	279	6112	2006 05 25 19 34 56 343	0	<NULL>	1		<NULL>	2362309606	<Binary>	<Binary>	<Binary>	<Binary>	0
10651	42	42	10	2006 06 02 12 21 55 593	16	<NULL>	<NULL>		<NULL>	4032119523	<Binary>	<Binary>	<Binary>	<Binary>	0
10652	42	42	10	2006 06 02 12 21 56 031	16	<NULL>	<NULL>		<NULL>	3221203856	<Binary>	<Binary>	<Binary>	<Binary>	0
10656	42	42	10	2006 06 02 12 21 57 828	16	<NULL>	<NULL>		<NULL>	3504297300	<Binary>	<Binary>	<Binary>	<Binary>	0
10657	42	42	10	2006 06 02 12 21 57 843	16	<NULL>	<NULL>		<NULL>	2929179465	<Binary>	<Binary>	<Binary>	<Binary>	0
9913	23	1	12	2006 05 26 18 15 09 968	0	<NULL>	<NULL>		<NULL>	2308525280	<Binary>	<Binary>	<Binary>	<Binary>	0
8600	1233	2	12	2006 05 16 15 59 19 921	0	<NULL>	<NULL>		<NULL>	3273259082	<Binary>	<Binary>	<Binary>	<Binary>	0
9189	42	42	10	2006 05 23 13 28 20 312	16	<NULL>	<NULL>		<NULL>	627073243	<Binary>	<Binary>	<Binary>	<Binary>	0
8838	6116	279	6113	2006 05 18 12 21 33 468	0	<NULL>	1		<NULL>	727733608	<Binary>	<Binary>	<Binary>	<Binary>	0
7528	42	42	10	2006 05 09 16 06 53 312	16	<NULL>	<NULL>		<NULL>	4238409208	<Binary>	<Binary>	<Binary>	<Binary>	0
8839	6119	279	6111	2006 05 18 12 21 33 500	0	<NULL>	1		<NULL>	2291337160	<Binary>	<Binary>	<Binary>	<Binary>	0
9479	9475	2	12	2006 05 24 20 30 58 609	16642	<NULL>	3		<NULL>	3326679246	<Binary>	<Binary>	<Binary>	<Binary>	1
10092	42	42	10	2006 05 29 00 54 47 656	16	<NULL>	<NULL>		<NULL>	844344297	<Binary>	<Binary>	<Binary>	<Binary>	0
9768	3929	276	12	2006 05 25 19 32 23 906	258	<NULL>	1		<NULL>	2671437172	<Binary>	<Binary>	<Binary>	<Binary>	1
8888	6116	279	6113	2006 05 18 12 22 28 203	0	<NULL>	1		<NULL>	2325015127	<Binary>	<Binary>	<Binary>	<Binary>	0
10130	10126	1	12	2006 05 29 12 42 01 109	0	<NULL>	<NULL>		<NULL>	1631537034	<Binary>	<Binary>	<Binary>	<Binary>	0
9772	3929	276	12	2006 05 25 19 34 18 640	258	<NULL>	3		<NULL>	366111739	<Binary>	<Binary>	<Binary>	<Binary>	1
9643	6116	265	6113	2006 05 25 15 37 52 578	0	<NULL>	1		<NULL>	3352593338	<Binary>	<Binary>	<Binary>	<Binary>	0
10098	23	1	12	2006 05 29 01 02 06 187	0	<NULL>	<NULL>		<NULL>	3743134567	<Binary>	<Binary>	<Binary>	<Binary>	0
10244	6119	279	6111	2006 05 29 14 46 57 218	0	<NULL>	1		<NULL>	406628213	<Binary>	<Binary>	<Binary>	<Binary>	0
9823	6119	279	6111	2006 05 25 19 34 56 281	0	<NULL>	1		<NULL>	2458089725	<Binary>	<Binary>	<Binary>	<Binary>	0
10496	23	1	12	2006 05 31 16 00 04 359	0	<NULL>	<NULL>		<NULL>	311786218	<Binary>	<Binary>	<Binary>	<Binary>	0
10689	278	265	12	2006 06 02 12 41 37 296	0	<NULL>	1		<NULL>	712994091	<Binary>	<Binary>	<Binary>	<Binary>	0
10660	42	42	10	2006 06 02 12 21 58 234	16	<NULL>	<NULL>		<NULL>	2359064967	<Binary>	<Binary>	<Binary>	<Binary>	0
7683	278	319	12	2006 05 10 15 53 36 171	0	<NULL>	1		<NULL>	3388983583	<Binary>	<Binary>	<Binary>	<Binary>	0
9633	6116	259	6113	2006 05 25 15 31 48 359	0	<NULL>	1		<NULL>	1277654440	<Binary>	<Binary>	<Binary>	<Binary>	0
10644	42	42	10	2006 06 02 12 21 55 500	16	<NULL>	<NULL>		<NULL>	1878588313	<Binary>	<Binary>	<Binary>	<Binary>	0
7718	6122	279	6112	2006 05 10 16 00 18 968	0	<NULL>	1		<NULL>	1524615338	<Binary>	<Binary>	<Binary>	<Binary>	0
10645	42	42	10	2006 06 02 12 21 55 500	16	<NULL>	<NULL>		<NULL>	1125339784	<Binary>	<Binary>	<Binary>	<Binary>	0
10646	42	42	10	2006 06 02 12 21 55 515	16	<NULL>	<NULL>		<NULL>	1299453184	<Binary>	<Binary>	<Binary>	<Binary>	0
9774	3929	276	12	2006 05 25 19 34 38 609	258	<NULL>	1		<NULL>	1442672644	<Binary>	<Binary>	<Binary>	<Binary>	0
9818	6116	279	6113	2006 05 25 19 34 56 203	0	<NULL>	1		<NULL>	4246916068	<Binary>	<Binary>	<Binary>	<Binary>	0
9837	6122	279	6112	2006 05 25 19 35 02 078	0	<NULL>	1		<NULL>	3752126241	<Binary>	<Binary>	<Binary>	<Binary>	0
10647	42	42	10	2006 06 02 12 21 55 515	16	<NULL>	<NULL>		<NULL>	1309637861	<Binary>	<Binary>	<Binary>	<Binary>	0

Figure 2-1. *CMS_InfoObjects5 table*

Such data elements as an object's ID, its type, or its GUID, for example, are stored in indexed columns. In Chapter 5, you'll see how to create SQL statements that extract this information through the InfoStore class. Using the indexed columns in the WHERE clause will make for the most efficient SQL query just as it would in any other RDBMS. If you're extracting a single object by referencing its SI_ID value in a WHERE clause—one of the most common SQL statements you'll write—the response will be very fast because SI_ID is indexed. Nonindexed data such as description, output format, printer information, etc., along with any properties you may create yourself (see Chapter 9), are stored collectively in binary (BLOB) columns and are unindexed. Caution must be used here when using unindexed properties exclusively in your WHERE clause as the search won't be as efficient.

FileStore

The FileStore refers to the disk directories where the actual report files reside. It can be found on your disk at \Program Files\Business Objects\BusinessObjects Enterprise 11.5\FileStore. The two main directories under this location are Input and Output. The Input directory stores the report templates and thumbnail images, while the Output directory stores the results from running those templates. Thus, the Output directory is normally many times larger than the Input directory. Each of these directories is managed by its own BO XI server, which is discussed in the next section.

The Report Properties page of the CMC shows you the location of the Input report files. The report shown in Figure 2-2 indicates that the RPT report template can be found at frs://Input/a_242/004/000/1266/aa04421b355c40.rpt.

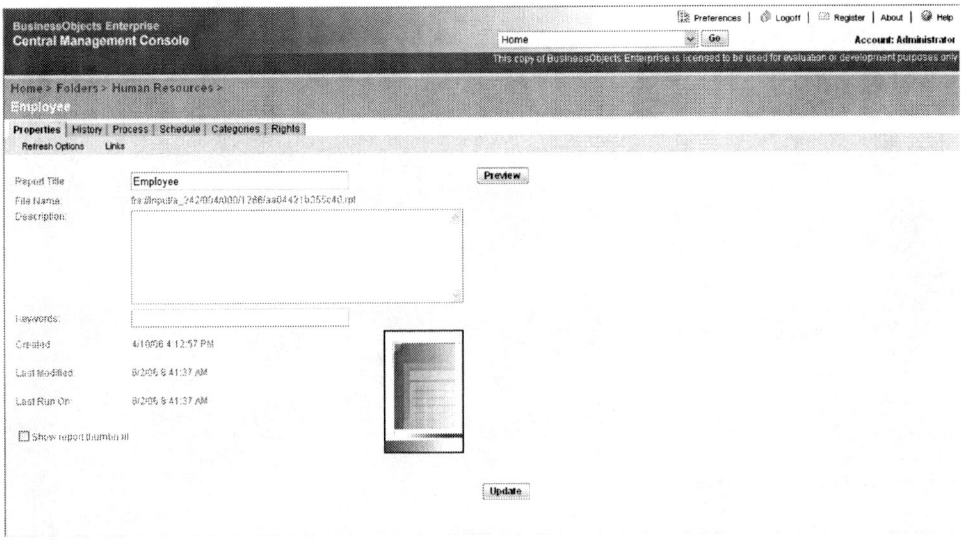

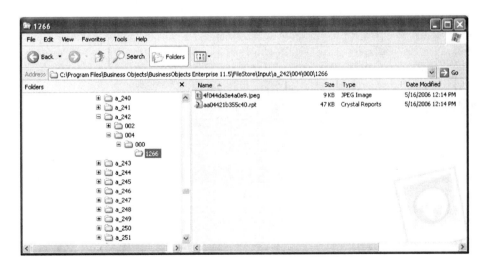

Figure 2-2. *Report Properties page*

An examination of this location (see Figure 2-3) shows two files: the RPT file with the name indicated on the report properties page of the CMC and a JPEG file, which serves as the thumbnail image.

Figure 2-3. *FileStore directory and files*

Report histories display their output files as well. Figure 2-4 shows the results of a successful run to a PDF file that was output to frs://Output/a_055/038/000/9783/~ce65445094ec639c.pdf.

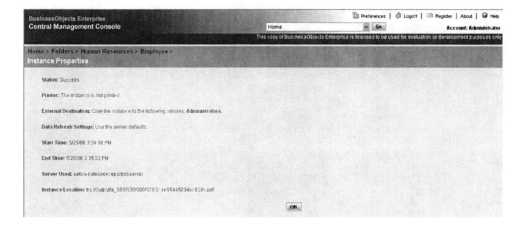

Figure 2-4. *Report results page*

When you delete report templates or report history entries, either programmatically or through the CMC, the associated file entries will be deleted as well.

BO XI handles the management of these disk locations through the File Repository servers. We'll discuss the individual servers in the next section.

Servers

You can manage the various servers that comprise a BO XI installation by selecting the Servers option from the main menu of the CMC. Some of these servers specifically handle BusinessObjects reports (like Desktop Intelligence and Web Intelligence) but we'll focus on the Crystal Reports servers only. You'll be presented with the screen shown in Figure 2-5.

Figure 2-5. *Server page*

From this page you can control the servers and manage their individual settings. You can also start and stop as well as enable and disable servers. There is a difference between stopping and disabling a server. *Stopping* a server terminates the server's process completely and results in a complete shutdown. *Disabling* a server prevents it from receiving any further requests but doesn't actually shut down the process. In production environments, it's a good practice to disable certain servers like the Job Server and Program Job Server prior to stopping them so that they can complete the processing of any pending jobs.

The BO XI servers may be grouped into two tiers—the intelligence tier and the processing tier. The intelligence tier manages security and audit information as well as handles server requests. The intelligence-tier servers are the Central Management Server, the Cache Server, both File Repository servers, and the Event Server. The processing tier consists of those servers that access the database and actually generate reports. These consist of the Report Job Server, the Program Job Server, the Web Intelligence Job and Report Servers, the Report Application Server, the Destination Job Server, the List of Values Job Server, the Page Server, and the Connection Server. Essentially, the intelligence-tier servers give the orders and the processing-tier servers obey them. The relationship of the servers is shown in Figure 2-6.

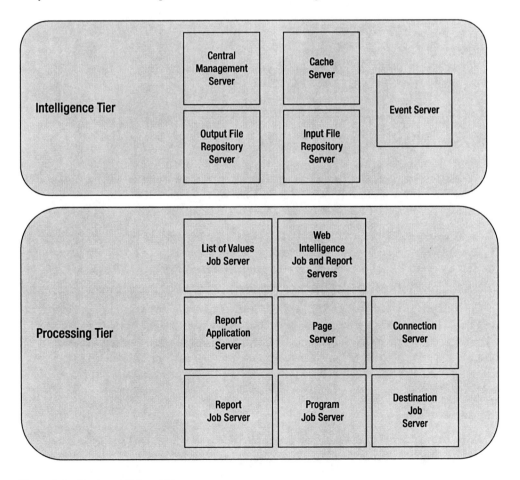

Figure 2-6. *BusinessObjects XI servers*

SERVER COMMAND-LINE PARAMETERS

If you open the Central Configuration Manager, right-click a server, and select the Properties option from the pop-up menu, you'll see a dialog that looks like Figure 2-7.

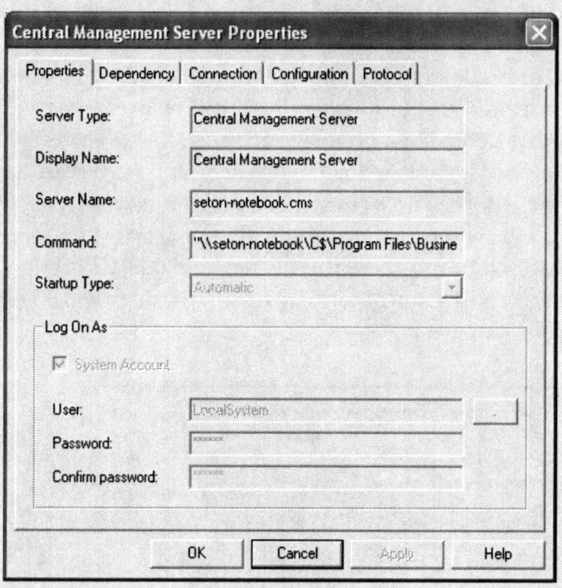

Figure 2-7. *Server properties*

The text boxes are all disabled because the server is running. You need to stop the server to make any edits. All servers are Windows Services, and the Command setting is the path and EXE name of that service. The command property of the Program Server, for example, looks like this:

```
"\\seton-notebook\C$\Program Files\Business Objects\BusinessObjects Enterprise
11.5\win32_x86\ProgramServer.exe" -service -name seton-notebook.programjobserver
-ns seton-notebook -objectType CrystalEnterprise.Program -lib procProgram
-restart -jsTypeDescription "Program Job Server"
```

The switches that appear after the EXE reference are placed there by default when BO XI is installed and should not be modified except on the instructions of technical support. These switches are not listed in any published documentation for this reason. The only switch setting that technical support may instruct you to add is the -trace option. Adding this to the command line will cause the server to write files to the \Program Files\Business Objects\BusinessObjects Enterprise 11.5\Logging directory. Should you wish to send the log files elsewhere, use the -loggingPath switch like this:

```
-loggingPath c:\temp
```

These files contain server activity and debugging information which you can send to technical support to aid them in diagnosing your problem. Each log file contains four columns: the time stamp; the process ID; the thread ID, which is the ID of the subprocess reporting the information; and the message which described what's happening. The output looks like this:

```
Timestamp                    ProcessID   ThreadID   Message
[Fri Jun 02 12:21:59 2006]   3228        848        (\backend\cms\include\Database
Indexers.h:166): trace message: Set property id 3 (SI_NAME) with value
[Fri Jun 02 12:21:59 2006]   3228        860           trace message: [UID=0;USID=0;
ID=10662 ] DoneCallbacks(id=10662,type=42,bef=false,aft=true,clus=false, ucode=1)
```

This sample was taken from a file called CMS_20060602_122140_3228.log. The file name itself has meaning. *CMS* refers to the process that created the file; *20060602* is the date the file was created, which in this example is June 2, 2006; *122140* refers to the time the file was created expressed as Greenwich Mean Time; and *3228* is the number of milliseconds past the second when the file was created. This assists in ensuring a unique name for the file.

Once your issue is resolved, make sure you remove the -trace switch, especially if you have it set in a production environment, as this will cause performance degradation and consume disk space through the continual writing of log files. These log files can build up fast. Each file contains up to a half megabyte of data before creating a backup of itself and starting a new file. After setting the -trace switch on the CMS, logging in, previewing a report, scheduling the same report to run immediately, and then shutting down the CMS, the following files were created all in a matter of three minutes:

File	Size
CMS_20060602_123940_5928.log	167KB
CMS_20060602_123940_5928_bak3.log	492KB
CMS_20060602_123940_5928_bak2.log	489KB
CMS_20060602_123940_5928_bak1.log	489KB

Programmatic Access

Server information is stored in the CI_SYSTEMOBJECTS category of the InfoStore. Here, server entries have an SI_KIND value of Server. The basic information about servers can be extracted with a SQL statement that requests the main server properties as shown in Listing 2-1.

Listing 2-1. *Extracting Basic Server Information*

```
//Connect to BO XI

szSQL = "SELECT SI_ID, SI_NAME, SI_DESCRIPTION, " +
  "SI_OWNER, SI_SERVER_ID, SI_SERVER_KIND, " +
  "SI_FRIENDLY_NAME, SI_SERVER_NAME, SI_NTSERVICE_NAME, " +
  "SI_REGISTER_TO_APS, SI_SERVER_DESCRIPTOR " +
  "FROM CI_SYSTEMOBJECTS " +
  "WHERE SI_KIND = 'Server' " +
  "ORDER BY SI_DESCRIPTION";

oInfoObjects = oInfoStore.Query(szSQL);
```

```
oDT = new DataTable();

oDT.Columns.Add(new DataColumn("ID"));
oDT.Columns.Add(new DataColumn("Name"));
oDT.Columns.Add(new DataColumn("Description"));
oDT.Columns.Add(new DataColumn("Owner"));
oDT.Columns.Add(new DataColumn("ServerID"));
oDT.Columns.Add(new DataColumn("ServerKind"));
oDT.Columns.Add(new DataColumn("FriendlyName"));
oDT.Columns.Add(new DataColumn("ServerName"));
oDT.Columns.Add(new DataColumn("NTServiceName"));
oDT.Columns.Add(new DataColumn("RegisterToAPS"));
oDT.Columns.Add(new DataColumn("ServerDescriptor"));

foreach (InfoObject oInfoObject in oInfoObjects)
{
    oDR = oDT.NewRow();

    oDR["ID"] =
        oInfoObject.Properties["SI_ID"].ToString();
    oDR["Name"] =
        oInfoObject.Properties["SI_NAME"].ToString();
    oDR["Description"] =
        oInfoObject.Properties["SI_DESCRIPTION"].ToString();
    oDR["Owner"] =
        oInfoObject.Properties["SI_OWNER"].ToString();
    oDR["ServerID"] =
        oInfoObject.Properties["SI_SERVER_ID"].ToString();
    oDR["ServerKind"] =
        oInfoObject.Properties["SI_SERVER_KIND"].ToString();
    oDR["FriendlyName"] =
        oInfoObject.Properties["SI_FRIENDLY_NAME"].ToString();
    oDR["ServerName"] =
        oInfoObject.Properties["SI_SERVER_NAME"].ToString();
    oDR["NTServiceName"] =
        oInfoObject.Properties["SI_NTSERVICE_NAME"].ToString();
    oDR["RegisterToAPS"] =
        oInfoObject.Properties["SI_REGISTER_TO_APS"].ToString();
    oDR["ServerDescriptor"] =
        oInfoObject.Properties["SI_SERVER_DESCRIPTOR"].ToString();

    oDT.Rows.Add(oDR);
}
```

This code will produce the DataTable displayed in Figure 2-8.

ID	Name	Description	Owner
288	seton-notebook.Web_IntelligenceReportServer.webiserver	Web Intelligence Report Server	System Account
546	seton-notebook.spcengine.spcEngine	AASPC	System Account
543	seton-notebook.rulesengine.rulesEngine	AARules	System Account
282	seton-notebook.RAS.rptappserver	Report Application Server	System Account
539	seton-notebook.repomgt.repomgt	AARepomgt	System Account
545	seton-notebook.setanalysisengine.queryManager	AAQueryManager	System Account
541	seton-notebook.probeengine.probeEngine	AAMetrics	System Account
538	seton-notebook.portfolioengine.portfolioEngine	AAAnalytics	System Account
285	seton-notebook.pageserver.pageserver	Crystal Reports Page Server	System Account
544	seton-notebook.miningengine.miningEngine	AAMinings	System Account
291	seton-notebook.reportjobserver.jobserver	Crystal Reports Job Server	System Account
280	seton-notebook.Desktop_IntelligenceJobServer.jobserver	Desktop Intelligence Job Server	System Account
287	seton-notebook.destinationjobserver.jobserver	Destination Job Server	System Account
301	seton-notebook.ListOfValuesJobServer.jobserver	List of Values Job Server	System Account
284	seton-notebook.programjobserver.jobserver	Program Job Server	System Account
303	seton-notebook.Web_IntelligenceJobServer.jobserver	Web Intelligence Job Server	System Account
542	seton-notebook.profileengine.iProfiler	AAIProfiler	System Account
289	Input.seton-notebook.fileserver	File Repository Server	System Account

Figure 2-8. *Basic server information*

The individual InfoObjects could be cast to the Server class in order to obtain the same information from the properties of the class like this:

```
oServer = ((Server) oInfoObject);

Console.Write(oServer.FriendlyName );
Console.Write(oServer.ServerName);
```

Each Server object has a ServerGeneralAdmin property that returns a ServerGeneralMetrics object. This object contains information that is common across all servers such as disk space available, CPU information, operating system information, and so on. The downloadable code has a method that will extract all the server information—the common properties as well as those specific to a given server—as XML. As we examine each server, we'll look at the classes specific to each one. The data contained by the ServerGeneralMetrics class is shown by the XML output in Listing 2-2.

Listing 2-2. *ServerGeneralAdmin Class Properties*

```
<CPU>Pentium</CPU>
<CPUCount>2</CPUCount>
<CurrentTime>5/17/2006 2:07:08 PM</CurrentTime>
<StartTime>5/16/2006 10:46:38 PM</StartTime>
<DiskSpaceAvailable>9298358272</DiskSpaceAvailable>
<DiskSpaceTotal>59954065408</DiskSpaceTotal>
<Memory>1047764</Memory>
<OperatingSystem>Windows .NET 5.1</OperatingSystem>
<Version>11.5.0.313</Version>
```

Because each server is very different, and in ways that are more pronounced than individual property settings, the BO XI object model offers a series of classes to encapsulate the main properties. In the following sections, we'll examine each server individually. We'll look at both how to configure the server through the CMC and how to access it programmatically.

Central Management Server

The aptly named Central Management Server (CMS) is the main server in the BO XI collection. Before the rebranding effort, it was known as the Crystal Management Server, and before that as the Automated Process Scheduler (APS). There are still a few active properties that are named for the old APS designation. One of these APS references is found in the ServerKind property of the Server class. The CMS ServerKind designation of the Central Management Server is still "aps".

The CMS handles communication with the RDBMS tables that store the metadata about the BO XI objects. Any commands issued by the SDK to the servers are communicated via the CMS. The CMS also manages the auditing database, should you choose to use one, as well as all schedule and custom events. File events alone are handled by the Event Server. The CMS manages security and controls authentication of all users as well as license management.

Because the Central Management Server is the principal server, it cannot be stopped from within the CMC. You must use the Central Configuration Manager. In a production environment, it's a good idea to disable all servers first so they can finish any pending requests before shutting them down, with the CMS being the last to close. If you're working with a cluster, shutting down one CMS will shift the workload to the other active ones—a feature that allows maintenance without causing downtime.

A CMS cluster consists of two or more CMS servers working in tandem. In mission-critical environments, you'll likely want to set up a cluster to handle failover so that if one server fails, the others will assume the workload without any loss of service. You can install multiple Central Management Servers on the same machine, but to establish proper redundancy they should be set up on separate server boxes.

When setting up a cluster, you need to make sure that each machine has the same version of BO XI with the same service packs and hot fixes applied to all instances. Also, each CMS server should use the same database account and connect to the same database using the same drivers. Ideally, all servers should have the same amount of memory. If you are using auditing, it must be enabled for each CMS server, which should then be connected to the same auditing database.

The CMS caches objects for efficient retrieval. How many objects it does cache is determined by the Windows registry key MaximumObjectsToKeepInMemory found at HKEY_LOCAL_MACHINE\SOFTWARE\Business Objects\Suite 11.5\CMS\Instances\ seton-notebook.cms. The default setting is 10,000, but you can raise this as high as 100,000. The more objects the CMS has in memory, the faster they can be retrieved. Of course, the more memory will be consumed as well. Like many of the server settings, you'll need to experiment to find the happy medium.

The attributes of the CMS are encapsulated in the CmsAdmin class. Once you instantiate a server object, you can instantiate a class that encapsulates its specific attributes by using the ServerAdmin property as a constructor parameter to the specific server class. ServerAdmin exists to provide an interface to a specific server. The instantiation of the CmsAdmin object is shown here:

```
oCmsAdmin = new CmsAdmin(oServer.ServerAdmin);
```

The CmsAdmin class handles the properties and methods specific to the CMS. The code to access the properties of this class is shown in Listing 2-3.

Listing 2-3. *CmsAdmin Class*

```
oCmsAdmin = new CmsAdmin(oServer.ServerAdmin);

Console.Write(oCmsAdmin.APSDatabaseName);
Console.Write(oCmsAdmin.APSDatabaseUserName);
Console.Write(oCmsAdmin.APSDataSourceName);
Console.Write(oCmsAdmin.APSPrivateBuildNumber.ToString());
Console.Write(oCmsAdmin.APSPrivateBuildNumber.ToString());
Console.Write(oCmsAdmin.APSProductVersion);
Console.Write(oCmsAdmin.PendingJobs.ToString());
Console.Write(oCmsAdmin.RunningJobs.ToString());
Console.Write(oCmsAdmin.SuccessJobs.ToString());
Console.Write(oCmsAdmin.WaitingJobs.ToString());
Console.Write(oCmsAdmin.FailedJobs.ToString());
Console.Write(oCmsAdmin.LicensesConcurrent.ToString());
Console.Write(oCmsAdmin.LicensesNamedUsers.ToString());
Console.Write(oCmsAdmin.LicensesProcessors.ToString());
Console.Write(oCmsAdmin.UserConnectedConcurrent.ToString());
Console.Write(oCmsAdmin.UserConnectedNamedUsers.ToString());
Console.Write(oCmsAdmin.UserExistingConcurrent.ToString());
Console.Write(oCmsAdmin.UserExistingNamedUsers.ToString());
Console.Write(oCmsAdmin.UserTokenConnections.ToString());

if (oCmsAdmin.ClusterMembers.Count != 0)
{
    foreach (string szClusterMembers in oCmsAdmin.ClusterMembers)
        Console.Write(szClusterMembers);
}
```

You can see the values for these CMS properties in the XML output shown in Listing 2-4.

Listing 2-4. *CmsAdmin Class Properties*

```
<Server SI_NAME="seton-notebook.cms.aps">
...
   <APSDatabaseName>
   </APSDatabaseName>
   <APSDatabaseUserName>
   </APSDatabaseUserName>
   <APSDataSourceName>CE10</APSDataSourceName>
   <APSPrivateBuildNumber>313</APSPrivateBuildNumber>
   <APSPrivateBuildNumber>313</APSPrivateBuildNumber>
   <APSProductVersion>11.5.0.313</APSProductVersion>
   <PendingJobs>2</PendingJobs>
   <RunningJobs>0</RunningJobs>
   <SuccessJobs>58</SuccessJobs>
   <WaitingJobs>0</WaitingJobs>
   <FailedJobs>16</FailedJobs>
   <LicensesConcurrent>2147483647</LicensesConcurrent>
   <LicensesNamedUsers>2147483647</LicensesNamedUsers>
   <LicensesProcessors>1</LicensesProcessors>
   <UserConnectedConcurrent>2</UserConnectedConcurrent>
   <UserConnectedNamedUsers>0</UserConnectedNamedUsers>
   <UserExistingConcurrent>3</UserExistingConcurrent>
   <UserExistingNamedUsers>4</UserExistingNamedUsers>
   <UserTokenConnections>0</UserTokenConnections>
   <ClusterMembers>
      <ClusterMember>SETON-NOTEBOOK</ClusterMember>
   </ClusterMembers>
  </Server>
```

Normally the data available in the properties of the specific server class is viewable in the CMC. The CMS is an exception.

File Repository Servers

The File Repository servers (FRSs) manage the FileStore directories, which are discussed at the beginning of the chapter. There are two servers involved here: the Output File Repository Server and the Input File Repository Server. Both manage their respective directories and handle all aspects of file management. When, for example, you delete an instance from the report history, the Output File Repository Server deletes the associated files from the FileStore automatically.

▪**Note** Sometimes after a deletion the folder structure is still present in the FileStore even though the associated files have been deleted. This has been a known problem since Crystal Enterprise 9. Make sure you have the latest service packs that will resolve this issue. You'll need to disable the Job Server and add the `-prune` switch to the command line of both FileStore servers. Doing so will make sure that the empty folders are deleted.

Both the Input and Output servers allow you to configure the disk location of the files. Because these servers manage disk files, it important to make sure that sufficient disk space is allocated for storage. Normally the Output server will require more space than the Input server— sometimes several orders of magnitude more. If you have 50 reports scheduled to run each business day, with each report writing a 100-kilobyte file to the Output directory, you're consuming 5 megabytes per day, 100 megabytes per month, and 1.2 gigabytes per year.

It's important not to assign the same root folder to both servers. The configuration for the Output server is shown in Figure 2-9. The Input server has a configuration screen just like it.

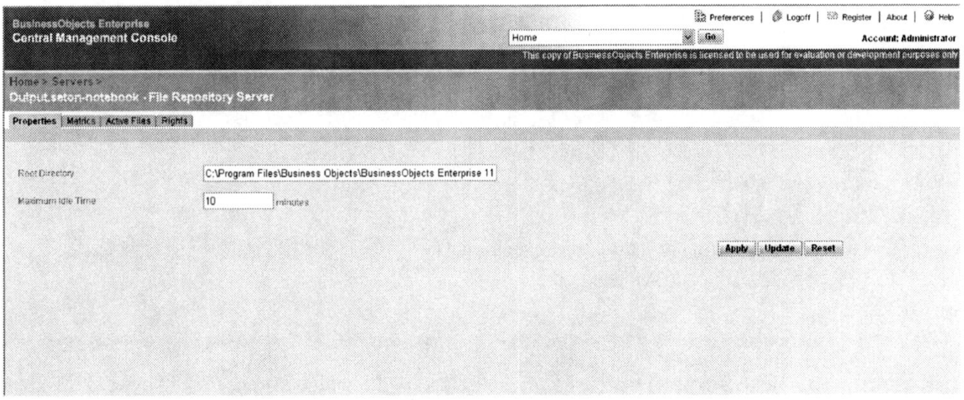

Figure 2-9. *Output Server configuration page*

The Maximum Idle Time setting establishes the amount of time the server will wait before closing any inactive connections. You'll likely want to keep the default setting here. Setting a value too low can prematurely close a user's request. Too high a setting can cause the server to unnecessarily consume system resources and waste processing time and disk space.

The Report Properties page in the CMC allows you to set options for refreshing reports against the original RPT file stored in the Input File Repository Server. *Refreshing reports* refers to saving modified reports from Crystal Reports directly to the InfoStore, the details of which are discussed further in Chapter 4. Here you can indicate what report elements will be updated so as to make it match the incoming RPT file. Where report elements are the same in the source report and the report object, the report refresh settings allow you to control which settings in the report object are updated with values from the version in the Input File Repository Server.

You can set up the File Repository servers as a cluster. If multiple instances of the same type are used, only one can be active at a time. A unique descriptor (SI_SERVER_DESCRIPTOR) is created the first time you start the File Repository servers. This descriptor will look something like this: fileserver.FileSystem.518005620609. Adding another File Repository server will create an entry with a higher numbered descriptor. Regardless of which server is started first, the one with the lower descriptor number will be primary, and the higher numbered one will be secondary.

The File Repository server is accessible programmatically via the FileServerAdmin class shown here:

```
oFileServerAdmin = new FileServerAdmin(oServer.ServerAdmin);
```

Both the Input server and Output server have the same set of properties as shown in the XML output in Listing 2-5.

Listing 2-5. *Output of FileServerAdmin Properties*

```
<Server SI_NAME="Input.seton-notebook.fileserver">
...
    <AvailableDiskPercent>11.2294046486823</AvailableDiskPercent>
    <AvailableDiskSpace>6732484608</AvailableDiskSpace>
    <TotalDiskSpace>59954065408</TotalDiskSpace>
    <BytesSent>0</BytesSent>
    <BytesWritten>0</BytesWritten>
    <ClientConnections>0</ClientConnections>
    <DiskSpaceLeft>6732484608</DiskSpaceLeft>
    <Hostname>seton-notebook</Hostname>
    <MaxIdleTime>10</MaxIdleTime>
    <RootDirectory>C:\Program Files\Business Objects\BusinessObjects Enterprise
    11.5\FileStore\Input\</RootDirectory>
</Server>
```

In addition to these properties, the FileServerAdmin class also contains a ListActiveFiles property, which returns a collection of active files currently in play by the servers. The code in Listing 2-6 shows this method in action.

Listing 2-6. *ListActiveFiles Property*

```
if (oFileServerAdmin.ListActiveFiles.Count > 0)
{
    foreach(FRSAdminFile oFRSAdminFile in oFileServerAdmin.ListActiveFiles)
    {
        Console.Write(oFRSAdminFile.Filename);
        Console.Write(oFRSAdminFile.Readers.ToString());
        Console.Write(oFRSAdminFile.Writers.ToString());
    }

}
```

Event Server

The Event Server is responsible for file events only (the CMS handles scheduled and custom events) and monitors the locations specified for the files to appear. A *file event* is a scheduled process you can set up in the CMC that will trigger only when a file of a given name appears in a given location. For example, a file event may be a prerequisite for permitting a report to run only after the data file that contains the report's daily information is updated to the database. When the file shows up, the Event Server informs the CMS, which then triggers any scheduled jobs that may have dependencies on that file. If possible, you should install the Event Server on the same machine where the monitored files will appear. Figure 2-10 shows the Metrics page of the Event Server where you can see that it is checking for the presence of the goreport.txt file in the c:\temp directory.

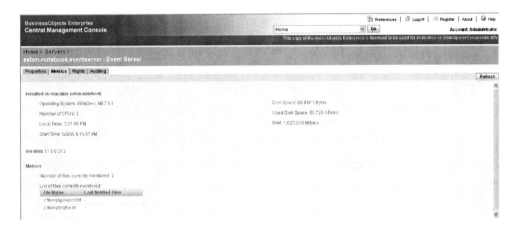

Figure 2-10. *Event Server metrics*

The Properties page allows you to specify the polling interval in seconds. This sets the frequency that the Event Server will check for the existence of the files it is trusted with monitoring.

Programmatic access to the Event Server is encapsulated within the EventServerAdmin class. The properties of this class will return the number of events the server is monitoring, the polling interval, the host name, and the files currently under surveillance along with the last time the CMS was notified of their existence. Listing 2-7 shows the EventServerAdmin properties.

Listing 2-7. *EventServerAdmin Class*

```
oEventServerAdmin = new EventServerAdmin(oServer.ServerAdmin);

Console.Write(oEventServerAdmin.Events.ToString());
Console.Write(oEventServerAdmin.FilePollTime.ToString());
Console.Write(oEventServerAdmin.Hostname);

if (oEventServerAdmin.ListFileMonitored.Count > 0)
{
    foreach (EventServerAdminFile oEventServerAdminFile in
        EventServerAdmin.ListFileMonitored)
        Console.Write(oEventServerAdminFile.Filename);
        Console.Write(oEventServerAdminFile.LastNotifiedTime.ToString());
}
```

A sample of the XML output of the EventServerAdmin class properties is shown in Listing 2-8.

Listing 2-8. *XML Output of EventServerAdmin Class*

```
<Server SI_NAME="seton-notebook.eventserver.eventserver">
    ...
    <Events>2</Events>
    <FilePollTime>2</FilePollTime>
    <Hostname>seton-notebook</Hostname>
    <MonitoredFiles>
        <Filename LastNotifiedTime="12/30/1899 12:00:00 AM">
        c:\temp\goreport.txt</Filename>
        <Filename LastNotifiedTime="12/30/1899 12:00:00 AM">
        c:\temp\myfile.txt</Filename>
    </MonitoredFiles>
</Server>
```

Sometimes the events will not trigger when the monitored file appears on a network drive. Usually this is because the server is running as the default "Local System" account. You can determine this by opening the Central Configuration Manager and right-clicking the Event Server name, selecting Properties from the pop-up menu, and examining the first tab as shown in Figure 2-11.

Figure 2-11. *Event Server Properties tab*

To resolve this, change the logon information to a domain account that has read access to the designated file share.

Page Server

The Page Server works in tandem with the Cache Server to process reports and respond to page requests by producing Encapsulated Page Format (EPF) pages. Each EPF file represents one page of a Crystal report. When a report is run, the Cache Server checks whether the pages necessary for the report already exist in the cache. If not, it requests them from the Page Server, which produces them as needed. The Page Server retrieves the report data from the data source and handles the necessary connections and disconnects as additional data is required. This process is illustrated in Figure 2-12.

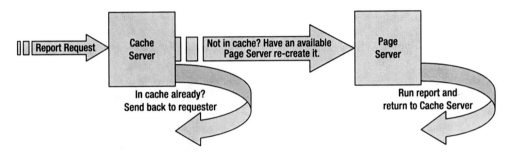

Figure 2-12. *Page Server process flow*

When the Page Server runs, it creates individual subprocesses, each of which load the Crystal Reports Print Engine (CRPE). These subprocesses in turn spawn threads that run report jobs. If a report job fails for any reason, only the threads within that particular subprocess are affected. Periodically, these subprocesses are shut down and new ones created so as to make most efficient use of resources. Starting with BO XI, the Page Server detects the number of processors on the server it is installed upon and scales itself accordingly. Page Servers work their best when they have an entire server dedicated to them.

The Properties page of the Page Server (shown in Figure 2-13) allows you to manage the various server settings. The Location of Temp Files option needs to be any directory with sufficient hard disk space available to handle the temporary files the server will need to create. Since this amount varies from installation to installation, it's helpful to monitor this location to make sure the limitations are not being reached.

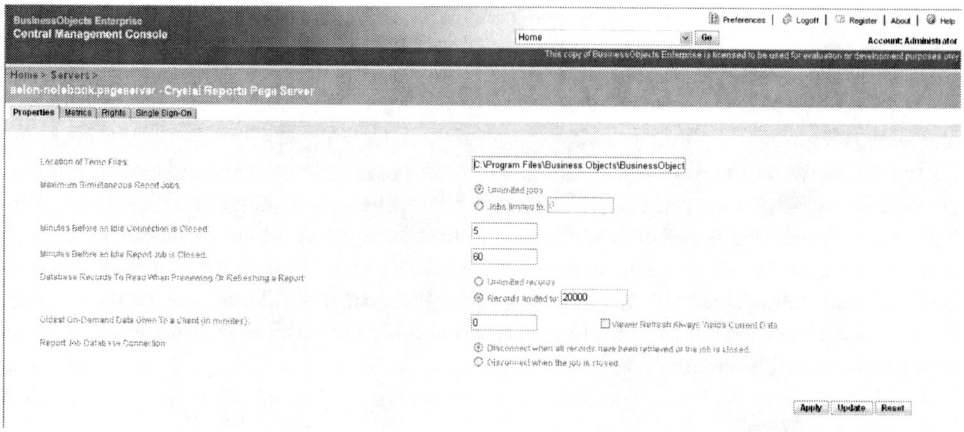

Figure 2-13. *Page Server properties*

The Maximum Simultaneous Report Jobs setting establishes the limit of the number of simultaneous reporting requests that any single Page Server may process. The default setting is unlimited.

The Minutes Before an Idle Connection is Closed setting limits the time the Page Server must wait for additional requests from an idle connection before closing it. Likewise, the Minutes Before an Idle Report Job is Closed setting establishes the length of time that the Page Server maintains a report job before closing it.

The Database Records to Read When Previewing Or Refreshing a Report option allows you to restrict the number of rows that the server retrieves when a user runs a query or report. This setting comes in handy when you wish to prevent users from performing on-demand reporting that contains queries that return large record sets. Since the Page Server is not involved in scheduled reports, you may prefer to schedule more data-intensive reports off-hours instead of allowing them to be run on demand during the course of the business day. If you expect a lot of on-demand reporting, you may want to install Page Servers on additional server boxes to allow for load balancing.

Ideally, there should only be one Page Server per machine, as they are designed for processor optimization on a machine-by-machine basis, and more than one on the same box would create a competition for resources that would thwart this optimization. This is where the Page Server differs in responsibility from the job servers. The Page Server is designed to handle a large number of smaller reports, whereas the job servers handle a smaller number of larger, more data-intensive reports. The former are usually run-on-demand, whereas the latter are scheduled.

■**Note** When a report is viewed with the Advanced DHTML viewer, the report is processed by the Report Application Server rather than the Page Server and the Cache Server.

The Oldest On-Demand Data Given To a Client setting determines how many minutes old previously retrieved data can be for it to be considered current by the Page Server. One of the key features of any report server like BO XI is the ability to know when more than one user requested the same data within a specified time period. If the Page Server receives a request that can be fulfilled using cached pages, and this data is not older than the setting in this property, these cached pages will be used to fulfill the request.

The setting on this value depends on how timely the report data needs to be. If you're dealing with rather static data that is updated only once a day, you could set this value relatively high. If you're dealing with a securities quote system, for example, you'll want to set this value to zero, as any data returned is obsolete as soon as it is presented to the user. You can override this setting by checking the Viewer Refresh Always Yields Current Data check box. This setting tells the Page Server to always pull reports data from the database and assume all existing report output is immediately obsolete.

The Report Job Database Connection option allows you to optimize your database connectivity. When a report is run, it needs to connect to the database to retrieve information. Sometimes, it needs to retrieve this information in stages by reading a chunk of data, processing the first report pages and sending them to the client, and then reading more data before processing additional pages while the user is reading the initial pages just sent. This setting will allow you to minimize database connectivity time, which is helpful when you have limited database licenses, so that the server connects to the database only before it retrieves a chunk of data and then disconnects again. Choosing this setting will slow performance, as the act of connecting to a data source is a resource-consuming process, but it may help you in these limited-license situations.

Note Because the Page Server accesses the database, you'll need to make sure that all native drivers and all OBDC connection entries are installed on the same machine as the Page Server. This is true of the Job Server as well.

The Page Server is encapsulated by the PageServerAdmin class as shown here:

```
oPageServerAdmin = new PageServerAdmin(oServer.ServerAdmin);
```

The XML output of the properties unique to this class is shown in Listing 2-9.

Listing 2-9. *PageServerAdmin Properties*

```
<Server SI_NAME="seton-notebook.pageserver.pageserver">
    ...
    <BytesTransferred>0</BytesTransferred>
    <Connections>0</Connections>
    <Directory>C:\Program Files\Business Objects\BusinessObjects
Enterprise 11.5\Data\seton-notebook.pageserver\</Directory>
    <MaxIdleTime>5</MaxIdleTime>
    <MaxIdleTimeUpdate>5</MaxIdleTimeUpdate>
    <MaxThreads>50</MaxThreads>
    <Threads>0</Threads>
    <QueuedRequests>0</QueuedRequests>
    <TotalRequests>0</TotalRequests>
</Server>
```

Job Servers

A look at the Server management page depicted in Figure 2-5 shows that there are a number of servers with "job server" in the title. A job server runs a scheduled action on an object at the behest of the CMS. There are different job servers for the different types of objects.

A Report Job Server executes scheduled actions on the reports registered in the CMC and produces the report instances. This server is responsible for opening the RPT template in the Input FRS, pulling the report data from the data source, and placing the output in the OutPut section of the FileStore as a report instance. There are also job servers for the BusinessObjects Web Intelligence and Desktop Intelligence reports, which work in a similar fashion.

The Program Job Server manages executable code such as EXE and Java applications stored in the CMC. The Destination Job Server handles instances stored in the FileStore. It sends these objects to the possible targets allowed by BO XI—unmanaged disk file, the Inbox, an FTP server, or an SMTP mail address. A List of Values Job Server processes the data used for dynamic prompts.

Job servers do not run as threads. Rather, each job server executes as an independent process. You can control this setting via the Properties page shown in Figure 2-14.

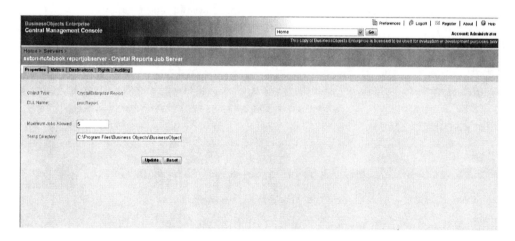

Figure 2-14. *Job Server Properties page*

Here, the Maximum Jobs Allowed setting sets the number of scheduled reports a job server can execute simultaneously as separate processes.

Programmatic access to the Job Server is available through the JobServerAdmin class as shown here:

```
oJobServerAdmin = new JobServerAdmin(oServer.ServerAdmin);
```

The properties of this class are shown in the XML output in Listing 2-10.

Listing 2-10. *JobServerAdmin Properties*

```
<Server SI_NAME="seton-notebook.Desktop_IntelligenceJobServer.jobserver">
    ...
    <CurrentJobs>0</CurrentJobs>
    <DLLName>pp_procFC</DLLName>
    <FailedCreated>0</FailedCreated>
    <MaxJobs>5</MaxJobs>
    <ObjectTypeName>CrystalEnterprise.FullClient</ObjectTypeName>
    <ProcType>3</ProcType>
    <TempDir>C:\Program Files\Business Objects\BusinessObjects Enterprise
    11.5\Data\procSched\seton-notebook.Desktop_IntelligenceJobServer</TempDir>
    <TotalJobs>0</TotalJobs>
    <SupportedDestination>
        <Name Enabled="False">CrystalEnterprise.DiskUnmanaged</Name>
        <Name Enabled="False">CrystalEnterprise.Ftp</Name>
        <Name Enabled="True">CrystalEnterprise.Managed</Name>
        <Name Enabled="False">CrystalEnterprise.Smtp</Name>
    </SupportedDestination>
</Server>
```

The supported destinations tag shows those destinations that are active for the Job Server. When you schedule a report to a destination like a disk file or FTP server, you may receive errors when the report runs. One of the issues that could cause these errors is that the destination is not active for the server. The code in Listing 2-11 shows how to use the Destinations property to determine which destinations are active.

Listing 2-11. *Iterating Job Server Destinations*

```
if (oJobServerAdmin.Destinations.Count > 0)
{
    foreach(JobServerDestination oJobServerDestination in
        oJobServerAdmin.Destinations)
        Console.Write(oJobServerDestination.Name);
        Console.Write(oJobServerDestination.Enabled.ToString());
}
```

These destinations can be activated via the Destinations page shown in Figure 2-15. Each destination name is a hyperlink that allows you to establish default settings particular to the destination. The SMTP mail option, for example, will accept an e-mail address, a message, a subject line, etc.

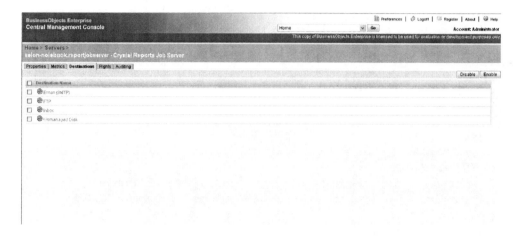

Figure 2-15. *Job Server Destinations page*

When you use the CMC to configure the destination settings for an individual report, the configuration page will offer you the option of using the Job Server settings or entering override settings specific to that report.

Cache Server

The Cache Server facilitates efficient delivery of reports. When a report request comes in, the Cache Server checks whether the request can be fulfilled with pages already in the cache. If one user requests a report with a set of parameters and then within a specified time frame a second request for the same report with the same parameters arrives, the Cache Server will retrieve the previously run report and send it to the client without needing to create it anew from the data source. Should the Cache Server be unable to fulfill the request, it informs the Page Server, which will re-create the report and send it back to the Cache Server. The Cache Server then passes it on to the requester. The Cache Server manages the Page Servers in this respect. This workflow is depicted in Figure 2-12.

As requests are passed along, the Cache Server performs load balancing by distributing the responsibilities proportionally among the multiple Page Servers. Neither the Cache Server nor the Page Server are employed, or needed, in the creation of scheduled reports. Their services are only needed for on-demand reports.

■**Note** Reports that are run through the Report Application Server (RAS) do not use the Cache Server, as the RAS has its own internal caching technology.

The Properties page, shown in Figure 2-16, allows you to manage the attributes of the Cache Server.

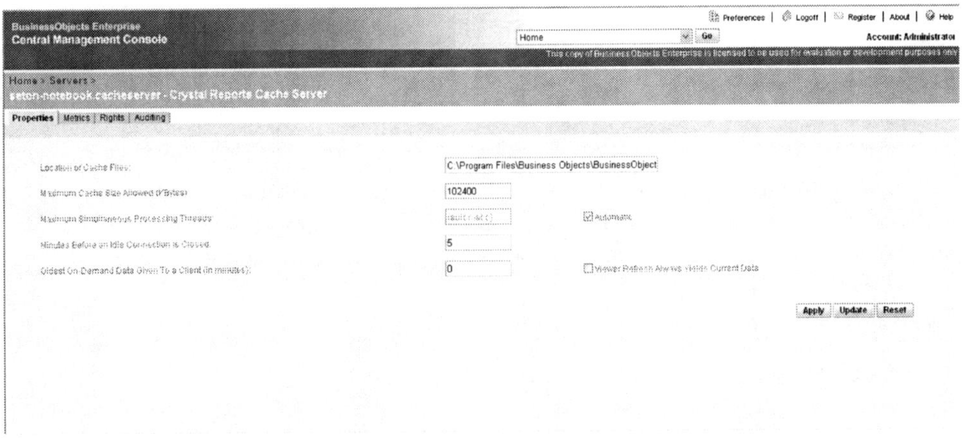

Figure 2-16. *Cache Server properties*

The Cache File Location refers to the directory where the EPF files will be stored. EPF file sizes vary depending on the report page they represent, so it's difficult to determine an average. Fortunately disk space is very cheap today, so make sure you allocate sufficient space. The default cache size is over 100 megabytes.

The Cache Server is handled by the CacheServerAdmin class as shown here:

```
oCacheServerAdmin = new CacheServerAdmin(oServer.ServerAdmin);
```

The output of the properties of this class is shown in Listing 2-12.

Listing 2-12. *CacheServerAdmin Class Properties*

```
<Server SI_NAME="seton-notebook.cacheserver.cacheserver">
    ...
    <BytesTransferred>0</BytesTransferred>
    <CacheSize>102400</CacheSize>
    <CacheSizeUpdate>102400</CacheSizeUpdate>
    <Connections>0</Connections>
    <Directory>C:\Program Files\Business Objects\BusinessObjects
    Enterprise 11.5\Data\seton-notebook.cacheserver\</Directory>
    <DriveSpaceUsed>0</DriveSpaceUsed>
    <HitRate>0</HitRate>
    <MaxIdleTime>5</MaxIdleTime>
    <MaxIdleTimeUpdate>5</MaxIdleTimeUpdate>
    <MaxThreads>0</MaxThreads>
    <QueuedRequests>0</QueuedRequests>
    <Refresh>0</Refresh>
    <RefreshAlwaysHitsDb>False</RefreshAlwaysHitsDb>
```

```
<Threads>21</Threads>
<TotalRequests>0</TotalRequests>
<PageServerConnections>
    <ServerName Connections="0">com.seagatesoftware.img.osca.pageserver.
"seton-notebook"-seton-notebook.pageserver</ServerName>
  </PageServerConnections>
</Server>
```

This class contains a PageServerConnection property that returns a collection of PageServerConnection objects. A PageServerConnection object encapsulates connections between a Cache Server to a Page Server. The code in Listing 2-13 shows how to access these objects.

Listing 2-13. *Iterating the PageServerConnections Collection*

```
if (oCacheServerAdmin.PageServerConnection.Count > 0)
{
    foreach(PageServerConnection oPageServerConnection in
        oCacheServerAdmin.PageServerConnection)

    Console.Write(oPageServerConnection.ServerName);
    Console.Write(oPageServerConnection.Connections.ToString());
}
```

You can see much of the same information in the Cache Server metrics page shown in Figure 2-17.

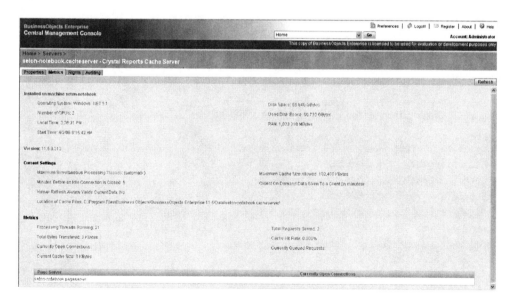

Figure 2-17. *Cache Server metrics*

Report Application Server

The Report Application Server (RAS) has multiple responsibilities. It allows you to create and modify reports at runtime using the RAS object model, a process to which Chapter 8 is dedicated. The RAS maintains its own cache and does not interact with the Cache Server. It also assumes the responsibilities of the Page Server by generating its own EPF pages. The RAS also processes reports that are viewed by the Advanced DHTML viewer.

The RAS has two sets of settings—Database and Server. The Database settings page is shown in Figure 2-18.

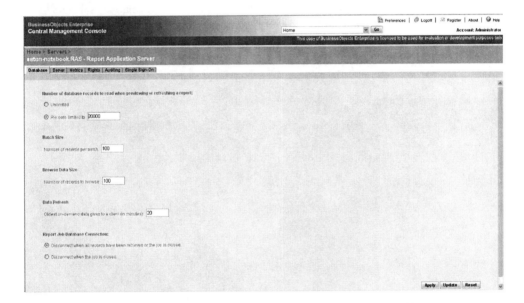

Figure 2-18. *Report Application Server Database settings*

Here you can set limitations on the number of records when extracting data from the RDBMS. The "Number of database records to read when previewing or refreshing a report" setting puts a ceiling on the number of rows that can be returned from the database in total. The default setting is 20,000. Assuming 50 rows of data per page, this still creates up to a 400-page report. Record extraction is managed in batches. You can also set the number of records in each batch that is returned.

The "Number of records to browse" setting allows you to establish the number of distinct records to browse when viewing a field's data. The RAS will look first to client's cache, then to the server's cache. If the requested data is in neither location, it is extracted from the data source.

Since the RAS must act as its own Page Server, it has the Oldest On-Demand Data Given To a Client and Report Job Database Connection Page Server settings. One of the key features of any report server like BO XI is the ability to know when more than one user requested the same data within a specified time period. If the RAS receives a request that can be fulfilled using data that was previously generated, and this data is not older than the setting in this property, this data will be used to fulfill the request.

The setting on this value depends on how timely the report data needs to be. If you're dealing with report data that is updated daily, you could set this value relatively high. If you're dealing with a securities quote system, you want to set this value to zero, as any data returned is obsolete as soon as it is presented to the user.

The Report Job Database Connection option allows you to optimize your database connectivity. When a report is run, it needs to connect to the database to retrieve information. Sometimes, it needs to retrieve this information in stages by reading a chunk of data, processing the first report pages and sending them to the client, and then reading more data before processing additional pages while the user is reading the initial pages just sent. This setting will allow you to minimize database connectivity time, which is helpful when you have limited database licenses, so that the server will connect to the database only before it retrieves a chunk of data and then disconnect again. Choosing this setting will slow performance as the act of connecting to a data source is a resource-consuming process, but it may help you in these limited license situations.

The Server pages settings shown in Figure 2-19 also permits you to set the number of minutes before an idle connection is closed and the number of simultaneous report jobs.

Figure 2-19. *Report Application Server settings*

The RAS is accessible programmatically by the `ReportAppServerAdmin` class. You can instantiate the class like this:

```
oReportAppServerAdmin = new ReportAppServerAdmin(oServer.ServerAdmin);
```

The properties of this class are shown in Listing 2-14.

Listing 2-14. *RAS Properties*

```
<Server SI_NAME="seton-notebook.RAS.rptappserver">
    ...
    <AgentTimeout>30</AgentTimeout>
    <AutomaticDBDisconnect>True</AutomaticDBDisconnect>
    <CurrentAgentCount>1</CurrentAgentCount>
    <CurrentDocumentCount>0</CurrentDocumentCount>
    <EnableAsyncQuery>False</EnableAsyncQuery>
    <EnablePushDownGroupBy>False</EnablePushDownGroupBy>
    <EnableSelectDistinctRecords>False</EnableSelectDistinctRecords>
    <MaxNumOfRecords>20000</MaxNumOfRecords>
    <MaxReportJobs>75</MaxReportJobs>
    <MinutesBetweenDBRefresh>20</MinutesBetweenDBRefresh>
    <NumOfBrowsingRecords>100</NumOfBrowsingRecords>
    <RowsetBatchSize>100</RowsetBatchSize>
    <TotalAgentCount>1</TotalAgentCount>
    <TotalDocumentCount>0</TotalDocumentCount>
</Server>
```

Server Groups

Server groups allow you to create collections of servers to manage them for different purposes. As you've seen in the preceding sections, servers can be configured with different options for different situations. Take, for instance, the Oldest On-Demand Data Given To a Client setting of the Page Server. If you have reports that run off a data source that is updated daily, setting this value high will work fine and allow the server to reuse report pages already generated to fulfill previous requests. Of course, this wouldn't work for a securities quote system where the data is immediately obsolete. But what if you need to support both types of reports in your BO XI installation? This is where a server group would come in handy. You could install two Page Servers. One has the Oldest On-Demand Data Given To a Client set rather high, while the other marks pages instantly obsolete. Then, you can create two server groups, each one with its own Page Server.

You can create a server group by selecting this option from the main menu. Then, click the New Server Group button, and you will be prompted to enter the name of the group and an optional description. Select the Servers tab to see the servers that are associated with this group. Clicking the Add/Remove Servers button will present you with the screen shown in Figure 2-20.

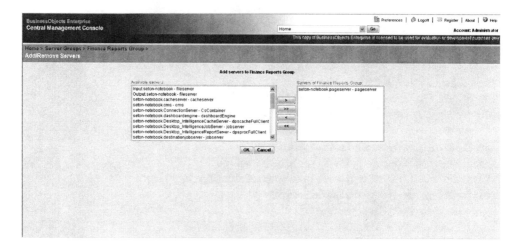

Figure 2-20. *Add/Remove Servers page*

To make sure a report will run on a designated server group, select the report template in the CMC and navigate to the Process tab shown in Figure 2-21.

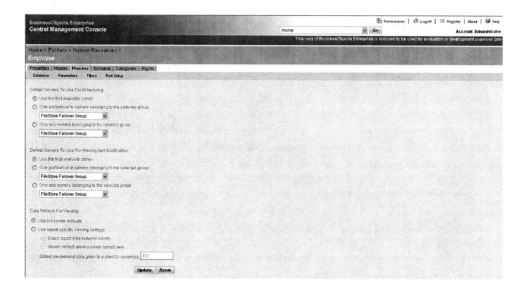

Figure 2-21. *Report Process tab*

Here you can assign the servers to be used for both scheduling and viewing. For both tasks, you can indicate whether the report should run on the first available server, give preference to servers in a designated server group, or run only on the servers in a designated group.

The BusinessObjects XI SDK gives you the ability to create server groups, add servers to them, and retrieve the members of a server group. Though you would likely only create such a front end if you were developing a third-party tool for BO XI, you'll see how to accomplish this in the next sections.

Creating a Server Group

Creating a server group is simple and is very similar to creating any other object type in the InfoStore. The code to create a group is shown in Listing 2-15.

Listing 2-15. *Creating a Server Group*

```
//Connect to BO XI

oInfoObjects = oInfoStore.NewInfoObjectCollection();

oPluginManager = oInfoStore.PluginManager;
oPluginInfo = oPluginManager.GetPluginInfo("ServerGroup");
oInfoObject = oInfoObjects.Add(oPluginInfo);
oServerGroup = ((ServerGroup) oInfoObject);

oServerGroup.Title = szServerGroupName;

oInfoStore.Commit(oInfoObjects);
```

After connecting to BO XI, we'll need to instantiate an empty InfoObjects collection by invoking the NewInfoObjectCollection() method of the InfoStore object. From the PluginManager object extract the plug-in for the type ServerGroup and add it to the InfoObjects collection so as to obtain an InfoObject that will reference the newly added group. Next, cast this InfoObject to a ServerGroup object type, and you're ready to assign a group name. Now that the group is set up, commit it to the InfoStore using the Commit() method and the new group is created.

Adding Servers to a Server Group

Once a server group is created, adding a server to it is also a simple process. The code in Listing 2-16 extracts a user group reference by its SI_ID value and adds a named server to it.

Listing 2-16. *Adding a Server to a Group*

```
szSQL = "SELECT SI_ID " +
    "FROM CI_SYSTEMOBJECTS " +
    "WHERE SI_ID = " + iServerGroupID.ToString();

oInfoObjects = oInfoStore.Query(szSQL);
oInfoObject = oInfoObjects[1];

oServerGroup = ((ServerGroup) oInfoObject);

szServerName = "seton-notebook.pageserver.pageserver";

oServerGroup.Servers.Add(szServerName);

oInfoStore.Commit(oInfoObjects);
```

Like all additions to or changes in the InfoStore, the Commit() method will save them.

Extracting the Servers in a Group

The names of the individual servers that comprise a server group can be found by extracting the SI_GROUP_MEMBERS property from the InfoStore. The code to extract the servers in a group is shown in Listing 2-17.

Listing 2-17. *Extracting the Members of a Server Group*

```
//Extract a server group object
szSQL = "SELECT SI_GROUP_MEMBERS " +
    "FROM CI_SYSTEMOBJECTS " +
    "WHERE SI_ID = " + szServerGroupID;

oInfoObjects = oInfoStore.Query(szSQL);

oDT = new DataTable();

oDT.Columns.Add(new DataColumn("Name"));

//Set a property bag reference so the code's not so long
oProperty = oInfoObjects[1].Properties["SI_GROUP_MEMBERS"];

//How many members does the group have?
iCnt = ((int) oProperty.Properties["SI_TOTAL"].Value);

//The names start with the second property as the SI_TOTAL value
//occupies the first property entry
for (int x = 2; x <= iCnt + 1; x++)
{
    oDR = oDT.NewRow();

    //Assign the server's information to the DataTable
    oDR["Name"] = oProperty.Properties[x].Value;

    oDT.Rows.Add(oDR);
}
```

By extracting all the group members, we can iterate through the members list and add the names of each server to the DataTable. The first property that is returned is called SI_GROUP_MEMBERS and lists the number of items in the collection.

The Auditing Database

BusinessObjects XI comes with a separate auditing package that allows you to track specific metrics about your servers and objects. You can enable auditing for individual servers and objects by turning it on selectively. Most of the servers have an Auditing page where you can specify the location of the audit log files (the default is C:\Program Files\Business Objects\ BusinessObjects Enterprise 11.5\Auditing\) as well as what aspects of the server you want recorded. The RAS, for example, uses the auditing page shown in Figure 2-22.

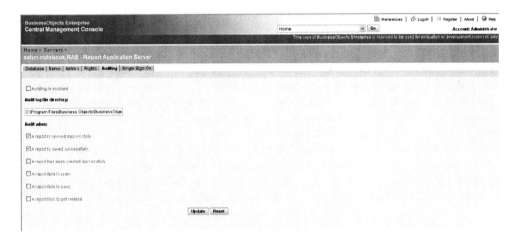

Figure 2-22. *RAS Auditing page*

Here you may determine whether auditing is even enabled for this server and if so, what actions are to be recorded. For reports, you can enable auditing from the Notification option of the Schedule tab. An audit record can be written both when a report succeeds and fails. The auditing data is written to a text file in the indicated directory and, periodically, these files are written to the auditing tables in the RDBMS. These tables are not part of the initial install unless you specifically choose to install auditing with BO XI. It is from these tables that the canned auditing reports that ship with BO XI derive their information.

The auditor allows you to record who logged into and out of the system and change their passwords, what reports they ran whether successful or unsuccessful, and what events were added, modified, deleted, or triggered, among other metrics.

Scalability

If you live a mile or two from work and don't drive much on weekends, a $300,000 Lamborghini Diablo probably wouldn't be a wise investment. Still, I've seen companies install a Lamborghini-level version of BO XI when their reporting needs could be handled by a Hyundai version of the tool. Too large a BO XI license can cost significantly more than a Lamborghini Diablo (and it won't help you pick up girls, either), so proper planning for scalability needs is vital in making a cost-efficient licensing decision.

BO XI is designed to be almost infinitely scalable. Since the product is comprised of multiple logical servers, you can install them all on one physical server, install them across several physical servers, or install multiple sets of logical servers across multiple physical servers. Technical support uses a 64-node cluster in their testing lab, and they have informed me of one customer who runs a BO XI installation across 23 globally distributed servers managed from a single CMS. Though there is no physical limit to this product, eventually there will be a performance hit on a massive installation from all the messages that need to pass back and forth between the various servers to keep them in sync.

Business Objects offers a series of recommended formulas you can use to determine the load on your BO XI installation based on the number of users, the number of reports, and the frequency that those users will hit those reports. You can read more about these estimation techniques by downloading the bo_xi_sizing_recommendations.pdf document from their web site.

Testing and quality assurance can also become an issue when your deployment is scaled across multiple servers. Ideally, your QA or UAT configuration will be the same as that of production. Sometimes elusive bugs can appear on a multiple server deployment that will not manifest themselves on a single-server installation. One example I experienced recently was a report that was installed on a production server where the Page Server was scaled across two machines. The report used a .NET assembly as its data source. When we tested the report by selecting Run Now on the CMC's report history page, the report failed every other time. On our development machines it always worked. The reason was that the CMC ordered the Page Servers to alternate report execution between machines. The first server had the .NET data access assembly installed on it and the second server did not. This explained the erratic behavior and is a prime example of how a distributed installation can make a difference.

Backups and Disaster Recovery

Creating backups to your BO XI installation requires consideration of several sets of data. There's the CMS system database that is installed into your existing RDBMS when BO XI is installed, an auditing database should you choose to use one, and the disk files that make up the Input and Output areas of the File Repository server. In addition, should you choose to store metadata related to your BO XI objects as discussed in Chapter 9, you'll need to make sure that data is backed up as well.

If your system is not mission critical and does not need to be online constantly, executing a backup is much easier. First, you'll need to disable your servers to permit them to complete any pending jobs. Disabling keeps them from accepting any new requests. Then, once all pending jobs are complete, you can shut down the servers completely and run a backup of both the RDBMS and FileStore information. This will keep all your data in sync so that if a restore from the backup becomes necessary, the RDBMS information will match the FileStore and vice versa. All of this can be scheduled off-hours so few, if any, users are affected. Probably the hardest part of doing this synchronized backup is cutting through the corporate bureaucracy to get both data sets backed up at once.

Should you need to support a system that cannot permit any downtime, things get a little trickier. You could set up your BO XI servers to write to redundant SANs in separate data centers. If the latency period between them is less than ten milliseconds, the chance of there being data out of sync between them is very much remote. Nevertheless, it's still possible that one of two scenarios would occur. If the repository transaction completes before the file transaction, this will result in an entry in the InfoStore that does not have a corresponding entry in the FileStore. The entry will be visible in the CMC but will generate an error when the file is viewed.

This problem is easy to solve, as you can copy the missing file into the FileStore location and everything will return to normal function. The other scenario happens when the opposite occurs. If the repository transaction completes after the file transaction succeeds, then you'll end up with a FileStore entry with no corresponding entry in the InfoStore. This causes a bigger problem, as you won't be able to make an entry into the InfoStore to restore the relationship.

BusinessObjects does not have an integrity checker that reconciles the InfoStore and the File-Store to determine an out-of-sync situation. At this time there is no solution for this problem, but this is expected to be addressed in a future version of the product.

Summary

This chapter covered the various BO XI servers and how to access them programmatically. We discussed the difference between the InfoStore and FileStore and the tasks and responsibilities of the individual servers that together comprise a BusinessObjects XI deployment. We also looked at scalability issues, backup issues, and server groups. Coming up, we'll look at the tools and utilities needed to manage your BusinessObjects XI installation.

CHAPTER 3

▪▪▪

Administration Tools

BusinessObjects XI offers a set of administration tools that allow you to manage your deployment. These tools offer a visual interface to your reports, report instances, schedules, and servers. Some of these tools, such as the Central Management Console and InfoView, are front ends to the InfoStore and FileStore, and their functionality can largely be replicated by using the SDK. Other tools such as the Import Wizard are utilities designed for a very narrow purpose (such as the BusinessObjects XI migration example listed later in this chapter), and their functionality is not intended to be replicated programmatically. In this chapter, we'll examine these tools and utilities, and you'll learn how you can leverage them in your daily administrative responsibilities.

Central Configuration Manager

The Central Configuration Manager (CCM) is the user interface for the Windows services that collectively comprise BusinessObjects XI. From this interface you can start, restart, and stop the services, as well as add, delete, enable, and disable servers. The CCM display is shown in Figure 3-1.

Display Name	Version	Status	Description
AA Alert & Notification Server	11.5.3.417	Running	Provides Alerting services
AA Analytics Server	11.5.3.417	Running	Provides analytic processing, rendering and transformation services
AA Dashboard Server	11.5.3.417	Running	Provides dashboard management services
AA Individual Profiler Server	11.5.3.417	Running	Provides individual analytic services
AA Metric Aggregation Server	11.5.3.417	Running	Provides metrics services
AA Predictive Analytic Server	11.5.3.417	Running	Provides predictive analytics services
AA Repository Management Server	11.5.3.417	Running	Provides AF repository services
AA Set Analyzer Server	11.5.3.417	Running	Provides set analytic services
AA Statistical Process Control Server	11.5.3.417	Running	Provides process control analytic services
Central Management Server	11.5.0.313	Running	Provides scheduling, security, and system management services.
Connection Server	11.5.3.417	Running	Connection Server
Crystal Reports Cache Server	11.5.3.417	Running	Stores report pages frequently requested by report viewers.
Crystal Reports Job Server	11.5.3.417	Running	Handles off-loaded processing of Crystal Reports documents.
Crystal Reports Page Server	11.5.3.417	Running	Generates report pages requested by report viewers.
Desktop Intelligence Cache Server	11.5.3.417	Running	Desktop Intelligence Cache Server
Desktop Intelligence Job Server	11.5.0.313	Running	Handles off-loaded processing of Desktop Intelligence documents.
Desktop Intelligence Report Server	11.5.3.417	Running	Desktop Intelligence Report Server
Destination Job Server	11.5.0.313	Running	Processes destination objects

Figure 3-1. *Central Configuration Manager*

By selecting any one server in the CCM, you view and set the properties that are managed on the tabbed dialog shown later in Figure 3-2. In order to edit any of these properties you'll need to stop the server. Though this example uses the Central Management Server, most of the tabs in this dialog are common across servers.

Each server has a series of settings. Should you ever wish to make a backup of these settings or send them to technical support, you can do so by selecting one or more servers in the CCM and clicking the Copy button on the toolbar. Doing so will produce output similar to that shown here:

```
1) Display Name: BOBJCentralMS
   Server Display Name: Central Management Server
   Version: 11.5.0.313
   Command Line: "\\seton-notebook\C$\Program Files\Business Objects\
   BusinessObjects Enterprise 11.5\win32_x86\CMS.exe"
   -service -name seton-notebook.cms  -restart -noauditor
   Status: Stopped
   Description: Provides scheduling, security, and system management services.
   Dependency: EventLog, Tcpip, RpcSs, NtLmSsp
   CMS Data Source: BusinessObjectsXI
   CMS belongs to cluster: SETON-NOTEBOOK
```

■**Note** Since each server runs as a Windows service, the problems usually associated with Windows services often manifest themselves. The main problem arises when the service stops running, commonly caused when the server reboots and the service fails to start automatically. Since this situation can completely or partially paralyze your BO XI installation, it makes sense to continually monitor your Windows services to ensure they are still running. One way to do this is with another Windows service that periodically checks the different BO XI services to see if all is well. This BO XI monitoring service is discussed in Chapter 9.

Properties Tab

This Central Management Server Properties dialog, shown in Figure 3-2, displays the server type and display name (which you can't edit) as well as the server name (which you shouldn't edit, as BusinessObjects determines the name during the installation).

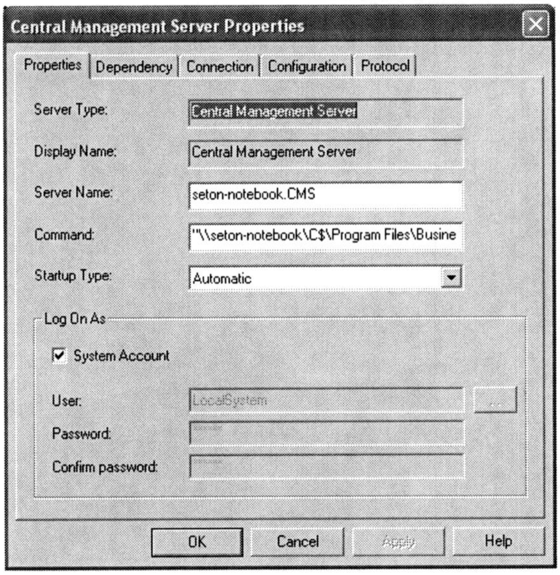

Figure 3-2. *Central Management Server Properties tab*

The only properties you may edit are the Command property, the Startup Type, and the Log On As properties. On the instructions of technical support, you may add a -trace switch to the command line, which will write out log files tracking server activity. This command-line switch and its caveats are covered in detail in Chapter 2. Otherwise, the command line should be left alone.

The Startup Type offers three options—Automatic, Disabled, and Manual. The default is set to Automatic, as the BO XI servers all need to be up and running in order for their different features to work properly or work at all. You may wish to set this to Manual on your development machine depending on how often you'll need to keep the servers running and consuming resources.

The Log On As property defaults to the local system account. This account sets the permissions of the service on the local machine, not on the network. The main reason for changing this is that the processing servers may require specific permissions or a specific user account to access the BO XI InfoStore database.

Dependency Tab

The Dependency tab lists the services upon which the selected server is dependent. All BO XI servers rely on the Event Log, NT LM Security Support Provider, and Remote Procedure Call (RPC) services, and these are set for you by default. If you wish, you can add additional dependencies as well by clicking the Add button shown in Figure 3-3. You may wish, for example, to make the MSSQLSERVER service a prerequisite for starting certain servers that will need to use it.

Figure 3-3. *Dependency tab*

Connection Tab

The Connection tab allows you to set SOCKS proxy servers for your firewall. *SOCKS* is a networking protocol that enables machines on different sides of a SOCKS server to communicate with one another without requiring a direct IP connection. Support for SOCKS servers is in the process of being deprecated in BO XI and eventually will not be supported in future releases of the product. It does exist in BO XI, and may exist in the next version, only for backward compatibility. You'll need to plan for another firewall in the future.

Note It is Business Objects's policy to provide at least two versions' notice for a feature to be completely deprecated. Thus, once a feature is declared deprecated, it will be supported in two versions of the tool beyond the one currently available. This should give you at least a few years' notice so you have time to rework any code dependent on these features.

Configuration Tab

The Configuration tab, shown in Figure 3-4, offers a set of options unique to the server you are working with. For the CMS, it allows you to manage the port number of back-end database connectivity for the InfoStore data. Note that the data source named here is called CE10. The reason is that the computer upon which BO XI was installed was a Crystal Enterprise 10 server. The upgrade respected the former name of the existing InfoStore. When BO XI installs, it reserves port numbers 6400 through 6410 for its own purposes. The default port for the CMS is 6400, and you'll see this when you reference the system name during a log on, which will look something like this: SETON-NOTEBOOK:6400.

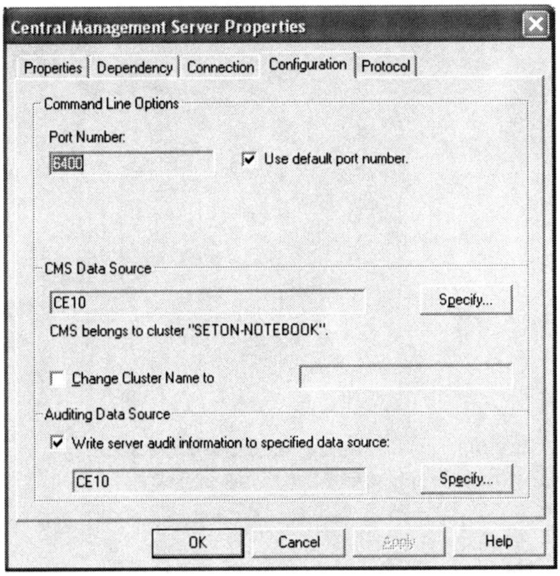

Figure 3-4. *Configuration tab*

Using the Configuration tab, you can alter your data source to another RDBMS or re-create the data source you currently have and start fresh with blank tables. This is accomplished by clicking the Specify button next to the CMS data source name, which will display the dialog shown in Figure 3-5.

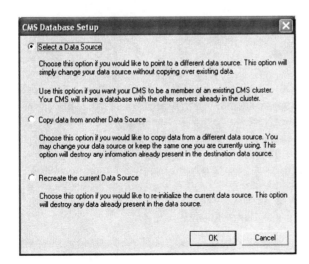

Figure 3-5. *Specifying the data source*

Here you may elect to point your BO XI installation to a completely different data source. You'll need to choose this option when you are clustering distributed CMS servers around a common database. After choosing this option, you'll need to select one of the database drivers in the dialog in Figure 3-6 to continue entering your connection information.

Figure 3-6. *Choosing a database driver*

Copying your data from an existing version of Crystal Enterprise or BusinessObjects is also possible. The dialog in Figure 3-7 shows how you can select the data source.

Figure 3-7. *Choosing a data source to copy from*

Note that copying data in this fashion will completely overwrite the data in the target installation. Note that it does not move the FileStore. To accomplish that, you'll need to use the Import Wizard, which is discussed in the next section. Never try to move a BusinessObjects installation by backing up and restoring the database using your RDBMS utilities or copying the FileStore from one location to another.

Finally, you can choose to re-create the data source of your existing installation. This process will re-create the database tables and in doing so destroy all existing data, leaving you with a deployment as if it were a first-time install. Depending on what you're working with in your development copy, this option can come in handy for starting fresh.

Protocol Tab

The Protocol tab allows you to configure the Secure Sockets Layer (SSL) certificates you may optionally use for communication between clients and servers. The configuration screen is shown in Figure 3-8.

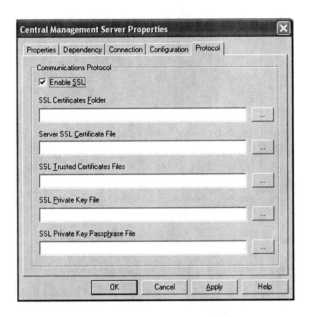

Figure 3-8. *Configuring Secure Sockets Layer*

You'll need to create key and certificate files for each machine in the BO XI deployment. This is done via the sslc.exe command-line utility located at \Program Files\Business Objects\ BusinessObjects Enterprise 11.5\win32_x86.

Import Wizard

The Import Wizard is a utility that allows you to migrate data from one installation/version of BO XI or Crystal Enterprise to another. You will commonly use this tool when you've completed testing and evaluating your development version and are ready to move into production. The Import Wizard will move your folders, reports, report instances, object packages, Inbox documents, categories, security settings, events, server groups, calendars, property settings, and all FileStore and InfoStore data from one installation to another. Should the objects you choose to import have any rights attached to them, you'll also need to import the associated users and groups. You can select exactly which items you want to import using the dialog shown in Figure 3-9.

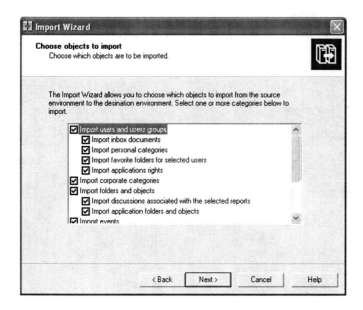

Figure 3-9. *Choosing objects to import*

BIAR FILES

BIAR (pronounced "beer," but let's skip the Budweiser jokes) is an acronym for Business Intelligence Archive Resource. A BIAR file is a portable, self-contained archive of a BO XI installation. These files are akin to database dumps. Just as a database dump contains all the tables, indices, relationships, stored procedures, etc., from a database, so the BIAR file contains all the InfoStore and FileStore information in a BO XI installation. Now you don't need to have access to both the source and the destination installations simultaneously. You can export your BO XI deployment to a BIAR file and then import it later or e-mail to another location for import.

   You can create a BIAR file by selecting BIAR as the destination in the Import Wizard. The wizard will prompt you to enter a file name with a .biar extension. The output file is really a ZIP file. If you rename the BIAR file to a .zip extension, you can open it in WinZip and view the contents. Except for a deployment manifest file called BusinessObjects.xml, all the files contained within are binary and store the objects in your BO XI deployment.

When updating existing objects in a target destination, there are two import options from which you must choose. You can opt to merge the source and target data by comparing the titles to determine whether a match exists. Optionally, you can automatically rename the top-level folders in the target. Rather than match on name, you can use the CUID of the objects to determine whether a match exists with the source. The CUID is stored in the InfoStore as the SI_CUID property and serves as a unique cluster ID on the object. When InfoStore objects are moved from one platform to another, the CUID remains the same though the SI_ID value will likely change. Note that if you are importing server groups, you'll need to once again add the member servers in the destination system first.

The next step is to choose which users you wish to import. You can do so through the screen shown in Figure 3-10.

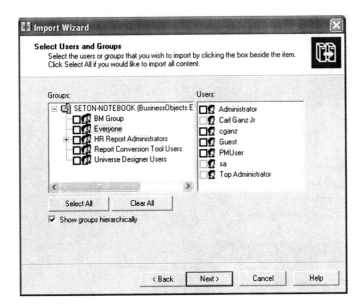

Figure 3-10. *Choosing users to import*

Your licensing plan will affect how the Import Wizard migrates users. If the source environment uses concurrent licensing, the wizard imports everyone as concurrent users. However, if the source environment employs named user licensing, the wizard first checks the destination for sufficient named user license keys. If enough are available to support the users about to be imported, the wizard imports everyone as a named user. Otherwise, the wizard imports all users as concurrent users.

If you employ categories in BO XI, you can choose which ones to import as shown in Figure 3-11.

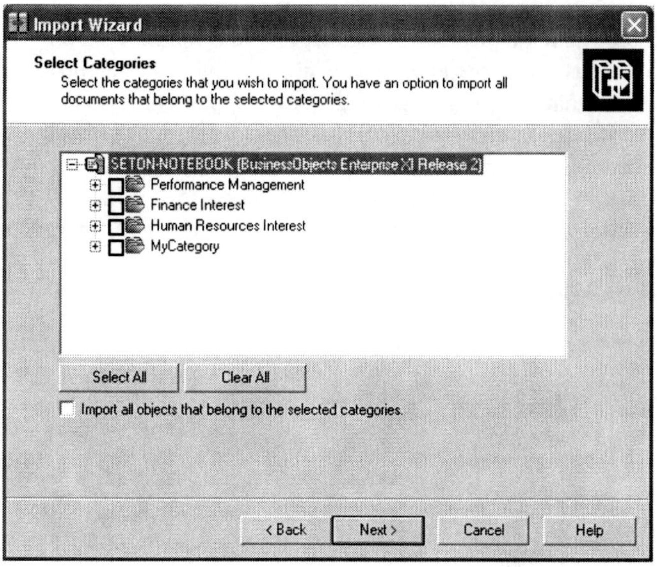

Figure 3-11. *Choosing categories to import*

Each folder, and objects within a folder, can be imported individually. Figure 3-12 shows the screen where you can choose what folders and objects are to be imported. The check box at the bottom of the screen lets you specify whether report histories are to be imported or just the report templates (SI_INSTANCE = 0) themselves.

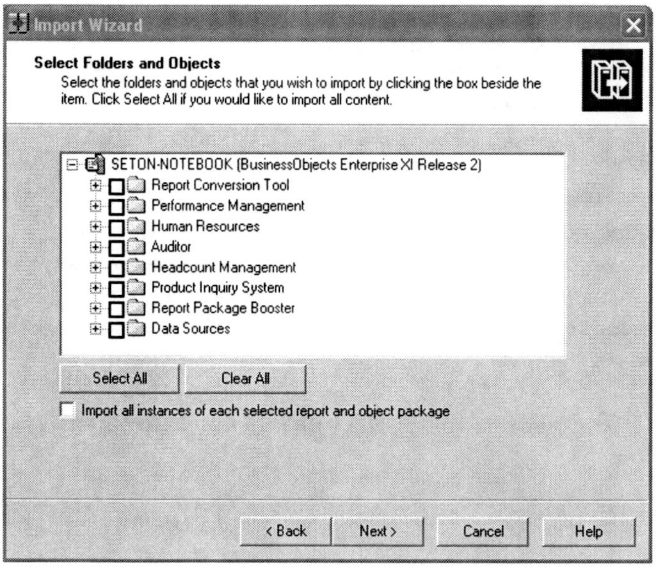

Figure 3-12. *Choosing folders and objects to import*

Your next option is to choose the import options for repository objects. Your choices are shown in Figure 3-13.

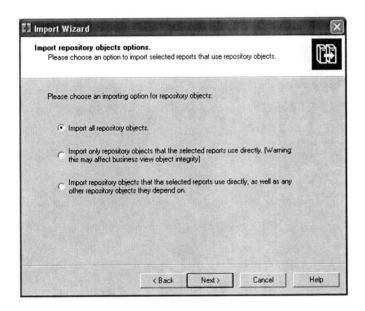

Figure 3-13. *Importing repository objects*

The Import Wizard unfortunately does not offer scripting capabilities nor does it expose an object model for programmatic access. Likewise, there are no command-line switches that would allow the creation of batch files to automate imports. Technical support has confirmed that such features have been submitted to Business Objects as an enhancement request and are under consideration for a future version.

■**Note** User e-mail addresses and custom functions in Crystal Reports are sometimes not imported when using the Import Wizard. These are known issues with BusinessObjects XI and are addressed by the service packs. Make sure you have the latest service packs installed should you experience either of these problems. Also, reports that are imported are sorted by the modified date in the target deployment and not alphabetically. This is also a known issue addressed by the service packs. Consult the documentation for the service pack for a list of bugs that are fixed.

Publishing Wizard

The Publishing Wizard is a tool that allows you to add files to the BO XI repository as a batch. Any file that BO XI supports—Crystal Reports, Desktop Intelligence reports, Word documents, PDFs, etc.—can be added via the Publishing Wizard. Suppose you wanted to make some of the BO XI technical papers available to your developers. You could create a folder called

BusinessObjects XI Technical Papers and then run the Publishing Wizard. After logging on, you'll be presented with an interface that allows you to select the files to be published. You can even select the contents of a directory. After selecting some of the BO XI documents, you'll see a screen that looks something like Figure 3-14.

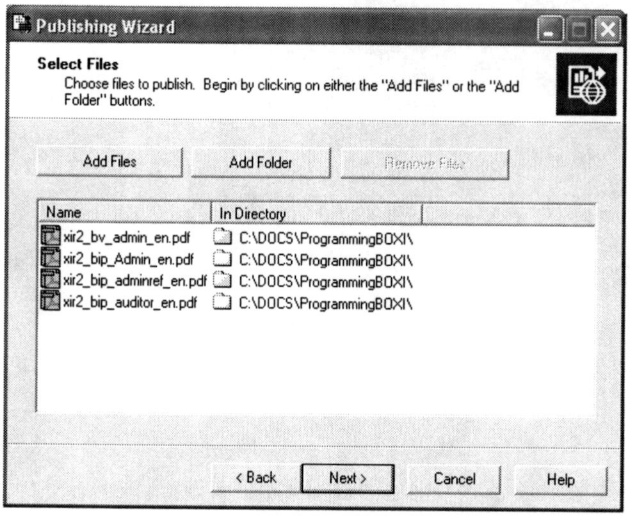

Figure 3-14. *Adding files*

In the next screen you can specify the target folder for the files you've just selected and optionally move some of the files to different folders. Next, you can assign categories to the batch of files you're publishing, and after that you can change the properties of the objects being imported. For the case of these PDF files as well as other static documents, the property options consist of title and description as shown in Figure 3-15.

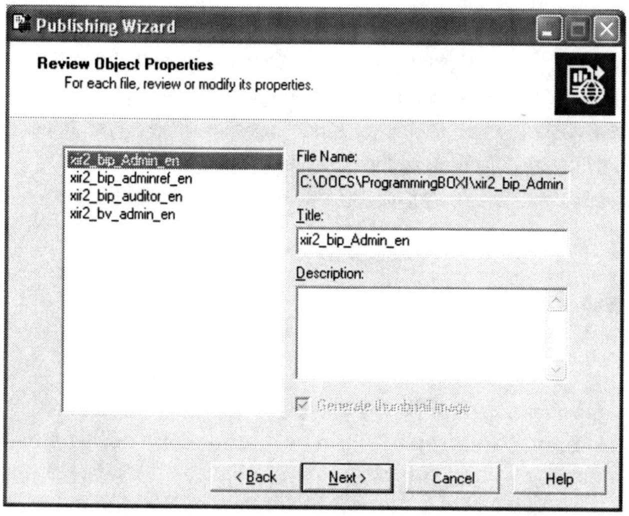

Figure 3-15. *Changing property options for PDF files*

Once you've confirmed the property changes, you can then commit the objects to the InfoStore.

Setting the properties of PDF files is very straightforward, as such documents cannot be scheduled or modified in any way since they are static. Crystal reports are a different story. Here the Publishing Wizard allows you to set the properties for scheduling, destination, and format. The schedule options offer you the ability to set the reports to all run once or on a recurring schedule either daily, weekly, or monthly. The scheduling dialog is shown in Figure 3-16.

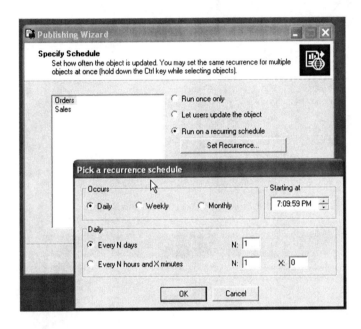

Figure 3-16. *Scheduling a batch of reports*

Next, you'll be asked if you wish to use the Object Repository when refreshing the reports and whether or not you wish to keep the saved data when running. Normally reports that are refreshed from the data source every time they are run do not need to be stored in BO XI with their data saved.

You'll now be prompted to set default values for the reports. Like the previously described PDF files, you can edit the title, description, and indicate whether a thumbnail is desired. Because these are reports, you can also specify the database connectivity information for each report as shown in Figure 3-17.

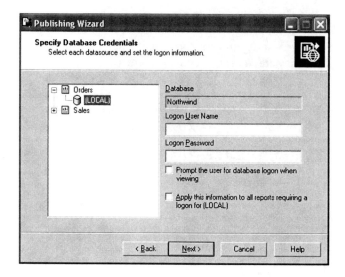

Figure 3-17. *Setting database defaults*

Next, you can set default parameters for each report as shown in Figure 3-18.

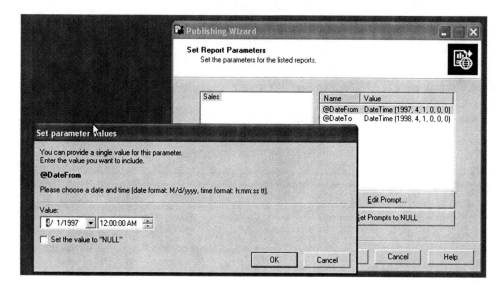

Figure 3-18. *Setting default parameters*

Finally, you can select an output format type and set the options specific to each type. Setting the Excel options is shown in Figure 3-19.

Figure 3-19. *Setting output format to Excel*

Administration Launchpad

The Administration Launchpad is the main screen that guides you to almost all other areas of BusinessObjects XI. In addition to the main administrative tools—the Central Management Console and InfoView—it offers a number of very handy administrative utilities. These tools perform much the same functions as the Central Management Console and InfoView but allow you to do them more efficiently in some cases, especially when working with batches of reports. If this type of batch functionality is important to you, there are some third-party tools described in Chapter 12 that also provide batch-management features over and above the Central Management Console and the administrative tools described here.

Central Management Console

The Central Management Console (CMC) is the principal administrative tool for working with folders and reports. Here you can import reports and executable code, schedule them, maintain histories of the output, manage users and user groups, and assign security rights. Chapter 4 is entirely dedicated to the CMC. This interface is intended as an administrative command center and should ordinarily not be opened to the end user.

InfoView

InfoView performs largely the same tasks as the CMC but is intended as an end-user tool, and as such has an interface that allows users to personalize their reporting interface and manage their business intelligence reports directly. Since this book is aimed at developers and administrators, a complete discussion of InfoView is beyond its scope.

Administration Tool Console

The Administration Tool Console is simply a submenu for the utilities listed below it. While these utilities do replicate much of the functionality you have in the CMC, they do offer several features that the CMC does not have. The main menu is shown in Figure 3-20.

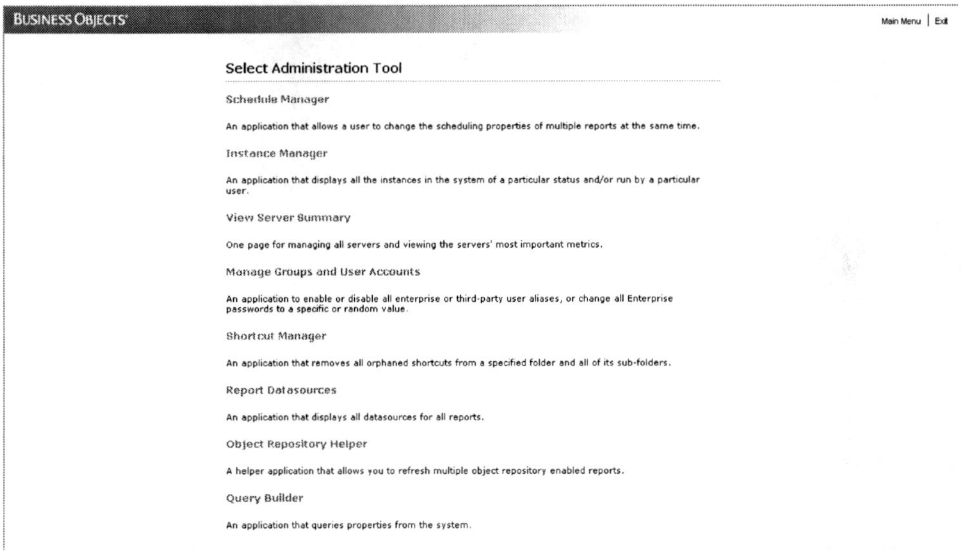

Figure 3-20. *Administration Tool Console*

Schedule Manager

While the CMC allows you to establish the schedules of reports one at a time, the Schedule Manager permits you to do this en masse. By selecting a folder, you can drill into the listing of objects within that folder and make multiple selections as shown in Figure 3-21.

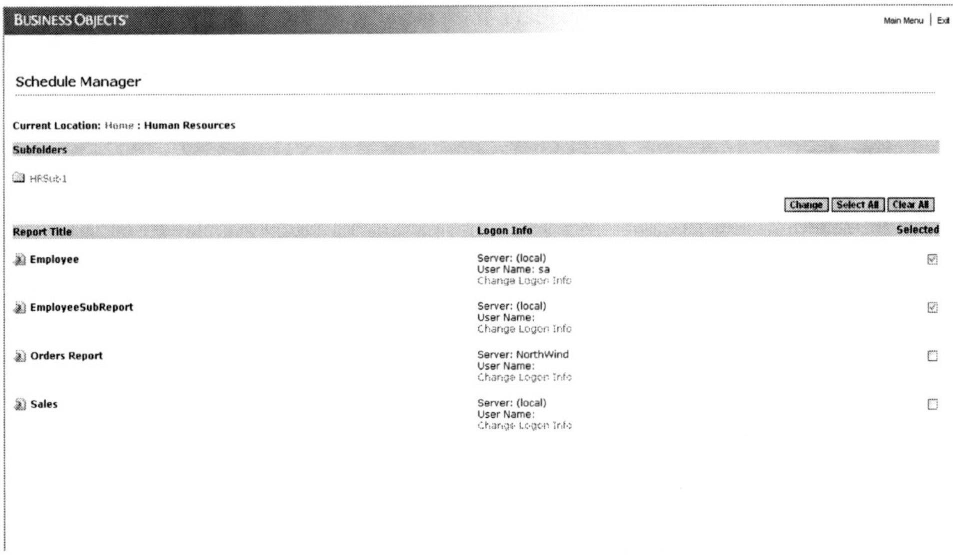

Figure 3-21. *Selecting reports with Schedule Manager*

Clicking the Change button will display a tab page that offers you an interface for setting the schedule, destination, and format. The offerings here are only a subset of what you have in the CMC. Unlike the CMC, the Schedule tab does not allow you to schedule with events or to set the number of retries or the retry interval. Nor does it allow you to set up notifications as you can in the CMC. The Schedule tab is shown in Figure 3-22.

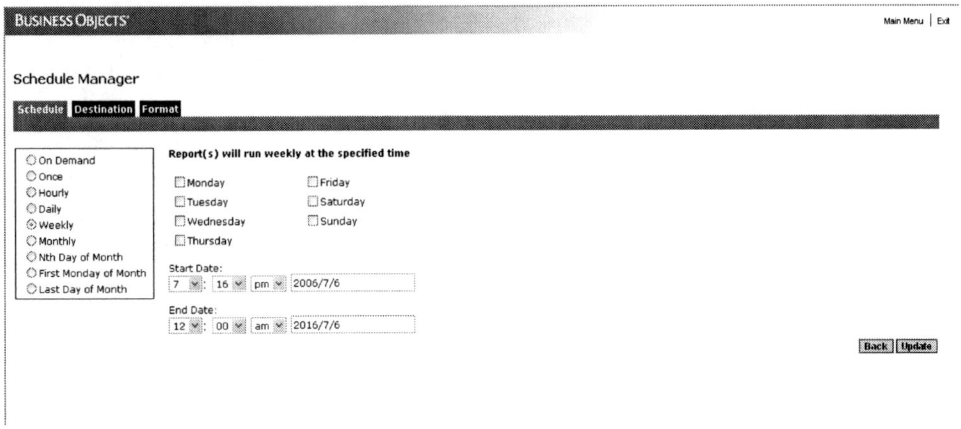

Figure 3-22. *Setting the report schedule*

The Destination tab has largely the same offerings as those offered in the CMC but the format options are more limited. For example, sending the report to Word, Acrobat, Plain Text, or Tab-Separated Text has no customization offerings at all, while Excel offers only the option to export headers and footers one per report or on each page and a tabular format option, which places all the objects in one area into one row.

Instance Manager

The Instance Manager displays all of your reports instances, filtered by user and optionally by report status (success, failed, pending, etc.). You can view or delete individual instances and the grid displays the run time in seconds, whereas the CMC displays the start and end times on the Status page. The Instance Manager is displayed in Figure 3-23.

Figure 3-23. *Instance Manager*

Other than being able to view all report instances without the need to drill down into a folder, there is not much more to the Instance Manager. It comes in handy when you need to delete all failed instances, but even then you need to do it on a user-by-user basis. Entering a user is mandatory for the filter.

View Server Summary

View Server Summary provides an interface to all your BO XI servers. Here you can start, stop, enable, disable, and restart servers as you can in the Central Configuration Manager or the Central Management Console. The advantage to this display is that you can view your server metrics on one page. There are two types of metrics offered—current and total, each existing on its own tab. The Current Metrics tab displays what is currently happening on the servers at the present time. For example, the Cache Server that you see in Figure 3-24 shows 21 processing threads running and a cache hit rate of 25 percent.

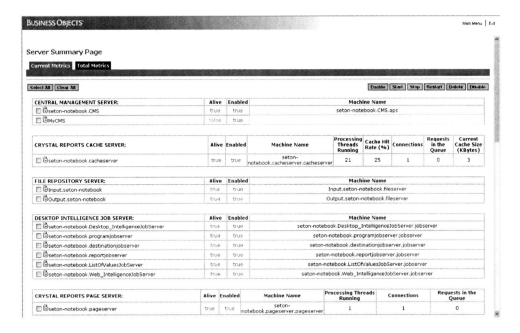

Figure 3-24. *Current metrics*

Total metrics show cumulative results for the servers. The Total Metrics tab shown in Figure 3-25 indicates that five requests have been fulfilled by the Cache Server.

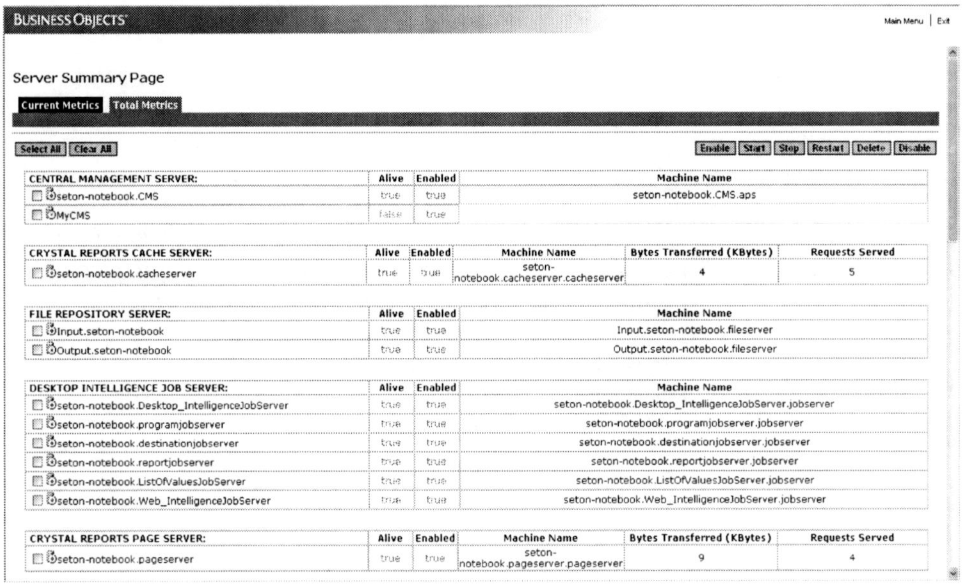

Figure 3-25. *Total metrics*

Manage Groups and User Accounts

The Manage Groups and User Accounts utility allows you to make mass changes to a set of users or to all the users in a set of user groups. You can reset passwords, enable and disable user aliases, and force a change of password at the next logon. The Manage Groups and User Accounts page is shown in Figure 3-26.

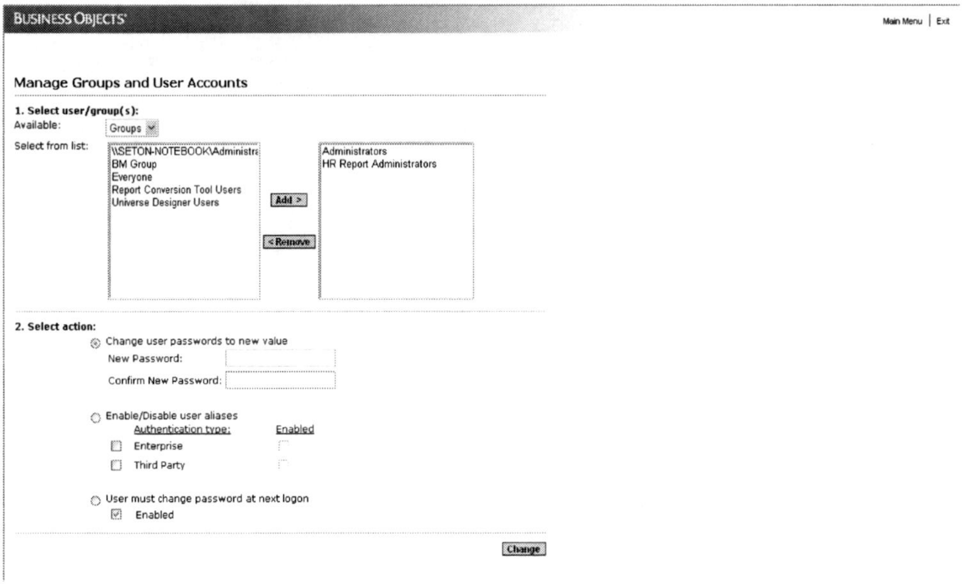

Figure 3-26. *Manage Groups and User Accounts tool*

Shortcut Manager

A shortcut is a link to an object that you can create in the CMC through the Object selection on the main menu. The purpose of a shortcut is to offer a user access to an object in another folder to which he ordinarily does not have access. The shortcut is located in a folder to which the user does have access. The CMC does not perform a cascading delete when the target object is deleted and thus you sometimes end up with orphaned shortcuts. The Shortcut Manager locates these orphaned shortcuts in the selected folder and prompts you to delete them. The Shortcut Manager interface is shown in Figure 3-27.

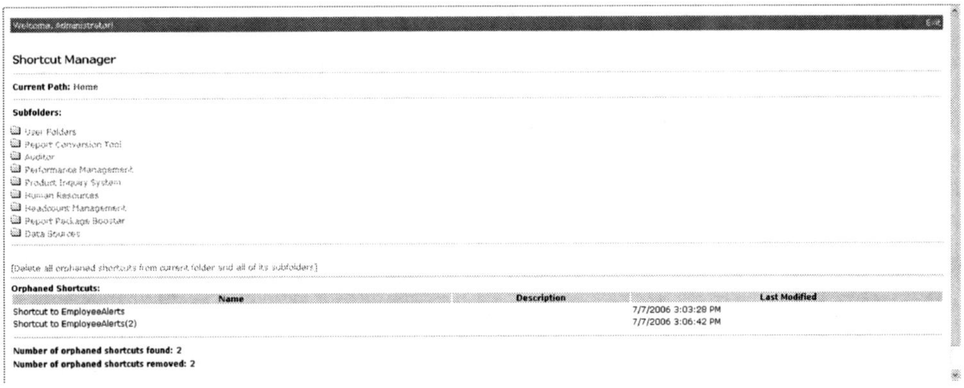

Figure 3-27. *Shortcut Manager*

You can create a shortcut by selecting Object from the main menu in the CMC. From there you can choose an object and select Copy/Move/Shortcut. You'll be presented with a screen that allows you to select a folder in which to create the shortcut.

Report Datasources

The Report Datasources utility presents you with a distinct list of data sources used by all the reports in your BO XI deployment. By clicking the hyperlinked data source name, another window will appear listing all the report instances that use that data source. Clicking the instance name will display the report. The data source window is shown in Figure 3-28.

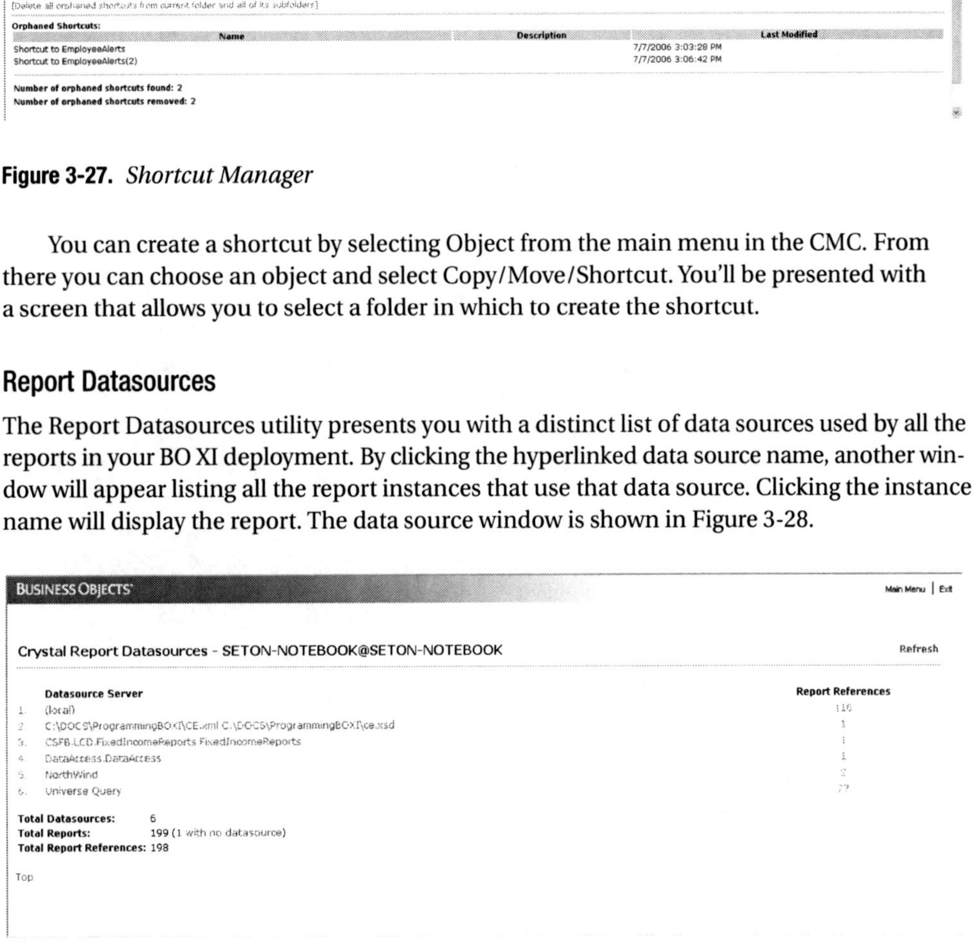

Figure 3-28. *Report Datasources*

Query Builder

The Query Builder is a simple interface that allows you to execute SQL statements against the InfoStore and displays the results in a separate page. It is the BO XI equivalent of SQL Server's Query Analyzer or Oracle's SQL Plus. If you are a beginner to the InfoStore SQL language, it offers a tool to create the SQL statement via a user interface. This utility and the SQL language particular to BusinessObjects XI are discussed in greater detail in Chapter 5.

Object Repository Helper

The Object Repository Helper allows you to make updates to the reports in the repository. If you check the "Use Object Repository when refreshing report" option on the Refresh Options tab in the CMC, your report will appear in this utility where you can refresh the reports individually or as a batch. As objects in the repository are updated, you'll likely want to update the Crystal Reports that reference those objects. When you update a report, the old objects stored in the report are then replaced with the latest versions from the repository.

MODULES IN MEMORY

There's a useful utility on the BusinessObjects web site called modules.exe. Though not officially supported, the purpose of the tool is to determine which DLL modules are loaded in memory at any point in time. This data can be saved to a file and shipped to technical support for further analysis. This tool is often used when there is an elusive bug that cannot easily be traced in the code and seems to be specific to one machine. By running your application to the error point, you can use modules.exe to capture what DLLs are in memory at the point the error occurred. This list can then be compared to one taken from another machine where the error is not occurring. Therefore, if technical support tells you, "But it works fine on our end," modules.exe can help determine why. Very often the problem turns out to be the lack of a service pack or hot fix. Though this is not intended as an end-user tool, it's helpful to have it on your machine in case technical support needs the output from it. This utility is a stand-alone EXE and does not require an installation. Search for modules.zip on the BusinessObjects support site at http://support.businessobjects.com.

Business Views Manager

Business Views are like the traditional BusinessObjects universes. They are metadata layers, also called semantic layers, through which you can abstract data sources to shield business analysts from the complexity of their RDBMSs. A detailed discussion of how Business Views (or universes for that matter) work is beyond the scope of this book and is a topic worth several chapters entirely unto itself.

Business Views allow you to create business-oriented cuts of data from your back-end databases. You can even create these semantic layers across heterogeneous systems from, for instance, SQL Server to Oracle to Sybase. All this will be transparent to the user. You can customize the different cuts of the data so that only those individuals permitted to view certain classified information will have the appropriate privileges.

Crystal Reports Explorer

Crystal Reports Explorer is essentially a web version of Crystal Reports. It is intended as a zero-client tool for end users to create their own reports from either Business Views or directly from the data sources themselves. You can obtain the administrator's guide and the user's guide by downloading xir2_crx_admin_en.pdf and xir2_crx_user_en.pdf, respectively, from www.businessobjects.com. In this section, I'll give you a brief walkthrough of the tool so you have an understanding of its features.

When users select the Crystal Reports Explorer option from the menu, they'll be offered two options: either define a report data source or create a report. If the Define Report Data Source option is disabled, you can enable it by opening the CMC and choosing BusinessObjects Enterprise Applications ➤ Crystal Reports Explorer from the main menu. Here you'll be presented with a list of the folders present in the CMC. One of these folders will need to be designated as the Data Source Folder by right-clicking the folder and selecting the Set as Data Sources Folder option from the pop-up menu as shown in Figure 3-29. The Data Sources folder holds the report data sources you'll create in the designer.

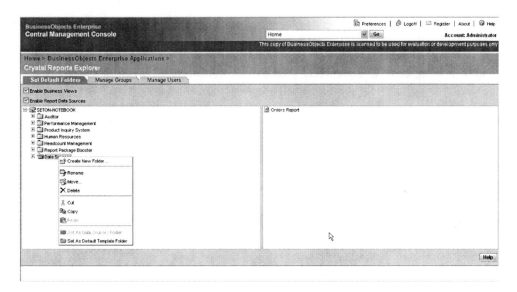

Figure 3-29. *Selecting the Data Sources folder*

While you're in the CMC, you may wish to determine which users and groups have which rights when designing reports. These rights include such features as the ability to create groups, filters, formulas, and summaries, sorting, charting, and using templates. This security screen is shown in Figure 3-30.

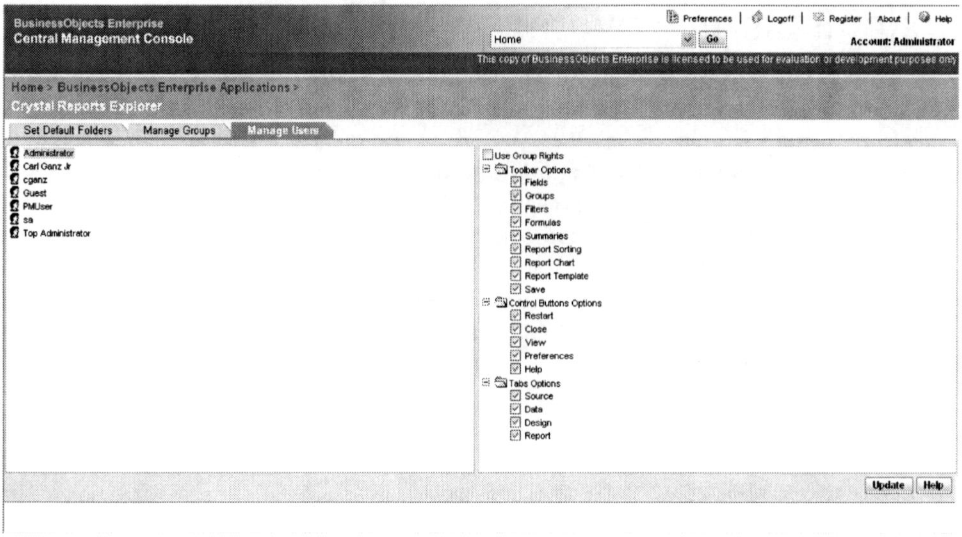

Figure 3-30. *Assigning user rights*

After enabling the Define Report Data Source option in the CMC, you can click the Define Report Data Source hyperlink in the Crystal Reports Explorer utility and choose the data source for your report. You'll be presented with a dialog that offers all the ODBC data sources registered in your system. This screen is shown in Figure 3-31.

Figure 3-31. *Selecting a data source*

Choose Northwind, and you'll be presented with a list of all the tables available in the database from which you can select the table you'll need in your report. What you are not presented with are the stored procedures and views that are available in the database, as you must create the links between the tables yourself. Select the tables as shown in Figure 3-32.

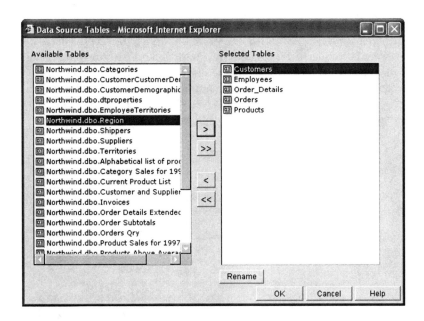

Figure 3-32. *Selecting tables*

Once you've selected the tables for the report, click the Link Tables option on the left menu to bring up the Table Linking dialog. You can select which tables link with which other tables and on what common key as shown in Figure 3-33.

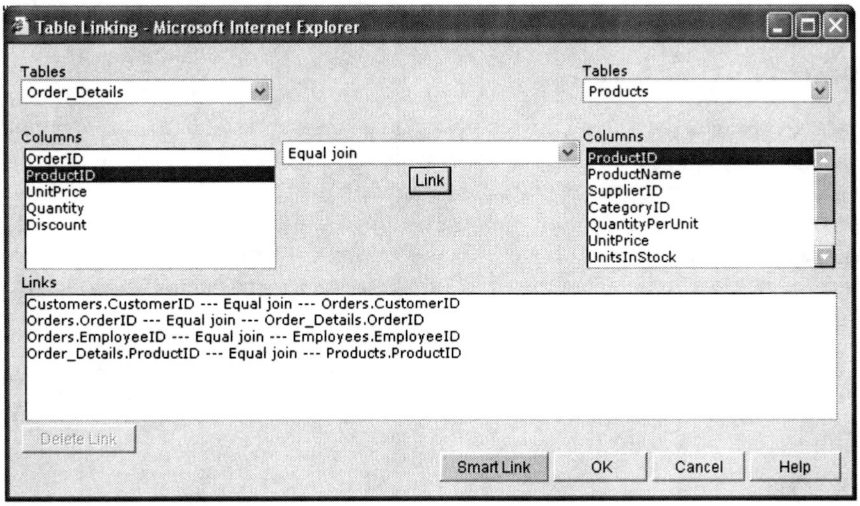

Figure 3-33. *Linking tables*

Once you've set up and saved your links, click the Design tab and you can begin creating your report. By dragging fields from the Groups list into the report design page, you can create a new group. Drag the entries from the Fields list to the Details section to show the report detail information. You can format fields and create formulas and summaries much in the same fashion as in Crystal Reports but with fewer options, as it is a slimmed down version of the tool. If you come from a long Crystal Reports background, using the web interface will take some getting used to. The report layout screen will look something like Figure 3-34.

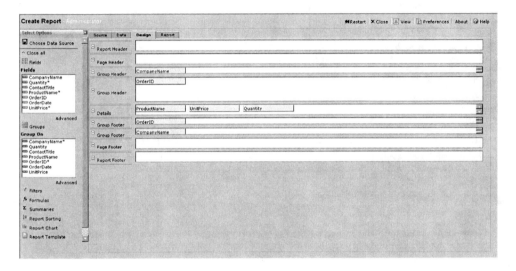

Figure 3-34. *Report layout*

Summary

BusinessObjects XI provides you with all the tools you'll need to administer it. Some are minor utilities that allow you to apply batch changes to the objects in the InfoStore, while others allow you to publish documents and migrate data from one BO XI installation to another. There are even utilities for the end user. InfoView is a web-based and user-friendly version of the CMC, while Crystal Reports Explorer is a web-based version of Crystal Reports. In the next chapter, we'll look at the most important of these tools in greater detail—the Central Management Console.

CHAPTER 4

■■■

Using the Central Management Console

As a system administrator, the first place you'll head to do anything with BusinessObjects XI is the Central Management Console (formerly the Crystal Management Console), commonly known as the CMC. It is here that you'll manage such things as folders, reports, servers, schedules, and users. Use of the tool is rather intuitive and highly navigable through the use of *breadcrumbs*, which are a series of hyperlinks that allow you to navigate back to any point you came from. This chapter will discuss how it is used to administer your BO XI installation. The tasks that you'll learn how to perform here will be shown programmatically in the Chapters 5, 6, and 9.

Folders and Reports

The main page of the CMC (see Figure 4-1) is a hyperlink menu that serves as your gateway to the various objects you can manage and tasks that you can perform. This is your starting point for accessing all the features offered by the CMC.

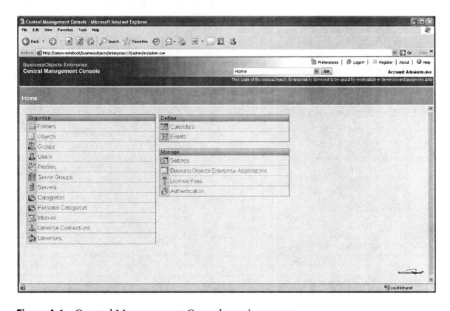

Figure 4-1. *Central Management Console main menu*

Folders

The first option, Folders, brings you to the list of folders (see Figure 4-2), which in turn may contain subfolders, reports, and other objects such as Excel or PDF files, and even executable code. An analogy here to Windows Explorer would be quite apt.

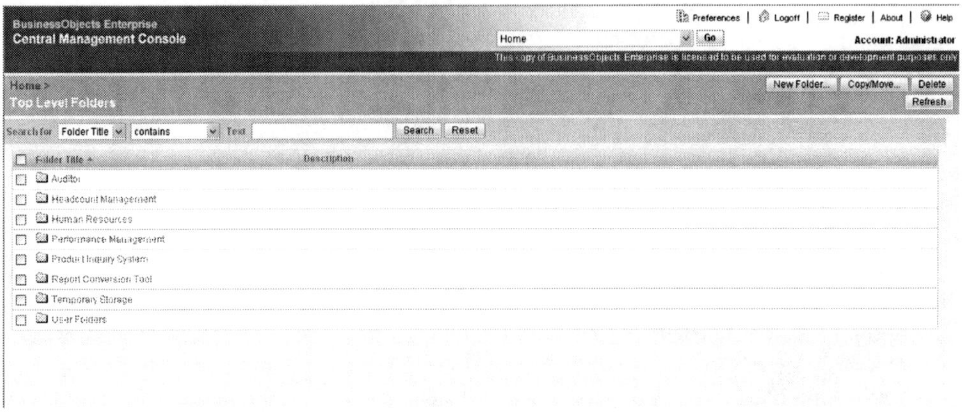

Figure 4-2. *Top-level folders*

To add a new folder, click the New Folder button and give your new folder a name and, optionally, a description. After you click OK, the name of the new folder will appear in the top-level folder list, and you can now add subfolders, reports, and many other objects to it.

When you display folders or objects within a folder, you don't necessarily want all the entries to be pulled from the InfoStore because of resource considerations. You can limit the number of entries extracted by choosing BusinessObjects Enterprise Applications from the main menu and then selecting Central Management Console. Here you can specify how many entries can be returned before the CMC tells the user to use the search tools instead (see Figure 4-3).

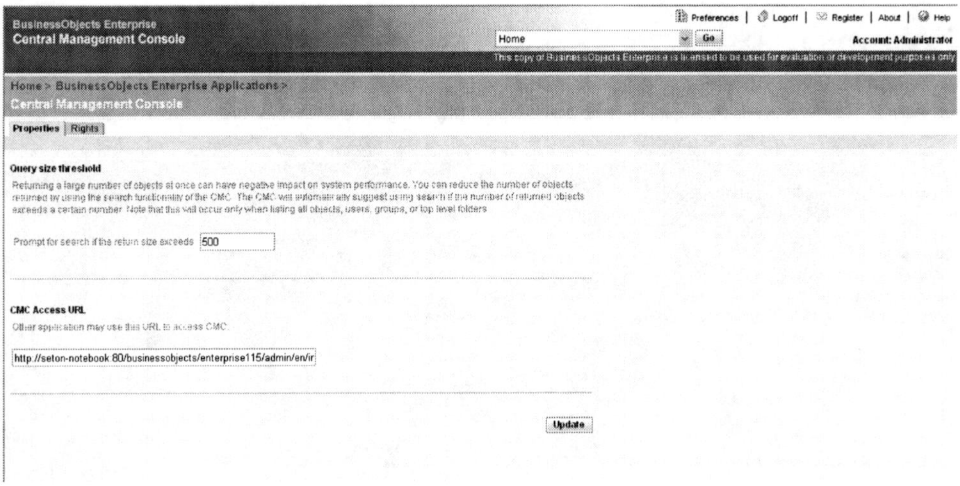

Figure 4-3. *Query size threshold*

Figure 4-4 shows what happens when I set the maximum size to five and then try to retrieve seven folders.

Figure 4-4. *Query size threshold reached*

Reports

To add a report to this folder, click the folder name hyperlink to enter it, select the Objects tab, and then click the New Object button. You will now see the screen shown in Figure 4-5.

Figure 4-5. *New Object page*

You'll see that you can add more that just Crystal reports. The CMC can serve as a repository for many objects, including Word, Excel, Acrobat, ASCII, and RTF files. If you have a document produced by another source that you wish to load and have available to the enterprise, you can add it here. The Program option allows you to install a piece of compiled executable code, say, a .NET assembly, which can be run on demand or scheduled. Program objects are one of the most powerful features in BO XI, and we'll discuss them at length in Chapter 9.

Click the Browse button to display the file dialog with which you can select your RPT file and click the Submit button in the lower right-hand corner to commit it to the InfoStore.

Properties

The main Properties tab allows you to create a report name, and add descriptive text and keywords. You can also see the Created, Last Modified, and Last Run dates for this report. The Properties tab is shown in Figure 4-6.

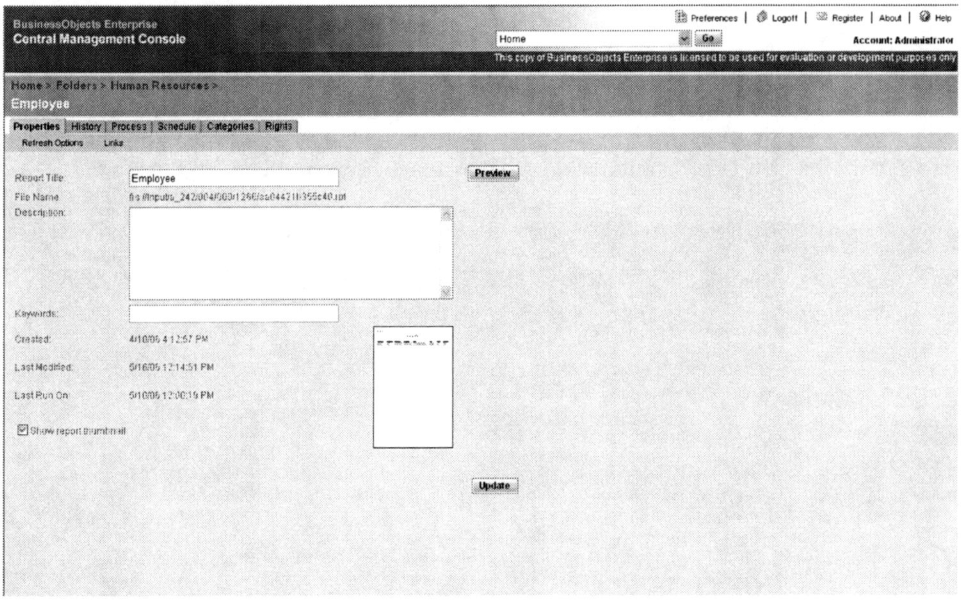

Figure 4-6. *Report Properties tab*

The Show report thumbnail check box determines whether a small preview of the report layout will display. This feature must be enabled in the RPT file itself. In Crystal Reports, select File ➤ Summary Info and select the Save Preview Picture check box. This will create a snapshot of the first page of the actual report that is embedded with the RPT, so make sure you don't inadvertently display any sensitive data by doing this.

The File Name entry is the location of the physical file in the InfoStore. From the directory location, you can see the SI_ID value of the report just before the file name. If the file name is frs://Input/a_059/017/000/4411/278447d0150890.rpt, the SI_ID value is 4411. The SI_ID is the unique primary key reference of the report in the InfoStore.

Refresh Options

The Refresh Options link under the Properties tab determines which properties of the report entry in the CMC are updated from the RPT file when a modified RPT file is saved to the Info-Store. The settings shown in Figure 4-7 are the default ones and the most common. You'll likely want to keep the more descriptive report name rather than overwrite it with the file name of the RPT. Depending on what you use the Description field for, you may want to check off this option.

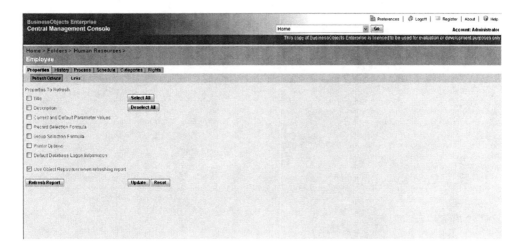

Figure 4-7. *Refresh Options page*

You can update CMC reports directly from Crystal Reports. Selecting File ➤ Save will present you with a file dialog. Choose the Enterprise option, and you'll be prompted to log on to BO XI. Then you'll be presented with a list of CMC folders to which you can save your new report or overwrite an existing one. Figure 4-8 shows this in action.

Figure 4-8. *File Save As dialog*

Links

Links refer to hyperlinks between reports intended as navigational aids that allow you to jump between reports. To establish these links, you'll need to open two reports from the InfoStore using Crystal Reports.

Crystal Reports makes the decision as to the type of link to establish. Links can be either relative or absolute. *Relative links* are those between reports in the same *object package* (which is a collection of objects that can be dealt with as a batch), whereas *absolute links* point to specific report objects or instances. The Links page is shown in Figure 4-9.

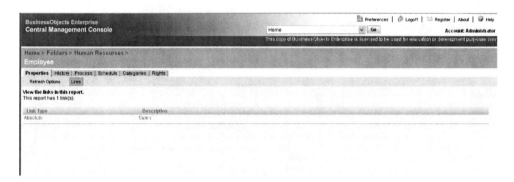

Figure 4-9. *Report Links page*

History

When reports execute via a schedule, even if they are set to run immediately, an entry is made in the report history that shows the name of the report, the date and time it was run, the status (Pending, Running, Success, or Failed), the output format, who ran it, and the parameter list. To view any instance of the report, simply click the hyperlinked report name. The report history page is shown in Figure 4-10.

Figure 4-10. *Report history page*

The report history records every instance of the report that was run through the scheduler. Even the Run Now button on the History tab is a shortcut to the scheduler, as it schedules the report to run immediately with the default parameters. This means that if you run a report programmatically by using the Report Application Server (RAS), as shown in Listing 4-1, no entry will be made in the report history. This may not be desirable, as your company security policy may require an audit trail history of all reports.

Listing 4-1. *Using the RAS to Run a Report*

```
SessionMgr oSessionMgr;
EnterpriseSession oEnterpriseSession;
EnterpriseService oEnterpriseService;
ReportAppFactory oReportAppFactory;
ReportClientDocument oReportClientDocument;

oSessionMgr = new SessionMgr();
oEnterpriseSession = oSessionMgr.Logon("administrator",
    "", "SETON-NOTEBOOK:6400", "secEnterprise");
oEnterpriseService = oEnterpriseSession.GetService("","RASReportFactory");

oReportAppFactory = ((ReportAppFactory) oEnterpriseService.Interface);

oReportClientDocument =
    oReportAppFactory.OpenDocument(int.Parse(szReportID), 0);

crystalReportViewer1.ReportSource = oReportClientDocument;
```

Clicking the Status hyperlink will provide the status information for that report. If successful, it will display the output specifications, such as what BO XI server handled the report. In addition, it indicates the location of the physical output in the FileStore. A successful status page is shown in Figure 4-11.

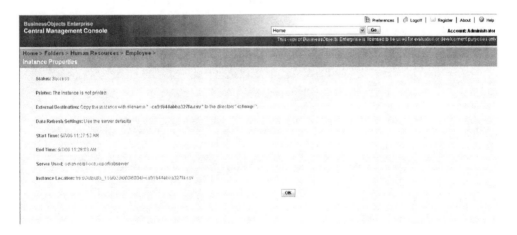

Figure 4-11. *Successful status page*

Should the report fail, you can retrieve the error information to determine what went wrong. A failed status page is shown in Figure 4-12.

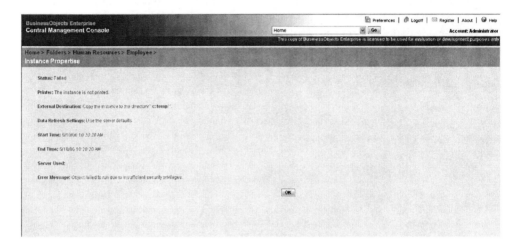

Figure 4-12. *Failed status page*

The Send To button will allow you to send the existing report instance to a disk file, an FTP server, SMTP mail, or an Inbox. Each option requires specific parameters to be entered, which are discussed later in the "Destinations" section.

Limits

Report limits allow you to determine how long or how many reports are to be kept in the report history. The CMC can act as an archiving system for your reports as long as you have disk space. You may not want to keep your report history around forever. Using the limits screen (shown in Figure 4-13), you can instruct the CMC to delete more than a specified number of report instances or any instances older than a specified number of days.

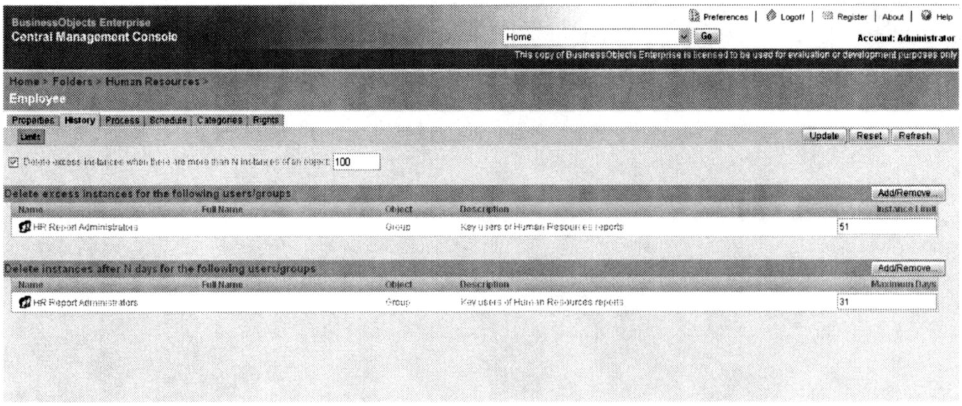

Figure 4-13. *Limits page*

Of course, you may not want any reports deleted at all since this would eliminate your audit trail. In this case, just don't set any limits, and the report history will build indefinitely. Some of my investment banking clients have an eight-year retention period, while my pharmaceutical clients, per FDA mandate, need to maintain reports for much longer. Given the limits of disk space, you may not want to have a decade's worth or more of reports, possibly comprising several million FileStore documents and InfoStore entries, clogging up your BO XI server. Commonly, reports need to be moved to a separate archiving system depending on your company's records-retention requirements.

Since limits are a security-related feature, they are discussed in detail in Chapter 10, which contains examples and explanations of programmatic access to them.

Process

The Process tab manages all the information that your report will need to run. This includes database connectivity, default parameters, filters, and printer information. The tab itself, shown in Figure 4-14, allows you to specify server management settings for report scheduling, viewing, and modification.

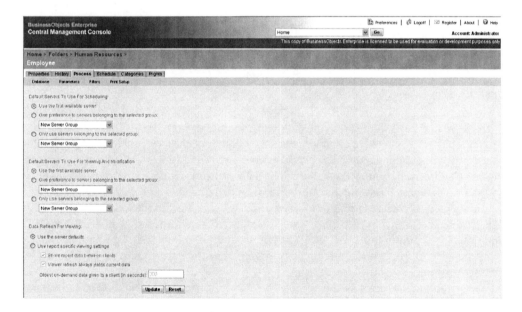

Figure 4-14. *Process tab*

Here you can indicate whether processing of these respective tasks goes to the first available server or a server in one of the server groups that you can create off the main CMC page. By selecting these options, you can perform load balancing down to the level of the individual report.

Database

The Database link on the Process tab displays the database information page shown in Figure 4-15.

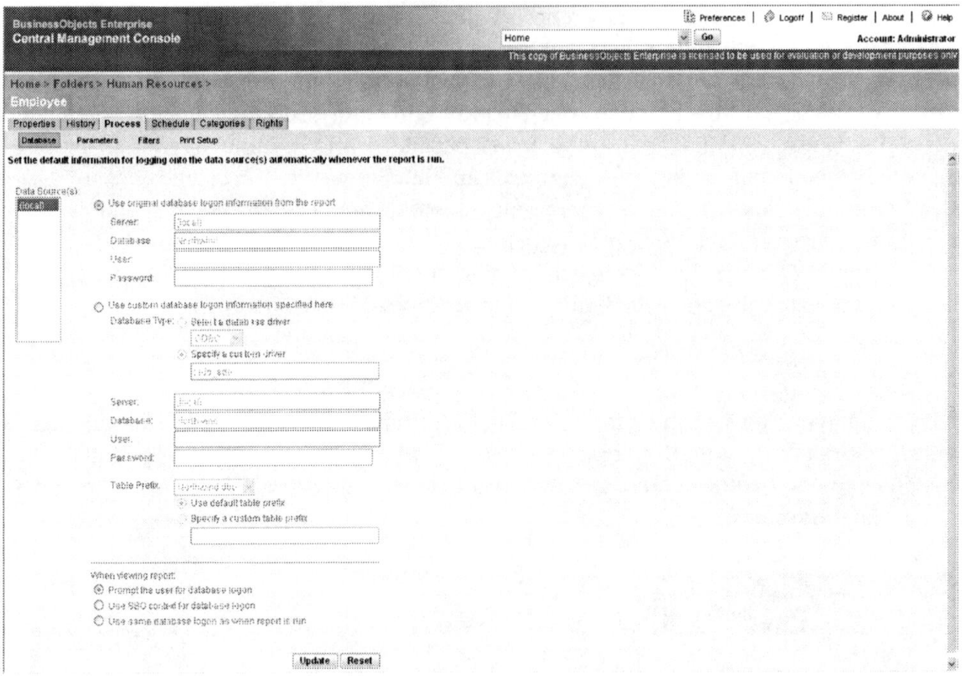

Figure 4-15. *Process tab/Database page*

You'll see that the CMC picks up the database information from the RPT file. All except the password, that is. You'll need to enter that here. As a matter of corporate security policy with all my clients, production passwords are not entered into the CMC by the BO XI administrator, as he is not authorized to know them. Rather, he'll enter the development or user-acceptance-testing (UAT) database password. If a report is run on demand via a web service invocation, the production password is contained in a server-based XML file that the web service opens on the production server, to which the developers and BO XI administrators do not have access. If you need to accommodate CMC access to the production database to handle scheduled reports, you can have the corporate security officer enter the password in the production version of the tool.

Another option is to use a .NET assembly as the data source for the report. At runtime, this assembly will access an XML file that contains the production password. The main drawback to this approach arises when you need to deploy a new version of the report to a production server. If you only need to deploy a modified report to the production installation of BO XI, you're simply using an application interface (the CMC), the use of which is relatively easy to get permissions for at most firms. Updating a disk file like a data access DLL often requires a great deal more bureaucracy. We'll discuss data access DLLs in further detail in Chapter 6.

The "Use custom database logon information specified here" radio button option allows you to specify a completely new data source for your report from the original one entered. You can toggle between them in the CMC simply by selecting the appropriate radio button.

Parameters

Selecting the Parameters link will display the page shown in Figure 4-16. Here you can set default parameters for the report. If you have parameters set in your RPT file, they will appear here by default; otherwise each option will display "[Empty]". You'll need to fill in something here in order to run the report in the CMC.

■**Note** As a general rule, if the report runs successfully in the CMC, it will run successfully when you access it programmatically. Always run your reports in the CMC first by clicking the Preview button, and you'll save yourself numerous debugging headaches.

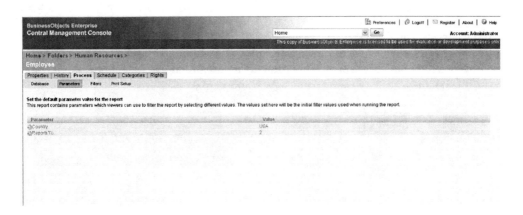

Figure 4-16. *Process tab/Parameters page*

When you schedule a report, the parameters you have stored here at the time will become the default parameters for the scheduled report. If you later change the default parameters, the scheduled report will retain the parameters it had at the time it was scheduled.

Note that date parameters in the CMC require special handling. Though your database stored procedure may be happy with the mm/dd/yyyy format, or some regional variant thereof, BO XI requires a very specific date format, specifically yyyy-mm-dd hh:mm:ss. Date parameters in the CMC automatically display with their own pop-up calendars to make date selection easy. Still, you need to be careful when passing in dates programmatically. The MakeDateParameter() method in Listing 4-2 will convert a date for you to the proper BO XI format.

Listing 4-2. *MakeDateParameter() Method*

```
private string MakeDateParameter(DateTime dDate)
{
   string szResult;

   szResult = "DateTime(" + dDate.Year.ToString() + "," +
      dDate.Month.ToString() + "," +
      dDate.Day.ToString() + ",0,0,0)";
```

```
        return szResult;
}
```

Filters

The Filters tab, shown in Figure 4-17, allows you to specify formulas for both record and group filtering. These formulas function like parameters in that they both filter data. Where they differ is that parameters are conduits to the data source, whereas formulas are filters for the data returned. If you have an employee report that prints data from the Northwind database, and are using a parameter of Country = "USA", the database will retrieve employee records only where the country is equal to "USA" and return just those rows to the reporting engine. A formula does not affect the retrieval of these records. By specifying a formula that limits the records retrieved to those where the city is Seattle, then of all the USA records are retrieved, but the report will only show those located in Seattle. The non-Seattle records are still brought back from the database even if they are not displayed. You can set both group and record formulas in Crystal Reports, and these settings will become the default in the CMC. This filtering feature often comes into play when performing report bursting. *Report bursting* allows you to retrieve all records in a given set once and then break up the report into individual reports by applying filters and not hitting the database to extract every subset of data.

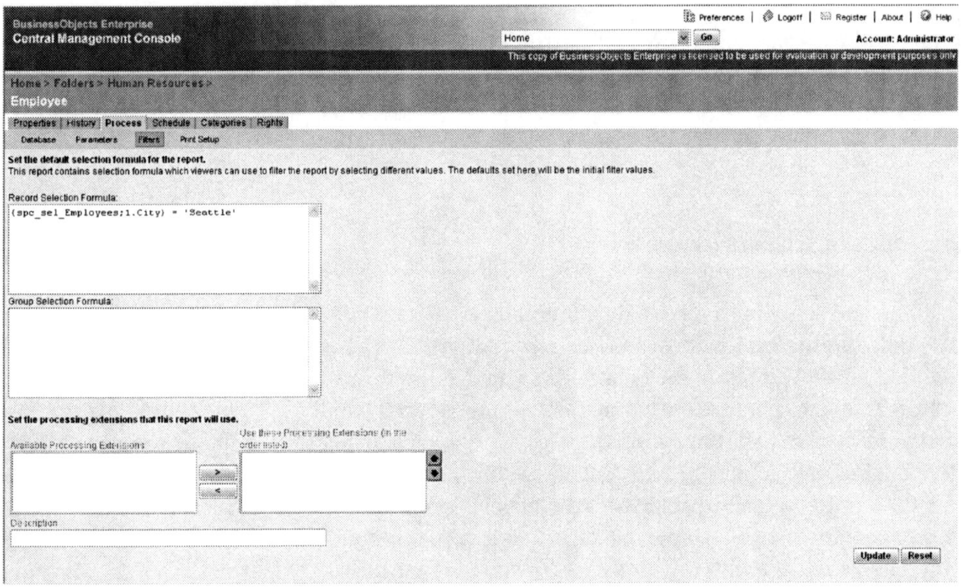

Figure 4-17. *Process tab/Filters page*

Processing extensions allow you to create compiled code that can apply custom business logic against the data being processed in your report. You can only write processing extensions in unmanaged C++ code, so unfortunately your .NET languages won't be helpful here. The extension manager offers a handle that enables the developer to intercept requests before they are processed by the job server. By doing this you can alter such settings as parameter values and filters.

One reason you may want to do this is to apply row-level security to a report. For example, if user A and user B may both run the Salary Report, but user A can see only departments 1 and 2, whereas user B can see departments 3 and 4, a processing extension can determine the identity of the currently logged-in user when the report is run and filter the data appropriately. Be aware that you can also accomplish such tasks by writing and scheduling .NET assemblies where you can also place the same row-level security logic, so the need for processing extensions has largely been rendered obsolete.

Print Setup

The Print Setup page controls the printer specification for the report. Here you can specify the target printer, number of copies, and page ranges. If you set your scheduled report to a printer destination, this page controls where it will print. The Print Setup page is shown in Figure 4-18.

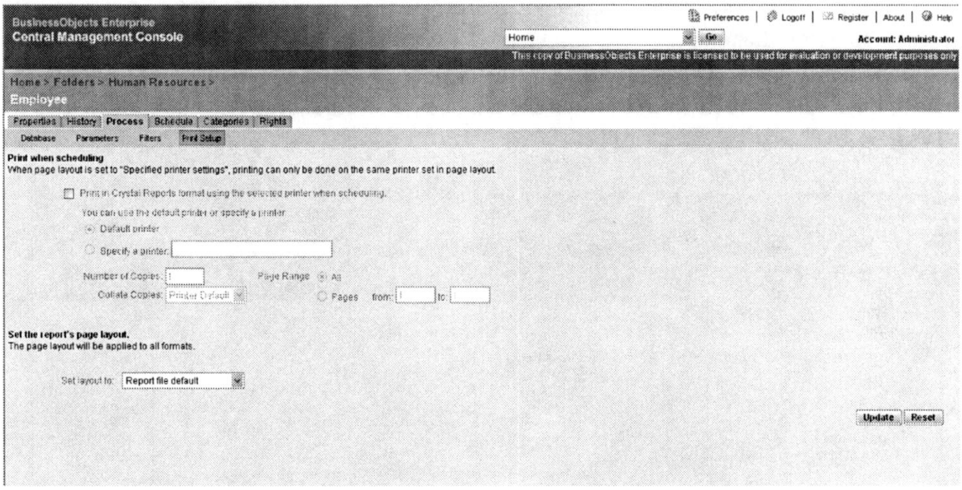

Figure 4-18. *Process tab/Print Setup page*

Normally a report's page layout settings are determined in Crystal Reports when the RPT is first created. BO XI offers you two page layout override options as shown in the sections that follow.

Specified Printer Settings Choosing Specified printer settings will change your Print Setup page options to look like Figure 4-19.

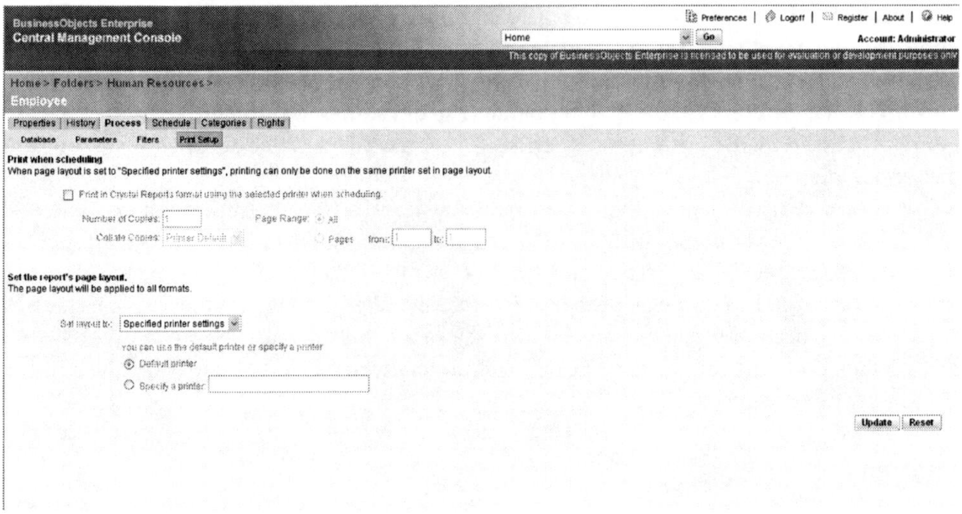

Figure 4-19. *Specified printer settings option/Print Setup page*

This option will conform your page layout setting—orientation, page size, paper type—to that of the printer indicated.

Custom Settings Choosing Custom settings will change your Print Setup page options to look like Figure 4-20.

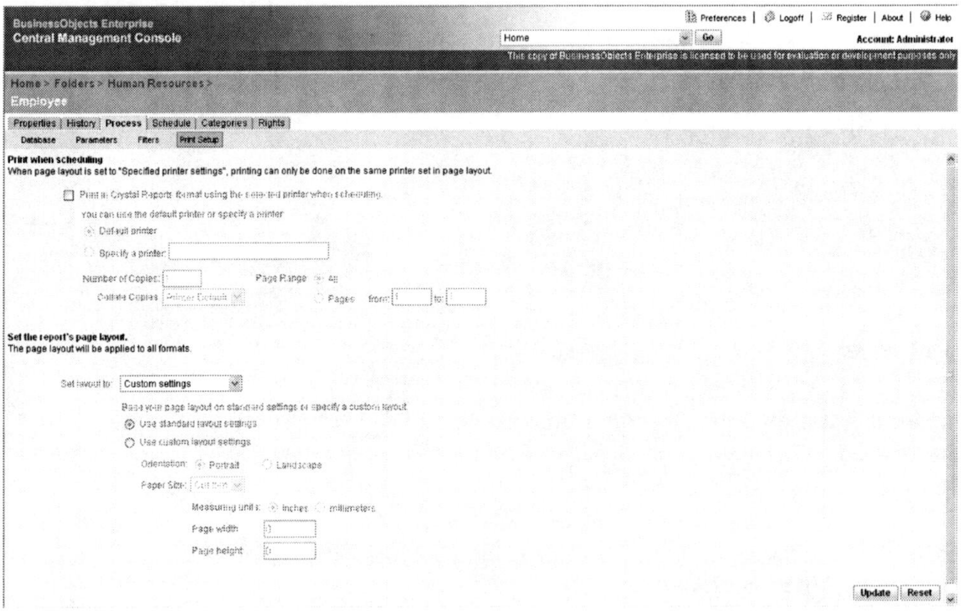

Figure 4-20. *Custom settings option/Print Setup page*

Here you can enter the specific page layout parameters customized exactly the way you want them.

Schedule

The Schedule tab allows you to choose the frequency and time of day your reports can be scheduled, the destination (disk file, e-mail, FTP server, Inbox), and the format (Crystal Report, Excel, PDF, etc.). A report can be run On Demand (meaning run it immediately), Once (either immediately or at a specified time), Daily, Weekly, Monthly, or through a custom Calendar. Selecting each radio button will display a different set of date/time selection options appropriate to it. The Weekly options are shown in Figure 4-21.

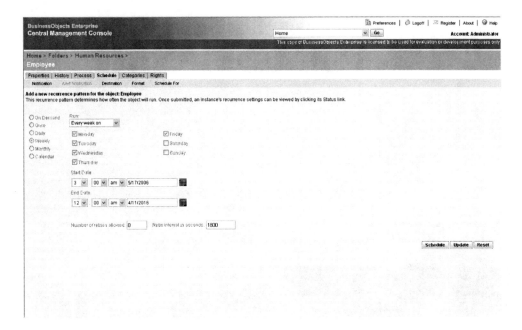

Figure 4-21. *Schedule report weekly*

▓**Note** If you like this interface and wish to provide it to users without giving them access to the CMC, you can easily do so. BO XI offers web controls that allow you to embed the Schedule tab, and many other CMC reporting options, in your custom application. This topic will be discussed further in Chapter 6.

The Calendar option allows you to tie your reports to a custom calendar should one of the listed options be too constraining. If you need a report that runs, say, on major holidays only, you can construct a calendar object that will handle these very specific days.

Notifications

The Notification feature allows you to determine how information about successful and failed reports will be handled. There are two types of notifications—audit and e-mail.

Audit Notifications Audit notifications write information about an object's execution to an auditing database. The only thing to do here is to check the boxes (see Figure 4-22) indicating whether successful or failed jobs (or both) should be written to the auditing database. The auditing database is covered in greater detail in Chapter 2.

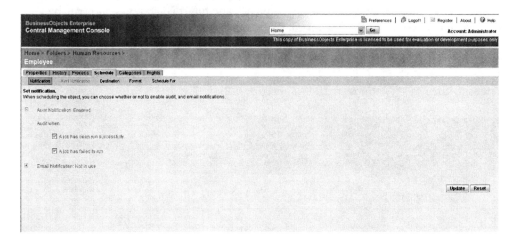

Figure 4-22. *Audit notifications*

E-mail Notifications Here you can create e-mails to notify users that their scheduled jobs have completed running. It's helpful to include links in these e-mails so that users can click them to see their report without ever needing to log in to your reporting front-end application or opening the CMC. The Email Notification page is shown in Figure 4-23.

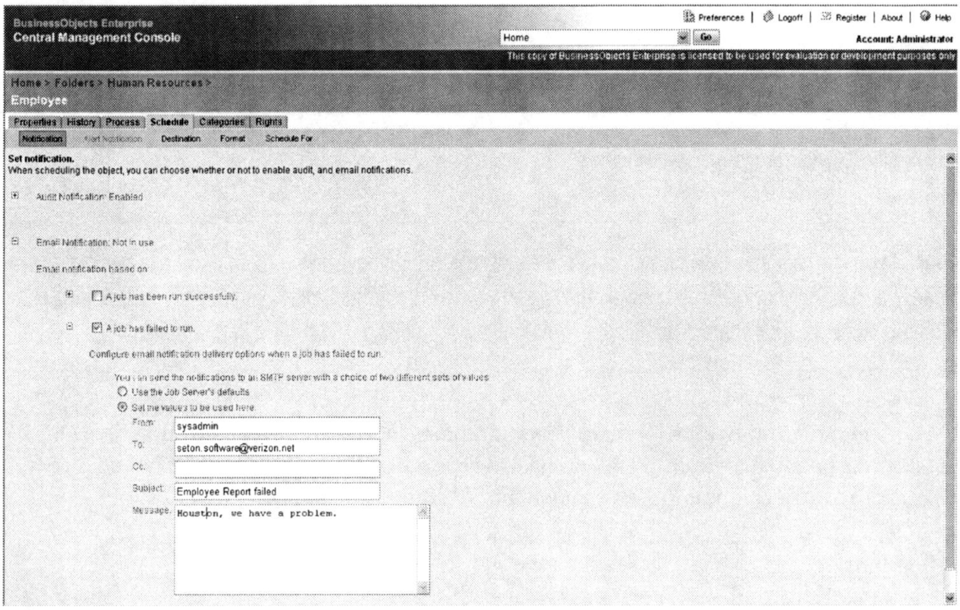

Figure 4-23. *E-mail notifications*

Alert Notification

Alerts are devices for indicating that the data in a generated report meet a set of criteria that you define through Crystal Reports. For example, you might set up an alert to trigger if the bottom line on a sales report was below a certain amount or if the average purchase order approval amount for a manager was outside of an acceptable range. The Alert Notification page allows you to enter the e-mail information for those users who are to be alerted to the triggering of the alert when the report is run. This e-mail will list individually the details of each record that met the alert condition. For each alert criteria established, you may set limits on the number of detail records printed in the e-mail. This e-mail will contain a list of the records that met the alert criteria along with a web link that displays the report filtered to only those records that meet the alert criteria. The Alert Notification page is shown in Figure 4-24.

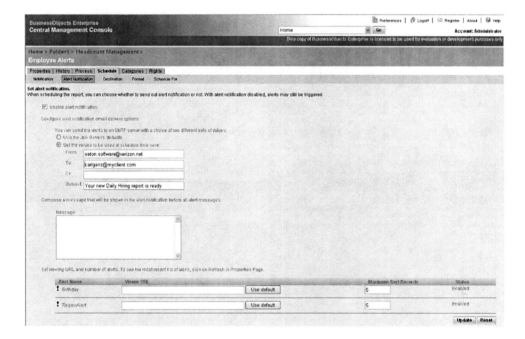

Figure 4-24. *Alert notifications*

Destination

The Destination page allows you to determine where the report will be sent—Unmanaged Disk, FTP, Email, or the Inbox. In order for these options to work, you need to enable them in the Destination tab of the Program Job Server management page. Each one of these options has a "Clean up instance after scheduling" check box. By selecting this option, BO XI will automatically delete the instance from the report history so as to minimize the number of instances in the FileStore.

Unmanaged Disk The Unmanaged Disk option sends your report to a disk file with a name and location of your choosing. You can have the CMC customize a file name for you by using placeholder variables in the Specified File Name field. Your options are Title, ID, Owner, Date/Time, User Full Name, Email Address, and File Extension. For example, a file name of EmployeeReport_%SI_OWNER%.%EXT% will produce a file name that may look something like this: EmployeeReport_Administrator.PDF. The full list of placeholder variables is shown in Table 4-1.

Table 4-1. *Destination File Name Placeholder Variables*

Variable	Description
%SI_NAME%	Title
%EXT%	File extension
%SI_ID%	SI_ID value
%SI_OWNER%	Owner name
%SI_STARTTIME%	Date/Time report was run
%SI_USERFULLNAME%	User full name
%SI_EMAIL_ADDRESS%	E-mail address

The Unmanaged Disk option page is shown in Figure 4-25.

Figure 4-25. *Unmanaged Disk option/Destination page*

FTP The FTP options (see Figure 4-26) allow you to specify an FTP server as the destination for the report. You have the same file naming options as for an unmanaged disk file, but you can also specify the FTP host and port number along with the user name, password, and account name.

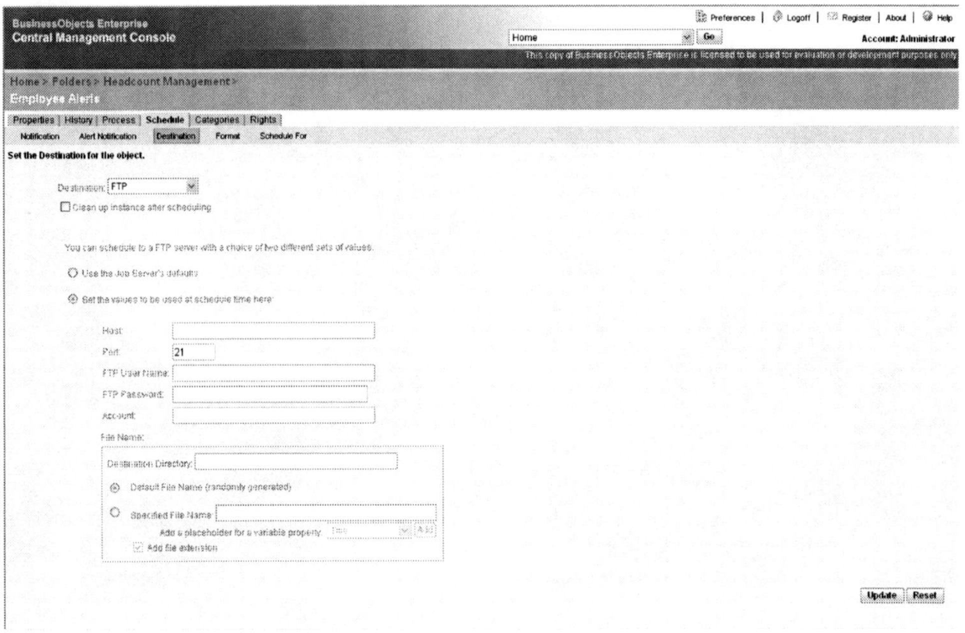

Figure 4-26. *FTP option/Destination page*

E-mail The Email option (see Figure 4-27) will send your report to the specified e-mail addresses upon completion with the file name you specify. You can even use placeholder variables—Title, ID, Owner, Date/Time, User Full Name, and Email Address—in both the subject and message body so that your e-mail could read, "Attached is the Daily Sales Report for 4/1/2007." In the body of the message, you also have the option to add a Viewer Hyperlink so the recipient can click this and see the report in the browser. You may wish to check with your e-mail administrator before attaching report output to e-mails. Too many large reports will tax the e-mail servers. I was warned once about this myself.

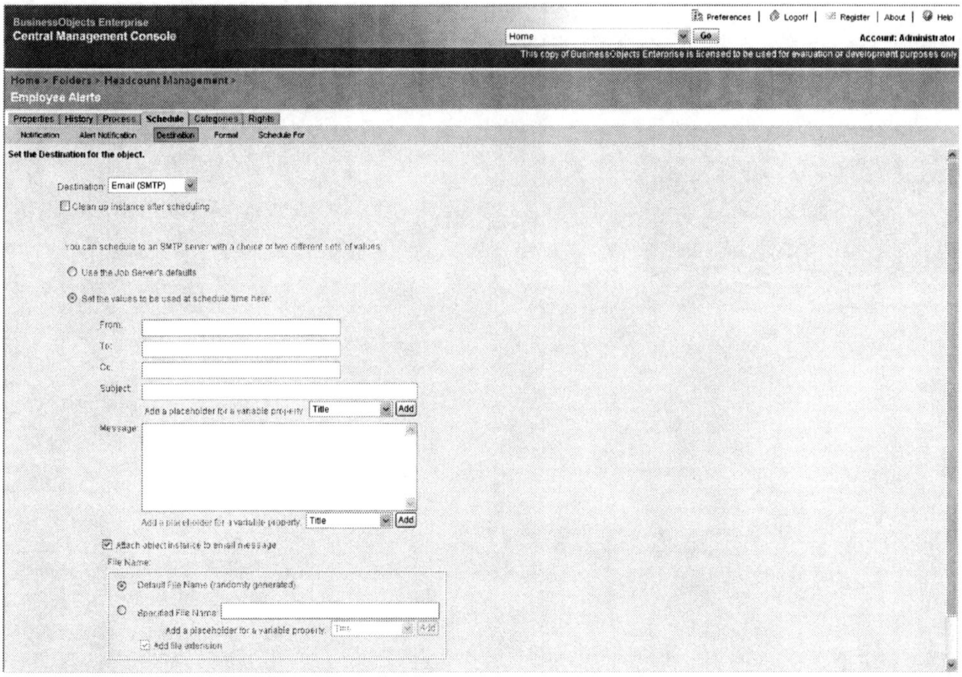

Figure 4-27. *Email option/Destination page*

Inbox The Inbox functions like the Microsoft Outlook Inbox. It serves as a destination for report output aimed at specific users. Every user automatically receives their own Inbox, and you don't need to do anything extra to create one. The Inbox will list the reports, who sent them, and when, along with a description. Users can then move these reports to other folders as they see fit. The Inbox destination setup is shown in Figure 4-28.

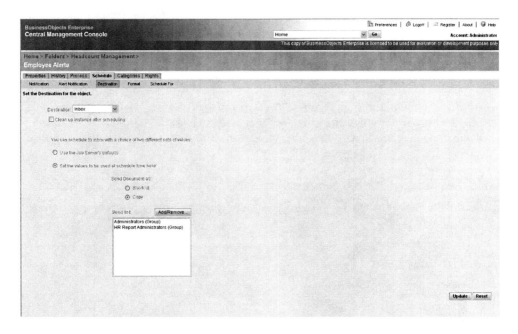

Figure 4-28. *Inbox option/Destination page*

Format

The Format tab establishes the output format for the report. Here you can determine whether the report should be created as a Crystal report, PDF, Excel, Word, or one of the many flavors of ASCII output. The format options are shown in Figure 4-29.

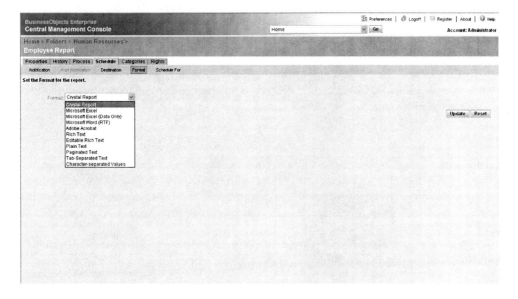

Figure 4-29. *Format page*

Most of the format options available have their own options particular to the output type. What the export options mean and how to access them programmatically is discussed in Chapter 6.

Schedule For

The Schedule For option shown in Figure 4-30 allows you to determine whether your scheduled report applies only to yourself or to a group or list of individual users. This option is intended for use with Crystal reports that use Business Views as their data sources and Web Intelligence documents that read from universes.

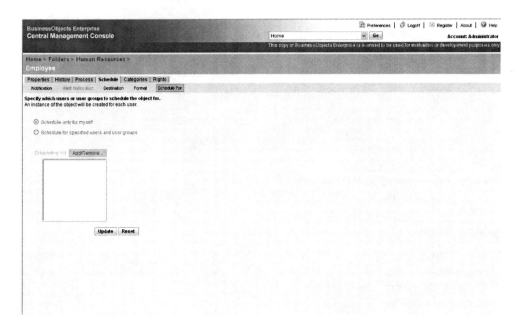

Figure 4-30. *Schedule For page*

Schedule For is geared toward report bursting. If, say, you have a status report that you wish to run by department, you can indicate that on this page. When the report runs, individual instances for each department will be created.

Categories

Categories are a feature new to the XI version. They are simply general collection names to which you can assign objects. You may have built a similar feature into your own applications in the past. One object can belong to multiple categories and one category may contain multiple objects. You can then ask BO XI to return all the objects that are members of a particular category.

Assigning categories is quite easy. To assign a corporate category, choose the Categories tab and click the Corporate link. Then click the Assign Categories button to display the page shown in Figure 4-31.

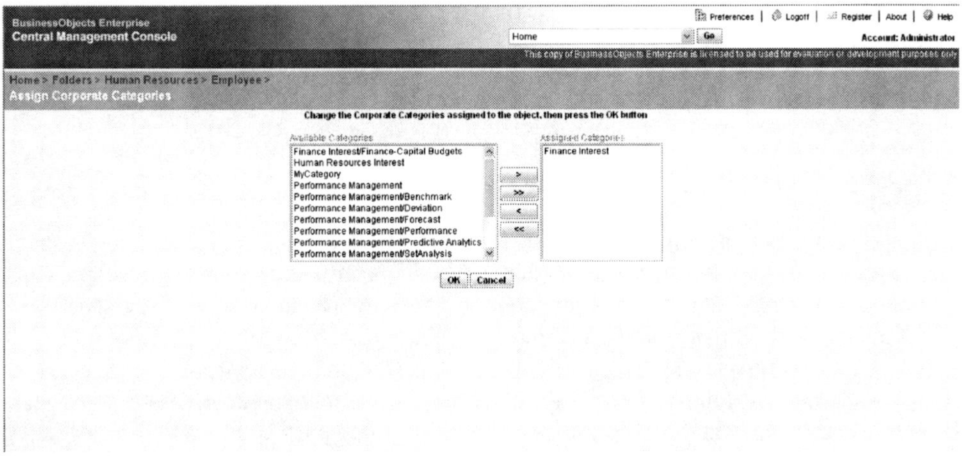

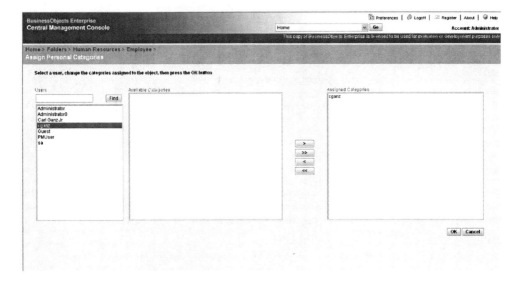

Figure 4-31. *Assigning corporate categories*

Use the arrows (double-clicking is not supported) to move your selections between the mutually exclusive list boxes and click OK.

Personal categories work a bit differently in that you need to select a user first and then you'll see the personal categories of that user, provided you have the rights to do so. Otherwise, you will only be able to select the user's name as a category. In Figure 4-32, I'm logged in as an administrator so I can see all the personal categories for an administrator. When I select cganz, I can only see the name and may assign only that.

Figure 4-32. *Assigning personal categories*

Rights

The Rights tab allows you to establish security rights over your reports. Security is discussed at length in Chapter 10.

Objects

The Objects option is more appropriately labeled Object Packages, for that is what it handles. An *object package* is a collection of objects that can be dealt with as a batch. For example, suppose you have a dozen sales reports that run daily at 2 p.m. and are e-mailed to the same group of people. Rather than create a dozen report schedules and set up the destination with the same e-mail addresses, you can place all these reports in an object package and set up the schedule and e-mail destination once. Any object that can be scheduled, like reports and executable code, can exist in an object package. The Objects main page is shown in Figure 4-33.

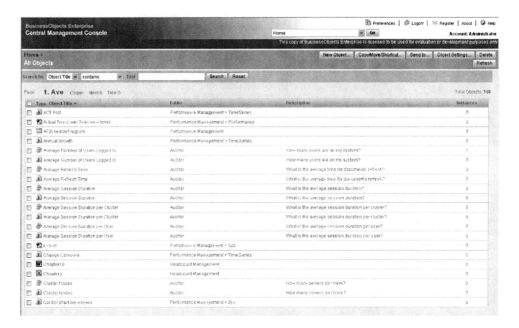

Figure 4-33. *Objects page*

Because BO XI ships with a number of auditing reports, the Objects page will be well populated. The links at the top—Ave, Corpor, Most A, and Tree O—are navigation aids so you can skip to the desired part of the alphabetized list.

To create a new object package, click the New Object button and then choose Object Package. You'll be prompted for a name, a description, and a target folder. Click Submit to create your new object package and begin adding objects to it. Should you attempt to load anything other than a report template or executable code to your object package, you'll receive an error, as report templates and executable code are the only items that can be scheduled.

Each time a scheduled object package runs, it creates an instance of that object package. This instance contains individual instances of the component objects. Because component instances are tied to object package instances, rather than to the base instance of the objects themselves, removing the base instance won't remove the historical instances.

Note the "Scheduled package fails upon individual component failure" check box. Choosing this option means that if one of the objects in the package fails, the entire package is marked as failed on the history page.

Calendars

Calendars are essentially custom schedules. You can create calendars to use any set of dates you wish. If your report scheduling requirements do not neatly fall into the periodic categories of daily, weekly, or monthly, you can create a calendar to set which days your report will print.

Calendars can be managed by selecting the Calendars option from the main CMC menu (refer back to Figure 4-1). Click the New Calendar button to see the screen shown in Figure 4-34, which allows you to name and describe your calendar.

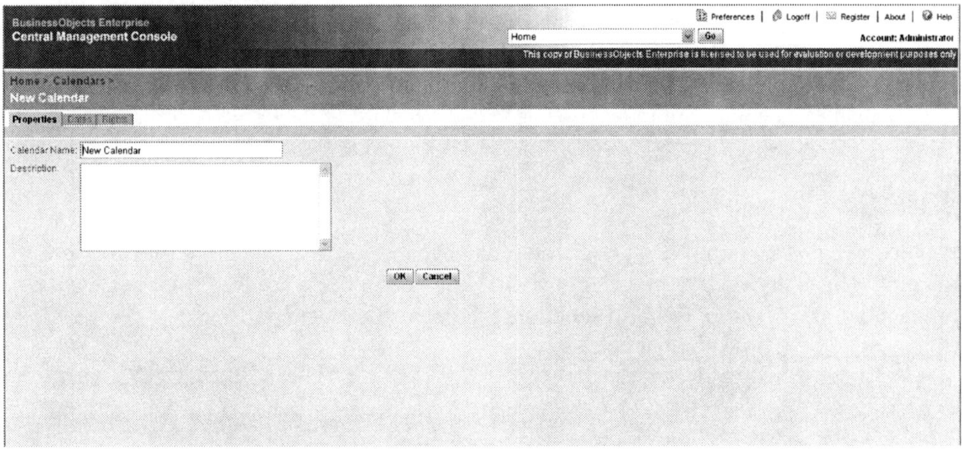

Figure 4-34. *Adding a calendar*

Click the OK button to commit your new calendar to the CMC and then select the Dates tab. You'll see a screen similar to the one shown in Figure 4-35.

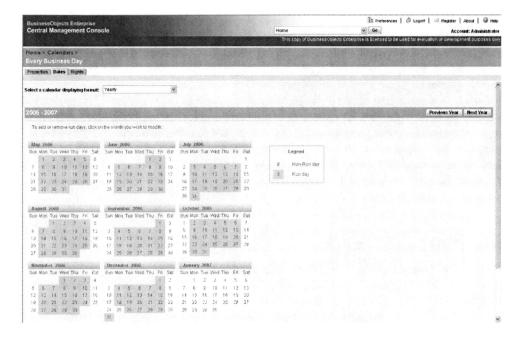

Figure 4-35. *Selecting dates*

Here you can select the dates you want for your calendar. You can do this by choosing individual dates or by using a generic monthly calendar that will apply to all days of that month going forward. I'm not sure if there is a limit to how far into the future you can set up schedules using a calendar, but in testing I've taken it well into the twenty-second century.

Events

Events are listeners that wait for a certain action to occur and then trigger another action based on it. The main Events screen is shown in Figure 4-36. There are three types of events: File, Schedule, and Custom. File and Schedule events are the most common.

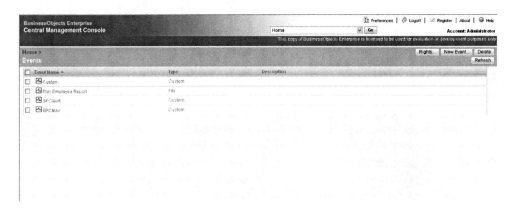

Figure 4-36. *Events*

File and Schedule Events

A File event acts like the .NET FileSystemWatcher class. It checks for the presence of a specified file name at a given location. Once this file appears, the action associated with the event triggers. You could set the event to watch for the import dump file that a database table will need to provide data to run a report. When the file appears, the scheduled program assembly will import the data and then run the report. More often, the file is simply an empty ASCII file that is used solely as a device to send a message to the event system to indicate that some outside process has met all the conditions necessary to run a report.

To create a File event, click the New Event button and then select a File event. You'll see the screen shown in Figure 4-37.

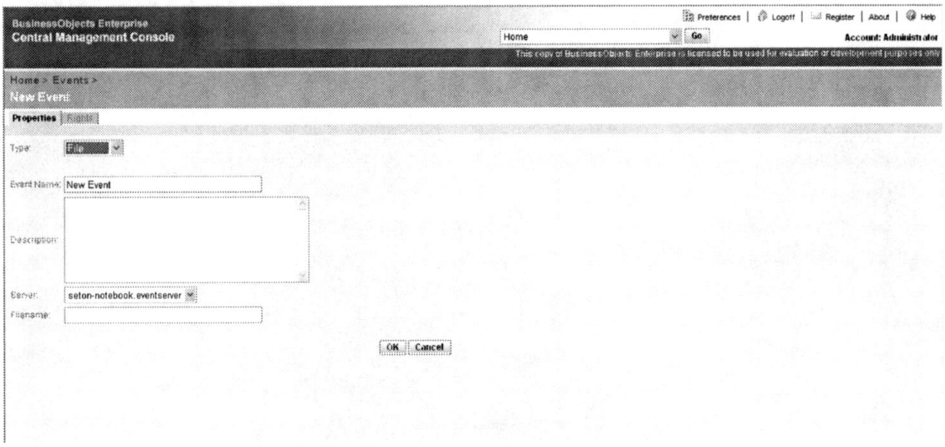

Figure 4-37. *Creating a File event*

Add the name of the file, click update, and your event is created.

Next, create another event of type Schedule. This event triggers upon completion of a scheduled task. Selecting this option will display the screen shown in Figure 4-38.

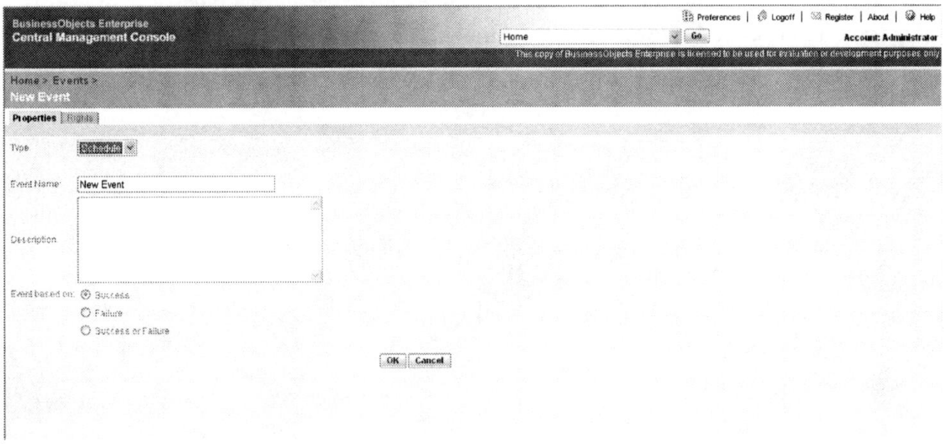

Figure 4-38. *Creating a Schedule event*

You can indicate whether the event should trigger when the scheduled task is successful, unsuccessful, or both. Since there is a special notifications screen that will send e-mails for both successfully and unsuccessfully completed tasks, you don't need to set up Schedule events to accomplish this.

Since an event won't do you much good unless it is associated with a process, you need to create a report schedule that anticipates the event. In the report schedule page the various frequency options have different run parameters. For example, the Weekly selection offers the options shown in Figure 4-39.

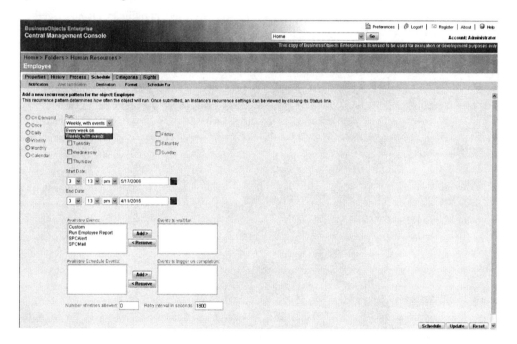

Figure 4-39. *Schedule option with and without events*

You can see that you have the choice of running "Every week on" or "Weekly, with events." Selecting the event option displays the screen shown in Figure 4-40.

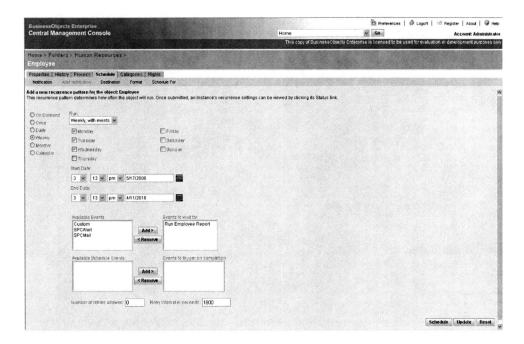

Figure 4-40. *Creating a schedule with an event*

You can schedule an event to wait for so the report doesn't make its weekly run without the event occurring. In addition, you can select a Schedule event that will execute after the report has completed. Here you may wish to associate the Schedule event with a piece of executable code, as you can then make the completion event do almost anything you want.

Custom Events

A Custom event isn't really an event. It's more like a shortcut to a piece of code. You can trigger it by clicking the Trigger this Event button (which will only appear once you've created a custom event) on the Event creation page as shown in Figure 4-41 or most likely by triggering it programmatically in your front-end application.

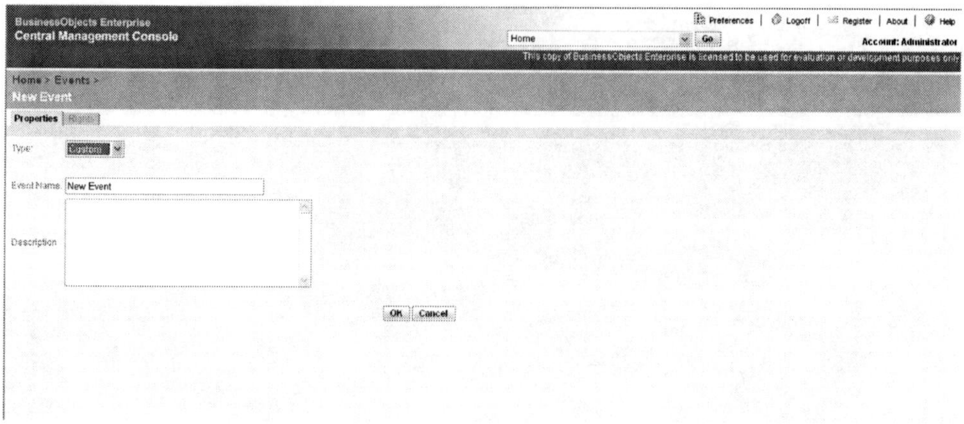

Figure 4-41. *Adding a custom event*

Summary

The Central Management Console allows you to administer every object in your BusinessObjects XI deployment. You learned how to work with folders and reports as well as how to schedule objects and send them to designated destinations with specific formatting options applied. Now that you understand the Central Management Console, you can handle almost all report-related aspects of BusinessObjects XI. In the next chapters, you'll learn how to perform programmatically the tasks covered interactively in this chapter.

CHAPTER 5

BusinessObjects XI SDK Programming I

The BusinessObjects XI object model is your gateway to accessing the full functionality of the product itself. Like the Microsoft Office Suite, almost anything that you can do interactively through the Central Management Console you can accomplish programmatically via the SDK. Most of the code discussed is backwardly compatible with versions 9 and 10 of Crystal Enterprise. Those features that are not are indicated as such.

Most of the programming examples we will look at are wrapped in a web service. Since BO XI is a server-based middleware application, it makes sense to expose its functionality through web services so that any application that can consume a web service—web and Windows front ends—can seamlessly access its features.

Connecting to BusinessObjects XI

Regardless of the task you wish to perform with the SDK, the first thing you'll need to do is establish a connection to the BO XI InfoStore. Connecting to the InfoStore is just like connecting to a SQL Server or Oracle database. Each web service method profiled in this book is overloaded so as to allow the developer to pass in all the connection information from the proxy application or a connection indicator string value—Development, QA, UAT, Production—so the web service can extract the connection information from a server-based XML file. Clearly, the latter approach is more secure, as your connection information does not need to be passed over the network.

The code in Listing 5-1 illustrates an overloaded web service method.

Listing 5-1. *Overloaded Web Service Method*

```
[WebMethod(MessageName="GetApplicationsViaLogonID")]
public DataSet GetApplications(string szUserID,
            string szPassword,
            string szSystem,
            string szAuthentication)
{
   return GetApplications(szUserID, szPassword, szSystem, szAuthentication, null);
}
```

```
[WebMethod(MessageName="GetApplicationsViaServer")]
public DataSet GetApplications(string szServer)
{
    return GetApplications(null, null, null, null, szServer);
}
```

MessageName is a web method attribute that allows the web service to use an alias that uniquely identifies overloaded method names. The GetApplicationsViaLogonID and the GetApplicationsViaServer names are never seen by the developer (outside of the WSDL), as they are only used by the autogenerated proxy class that acts as an intermediary between the application and the web service. IntelliSense will display only two signature sets for the GetApplications() method. All the web methods in this book use the same set of overloaded connection options, so for the sake of brevity they will not be repeated with every code sample.

■**Note** The SDK components are supported for a thin client/fat server architecture. All the SDK components should be installed on the server. If you wish to install the SDK components on the individual client machines, everything should work just fine, but technical support cannot help you should any problems arise. Business Objects has published this disclaimer in KnowledgeBase article c2018198.

There are three ways to establish connections to BusinessObjects XI: connect using either a user ID/password combination every time, tokens, or a trusted connection.

Connecting with User IDs

Connecting using the user ID/password every time is akin to connecting to an RDBMS. Each time the user ID and password must be validated against the database before a connection is established. Listing 5-2 shows how a connection to the InfoStore is made. The InfoStore is a class that acts as a communications link to the RDBMS where the BO XI data is stored. The first step is to instantiate a SessionMgr object. The Logon() method of this object receives the user ID, password, server name, and security authentication type to return an EnterpriseSession object. Working in tandem, they function as the BO XI equivalents of the SqlConnection or OracleConnection objects of ADO.NET. It is through the EnterpriseSession object that you can instantiate the InfoStore object through which you can interact with the BO XI database.

Listing 5-2. *Connecting to BO XI*

```
private EnterpriseSession GetIdentity(string szUserID,
        string szPassword,
        string szSystem,
        string szAuthentication,
        string szServer)
{
    EnterpriseSession oEnterpriseSession = null;
    SessionMgr oSessionMgr = null;
```

```
//Instantiate new SessionMgr object
oSessionMgr = new SessionMgr();

//If server code - Dev, QA, Prod, etc. - was used, obtain
//connection information from XML file
if (szServer != null  && szServer.Length > 0)
   GetLoginInfo(szServer,
       ref szUserID,
       ref szPassword,
       ref szSystem,
       ref szAuthentication);

//Use your decryption technology to decrypt password
//szPassword = DecryptData(szPassword);

//Connect to BO XI
oEnterpriseSession = oSessionMgr.Logon(szUserID, szPassword,
       szSystem, szAuthentication);

oSessionMgr.Dispose();

return oEnterpriseSession;

}
```

The XML file—should you choose to use one—that stores the connection information is shown in Listing 5-3. Each connection indicator has a `WorkingDirectory` element that refers to a physical location on the server to which files can be written. In case a connection indicator is not used, that is, all the connection information is passed in from the proxy, the `DefaultWorkingDirectory` element will provide the location of the working directory.

Listing 5-3. *Sample XML File with Connection Information*

```
<BOXI>
  <DefaultWorkingDirectory>c:\Temp\</DefaultWorkingDirectory>
  <Dev>
    <UserID>administrator</UserID>
    <Password></Password>
    <Server>seton-notebook:6400</Server>
    <Authentication>secEnterprise</Authentication>
    <WorkingDirectory>c:\Temp\</WorkingDirectory>
  </Dev>
  <QA>
    <UserID>administrator</UserID>
    <Password>kj134hkj34bkG13K4gv==</Password>
    <Server>myservername</Server>
    <Authentication>secEnterprise</Authentication>
    <WorkingDirectory>c:\Temp\</WorkingDirectory>
```

```
    </QA>
...
</BOXI>
```

After any interaction with BO XI, you'll need to log off, just as you would close an open connection to a database once your transaction is complete. If you don't log off, the connection will remain open for 20 minutes by default. Logging off simply involves invoking the LogOff() method of the EnterpriseSession object like this:

```
oEnterpriseSession.Logoff()
```

In case you have a license to only a limited number of concurrent users, you reduce conflicts by cleaning up after yourself. When ending a web session, be sure to invoke the Session.Abandon() method to destroy the ASP.NET session. Then, call the Clear() method of the Cookies collection to open the way for future logons:

```
Session.Abandon();
Response.Cookies.Clear();
```

Connecting with Tokens

You can also connect to the InfoStore using a token. Doing so will save the validation process of passing the user ID and password every time. Though tokens will reduce the number of resources needed to validate a user, they don't necessarily work any faster. A token is a string value that you can designate as valid for a certain number of minutes and/or a certain number of login attempts. Using a token is more efficient than opening an EnterpriseSession object at the beginning of your application's lifetime and not closing it again until the user is done. On web applications, it's best not to assign an EnterpriseSession object to a session variable, as this will consume too many resources in high concurrency systems. You can't assume that all BO XI installations operate on an unlimited license scheme. You'd be better off storing the token as a cookie.

The code to obtain a token is shown in Listing 5-4. Just to obtain the token the first time you still need to log on using SessionMgr and EnterpriseSession objects, but after that the token will suffice.

Listing 5-4. *Obtaining a Token*

```
private string GetToken(string szUserID,
    string szPassword,
    string szSystem,
    string szAuthentication,
    string szServer)
{
    EnterpriseSession oEnterpriseSession = null;
    SessionMgr oSessionMgr = null;
    string szToken;

    //Instantiate new SessionMgr object
    oSessionMgr = new SessionMgr();
```

```
//If server code - Dev, QA, Prod, etc. - was used, obtain
//connection information from XML file
if (szServer != null  && szServer.Length > 0)
   GetLoginInfo(szServer,
       ref szUserID,
       ref szPassword,
       ref szSystem,
       ref szAuthentication);

//Use your decryption technology to decrypt password
//szPassword = DecryptData(szPassword);

//Connect to BO XI
oEnterpriseSession = oSessionMgr.Logon(szUserID, szPassword,
   szSystem, szAuthentication);

        //WCA is an abbreviation for Web Component Adapter
szToken = oEnterpriseSession.LogonTokenMgr.
   CreateWCATokenEx (Environment.MachineName, 10, 100);

oSessionMgr.Dispose();

return szToken;
}
```

In this code, the `CreateWCATokenEx()` method (the `CreateLogonTokenEx()` method has been deprecated but is retained for backward compatibility) receives the machine name, the number of minutes the token may remain active, and the number of connections the token can make before it expires. By passing the machine name, the generated token can only be used to connect from that machine. If an empty string is passed instead, the token will be valid from all machines. The maximum number of minutes for a token life is 1440, or one full day. By comparison, the `LogonTokenMgr.DefaultToken` property provides a token specific to the session in which it was requested. Once that session ends, so does the default token. A token string will look something like this:

```
SETON-NOTEBOOK@3596JGJY78PkxCnGDiDO3594JbebCLEBOJ8JEXUPONEOFF
```

Once you have the token, you can log in using the code in Listing 5-5.

Listing 5-5. *Connecting via a Token*

```
private EnterpriseSession GetIdentityWithToken(string szToken)
{
   EnterpriseSession oEnterpriseSession = null;
   SessionMgr oSessionMgr = null;

   //Instantiate new SessionMgr object
   oSessionMgr = new SessionMgr();
```

```
//Connect to BO XI
oEnterpriseSession = oSessionMgr.LogonWithToken(szToken);

oSessionMgr.Dispose();

return oEnterpriseSession;
}
```

Connecting with Trusted Connections

You also have the option of connecting to BO XI using a trusted connection. This approach enables you to log on without a password because you've already established trust with CMC ahead of time. To establish a trusted connection, select the Authentication option from the main menu and choose the Enterprise tab. You'll see the page shown in Figure 5-1.

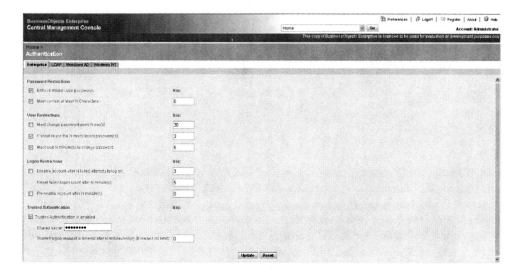

Figure 5-1. *Enterprise authentication tab*

Toward the bottom of this page you'll see a check box labeled "Trusted Authentication is enabled". Check this box and enter some text for the Shared Secret text box. The next step is to create a text file called TrustedPrincipal.conf that contains the text you entered in the Shared Secret text box in this format:

```
SharedSecret=MyDogElke
```

You'll need to save this text file in the \Program Files\Business Objects\BusinessObjects Enterprise 11.5\win32_x86\plugins\auth\secEnterprise directory. The code in Listing 5-6, which creates a trusted connection, will look to the TrustedPrincipal.conf file in this directory, compare the SharedSecret tag value with that you entered in the CMC, and validate you as a user.

Listing 5-6. *Using a Trusted Connection*

```
private EnterpriseSession ConnectTrusted()
{
    SessionMgr oSessionMgr = null;
    TrustedPrincipal oTrustedPrincipal = null;
    EnterpriseSession oEnterpriseSession = null;

    oSessionMgr = new SessionMgr();
    oTrustedPrincipal =
        oSessionMgr.CreateTrustedPrincipal("Administrator",
        "SETON-NOTEBOOK:6400");
    oEnterpriseSession =
        oSessionMgr.LogonTrustedPrincipal(oTrustedPrincipal);

    return oEnterpriseSession;
}
```

Examining the Connection Objects

There are a few properties of the EnterpriseSession object that may prove helpful in your application development and debugging. The CMSName property stores the name of the CMS machine to which the connection is currently made. The APSName property stores the name of the CMS server. In many cases this will be the same value, and on my development machine it is SETON-NOTEBOOK. APS refers to Automated Process Server, the original name for the Crystal Enterprise repository in the original versions of the product. The APSVersion property will return an enumerated value indicating the version of the software. The value for the current incarnation is ceAPSVersion11_5. ClusterName stores the name of the CMS cluster of the current connection. ClusterMembers returns the names of the CMS machines in the named cluster.

The SystemInfoProperty class returns a list of the functionality supported (or not) by your install of BO XI. Listing 5-7 shows this collection in action.

Listing 5-7. *SystemInfoProperty Class*

```
oStringBuilder = new System.Text.StringBuilder();

foreach(SystemInfoProperty oSystemInfoProperty in
    oEnterpriseSession.SystemInfoProperties)
    oStringBuilder.AppendFormat("{0} = {1}\n",
        oSystemInfoProperty.Name, oSystemInfoProperty.Value);
```

This code will produce the output shown in Listing 5-8.

Listing 5-8. *SystemInfoProperty Class Values*

```
SI_CAN_CREATE_GROUPS = True
SI_CAN_CREATE_USERS = True
SI_IS_VALID_PRODUCT = True
SI_PRODUCT_ID = 49972
SI_PRODUCT_DESCRIPTION = BusinessObjects Enterprise Premium Version
SI_CAN_PRINT_REPORTS = True
SI_RAS_KEYCODE_PRESENT = True
SI_CAN_SCHEDULE_TO_DEST = True
SI_CAN_USE_EVENTS = True
SI_CAN_SET_LIMITS = True
SI_CAN_USE_THIRD_PARTY_AUTHEN = True
SI_CAN_USE_NOTIFICATION = True
SI_CAN_USE_CLUSTERING = True
SI_CAN_USE_PROCESSING_EXT = True
SI_CAN_USE_PROGRAM_OBJECTS = True
SI_CAN_USE_METADATA =   True
SI_CAN_USE_SERVER_GROUPS = True
SI_IS_EVAL_PRODUCT = True
SI_CAN_CREATE_NEWUSERS = True
SI_PREMIUM_KEYCODE_PRESENT = True
SI_PRO_KEYCODE_PRESENT = False
SI_STD_KEYCODE_PRESENT  = False
SI_OEM_KEYCODE_PRESENT = False
SI_ENABLE_WEBI = True
SI_ENABLE_PORTAL = True
SI_ENABLE_PIKS = True
SI_ENABLE_DASHBOARD_MANAGER = True
SI_ENABLE_PERFORMANCE_MANAGER = True
SI_ENABLE_SETS = False
SI_ENABLE_SPC = False
SI_ENABLE_PREDICTION = False
SI_ENABLE_LIVEOFFICE = True
SI_ENABLE_SCHEDULE =   True
SI_ENABLE_AUDIT True
SI_ENABLE_INTERACTIVE_REPORTING True
SI_ENABLE_MYINFOVIEW_DASHBOARD = True
SI_ENABLE_PUBLISH_CR = True
SI_ENABLE_PUBLISH_CA = True
SI_ENABLE_BCAP = True
SI_CAN_USE_FULLCLIENT = True
BOE.BOEFamily = 1
BOE.EnableBOE = 1
BOE.EnableEncyclopedia = 1
BOE.EnableMultipleMachines = 1
BOE.EnableProcessTracker = 1
```

```
BOE.EnablePublish.CrystalEnterprise.Profile = 1
BOE.EnablePublishing = 1
BOE.Processors = 1
```

You can determine who's connected to BO XI by extracting the Connection entries from the InfoStore. The code shown in Listing 5-9 extracts the currently logged in users and stores the information to a DataTable.

Listing 5-9. *Extracting Currently Logged-In Users*

```
szSQL = "SELECT SI_ID, SI_NAME, SI_AUTHEN_METHOD, " +
   "SI_LAST_ACCESS, SI_USERID, SI_LOGON_ALIAS " +
   "FROM CI_SYSTEMOBJECTS " +
   "WHERE SI_KIND = 'Connection'";

oInfoObjects = oInfoStore.Query(szSQL);

oDT = new DataTable();

oDT.Columns.Add(new DataColumn("ID"));
oDT.Columns.Add(new DataColumn("Name"));
oDT.Columns.Add(new DataColumn("AuthenticationMethod"));
oDT.Columns.Add(new DataColumn("LastAccess"));
oDT.Columns.Add(new DataColumn("UserID"));
oDT.Columns.Add(new DataColumn("LogonAlias"));

foreach (InfoObject oInfoObject in oInfoObjects)
{
   oConnection = ((CrystalDecisions.Enterprise.Desktop.Connection) oInfoObject);

   oDR = oDT.NewRow();

   oDR["ID"] = oConnection.ID;
   oDR["Name"] = oConnection.Title;
   oDR["AuthenticationMethod"] = oConnection.AuthenticationMethod;
   oDR["LastAccess"] = oConnection.LastAccess;
   oDR["UserID"] = oConnection.UserID;
   oDR["LogonAlias"] = oConnection.UserAlias;

   oDT.Rows.Add(oDR);
}
```

The data returned by this SQL statement will look something like Figure 5-2.

	ID	Name	AuthenticationMethod	LastAccess	UserID	LogonAlias
►	8925	System Account	server-token	5/19/2006 8:17:12 AM	10	
	8937	Administrator	secEnterprise	5/19/2006 8:19:27 AM	12	secEnterprise:Administrator
	8940	Administrator	secEnterprise	5/19/2006 8:21:38 AM	12	secEnterprise:Administrator
	8946	Administrator	secEnterprise	5/19/2006 8:23:11 AM	12	secEnterprise:Administrator
	8953	Administrator	secEnterprise	5/19/2006 8:50:38 AM	12	secEnterprise:Administrator
✱						

Figure 5-2. *Currently logged-in users*

Querying the InfoStore

The starting point for extracting information from the InfoStore is to create an InfoObjects collection object that contains the results of an SQL query. This can be done via the Query() method like this:

```
oInfoObjects = oInfoStore.Query(szSQL);
```

The BO XI query language is syntactically modeled after SQL, and often it's difficult to remember that you're not dealing with real SQL. BO XI even provides a Query Builder tool where you can create and execute these SQL statements. Query Builder is the equivalent of SQL Server's Query Analyzer or Oracle's SQL Plus, though not nearly as versatile because of its HTML interface. The Query Builder page is shown in Figure 5-3.

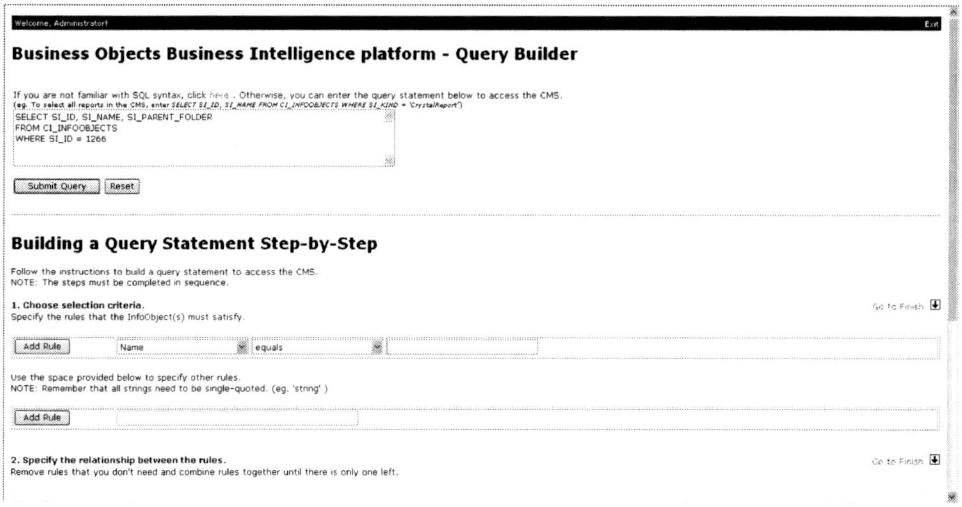

Figure 5-3. *Query Builder*

The results of this query are shown in Figure 5-4.

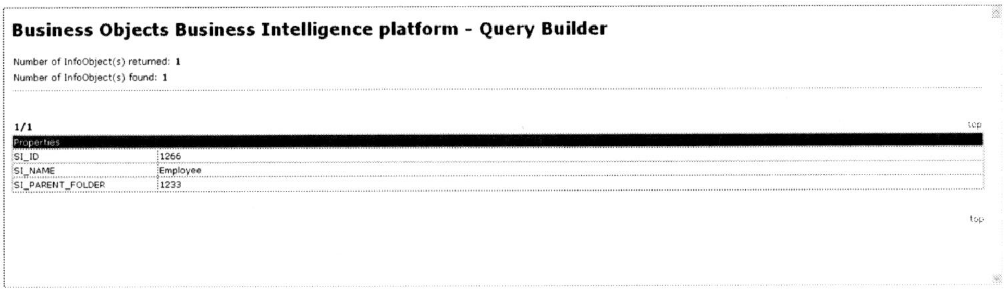

Business Objects Business Intelligence platform - Query Builder

Number of InfoObject(s) returned: 1
Number of InfoObject(s) found: 1

1/1   top
Properties
SI_ID   1266
SI_NAME   Employee
SI_PARENT_FOLDER   1233

                                                                                                  top

Figure 5-4. *Query results*

The InfoStore SQL Language

The InfoStore SQL language only functions as in-line SQL, and there is no equivalent of a stored procedure. Nevertheless, it still makes sense to encapsulate your SQL commands in parameterized methods that can return a properly formatted query string so as to isolate your data access layer. I have not done this in the examples in this book solely to make the code examples more readable. In my production applications, I've created a BO XI access layer that encapsulates the connectivity to the InfoStore and retrieval of InfoStore objects much like the Microsoft Data Access Application blocks encapsulate connectivity to your RDBMS and returns DataTables. You can think of an InfoObjects collection as you would a DataTable. Both contain disconnected data, meaning that the data is accessible from the object even after the connection that first created it is closed.

The InfoStore SQL language supports all the basic SQL commands: SELECT, FROM, WHERE, and ORDER BY. You cannot INSERT, UPDATE, or DELETE into the InfoStore, and such actions must be performed through the various properties and methods of the object model.

▓Note Before examining any SQL commands, please understand that the same rules of efficient database application design apply equally to the BO XI InfoStore as they do to any other RDBMS. This means that executing SELECT * is considered sloppy, and allowing your users to pull too much information about too many reports will slow the response time to a crawl. You'll need to experiment a bit to see what your system performance is, given concurrency and the number of processors.

SQL Basics

Let's try a few examples to get started. To pull the ID and name of all the Crystal Report objects in the InfoStore, you can execute the following command:

```
SELECT SI_ID, SI_NAME
FROM CI_INFOOBJECTS
WHERE SI_KIND = 'CrystalReport'
ORDER BY SI_UPDATE_TS
```

Should you want the results in descending date order, you can use the DESC keyword like this:

```
SELECT SI_ID, SI_NAME
FROM CI_INFOOBJECTS
WHERE SI_KIND = 'CrystalReport'
ORDER BY SI_UPDATE_TS DESC
```

The LIKE statement is supported, so you can extract data using wildcards. For example, to extract all reports whose names begin with "Emp", use

```
SELECT SI_NAME
FROM CI_INFOOBJECTS
WHERE SI_KIND = 'CrystalReport'
AND SI_NAME LIKE 'Emp%'
```

Likewise, you can search for text within text like this:

```
SELECT SI_NAME
FROM CI_INFOOBJECTS
WHERE SI_KIND = 'CrystalReport'
AND SI_NAME LIKE '%Label%'
```

The underscore is a wildcard character. In this SQL, all reports whose SI_NAMEs have a space as their second character, a dot as the third, and a *J* as the fourth will be returned regardless of what the first character is.

```
SELECT SI_ID, SI_NAME
FROM CI_INFOOBJECTS
WHERE SI_KIND = 'CrystalReport'
AND SI_NAME LIKE '_. J%'
```

Ranges can be handled with brackets. This SQL will return all reports whose SI_NAMEs begin with 1 or 2.

```
SELECT SI_ID, SI_NAME
FROM CI_INFOOBJECTS
WHERE SI_KIND = 'CrystalReport'
AND SI_NAME LIKE '[1-2]. J%'
```

Finally, the caret indicates negation. This SQL will return all reports whose SI_NAMEs are anything other than 1.

```
SELECT SI_ID, SI_NAME
FROM CI_INFOOBJECTS
WHERE SI_KIND = 'CrystalReport'
AND SI_NAME LIKE '[^1]. J%'
```

Boolean Values

Real Boolean values don't exist in the InfoStore. Rather, you can use 1 for True and 0 for False like this:

```
SELECT SI_ID, SI_NAME, SI_INSTANCE
FROM CI_INFOOBJECTS
WHERE SI_KIND = 'CrystalReport'
AND SI_INSTANCE = 1
```

Though the displayed results from the Query Builder show the words *True* and *False*, using them in SQL will return misleading queries. The following SQL statement:

```
SELECT SI_ID, SI_NAME, SI_INSTANCE
FROM CI_INFOOBJECTS
WHERE SI_KIND = 'CrystalReport'
AND SI_INSTANCE = 'False'
```

will return the same result set as this one:

```
SELECT SI_ID, SI_NAME, SI_INSTANCE
FROM CI_INFOOBJECTS
WHERE SI_KIND = 'CrystalReport'
AND SI_INSTANCE = 'True'
```

The reason is that the strings True and False both evaluate to 0, so both of these statements will respond as if you used this:

```
SELECT SI_ID, SI_NAME
FROM CI_INFOOBJECTS
WHERE SI_KIND = 'CrystalReport'
AND SI_INSTANCE = 0
```

Subqueries

Subqueries are not supported, so you can't retrieve the reports for a given folder number like this:

```
SELECT SI_ID, SI_NAME
FROM CI_INFOOBJECTS
WHERE SI_KIND = 'CrystalReport'
AND SI_PARENTID IN (SELECT SI_ID
   FROM CI_INFOOBJECTS
   WHERE SI_KIND = 'Folder'
   AND SI_ID = 1233)
```

but IN clauses (and NOT IN clauses also) are supported, so if you obtain the SI_IDs of these reports, you can retrieve them like this:

```
SELECT SI_ID, SI_NAME
FROM CI_INFOOBJECTS
WHERE SI_KIND = 'CrystalReport'
AND SI_ID IN (1266, 1272)
```

Note, however, that BETWEEN is also supported.

```
SELECT SI_ID, SI_CREATION_TIME
FROM CI_INFOOBJECTS
WHERE SI_ID BETWEEN 1 AND 100
```

AS Clause and Aliasing

Neither column nor table aliasing is available. This next SQL statement will generate an error:

```
SELECT SI_NAME AS Name, SI_ID AS ID
FROM CI_INFOOBJECTS
WHERE SI_KIND = 'CrystalReport'
```

However, the following one will return blank information for every Crystal Report entry in the system:

```
SELECT i.SI_NAME, i.SI_ID
FROM CI_INFOOBJECTS i
WHERE SI_KIND = 'CrystalReport'
```

MISSING COLUMN DATA

Here is a pitfall to be alert for. We are all accustomed to having a SQL statement fail when mistyping a column or table name. This does not always happen with BO XI. For example, the following SQL will execute without error:

```
SELECT SI_ID, SI_NAME, SI_THIS_DOESNT_EXIST
FROM CI_INFOOBJECTS
WHERE SI_KIND = 'CrystalReport'
```

even though SI_THIS_DOESNT_EXIST is obviously not a data element. No data will return for this nonexistent column. This is not a design defect in the SDK. The reason for this is that some objects may have a given property, while another object may not. Unfortunately, there is no AS clause available that would permit you to create a virtual column. If an object does not have the requested property, then nothing is returned. If you need to return data that is specifically missing a certain property, say, reports that don't have any notifications assigned, you can accomplish this by checking for = NULL as shown here:

```
SELECT SI_ID, SI_NAME, SI_SCHEDULEINFO.SI_NOTIFICATION
FROM CI_INFOOBJECTS
WHERE SI_SCHEDULEINFO.SI_NOTIFICATION = NULL
AND SI_KIND = 'CrystalReport'
```

Aggregates

GROUP BY and HAVING are not supported, and the only aggregate function is COUNT. For example, the following will return the number of Crystal Reports in the system:

```
SELECT COUNT(SI_ID)
FROM CI_INFOOBJECTS
WHERE SI_KIND='CrystalReport'
```

To extract this property in code, use the SI_AGGREGATE_COUNT property as shown in Listing 5-10.

Listing 5-10. *Extracting the SI_AGGREGATE_COUNT Property*

```
int iCount;

szSQL = "Select COUNT(SI_ID) " +
    "From CI_INFOOBJECTS " +
    "Where SI_KIND='CrystalReport'";

oInfoObjects = oInfoStore.Query(szSQL);

iCount = ((int) oInfoObjects[1].
    Properties["SI_AGGREGATE_COUNT"].Properties["SI_ID"].Value);
```

COUNT(*) is not supported, but if you try to execute

```
SELECT COUNT(*)
FROM CI_INFOOBJECTS
WHERE SI_KIND='CrystalReport'
```

it will return zero, making you think that there are no matching records. Obviously, this lack of error generation can be quite confusing.

MIN and MAX are not directly supported, but the same effect can be achieved via the ALL keyword. For example, to find the InfoStore entry with the lowest SI_ID value, use the following SQL:

```
SELECT SI_ID, SI_NAME
FROM CI_INFOOBJECTS
WHERE SI_ID <= ALL SI_ID
```

Conversely, to find the one with the highest value, or the most recent addition to the Info-Store, simply reverse the operator like this:

```
SELECT SI_ID, SI_NAME
FROM CI_INFOOBJECTS
WHERE SI_ID <= ALL SI_ID
```

ALL compares the properties of one object with those of all others, including itself.

Distinct

The DISTINCT keyword is ignored so the statement

```
SELECT DISTINCT SI_KIND
FROM CI_INFOOBJECTS
```

will return the same results as

```
SELECT SI_KIND
FROM CI_INFOOBJECTS
```

It looks like Business Objects may have intended to activate the DISTINCT feature at one point because the following statement will cause an error:

```
SELECT DISTINCTX SI_KIND
FROM CI_INFOOBJECTS
```

DISTINCT seems to have some meaning, but it is not active in the query language.

Top n

TOP n is also supported as shown here:

```
SELECT TOP 10 SI_NAME
FROM CI_SYSTEMOBJECTS
WHERE SI_KIND = 'User'
ORDER BY SI_NAME
```

By default, SQL queries return a maximum of 1000 records. Should you ever wish to extract more records than this, you can specify an arbitrary number using a TOP n statement, say, SELECT TOP 5000 FROM CI_SYSTEMOBJECTS. The 1000-record default is set in the Windows registry in a value named InfoStoreDefaultTopNValue, which can be found at HKEY_LOCAL_MACHINE\SOFTWARE\Business Objects\Suite 11.5\CMS\Instances\<CMS server name>. If you alter this value, you'll need to stop and restart the Central Management Server for the change to take effect.

SELECTUSINGPROPERTY

One undocumented feature is the SELECTUSINGPROPERTY command, which I learned somewhat unintentionally from technical support. In a discussion as to how far the SQL commands can go before needing to resort to the object model, I asked about pulling a list of user groups from the InfoStore, selecting a group, and then retrieving the list of users within that selected group. The following command accomplishes this quite nicely:

```
SELECT SI_ID, SI_NAME, SI_DESCRIPTION, SI_USERFULLNAME
FROM CI_SYSTEMOBJECTS
WHERE SI_KIND='User'
AND SELECTUSINGPROPERTY(101,SI_ID,SI_GROUP_MEMBERS,SI_ID)
ORDER BY SI_NAME
```

Here 101 is the SI_ID of the requested group. Since this command is not documented anywhere in cyberspace, I have no idea what the other parameters mean, and technical support says they're not sure either. Technical support has told me time and again that undocumented features are not officially supported and there is no guarantee that they will be available in future releases. Use them at your own risk.

Property Storage

Just like any RDBMS, some data elements are indexed and some are not. Of course, it's more efficient to conduct searches against indexed elements. What constitutes an indexed property in the BO XI InfoStore is an entry that has its own column in the database underlying the

InfoStore. This database is created when the product is first installed. Most of the properties are stored in a binary column, and though searchable, are not as speedily searched as an indexed property stored in a column. This architecture is explained in more detail in Chapter 2. The list of indexed columns is shown in Table 5-1.

Table 5-1. *Indexed Properties*

Property
SI_CUID
SI_GUID
SI_HIDDEN_OBJECT
SI_ID
SI_INSTANCE_OBJECT
SI_KIND
SI_NAME
SI_NAMEDUSER
SI_NEXTRUNTIME
SI_OWNERID
SI_PARENTID
SI_PLUGIN_OBJECT
SI_PROGID
SI_RECURRING
SI_RUID
SI_RUNNABLE_OBJECT
SI_SCHEDULE_STATUS
SI_UPDATE_TS

Working with Dates

Date and time values are stored as UTC—universal time—values, that is, Greenwich Mean Time. A report that is created at 9:30 p.m. on December 1, 2006, EST is stored in the SI_CREATION_TIME property as 2:30 a.m. on December 2, 2006, as Greenwich, England, is five hours ahead of the eastern coast of the United States. To realign the dates and times, the SDK provides a UTCConverter class that will perform this translation for you. Listing 5-11 shows it in action.

Listing 5-11. *UTCConverter Class*

```
public string ConvertToUTC(string szUserID,
        string szPassword,
        string szSystem,
        string szAuthentication,
        string szServer,
        DateTime dDateTime)
```

```
{
  CrystalDecisions.Enterprise.Utils.UTCConverter oUTCConverter;
  EnterpriseSession oEnterpriseSession = null;
  string szResult;

  oEnterpriseSession = GetIdentity(szUserID, szPassword, szSystem,
          szAuthentication, szServer);

  oUTCConverter = new CrystalDecisions.Enterprise.Utils.UTCConverter();

  szResult = oUTCConverter.ConvertToUTC(dDateTime,
     oEnterpriseSession.TimeZone);

  return szResult;
}
```

The code in Listing 5-12 invokes the web service method that encapsulates this conversion utility.

Listing 5-12. *Converting Dates to UTC*

```
localhost.CEWebService oCEWebService;
DateTime dDateFrom;
DateTime dDateTo;
string szDateFrom;
string szDateTo;
string szSQL;

dDateFrom = new DateTime(2006, 12, 1, 0, 0, 0);
dDateTo = new DateTime(2006, 12, 1, 23, 59, 59);

oCEWebService = new localhost.CEWebService();
oCEWebService.Credentials = System.Net.CredentialCache.DefaultCredentials;

szDateFrom = oCEWebService.ConvertToUTC("Dev", dDateFrom);
szDateTo = oCEWebService.ConvertToUTC("Dev", dDateTo);

szSQL = "SELECT SI_ID, SI_CREATION_TIME " +
   "FROM CI_INFOOBJECTS " +
   "WHERE SI_CREATION_TIME >= '" + szDateFrom + "' " +
   "AND SI_CREATION_TIME <= '" + szDateTo + "'";
```

This code will produce a SQL string that looks something like this:

```
SELECT SI_ID, SI_CREATION_TIME
FROM CI_INFOOBJECTS
WHERE SI_CREATION_TIME >= '2006-12-01 05:00:00.000'
AND SI_CREATION_TIME <= '2006-12-02 04:59:59.000'
```

Properties

There are three main virtual tables, also known as categories, in BO XI—CI_INFOOBJECTS, CI_SYSTEMOBJECTS, and CI_APPOBJECTS:

- CI_INFOOBJECTS stores information pertaining to the user desktop. You'll likely use this table the most. It contains data for report templates as well as report instances regardless of the format to which they are output. It also stores information relating to the FTP, SMTP, and disk file capabilities of BO XI. All executable programs that are stored in the InfoStore are managed through CI_INFOOBJECTS as well.

- CI_SYSTEMOBJECTS stores information pertaining to the administrative desktop. This includes folders, servers, users, and user groups. It also handles calendars, events, license keys, and information about the four types of authentication—secEnterprise, secLDAP, secWindowsNT, and secWinAD.

- CI_APPOBJECTS holds information about application objects as well as metric information about universes.

Since these are not real tables, there are no common keys between them. Thus, there is no concept of a JOIN in this flavor of SQL. It would come in handy to be able to join a table to itself so as to retrieve the name of a parent folder given the ID of a report. Unfortunately, this is not possible, and you'll need to execute two queries to obtain this information.

The SQL statements examined in the preceding section show some of the most commonly used properties, and it's important to understand exactly how they work. SI_ID is a unique identifier that functions essentially as a primary key. Like a primary key, it is assigned when a new entry, say a report or a user, is saved to the InfoStore and exists until the object it is associated with is destroyed. Unlike most other primary keys, you cannot set a starting value nor can you determine the increment.

You'll use the SI_ID property often. For example, you may wish to populate a combo box with report names and then use the SI_ID value to retrieve the report history. Just as with any RDBMS, the SI_ID will be lost of you delete the object it references with all related data like report instances. Thus, the InfoStore enforces referential integrity and cascading deletes. Should you wish to update the zero instance of a report, that is, the RPT template, you can choose File ➤ Save in Crystal Reports and select Enterprise from the Save dialog. This will allow you to save the modified report to BO XI without altering the SI_ID value.

Note The SI_ID does not retain its value when you migrate your reports from one server installation to another. Therefore, avoid hard coding any SI_ID values in your applications, as they will not work when migrating from one server to another. The same goes for the SI_GUID property. SI_GUID is a globally unique identifier—which means that while it is unique across space and time, it is still theoretically possible to generate a duplicate—and therefore will also change when the object it references moves from one server to another. SI_CUID, on the other hand, is a cluster identifier. This value will remain the same from server to server. Note that where the SI_ID is always a numeric value, SI_GUID, SI_CUID, and SI_RUID (the unique ID of the InfoObject in the object package) are all alphanumeric and look something like this: AXUDhPUtPvNBvGB.pQOrxC8.

The SI_NAME property holds the name of the object and acts as a one-line description of up to 100 characters. Use SI_DESCRIPTION if you need a longer description, as you can store up to 1024 characters there.

Note These 100- and 1024-character limits are enforced client side by JavaScript code in the CMC. In reality, you can store much more information in these properties. Since SI_NAME and SI_DESCRIPTION are stored in binary fields in the RDBMS, they could potentially hold millions of bytes of information. Of course, when you edit the entry in the CMC, the size limits will be enforced, and you won't be able to save without truncating your data. It's best to use a custom property in such cases. Custom properties are covered in Chapter 9.

SI_INSTANCE indicates whether an entry is a report instance. It's actually a Boolean value that recognizes zero for False and one for True. The InfoStore handles all True/False values in this fashion and does not support a true Boolean data type. After you develop a report with Crystal Reports and upload the RPT file through the CMC, the entry for this report will have an SI_INSTANCE value of zero. This is because this report contains no data and is just a template that can be run repeatedly in the future. When you run the report, an entry will be made in the Report history, and this entry will have an SI_INSTANCE value of one.

SI_PROGID and SI_KIND are two similar properties that indicate the type of entry in the InfoStore. They perform essentially the same function, and they differ only in their wording. SI_PROGID prefixes all the object types with "CrystalEnterprise". Since Business Objects now owns the product, all vestiges of the word *Crystal* are being purged from the product as part of the rebranding effort, and the SI_PROGID property is being deprecated and offered here only for backward compatibility, though there are a few places where it is still needed over SI_KIND as you'll see later on. Both of these SQL statements are the same:

```
SELECT SI_ID, SI_NAME, SI_DESCRIPTION, SI_USERFULLNAME
FROM CI_SYSTEMOBJECTS
WHERE SI_PROGID='CrystalEnterprise.User'
```

and

```
SELECT SI_ID, SI_NAME, SI_DESCRIPTION, SI_USERFULLNAME
FROM CI_SYSTEMOBJECTS
WHERE SI_KIND='User'
```

Table 5-2 lists all the possible values for SI_KIND.

Table 5-2. *SI_KIND Values*

AuditAdmin	FullClient	ReportAppServerAdmin
CacheServerAdmin	Hyperlink	Rtf
Calendar	Inbox	Server
Category	JobServerAdmin	Shortcut
CMSAdmin	LicenseKey	Smtp
Connection	Managed	SSOAdmin
CrystalReport	ObjectPackage	Txt
Diskunmanaged	Overload	Universe
Event	PageServerAdmin	User
EventServerAdmin	PersonalCategory	Usergroup
Excel	Pdf	Webi
FavoritesFolder	Powerpoint	WebiServerAdmin
Folder	Profile	Word
FileServerAdmin	Program	
Ftp	Publication	

Another important property is SI_PARENTID, which must not be confused with SI_PARENT_FOLDER. Objects in the InfoStore exist in a hierarchy. There is a top-level folder, which in turn can hold many sub-level folders or reports. Each sub-level folder can also hold many other sub-level folders or reports. Each of these objects has an SI_PARENT_FOLDER that allows you to determine its place in the hierarchy. For example, if you store your reports and folders in the InfoStore using the same structure that you wish them to appear in a menu, then by using SI_PARENT_FOLDER and a recursive function, you can dynamically create a menu that matches your InfoStore. (Such a recursive function is discussed in Chapter 9.) By comparison, SI_PARENTID refers to an object's parent. You'll commonly see this used in extracting report histories. Each report template (SI_INSTANCE = 0) may have many report instances (SI_INSTANCE = 1). The SI_PARENTID of these report instances is the SI_ID of the report template from which they were spawned.

By comparison, SI_ANCESTOR can be used to extract all the objects that are descendants of a specified object, regardless of how many generations removed. If you wanted to pull a list of all the Crystal Reports under a given folder regardless of their level of nesting, you could do so with the following SQL:

```
SELECT SI_ID, SI_NAME
FROM CI_INFOOBJECTS
WHERE SI_KIND = 'CrystalReport'
AND SI_ANCESTOR = 101
ORDER BY SI_UPDATE_TS
```

The `SI_CHILDREN` property indicates how many child objects another object owns. For example, the following SQL shows each folder and how many report templates and subfolders are directly under it:

```
SELECT SI_ID, SI_NAME, SI_CHILDREN
FROM CI_INFOOBJECTS
WHERE SI_KIND = 'Folder'
```

Report history instances are not included in this number. They would be the children of the report template that generated them and not the folder they're stored in.

`SI_RECURRING` is a True/False property that indicates whether an entry is a scheduled instance of a report or an executable binary. When you add an RPT through the CMC, the `SI_RECURRING` property is zero (False). When you schedule it to run periodically, another entry for that scheduled report is created with an `SI_RECURRING` property of one (True).

■**Note** If you're thinking that you'd like to create your own custom properties, you can! This is discussed further in Chapter 9.

All of the SQL examples examined thus far have related to processing information. Those pertaining to scheduling information need to have `SI_SCHEDULEINFO` prefixed to the property name as shown in the following example:

```
SELECT SI_SCHEDULEINFO.SI_NOTIFICATION
FROM CI_INFOOBJECTS
WHERE SI_KIND = 'CrystalReport'
```

This code will retrieve all the notification information for all the reports in the system. Unfortunately, property references in SQL do not reference as easily as they do when using the property bags programmatically. For example, you can't retrieve the information about the notifications sent when a report is successfully run by executing the following code:

```
SELECT SI_SCHEDULEINFO.SI_NOTIFICATION.SI_DESTINATION_SUCCESS
FROM CI_INFOOBJECTS
WHERE SI_KIND = 'CrystalReport'
```

Like many other erroneous SQL commands, this query will execute without error and simply not return any data.

Deprecated Properties

As in any system that has been on the market for a few versions, certain features become obsoleted over the years. Table 5-3 lists the deprecated properties of the query language.

Table 5-3. *Deprecated Properties*

Property Name	Deprecated As of Version	Comments
SI_DAYLIGHT	8.5	No replacement.
SI_ERROR_MESSAGE	8.5	Use SI_SCHEDULEINFO.SI_OUTCOME and SI_SCHEDULEINFO.STATUSINFO instead, which allows you to access SchedulingInfo. ErrorMessage. This property originally stored an unlocalized error message. Current version stores an error message in the language specified by the user's regional settings.
SI_INTERVAL_TYPE	8.5	No replacement.
SI_ISMACHINE	8.5	Replaced by SI_MACHINE_USED.
SI_OBJECT_IS_CONTAINER	8.5	Exists only for backward compatibility.
SI_OBTYPE	8.5	Exists only for backward compatibility.
SI_PLUGIN_CAT	10	No replacement.
SI_PLUGIN_NAME	10	No replacement.
SI_PLUGIN_OBJECTTYPENAME	8.5	Exists only for backward compatibility.
SI_PLUGIN_PROGID	10	No replacement.
SI_PLUGIN_SETUPCMD	10	No replacement.
SI_PLUGIN_SETUPFILE	10	No replacement.
SI_PLUGIN_SETUPPROGRAM	10	No replacement.
SI_PLUGIN_UNINSTALLCOMMAND	10	No replacement.
SI_PLUGIN_UNINSTALLFILE	10	No replacement.
SI_RUN_NOW	8.5	Exists only for backward compatibility.
SI_TARGETID	8.5	Exists only for backward compatibility.
SI_TIMEZONE	8.5	No replacement.
SI_TIMEZONE_NAME	8.5	Use SI_SCHEDULE.SI_TIMEZONE_ID instead, which allows you to access SchedulingInfo. TimeZone. This property originally stored the name of the time zone in which the report was run. In this version, this property returns the ID of the time zone in which the report was run.
SI_UISTATUS	8.5	Replaced by SI_SCHEDULE_STATUS, which is a subset of the original property. In this version, this property remains only to preserve backward compatibility.
SI_VERSIONS	8.5	No replacement.

Working with the InfoStore

Now that you understand the InfoStore query language, let's look at how to leverage it to manipulate objects in the InfoStore. We'll look at folders first, and then examine reports. You'll see the commonality of the code emerge as we look at the different objects. The object model may not be very intuitive, but at least it's consistent.

Extracting Folder Information

A folder with an SI_PARENTID of zero is a top-level folder. It is commonly known as an *application folder* since it is often named after the application whose reports it is storing. Suppose you want to extract all the top-level folders and return them in a DataTable. We'll examine a web service method that will do this for you. Since this is the first web service examined in this book, we'll review every line of code including variable declarations, the BusinessObjects XI logon, error handling, and cleanup code. For the sake of brevity, we'll omit these parts for the other examples shown in this book, as they are rather repetitive.

First, declare the needed variables as shown in Listing 5-13.

Listing 5-13. *Declaring Variables*

```
EnterpriseSession oEnterpriseSession = null;
EnterpriseService oEnterpriseService = null;
InfoStore oInfoStore = null;
InfoObjects oInfoObjects = null;
DataSet oDS;
DataTable oDT;
DataRow oDR;
string szSQL;
```

Next, we'll connect to BO XI and derive an InfoStore object as shown in Listing 5-14. The InfoStore object is the main access class to the BO XI object model. The code for the GetIdentity() method is shown and explained earlier in Listing 5-2.

Listing 5-14. *Connecting to the InfoStore*

```
oEnterpriseSession = GetIdentity(szUserID, szPassword,
        szSystem, szAuthentication, szServer);

oEnterpriseService = oEnterpriseSession.GetService("", "InfoStore");

oInfoStore = new InfoStore(oEnterpriseService);
```

The next step is to pull all the folders that have an SI_PARENTID of zero as shown in Listing 5-15. Any time you pull data from the InfoStore, the results are returned in an InfoObjects collection. An InfoObject (singular) represents one element of the InfoObjects (plural) collection. Should you need to access object-specific properties or methods of the object type that comprise an individual item in the InfoObjects collection, you could accomplish this via a type conversion like this:

```
oReport = ((Report) oInfoObject)
```

There are many examples of this later in the chapter, and it's something you'll use quite frequently in your code.

Listing 5-15. *Extracting the Top-Level Folders*

```
szSQL = "Select SI_ID, SI_NAME " +
   "From CI_INFOOBJECTS " +
   "Where SI_KIND = 'Folder' " +
   "And SI_PARENTID = 0 " +
   "Order By SI_NAME";

oInfoObjects = oInfoStore.Query(szSQL);
```

Once the folder references are in an InfoObjects collection, you can iterate through them and populate a DataTable as shown in Listing 5-16. Some of the properties of an InfoObject are available through named property access. In this case, the ID and name could be extracted by referring to oInfoObject.ID and oInfoObject.Name, respectively. Certain sets of properties, like the scheduling or security information, will only populate in the InfoObject if this data is requested in the query that created the InfoObject. Here, you can see how to use the property bag to extract the same data.

Listing 5-16. *Adding Properties to DataTable*

```
oDT = new DataTable();

oDT.Columns.Add(new DataColumn("ID"));
oDT.Columns.Add(new DataColumn("Name"));

foreach (InfoObject oInfoObject in oInfoObjects)
{
    oDR = oDT.NewRow();

    oDR["ID"] = oInfoObject.Properties["SI_ID"];
    oDR["Name"] = oInfoObject.Properties["SI_NAME"];

    oDT.Rows.Add(oDR);
}
```

Once the DataTable has been constructed, we can then log off from BO XI, mark the objects destroyed, add the DataTable to a DataSet object, and return it to the proxy application. This is illustrated in Listing 5-17.

Listing 5-17. *Log Off and Clean Up*

```
oEnterpriseSession.Logoff();

oInfoStore.Dispose();
oInfoObjects.Dispose();
oEnterpriseSession.Dispose();
oEnterpriseService = null;
```

```
oDS = new DataSet();

oDS.Tables.Add(oDT);

return oDS;
```

Note This web method is returning a DataSet from which a DataTable is extracted client side. The reason is that in the .NET Framework 1.1 and earlier, DataSets are serializable and DataTables are not. This changed in version 2.0, and you can return DataTables directly from your web methods. This DataSet approach is described here solely for the sake of backward compatibility.

Once a user selects a top-level application folder, you can use the SI_ID of this folder to extract the reports associated with it. The code that accomplishes this is shown in Listing 5-18.

Listing 5-18. *Extracting Reports from Folder*

```
szSQL = "SELECT SI_ID, SI_NAME " +
    "FROM CI_INFOOBJECTS " +
    "WHERE SI_KIND = 'CrystalReport' " +
    "AND SI_INSTANCE = 0 " +
    "AND SI_PARENTID = " + szReportID +
    " ORDER BY SI_NAME";

oInfoObjects = oInfoStore.Query(szSQL);
```

Here, given the SI_ID value of a report assigned to the szReportID variable, all the template instances (SI_INSTANCE = 0) are extracted into an InfoObjects collection.

INFOOBJECTS

InfoObjects are something you see a lot of in your BO XI development, so it's vital to understand their features. An InfoObject encapsulates an object within the InfoStore, such as a report, folder, user, or server. To this end, there are a number of common properties that are helpful. The ID property holds the SI_ID of the object being referenced, and Description contains any text description entered. The Actions collection lists the Windows actions that are supported. For example:

```
?oInfoObject.Actions[1].Name
"View"


?oInfoObject.Actions[2].Name
"Schedule"
```

```
?oInfoObject.Actions[3].Name
"Refresh"

?oInfoObject.Actions[4].Name
"Properties"

?oInfoObject.Actions[5].Name
"History"

?oInfoObject.Actions[6].Name
"Modify"
```

Creating Folders

Let's move to a more involved example by programmatically creating a folder and then returning the SI_ID of the newly created folder. The pertinent code is shown in Listing 5-19. The variable szFolderName is a parameter value containing the name of the folder to be created.

Listing 5-19. *Creating a New Folder*

```
PluginManager oPluginManager = null;
PluginInfo oPluginInfo = null;
Folder oFolder = null;
string szResult;

//Connect to BO XI

oInfoObjects = oInfoStore.NewInfoObjectCollection();

oPluginManager = oInfoStore.PluginManager;
oPluginInfo = oPluginManager.GetPluginInfo("Folder");
oInfoObject = oInfoObjects.Add(oPluginInfo);
oFolder = ((Folder) oInfoObject);

oFolder.Title = szFolderName;
oFolder.Properties.Add ("SI_PARENTID", iParentFolderID.ToString());

oInfoStore.Commit(oInfoObjects);

szResult = oFolder.ID.ToString();
```

PLUG-INS

Here we begin working with the plug-in objects. A *plug-in* is simply a class that encapsulates functionality specific to BO XI such as folders, reports, schedules, destinations, or users. After connecting to BO XI, you need to instantiate an empty `InfoObjects` collection to act as a repository for the object you're working with, in this case a `Folder` object. The previous examples used an `InfoObjects` collection by extracting a report entry from the InfoStore. Here, the `NewInfoObjectCollection()` method creates this empty collection. Then, the `PluginManager` object extracts a `PluginInfo` object that stores folder information and adds it to the `InfoObjects` collection. A type conversion was then used to cast the `InfoObject` object into an object of type `Folder`. This is not the most intuitive way of doing things, but it's important to understand the process here, as you'll be using it a lot as you work with the various objects in the BO XI SDK.

Plug-ins contain a number of useful properties that can tell you something about them. For example, suppose you create a `PluginInfo` object via the following code:

```
oPluginManager = oInfoStore.PluginManager;
oPluginInfo = oPluginManager.GetPluginInfo("Folder");
```

Before using the plug-in, you can determine whether it's fully functional by querying the `oPluginInfo.IsFunctional` property. The `oPluginInfo.Category` property will tell you this is a plug-in of type "desktop", and the `oPluginInfo.ObjectTypeName` indicates that it's of type "Folder". Since plug-ins are compiled code that reside in DLLs, the `oPluginInfo.InstallDirectory` will tell you where. In this case, the values would be @"C:\Program Files\Business Objects\BusinessObjects Enterprise 11.5\win32_x86\plugins\desktop\CrystalEnterprise.Folder".

Once a `Folder` object is created, assign the name to the `Title` property, and then add the parent ID value so it knows what top folder it belongs to. Remember that a parent ID of zero will make this a top-level folder. Once this is accomplished, commit the change to the `InfoObjects` collection—with the newly created folder—and you're done. The ID property of the `Folder` object contains the `SI_ID` of the newly created folder. You can return this value from the web service just like you would the newly created primary key in any `INSERT` stored procedure.

Deleting Folders

The code to delete a folder should by now look rather familiar. Listing 5-20 shows what needs to be done.

Listing 5-20. *Deleting a Folder*

```
szSQL = "SELECT SI_ID " +
   "FROM CI_INFOOBJECTS " +
   "WHERE SI_ID = " + iFolderID.ToString();

oInfoObjects = oInfoStore.Query(szSQL);
oInfoObject = oInfoObjects[1];

oFolder = ((Folder) oInfoObject);
```

```
oFolder.DeleteNow();

oInfoStore.Commit(oInfoObjects);
```

Here we're pulling the specific folder object, casting the `InfoObject` of the one matching report to a `Folder` object, and executing the `DeleteNow()` method against this object. You will note that the indexing of BO XI collections starts with one. As always, committing the `InfoObjects` collection back to the InfoStore will permanently delete the folder. Like the examples given to add a folder, this deletion approach works pretty much the same way against the other object types in the BO XI repository. Note that the `DeleteNow()` method is new to BO XI.

Report Refresh Options

When you save a modified report to BO XI from Crystal Reports by selecting File ➤ Save and then choosing the Enterprise option, some of the data from the report is updated in the CMC based on options of your choosing. The Refresh Options link of the Properties tab governs this behavior. You can manipulate this programmatically via the `ReportRefreshOptions()` method of the `Report` object. You'll need to assign one of the enumerated values in Table 5-4 as shown here:

```
oReport.ReportRefreshOptions = CeReportRefreshOption.ceRefreshAll;
```

Table 5-4. *CeReportRefreshOption Enumerator Members*

Member	Value	Description
ceRefreshAll	-1	Refresh all custom properties.
ceRefreshDefaultLogon	5	Refresh default report logon information.
ceRefreshDescription	1	Refresh report's description.
ceRefreshGroupFormula	4	Refresh report's group selection formula.
ceRefreshPrinterOptions	6	Refresh report's printer options.
ceRefreshPromptValues	2	Refresh report's prompt values.
ceRefreshRecordFormula	3	Refresh report's record selection formulas.
ceRefreshTitle	0	Refresh report's title.

To select multiple options, use the + operator like this:

```
oReport.ReportRefreshOptions =
    CeReportRefreshOption.ceRefreshDescription  +
    CeReportRefreshOption.ceRefreshPrinterOptions;
```

Scheduling Reports

One of the principal features of BO XI is the ability to schedule reports. Commonly users will want to run a report at a certain time and with a certain frequency—daily, weekly, etc.—and have that report sent to a specified destination in a desired format. The Schedule tab in the CMC allows you to set up all these parameters. In the following sections (and continuing into Chapter 6), you'll learn how to perform them programmatically.

Report History in the CMC

When you add a report, say, the New Hires report, to the InfoStore using the CMC, schedule that report, and that report runs for the first time, three instances of the same report will be found in the InfoStore. The first is the initial entry of the New Hires report. It has an SI_INSTANCE value of zero (False) because it is the original Crystal Reports RPT template. The second entry appears when the report is scheduled. This entry has an SI_RECURRING value of one (True), as it is a repeating report. When the report runs at the scheduled time, a third entry is made into the InfoStore with an SI_INSTANCE value of one, indicating that it is an instance of the original template and therefore part of the report history.

Be careful here not to become confused by the SI_KIND value. The SI_KIND of the original report is "CrystalReport" because that is exactly what the original RPT file is. By default, all scheduled reports will output as type CrystalReport, that is, they will be saved in the InfoStore as RPT files with data. However, you may very well wish to output your reports as Excel or PDF files, in which case the SI_KIND property will contain "Excel" or "Pdf", respectively. Therefore the following statement may or may not get you your complete report history:

```
SELECT SI_ID, SI_NAME
FROM CI_INFOOBJECTS
WHERE SI_KIND = 'CrystalReport'
AND SI_PARENTID = 123
```

However, the following will:

```
Select SI_ID, SI_NAME
From CI_INFOOBJECTS
Where SI_INSTANCE != 0
AND SI_PARENTID = 123
```

If SI_INSTANCE does not equal zero, then by definition the entry is part of the report history for a given report.

Figure 5-5 shows the report history page from BO XI.

Figure 5-5. *CMC Report History tab*

Building Your Own Report History

You will likely want to replicate the CMC's report history functionality in your own front-end application. Extracting the report history can be accomplished by requesting all the entries where SI_INSTANCE does not equal zero for a given SI_PARENTID. Determining the report name and create date are fairly straightforward property reads. The name should be the same for each instance unless the report was renamed since it was first loaded into the InfoStore. You may wish to omit the SI_NAME property altogether and let the SI_NAME of the zero instance govern. The code to extract the report history is shown in Listing 5-21.

Listing 5-21. *Extracting Report History*

```
//no need to filter SI_KIND as SI_INSTANCE != 0 guarantees a report history
szSQL = "SELECT SI_ID, SI_NAME, SI_CREATION_TIME, " +
    " SI_SCHEDULE_STATUS, SI_KIND, SI_PROCESSINFO.SI_PROMPTS " +
    "FROM CI_INFOOBJECTS " +
    "WHERE SI_PARENTID = " + szParentID +
    "AND SI_INSTANCE != 0 " +
    "ORDER BY SI_CREATION_TIME DESC";

oInfoObjects = oInfoStore.Query(szSQL);

oDT = new DataTable();

oDT.Columns.Add(new DataColumn("ID"));
oDT.Columns.Add(new DataColumn("Name"));
oDT.Columns.Add(new DataColumn("CreationDate"));
oDT.Columns.Add(new DataColumn("Status"));
oDT.Columns.Add(new DataColumn("Format"));
oDT.Columns.Add(new DataColumn("Parameters"));

foreach (InfoObject oInfoObject in oInfoObjects)
{
    //Could also use oInfoObject.Kind
    switch (oInfoObject.Properties["SI_KIND"].ToString())
    {
        case "CrystalReport":
            szFormat = "Crystal Report";
            break;

        case "Pdf":
            szFormat = "Acrobat PDF";
            break;

        case "Excel":
            szFormat = "Microsoft Excel";
            break;
```

```
    case "Word":
        szFormat = "Microsoft Word";
        break;
}

oDR = oDT.NewRow();

oDR["ID"] = oInfoObject.Properties["SI_ID"].ToString();
oDR["Name"] = oInfoObject.Properties["SI_NAME"].ToString();
oDR["CreationDate"] = oInfoObject.Properties["SI_CREATION_TIME"].ToString();
oDR["Status"] = GetScheduleStatus(((CeScheduleStatus)
    int.Parse(oInfoObject.Properties["SI_SCHEDULE_STATUS"].ToString()))));
oDR["Format"] = szFormat;
oDR["Parameters"] = GetParameters(oInfoObject.ProcessingInfo);

oDT.Rows.Add(oDR);
}
```

In this code, it's the output format, status, and the parameters that take a little work. Since a report may be run to a number of formats—PDF, Word, Excel, ASCII, RTF, among others—you'll need to refer to the SI_KIND property to determine the format the given instance of the report is in. In this example, a switch block is checking the SI_KIND property of the InfoObject to determine the format. Then, this data is translated to a friendly name description for presentation to the user. For the sake of the readability of this code example, I'm only checking for an abbreviated list of format types, so you'd be better off invoking the GetFormatType() method, found in the downloadable code, which handles all possible types.

The Status column is derived from the SI_SCHEDULE_STATUS property. This property evaluates to the CeScheduleStatus enumerator, which is listed in Table 5-5. The GetScheduleStatus() method translates this enumerator to a string value.

Table 5-5. *CeScheduleStatus Enumerator Members*

Member	Value	Description
ceStatusFailure	3	The job failed. Use error message or outcome to get more information.
ceStatusPaused	8	The job is paused.
ceStatusPending	9	The job has not started because dependencies, such as time constraints and events, are not satisfied.
ceStatusRunning	0	The job is currently being processed by the job server.
ceStatusSuccess	1	The job completed successfully.

Parameters require even more work. There may be none, one, or multiple parameter values used. To extract them, we need to reference the `SI_PROCESSINFO.SI_PROMPTS` property in the query string and drill down into several layers of nested properties. Figure 5-6 shows the structure of the data set.

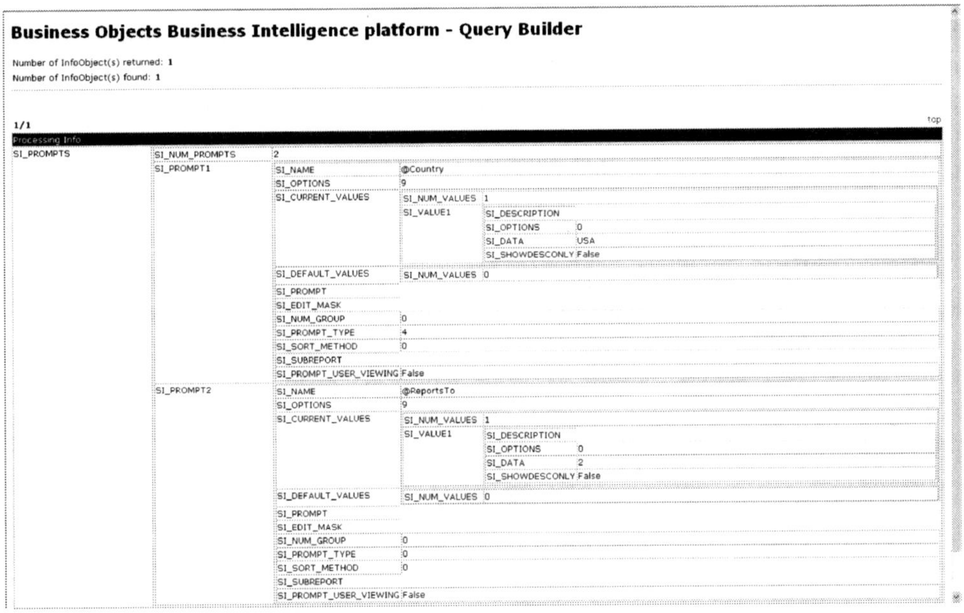

Figure 5-6. *Extracting SI_PROCESSINFO.SI_PROMPTS data*

Here we want to obtain a paired list of <parameter name>:<parameter value> entries delimited with a carriage return. By doing so, we can present a report history to the user that shows even more information than the BO XI report history interface, which only shows the parameter values used, not the names. Our goal is to display a screen like the one shown in Figure 5-7.

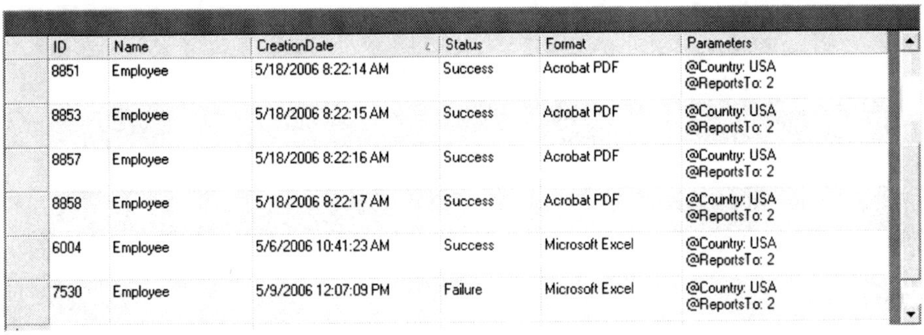

ID	Name	CreationDate	Status	Format	Parameters
8851	Employee	5/18/2006 8:22:14 AM	Success	Acrobat PDF	@Country: USA @ReportsTo: 2
8853	Employee	5/18/2006 8:22:15 AM	Success	Acrobat PDF	@Country: USA @ReportsTo: 2
8857	Employee	5/18/2006 8:22:16 AM	Success	Acrobat PDF	@Country: USA @ReportsTo: 2
8858	Employee	5/18/2006 8:22:17 AM	Success	Acrobat PDF	@Country: USA @ReportsTo: 2
6004	Employee	5/6/2006 10:41:23 AM	Success	Microsoft Excel	@Country: USA @ReportsTo: 2
7530	Employee	5/9/2006 12:07:09 PM	Failure	Microsoft Excel	@Country: USA @ReportsTo: 2

Figure 5-7. *Custom report history*

▓**Note** Since many parameters consist of nothing more than a unique ID, such as a personnel or department primary key reference, viewing the raw parameters list may not be that helpful to the end user. You'll likely want to construct a generic tool to display report information without resorting to custom JOINs to extract the description information associated with these primary keys. Therefore it makes sense to get this information to the report before it is executed. One way to accomplish this is to add parameters such as "Employee Name" or "Department" to either the report or to the stored procedure that can accept these text descriptions, which are usually known when the unique ID is sent to the report. These parameters will be ignored by both the report and the stored procedure logic. Their sole purpose is to make available the descriptive values of the numeric references that RDBMSs prefer for display in the report history.

To extract the parameters, we need to reference the ProcessingInfo plug-in. The SI_PROMPTS property in turn contains a property called SI_NUM_PROMPTS, which indicates how many prompts are in the report. At the same property level is the report information. This is why the iteration begins at the second property. The code in Listing 5-22 shows the prompt extraction process.

Listing 5-22. *Extracting Parameters from the InfoStore*

```
private string GetParameters(ProcessingInfo oProcessingInfo)
{
    System.Text.StringBuilder oResult = null;
    Property oProperty;
    int iCnt = 0;
    string szPromptName;
    string szPromptValue;

    oResult = new System.Text.StringBuilder();

    //How many prompts are there
    iCnt = ((int) oProcessingInfo.Properties["SI_PROMPTS"].
        Properties["SI_NUM_PROMPTS"].Value);

    if (iCnt != 0)
    {
        //start iterating at the second property
        for (int i=2; i<=iCnt+1; i++)
        {
            //Let's abbreviate our code a bit
            oProperty = oProcessingInfo.Properties["SI_PROMPTS"].Properties[i];

            //Get the name
            szPromptName = ((string) oProperty.Properties["SI_NAME"].Value);

            try
            {
                szPromptValue = ((string) oProperty.Properties["SI_CURRENT_VALUES"].
```

```
                              Properties["SI_VALUE1"].Properties["SI_DATA"].Value);
        }
        catch
        {
            szPromptValue = string.Empty;
        }

        oResult.Append(szPromptName);
        oResult.Append(": ");
        oResult.Append(szPromptValue);
        oResult.Append("\n");

      }
    }

    return oResult.ToString();
}
```

You may have noticed some rather deeply nested property bag references. To minimize this I created a Property object and set it equal to the property bag containing the prompt information. This is a situation you'll need to get used to. To illustrate what's coming, here is the full reference to check the number of e-mail addresses that will receive a report success notification:

```
oInfoObject.SchedulingInfo.Properties["SI_NOTIFICATION"].Properties["SI_DESTINATION_
SUCCESS"].Properties["1"].Properties["SI_DEST_SCHEDULEOPTIONS"].Properties["SI_MAIL_
ADDRESSES"].Properties["SI_TOTAL"].Value;
```

PARAMETERIZED SORT ORDERS

One of the many items you can pass to a stored procedure is a numeric value indicating sort order. Crystal Reports has a sorting capability, but it's more efficient for the database to sort the data server side using its own optimized sorting technology. One way to accomplish this in a Microsoft SQL Server stored procedure is to pass a value indicating the sort order and then change the ORDER BY clause using a CASE...END statement. The following example illustrates this technique:

```
Declare @SortCol int

SET @SortCol = 2

SELECT CompanyName, ContactName, ContactTitle
FROM Customers
ORDER BY CASE
    WHEN @SortCol=1 THEN CompanyName
    WHEN @SortCol=2 THEN ContactName
END
```

> Oracle handles this a bit differently. The DECODE function will handle the translation of your parameter value as the following example illustrates:
>
> ```
> P_SORTCOL IN NUMERIC(1);
>
>
> P_SORTCOL = 2;
>
> SELECT LAST_NAME, FIRST_NAME
> FROM T_LCD_EMPLOYEE
> ORDER BY
>     decode(P_SORTCOL, 1, LAST_NAME||FIRST_NAME,
>                       2, FIRST_NAME||LAST_NAME);
> ```
>
> Either way, dynamic SQL is not necessary.

Adding New Reports

Now that you've seen how to extract report data, I'll show you how to programmatically load a new report into the InfoStore. First we'll need to extract a reference to the parent folder. Then, instantiate an empty InfoObjects collection by invoking the NewInfoObjectCollection() method of the InfoStore object. From the PluginManager object, extract the plug-in for the type Report and add it to the InfoObjects collection so as to obtain an InfoObject that will reference the newly added report. Cast this to a Report object type and we're ready to add the RPT file. Then, we can assign the SI_ID of the parent folder and commit the new report to the InfoStore. Listing 5-23 shows how this is accomplished.

Listing 5-23. *Adding a New Report*

```
szSQL = "SELECT SI_ID " +
   "FROM CI_INFOOBJECTS " +
   "WHERE SI_ID = " + iFolderID.ToString() +
   "AND SI_KIND = 'Folder'";

oInfoObjects = oInfoStore.Query(szSQL);
oInfoObject = oInfoObjects[1];

oInfoObjects = oInfoStore.NewInfoObjectCollection();

oPluginManager = oInfoStore.PluginManager;
oPluginInfo = oPluginManager.GetPluginInfo("Report");
oInfoObject = oInfoObjects.Add(oPluginInfo);
oReport = ((Report) oInfoObject);

oReport.Files.Add(szReportName);
oReport.Properties.Add ("SI_PARENTID", iFolderID.ToString());
oReport.EnableThumbnail = true;
```

```
oInfoStore.Commit(oInfoObjects);

szResult = oReport.ID.ToString();
```

Though you can add reports and establish their parent folders, you cannot use the same technique to populate a report history. Suppose you have a report template in a folder and you have some PDF or XLS files that were generated outside of BO XI that you wish to become part of the report history for that template. Unfortunately, you will not be able to do this. This is why the Report.Instance property is read-only. Adding anything else other than a Crystal Report file to the Report.Files collection will generate an error. If you do upload a Crystal Report file and assign to the SI_PARENTID property the SI_ID of another report, the new report will be stored in the report history for the indicated report with a status that perpetually indicates Running. Though no error will be generated, such an attempt is not supported by BO XI.

Run Now

A Run Now action will schedule a report to run immediately using the default parameters set in the zero instance. When you have a series of scheduled reports, it's often helpful to provide at least the local report administrator with the facilities to run these reports as a batch. I often give this facility to the users as well unless the reports are so data intensive that they put too much strain on the server if not handled with care. You can provide the users with a checked list box from which they can select individual scheduled reports to run immediately and then pass these selections to your RunNow() method to be used with an IN clause. The code to run an individual report immediately is shown in Listing 5-24.

Listing 5-24. *Run Now*

```
//Get Top Application folder
szSQL = "SELECT SI_ID, SI_NAME " +
    "FROM CI_INFOOBJECTS " +
    "WHERE SI_NAME = '" + szApplication + "' " +
    "AND SI_KIND = 'Folder'";

oInfoObjects = oInfoStore.Query(szSQL);

szID = oInfoObjects[1].Properties["SI_ID"].ToString();

//Get all reports of specified name that belong under the top folder
szSQL = "SELECT SI_ID, SI_NAME " +
    "FROM CI_INFOOBJECTS " +
    "WHERE SI_NAME = '" + szReportName + "' " +
    "AND SI_KIND = 'CrystalReport' " +
    "AND SI_INSTANCE = 0 " +
    "AND SI_ANCESTOR = " + szID;

oInfoObjects = oInfoStore.Query(szSQL);
```

```
oInfoObjects[1].SchedulingInfo.RightNow = true;
oInfoObjects[1].SchedulingInfo.Type = CeScheduleType.ceScheduleTypeOnce;
oInfoStore.Schedule(oInfoObjects);
```

Retrieving and Saving Schedules

Suppose you wish to offer your users a data entry screen that permits them to view and modify the schedule for a report. The code shown in Listing 5-25 assumes a report scheduled on a weekly basis. A weekly schedule means that you may select any one, some, or all seven days of the week, plus a start and end date for the schedule and the time of day you wish the scheduled report to run. This example assumes that a schedule already exists for the report and is being made available to the user for editing. The SQL command SI_RECURRING = 1 indicates a scheduled entry for the report.

Listing 5-25. *Extracting Schedule Information*

```
//Logon to BO XI

//Pull the report schedule
szSQL = "SELECT SI_ID, SI_SCHEDULEINFO.SI_STARTTIME, " +
    "SI_SCHEDULEINFO.SI_ENDTIME, " +
    "SI_SCHEDULEINFO.SI_RUN_ON_TEMPLATE " +
    "FROM CI_INFOOBJECTS  " +
    "WHERE SI_PARENTID = " + szReportID +
    " AND SI_RECURRING = 1";

oInfoObjects = oInfoStore.Query(szSQL);

oReport = ((Report) oInfoObjects[1]);

//Create a DataTable for a weekly schedule
oDT = new DataTable();

oDT.Columns.Add(new DataColumn("ID"));
oDT.Columns.Add(new DataColumn("StartDate"));
oDT.Columns.Add(new DataColumn("EndDate"));
oDT.Columns.Add(new DataColumn("Sunday"));
oDT.Columns.Add(new DataColumn("Monday"));
oDT.Columns.Add(new DataColumn("Tuesday"));
oDT.Columns.Add(new DataColumn("Wednesday"));
oDT.Columns.Add(new DataColumn("Thursday"));
oDT.Columns.Add(new DataColumn("Friday"));
oDT.Columns.Add(new DataColumn("Saturday"));

oDR = oDT.NewRow();
```

```
//Assign the start and end dates and default each day to false
oDR["ID"] = oReport.Properties["SI_ID"];
oDR["StartDate"] = oReport.SchedulingInfo.Properties["SI_STARTTIME"];
oDR["EndDate"] = oReport.SchedulingInfo.Properties["SI_ENDTIME"];
oDR["Sunday"] = false;
oDR["Monday"] = false;
oDR["Tuesday"] = false;
oDR["Wednesday"] = false;
oDR["Thursday"] = false;
oDR["Friday"] = false;
oDR["Saturday"] = false;

oPropertyBag = oReport.SchedulingInfo.
    Properties["SI_RUN_ON_TEMPLATE"].Properties;

//Iterate through the daily schedule listing and assign the day's schedule
iCnt = ((int) oPropertyBag["SI_NUM_TEMPLATE_DAYS"].Value);

for (int x=1; x<=iCnt; x++)
{
iDay = ((int) oPropertyBag["SI_TEMPLATE_DAY" + x.ToString()].
    Properties["SI_DAYS_OF_WEEK"].Value);

switch (iDay)
{
    case 1:
        oDR["Sunday"] = true;
        break;

    case 2:
        oDR["Monday"] = true;
        break;

    //...and so on, you get the point
}
}
```

This sample retrieves the schedule information for a specified report and loads it into a DataTable. The SI_NUM_TEMPLATE_DAYS property indicates how many days in a week the report is scheduled to run. This value can govern the for loop, which will iterate through the individual days whose matching field values are set to true in the DataTable. BusinessObjects XI stores the individual days as numeric values that match to a member of the CeDayOfWeek enumerator. The members of this enumerator are shown in Table 5-6.

Table 5-6. *CeDayOfWeek Enumerator Members*

Member	Value
ceDaySunday	1
ceDayMonday	2
ceDayTuesday	3
ceDayWednesday	4
ceDayThursday	5
ceDayFriday	6
ceDaySaturday	7
ceDayAll	0

Be careful here not to confuse the members of this BO-supplied enumerator with the System.DayOfWeek enumerator supplied by .NET. The matching numbers in the .NET enumerator (see Table 5-7) are one less than their BO XI equivalents, and using the wrong enumerator can obviously cause major problems with your report schedules.

Table 5-7. *System.DayOfWeek Enumerator Members*

Member	Value
Sunday	0
Monday	1
Tuesday	2
Wednesday	3
Thursday	4
Friday	5
Saturday	6

After displaying the report's schedule information on a data entry form, the user can now modify that information and save the changes back to the InfoStore. Listing 5-26 accepts a report ID, a start and end date, a daily run time, and a string indicating the days to run in the format "246", which would indicate Monday, Wednesday, and Friday, as per the values in Table 5-6. Then, utilizing the SchedulingInfo object of the Report object, you can schedule the individual days the report should be run. The BeginDate property receives a combination of the start date and daily run time, and the CalendarRunDays property of the SchedulingInfo object receives the start and end month, day, and year for each day of the week the schedule should run.

Listing 5-26. *Saving Schedule Information*

```
public void SaveSchedule(string szServer,
    string szReportID,
    System.DateTime dTime,
    System.DateTime dStartDate,
    System.DateTime dEndDate,
    string szDays)
```

```
{
   //Logon to BO XI

   szSQL = "SELECT * " +
      "FROM CI_INFOOBJECTS " +
      "WHERE SI_ID = " + szReportID;

   oInfoObjects = oInfoStore.Query(szSQL);

   oReport = ((Report) oInfoObjects[1]);

   oReport.SchedulingInfo.BeginDate =
      DateTime.Parse(dStartDate.ToShortDateString() + " " +
      dTime.ToShortTimeString());
   oReport.SchedulingInfo.EndDate = dEndDate;
   oReport.SchedulingInfo.Type = CeScheduleType.ceScheduleTypeCalendar;
   oReport.SchedulingInfo.RightNow = false;

   if (szDays.IndexOf("1") != -1)
      oReport.SchedulingInfo.CalendarRunDays.Add(
         dStartDate.Day, dStartDate.Month, dStartDate.Year,
         dEndDate.Day, dEndDate.Month, dEndDate.Year,
         CeDayOfWeek.ceDaySunday);

   if (szDays.IndexOf("2") != -1)
      oReport.SchedulingInfo.CalendarRunDays.Add(
         dStartDate.Day, dStartDate.Month, dStartDate.Year,
         dEndDate.Day, dEndDate.Month, dEndDate.Year,
         CeDayOfWeek.ceDayMonday);

   //...and so on, you get the point

   //schedule the report
   oInfoStore.Schedule(oInfoObjects);

}
```

To see the SaveSchedule() method in action, look at the method call shown in Listing 5-27. This code will produce the schedule shown in Figure 5-8.

Listing 5-27. *Invoking the SaveSchedule() Method*

```
string szServer = "Dev";
string szReportID = "1266";
System.DateTime dTime = System.DateTime.Parse("1:00:00 PM");
System.DateTime dStartDate = System.DateTime.Parse("6/1/2006");
System.DateTime dEndDate = System.DateTime.Parse("12/31/2010");
string szDays = "135";
```

```
oBOXIWebService.SaveSchedule(szServer, szReportID,
    dTime, dStartDate, dEndDate, szDays);
```

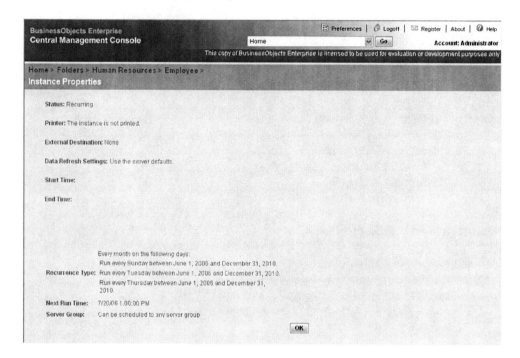

Figure 5-8. *Scheduled report*

Adding Executable Code

Just as you can add reports and other static documents to the InfoStore, you can also add executable code. The approach is very similar to that of adding a report. The Program class allows you to specify properties specific to a code file. First, you'll need to indicate what type of executable code you're adding by setting the ProgramType property to a member of the CeProgramType enumerator. The members of CeProgramType are listed in Table 5-8.

Table 5-8. *CeProgramType Enumerator Members*

Member	Value	Description
ceBinary	1	Binary
ceJavaProgram	2	Java program
ceScript	3	Script
ceUndefined	0	Undefined

In this example, we're adding a .NET executable, so the setting is ceBinary. Next, you'll need to specify the full file name of the program file on disk. You can also set any command-line arguments that the code will expect. These arguments are editable through the CMC and can be used to indicate such things as a report name that will run at the scheduled time. Finally, you'll need to specify your network user ID and password so BO XI can run the executable code under your login ID. The code to import an executable program is shown in Listing 5-28.

Listing 5-28. *Importing Executable Code*

```
//Logon to BO XI

oInfoObjects = oInfoStore.NewInfoObjectCollection();

oPluginManager = oInfoStore.PluginManager;
oPluginInfo = oPluginManager.GetPluginInfo("Program");
oInfoObject = oInfoObjects.Add(oPluginInfo);
oProgram = ((Program) oInfoObject);

oProgram.ParentID = iFolderID;
oProgram.Title = szTitle;
oProgram.ProgramType = CeProgramType.ceBinary;
oProgram.BinaryProgram.File = szProgramFileName;
oProgram.BinaryProgram.AddFile(szAuxiliaryFileName);
oProgram.BinaryProgram.Args = szArgs;
oProgram.BinaryProgram.UserName = szUserName;
oProgram.BinaryProgram.Password = szUserPassword;

oInfoStore.Commit(oInfoObjects);

szResult = oProgram.ID.ToString();
```

Handling Report Parameters Generically

When you navigate to the Parameters page in the CMC, you are presented with a generic data entry page for your report parameters. There may be occasions when you wish to replicate this functionality, to some greater or lesser degree of user interface sophistication, in your own front end. You can accomplish this by extracting the prompt information from the InfoStore using the following SQL:

```
SELECT SI_ID, SI_NAME, SI_PROCESSINFO.SI_PROMPTS
FROM CI_INFOOBJECTS
WHERE SI_ID = 123;
```

The goal is to iterate through the individual prompts and dynamically display a label and a text box for each parameter. The data type of each parameter field is identified by the SI_PROMPT_TYPE property. Unfortunately, the values of SI_PROMPT_TYPE are not explained anywhere in the documentation, and they can only be determined by setting up a report with different data types and looking at the equivalent values in the Query Builder results. So far, I have exegeted the values shown in Table 5-9 using a SQL Server stored procedure.

Table 5-9. *SI_PROMPT_TYPE Values*

Value	Type
0	Numeric (int, smallint, tinyint)
1	money
2	Boolean (bit)
4	string (varchar and char)
7	date

Technical support has informed me that the developers themselves don't know what the values of this property mean, as it isn't even documented internally.

In your code, you may wish to check the SI_PROMPT_TYPE property and display something more user friendly than a text box, like a check box for a Boolean or a date control for a date value. Using the SQL statement shown previously, you can create a DataTable containing each parameter and the current value setting using the code in Listing 5-29.

Listing 5-29. *Extracting Prompts*

```
oDT = new DataTable();

oDT.Columns.Add(new DataColumn("Name"));
oDT.Columns.Add(new DataColumn("PromptType"));
oDT.Columns.Add(new DataColumn("DefaultValue"));

if (oInfoObjects.Count != 0)
{
   oInfoObject = oInfoObjects[1];

   //Abbreviate the code a bit
   oPropertyBag = oInfoObject.ProcessingInfo.Properties["SI_PROMPTS"].Properties;

   //How many prompts?
   iCnt = ((int) oPropertyBag["SI_NUM_PROMPTS"].Value);

   for (int x=1; x<=iCnt; x++)
   {
      szCnt = x.ToString();

      oDR = oDT.NewRow();

      oDR["Name"] = GetPropertyValue(oPropertyBag["SI_PROMPT" + szCnt].
         Properties, "SI_NAME", string.Empty);
      oDR["PromptType"] = GetPropertyValue(oPropertyBag["SI_PROMPT" + szCnt].
         Properties, "SI_PROMPT_TYPE", "0");

      if (HasMember(oPropertyBag["SI_PROMPT" + szCnt].
         Properties["SI_CURRENT_VALUES"].Properties, "SI_VALUE1"))
```

```
    {
        szDefaultValue = GetPropertyValue(oPropertyBag["SI_PROMPT" + szCnt].
            Properties["SI_CURRENT_VALUES"].Properties["SI_VALUE1"].
    Properties, "SI_DATA", string.Empty);

        //If it's a date in the BO "DateTime(2006,12,21,0,0,0)"
        //format let's make it presentable as "12/21/2006"
        if (szDefaultValue.Length > 9 &&
            szDefaultValue.Substring(0, 8) == "DateTime")
            szDefaultValue = FormatInfoStoreDate(szDefaultValue);

        oDR["DefaultValue"] = szDefaultValue;
    }

    oDT.Rows.Add(oDR);
  }
}
```

The `SI_NUM_PROMPTS` property tells us exactly how many prompts the report has before we even start so we can use that value to govern the for loop. Then, we extract the name of the prompt (`SI_NAME`), the data type (`SI_PROMPT_TYPE`), and the value setting (`SI_VALUE1`). The `GetPropertyValue()` and `HasMember()` methods can be found in the downloadable code.

Special care is taken for date values, as BO XI stores dates in the format "DateTime (2006,12,21,0,0,0)" when the user would rather see "12/21/2006". The `FormatInfoStoreDate()` method, also found in the downloadable code, handles this transformation. Once the DataTable object is built, you can dynamically create a data entry screen to accept the user changes. When the user is done with his edits, the code shown in Listing 5-30 will save the new value settings back to the InfoStore.

Listing 5-30. *Saving Prompt Value Settings*

```
szSQL = "SELECT SI_ID, SI_NAME, SI_PROCESSINFO.SI_PROMPTS " +
    "FROM CI_INFOOBJECTS " +
    "WHERE SI_ID = " + szReportID;

oInfoObjects = oInfoStore.Query(szSQL);

if (oInfoObjects.Count != 0)
{
    oInfoObject = oInfoObjects[1];

    //Abbreviate the code a bit
    oPropertyBag = oInfoObject.ProcessingInfo.Properties["SI_PROMPTS"].Properties;

    //How many prompts?
    iCnt = ((int) oPropertyBag["SI_NUM_PROMPTS"].Value);
```

```
    for (int x=1; x<=iCnt; x++)
    {
        szCnt = x.ToString();

        if (szField == GetPropertyValue(oPropertyBag["SI_PROMPT" + szCnt].
            Properties, "SI_NAME", string.Empty))
        {
            oPropertyBag["SI_PROMPT" + szCnt].Properties["SI_CURRENT_VALUES"].
                Properties["SI_VALUE1"].Properties["SI_DATA"].Value = szValue;
            break;
        }
    }
}
```

```
oInfoStore.Commit(oInfoObjects);
```

The code to save the prompt changes is similar to the code to extract them. First, pull all the prompts for the report and iterate through the resulting InfoObjects collection until locating the prompt whose value is being saved. Once this is done, you can assign the SI_DATA property value to the new setting and commit the InfoObjects collection back to the InfoStore. You could also modify this method to accept an array of all the prompts and their values. Then, by iterating the array, you could make all the changes at once and avoid the need to extract and commit the InfoObjects collection for each parameter.

Summary

This chapter introduced the InfoStore query language and showed how to work with InfoObjects. We looked at how to connect to the InfoStore and examined the creation and deletion of folders and reports and the basics of scheduling reports. In addition, we looked at report histories and how to work with report parameters. We also explored how to load executable code into the InfoStore. As a bonus, we even looked at a few undocumented features with the SELECTUSINGPROPERTY SQL function and the SI_PROMPT_TYPE property. Coming up, we'll look at some of the more complex objects offered by the BusinessObjects XI SDK.

■■■

CHAPTER 6

BusinessObjects XI SDK Programming II

In the previous chapter, we examined the fundamentals of the BusinessObjects XI object model and how the query language works. The examples showed how to extract information from the InfoStore and how to programmatically manipulate Folder and Report objects. In this chapter, we'll build on that knowledge and look at some more advanced topics such as scheduling, notifications, export formats, destinations, printing, calendars, events, data access techniques, and the BO XI web server controls.

Scheduling

The ability to schedule reports to run at specific times and dates is one of the principal features in any report server. It is also one of the key reasons to even have a report server. It should come as no surprise that the object model that encapsulates the scheduling functionality is quite extensive. This is what we will discuss in the following sections.

Notifications

As the name implies, notifications inform you when something happens. This event will be either a success or a failure. When scheduling an object, you are instructing the BO XI server to run reports unattended. You'll likely want to know if they actually ran or not. For this purpose, there are two types of notifications to choose from—e-mail and audit. We'll examine both in the next sections.

E-Mail Notifications

E-mail notifications allow the system administrator to instruct BO XI to send e-mails to designated individuals when a scheduled report succeeds or fails. You can enter this information directly in the CMC or handle it programmatically. Listing 6-1 shows how to create an e-mail notification for a report.

Listing 6-1. *Creating an E-Mail Notification*

```
szSQL = "SELECT SI_ID " +
    "FROM CI_INFOOBJECTS " +
    "WHERE SI_ID = " + szReportID;

oReportInfoObjects = oInfoStore.Query(szSQL);
oReport = ((Report) oReportInfoObjects[1]);

//You need to pull both SI_DEST_SCHEDULEOPTIONS and
//SI_PROGID in order for the SetFromPlugin() method to write
//the DestinationPlugin object
szSQL = "SELECT SI_DEST_SCHEDULEOPTIONS, SI_PROGID " +
    "FROM CI_SYSTEMOBJECTS " +
    "WHERE SI_PARENTID=29 " +
    "AND SI_NAME = 'CrystalEnterprise.Smtp'";

oInfoObjects = oInfoStore.Query(szSQL);
oInfoObject = oInfoObjects[1];

oDestinationPlugin = new DestinationPlugin(oInfoObject.PluginInterface);

oSmtpOptions = new SmtpOptions(oDestinationPlugin.ScheduleOptions);

oSmtpOptions.ServerName = "MyServer";
oSmtpOptions.Port = 25;
oSmtpOptions.DomainName = "mydomain.com";
oSmtpOptions.SenderAddress = "seton.software@verizon.net";
oSmtpOptions.ToAddresses.Add("carlganz@myclient.com");
oSmtpOptions.Subject = "Your Employee report is now ready";
oSmtpOptions.Message = "Please click on the link below to see your report.";
oSmtpOptions.SMTPAuthentication = CeAuthentication.ceAuthNone;
oSmtpOptions.SMTPUserName = "myname";
oSmtpOptions.SMTPPassword = "mypass";

//Pass in a string value to name the new notification
oDestination = oReport.SchedulingInfo.Notifications.
    DestinationsOnSuccess.Add("new");

oDestination.SetFromPlugin(oDestinationPlugin);

oInfoStore.Commit(oReportInfoObjects);
```

In this sample, we are extracting a report InfoObject based on a specific report ID. Because these notifications are sent via SMTP mail, we need to create an SmtpOptions object to hold the e-mail settings. To obtain this SmtpOptions object, you need to extract an InfoObject reference to the Smtp plug-in entry in the InfoStore. The SQL to accomplish this is shown here:

```
SELECT SI_DEST_SCHEDULEOPTIONS, SI_PROGID
FROM CI_SYSTEMOBJECTS
WHERE SI_PARENTID=29
AND SI_NAME = 'CrystalEnterprise.Smtp'
```

This statement will extract the result set shown in Figure 6-1.

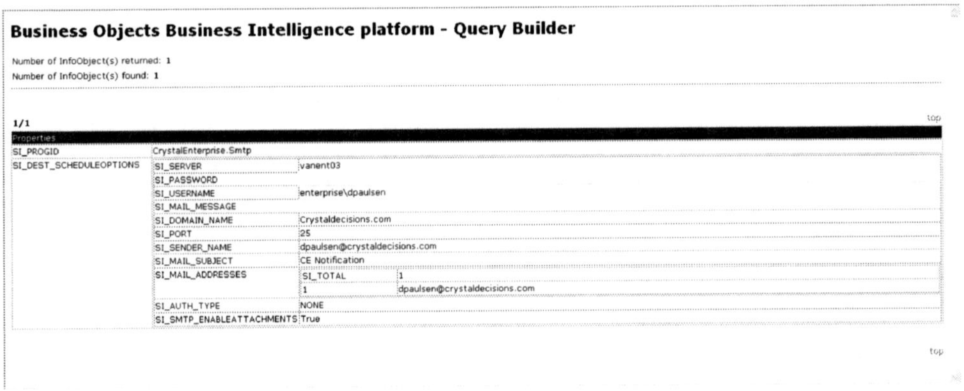

Figure 6-1. *Smtp plug-in entry from InfoStore*

The reason SI_PARENTID = 29 is hard-coded into the SQL query is that the entry with an SI_ID value of 29 is the topmost folder entry for all the destination plug-ins. The following SQL illustrates this:

```
SELECT SI_NAME
FROM CI_SYSTEMOBJECTS
WHERE SI_PARENTID=29
```

This SQL query returns the result set shown in Figure 6-2, which lists the various destination plug-ins available.

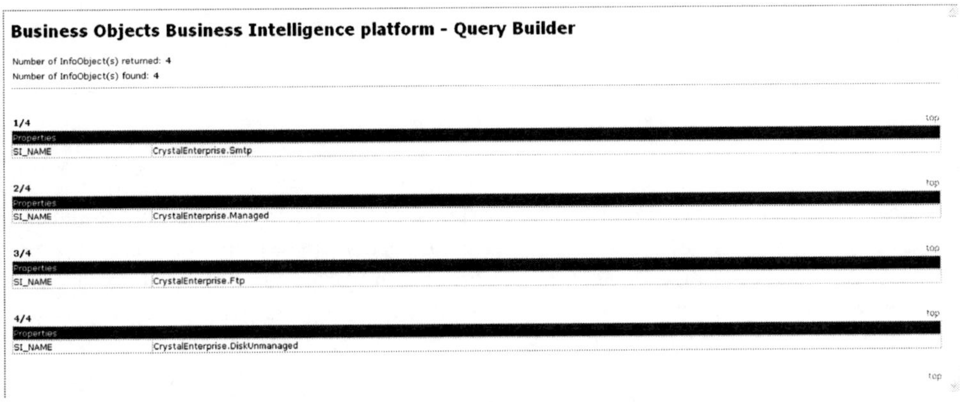

Figure 6-2. *Destination plug-in entries from InfoStore*

Remember, since subqueries are not supported in the BO XI brand of SQL, you can't reference the SI_NAME entry of the parent folder and therefore need to use the more cryptic SI_PARENTID = 29.

After obtaining the InfoObject reference to the Smtp plug-in, you'll need to obtain a DestinationPlugin object. From this DestinationPlugin object we can obtain an SmtpOptions object, through which we can set the properties of the e-mail. If you're thinking that this approach seems convoluted, then you're not alone. BO XI has always had a rather obtuse and nonintuitive object model.

This example creates an e-mail for a successful run of a report as it was added to the Notifications collection through the DestinationsOnSuccess property. To create an e-mail for a failed report, use the DestinationsOnFailure property instead. Otherwise, the rest of the code remains the same.

Audit Notifications

Audit notifications will write information about the scheduled object to the auditing database if you have one installed. To enable this option for both successful and failed reports, use the following line of code:

```
oReport.SchedulingInfo.Notifications.AuditOption =
  CeAuditOnResult.ceAuditOnBoth;
```

You can indicate whether auditing should be enabled for just failures, just successes, or not at all. Auditing information and database configuration is discussed in greater detail in Chapter 2.

■**Note** Once notifications are set up, they cannot, unlike schedules, explicitly be suspended and reactivated. If you want your report to run but wish to suspend notifications for a specific period of time, you'll need to remove the e-mail and message information for the notifications. Even the CMC works this way. If you uncheck the e-mail notifications on the Notifications tab of the Schedule dialog and click Update, the notification filter will blank out. If you'd like to save the notification information so the user does not need to reenter everything when the notification is reenabled, consider the use of custom properties to store the data while the notification is suspended. Custom properties are explained in Chapter 9.

Alerts

Alerts are devices for indicating that the data in a generated report met a set of predefined criteria. Commonly, you might set up an alert to trigger if the bottom line on a sales report were below a certain amount; if the average purchase order approval amount for a manager were outside of an acceptable range; or even if an employee were celebrating a birthday. This criteria is defined in Crystal Reports by selecting Report ➤ Alerts ➤ Create or Modify Alerts from the menu. In the example shown in Figure 6-3, selecting New from the Create Alerts dialog brings up the Edit Alerts dialog, where you can name and describe the event.

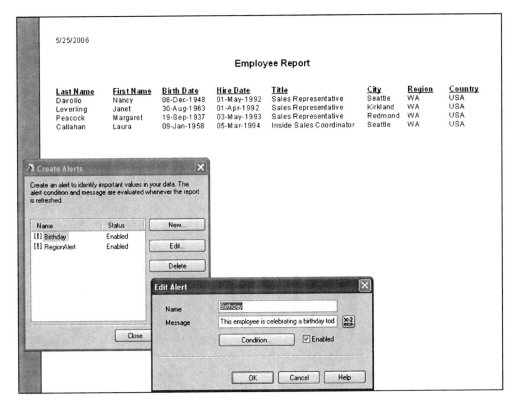

Figure 6-3. *Setting up an alert in Crystal Reports*

The Condition button will display the code editing dialog shown in Figure 6-4 where you can enter the logic that will trigger the alert. In this example, we're looking to see who has a birthday today.

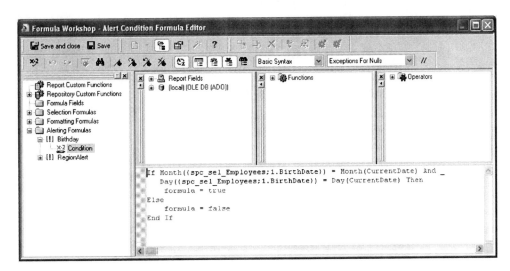

Figure 6-4. *Alert condition*

When the report is imported into the CMC, the presence of the alert is detected and the Alert Notification option on the Schedule tab is enabled as shown in Figure 6-5.

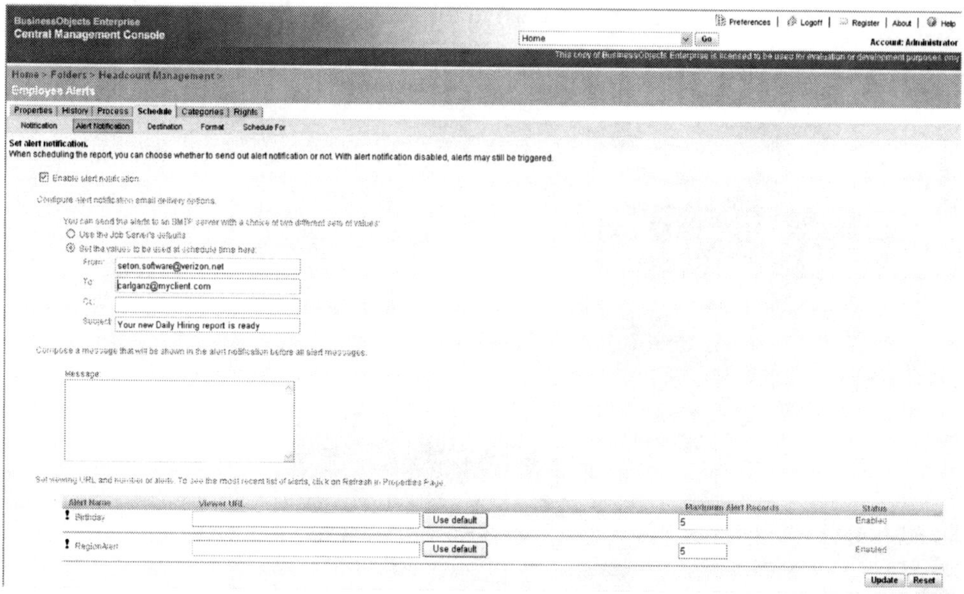

Figure 6-5. *Alert Notification page*

The Alert Notification page allows you to enter the e-mail information for those users who are to be alerted to the triggering of the alert when the report is run. This e-mail will list individually the details of each record that met the alert condition. For each alert criteria established, you may set limits on the number of detail records printed in the e-mail. This email—similar to the one shown in Figure 6-6—will contain a list of the records that met the alert criteria along with a web link that displays the report filtered to only those records that meet the alert criteria.

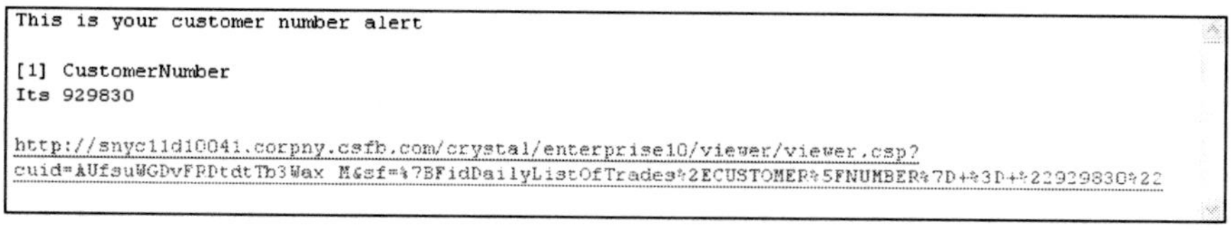

Figure 6-6. *Alert Notification e-mail*

Accomplishing this task programmatically is very similar to programming notifications and is shown in Listing 6-2.

Listing 6-2. *Creating Alert Notifications*

```
szSQL = "SELECT SI_ID " +
    "FROM CI_INFOOBJECTS " +
    "WHERE SI_ID = " + szReportID;

oReportInfoObjects = oInfoStore.Query(szSQL);
oReport = ((Report) oReportInfoObjects[1]);

//You need to pull both SI_DEST_SCHEDULEOPTIONS and
//SI_PROGID in order for the SetFromPlugin() method to write
//the DestinationPlugin object
szSQL = "SELECT SI_DEST_SCHEDULEOPTIONS, SI_PROGID " +
    "FROM CI_SYSTEMOBJECTS " +
    "WHERE SI_PARENTID=29 " +
    "AND SI_NAME = 'CrystalEnterprise.Smtp'";

oInfoObjects = oInfoStore.Query(szSQL);
oInfoObject = oInfoObjects[1];

oDestinationPlugin = new DestinationPlugin(oInfoObject.PluginInterface);

oSmtpOptions = new SmtpOptions(oDestinationPlugin.ScheduleOptions);

oSmtpOptions.ServerName = "MyServer";
oSmtpOptions.Port = 25;
oSmtpOptions.DomainName = "mydomain.com";
oSmtpOptions.SenderAddress = "seton.software@verizon.net";
oSmtpOptions.ToAddresses.Add("carlganz@myclient.com");
oSmtpOptions.Subject = "Here are today's alerts:";
oSmtpOptions.Message = "Please click on the link below to see your report.";
oSmtpOptions.SMTPAuthentication = CeAuthentication.ceAuthNone;
oSmtpOptions.SMTPUserName = "myname";
oSmtpOptions.SMTPPassword = "mypass";
```

oReport.SchedulingInfo.AlertDestination.SetFromPlugin(oDestinationPlugin);

oInfoStore.Commit(oReportInfoObjects);

The similarities are striking, and the code for alerts and notifications (shown in Listing 6-1) is almost exactly the same. The difference is simply the property to which the SmtpOptions object is written. For a notification, it is written to oReport.SchedulingInfo.Notifications. DestinationsOnSuccess (or DestinationsOnFailure), whereas for alerts it's written to oReport. SchedulingInfo.AlertDestination.

The alerts themselves are managed through the Report object and not through the SchedulingInfo plug-in. The following code shows how to check the name of the alert as well as how to enable an individual alert and set the alert size as shown in Figure 6-5.

```
oReport.ReportAlerts[1].Name;
oReport.ReportAlerts[1].Enabled = true;
oReport.ReportAlerts[1].AlertSetSize = 5;
```

Report Format Options

In Chapter 4, we looked at the various output format options that exist for reports—Microsoft Word, ASCII, PDF, Excel, etc. Here we'll see how these options may be set programmatically. In a few cases, you'll see more formatting options accessible programmatically through the object model than are available in the CMC.

The BO XI object model has a class called ReportFormatOptions that encapsulates the settings for the various output formats. Table 6-1 lists the methods for the ReportFormatOptions class, which governs these formats. The export format options fall into two categories—page-based and record-based. Paged-based formats focus on maintaining the presentation (fonts, colors, position, graphics, etc.) of the report output. Formats such as PDF and Word are examples of this. Record-based formats emphasize the data itself without regard to the presentation and are usually used for data transfer. PlainText and ExcelDataOnly are examples of this.

Table 6-1. *ReportFormatOptions Formats*

Method Name
ExcelDataOnyFormat
ExcelFormat
PDFFormat
PlainTextFormat
RichTextEditableFormat
RichTextFormat
TextFormatCharacterSeparated
TextFormatPaginated
TextFormatTabSeparated
WordFormat

Setting the format options involves obtaining an InfoObject reference to a report and creating an object of type ReportFormatOptions. Working through the ReportFormatOptions object, you can reference one of the properties collections listed in Table 6-2 to set the particulars of a given format. The first task is to set the Format property so the SDK knows what the format governs. The Format property receives one of the enumerations shown in Table 6-2.

Table 6-2. *CeReportFormat Enumerator Members*

Member	Value	Description
ceFormatCrystalReport	0	Crystal Report file
ceFormatExcel	1	Microsoft Excel spreadsheet
ceFormatWord	2	Microsoft Word document
ceFormatPDF	3	Adobe PDF document
ceFormatRTF	4	Rich Text Format document
ceFormatRTFEditable	11	Editable RTF file
ceFormatTextPlain	5	Plain text file
ceFormatTextPaginated	6	Paginated text file
ceFormatTextTabSeparated	7	Text file with tab-separated values
ceFormatTextCharacterSeparated	8	Text file with character-separated values
ceFormatTextTabSeparatedText	10	Text file with tab-separated text values
ceFormatExcelDataOnly	9	Raw data values
ceFormatUserDefined	1000	User-defined type

The code in Listing 6-3 shows how to set the report format for Microsoft Word and assign the properties particular to the Word format.

Listing 6-3. *Using ReportFormatOptions*

```
//Connect to BO XI
szSQL = "SELECT SI_ID " +
    "FROM CI_INFOOBJECTS " +
    "WHERE SI_ID = " + szReportID;

oReportInfoObjects = oInfoStore.Query(szSQL);
oReport = ((Report) oReportInfoObjects[1]);

oReportFormatOpts = oReport.ReportFormatOptions;
oReportFormatOpts.Format = CeReportFormat.ceFormatWord;

WordFormat oWordFormat;

oWordFormat = oReportFormatOpts.WordFormat;

oWordFormat.StartPageNumber = 1;
oWordFormat.EndPageNumber = 10;
oWordFormat.ExportAllPages = false;
```

The Word format is very simple. You can choose a starting page, an ending page, or indicate that all pages should be exported. The output will be a traditional Word document like the one shown in Figure 6-7. Each entry in the output is stored in its own separate frame.

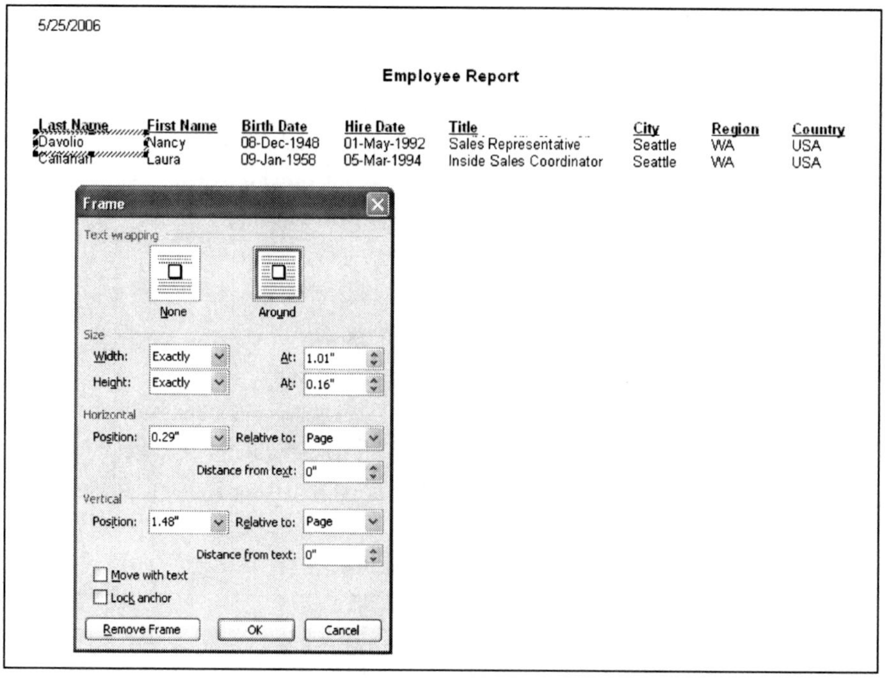

Figure 6-7. *Word format*

In the sections that follow, we'll examine some of the different options. There are some options that are common between many of the formatting options. One property of the ReportFormatOptions object—UseOptionsInReportFile—takes a Boolean that determines whether the formatting options saved with the report in Crystal Reports will govern. You can access these options by selecting File ➤ Export ➤ Report Export Options from the Crystal Reports menu. The options for exporting to the Excel format is shown in Figure 6-8.

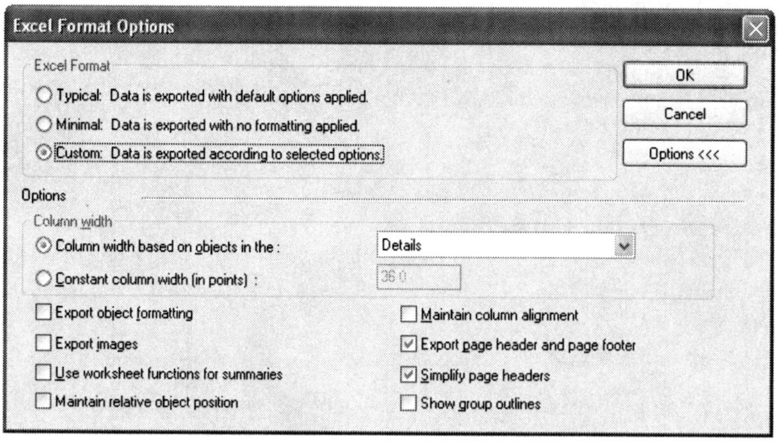

Figure 6-8. *Export to Excel options*

■**Note** You may notice that there are a few formatting options available to you in Crystal Reports that are not available to you in BO XI either through the CMC or programmatically. The only way to overcome this limitation is to set your formatting option to the required value in Crystal Reports and then import the RPT into BO XI. Though the formatting option may not be programmatically available through the BO XI SDK, the setting will be respected.

Other `ReportFormatOptions` properties that are used frequently are `IsSameDate` and `IsSameNumber`. These Boolean properties allow you to indicate whether the exported text uses the same date and number formats, respectively, as the main report. `StartPageNumber` and `EndPageNumber` specify a page range for printing, but setting `ExportAllPages` to True will override these page range settings.

In the sections that follow, we'll look at the settings available for each export format.

TextFormatTabSeparated

The `TextFormatTabSeparated` format (see Listing 6-4) allows you to indicate whether the exported text uses the same date and number formats as the main report. Multiline text objects are exported in a single line, all strings are surrounded by double quotes, and the values are separated by tab characters (as the name would suggest).

Listing 6-4. *Using TextFormatTabSeparated*

```
oReportFormatOpts.Format = CeReportFormat.ceFormatTextTabSeparated;

TextFormatTabSeparated oTextFormatTabSeparated;

oTextFormatTabSeparated = oReportFormatOpts.TextFormatTabSeparated;

oTextFormatTabSeparated.IsSameDate = true;
oTextFormatTabSeparated.IsSameNumber = true;
```

TextFormatPaginated

The `TextFormatPaginated` format (see Listing 6-5) permits you to set the characters and lines per inch. Figure 6-9 shows a setting of 8 characters per inch, and Figure 6-10 shows 20 characters per inch. The `CharactersPerInch` property specifies the number of characters that will fit in a linear inch of horizontal space, and therefore determines the font dimension. The other font properties set in Crystal Reports will be respected by BO XI.

Listing 6-5. *Using TextFormatPaginated*

```
oReportFormatOpts.Format = CeReportFormat.ceFormatTextPaginated;

TextFormatPaginated oTextFormatPaginated;

oTextFormatPaginated = oReportFormatOpts.TextFormatPaginated;

oTextFormatPaginated.CharactersPerInch = 10;
oTextFormatPaginated.LinesPerPage = 50;
```

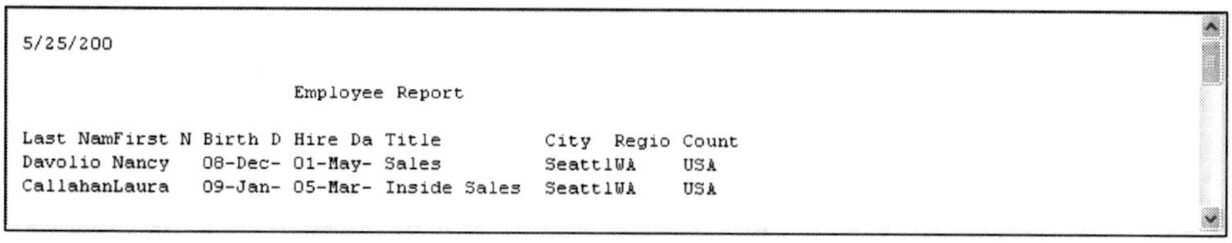

```
5/25/200

                    Employee Report

Last NamFirst N Birth D Hire Da Title         City  Regio Count
Davolio Nancy   08-Dec- 01-May- Sales         Seatt1WA    USA
CallahanLaura   09-Jan- 05-Mar- Inside Sales  Seatt1WA    USA
```

Figure 6-9. *Eight characters per inch*

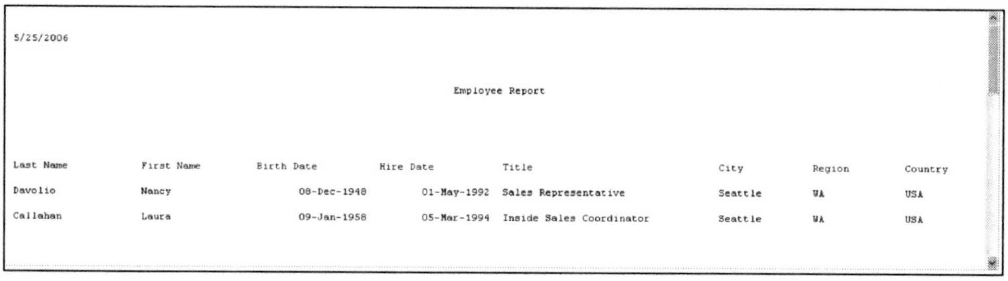

```
5/25/2006

                                         Employee Report



Last Name       First Name    Birth Date      Hire Date      Title                City      Region    Country

Davolio         Nancy              08-Dec-1948    01-May-1992  Sales Representative     Seattle   WA        USA

Callahan        Laura              09-Jan-1958    05-Mar-1994  Inside Sales Coordinator Seattle   WA        USA
```

Figure 6-10. *Twenty characters per inch*

TextFormatCharacterSeparated

The TextFormatCharacterSeparated format (see Listing 6-6) offers a number of options. Because this is a character-separated file, you get to choose the character that separates the fields.

Listing 6-6. *Using TextFormatCharacterSeparated*

```
oReportFormatOpts.Format = CeReportFormat.ceFormatTextCharacterSeparated;

TextFormatCharacterSeparated oTextFormatCharacterSeparated;

oTextFormatCharacterSeparated =
    oReportFormatOpts.TextFormatCharacterSeparated;

oTextFormatCharacterSeparated.Delimiter = "'";
oTextFormatCharacterSeparated.Separator = ",";
oTextFormatCharacterSeparated.Quote = "'";
```

```
oTextFormatCharacterSeparated.ExportMode =
   CeSVExportMode.ceSVExportModeStandard;
oTextFormatCharacterSeparated.GroupSectionsOption =
   CeGroupSectionsOption.ceGroupSectionsExportIsolated;
oTextFormatCharacterSeparated.ReportSectionsOption =
   CeReportSectionsOption.ceReportSectionsExportIsolated;
oTextFormatCharacterSeparated.IsSameDate = true;
oTextFormatCharacterSeparated.IsSameNumber = true;
```

The Delimiter property determines how the nonnumeric fields are enclosed, which is usually by single or double-quotes. You can use any string for the Delimiter value, but be aware that the application reading the ASCII output may not always like it. By comparison, the Separator property separates one field from another. Usually a comma is assigned here, but any string value will be accepted. The same caveat applies here as for the Delimiter property. Make sure the target application will understand the meaning of the separator value.

The ReportSectionsOption property, here set to ceReportSectionsExportIsolated, exports the report and page header sections to their own records at the beginning of the file. The report and page footer sections are exported to their own records at the end of the file. The output looks like this:

```
"RH S1 F1", "RH S1 F2"
"RH S2 F1", "RH S2 F2"
"PH S1 F1", "PH S1 F2"
"GH1 F1", "D F1", "D F2", "D F3", "GF1 F1"
"GH1 F1", "D F1", "D F2", "D F3", "GF1 F1"
"PF S1 F1", "PF S1 F2"
"RF S1 F1", "RF S1 F2"
"RF S2 F1", "RF S2 F2"
```

Table 6-3 lists the meanings of each abbreviation.

Table 6-3. *Report Section Abbreviations*

Abbreviation	Meaning
RH	Report Header
S1	Section 1
PH	Page Header
GH	Group Header
D	Detail
F1	Field 1
GF	Group Footer
PF	Page Footer
RF	Report Footer

When the GroupSectionsOption property is set to ceGroupSectionsExportIsolated, the output is similar to the ceReportSectionsExportIsolated option, but with group information segregated from detail rows as in the following layout:

```
"RH S1 F1", "RH S1 F2"
"RH S2 F1", "RH S2 F2"
"PH S1 F1", "PH S1 F2"
"GH1 F1",
"D F1", "D F2", "D F3",
"D F1", "D F2", "D F3",
"GF1 F1"
"GH1 F1",
"D F1", "D F2", "D F3",
"D F1", "D F2", "D F3",
"GF1 F1"
"PF S1 F1", "PF S1 F2"
"RF S1 F1", "RF S1 F2"
"RF S2 F1", "RF S2 F2"
```

RichTextFormat

The `RichTextFormat` format (see Listing 6-7) is very simple and has the same options as the Word format. You can choose starting and ending pages, or indicate that all pages should be exported. This format exports data elements as individual objects and is commonly employed for output intended for use as fill-in-the-blank forms. `RichTextFormat` preserves most of the formatting. Be advised that text objects cannot be located beyond the left edge of the page. Those that are will be pushed right.

Listing 6-7. *Using RichTextFormat*

```
oReportFormatOpts.Format = CeReportFormat.ceFormatRTF;

RichTextFormat oRichTextFormat;

oRichTextFormat = oReportFormatOpts.RichTextFormat;

oRichTextFormat.StartPageNumber = 1;
oRichTextFormat.EndPageNumber = 1;
oRichTextFormat.ExportAllPages = true;
```

This format will produce an RTF file that opens in Word as shown in Figure 6-11.

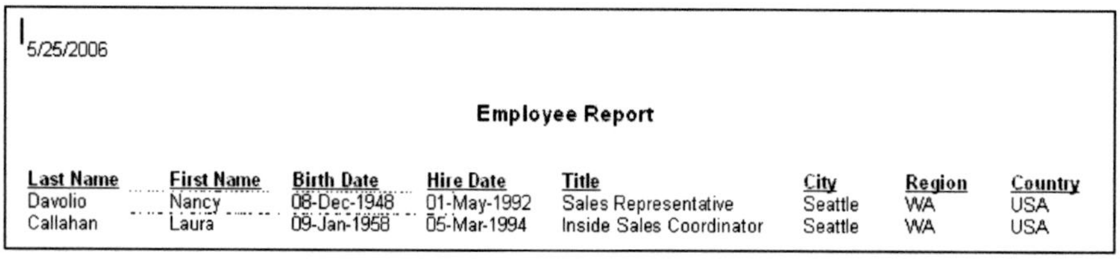
5/25/2006

Employee Report

Last Name	First Name	Birth Date	Hire Date	Title	City	Region	Country
Davolio	Nancy	08-Dec-1948	01-May-1992	Sales Representative	Seattle	WA	USA
Callahan	Laura	09-Jan-1958	05-Mar-1994	Inside Sales Coordinator	Seattle	WA	USA

Figure 6-11. *Export RTF option*

RichTextEditableFormat

The `RichTextEditableFormat` format shown in Listing 6-8 converts all of the report object contents to text lines. It differs from the Microsoft Word (RTF) format in that it does not employ text frames. Text formatting is preserved, but attributes such as background color and fill pattern may not be. All report images are inlined with the textual content, and as a result the images automatically shift to accommodate text when the document is opened in Word. `RichTextEditableFormat` does not export line and box objects from your report.

The `PageBreakAfterEachReportPage` property permits you to indicate whether or not to insert page breaks after each report page. This option may not correspond to the page breaks created by Microsoft Word and is used primarily to separate report page contents.

Listing 6-8. *Using RichTextEditableFormat*

```
oReportFormatOpts.Format = CeReportFormat.ceFormatRTFEditable;

RichTextEditableFormat oRichTextEditableFormat;

oRichTextEditableFormat = oReportFormatOpts.RichTextEditableFormat;

oRichTextEditableFormat.StartPageNumber = 1;
oRichTextEditableFormat.EndPageNumber = 1;
oRichTextEditableFormat.ExportAllPages = true;
oRichTextEditableFormat.PageBreakAfterEachReportPage = true;
```

PlainTextFormat

`PlainTextFormat` outputs a simple text dump of the report data without any formatting. The `CharactersPerInch` property specifies the number of characters that will fit in a linear inch of horizontal space, and therefore determines the font dimension. The use of `PlainTextFormat` is shown in Listing 6-9.

Listing 6-9. *Using PlainTextFormat*

```
oReportFormatOpts.Format = CeReportFormat.ceFormatTextPlain;

PlainTextFormat oPlainTextFormat;

oPlainTextFormat = oReportFormatOpts.PlainTextFormat;

oPlainTextFormat.CharactersPerInch = 10;
```

PDFFormat

Adobe Acrobat is probably the most common format for report distribution, as the Adobe Reader is available on almost every corporate desktop and is free of charge. `PDFFormat` will embed the TrueType fonts that appear in the document, as non-TrueType fonts are not supported. Listing 6-10 shows the PDF export in action.

Listing 6-10. *Using PDFFormat*

```
oReportFormatOpts.Format = CeReportFormat.ceFormatPDF;

PDFFormat oPDFFormat;

oPDFFormat = oReportFormatOpts.PDFFormat;

oPDFFormat.StartPageNumber = 1;
oPDFFormat.EndPageNumber = 1;
oPDFFormat.ExportAllPages = true;
oPDFFormat.CreateBookmarksFromGroupTree  = true;
```

The `CreateBookmarksFromGroupTree()` method determines whether the group tree items are translated into PDF bookmarks. Bookmarks are navigation aids that allow the user to jump to various points in the documents quickly without scrolling through all the detail information first.

ExcelFormat

The Excel format shown in Listing 6-11 is most commonly requested by my investment banking clients. Often they want their reports in Excel—and sometimes only in Excel—in order to perform additional analysis and to add additional data before distributing them. The `ExcelFormat` tries to put all the information across all pages into one worksheet and only uses another worksheet when more space is needed. Should you have a report with more than 256 columns, note that these additional columns will not export, as this is Excel's column limit. Though it preserves the formatting, lines and boxes are not exported.

If it's important to export your reports to Excel, then it's helpful to understand how Crystal Reports handles the report layout internally. Crystal employs an insertion point interface. When you drop an object on your report, this object is given an XY coordinate calculated from the top-left corner of the page. By comparison, Excel uses a line-by-line interface, which does not permit placement of objects between the lines. This means that when you export a report to Excel, objects placed between lines will be moved to the nearest line. If Excel is your ultimate destination, you'll have the best results if you format the report as closely as possible to the layout of an Excel spreadsheet.

Listing 6-11. *Using ExcelFormat*

```
oReportFormatOpts.Format = CeReportFormat.ceFormatExcel;

ExcelFormat oExcelFormat;

oExcelFormat = oReportFormatOpts.ExcelFormat;

oExcelFormat.BaseAreaGroupNum = 1;
oExcelFormat.BaseAreaType = CeSectionType.ceDetail;
oExcelFormat.ConstColWidth = 30;
oExcelFormat.ConvertDateToString = true;
oExcelFormat.CreatePageBreak = true;
oExcelFormat.ExportAllPages = true;
```

```
oExcelFormat.ExportPageHeader = true;
oExcelFormat.ExportPageHeaderFooter =
    CeReportHeaderFooterOption.ceReportHeaderFooterForEachPage;
oExcelFormat.ExportShowGridlines = true;
oExcelFormat.HasColumnHeadings = true;
oExcelFormat.IsTabularFormat = true;
oExcelFormat.StartPageNumber = 1 ;
oExcelFormat.EndPageNumber = 1;
oExcelFormat.UseConstColWidth = true;
```

Sometimes Crystal reports that are not formatted with Excel output in mind export with blank lines. To reduce this problem, use the report designer to minimize the height of each section via the Fit Section option available by right-clicking over the section. The Fit Section option will resize a section by moving the bottom border up to the point of the lowest object in that section. Therefore, it's best to position fields at the top of the section to minimize space between the tops of the fields and the top of the section. All objects that you wish to have appear in the same row in Excel must be the same height in Crystal Reports. Likewise, all objects you wish to appear in the same column in Excel must have the same width. Sometimes text that spans two lines on the report will appear as one line in the export. Should this occur, look to the Can Grow option in Crystal Reports under the Format text option of the text box. Select this option and the text wrapping problem should resolve itself.

ExcelDataOnlyFormat

The ExcelDataOnly format is similar to the Excel format, as it preserves much of the formatting even though it is a record-based export format. Listing 6-12 shows the ExcelDataOnlyFormat method at work.

Listing 6-12. *Using ExcelDataOnlyFormat*

```
oReportFormatOpts.Format = CeReportFormat.ceFormatExcelDataOnly;

ExcelDataOnlyFormat oExcelDataOnlyFormat;

oExcelDataOnlyFormat = oReportFormatOpts.ExcelDataOnlyFormat;

oExcelDataOnlyFormat.BaseAreaGroupNum = 1;
oExcelDataOnlyFormat.BaseAreaType = CeSectionType.ceGroupHeader;
oExcelDataOnlyFormat.ConstColWidth = 10;
oExcelDataOnlyFormat.ExportImage = true;
oExcelDataOnlyFormat.ExportPageHeader = true;
oExcelDataOnlyFormat.MaintainColAlignment = true;
oExcelDataOnlyFormat.MaintainRelativeObjPosition = true;
oExcelDataOnlyFormat.ShowGroupOutlines = true;
oExcelDataOnlyFormat.SimplifyPageHeader = true;
oExcelDataOnlyFormat.UseConstColWidth = true;
oExcelDataOnlyFormat.UseFormat = true;
oExcelDataOnlyFormat.UseWorksheetFunc = true;
```

The UseWorksheetFunc property indicates whether worksheet summaries should be exported as Excel functions. If your report displays a column of numbers and you've created a Summary value to show the total, setting this property to true will export that summary value as an @SUM function in Excel. This feature will allow your users to perform "what-if" analysis whereby they can change detail values in the spreadsheet and examine its effects on the rest of the report. There is, unfortunately, a catch here. Only database field summaries may be exported as functions. Formula summaries cannot be. Moreover, only group-level summaries are available for export as Excel functions regardless of whether they are database or formula summaries. Therefore, you could not export a grand total. If producing "what-if" reports where every summary field is an Excel function is your goal, check out some of the third-party Excel solutions discussed in Chapter 12.

Destination Options

Also in Chapter 4, we saw how to use the CMC to set various destinations for your reports. Reports can go to SMTP mail, an FTP server, a disk file, or an Inbox. These settings can be established programmatically as well. Listings 6-13 and 6-14 show the how SMTP mail can be set as the destination source. The approach to setting SMTP mail is structurally very similar to setting destinations for unmanaged disk files, FTP servers, and Inboxes.

■**Note** Should you experience errors when attempting to run a report to a particular destination, make sure that the specified destination is enabled in the Destinations tab of the Program Job Server. This topic is covered in greater detail in Chapter 2.

Listing 6-13. *Extracting the Report and SMTP Plug-In Objects*

```
szSQL = "SELECT SI_ID " +
   "FROM CI_INFOOBJECTS " +
   "WHERE SI_ID = " + szReportID;

oReportInfoObjects = oInfoStore.Query(szSQL);
oReport = ((Report) oReportInfoObjects[1]);

//You need to pull both SI_DEST_SCHEDULEOPTIONS and
//SI_PROGID in order for the SetFromPlugin() method
//to write the DestinationPlugin object
szSQL = "SELECT SI_DEST_SCHEDULEOPTIONS, SI_PROGID " +
   "FROM CI_SYSTEMOBJECTS " +
   "WHERE SI_PARENTID=29 " +
   "AND SI_NAME = 'CrystalEnterprise.Smtp'";

oInfoObjects = oInfoStore.Query(szSQL);
oInfoObject = oInfoObjects[1];
```

Listing 6-13 extracts the report InfoObject that is cast to an object of type Report. Then, you'll need to extract into an InfoObject the InfoStore entry for Smtp mail. Listing 6-14 shows how to create a DestinationPlugIn object through which an object of type SmtpOptions can be instantiated.

Listing 6-14. *Creating the SmtpOptions Object*

```
oDestinationPlugin = new DestinationPlugin(oInfoObject.PluginInterface);

oSmtpOptions = new SmtpOptions(oDestinationPlugin.ScheduleOptions);

oSmtpOptions.EnableAttachments = true;
oSmtpOptions.SMTPAuthentication = CeAuthentication.ceAuthLogin;
oSmtpOptions.SMTPPassword = "mypassword";
oSmtpOptions.SMTPUserName = "myuserName";
oSmtpOptions.ServerName = "mysmtpserver";
oSmtpOptions.DomainName = "mydomain";
oSmtpOptions.Port = 80;
oSmtpOptions.SenderAddress = "BOXIAdmin@mycompany.com";
oSmtpOptions.ToAddresses.Add("seton.software@verizon.net");
oSmtpOptions.CCAddresses.Add("youraddress@verizon.net");
oSmtpOptions.Delimiter = ";";
oSmtpOptions.Subject = "Daily Sales Report";
oSmtpOptions.Message = "Click here %SI_VIEWER_URL% to view your report." ;
oSmtpOptions.Attachments.Add("mimeType", "myfile.txt");

oDestination = oReport.SchedulingInfo.Destination;

oDestination.SetFromPlugin(oDestinationPlugin);

oInfoStore.Commit(oReportInfoObjects);
```

Once you've instantiated your SmtpOptions object, you can assign to it the properties you would expect to be associated with an e-mail—from and to addresses, CC addresses, server and connectivity information, as well as subject and message body. Notice that the message in this example uses the variable indicator %SI_VIEWER_URL%. This hard-coded variable has special meaning to the BO XI object model and will cause it to replace this value with the URL of the report so the user can simply click the link and see the output. Table 6-4 lists the other variables available to you. Except for %SI_VIEWER_URL%, which is available only for the body of the e-mail, all the options shown are available for both the subject and the body.

Table 6-4. *Placeholder Variables*

Variable	Description
%SI_NAME%	Report title
%SI_ID%	InfoStore SI_ID value
%SI_OWNER%	Owner
%SI_STARTTIME%	Date and time report was run
%SI_USERFULLNAME%	User name
%SI_EMAIL_ADDRESS%	E-mail address
%SI_VIEWER_URL%	URL to view report

The code for sending report output to an FTP server is structurally very similar to that for sending output to an Smtp mail destination. After extracting the report reference, you need to extract the Ftp reference stored in the InfoStore. Then, assign all the properties that are specific to an FTP server as shown in Listing 6-15.

Listing 6-15. *FTP Server Destination*

```
szSQL = "SELECT SI_ID " +
    "FROM CI_INFOOBJECTS " +
    "WHERE SI_ID = " + szReportID;

oReportInfoObjects = oInfoStore.Query(szSQL);
oReport = ((Report) oReportInfoObjects[1]);

//You need to pull both SI_DEST_SCHEDULEOPTIONS and
//SI_PROGID in order for the SetFromPlugin() method
//to write the DestinationPlugin object
szSQL = "SELECT SI_DEST_SCHEDULEOPTIONS, SI_PROGID " +
    "FROM CI_SYSTEMOBJECTS " +
    "WHERE SI_PARENTID=29 " +
    "AND SI_NAME = 'CrystalEnterprise.Ftp'";

oInfoObjects = oInfoStore.Query(szSQL);
oInfoObject = oInfoObjects[1];

oDestinationPlugin = new DestinationPlugin(oInfoObject.PluginInterface);

oFtpOptions = new FtpOptions(oDestinationPlugin.ScheduleOptions);

oFtpOptions.ServerName = "myServerName";
oFtpOptions.UserName = "myUserName";
oFtpOptions.Password = "myPassword";
oFtpOptions.Port = 21;
oFtpOptions.Account = "myAccount";
```

```
oFtpOptions.DestinationFiles.Add("thisfile.rpt");
oFtpOptions.DestinationFiles.Add("thatfile.rpt");

oDestination = oReport.SchedulingInfo.Destination;

oDestination.SetFromPlugin(oDestinationPlugin);

oInfoStore.Commit(oReportInfoObjects);
```

Next we'll look at how to send a report to an unmanaged disk file destination. This code, shown in Listing 6-16, is much simpler than the previous examples, as it only requires you to specify a file name.

Listing 6-16. *Unmanaged Disk File Destination*

```
szSQL = "SELECT SI_ID " +
   "FROM CI_INFOOBJECTS " +
   "WHERE SI_ID = " + szReportID;

oReportInfoObjects = oInfoStore.Query(szSQL);
oReport = ((Report) oReportInfoObjects[1]);

//You need to pull both SI_DEST_SCHEDULEOPTIONS and
//SI_PROGID in order for the SetFromPlugin() method
//to write the DestinationPlugin object
szSQL = "SELECT SI_DEST_SCHEDULEOPTIONS, SI_PROGID " +
   "FROM CI_SYSTEMOBJECTS " +
   "WHERE SI_PARENTID=29 " +
   "AND SI_NAME = 'CrystalEnterprise.DiskUnmanaged'";

oInfoObjects = oInfoStore.Query(szSQL);
oInfoObject = oInfoObjects[1];

oDestinationPlugin = new DestinationPlugin(oInfoObject.PluginInterface);

oDiskUnmanagedOptions =
   new DiskUnmanagedOptions(oDestinationPlugin.ScheduleOptions);

oDiskUnmanagedOptions.DestinationFiles.Add("targetfile.pdf");

oDestination = oReport.SchedulingInfo.Destination;

oDestination.SetFromPlugin(oDestinationPlugin);

oInfoStore.Commit(oReportInfoObjects);
```

Printer Options

You can handle customization of the printer options through the `ReportPrinterOptions` method of the `Report` class. Listing 6-17 shows the printer setup for a `Report` object.

Listing 6-17. *Setting Up the Printer*

```
oReport.ReportPrinterOptions.Copies = 1;
oReport.ReportPrinterOptions.PrinterName = @"\\servername\printername";
oReport.ReportPrinterOptions.LandscapeMode = false;
oReport.ReportPrinterOptions.PrintCollationType =
    CePrintCollateType.cePrintCollateTypeCollated;
oReport.ReportPrinterOptions.PageSize = CePageSize.cePageSizeLegal;
oReport.ReportPrinterOptions.FromPage = 1;
oReport.ReportPrinterOptions.ToPage = 2;
```

This code shows that you can set the paper size to which the report will be formatted. The enumerated values for paper size are shown in Table 6-5.

Table 6-5. *CePageSize Enumerator Members*

Member	Value	Description
ceCustomPageSize	0	Custom page size
cePageSizeA4	9	A4
cePageSizeA5	11	A5
cePageSizeB5	13	B5
cePageSizeLegal	5	Legal
cePageSizeLetter	1	Letter

The `PageLayout` property determines the source from which the page will derive its formatting. The enumerated values available for this property are listed in Table 6-6.

Table 6-6. *CeReportLayout Enumerator Members*

Member	Value	Description
ceReportFileSettings	0	Default page layout from the report file.
ceDefaultPrinterSettings	1	Page layout settings from the default printer.
ceNoPrinterSettings	2	Page layout settings from the system default device.
ceSpecifiedPrinterSettings	3	Page layout from a specified printer. Printing can then only be done on this printer.
ceCustomSettings	4	Custom page layout.

Programming Categories

Categories are all-purpose identifiers by which you can better organize your objects. There are two types of categories—corporate and personal. The former is created by an administrator and available to multiple users, while the latter is created by a user for his own purposes. The code for creating a corporate category is very similar to that for creating a folder. Listing 6-18 shows it in action.

Listing 6-18. *Creating a Corporate Category*

```
//Log on to BO XI

oInfoObjects = oInfoStore.NewInfoObjectCollection();

oPluginManager = oInfoStore.PluginManager;
oPluginInfo = oPluginManager.GetPluginInfo("Category");
oInfoObject = oInfoObjects.Add(oPluginInfo);
oCategory = ((Category) oInfoObject);

oCategory.Title = szCategoryName;

oInfoStore.Commit(oInfoObjects);

szResult = oCategory.ID.ToString();
```

Creating a personal category is slightly different. Because a personal category belongs to a particular user, you need to specify a parent ID as shown in Listing 6-19. This parent ID value is the SI_ID of the user who owns it.

Listing 6-19. *Creating a Personal Category*

```
//Log on to BO XI

oInfoObjects = oInfoStore.NewInfoObjectCollection();

oPluginManager = oInfoStore.PluginManager;
oPluginInfo = oPluginManager.GetPluginInfo("PersonalCategory");
oInfoObject = oInfoObjects.Add(oPluginInfo);
oPersonalCategory = ((PersonalCategory) oInfoObject);

oPersonalCategory.Title = szCategoryName;
oPersonalCategory.ParentID = iBOUserID;

oInfoStore.Commit(oInfoObjects);
```

Since the whole idea behind using categories is to implement an all-purpose grouping mechanism, it would seem likely that you would either want to retrieve all the objects associated to a particular category, or retrieve all the categories associated with a particular object.

The code in Listing 6-20 shows how to retrieve a DataTable containing both the corporate and personal categories associated with a given object.

Listing 6-20. *Retrieving Categories for an Object*

```
//Connect to BO XI

oDT = new DataTable();

oDT.Columns.Add(new DataColumn("ID"));
oDT.Columns.Add(new DataColumn("Description"));
oDT.Columns.Add(new DataColumn("Type"));

//Run the same code once for each category type
for (int x=1; x<=2; x++)
{
   if (x == 1)
   {
      szField = "SI_CORPORATE_CATEGORIES";
      szType = "Corporate";
   }
   else
   {
      szField = "SI_PERSONAL_CATEGORIES";
      szType = "Personal";
   }

   szSQL = "SELECT " + szField +
      " FROM CI_INFOOBJECTS " +
      "WHERE SI_INSTANCE=0 " +
      "AND SI_ID= " + szID;

   oInfoObjects = oInfoStore.Query(szSQL);

   //How many categories were found?
    oPropertyBag = oInfoObjects[1].Properties[szField].Properties;
    iCnt = ((int) oPropertyBag["SI_TOTAL"].Value);

   //For each one extract the name
   //and add everything to the DataTable
   for (int y=1; y<=iCnt; y++)
   {
      oDR = oDT.NewRow();

      szSQL = "SELECT SI_NAME " +
         "FROM CI_INFOOBJECTS " +
         "WHERE SI_ID= " + oPropertyBag[y.ToString()].Value;
```

```
    oCategories = oInfoStore.Query(szSQL);

    oDR["ID"] = oCategories[1].ID;
    oDR["Description"] = oCategories[1].Title;
    oDR["Type"] = szType;

    oDT.Rows.Add(oDR);
  }
}
```

The DataTable produced by this code is shown in Figure 6-12.

ID	Description	Type
4138	Finance Interest	Corporate
1043	cganz	Personal
5094	Human Resource Interest	Personal

Figure 6-12. *Categories of an object*

Categories can easily be extracted from the InfoStore via a simple SQL statement. This statement retrieves the personal categories for a given report:

```
SELECT SI_PERSONAL_CATEGORIES
FROM CI_INFOOBJECTS
WHERE SI_ID = 1266
AND SI_ID=1266
```

whereas this statement retrieves the corporate ones:

```
SELECT SI_CORPORATE_CATEGORIES
FROM CI_INFOOBJECTS
WHERE SI_ID = 1266
AND SI_ID=1266
```

Programming Events

Events allow you to make the execution of scheduled tasks in the CMC contingent on the performance of certain actions. There are three types of events—file, schedule, and custom. You can create events programmatically using the event classes. The code in Listing 6-21 shows how a file event is created.

Listing 6-21. *Creating Events*

```
oInfoObjects = oInfoStore.NewInfoObjectCollection();

oPluginManager = oInfoStore.PluginManager;
oPluginInfo = oPluginManager.GetPluginInfo("Event");
oInfoObject = oInfoObjects.Add(oPluginInfo);
oEvent = ((Event) oInfoObject);
```

```
oEvent.Title = "My New File Event";
oEvent.EventType = CeEventType.ceFile;
oEvent.FileEvent.FileName = @"c:\temp\myfile.txt";
oEvent.FileEvent.ServerFriendlyName = "seton-notebook.eventserver";

oInfoStore.Commit(oInfoObjects);
```

This example creates the base event object just like any other InfoStore object is created. A new InfoObjects collection is created by invoking the NewInfoObjectCollection() method, and a plug-in of type "Event" is added to it. Then, the new entry is type cast to an Event object, and the file and event server references set appropriately. Finally, the modified InfoObjects collection is committed back to the InfoStore.

Creating a custom event is even easier. The following code shows how it's done:

```
oEvent.Title = "My New Custom Event";
oEvent.EventType = CeEventType.ceUser;
```

Then, to trigger the event, invoke the Trigger() method like this:

```
oEvent.UserEvent.Trigger();
```

Once you've created an event, it's easy to assign it to a scheduled report. The code in Listing 6-22 extracts a report object and schedules it to run every day at 1:00 p.m. for the next decade. The Dependencies collections of the report's SchedulingInfo object has an Add() method that accepts the SI_ID values of the events upon which it is dependent.

Listing 6-22. *Assigning Events*

```
szSQL = "SELECT SI_ID " +
   "FROM CI_INFOOBJECTS " +
   "WHERE SI_ID=" + szReportID;

oInfoObjects = oInfoStore.Query(szSQL);

oReport = ((Report) oInfoObjects[1]);

//Assign the event
oReport.SchedulingInfo.Dependencies.Add(iEventID);

//Schedule the report
szStartDateTime = DateTime.Today.ToShortDateString() + " 1:00:00 PM";

oReport.SchedulingInfo.IntervalDays = 1;
oReport.SchedulingInfo.BeginDate = DateTime.Parse(szStartDateTime);
oReport.SchedulingInfo.EndDate = DateTime.Today.AddYears(10);
oReport.SchedulingInfo.Type = CeScheduleType.ceScheduleTypeDaily;
oReport.SchedulingInfo.RightNow = false;

//Write the new schedule to the InfoStore
oInfoStore.Schedule(oInfoObjects);
```

Programming Calendars

Calendar objects allow you to specify a collection of dates when a report can be run. Creating a Calendar object is very similar to the code you've already seen for creating folders and reports. The difference is the addition of the dates. Listing 6-23 shows how to add a new Calendar object.

Listing 6-23. *Calendar Creation*

```
public void CreateCalendar(string szServer, string szCalendarName)
{
   //Log on to BO XI

   szSQL = "Select SI_ID " +
      "From CI_SYSTEMOBJECTS " +
      "Where SI_NAME = '" + szCalendarName + "' " +
      "And SI_KIND='Calendar'";

   oInfoObjects = oInfoStore.Query(szSQL);

   //If calendar of this name exists, delete and re-create
   if (oInfoObjects.Count != 0)
   {
      oCalendar = ((Calendar) oInfoObjects[1]);
      oCalendar.DeleteNow();
   }

   oPluginManager = oInfoStore.PluginManager;
   oPluginInfo = oPluginManager.GetPluginInfo("CrystalEnterprise.Calendar");
   oInfoObjects = oInfoStore.NewInfoObjectCollection();
   oInfoObjects.Add(oPluginInfo);

   oInfoObject = oInfoObjects[1];
   oCalendar = ((Calendar) oInfoObject);

   oCalendar.Title = szCalendarName;

   oInfoStore.Commit(oInfoObjects);

}
```

Writing the dates to the Calendar object is done via the Add() method of the Days collection. The first two sets of parameters are the "from" and "to" dates the new days apply to. Then, add an enumerated value that indicates the day of week, and finally indicate the week of month the change applies to. A zero value for week of month means all weeks. Likewise, a zero value for a day, month, or year also means all values for those calendar categories. For example, to create a calendar for the first Monday of the month for all of 2006, use the following line of code:

```
oCalendar.Days.Add(1,1,2006,31,12,2006,CeDayOfWeek.ceDayMonday,1);
```

A calendar that runs every Monday for all of 2006 can be had with this line of code:

```
oCalendar.Days.Add(1,1,2006,31,12,2006,CeDayOfWeek.ceDayMonday,0);
```

To run every business day for all of 2006, use the code in Listing 6-24.

Listing 6-24. *Calendar for Every Business Day of 2006*

```
oCalendar.Days.Add(1,1,2006,31,12,2006,CeDayOfWeek.ceDayMonday,0);
oCalendar.Days.Add(1,1,2006,31,12,2006,CeDayOfWeek.ceDayTuesday,0);
oCalendar.Days.Add(1,1,2006,31,12,2006,CeDayOfWeek.ceDayWednesday,0);
oCalendar.Days.Add(1,1,2006,31,12,2006,CeDayOfWeek.ceDayThursday,0);
oCalendar.Days.Add(1,1,2006,31,12,2006,CeDayOfWeek.ceDayFriday,0);
```

To create exceptions to this Monday through Friday schedule, use the Remove() method to skip certain days, say, Christmas, as shown here:

```
oCalendar.Remove(25,12,2006,25,12,2006);
```

But suppose we need a report for New Year's Eve even though it's a Saturday. This individual day can be added here:

```
oCalendar.Days.Add(31,12,2006,31,12,2006);
```

What we end up with is a Calendar object that looks like Figure 6-13.

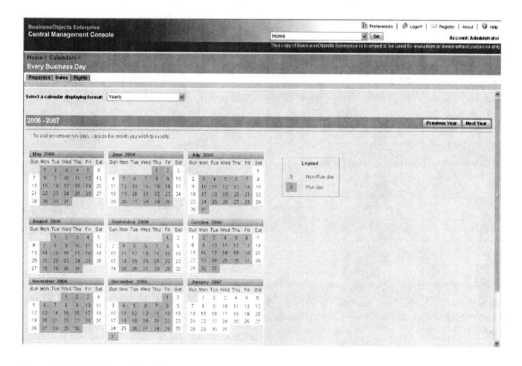

Figure 6-13. *Custom calendar*

Data Access Techniques

When you load a report into the CMC, you still have as much control over the data access as when you originally developed it using Crystal Reports. One of the most flexible methods of data access for your reports is the use of a custom DLL that serves as an intermediary layer between your report and the back-end database. The option to choose in Crystal Reports when creating your RPT is ADO.NET (XML). This will present you with a dialog (see Figure 6-14) through which you can select the DLL and the class name within the DLL whose methods return a DataTable object.

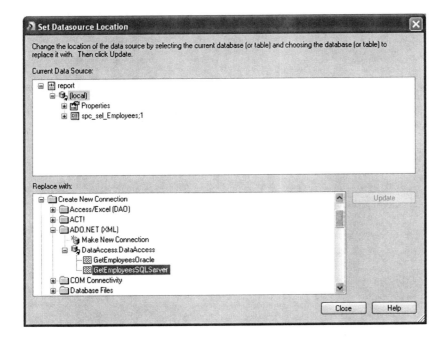

Figure 6-14. *Selecting assembly methods as data source*

Why do you need this flexibility? One reason may be security. Your data access DLL can reside on a server machine and obtain its connectivity information from a server-based XML file. The developers will have the development server information, but the production machine will be kept off limits to them. Moreover, using this approach, no production user IDs or password need be entered in the CMC.

Another reason is the requirement for decryption. Some of my clients store their most sensitive information—birth dates, social security numbers, salaries—in the database in encrypted format. Using a data access DLL, you can extract this data, iterate through the data set, and decrypt the data before passing it to the reporting engine as a return value from the data source method. It's possible to invoke your decryption software from the stored procedure that extracts it. Both SQL Server and Oracle can invoke executable code from within stored procedures that would be used to handle the decryption. This may not be permissible due to corporate security policy or because the DBAs won't allow executable code to be invoked from their RDBMSs.

The code to extract a DataTable from SQL Server is shown in Listing 6-25.

Listing 6-25. *Extracting Data from SQL Server*

```
public static DataTable GetEmployeesSQLServer(string szCountry, int iReportsTo)
{
    DataTable oDT = null;

    string connectionString = "Data Source=(local);Initial catalog=Northwind;" +
        "Integrated security=SSPI;Persist security info=False";

    using (SqlConnection connection = new SqlConnection(connectionString))
    {
        using (SqlCommand oCmd = new SqlCommand("spc_sel_Employees", connection))
        {
            DataSet oDS = new DataSet();

            oCmd.CommandType = CommandType.StoredProcedure;
            oCmd.Parameters.Add("@Country", SqlDbType.NVarChar).Value = szCountry;
            oCmd.Parameters.Add("@ReportsTo", SqlDbType.Int).Value = iReportsTo;

            using (SqlDataAdapter oAdapter = new SqlDataAdapter(oCmd))
            {
                oAdapter.MissingSchemaAction = MissingSchemaAction.AddWithKey;
                oAdapter.Fill(oDS);

                if (oDS != null)
                    oDT = oDS.Tables[0];
            }
        }
    }

    return oDT;
}
```

As you can plainly see, this is familiar data access code wrapped in a method that returns a DataTable. The difference is that before this DataTable is returned, you can perform any programmatic manipulation of the data that you need. The code for Oracle access is available in the code download along with the scripts to create the package and stored procedure. Except for some Oracle-specific syntax, the approach is exactly the same.

Another reason to use a DataTable is to allow an easy and secure change of data source at runtime. Suppose you have a report that can run against different data sources of the same structure. An easy way to handle this is to set up a report parameter that indicates the data source. Then, the data access DLL can connect to different data sources before executing any stored procedures and so return data specific to that data source.

I've occasionally had some difficulty using the data access DLL approach whereby the Crystal Reports designer would not recognize the data structure of the resulting DataTable so as to populate the Database Field section of the Fields Explorer. The workaround was to instantiate a DataTable object first and then add the DataColumn objects to it individually as shown in Listing 6-26.

Listing 6-26. *Workaround When DataTable Structure Is Not Recognized*

```
DataTable oEmployeeDT = new DataTable();
oEmployeeDT.Columns.Add(new DataColumn("EMPNO", typeof(string)));
oEmployeeDT.Columns.Add(new DataColumn("ENAME", typeof(string)));
oEmployeeDT.Columns.Add(new DataColumn("JOB", typeof(string)));
oEmployeeDT.Columns.Add(new DataColumn("HIREDATE", typeof(System.DateTime)));
oEmployeeDT.Columns.Add(new DataColumn("SAL", typeof(string)));
//Here iterate through the original DataTable and
//copy the contents to oEmployeeDT

return oEmployeeDT;
```

BO XI Web Controls

If you're presenting a web front end to your users, you may want to offer them some of the power you have with the CMC without actually giving them access to the CMC itself. Programming the interfaces offered by the CMC from scratch can be a prodigious task. Look at the CMC scheduling page as just one example. When the users select a frequency of Once, they're presented with one set of options. When they select Weekly, another set of options appears, and so on. This complex an interface, with managing the appearance and disappearance of the different component controls, would be a substantial amount of work to program yourself. Fortunately, BO XI offers you a solution in the form of web controls that do what the various pages of the CCM can do.

■**Note** The BO XI web controls were only recently marked as deprecated. They will be supported for the next two versions, and therefore we are covering them here. In the next section, we'll examine the successor technology for these web controls, called the *.NET Providers*, which are compatible with Visual Studio 2005.

Getting Started

To get started using the BO XI web controls, add the web components to your toolbox by creating a new toolbox tab and selecting the components as shown in Figure 6-15.

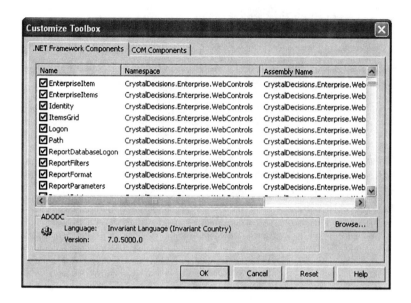

Figure 6-15. *Adding BO XI web components to the toolbox.*

Connecting to BO XI

The first component to examine is the Identity control. An Identity manages a connection to the InfoStore. To pass the connection information to the Identity control, you can use the Logon visual interface component shown in Figure 6-16. When you first drag this, or any of the visual controls, onto the page designer, it does not take on its final visual appearance until the Identity property on the Property dialog is set to the name of the visual Identity control. You can default the logon information by setting the values in the Page_Load event as shown in Listing 6-27.

Listing 6-27. *Page_Load Event*

```
private void Page_Load(object sender, System.EventArgs e)
{
    if (!Page.IsPostBack)
    {
        identity1.UserName ="Administrator";
        identity1.System = "seton-notebook:6400";
        identity1.SelectedAuthentication = "Enterprise";

        //Let's get creative with the button text
        Logon1.LogonButton.Text = "Enter BO XI";
        Logon1.LogoffButton.Text = "Say goodbye to BO XI";

        Logon1.DataBind();
    }
}
```

This will produce the page shown in Figure 6-16.

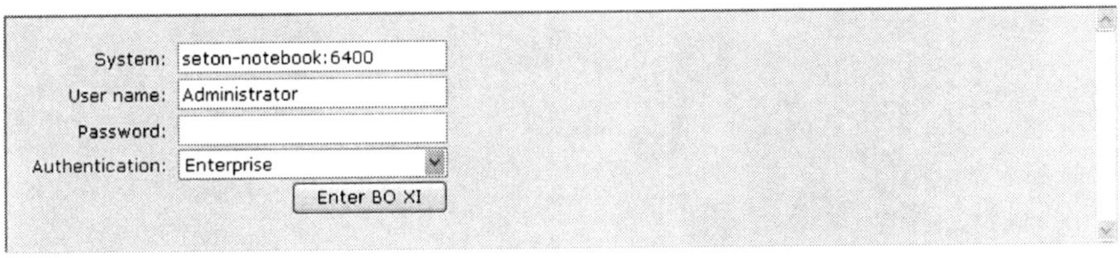

Figure 6-16. *Logon page*

Clicking the Enter BO XI button will attempt to log on to the InfoStore using the information entered into the Logon control. If successful, the LoggedOn event will trigger, and you can take the user into the other areas of the application as shown in Listing 6-28.

Listing 6-28. *LoggedOn Event*

```
private void identity1_LoggedOn(object sender, System.EventArgs e)
{
    Response.Redirect("Folders.aspx");
}
```

Of course, you may not successfully log on. If this is the case, it may be for one of two reasons. Either you entered an invalid password or your password is expired. In the case of an invalid password, the LogonFailed event will trigger as shown in Listing 6-29. From here you can direct the users to a message page informing them as to the nature of the problem.

Listing 6-29. *LogonFailed Event*

```
private void identity1_LogonFailed(object sender,
    CrystalDecisions.Enterprise.ExceptionEventArgs e)
{
    Response.Redirect("Error.aspx?Error=Not%20authorized");
}
```

Should the password entered be expired, the PasswordExpired event will trigger as shown in Listing 6-30.

Listing 6-30. *PasswordExpired Event*

```
private void identity1_PasswordExpired (object sender,
    System.EventArgs e)
{
    Response.Redirect("NewPassword.aspx");
}
```

From this event you can direct the user to a change password page where you can use the ChangePassword control, shown in Figure 6-17, to accept the new password information and commit it to the InfoStore using the following line of code:

```
ChangePassword1.Submit(identity1);
```

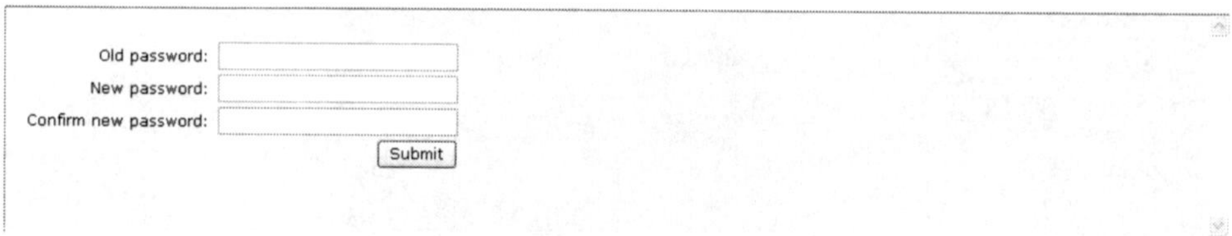

Figure 6-17. *ChangePassword control*

EnterpriseItems and ItemsGrid Controls

The Folders page contains three BO XI web controls: an ItemsGrid, an EnterpriseItems control, and an Identity control. The Identity control goes on first. This control will transport the valid connection made on the logon page throughout the application. The EnterpriseItems control represents a collection of objects extracted from the InfoStore and their associated properties. It is, in essence, the visual representation of an InfoObjects collection. You can even determine the object types that belong to it by setting the ItemTypes collection property in the Property dialog as shown in Figure 6-18.

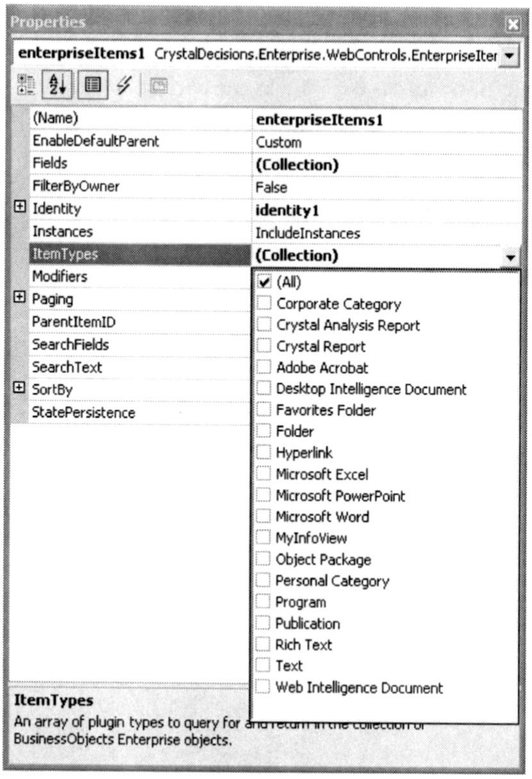

Figure 6-18. *ItemTypes property*

For each of these objects, you can determine what fields display as columns in the ItemsGrid by setting the `EnterpriseItems.Fields` collection shown in Figure 6-19.

Figure 6-19. *Fields property*

For the EnterpriseItems control to extract any data, the `Identity` property needs to be set to the name of the Identity control. Then, the `ItemSource` property of the ItemsGrid needs to be set to the name of the EnterpriseItems control. This is the pattern for any of the other controls as well: <Control>.ItemSource ➤ EnterpriseItem(s) control and EnterpriseItem(s).Identity ➤ Identity.

An ItemsGrid control is the visual display of the data extracted from the InfoStore via the EnterpriseItems control. It is essentially an ASP.NET DataGrid control specifically designed to work with InfoStore data. This control has properties that, if configured properly, could produce a screen that looks very much like the CMC itself. Since the ItemsGrid is bound to an EnterpriseItems control, you can restrict which properties returned by the EnterpriseItems control will display in the ItemsGrid. You can accomplish this by selecting the dialog box in the Columns property (see Figure 6-20) and adding the properties individually. For each property, you can indicate whether it is to be displayed as a hyperlink or not. If a hyperlink, clicking it will trigger the `ItemClicked` event of the ItemGrid control where you can take further action of the object entry that was selected.

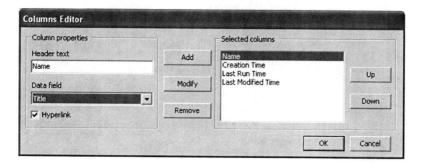

Figure 6-20. *Columns property dialog box*

The ItemsGrid also offers paging, the ability to set custom styles for alternating grid rows, and the option to allow drilldown to sublevels. In essence, it offers all the properties you would expect with any other grid control.

There are additional controls that allow you to view reports, schedule reports, maintain database logon information, set filters, determine format, apply parameters, and set up printing and destination options. Though these controls all have their own unique functions, each is set up in the same fashion.

Suppose you've selected a report from the ItemsGrid and wish to schedule it. Clicking the report hyperlink in the grid will invoke the ItemClicked event. Here you can check the ItemType property of the ItemEventArgs parameter to determine whether you clicked a report reference. ItemType encapsulates the SI_KIND property. Then, you can pass the ID of the report to the web page that contains the scheduling control using the ItemID property, which encapsulates SI_ID. This code is shown in Listing 6-31.

Listing 6-31. *ItemClicked Event*

```
private void ItemsGrid1_ItemClicked(object sender,
    CrystalDecisions.Enterprise.WebControls.ItemEventArgs e)
{
    if (e.ItemType == "CrystalEnterprise.Report")
    {
        if (rbScheduleReport.Checked)
            Response.Redirect("Schedule.aspx?ID=" + e.ItemID.ToString());
    }
}
```

Using the Schedule Control

The Schedule.aspx page has an Identity control on it that is bound to an EnterpriseItem (singular) control. This is the visual equivalent of an InfoObject property and encapsulates one object only. In the Form_Load event, you can assign the value of the ItemID passed in as a URL parameter to the EnterpriseItem control like this:

```
enterpriseItem1.ItemID = Request["id"];
```

The page will display, and you can then use the control to set up scheduling for your report. Every time the user selects a different scheduling option, a postback is required for the control to refresh with the options particular to that choice. When finished, click the Submit button. Doing so will trigger the SubmitClicked event shown in Listing 6-32.

Listing 6-32. *SubmitClicked Event*

```
private void Schedule1_SubmitClicked(object sender, System.EventArgs e)
{
    Schedule1.Submit(enterpriseItem1);
}
```

The Submit() method of the Schedule control will commit the changes to the InfoStore and the report will be scheduled (see Figure 6-21). It's that easy.

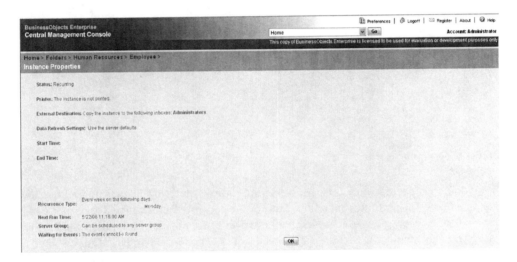

Figure 6-21. *CMC Schedule page*

The web controls are intended to act as interfaces to the CMC, and they transfer the selections entered by the user directly to the InfoStore via the Submit() method. There is no way to either set or query the properties of a given control to default or obtain the selections made by the user. The user settings exist in an unreachable black box that can only communicate with the InfoStore directly. Therefore, you can easily use these controls as user interface shortcuts to build your own customized front ends where you wish to manipulate the user settings before sending to the InfoStore. You may want to do this in order to send an e-mail to a manager requesting approval before the change is made or to indicate to the manager that a scheduling change took place. One possible way around this limitation is to submit the control to another report in the InfoStore and then read the properties back out via an SQL query like this:

```
SELECT SI_PROCESSINFO.SI_FORMAT_INFO
FROM CI_INFOOBJECTS
WHERE SI_ID = 1266
```

This query will return a result set that looks something like Figure 6-22. In this example, the report is set to character-separated values.

1/1 top

Processing Info		
SI_FORMAT_INFO	SI_FORMAT	u2fsepv:3
	SI_QUOTE	~
	SI_SEPARATOR	,
	SI_SAME_NUMBER	1
	SI_SAME_DATE	1
	SI_FORMAT_XLS_COLHEADINGS	True
	SI_FORMAT_XLS_USECONSTCOLWIDTH	False
	SI_FORMAT_XLS_CONSTCOLWIDTH	10
	SI_FORMAT_XLS_TABULARFORMAT	True
	SI_FORMAT_XLS_BASEAREATYPE	255
	SI_FORMAT_XLS_BASEAREAGROUPNUM	1
	SI_LINES_PER_PAGE	60
	SI_FORMAT_XLS_CREATE_PAGEBREAK	False
	SI_FORMAT_XLS_CONVERT_DATE	False
	SI_FORMAT_XLS_EXPORT_PAGEHEADER	True
	SI_FORMAT_XLS_SIMPLIFY_PAGEHEADER	True
	SI_FORMAT_XLS_USE_WORKSHEETFUNC	True
	SI_FORMAT_XLS_EXPORT_IMAGE	True
	SI_FORMAT_XLS_USE_FORMAT	True
	SI_FORMAT_XLS_MAINTAIN_COLALIGNMENT	True
	SI_FORMAT_EXPORT_ALLPAGES	True
	SI_FORMAT_STARTPAGE	1
	SI_FORMAT_ENDPAGE	1
	SI_FORMAT_XLS_EXPORT_PAGEAREAPAIR	0
	SI_FORMAT_XLS_MAINTAIN_RELATIVE_OBJ_POSITION	True
	SI_FORMAT_XLS_SHOW_GRIDLINES	False
	SI_FORMAT_CHARACTERS_PERINCH	20
	SI_USE_OPTION_IN_REPORT	False
	SI_PAGEBREAK_AFTER_EACH_REPORTPAGE	True
	SI_FORMAT_XLS_SHOW_GROUP_OUTLINES	True
	SI_FORMAT_CREATE_BOOKMARKS_FROM_GROUPTREE	False
	SI_FORMAT_FIELD_DELIMITER	"
	SI_FORMAT_EXPORT_MODE	1
	SI_FORMAT_REPORT_SECTIONS_OPTION	0
	SI_FORMAT_GROUP_SECTIONS_OPTION	0

Figure 6-22. *Format properties*

You do have a degree of customization over the controls, and we'll discuss their individual characteristics in the sections that follow. Most of the controls contain labels to describe the individual controls or groups of controls contained within them. For example, in the Printer control, you can specify the text for the labels that say "Printer:", "Range:", "Copies:", and "Collate:". You cannot, however, change the text of the controls labeled "Default printer", "Custom Printer", "All pages(s)", "From", and "To".

Other common properties include `EmptyText` and `LoggedOffText`. These properties hold the message to be displayed on the control when there are no reports in the EnterpriseItems control or the control is not logged on to the InfoStore, respectively. In addition, there is a `NotReportText` property for controls that work with reports only that will hold the text displayed when one of the items to which it is bound is not of `SI_KIND = CrystalReport`.

Each control has a Submit button that can be customized as well. You can change the button text from "Submit" to another phrase. You can also indicate whether you really want a standard command button as opposed to an image button or a link button. The following code shows these properties in action for the ReportFormat control:

```
ReportFormat1.SubmitButton.Text = "Save Changes";
ReportFormat1.SubmitButton.Type = ButtonType.LinkButton;
```

Having covered the Schedule control in detail, you now largely know how the other controls work as well, as they all have a similar implementation.

Web Controls

The remaining BO XI web controls are discussed in the following sections. We'll look at their idiosyncrasies in detail.

Database Logon

The Database Logon control shown in Figure 6-23 allows you to pass login information to the data source of your report. Even with a control this simple, you can change only the text labels describing each field and cannot programmatically access the contents of the fields themselves.

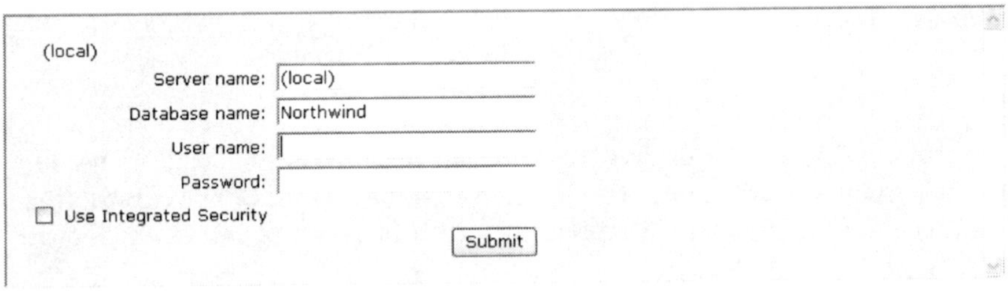

Figure 6-23. *Database Logon control*

Destination

The Destination control (see Figure 6-24) handles the settings found on the Destination page of the Schedule tab. Here you can determine whether the report will output to a disk file, e-mail recipients, Inbox, or FTP server and what the settings are for each option.

Figure 6-24. *Destination control*

Filters

The Filter control (see Figure 6-25) serves as an interface to the Filter page of the CMC's Process tab. Here you can edit the record and group filters that determine what data returned from the data source is displayed in the report.

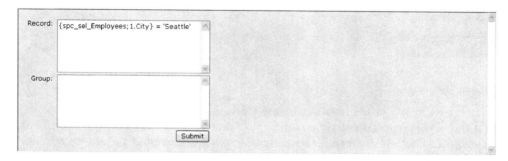

Figure 6-25. *Filters control*

Format

The Format control (see Figure 6-26) allows a greater degree of customization in that it permits you to control the options it offers. Suppose you want to offer the user the options of exporting only to PDF or Excel. You could accomplish this using the VisibleFormats property as shown here:

```
ReportFormat1.VisibleFormats = "AdobeAcrobat,MicrosoftExcel";
```

The Formats property will return a collection of all the formats that are available as shown here:

```
Response.Write(ReportFormat1.Formats[0] + "<BR>");
CrystalReport
```

```
Response.Write(ReportFormat1.Formats[1] + "<BR>");
AdobeAcrobat
```

```
Response.Write(ReportFormat1.Formats[2] + "<BR>");
EditableRichText
//...and so on.
```

This control allows you to extract at least some of the user-selected information as shown here:

```
//Returns default selection
ReportFormatType sSelectedFormat = ReportFormat1.SelectedFormat;
```

```
//Returns choice selected by user
ReportFormatType sSelectedType = ReportFormat1.SelectedType;
```

```
//returns "Document Settings"
string szSelectedPageLayout = ReportFormat1.SelectedPageLayout;
```

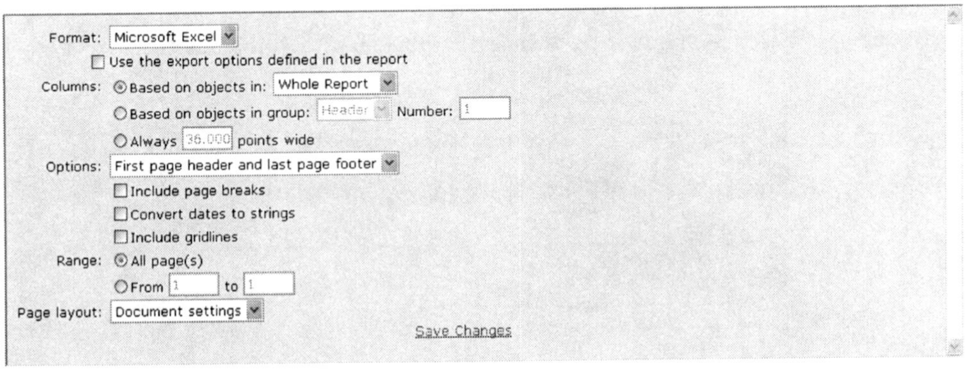

Figure 6-26. *Format control*

Parameters

The Parameters control (see Figure 6-27) handles the Parameters page of the CMC Process tab. Here you can specify the default parameters for your report.

Figure 6-27. *Parameters control*

Print

The Print control (see Figure 6-28) is an interface to the Print Setup page of the Process tab. To restrict the print options shown to just the Crystal Report format, you can use the VisiblePrintFormats property as shown here:

```
ReportPrint1.VisiblePrintFormats = "CrystalReport";
```

To see what print formats are available, you can use the PrintFormats property as shown in this example:

```
Response.Write(ReportPrint1.PrintFormats[0] + "<BR>");
CrystalReport

Response.Write(ReportPrint1.PrintFormats[1] + "<BR>");
None
```

Determining the default and user-selected options can be accomplished via the SelectedPrintFormat and SelectedType properties, respectively, as shown here.

```
//Default option
ReportPrintType sSelectedPrintFormat = ReportPrint1.SelectedPrintFormat;

//Selected option
ReportPrintType sSelectedType = ReportPrint1.SelectedType;
```

Both properties return a value of the `ReportPrintType` enumerator.

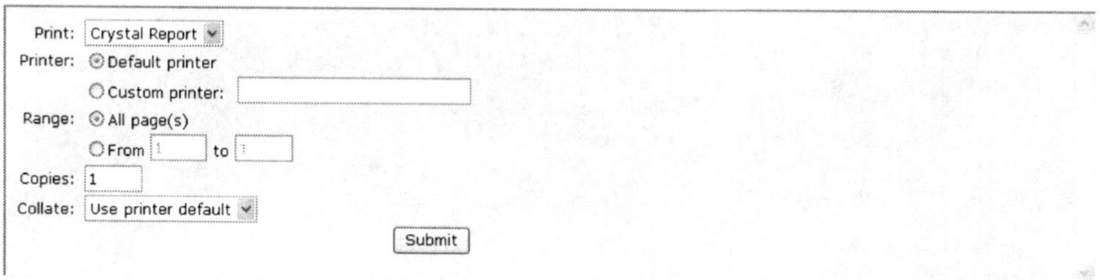

Figure 6-28. *Print control*

Path

The one control that differs the most from the others is the Path control. This control handles the *breadcrumbs*, a reference to the trail one leaves when navigating through a series of web pages. You'll notice this trail on the top left of the CMC. Like the other controls, Path is bound to an EnterpriseItem control. You can indicate the separator character (the default is >) or set the navigational display to either horizontal or vertical.

CrystalReportViewer

The CrystalReportViewer control is a visual container for Crystal report output. It provides page navigation, export options, tree view navigation, search functionality, and zooming. Using the properties of the control, you can turn these features on or off as you wish. Assuming the viewer page is invoked with the report ID as a URL parameter, let's take a look at how to extract a report and display it in the viewer. The code in Listing 6-33 shows the Page_Load event and how to extract a report and send it to the CrystalReportViewer control.

Listing 6-33. *Using the CrystalReportViewer*

```
private void Page_Load(object sender, System.EventArgs e)
{
    EnterpriseSession oEnterpriseSession = null;
    EnterpriseService oEnterpriseService = null;
    InfoStore oInfoStore = null;
    SessionMgr oSessionMgr = null;
    InfoObjects oInfoObjects;
    InfoObject oInfoObject;
    string szReportID;
    string szSQL;
```

```
szReportID = Request.QueryString["ID"];

//Connect to BO XI

szSQL = "SELECT SI_ID " +
        "FROM CI_INFOOBJECTS " +
        "WHERE SI_ID = " + szReportID;

oInfoObjects = oInfoStore.Query(szSQL);
  oInfoObject = oInfoObjects[1];

  CrystalReportViewer1.EnterpriseLogon = oEnterpriseSession;
  CrystalReportViewer1.ReportSource = oInfoObject;
}
```

Should you wish to connect using the visual controls, you can accomplish the same task as shown in Listing 6-34.

Listing 6-34. *Sending Report Encapsulated by the EnterpriseItem Control to CrystalReportViewer*

```
private void Page_Load(object sender, System.EventArgs e)
{
   enterpriseItem1.ItemID = Request["id"];

   CrystalReportViewer1.ReportSource = enterpriseItem1.
      GetReportSource(CrystalDecisions.Enterprise.WebControls.
      ReportServerType.PageServer);
}
```

The CrystalReportViewer control will only help you if your report has been output as a Crystal report. You may have very well output your report to PDF, Excel, or one of the many other formats available. If this is the case, you can stream the output of the report for viewing in the browser where it will display in its native viewer. The Report2Browser() method, shown in Listing 6-35, refers to the report encapsulated by an EnterpriseItem control. By referencing the InfoObject property of EnterpriseItem, you can determine the object type and handle it accordingly. This example shows only the Excel and PDF formats, but the others work in much the same fashion. The InfoObject is cast to a format-specific object, and the ByteStream array is extracted from this object and sent to the browser.

Listing 6-35. *Streaming Reports to the Browser*

```
private void Report2Browser()
{
   InfoObject oInfoObject;
   Excel oExcel;
   Pdf oPdf;
   byte[] aReportData = null;
   string szFilename = String.Empty;
   string szMimeType = String.Empty;
```

```
oInfoObject = enterpriseItem1.InfoObject;

switch(oInfoObject.Kind)
{
    case "Excel":
        oExcel = ((Excel) oInfoObject);
        aReportData = ((byte[]) oExcel.ByteStream);
        szFilename = oExcel.Title + ".xls";
        szMimeType = oExcel.MimeType;
        break;

    case "Pdf":
        oPdf = ((Pdf) oInfoObject);
        aReportData = ((byte[]) oPdf.ByteStream);
        szFilename = oPdf.Title + ".pdf";
        szMimeType = oPdf.MimeType;
        break;
}

Response.Clear();
Response.AddHeader("Content-Length", aReportData.Length.ToString());
Response.AddHeader("Content-Disposition",
    String.Format("inline; filename={0};", szFilename));
Response.ContentType = szMimeType;
Response.BinaryWrite(aReportData);
Response.Flush();
Response.End();
}
```

.NET Providers

After BusinessObjects XI Release 2 hit the market, Business Objects made its .NET Providers
available. This developer tool is compatible only with Visual Studio 2005 and was released without any major product announcements. Therefore, you may only have learned of their existence
by surfing the developer site or perhaps by reading this right now. Because the .NET Providers do
not ship with the installation CDs for BusinessObjects XI Release 2, they must be downloaded
from the BusinessObjects web site at www.businessobjects.com/products/downloadcenter/
boeproxi.asp.

   The .NET Providers act as data controls that extract information from the InfoStore and
make it available to your .NET Managed visual controls. There are two main data controls: the
BOEDataSource and the BOEHierarchicalDataSource. These controls can be bound to the .NET
Managed controls that ship with Visual Studio, specifically the GridView for the BOEDataSource
control and the TreeView for the BOEHierarchicalDataSource. The key advantage to these controls is that you can now bind your data sources to controls other than the ItemGrid provided
with the BusinessObjects .NET Server Controls discussed in the previous section. I've tried them

with the Infragistics tree and grid controls, and they do not work at all. Even if other third-party vendors make tools that support the .NET Providers, Business Objects doesn't officially support their use with any tools other than the Microsoft .NET Managed controls.

The .NET Server Controls that were introduced with Crystal Enterprise 10 are being deprecated and replaced with the .NET Providers. The .NET Providers do not provide visual controls like the Scheduling or Database controls offered with the .NET Server Controls, as it is expected that developers will use their own toolset to create these user interfaces.

The .NET Providers have been designed to work only with the .NET Managed controls like the GridView and TreeView.

Membership Provider

The .NET Providers can connect with BusinessObjects XI via membership providers. The BOEMembershipProvider class is used to validate BusinessObjects XI users. It works with the new ASP.NET 2.0 membership functionality, which is designed to validate and store user credentials. You can accomplish this by binding it to the new ASP.NET 2.0 Logon controls or by invoking the BOEMembershipProvider object's ValidateUser() method as shown here:

```
BOEMembershipProvider oBOEMembershipProvider =
((BOEMembershipProvider) Membership.Provider);
oBOEMembershipProvider.ValidateUser(szUserName, szPassword);
```

You'll need to configure the BOEMembershipProvider object by setting the properties in code or making an entry in the web.config file as shown in Listing 6-36.

Listing 6-36. *Setting Up BOEMembershipProvider in web.config*

```
<connectionStrings>
  <add name="LocalCMS" connectionString="localhost:6400"/>
</connectionStrings>
<system.web>
  <membership defaultProvider="BOEMembershipProvider1"
                          userIsOnlineTimeWindow="15">

    <providers>
      <add name="BOEMembershipProvider1"
       type="BusinessObjects.Enterprise.Providers.BOEMembershipProvider"
       applicationName="DotNetProviderDemo"
       connectionStringName="LocalCMS"
       authentication="secEnterprise"
       enableCookies="true"
       tokenExpiry="540"/>
    </providers>
  </membership>

  ...

</system.web>
```

The connectionString tag names a reference to a BusinessObjects XI server, which in this example is running on the localhost server using port 6400. You can create multiple membership provider entries and set a default with a userIsOnlineTimeWindow tag to specify a timeout period, in minutes, after which a user is no longer considered to be online.

The applicationName attribute is stored in the data source with related user information to associate a user with a particular application. Since membership providers store user information uniquely for each application, multiple applications can access the same data source if duplicate user names are created. Likewise, multiple ASP.NET applications can use the same user data source by specifying the same applicationName attribute value. The connectionStringName attribute stores the name of the connection string defined in the connectionStrings element to which the particular membership provider will connect.

The enableCookies attribute instructs the BOEMembershipProvider to store session information in a cookie. This will allow it to automatically log a user back into BO XI after the session times out. You can use the tokenExpiry attribute to set the number of minutes that this session information remains valid. The default value is 540, and the maximum is 1440. The lower the setting, the more efficient the system performance.

The type attribute indicates the type that is implementing the MembershipProvider abstract base class. This attribute is always set to "BusinessObjects.Enterprise.Provider. BOEMembershipProvider". Finally, set the authentication attribute to the BO XI security protocol used to handle authentication. The valid values are secEnterprise, secWinAD, and secWindowsNT.

Using the .NET Providers

To get started with the .NET Providers, drag a TreeView and a BOEHierarchicalDataSource control onto a web page and set the DataSourceID property of the TreeView control to the BOEHierarchicalDataSource control. In the Page_Load event, set the control properties as shown in Listing 6-37.

Listing 6-37. *Setting Properties for BOEHierarchicalDataSource*

```
BOEHierarchicalDataSource1.Mode = HierarchyMode.Folder;
BOEHierarchicalDataSource1.Home = "Top Level";
BOEHierarchicalDataSource1.QueryFilter = "SI_KIND = 'Folder'";
BOEHierarchicalDataSource1.Roots.Clear();

TreeView1.DataBind();
```

This code will populate the .NET provider with the hierarchy of folders—the other alternative is categories—and set the text of the highest level node to the string Top Level. Note that the Mode, Home, and QueryFilter properties can also be set using declarative syntax in the .aspx page.

When a control is loaded with data, usually you'll want to load each entry with two pieces of information. The first is a text description that the user will see, and the second is a unique ID that identifies the entry. This is what the BOEHierarchicalDataSource does for you. It loads the SI_ID and SI_NAME properties into each node, but not into the Text and Value properties as you would expect. Therefore, when you select a node and wish to extract the SI_ID value, you can use the code shown in Listing 6-38.

Listing 6-38. *Drilling from Folder to Reports*

```
protected void TreeView1_SelectedNodeChanged(object sender, EventArgs e)
{
    string szSQL;
    string szDataPath;
    int iID;

    szDataPath = TreeView1.SelectedNode.DataPath;

    iID = BOEHierarchicalDataSourceView.ExtractIDFromViewPath(szDataPath);

    szSQL = "select SI_ID, SI_NAME, SI_LAST_RUN_TIME " +
            "from CI_INFOOBJECTS " +
            "where SI_PARENTID = " + iID.ToString() +
            "and SI_KIND = 'CrystalReport' " +
            "and SI_INSTANCE = 0";

    BOEDataSource1.SelectCommand = szSQL;
}
```

Here, the SelectedNodeChanged event is extracting the DataPath value of the selected Tree-view node. This value looks something like this: Home_23_790. You can extract the SI_ID value of the selected folder by passing the DataPath value to the ExtractIDFromViewPath() method of the BOEHierarchicalDataSourceView class. In this example, this method will return 790. The DataPath property contains an underscore-separated list of the folder IDs from the root directory to the currently selected folder. For example, if your report is nested like this:

```
Root Folder
    Human Resources Reports
        Employee Report
```

the DataPath string will look something like this: 100_200_300, where 100 is the SI_ID of the Root folder, 200 is the SI_ID of the Human Resources Reports folder, and 300 is the SI_ID of the Employee Report itself.

You can then use this SI_ID value to create a SQL statement and set it to the SelectCommand property of a BOEDataSource object. This BOEDataSource objects serves as the data source of a GridView control. The results will give you a web page that looks something like Figure 6-29.

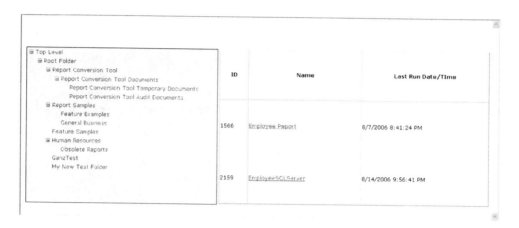

Figure 6-29. *Data delivered by .NET Providers*

In this example, the report name is a hyperlink that brings the user to another page that displays the report history for the report. The report history grid is loaded in much the same way as the report list grid. Alter the SQL statement to show all the instances of a given report and set this SQL string to the SelectCommand property of a BOEDataSource, which is bound to a GridView control. The code to accomplish this is shown in Listing 6-39.

Listing 6-39. *Extracting Report History*

```
szID = Request.QueryString["ID"];

szSQL = "select SI_ID, SI_NAME, SI_LAST_RUN_TIME " +
        "from CI_INFOOBJECTS " +
        "where SI_PARENTID = " + szID +
        "and SI_INSTANCE = 1 " +
        "order by SI_LAST_RUN_TIME desc";

BOEDataSource1.SelectCommand = szSQL;
```

Here, the BOEDataSource is set to retrieve the SI_ID, SI_NAME, and SI_LAST_RUN_TIME properties from the InfoStore. If you create a GridView and bind the columns to these properties, you face a potential problem. Though every report has SI_ID and SI_NAME properties, only reports that have been run at least once have the SI_LAST_RUN_TIME property. If you pull a list of reports that have never been run before, no SI_LAST_RUN_TIME property will be returned, and the GridView will throw an error. One way to avoid this is to set the GridView's AutoGenerateColumns property to True and set the column formatting programmatically, first checking for the existence of the SI_LAST_RUN_TIME column.

Once you've identified the report you want, you can display it in a CrystalReportsViewer control using the code in Listing 6-40.

Listing 6-40. *Viewing a Report*

```
BOEMembershipProvider oBOEMembershipProvider = null;
SessionMgr oSessionMgr = null;
EnterpriseSession oEnterpriseSession = null;
EnterpriseService oEnterpriseService = null;
PSReportFactory oPSReportFactory = null;
ISCRReportSource oISCRReportSource = null;
string szID;
string szSessionID;
int iReportID;

szID = Request.QueryString["ID"];
iReportID = Int32.Parse(szID);

oBOEMembershipProvider = ((BOEMembershipProvider) Membership.Provider);
szSessionID = oBOEMembershipProvider.BOESessionID;

oSessionMgr = new SessionMgr();
oEnterpriseSession = oSessionMgr.GetSession(szSessionID);
oEnterpriseService = oEnterpriseSession.GetService("PSReportFactory");
oPSReportFactory = ((PSReportFactory) oEnterpriseService.Interface);

oISCRReportSource = oPSReportFactory.OpenReportSource(iReportID);

CrystalReportViewer1.ReportSource = oISCRReportSource;
```

Since the existing membership provider has already authenticated the user, there is no need to invoke any of the Logon methods of the SessionMgr class. Rather, you need only obtain the BOESessionID string and pass that to the SessionMgr class's GetSession() method. From there you can open a PSReportFactory service, set an ISCRReportSource object reference to the report via its SI_ID number, and display it in the viewer.

Though the .NET Providers can be a useful tool, they do have a few drawbacks. The first is that Business Objects has not been actively pushing their use, and it remains to be seen how this technology will be adopted by the marketplace. Since they can only be used with the .NET Managed controls, you may not be able to use your favorite third-party toolset to create BO XI data–aware user interfaces.

Summary

In this chapter, we covered the more advanced aspects of BusinessObjects XI SDK programming. Starting with notifications and alerts, we moved on to the report format option classes, which allow you to customize the report output. Next, we looked at how to send reports to various destinations and how to programmatically create events and calendars. We also examined customized data access techniques that give you much more flexibility when working with data sources. Finally, we examined the deprecated BO XI web controls and their successor technology, the new .NET Providers.

CHAPTER 7

Crystal Reports and BusinessObjects XI

While this book is aimed at BusinessObjects XI development and not Crystal Reports, there is still a bit of overlap between the two products. This chapter will focus mostly on integrating your desktop-based applications with BusinessObjects XI and running reports locally without using the server tool. We'll discuss the Crystal Reports viewer control, accessing reports from BusinessObjects XI, embedded reports, accessing disk-based reports, the `CrystalDecisions.CrystalReports.Engine` object model, and how to integrate with Crystal Reports web services.

Crystal Reports Viewer Control

Crystal Reports ships with a viewer control that is intended to allow users to preview reports on the desktop. It also ships with a web viewer control that is discussed in Chapter 6. Whether your report originates from BO XI or from a local RPT file, the viewer control will display it to the user. The control has all the navigational features you would expect: a tree view for quickly finding data in grouped reports, the ability to export to other formats, text search capability, page navigation, zooming, and printing options.

Setting Up the Control

The viewer control allows you to show or hide almost every feature displayed on it. Figure 7-1 shows the full viewer control displaying a report. The properties that control each of these features are shown as well.

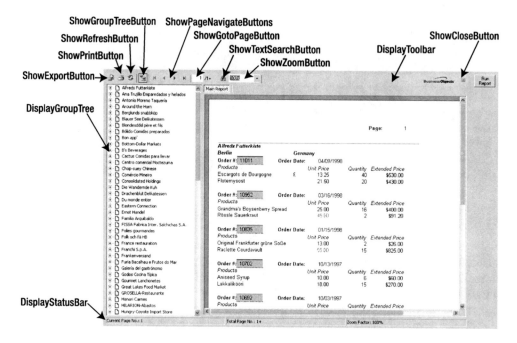

Figure 7-1. *Crystal Reports viewer control*

When you first drop the CrystalReportsViewer control onto your Windows form, it automatically sizes itself to the area of the screen. You can adjust this by opening the dialog menu indicated by the right arrow button, known as a *Smart Tag*, in the upper-right corner of the control as shown in Figure 7-2.

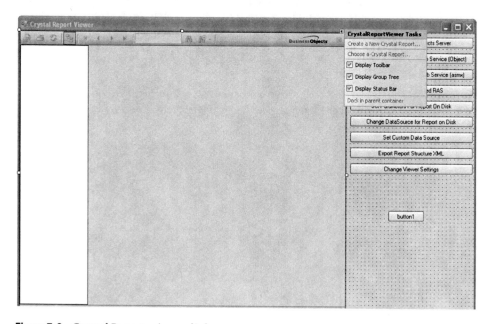

Figure 7-2. *Crystal Reports viewer dialog menu*

The last option, Dock in Parent Container, will toggle between a viewer control that is set to the dimension of the owner form and one whose size you can control.

The code shown in Listing 7-1 shows how to toggle the various viewer control buttons and features as needed.

Listing 7-1. *Configuring the Viewer Control*

```
crystalReportViewer1.DisplayGroupTree = false;
crystalReportViewer1.DisplayBackgroundEdge = false;
crystalReportViewer1.DisplayStatusBar = false;

crystalReportViewer1.DisplayToolbar = true;
crystalReportViewer1.ShowCloseButton = true;
crystalReportViewer1.ShowExportButton = true;
crystalReportViewer1.ShowGotoPageButton = true;
crystalReportViewer1.ShowGroupTreeButton = true;
crystalReportViewer1.ShowPageNavigateButtons = true;
crystalReportViewer1.ShowPrintButton = true;
crystalReportViewer1.ShowRefreshButton = true;
crystalReportViewer1.ShowTextSearchButton = true;
crystalReportViewer1.ShowZoomButton = true;
```

Methods

There is a collection of methods for implementing your own interface options. Should you wish to create your own user interface to control report navigation, you can do so by wiring your controls to the appropriately named methods shown here:

```
crystalReportViewer1.ShowFirstPage();
crystalReportViewer1.ShowNextPage();
crystalReportViewer1.ShowPreviousPage();
crystalReportViewer1.ShowLastPage();
```

The ShowNthPage() method receives an integer value as a parameter that will take you to the page number specified like this:

```
crystalReportViewer1.ShowNthPage(10);
```

You can determine what page you are actually viewing by invoking the GetCurrentPageNumber() method.

The SearchForText() method receives a text string to look for in the report. If it finds it, the first occurrence of the text will be highlighted in red. This method returns a Boolean indicating whether the search was successful or not as illustrated in the following code:

```
if (! crystalReportViewer1.SearchForText("London"))
    MessageBox.Show("Text not found.");
```

You can control the zoom via the Zoom( ) method. Zoom( ) accepts an integer value that sets the zoom percentage and recognizes values between 25 and 400. The Zoom( ) method is shown here:

```
crystalReportViewer1.Zoom(300);
```

Note If you pass 1 to the Zoom( ) method, the report will fit the entire width of the page. Passing the value 2 will fit the entire page in the window.

The ExportReport( ) method displays a Save As dialog where you can specify the output type of the report. This dialog and its export options are shown in Figure 7-3.

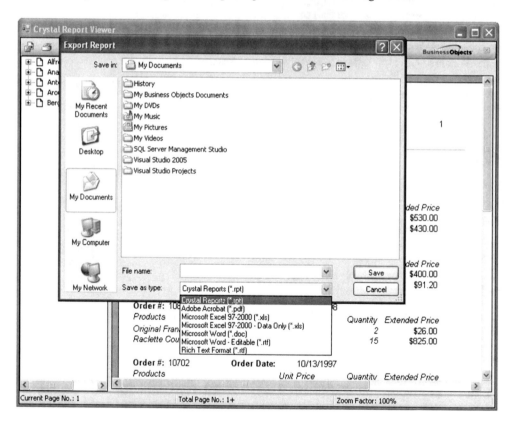

Figure 7-3. *Save As dialog from ExportReport method*

You can even apply filters to your report using the SelectionFormula property. In this example we're restricting the report output to one company's information:

```
crystalReportViewer1.ReportSource = @"c:\temp\myreport.rpt";
crystalReportViewer1.SelectionFormula =
  "{spc_SalesOrders;1.CompanyName} = 'Around the Horn'";
```

Should you need to implement row-level security based on the ID of the currently logged-in user, use of the SelectionFormula property is one way to accomplish it by filtering only those rows to which a given user has access.

Finally, you can display the printer dialog by invoking the PrintReport() method like this:

```
crystalReportViewer1.PrintReport();
```

Events

The viewer control offers several events, which are listed in Table 7-1. Some of these events receive custom argument objects in their event handlers. For example, the Navigate event receives a NavigateEventArgs object that indicates the current page number, the new page number, and a Handled property which, if set to True in the event handlers, will abort the action that caused the event.

Table 7-1. *CrystalReportViewer Events*

Event	Description
Drill	Fired when user drills down on data in report
DrillDownSubreport	Fired when user drills down on data in subreport
Error	Fired when error occurs in control
Navigate	Fired when user navigates (changes page) in report
ReportRefresh	Fired when report data is refreshed
Search	Fired when search is performed on report data
ViewZoom	Fired when zoom changes

The Drill and DrillDownSubreport events receive DrillEventArgs and DrillSubreportEventArgs, respectively. The DrillEventArgs indicate the current and new group levels, the current group name, and the current and new group paths. Similarly, DrillSubreportEventArgs provides you with the current and new subreport names, and the current and new page numbers and positions.

The code in Listing 7-2 sets up the delegate for a ViewZoom event handler. The event handler itself receives a ZoomEventArgs object as a parameter, which contains the old and new zoom settings.

Listing 7-2. *Setting Up Events*

```
crystalReportViewer1.ViewZoom +=
    new CrystalDecisions.Windows.Forms.
    ZoomEventHandler(CrystalReportViewer1_ViewZoom);

void CrystalReportViewer1_ViewZoom(object source,
    CrystalDecisions.Windows.Forms.ZoomEventArgs e)
{
    MessageBox.Show("You're about to zoom from " +
        e.CurrentZoomFactor.ToString() +
        "% to " + e.NewZoomFactor.ToString() +"%");
}
```

Communicating with the BusinessObjects XI Server

If you have a desktop application, there are a number of ways to display a report that resides in the BO XI InfoStore. You could use the run-on-demand web service discussed in Chapter 9 to execute the report and return its output as a base64-encoded string to the desktop, where it can be decoded and opened as a native file. You could also use the .NET SDK to extract the report, set the parameters, and return it to the Crystal Reports viewer. From there you can export it to any format you wish. The code to extract a report from BO XI and display it using the .NET SDK is shown in Listing 7-3.

Listing 7-3. *Running a BusinessObjects XI Report*

```
SessionMgr oSessionMgr;
EnterpriseSession oEnterpriseSession;
EnterpriseService oEnterpriseService;
InfoStore oInfoStore;
InfoObjects oInfoObjects;
ReportParameter oReportParameter;
ReportParameterSingleValue oReportParameterSingleValue;
Report oReport;
string szSQL;

//Log on to BO XI
oSessionMgr = new SessionMgr();
oEnterpriseSession = oSessionMgr.Logon("Administrator", "",
    "SETON-NOTEBOOK:6400", "secEnterprise");
oEnterpriseService = oEnterpriseSession.GetService("InfoStore");
oInfoStore = new InfoStore(oEnterpriseService);

//Pull the needed report information and cast as a Report object
szSQL = "SELECT SI_ID, SI_PROCESSINFO.SI_PROMPTS " +
        "FROM CI_INFOOBJECTS " +
        "WHERE SI_ID = 1266";

oInfoObjects = oInfoStore.Query(szSQL);
oReport = ((Report)oInfoObjects[1]);

//Set the value of the first parameter
oReportParameter = oReport.ReportParameters[1];
oReportParameterSingleValue = oReport.ReportParameters[1].CreateSingleValue();
oReportParameterSingleValue.Value = "UK";
oReport.ReportParameters[1].CurrentValues.Clear();
oReport.ReportParameters[1].CurrentValues.Add(oReportParameterSingleValue);

//Set the value of the second parameter. Even though this is a numeric value
//it must be set as a string
oReportParameter = oReport.ReportParameters[2];
oReportParameterSingleValue = oReport.ReportParameters[2].CreateSingleValue();
```

```
oReportParameterSingleValue.Value = "5";
oReport.ReportParameters[2].CurrentValues.Clear();
oReport.ReportParameters[2].CurrentValues.Add(oReportParameterSingleValue);

//Commit the report to the Infostore
oInfoStore.Commit(oInfoObjects);

//Set the session connection to the Crystal viewer
crystalReportViewer1.EnterpriseLogon = oEnterpriseSession;

//Set the report object as the ReportSource and the report will display
crystalReportViewer1.ReportSource = oReport;
```

If you've read Chapter 5 first, this code should look very familiar. First, you establish a connection to BO XI and extract the Report object reference. Then, using the ReportParameters collection of the Report object, you set the individual parameter values. Finally, you commit the changes to the InfoStore and then set the EnterpriseLogon property of the Crystal Reports viewer control to your EnterpriseSession object. Once this is done, you can assign the Report object to the ReportSource property of the viewer control, and the report will display.

Running a Report on Disk

If your organization does not have BusinessObjects XI, or you need to be prepared for those periods when the BO XI server is unavailable for any reason, you can run RPT files directly on the disk. The code in Listing 7-4 shows how to open a Crystal report file at a designated directory location, pass parameters to it, and display the report in the viewer.

Listing 7-4. *Running a Crystal Report from an RPT File*

```
//If the report is local to a web project, use Server.MapPath here
//to get an absolute reference to the file
crystalReportViewer1.ReportSource =
    @"C:\DOCS\ProgrammingBOXI\EmployeeSQLServer.rpt";

ParameterFields oParameterFields;
ParameterDiscreteValue oParameterDiscreteValue;

oParameterFields = crystalReportViewer1.ParameterFieldInfo;

oParameterDiscreteValue = new ParameterDiscreteValue();
oParameterDiscreteValue.Value = "UK";

oParameterFields[0].CurrentValues.Clear();
oParameterFields[0].CurrentValues.Add(oParameterDiscreteValue);

oParameterDiscreteValue = new ParameterDiscreteValue();
oParameterDiscreteValue.Value = 5;
```

```
oParameterFields[1].CurrentValues.Clear();
oParameterFields[1].CurrentValues.Add(oParameterDiscreteValue);

crystalReportViewer1.ParameterFieldInfo = oParameterFields;
```

The viewer control itself exposes an interface to the parameter fields of the report via the ParameterFieldInfo property. By setting the ReportSource to the RPT file first, the control is able to read the parameters that the report is expecting. In this example, it is @Country and @ReportsTo. By instantiating objects of the ParameterDiscreteValue class, you can assign these values and add them to the ParameterFields object. Once both parameters are set, the ParameterFields object is assigned back to the ParameterFieldInfo property of the report viewer, and the report will execute using those parameters to filter the data source.

Note It is important to understand that when reports are executed in the fashions just described, no record is made of them ever having been executed. This may not meet the security policies of your company. Moreover, you may wish to track report metrics to see which reports are being used the most. If a record of every report run needs to be made, use the .NET SDK to schedule the report to run immediately. Doing so will create an entry in the report history that can be tracked for auditing purposes. Chapter 9 describes how reports can be scheduled to run immediately.

When a report is run on a disk file, it is very likely that the embedded database connectivity information is pointing to a development instance of the server. If you are not using integrated security, then you'll also need to send the password to the RPT file so it can connect. The code in Listing 7-5 shows how to pass connectivity information to the RPT file at runtime.

Listing 7-5. *Passing Connectivity Information to an RPT File*

```
ReportDocument oReportDocument;
ConnectionInfo oConnectionInfo;
TableLogOnInfo oTableLogOnInfo;
Tables oTables;

//Create a ConnectionInfo object and add the database information
oConnectionInfo = new ConnectionInfo();
oConnectionInfo.ServerName = "(local)";
oConnectionInfo.DatabaseName = "Northwind";
oConnectionInfo.IntegratedSecurity = true;

//Create a ReportDocument object to encapsulate the RPT file
oReportDocument = new ReportDocument();
oReportDocument.Load(@"c:\temp\myreport.rpt");
```

```
//Reference the tables collection, which in this
//example consists of one stored procedure
oTables = oReportDocument.Database.Tables;

//Iterate through the individual Table objects
//and set the connectivity information
foreach (Table oTable in oTables)
{
    oTableLogOnInfo = oTable.LogOnInfo;
    oTableLogOnInfo.ConnectionInfo = oConnectionInfo;
    oTable.ApplyLogOnInfo(oTableLogOnInfo);
}

crystalReportViewer1.ReportSource = oReportDocument;
```

Of course, if you're not using integrated security as in this example, you can also pass the user ID and password to the ConnectionInfo object as shown here:

```
oConnectionInfo.UserID = "myname";
oConnectionInfo.Password = "mypass";
```

Passing Parameters

Reports invoked by web applications will need a way of having the criteria parameters passed to them. One way to accomplish this is to pass the parameters via the URL like this:

```
myreport.aspx?datefrom='01/01/2007'&
    dateto='01/31/2007'&deptid='(12345, 45678)'
```

The problem with this approach is that the user gets to see the entire URL call in the browser where it is available for editing. There is nothing to stop a curious or malicious user from changing one of the department ID parameters from 12345 to another value that could very well be a department to which he is not intended to have access. One way to avoid this problem is to write the criteria information to invisible text controls and then retrieve it server side when the page is posted back to the server like this:

```
private void Page_Load(object sender, System.EventArgs e)
{
    szDateFrom = txtDateFrom.Value;
    szDateTo = txtDateTo.Value;
    szDeptID = txtDeptID.Text;
}
```

If you need to transmit the report criteria via URL, say, because you're sending out prefiltered report links via e-mail, you can do so using encryption. One of my clients sends commission statements electronically to his sales associates. The web link looks something like this:

```
www.companyname.com/commrpt.aspx?id=6D738FT344H764EF2&checksum=87136487613
```

By clicking this URL, the sales associate can view his personal sales report for the current or any previous month. In order to avoid a user tampering with the ID parameter and seeing someone else's report, the ID is encrypted and the decryption key stored on the server. To further complicate matters for someone who wants to write a loop that tries various combinations of the alphanumeric encrypted user ID, a checksum value is added that corresponds to a server-based checksum algorithm. If the checksum does not match a valid user ID, access will not be granted. While this system is not foolproof, the odds of someone obtaining access this way are astronomical.

Passing an Entire SQL Statement to Crystal Reports

Sometimes your report criteria are not as simple as a predefined set of stored procedure parameters like DepartmentID or order date range. If you're building a general search screen, the user could potentially enter a dozen or more criteria elements, any of which are optional. It's not realistic for you to have every possible permutation of criteria represented as a SQL statement in a stored procedure, as this could lead to an unmanageable list of hundreds of possibilities. This is where dynamic SQL comes in. In cases such as this, you'll need to create your SQL statement as a string and then execute it. You can create this string either in your application or in your stored procedure as you see fit. Should you create it in your application and pass it to a stored procedure, executing it is as simple as the following SQL Server stored procedure illustrates:

```
CREATE PROCEDURE dbo.spc_ExecuteSQL

@SQL varchar(8000)

AS

EXEC(@SQL)
```

> **Note** You may also wish to look at the sp_ExecuteSQL procedure when executing dynamic SQL. Many developers prefer it over the EXECUTE command as it generates execution plans that SQL Server can reuse and thereby result in a performance gain.

Both your programming language and your stored procedure language will offer you string manipulation functions to enable you to do your work. There are two main dangers to taking this approach. The first is that it's much easier to introduce bugs (data type mismatches are the most common) that will not be caught at compile time. This means that your SQL creation logic will require some very extensive testing. The second problem is the risk of SQL injection, which is explained in the following sidebar. Given the number of optional parameters you are dealing with, however, you may not have a choice but to use dynamic SQL.

SQL INJECTION

One major security flaw in web reporting is the problem of SQL injection. This nefarious practice usually occurs when a user enters a SQL statement into a criteria input field rather than the discrete value that is intended for the field. For example, suppose you have a textbox that receives as a parameter an employee number. This value is then posted to another page that concatenates the value to a SQL statement (using SQL Server syntax) such as

```
string szSQL = "SELECT * FROM Employee WHERE ID = " + txtEmpID.Text;
```

Suppose the user enters a piece of another SQL statement for the `txtEmpID` value such as this one:

```
"O UNION SELECT * FROM Employee"
```

The statement that gets executed is

```
SELECT * FROM Employee WHERE ID = O
UNION
SELECT * FROM Employee
```

which effectively returns all the records. This is probably not what you intended. Users could also use the semicolon, which separates multiple SQL statements to do such nasty things as entering this line:

```
O; TRUNCATE TABLE Employee
```

Another security flaw lies in the use of the SQL Server stored procedure `sp_makewebtask`, which produces an HTML document containing data returned by executed queries, and `xp_cmdshell`, which opens a command window. A user could easily inject the following, which produces a local copy of the entire Employee table:

```
; EXEC makewebtask 'c:\\Inetpub\\wwwroot\\bendoverandsmile.html',
'SELECT * FROM Employee'
```

Using `xp_cmdshell`, he could easily execute the command to, say, reformat the hard disk.

To guard against SQL injection, you have a number of options. Because a user can modify the HTTP header of the page that posts non–free-form criteria to the server, most of these options are server based. First, you'll need to filter any criteria before they are concatenated to an in-line SQL statement or passed to a stored procedure to make sure nothing is amiss. You'll need to verify that only the proper data types are being passed. If a parameter is supposed to be a string composed only of numbers, verify that this is the case. Likewise, the `String.Length` property will indicate whether discrete values are longer than they are expected to be. Also, the `String.IndexOf()` method will indicate if any unexpected keywords get passed in. The best defense is to restrict permissions to the tables so that the user created for the web application has only the minimum rights necessary for `SELECT`, `UPDATE`, and `DELETE` on only those tables that are needed.

Embedded vs. Nonembedded Reports

When you develop a report using the version of Crystal Reports that ships with Visual Studio for .NET, you have a choice of creating separate RPT files or embedding the reports directly in your compiled application. The advantage of embedding your reports directly is that .NET will create a class wrapper for you to interact with your reports, and you will no longer need to deal with the disk file programmatically. The report itself will be embedded within the compiled application assembly and not function as a separate RPT.

The downside to this approach is that every time you wish to update a report, you need to recompile and distribute an EXE rather than just a separate RPT file. Moreover, getting an individual RPT file through your company's change control process for installation on a production box is usually much easier than pushing through a full EXE.

■**Note** Starting with Visual Studio 2005, Crystal Reports report files are no longer embedded in web applications and the IDE doesn't need to generate class wrappers. Rather, the reports are stored in a folder where they must be referenced by their file directory path.

Visual Studio ships with its own version of Crystal Reports so you can create and edit reports from within the IDE. The interface for the report designer is shown in Figure 7-4.

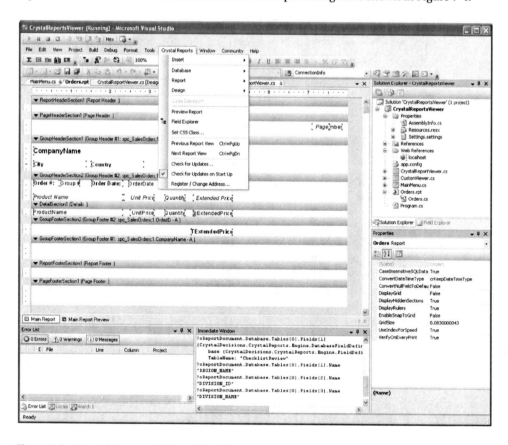

Figure 7-4. *Crystal Reports in Visual Studio*

You have the same functionality for designing reports here as you do in the stand-alone version of Crystal. The only difference is that it is integrated into your development environment. If you wish to continue using your stand-alone version, you are certainly free to do so.

The class wrapper that the IDE generates for each RPT file associated with a solution inherits from ReportClass, which contains the methods and properties you'll need to control almost every aspect of the report. Listing 7-6 shows an abbreviated report class wrapper that creates a public method for every section in the report.

Listing 7-6. *Abbreviated Report Class Wrapper*

```
public class Orders : ReportClass {

    public Orders() {
    }

    public override string ResourceName {
        get {
            return "Orders.rpt";
        }
        set {
            // Do nothing
        }
    }

    [Browsable(false)]
    [DesignerSerializationVisibilityAttribute(
        System.ComponentModel.DesignerSerializationVisibility.Hidden)]
    public CrystalDecisions.CrystalReports.Engine.Section ReportHeaderSection1 {
        get {
            return this.ReportDefinition.Sections[0];
        }
    }

...
}

[System.Drawing.ToolboxBitmapAttribute(typeof(
    CrystalDecisions.Shared.ExportOptions), "report.bmp")]
public class CachedOrders : Component, ICachedReport {

...

    [Browsable(false)]
    [DesignerSerializationVisibilityAttribute(
        System.ComponentModel.DesignerSerializationVisibility.Hidden)]
    public virtual System.TimeSpan CacheTimeOut {
```

```
        get {
            return CachedReportConstants.DEFAULT_TIMEOUT;
        }
        set {
            //
        }
    }

    public virtual CrystalDecisions.CrystalReports.
        Engine.ReportDocument CreateReport() {
        Orders rpt = new Orders();
        rpt.Site = this.Site;
        return rpt;
    }

    public virtual string GetCustomizedCacheKey(RequestContext request) {
        String key = null;
        // // The following is the code used to generate the default
        // // cache key for caching report jobs in the ASP.NET Cache.
        // // Feel free to modify this code to suit your needs.
        // // Returning key == null causes the default cache key to
        // // be generated.
        //
        // key = RequestContext.BuildCompleteCacheKey(
        //      request,
        //      null,        // sReportFilename
        //      this.GetType(),
        //      this.ShareDBLogonInfo );
        return key;
    }
}
```

You can instantiate this class as you would any other. To display the report to the viewer without applying any special settings, you can use the following code:

```
Orders oOrders;

oOrders = new Orders();

crystalReportViewer1.ReportSource = oOrders;
```

The Orders object encapsulates the properties and methods needed to examine the structure of the report. This structure is exposed through the objects of the CrystalDecisions. CrystalReports.Engine namespace. If you are familiar with the managed RAS (covered in Chapter 8), you'll immediately see many structural similarities here. The two object models are not exactly the same, however. The RAS is designed to create reports and modify the structure of existing reports. This is not possible using the objects of the CrystalDecisions. CrystalReports.Engine namespace. Though you can see the information about every area, section, and field in the report, you cannot add new objects or delete existing ones.

The Crystal object model does allow you to control many aspects of your report programmatically, which we will cover in the next sections.

Exporting Reports

Suppose you'd like to export the Orders report to a disk file instead; you can use the code shown here to accomplish that:

```
oOrders.ExportToDisk(ExportFormatType.Excel, @"c:\temp\myreport.xls");
```

■**Note** Make sure to obtain the required permissions so the user account your application is running under can write to the target directory. In ASP.NET, you would have to provide write permission to (IIS 5) ASPNET or the (IIS 6) NetworkService account if you're not using Windows Authentication. If you are using Windows Authentication, you could create a group that has write permission to this directory.

The ExportToDisk() method takes an ExportFormatType enumerator and a location string to which to write the output. The members of the ExportFormatType enumerator are listed in Table 7-2.

Table 7-2. *ExportFormatType Enumerator Members*

Member	Value	Description
CharacterSeparatedValues	10	Character-separated values
CrystalReport	1	Crystal Report
EditableRTF	12	Editable RTF
Excel	4	Excel
ExcelRecord	8	Excel record
HTML32	6	HTML 3.2
HTML40	7	HTML 4.0
NoFormat	0	No format
PortableDocFormat	5	Adobe PDF
RichText	2	Rich Text
TabSeperatedText	11	Tab-separated text (that's right, it's misspelled!)
Text	9	Text
WordForWindows	3	Word

Exporting to a particular file format is not a generic function. You have the same format-specific customizations as you do in Crystal Reports. Suppose you wish to customize the Excel export options used in the previous example. You can accomplish this via the ExcelDataOnlyFormatOptions class shown in Listing 7-7.

Listing 7-7. *Setting Export Options*

```
ExportOptions oExportOptions;
ExcelDataOnlyFormatOptions oExcelDataOnlyFormatOptions;
DiskFileDestinationOptions oDiskFileDestinationOptions;

oDiskFileDestinationOptions = new DiskFileDestinationOptions();
oDiskFileDestinationOptions.DiskFileName = @"c:\temp\mydata.xls";

oExcelDataOnlyFormatOptions = new ExcelDataOnlyFormatOptions();
oExcelDataOnlyFormatOptions.ExcelConstantColumnWidth = 20;
oExcelDataOnlyFormatOptions.ExcelUseConstantColumnWidth = true;
oExcelDataOnlyFormatOptions.ExportImages = true;
oExcelDataOnlyFormatOptions.ExportPageHeaderAndPageFooter = true;
oExcelDataOnlyFormatOptions.MaintainColumnAlignment = true;
oExcelDataOnlyFormatOptions.MaintainRelativeObjectPosition = true;
oExcelDataOnlyFormatOptions.ShowGroupOutlines = true;
oExcelDataOnlyFormatOptions.SimplifyPageHeaders = false;
oExcelDataOnlyFormatOptions.UseWorksheetFunctionsForSummaries = true;

oExportOptions = new ExportOptions();
oExportOptions.ExportFormatOptions = oExcelDataOnlyFormatOptions;
oExportOptions.ExportDestinationType = ExportDestinationType.DiskFile;
oExportOptions.ExportDestinationOptions = oDiskFileDestinationOptions;
oExportOptions.ExportFormatType = ExportFormatType.ExcelRecord;

oOrders.Export(oExportOptions);
```

As Figure 7-5 proves, the ExcelDataOnlyFormatOptions class mirrors the export options offered by Crystal Reports for this same data format.

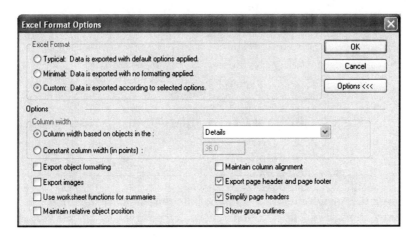

Figure 7-5. *Excel Format Options screen from Crystal Reports*

The `DiskFileDestinationOptions` class matches the `ExportDestinationType` property settings of the `ExportOptions` object, which is set to `ExportDestinationType.DiskFile`. Since it is going to a disk file, it makes sense that the format options pertain to a disk file. The output can also go to an Exchange folder or Microsoft Mail. In the example shown in Listing 7-8, the destination is Microsoft Mail and the format is a PDF file.

Listing 7-8. *Setting Destination Options*

```
ExportOptions oExportOptions;
PdfFormatOptions oPdfFormatOptions;
MicrosoftMailDestinationOptions oMicrosoftMailDestinationOptions;

oMicrosoftMailDestinationOptions =
    new MicrosoftMailDestinationOptions();
oMicrosoftMailDestinationOptions.UserName = "myname";
oMicrosoftMailDestinationOptions.Password = "mypass";
oMicrosoftMailDestinationOptions.MailToList =
    "seton.software@verizon.net";
oMicrosoftMailDestinationOptions.MailCCList =
    "wendy.p.ganz@verizon.net";
oMicrosoftMailDestinationOptions.MailSubject =
    "Here's your report";
oMicrosoftMailDestinationOptions.MailMessage =
    "Please review this report and get back to me ASAP";

oPdfFormatOptions = new PdfFormatOptions();
oPdfFormatOptions.UsePageRange = false;

oExportOptions = new ExportOptions();
oExportOptions.ExportFormatOptions = oPdfFormatOptions;
oExportOptions.ExportDestinationType =
    ExportDestinationType.MicrosoftMail;
oExportOptions.ExportDestinationOptions =
    oMicrosoftMailDestinationOptions;
oExportOptions.ExportFormatType =
    ExportFormatType.PortableDocFormat;

oOrders.Export(oExportOptions);
```

Filtering

To filter the records to a particular set of data, use the `RecordSelectionFormula` property as shown here:

```
oOrders.RecordSelectionFormula =
    "{spc_SalesOrders;1.CompanyName} = 'Around the Horn'";
```

You can use the RecordSelectionFormula property to implement report bursting. By extracting all the possible data for a report, you can set filters to restrict the data to those records that are specific to the recipient. Suppose you want to send a weekly sales report to each employee. Rather than execute the full report once per employee with a database hit occurring each time, you could pull all the data at once and apply a filter for each individual employee, saving each filtered instance to a separate report file.

Field Structure

The field structure of the report is open to you as well. The example shown in Listing 7-9 uses the ReportObjects collection of the ReportDefinition class to iterate through all the objects on the report. If an object is a field, the color is set to aqua. The ReportObjects collection includes text objects, line and box objects, field objects, and so on. Each ReportObject is identified through its Kind property by a member of the ReportObjectKind enumerator.

Listing 7-9. *Iterating the ReportObjects Collection*

```
FieldObject oFieldObject;

//oOrders is the generated class wrapper object for the Orders report
foreach (ReportObject oReportObject in
    oOrders.ReportDefinition.ReportObjects)
{
    if (oReportObject.Kind == ReportObjectKind.FieldObject)
    {
        oFieldObject = ((FieldObject) oReportObject);
        oFieldObject.Color = Color.Aqua;
    }
}
```

The full list of the ReportObjectKind enumerator's members is given in Table 7-3.

Table 7-3. *ReportObjectKind Enumerator Members*

Member	Value	Description
BlobFieldObject	9	Blob field
BoxObject	4	Box
ChartObject	7	Chart
CrossTabObject	8	Cross tab
FieldHeadingObject	12	Field heading
FieldObject	1	Field
LineObject	3	Line
MapObject	10	Map
OlapGridObject	11	OLAP grid
PictureObject	6	Picture
SubreportObject	5	Subreport
TextObject	2	Text

You can iterate through all the data fields available in the report via the Fields collection. In the example shown in Listing 7-10, each DatabaseFieldDefinition object is checked for the name and field type.

Listing 7-10. *Viewing the Database Field Information*

```
string szName;
FieldValueType sFieldValueType;

foreach (DatabaseFieldDefinition oDatabaseFieldDefinition in
    oOrders.Database.Tables[0].Fields)
{
    szName = oDatabaseFieldDefinition.Name;
    sFieldValueType = oDatabaseFieldDefinition.ValueType;
}
```

Sections

Sections are predefined areas in a report. Specifically they are the Report Header, Page Header, Group Header, Details, Group Footer, Page Footer, and Report Footer. Like ReportsObjects, Section objects have a Kind property, which is set to a member of the AreaSectionKind enumerator that distinguishes the type of section from another. The members of AreaSectionKind are listed in Table 7-4.

Table 7-4. *AreaSectionKind Enumerator Members*

Member	Value	Description
Detail	4	Details section
GroupFooter	5	Group Footer section
GroupHeader	3	Group Header section
Invalid	0	Invalid
PageFooter	7	Page Footer section
PageHeader	2	Page Header section
ReportFooter	8	Report Footer section
ReportHeader	1	Report Header section
WholeReport	255	Whole report

You can add additional sections within a section. For example, there are as many Group Header and Group Footer sections as there are groups. You can also add a section to, say, a Report Header and so produce Report Header A and Report Header B. In the following code shown, we're changing some of the settings for a section using the SectionFormat object.

```
SectionFormat oSectionFormat;

oSectionFormat = oOrders.ReportDefinition.Sections[1].SectionFormat;

SectionSettings(oSectionFormat);
```

Listing 7-11 shows the SectionSettings() method that makes the requested changes.

Listing 7-11. *Using the SectionFormat Object*

```
public void SectionSettings(SectionFormat oSectionFormat)
{
    oSectionFormat.EnableKeepTogether = true;
    oSectionFormat.EnableNewPageAfter = true;
    oSectionFormat.EnablePrintAtBottomOfPage = true;
    oSectionFormat.EnableResetPageNumberAfter = true;
    oSectionFormat.EnableSuppress = true;
    oSectionFormat.EnableSuppressIfBlank = true;
    oSectionFormat.EnableUnderlaySection = true;
}
```

Here you can determine whether new pages should appear before or after the section is printed, whether the section should always be suppressed or only if blank, and whether the page number should reset itself after printing. You can also determine whether the section should be printed on one page and not split across two pages or suppressed completely if there is no information to be printed in it.

To illustrate the use of the Report and Section objects that we've discussed, we can use these objects to create an XML file that describes the structure of a report. The output of this XML file would look something like Listing 7-12.

Listing 7-12. *Exporting Report Structure*

```
<Orders.rpt>
  <ReportHeader Name="ReportHeaderSection1" />
  <PageHeader Name="PageHeaderSection1">
    <PageNumber1 />
       <Text17 />
  </PageHeader>
  <FieldObject>PageNumber1</FieldObject>
  <FieldHeadingObject>Text17</FieldHeadingObject>
   <GroupHeader Name="GroupHeaderSection1">
   <CompanyName1 />
   <City1 />
   <Country1 />
  </GroupHeader>
  <FieldObject>CompanyName1</FieldObject>
  <FieldObject>City1</FieldObject>
  <FieldObject>Country1</FieldObject>
...
<Orders.rpt>
```

In order to produce such a file, we would need to iterate through the Sections collection of the report object. For each section, we'll extract the type and name and use that for the section tag of the XML output. Within each section, we'll iterate through the ReportObjects collection to extract the name and type of each field on the report. This information will also be used for creating XML tags. The code to produce this XML output is shown in Listing 7-13.

Listing 7-13. *Exporting Report Structure to XML*

```
XmlDocument oXmlDocument = null;
XmlElement oXmlElement = null;
XmlElement oXmlSubElement = null;
XmlElement oXmlReportElement = null;
XmlElement oXmlChildElement;
XmlText oXmlChildText;

oXmlDocument = new XmlDocument();

oXmlElement = oXmlDocument.CreateElement("", oOrders.ResourceName, "");

oXmlDocument.AppendChild(oXmlElement);

foreach (Section oSection in oOrders.ReportDefinition.Sections)
{

    oXmlSubElement =
        oXmlDocument.CreateElement("", oSection.Kind.ToString(), "");
    oXmlSubElement.SetAttribute("Name", oSection.Name);

    oXmlElement.AppendChild(oXmlSubElement);

    foreach (ReportObject oReportObject in oSection.ReportObjects)
    {
        oXmlReportElement =
            oXmlDocument.CreateElement("", oReportObject.Name, "");

        oXmlChildElement =
            oXmlDocument.CreateElement(oReportObject.Kind.ToString());
        oXmlChildText = oXmlDocument.CreateTextNode(oReportObject.Name);

        oXmlElement.AppendChild(oXmlChildElement);
        oXmlElement.LastChild.AppendChild(oXmlChildText);

        oXmlSubElement.AppendChild(oXmlReportElement);
    }
}

oXmlDocument.Save(@"c:\temp\report.xml");
```

Database Connectivity

The Database class provides an interface to the report's data source. You can extract the name of the data source like this:

```
oOrders.Database.Tables[0].Name;
```

which in the examples used in this chapter will return the name of the stored procedure or ascertain that there is a valid database connection by making sure the report can actually connect as shown in Listing 7-14.

Listing 7-14. *Making Sure the Report Can Connect*

```
if (oOrders.Database.Tables[0].TestConnectivity())
 MessageBox.Show("We're in");
else
 MessageBox.Show("We're not in");
```

Printer Options

Part and parcel of printing reports is establishing the type of page you'll be working with. In Crystal Reports, the first thing you'll need to do when creating a new report is to determine the margins, paper size, and orientation. This will determine the size and shape of the layout page in the report designer. These settings may be handled programmatically as well via the PrintOptions object. The code shown in Listing 7-15 illustrates how to set up a typical letter-size report. Note that the PageMargins settings are read-only.

Listing 7-15. *Setting Printer Options*

```
oOrders.PrintOptions.PaperOrientation = PaperOrientation.Landscape;
oOrders.PrintOptions.PaperSize = PaperSize.PaperLetter;
oOrders.PrintOptions.PaperSource = PaperSource.Upper;
oOrders.PrintOptions.PrinterDuplex = PrinterDuplex.Default;

Console.Write(oOrders.PrintOptions.PageMargins.leftMargin);
Console.Write(oOrders.PrintOptions.PageMargins.rightMargin);
Console.Write(oOrders.PrintOptions.PageMargins.topMargin);
Console.Write(oOrders.PrintOptions.PageMargins.bottomMargin);
```

Summary Information

Crystal Reports stores summary information for each report. This feature allows you to set descriptive properties for a report like the author's name, the title, keywords, etc. Except for the Template field, this same information is available to you programmatically through the SummaryInfo object. You can instantiate this object and assign the properties via the code shown in Listing 7-16.

Listing 7-16. *Setting Summary Information*

```
oOrders.SummaryInfo.ReportAuthor = "Carl Ganz, III";
oOrders.SummaryInfo.ReportComments = "These are comments";
oOrders.SummaryInfo.ReportSubject = "This is the subject";
oOrders.SummaryInfo.ReportTitle = "My title";
```

Unmanaged RAS

Like the managed RAS that will be covered in Chapter 8, the unmanaged RAS revolves around the ReportClientDocument object. The RAS allows you to create new reports and modify existing ones. Listing 7-17 shows how you can extract a ReportClientDocument object from an embedded report.

Listing 7-17. *Extracting the ReportClientDocument Object from an Embedded Report*

```
ISCDReportClientDocument oReportClientDocument;
Orders oOrders;

oOrders = new Orders();
oOrders.ReportAppServer = "localhost";
oOrders.Load();
oReportClientDocument = oOrders.ReportClientDocument;

crystalReportViewer1.ReportSource = oReportClientDocument;
```

Should you wish to open a report from a disk file, use the code shown in Listing 7-18.

Listing 7-18. *Extracting the ReportClientDocument Object from a Disk File*

```
ISCDReportClientDocument oReportClientDocument;
object oTarget;

oTarget = @"C:\DOCS\ProgrammingBOXI\EmployeeSQLServer.rpt";

oReportClientDocument = new ReportClientDocumentClass();

//The Open method requires the path set to an object variable and passed by ref
oReportClientDocument.Open(ref oTarget, 1);

crystalReportViewer1.ReportSource = oReportClientDocument;
```

Most of the functionality that you have in the managed RAS is available to you in the unmanaged RAS. Since the similarity is so great, and since the unmanaged RAS is only tangential to the subject of this book, I will not cover it in detail here. The coverage of the managed RAS in Chapter 8 will tell you most of what you need to know.

Passing Data Sources

Simply because the RPT file points to a data source like an RDBMS or an XML file doesn't mean that you are bound to use that data source. Nor are you obligated to point the RPT to another data source of the same type as you would in a development-to-production migration. An RPT file is like a template. It needs to point to a data source at design time so as to retrieve the structure of the underlying data, which enables you to drop fields onto the report page. As long as any future data source matches this structure, the RPT file will accept it. This includes ADO.NET DataTable and DataSet objects. Suppose you created an orders report using the following SQL statement, which extracts data from SQL Server's Northwind database:

```
SELECT c.CustomerID, c.CompanyName, c.City, c.Country,
o.OrderID, o.OrderDate, e.FirstName + ' ' + e.LastName AS Employee,
p.ProductName, od.UnitPrice, od.Quantity
FROM Customers c
LEFT OUTER JOIN Orders o ON c.CustomerID = o.CustomerID
LEFT OUTER JOIN Employees e ON o.EmployeeID = e.EmployeeID
LEFT OUTER JOIN [Order Details] od ON o.OrderID = od.OrderID
LEFT OUTER JOIN Products p ON od.ProductID = p.ProductID
ORDER BY c.CompanyName, o.OrderID, p.ProductName
```

This obligates you to use only a data source that has the same column names and data types. Once you create this data source, you can pass it to the report using the SetDataSource() method as shown in Listing 7-19. In this example, a DataTable object is being passed to the report.

Listing 7-19. *Using SetDataSource*

```
Orders oOrders;
DataTable oDT;

oDT = GetData();

oOrders = new Orders();

oOrders.SetDataSource(oDT);

crystalReportViewer1.ReportSource = oOrders;
```

How you populate this DataTable object is up to you. This example obtains a DataTable from the GetData() method shown in Listing 7-20. You need only pass the DataTable to the SetDataSource() method and display the report.

Listing 7-20. *Creating a Data Source*

```
public static DataTable GetData()
{
    DataTable oDT;
    DataRow oDR;

    oDT = new DataTable("spc_SalesOrders");

    oDT.Columns.Add(new DataColumn("CustomerID", typeof(string)));
    oDT.Columns.Add(new DataColumn("CompanyName", typeof(string)));
    oDT.Columns.Add(new DataColumn("City", typeof(string)));
    oDT.Columns.Add(new DataColumn("Country", typeof(string)));
    oDT.Columns.Add(new DataColumn("OrderID", typeof(int)));
    oDT.Columns.Add(new DataColumn("OrderDate", typeof(DateTime)));
    oDT.Columns.Add(new DataColumn("Employee", typeof(string)));
    oDT.Columns.Add(new DataColumn("ProductName", typeof(string)));
    oDT.Columns.Add(new DataColumn("UnitPrice", typeof(int)));
    oDT.Columns.Add(new DataColumn("Quantity", typeof(int)));

    oDR = oDT.NewRow();

    oDR["CustomerID"] = "12345";
    oDR["CompanyName"] = "Seton Software Development, Inc.";
    oDR["City"] = "Raritan, NJ";
    oDR["Country"] = "USA";
    oDR["OrderID"] = 10001;
    oDR["OrderDate"] = "10/21/2006";
    oDR["Employee"] = "Carl Ganz, Jr.";
    oDR["ProductName"] = "BusinessObjects XI Book";
    oDR["UnitPrice"] = 59.99;
    oDR["Quantity"] = 5;

    oDT.Rows.Add(oDR);

    return oDT;
}
```

You can see that the DataTable is named after the stored procedure to which it was originally bound. The reason is that the RPT will have references to this stored procedure as a prefix to the field information. Then, create a DataTable with the same structure as the stored procedure against which the report was originally created. This will avoid any data type mismatch errors. You can populate your data table as you see fit. The final output of the report is shown in Figure 7-6.

```
Seton Software Development, Inc.

Raritan, NJ          USA
Order #:   10001     Order Date:   10/21/2006

Product Name                    Unit Price    Quantity    Extended Price
BusinessObjects XI Book            $59.99            5          $299.95
                                                               $299.95
```

Figure 7-6. *Report output from external data source*

Crystal Reports Web Services

You can expose your Crystal reports as web services to be invoked by proxy applications. Unfortunately, these web services are not cross-platform and are not scalable. In order to accomplish this, create a web service project and call it CrystalReportsWebServices. Then, add the RPT files you wish to expose to this project. Right-click an RPT file and select the Publish as Web Service option. Doing so will generate a web service wrapper for the RPT file. The code for this wrapper is shown in Listing 7-21.

Listing 7-21. *Crystal Reports Web Service Wrapper*

```csharp
<%@ webservice language="C#" class="EmployeeSQLServerService" %>

using System;
using System.Web.Services;
using CrystalDecisions.Shared;
using CrystalDecisions.CrystalReports.Engine;
using CrystalDecisions.ReportSource;
using CrystalDecisions.Web.Services;

[ WebService(
    Namespace="http://crystaldecisions.com/reportwebservice/9.1/" ) ]
public class EmployeeSQLServerService : ReportServiceBase
{
    public EmployeeSQLServerService()
    {
        this.ReportSource = this.Server.MapPath("EmployeeSQLServer.rpt");
    }
}
```

Note that this code inherits from ReportServiceBase and not System.Web.Services. WebService, as other web services do by default. ReportServiceBase exposes the necessary methods that make it possible for the report to be published as a web service. The additional methods added by ReportServiceBase are shown in Figure 7-7.

Figure 7-7. *Default web methods*

You'll generate a new ASMX file for every RPT file you wish to expose as a web service. Once the report is exposed as a web service, invoking it from the proxy application is very simple, and you would handle it as you would any other web service. Set the report source to the URL of the web service and continue to set the parameter properties accordingly. In the example shown in Listing 7-22, a report exposed as a web service is referenced via its ASMX file. After this, setting the parameters and viewing the report are the same as if the report were referenced as a local RPT.

Listing 7-22. *Invoking the Crystal Reports Web Service*

```
crystalReportViewer1.ReportSource =
"http://localhost:2662/CrystalReportsWebServices/EmployeeSQLServerService.asmx";

ParameterFields oParameterFields;
ParameterDiscreteValue oParameterDiscreteValue;

oParameterFields = crystalReportViewer1.ParameterFieldInfo;

oParameterDiscreteValue = new ParameterDiscreteValue();
oParameterDiscreteValue.Value = "UK";
```

```
oParameterFields[0].CurrentValues.Clear();
oParameterFields[0].CurrentValues.Add(oParameterDiscreteValue);

oParameterDiscreteValue = new ParameterDiscreteValue();
oParameterDiscreteValue.Value = 5;

oParameterFields[1].CurrentValues.Clear();
oParameterFields[1].CurrentValues.Add(oParameterDiscreteValue);

crystalReportViewer1.ParameterFieldInfo = oParameterFields;
```

This web service reference was made directly in the code by setting the URL of the ASMX file. You can also add a web service reference to your application by right-clicking the Web References item in the Solution Explorer. Then, you can instantiate it as an object as you would any other web service reference. The code in Listing 7-23 illustrates how this is accomplished.

Listing 7-23. *Using a Web Service Reference*

```
localhost.EmployeeSQLServerService oEmployeeSQLServerService;

oEmployeeSQLServerService =
    new CrystalReportsViewer.localhost.EmployeeSQLServerService();

crystalReportViewer1.ReportSource = oEmployeeSQLServerService;

ParameterFields oParameterFields;
ParameterDiscreteValue oParameterDiscreteValue;

oParameterFields = crystalReportViewer1.ParameterFieldInfo;

oParameterDiscreteValue = new ParameterDiscreteValue();
oParameterDiscreteValue.Value = "USA";

oParameterFields[0].CurrentValues.Clear();
oParameterFields[0].CurrentValues.Add(oParameterDiscreteValue);

oParameterDiscreteValue = new ParameterDiscreteValue();
oParameterDiscreteValue.Value = 2;

oParameterFields[1].CurrentValues.Clear();
oParameterFields[1].CurrentValues.Add(oParameterDiscreteValue);

crystalReportViewer1.ParameterFieldInfo = oParameterFields;
```

Except for the first lines where the web service object is instantiated, the remainder of the code is the same as in Listing 7-22.

When referencing a web service in your code as shown in Listing 7-22, you can store the server location in an XML file that is read out at runtime to concatenate to the name of the report ASMX.

Referencing a web service by adding a web reference to your Solution Explorer and later instantiating it as an object reference requires a different approach. Since you won't be referring to the localhost on your production server, you can set up the translation in the web.config or app.config files as shown in Listing 7-24.

Listing 7-24. *Setting Up the web.config or app.config*

```
...
</system.web>

<appSettings>
    <add key="CrystalReportsWebServices.EmployeeSQLServerService"
value="http://prodserver/CrystalReportsWebServices/EmployeeSQLServerService.asmx"/>
</appSettings>

</configuration>
```

Summary

This chapter explained the relationship between Crystal Reports and BusinessObjects XI. We looked at how to use the viewer control and how to work with Crystal reports that are not managed by BO XI. We also covered Crystal web services and how to develop with the `CrystalDecisions.CrystalReports.Engine` object model and unmanaged RAS. Coming up, we'll examine how to create and modify Crystal reports programmatically using BO XI's Report Application Server (RAS) SDK, also known as the managed RAS.

CHAPTER 8

■ ■ ■

Programming the Report Application Server

The Report Application Server (RAS) is both a server that manages the delivery of reports (and as such handles its own page caching) and an SDK that allows you to create and modify reports at runtime. There are two types of RAS SDK models available. One ships with the Crystal Reports Advanced Edition and is known as the *unmanaged RAS*, and the other ships with BusinessObjects XI and is called the *managed RAS*. Unmanaged refers to the direct access the programming language provides to Crystal report files on disk. Managed refers to reports that are managed within the InfoStore. The unmanaged RAS is covered in Chapter 7.

In this chapter, we'll examine how to build and modify reports programmatically. There are several reasons you may wish to do this. Once your report is created and loaded into BO XI, you may wish to allow the user to make permanent modifications to the structure of the reports without requiring them to open Crystal Reports and use an interface they may perhaps be unfamiliar with. Rather, these change options can be offered to the user via a custom interface of your own design.

Introduction to RAS Programming

One of the main reasons you would need to build a report programmatically is to handle situations where the columns or groups are unknown at design time. Suppose you have an employee report that will display an employee's name and maybe up to one dozen out of several hundred columns of information stored in an employee table. Each user may be interested in creating a custom report that includes only certain pieces of relevant information. One user may wish to create an emergency contact list and therefore request off-site contact addresses and phone numbers. Another user may be looking to determine space and resource utilization and request building, floor, desk, extension, and e-mail within an office complex. Regardless of the choices made, these columns can be added to the report programmatically.

Report programming doesn't stop here, however. Using the RAS you can programmatically attach to data sources, create groups and formulas, add fields to the detail and group sections, create summary fields, and manage report setup and printing. You could essentially construct your own report-writing front end and use the RAS behind the scenes to convert the visual settings into a report. In short, almost anything you can accomplish with the user interface of Crystal Reports you can accomplish via the RAS. Simply put, the RAS is to Crystal Reports what the VBA programming language is to Microsoft Office.

■Note Unfortunately, Crystal Reports does not have a macro recorder like Microsoft Office. However, it is technically possible to decompile an RPT file into the RAS code that can reconstruct it. Crystal's technical support had such a tool for version 9 but never released it to the public and only decompiled reports on request. I only learned of its existence because I asked about it during a support call. They do not have one available for the current version of the tool.

Working with Reports

Any discussion of the RAS must start with the ReportClientDocument class. It is through ReportClientDocument that you may access any part of a report, as its component classes act as a gateway to everything contained within a Crystal Reports RPT file.

Before you can get to a report, however, you must first connect to BO XI in a fashion similar to the way you connect using the SDK. The code in Listing 8-1 illustrates how this is done.

Listing 8-1. *Connecting to BO XI*

```
SessionMgr oSessionMgr;
EnterpriseSession oEnterpriseSession;
EnterpriseService oEnterpriseService;
ReportAppFactory oReportAppFactory;
ReportClientDocument oReportClientDocument;

oSessionMgr = new SessionMgr();
oEnterpriseSession = oSessionMgr.Logon("administrator",
    "", "SETON-NOTEBOOK:6400", "secEnterprise");
oEnterpriseService = oEnterpriseSession.GetService("","RASReportFactory");

oReportAppFactory = ((ReportAppFactory) oEnterpriseService.Interface);
```

■Note BO XI still offers the PSReportFactory service to connect to and retrieve a report directly from the Page Server. This was done to provide the most efficient performance. Because the InfoObject class now retrieves reports from the Page Server directly (as of the R2 release), use of this service is no longer necessary, and it is provided only for backward compatibility.

The first step is to instantiate a `SessionMgr` object and use the `Logon()` method to connect. You may also log on using a token or a trusted principal as explained in Chapter 5. Then, use the `GetService()` method of the `EnterpriseSession` object to return an `EnterpriseService` object that returns a `RASReportFactory`, as opposed to an InfoStore reference. This object is then cast to one of type `ReportAppFactory`, and from here we can create a new report document as follows:

```
oReportClientDocument = oReportAppFactory.NewDocument();
```

You may also open an existing report using the `OpenDocument()` method as shown here:

```
oReportClientDocument =
    oReportAppFactory.OpenDocument(int.Parse(szReportID), 0);
```

If you wish to open a Crystal report from a disk file, you can do so with the `Open()` method:

```
object oTarget;
oTarget = @"c:\temp\myreport.rpt";
oReportClientDocument = new ReportClientDocumentClass();
oReportClientDocument.Open(ref(oTarget), 1);
```

When you wish to display the report, you can do so by setting the `ReportSource` property of the Crystal view control to the `ReportClientDocument` object like this:

```
crystalReportViewer1.ReportSource = oReportClientDocument;
```

Connecting to the Data Source

There are two ways you can set up the data for your report. You can add a series of tables to the `Tables` collection of the `Database` property and then link them together on a common key, or you can create a stored procedure that returns all your data in a data set. We'll look at the table approach first. Either way, you'll need to reference the connectivity information that opens a connection to the database.

Using Tables

Suppose you want to create a report that lists all the companies in the `Northwind` database. Each company grouping displays the individual orders, the order date, and the employee who made the sale. Within each order you can list the product name, price, quantity, and extended price with a subtotal at the end of each order. The final output is shown in Figure 8-1.

		Page:	1

Alfreds Futterkiste
Berlin   *Germany*

Order #: 11011   **Order Date:**   04/09/1998
Products		*Unit Price*	*Quantity*	*Extended Price*
Escargots de Bourgogne	£	13.25	40	$530.00
Flotemysost		21.50	20	$430.00

Order #: 10952   **Order Date:**   03/16/1998
Products	*Unit Price*	*Quantity*	*Extended Price*
Grandma's Boysenberry Spread	25.00	16	$400.00
Rössle Sauerkraut	45.60	2	$91.20

Order #: 10835   **Order Date:**   01/15/1998
Products	*Unit Price*	*Quantity*	*Extended Price*
Original Frankfurter grüne Soße	13.00	2	$26.00
Raclette Courdavault	55.00	15	$825.00

Order #: 10702   **Order Date:**   10/13/1997
Products	*Unit Price*	*Quantity*	*Extended Price*
Aniseed Syrup	10.00	6	$60.00
Lakkalikööri	18.00	15	$270.00

Order #: 10692   **Order Date:**   10/03/1997
Products	*Unit Price*	*Quantity*	*Extended Price*
Vegie-spread	43.90	20	$878.00

Order #: 10643   **Order Date:**   08/25/1997
Products	*Unit Price*	*Quantity*	*Extended Price*
Chartreuse verte	18.00	21	$378.00
Rössle Sauerkraut	45.60	15	$684.00
Spegesild	12.00	2	$24.00

$4,596.20

Figure 8-1. *Sales order report*

To accomplish this, we'll need data from the Customers, Orders, Order Details, Employees, and Products tables. Each table is added to the report by specifying the connectivity information, setting a reference to the required table, and adding it to the DatabaseController object. The AddTable() method in Listing 8-2 illustrates the data that is required in order for a table to be added to a report.

Listing 8-2. *Adding Tables to a Report*

```
private void AddTable(ReportClientDocument oReportClientDocument,
                string szDataSource,
                string szInitialCatalog,
                string szProvider,
                string szDatabaseDLL,
                string szDatabaseType,
                string szUserName,
                string szPassword,
                string szTableName)
```

```
{
    PropertyBag oLogonPropertyBag;
    PropertyBag oPropertyBag;
    ConnectionInfo oConnectionInfo;
    Table oTable;

    oLogonPropertyBag = new PropertyBagClass();
    oLogonPropertyBag["Data Source"] = szDataSource;
    oLogonPropertyBag["Initial Catalog"] = szInitialCatalog;
    oLogonPropertyBag["Provider"] = szProvider;

    oPropertyBag = new PropertyBagClass();
    oPropertyBag["Database DLL"] = szDatabaseDLL;
    oPropertyBag["QE_DatabaseType"] = szDatabaseType;
    oPropertyBag["QE_LogonProperties"] = oLogonPropertyBag;
    oPropertyBag["QE_SQLDB"] = "True";

    oConnectionInfo = new ConnectionInfoClass();
    oConnectionInfo.Attributes = oPropertyBag;
    oConnectionInfo.UserName = szUserName;
    oConnectionInfo.Password = szPassword;
    oConnectionInfo.Kind = CrConnectionInfoKindEnum.crConnectionInfoKindCRQE;

    oTable = new CrystalDecisions.ReportAppServer.DataDefModel.TableClass();
    oTable.Name = szTableName;
    oTable.ConnectionInfo = oConnectionInfo;

    oReportClientDocument.DatabaseController.AddTable(oTable, null);
}
```

The PropertyBag objects in this example contain the connection information necessary to connect to an OLE DB data source. The data source is the name of the SQL Server and the initial catalog is the name of the database—in this example "Northwind". The provider is SQLOLEDB. Since each connection type has its own Crystal Reports DLL supporting it, you'll need to specify it in the Database DLL property. Setting the QE_SQLDB element to True indicates that it's a SQL database that we're dealing with here. For the OLE DB connection, the DLL is crdb_ado.dll. Finally, we'll pass in the user ID and password to the database.

Each type of data source will require its own property bag setup. By comparison, an ODBC connection to the same data source would look like the code in Listing 8-3.

Listing 8-3. *Connecting via ODBC*

```
oPropertyBag = new PropertyBagClass();
oPropertyBag["Database DLL"] = "crdb_odbc.dll";
oPropertyBag["QE_DatabaseType"] = "ODBC (RDO)";
oPropertyBag["QE_SQLDB"] = true;
oPropertyBag["Server Name"] = "NorthWind";
```

```
oConnectionInfo = new ConnectionInfoClass();
oConnectionInfo.Attributes = oPropertyBag;
oConnectionInfo.Kind = CrConnectionInfoKindEnum.crConnectionInfoKindSQL;
```

The database type names match the data source names listed when you first connect a Crystal report to a data source using the dialog shown in Figure 8-2.

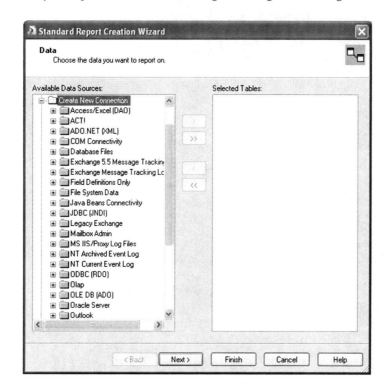

Figure 8-2. *Data source dialog*

Once the connectivity information has been established, instantiate a TableClass object to which the table name and the ConnectionInfo object are assigned. Then, add the table to the collection via the AddTable() method.

Linking Tables

Adding tables directly to a report does no good unless the data in those tables are somehow related. The primary keys in one table must be pointed at the matching foreign keys in another table in order for the referential relationships to take effect. The code in Listing 8-4 accepts the table and column names of a target and source table and sets a link between them.

Listing 8-4. *Setting Table Links*

```
public void AddTableLink(ReportClientDocument oReportClientDocument,
                string szSourceField,
                string szTargetField,
```

```
                    string szSourceTable,
                    string szTargetTable)
{
   TableLink oTableLink;

   oTableLink = new TableLinkClass();

   oTableLink.JoinType = CrTableJoinTypeEnum.crTableJoinTypeEqualJoin;

   oTableLink.SourceFieldNames.Add(szSourceField);
   oTableLink.TargetFieldNames.Add(szTargetField);

   oTableLink.SourceTableAlias = szSourceTable;
   oTableLink.TargetTableAlias = szTargetTable;

   oReportClientDocument.DatabaseController.AddTableLink(oTableLink);
}
```

Table linking is the equivalent of using a JOIN command in SQL, and the type of join is indicated by using the JoinType property. Since there are different types of joins—INNER, OUTER, LEFT, RIGHT, etc.—there are different ways the TableLinkClass can establish the link between the tables. The type of join is indicated by CrTableJoinTypeEnum, whose members are listed in Table 8-1.

Table 8-1. *CrTableJoinTypeEnum Enumerator Members*

Member	Value	Description
crTableJoinTypeAdvance	9	Advance
crTableJoinTypeEqualJoin	0	Equal join
crTableJoinTypeGreaterOrEqualJoin	6	Greater than or equal join
crTableJoinTypeGreaterThanJoin	4	Greater than join
crTableJoinTypeLeftOuterJoin	1	Left outer join
crTableJoinTypeLessOrEqualJoin	7	Less than or equal join
crTableJoinTypeLessThanJoin	5	Less than join
crTableJoinTypeNotEqualJoin	8	Not equal join
crTableJoinTypeOuterJoin	3	Outer join
crTableJoinTypeRightOuterJoin	2	Right outer join

Using Stored Procedures

Most likely you'll be developing your reports based on stored procedures rather than individual tables that need to be joined. Using a stored procedure as a data source is very similar to using a table. The key difference is that you need to add ";1" after any reference to the stored procedure name. For example, calling the AddTable() method shown in Listing 8-2 for use of a stored procedure instead of a table would look like this:

```
AddTable(oReportClientDocument, "(local)", "NorthWind", "SQLOLEDB",
    "crdb_ado.dll", "OLE DB (ADO)", "sa", "mypass", "spc_SalesOrders;1");
```

Because a stored procedure contains references to all the tables needed for a report and establishes the joins between them through the SQL syntax, there is no need to add the tables individually and no need to establish any links programmatically.

Since stored procedures are a far more common data source than individual tables, the remainder of the examples in this chapter will use one. Following is the stored procedure needed to produce the report shown in Figure 8-1:

```
SELECT c.CustomerID, c.CompanyName, c.City, c.Country,
o.OrderID, o.OrderDate, e.FirstName + ' ' + e.LastName AS Employee,
p.ProductName, p.UnitPrice, od.Quantity
FROM Customers c
LEFT OUTER JOIN Orders o ON c.CustomerID = o.CustomerID
LEFT OUTER JOIN Employees e ON o.EmployeeID = e.EmployeeID
LEFT OUTER JOIN [Order Details] od ON o.OrderID = od.OrderID
LEFT OUTER JOIN Products p ON od.ProductID = p.ProductID
ORDER BY c.CompanyName, o.OrderID, p.ProductName
```

Building the Body of the Report

Reports consist of multiple components. There are report header and footer sections, page header and footer sections, group sections, and detail sections. Any one of these sections can hold multiple objects. In the following sections, you'll learn how to reference these section objects and create the various parts of a report programmatically.

Working with Groups

Report data is often presented hierarchically, and each level of this hierarchy is called a *group*. In the Northwind database, a region may have many customers, each customer may have many orders, and each order may have many order items. Every level in this data set—regions, customers, and orders—constitutes a group, and you can list detail items within each group as well as summary amounts such as subtotals or averages, minimums or maximums. The code in Listing 8-5 shows how to add a group to a report.

Listing 8-5. *Adding a Group*

```
public void AddGroup(ReportClientDocument oReportClientDocument,
                    string szTableName,
                    string szFieldName)
{
    Group oGroup;
    Table oTable;
    ISCRTable oISCRTable;
    Field oField;

    oGroup = new GroupClass();
```

```
//Find the table or stored procedure in the table collection based on the name
oISCRTable = oReportClientDocument.Database.
    Tables.FindTableByAlias(szTableName);

//Extract the table or stored procedure and cast it to a Table object
oTable = ((Table) oISCRTable);

//Cast this field reference to a Field object
oField = ((Field) oTable.DataFields.FindField(szFieldName,
    CrFieldDisplayNameTypeEnum.crFieldDisplayNameName,
    CrystalDecisions.ReportAppServer.DataDefModel.
    CeLocale.ceLocaleUserDefault));

//Set the Field object as the group condition
oGroup.ConditionField = oField;

//Add the group to the report
oReportClientDocument.DataDefController.GroupController.Add(-1, oGroup);
}
```

A group is usually made on a field or virtual column name in a stored procedure. It could also be constructed on a formula as well. If you are working with a stored procedure—as you likely will be—even virtual columns can be used as group fields. In the AddGroup() method the table name is passed in and located in the Tables collection by the FindByAlias() method. The entry for that table is cast to an object of type Table. Then, the field name is located in the DataFields collection of the Table object and cast to an object of type Field. This Field object is set as the value of the ConditionField property of the Group object. Finally, the new Group object is added to the GroupController. The -1 parameter specifies that the new Group object should be added to the end of the Groups array.

Working with Sections

The different areas of a report are divided up into sections. Some sections come standard with all reports like the report and page header and footer sections or the details section. Other sections are created when groups are added to the report. Each group has a group header and a group footer. You can also add additional sections as needed to any of the sections just discussed. Most likely, you'll simply need to reference an existing section for the purpose of assigning objects to it. This can be accomplished through the ReportDefinition class.

ReportDefinition contains properties that offer access to the different areas of the report. Since each area can have many sections, there is a sections collection that you can use to reference the section you are dealing with. The code in Listing 8-6 shows how to set an object reference to the report header and footer sections and the page header and footer sections.

Listing 8-6. *Referencing Sections*

```
ReportDefinition oReportDefinition;

oReportDefinition = oReportClientDocument.ReportDefinition;

oSection = oReportDefinition.ReportHeaderArea.Sections[0];

oSection = oReportDefinition.ReportFooterArea.Sections[0];

oSection = oReportDefinition.PageHeaderArea.Sections[0];

oSection = oReportDefinition.PageFooterArea.Sections[0];
```

All of these Section objects refer to the zero element of the Sections collection. Usually there will be only one section per area of the report. The section breakdown for the Order Details report is shown in Figure 8-3.

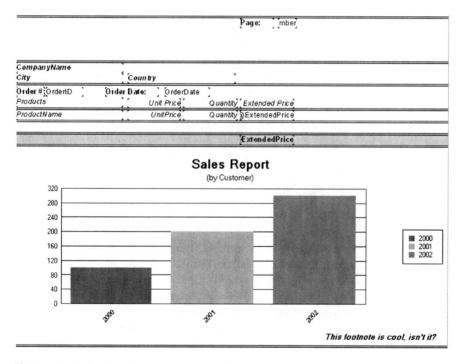

Figure 8-3. *Order Details report at design time*

Since there may be multiple groups, the group headers and footers are themselves referenced via a collection, the members of which each have their own section collections as shown in Listing 8-7.

Listing 8-7. *Referencing Header and Footer Sections*

```
ReportDefinition oReportDefinition;

oReportDefinition = oReportClientDocument.ReportDefinition;

oSection = oReportDefinition.get_GroupHeaderArea(0).Sections[0];

oSection = oReportDefinition.get_GroupFooterArea(0).Sections[0];
```

In Crystal Reports, the Section Expert option of the Properties item (see Figure 8-4) on the pop-up menu allows you to set different properties for a section.

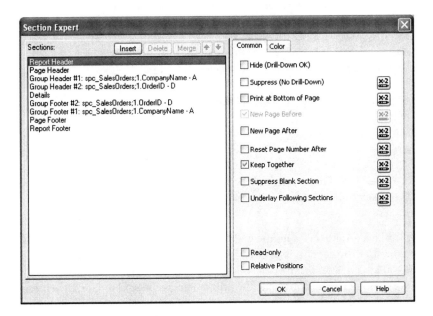

Figure 8-4. *Section Expert*

These same options are available programmatically through the SectionFormat class. The method shown in Listing 8-8 demonstrates how to set the various properties of a section through this class.

Listing 8-8. *Configuring Sections*

```
private void SetSectionSettings(ReportClientDocument oReportClientDocument,
    Section oSection,
    Color oBackgroundColor,
    bool bEnableKeepTogether,
    bool bEnableNewPageAfter,
    bool bEnableNewPageBefore,
    bool bEnablePrintAtBottomOfPage,
    bool bEnableResetPageNumberAfter,
```

```
        bool bEnableSuppress,
        bool bEnableSuppressIfBlank,
        bool bEnableUnderlaySection)
{
    SectionFormat oSectionFormat;
    ReportSectionController oReportSectionController;

    oSectionFormat = new SectionFormat();
    oSectionFormat.EnableKeepTogether = bEnableKeepTogether;
    oSectionFormat.EnableNewPageAfter = bEnableNewPageAfter;
    oSectionFormat.EnableNewPageBefore = bEnableNewPageBefore;
    oSectionFormat.EnablePrintAtBottomOfPage = bEnablePrintAtBottomOfPage;
    oSectionFormat.EnableResetPageNumberAfter = bEnableResetPageNumberAfter;
    oSectionFormat.EnableSuppress = bEnableSuppress;
    oSectionFormat.EnableSuppressIfBlank = bEnableSuppressIfBlank;
    oSectionFormat.EnableUnderlaySection = bEnableUnderlaySection;
    oSectionFormat.BackgroundColor =
        uint.Parse(ColorTranslator.ToWin32(oBackgroundColor).ToString());

    oReportSectionController =
        oReportClientDocument.ReportDefController.ReportSectionController;

    oReportSectionController.SetProperty(oSection,
        CrReportSectionPropertyEnum.crReportSectionPropertyFormat, oSectionFormat);
}
```

Here you can set the background color for the entire section, determine whether new pages should appear before or after the section is printed, whether the section should always be suppressed or only if blank, and whether the page number should reset itself after printing. You can also determine whether the section should be printed on one page and not split across two pages. Once the object properties have been set, you can use the SetProperty() method of the ReportSectionController class to apply the setting choices to the section object.

Section objects have a property called ReportObjects that contains a reference to every object in the section itself. You can iterate this collection to make changes across the section's objects. If you wanted to change the background color of every data field in the collection to gold, for example, you could do so using the code in Listing 8-9.

Listing 8-9. *Iterating the Objects in a Section*

```
oSection = oReportClientDocument.ReportDefinition.DetailArea.Sections[0];

foreach (ReportObject oReportObject in oSection.ReportObjects)
{
    if (oReportObject.Kind == CrReportObjectKindEnum.crReportObjectKindField)
        oReportObject.Border.BackgroundColor =
            uint.Parse(ColorTranslator.ToWin32(Color.Gold).ToString());
}
```

Creating Formulas

Crystal Reports allows you to create formulas and insert them into reports. A *formula* is a block of executable code within a report. All the data fields and even other formulas in the report are visible to your formulas as values. Using the RAS, you can create formulas programmatically as code strings and insert them into the report at runtime as well. Commonly, a formula may perform a mathematical function on two numbers, and in our example they will multiply the unit price by the quantity ordered to obtain the extended price. You could also use a formula to perform proper concatenation of a person's name from prefix, first, middle, last, and suffix fields or perform calculations between dates. Though you could handle many of these tasks using SQL statements and functions, formulas nevertheless allow you to perform them from within the report itself.

You can create a formula and add it to a report using the code in Listing 8-10.

Listing 8-10. *Creating a Formula*

```
private void AddFormula(ReportClientDocument oReportClientDocument,
    string szName,
    string szFormula)
{
    FormulaField oFormulaField;

    oFormulaField = new FormulaField();

    oFormulaField.Name = szName;
    oFormulaField.Text = szFormula;
    oFormulaField.Syntax = CrFormulaSyntaxEnum.crFormulaSyntaxCrystal;
    oFormulaField.Type = CrFieldValueTypeEnum.crFieldValueTypeStringField;

    oReportClientDocument.DataDefController.
        FormulaFieldController.Add(oFormulaField);
}
```

This method accepts the `ReportClientDocument` object, the name of the formula, and the formula code itself. In this example, we'll call the formula "ExtendedPrice" and set the formula text to

```
{spc_SalesOrders;1.Quantity} * {spc_SalesOrders;1.UnitPrice}
```

The code is passed as a string. If you have multiple lines of code, you can separate each one with carriage returns to make the code more readable when it is displayed inside the reports formula editor. The `Syntax` property allows you to designate the formula as adhering to the Crystal, Basic, or SQL syntax. When the report is created, you'll see the ExtendedPrice formulas listed under the formula fields as shown in Figure 8-5.

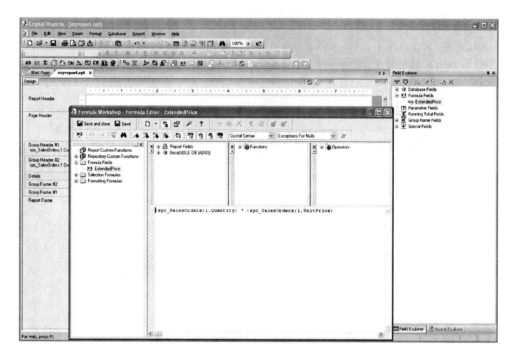

Figure 8-5. *ExtendedPrice formula in Crystal Reports*

Condition Formulas

Condition formulas are snippets of code that can control different aspects of your report display. The purpose of adding condition formulas is to allow you a much more granular level of control over your reports than is available by the mere presence of a field in a section. Condition formulas will allow you to do such things as display values over $100 in red, or suppress columns or entire sections based on parameter values. Using condition formulas, you can customize your report down to the level of the single data element.

Many of the configuration screens of Crystal Reports offer the condition formula icons. You can select these icons and display the Formula Workshop screen as shown in Figure 8-6.

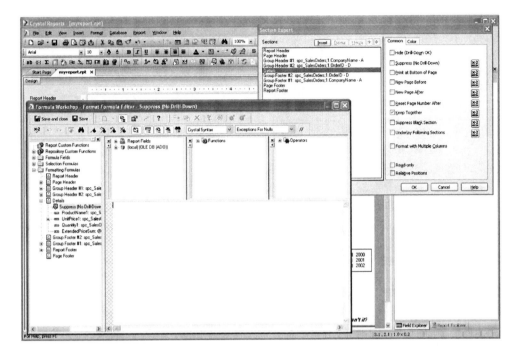

Figure 8-6. *Adding a condition formula*

The same code that you enter into these editing screens can be applied programmatically to your reports using the ConditionFormulas() method. First, you must define the object and event to which the conditional formatting applies. There are a series of enumerators that allow you to determine this, and these enumerated values correspond to the formula icons on the configuration screens. A list of these enumerators can be found in Table 8-2.

Table 8-2. *Formula Type Enumerators*

Enumerator	Description
CrBooleanFieldFormatConditionFormulaTypeEnum	Boolean field format
CrBorderConditionFormulaTypeEnum	Border condition
CrCommonFieldFormatConditionFormulaTypeEnum	Common field format
CrDateFieldFormatConditionFormulaTypeEnum	Date field format
CrDateTimeFieldFormatConditionFormulaTypeEnum	Date/time field format
CrNumericFieldFormatConditionFormulaTypeEnum	Numeric field format
CrObjectFormatConditionFormulaTypeEnum	Object format
CrSectionAreaFormatConditionFormulaTypeEnum	Section area format
CrTimeFieldFormatConditionFormulaTypeEnum	Time field format
CrFontColorConditionFormulaTypeEnum	Font color

Let's examine the members of one of these enumerators—
CrSectionAreaFormatConditionFormulaTypeEnum. The members of this enumerator, which correspond to the options shown in Figure 8-6, are listed in Table 8-3.

Table 8-3. *CrSectionAreaFormatConditionFormulaTypeEnum Enumerator Members*

Member	Value	Description
crSectionAreaConditionFormulaTypeBackgroundColor	8	Background color
crSectionAreaConditionFormulaTypeEnableHideForDrillDown	9	Hide for drilldown
crSectionAreaConditionFormulaTypeEnableKeepTogether	4	Keep together
crSectionAreaConditionFormulaTypeEnableNewPageAfter	2	New page after
crSectionAreaConditionFormulaTypeEnableNewPageBefore	3	New page before
crSectionAreaConditionFormulaTypeEnablePrintAtBottomOfPage	1	Print at bottom of page
crSectionAreaConditionFormulaTypeEnableResetPageNumberAfter	6	Reset page number after
crSectionAreaConditionFormulaTypeEnableSuppress	0	Suppress
crSectionAreaConditionFormulaTypeEnableSuppressIfBlank	5	Suppress if blank
crSectionAreaConditionFormulaTypeEnableUnderlaySection	7	Underlay section

If you wanted, say, to control whether or not a given footer section is suppressed under certain conditions, you could do so by referencing the CrSectionAreaFormatConditionFormulaTypeEnum. crSectionAreaConditionFormulaTypeEnableSuppress enumerator value. The approach to creating a condition formula is shown in Listing 8-11.

Listing 8-11. *Adding a Conditional Formula*

```
ReportObjectController oReportObjectController;
ReportObject oFieldReportObject = null;
ReportObjects oReportObjects;
FieldObject oFieldObject;
FieldObject oFieldObjectTemp;
string szFormula;

oReportObjectController = oReportClientDocument.
   ReportDefController.ReportObjectController;

oReportObjects = oReportObjectController.GetAllReportObjects();
```

```
foreach (ReportObject oReportObject in oReportObjects)
{
   string szName = oReportObject.Name;
   if (szName  == "UnitPrice1")
   {
      oFieldReportObject = oReportObject;
      break;
   }
}

oFieldObject = ((FieldObject) oFieldReportObject);
oFieldObjectTemp = ((FieldObject) oFieldObject.Clone(true));

szFormula = "if {spc_SalesOrders;1.UnitPrice} > 30 then crGreen";

oFieldObjectTemp.FontColor.
   ConditionFormulas[CrFontColorConditionFormulaTypeEnum.
   crFontColorConditionFormulaTypeColor].Text = szFormula;

oReportObjectController.Modify(oFieldObject, oFieldObjectTemp);
```

In this example, we want to display any unit prices that are greater than $30 in green letters. To test out your logic, you can use the Formula Editor in Crystal Reports to ascertain that your syntax is correct and then copy the code from your Formula Editor into the IDE. The logic to accomplish this is stored as a string and applies to the FontColor property of the FieldObject via the ConditionFormulas() method. To indicate that it is the font color that we're referring to, we'll specify the crFontColorConditionFormulaTypeColor member of the CrFontColorConditionFormulaTypeEnum enumerator. Then, the modified object is assigned to the ReportObjectController object.

■**Note** In your search through the RAS documentation, you may have come across such classes as NumericFieldFormatConditionFormulasClass and BooleanFieldFormatConditionFormulasClass. These and other similarly named classes do store condition formulas for the various object types but are intended for internal calls from within the SDK. Therefore, you should not invoke them directly in your own code.

Working with Fields

There are several types of fields that you can add to a report. The most common are data fields that display information located in the data source to which you are attached. Other fields display text that appears as labels on the report. You can also display predefined special fields like the page number or the date and time the report was printed. Finally, you can create summary fields that execute a summary calculation like a sum or an average on a column of numbers. In the sections that follow, we'll examine how to create each of these fields programmatically. Though each field type is encapsulated by its own specific object, you'll see that working with the various fields in the RAS uses a consistent body of logic.

Data Fields

Data fields display data from the columns in the underlying data source, including virtual columns created in stored procedures. In the AddField() method shown in Listing 8-12, the table name is passed in and located in the Tables collection by the FindByAlias() method. The entry for that table is cast to an object of type Table. Then, the field name is located in the DataFields collection of the Table object and cast to an object of type Field.

Listing 8-12. *Adding a Field Object*

```
private void AddField(ReportClientDocument oReportClientDocument,
                Section oSection,
                FontColor oFontColor,
                CrAlignmentEnum sAlignmentEnum,
                string szTableName,
                string szFieldName,
                int iLeft,
                int iTop,
                int iWidth,
                int iHeight)
{
    Table oTable;
    ISCRTable oISCRTable;
    FieldObject oFieldObject;
    Field oField;

    //Find the table or stored procedure in the table collection based on the name
    oISCRTable = oReportClientDocument.Database.Tables.
        FindTableByAlias(szTableName);

    //Extract the table or stored procedure and cast it to a Table object
    oTable = ((Table) oISCRTable);

    //Cast this field reference to a Field object
    oField = ((Field) oTable.DataFields.FindField(szFieldName,
        CrFieldDisplayNameTypeEnum.crFieldDisplayNameName,
        CrystalDecisions.ReportAppServer.DataDefModel.
        CeLocale.ceLocaleUserDefault));

    //Instantiate a FieldObjectClass and set the properties
    //and display the data and position on the page.
    oFieldObject = new FieldObjectClass();
    oFieldObject.Kind = CrReportObjectKindEnum.crReportObjectKindField;
```

```
oFieldObject.FieldValueType = oField.Type;
oFieldObject.DataSource = oField.FormulaForm;
oFieldObject.Left = iLeft;
oFieldObject.Top = iTop;
oFieldObject.Width = iWidth;
oFieldObject.Height = iHeight;
oFieldObject.FontColor = oFontColor;
oFieldObject.Format.HorizontalAlignment = sAlignmentEnum;

//Add the group to the report
oReportClientDocument.ReportDefController.
   ReportObjectController.Add(oFieldObject, oSection, 0);
}
```

Next you'll need to instantiate an object of type FieldObjectClass. This object encapsulates the visual display of the field on the report design page and specifies the size and position coordinates. The Kind property indicates the type of Crystal Reports field we're dealing with and is set to a member of the CrReportObjectKindEnum enumerator. In this example, we're working with a crReportObjectKindField. The other members of the CrReportObjectKindEnum enumerator are shown in Table 8-4.

Table 8-4. *CrReportObjectKindEnum Enumerator Members*

Member	Value	Description
crReportObjectKindBlobField	9	Blob field
crReportObjectKindBox	4	Box
crReportObjectKindChart	7	Chart
crReportObjectKindCrosstab	8	Crosstab
crReportObjectKindField	1	Field
crReportObjectKindFieldHeading	12	Field heading
crReportObjectKindInvalid	0	Invalid
crReportObjectKindLine	3	Line
crReportObjectKindMap	10	Map
crReportObjectKindOlapGrid	11	Olap grid
crReportObjectKindPicture	6	Picture
crReportObjectKindSubreport	5	Subreport
crReportObjectKindText	2	Text

The Type property of the Field object is assigned to the FieldValueType property of the FieldObject. This value is a member of CrFieldValueTypeEnum, and the other members are listed in Table 8-5. Finally, the new FieldObject is added to the ReportDefController.

Table 8-5. *CrFieldValueTypeEnum Enumerator Members*

Member	Value	Description
crFieldValueTypeBitmapField	20	Bitmap
crFieldValueTypeBlobField	14	Blob
crFieldValueTypeBooleanField	8	Boolean
crFieldValueTypeChartField	24	Chart
crFieldValueTypeCurrencyField	7	Currency
crFieldValueTypeDateField	9	Date
crFieldValueTypeDateTimeField	15	Date/time
crFieldValueTypeDecimalField	16	Decimal
crFieldValueTypeIconField	21	Icon
crFieldValueTypeInt16sField	2	Signed 16-bit integer
crFieldValueTypeInt16uField	3	Unsigned 16-bit integer
crFieldValueTypeInt32sField	4	Signed 32-bit integer
crFieldValueTypeInt32uField	5	Unsigned 32-bit integer
crFieldValueTypeInt64sField	17	Signed 64-bit integer
crFieldValueTypeInt64uField	18	Unsigned 64-bit integer
crFieldValueTypeInt8sField	0	Signed 8-bit integer
crFieldValueTypeInt8uField	1	Unsigned 8-bit integer
crFieldValueTypeInterfacePointerField	101	Interface pointer
crFieldValueTypeNumberField	6	Number
crFieldValueTypeOleField	23	OLE
crFieldValueTypePersistentMemoField	13	Persistent memo
crFieldValueTypePictureField	22	Picture
crFieldValueTypePointerField	100	Pointer
crFieldValueTypeSameAsInputField	25	Same as input
crFieldValueTypeStringField	11	String
crFieldValueTypeTimeField	10	Time
crFieldValueTypeTransientMemoField	12	Transient memo
crFieldValueTypeUnknownField	255	Unknown

Text Fields

Adding a text field like a report title is a rather convoluted process involving a number of objects—five to be exact—just to display a piece of text on the report. First you'll need a ParagraphTextElement object that contains the text you wish to display, which you then need to add to a ParagraphElements collection object. This collection is then added to the ParagraphElements property of a Paragraph object, which in turn is added to a Paragraphs collection. Finally, the Paragraphs collection object is added to the Paragraphs property of a TextObject. The TextObject is the visual element that holds settings for size and position.

Whew! Working with TextObjects is one of the less intuitive parts of the RAS SDK. It's best to use the prebuilt method in Listing 8-13 to shield yourself from the complexity.

Listing 8-13. *Adding a Text Field*

```
private void AddTextField(ReportClientDocument oReportClientDocument,
    Section oSection,
    string szText,
    FontColor oFontColor,
    CrAlignmentEnum sAlignmentEnum,
    int iLeft,
    int iTop,
    int iWidth,
    int iHeight)
{

    TextObject oTextObject;
    Paragraphs oParagraphs;
    Paragraph oParagraph;
    ParagraphElements oParagraphElements;
    ParagraphTextElement oParagraphTextElement;

    //Instantiate the necessary objects
    oTextObject = new TextObject();
    oParagraphs = new Paragraphs();
    oParagraph = new Paragraph();
    oParagraphElements = new ParagraphElements();
    oParagraphTextElement = new ParagraphTextElement();

    //Set the displayed text to the ParagraphTextElement object
    oParagraphTextElement.Text = szText;
    oParagraphTextElement.Kind =
        CrParagraphElementKindEnum.crParagraphElementKindText;

    //Add the ParagraphTextElement to the ParagraphTextElements collection
    oParagraphElements.Add(oParagraphTextElement);

    //Set the ParagraphTextElements collection to the ParagraphElements
    //property of the Paragraph object and set the text alignment
    oParagraph.ParagraphElements = oParagraphElements;
    oParagraph.Alignment = sAlignmentEnum;

    //Add the Paragraph object to the Paragraphs collection
    oParagraphs.Add(oParagraph);

    //Set up the TextObject by assigning the Paragraphs collection object to
    //its Paragraphs property. Also, set the size and position.
    oTextObject.Kind = CrReportObjectKindEnum.crReportObjectKindText;
    oTextObject.Paragraphs = oParagraphs;
```

```
oTextObject.Left = iLeft;
oTextObject.Top = iTop;
oTextObject.Width = iWidth;
oTextObject.Height = iHeight;
oTextObject.FontColor = oFontColor;

//Finally, add the TextObject to the report
oReportClientDocument.ReportDefController.
    ReportObjectController.Add(oTextObject, oSection, -1);
}
```

Special Fields

A *special field* contains a predefined piece of information that you can display on the report. Some of the more common ones are page number, page n of m, and the print date and time. The purpose of a special field is to shield you from determining programmatically the repetitive information that is repeated in almost every report. You could, for example, create a variable in your Crystal report that is incremented every time a new page begins and then display this variable at the top of every page to provide a page number. To avoid making you do such unnecessary and error prone coding, Business Objects has added these predefined fields that do the same things for you. The code to display a special field is shown in Listing 8-14.

Listing 8-14. *Adding a Special Field*

```
private void AddSpecialField(ReportClientDocument oReportClientDocument,
    Section oSection,
    CrSpecialFieldTypeEnum sSpecialFieldTypeEnum,
    int iLeft,
    int iTop,
    int iWidth,
    int iHeight)
{
    SpecialField oSpecialField;
    FieldObject oFieldObject;

    //Instantiate a SpecialField object
    oSpecialField = new SpecialField();

    //...and use the enumerator to indicate the type of special field
    oSpecialField.SpecialType = sSpecialFieldTypeEnum;

    //Ultimately you'll be displaying a field type
    //that references the SpecialField object.
    oFieldObject = new FieldObject();

    oFieldObject.Kind = CrReportObjectKindEnum.crReportObjectKindText;
    oFieldObject.FieldValueType = oSpecialField.Type;
    oFieldObject.DataSource = oSpecialField.FormulaForm;
```

```
oFieldObject.Left = iLeft;
oFieldObject.Top = iTop;
oFieldObject.Width = iWidth;
oFieldObject.Height = iHeight;

//Finally, add the FieldObject to the report
oReportClientDocument.ReportDefController.
   ReportObjectController.Add(oFieldObject, oSection, -1);
}
```

The type of field to be displayed—page number, print date, etc.—is determined by the SpecialType property of the SpecialField object, which is set to a member of the CrSpecialFieldTypeEnum enumerator. The members of this enumerator are listed in Table 8-6.

Table 8-6. *CrSpecialFieldTypeEnum Enumerator Members*

Member	Value	Description
crSpecialFieldTypeDataDate	6	Date
crSpecialFieldTypeDataTime	7	Time
crSpecialFieldTypeFileAuthor	17	Author
crSpecialFieldTypeFileCreationDate	18	Creation date
crSpecialFieldTypeFileName	16	File name
crSpecialFieldTypeGroupNumber	10	Group number
crSpecialFieldTypeGroupSelection	15	Group selection
crSpecialFieldTypeModificationDate	4	Modification date
crSpecialFieldTypeModificationTime	5	Modification time
crSpecialFieldTypePageNOfM	19	Page n of m
crSpecialFieldTypePageNumber	9	Page number
crSpecialFieldTypePrintDate	2	Print date
crSpecialFieldTypePrintTime	3	Print time
crSpecialFieldTypeRecordGroupNamePath	21	Record group name path
crSpecialFieldTypeRecordGroupPath	1	Record group path
crSpecialFieldTypeRecordKey	0	Record key
crSpecialFieldTypeRecordNumber	8	Record number
crSpecialFieldTypeRecordSelection	14	Record selection
crSpecialFieldTypeReportComments	13	Report comments
crSpecialFieldTypeReportPath	20	Report path
crSpecialFieldTypeReportTitle	12	Report title
crSpecialFieldTypeTotalPageCount	11	Total page count

Formula Fields

Earlier in the chapter we looked at how to create formulas. Formulas have limited usefulness unless they are displayed on a report. Adding a formula field is similar to adding any other field except that it works through a FormulaField object. The code to display a formula field is shown in Listing 8-15.

Listing 8-15. *Adding a Formula Field*

```
private void AddFormulaField(ReportClientDocument oReportClientDocument,
    Section oSection,
    string szFieldName,
    CrFieldValueTypeEnum sFieldValueTypeEnum,
    int iLeft,
    int iTop,
    int iWidth,
    int iHeight)
{
    FormulaField oFormulaField;
    Fields oFields;
    ISCRField oISCRField;
    FieldObject oFieldObject;

    oFormulaField = new FormulaFieldClass();

    oFields = oReportClientDocument.DataDefinition.FormulaFields;

    oISCRField = oFields.FindField(szFieldName,
        CrFieldDisplayNameTypeEnum.crFieldDisplayNameName,
        CrystalDecisions.ReportAppServer.DataDefModel.CeLocale.ceLocaleUserDefault);

    oFormulaField = ((FormulaField) oISCRField);
    oFormulaField.Type = sFieldValueTypeEnum;

    oFieldObject = new FieldObjectClass();
    oFieldObject.Kind = CrReportObjectKindEnum.crReportObjectKindField;
    oFieldObject.FieldValueType = oFormulaField.Type;
    oFieldObject.DataSource = oFormulaField.FormulaForm;
    oFieldObject.Left = iLeft;
    oFieldObject.Top = iTop;
    oFieldObject.Width = iWidth;
    oFieldObject.Height = iHeight;

    oReportClientDocument.ReportDefController.
        ReportObjectController.Add(oFieldObject, oSection, 1);
}
```

The sFieldValueTypeEnum parameter must be set to an enumerator value that appropriately matches the formula output. If you are multiplying two numbers, for example, the parameter should be set to crFieldValueTypeNumberField. Failure to use the proper type designation will cause a runtime error.

Summary Fields

A summary field provides a calculation on a series of numbers. You'll commonly use a summary field in a group footer to show a sum, average, or median of a column of numbers displayed in the preceding detail section. A summary field is encapsulated by a SummaryField object. The field you wish to summarize, say, Extended Price, is referenced via a Field object, and then that Field object is set to the SummarizedField property of the SummaryField object. Since you'll need an object of the FieldObject class to visually display the data, you'll need to instantiate one and set the FieldObject's DataSource property to the SummaryField object as shown in Listing 8-16.

Listing 8-16. *Adding a Summary Field*

```
public void AddSummaryField(ReportClientDocument oReportClientDocument,
    Section oSection,
    string szTableName,
    string szFieldName,
    CrSummaryOperationEnum sSummaryOperationEnum,
    int iLeft,
    int iTop,
    int iWidth,
    int iHeight)
{
    SummaryField oSummaryField;
    Table oTable;
    ISCRTable oISCRTable;
    FieldObject oFieldObject;
    Field oField;
    int iIndex;

    //If you pass a table prefix, then you are summarizing a data field
    //(like unit price).
    //Otherwise assume you are summarizing a formula (like unit price * quantity)
    if (szTableName != string.Empty)
    {
        iIndex = oReportClientDocument.Database.Tables.FindByAlias(szTableName);
        oISCRTable = oReportClientDocument.Database.Tables[iIndex];
        oTable = ((Table) oISCRTable);

        iIndex = oTable.DataFields.Find(szFieldName,
            CrFieldDisplayNameTypeEnum.crFieldDisplayNameName,
            CrystalDecisions.ReportAppServer.DataDefModel.
            CeLocale.ceLocaleUserDefault);
        oField = ((Field) oTable.DataFields[iIndex]);
    }
    else
    {
        iIndex = oReportClientDocument.DataDefinition.FormulaFields.Find(szFieldName,
```

```
            CrFieldDisplayNameTypeEnum.crFieldDisplayNameName,
            CrystalDecisions.ReportAppServer.DataDefModel.
            CeLocale.ceLocaleUserDefault);

        oField = ((Field) oReportClientDocument.DataDefinition.FormulaFields[iIndex]);
    }

    oSummaryField = new SummaryFieldClass();
    oSummaryField.Group = oReportClientDocument.DataDefinition.Groups[0];
    oSummaryField.SummarizedField = oField;
    oSummaryField.Operation = sSummaryOperationEnum;
    oSummaryField.Type = oField.Type;

    oFieldObject = new FieldObjectClass();
    oFieldObject.Kind = CrReportObjectKindEnum.crReportObjectKindField;
    oFieldObject.FieldValueType = oSummaryField.Type;
    oFieldObject.DataSource = oSummaryField.FormulaForm;
    oFieldObject.Left = iLeft;
    oFieldObject.Top = iTop;
    oFieldObject.Width = iWidth;
    oFieldObject.Height = iHeight;

    oReportClientDocument.ReportDefController.
        ReportObjectController.Add(oFieldObject, oSection, 1);
}
```

The type of summary you wish to create is determined by the Operation property of the SummaryField object. This property takes a member of the CrSummaryOperationEnum enumerator listed in Table 8-7.

Table 8-7. *CrSummaryOperationEnum Enumerator Members*

Member	Value	Description
crSummaryOperationAverage	1	Average
crSummaryOperationCorrelation	10	Correlation
crSummaryOperationCount	6	Count
crSummaryOperationCovariance	11	Covariance
crSummaryOperationDistinctCount	9	Distinct count
crSummaryOperationMaximum	4	Maximum
crSummaryOperationMedian	13	Median
crSummaryOperationMinimum	5	Minimum
crSummaryOperationMode	17	Mode
crSummaryOperationNthLargest	15	Nth largest
crSummaryOperationNthMostFrequent	18	Nth most frequent
crSummaryOperationNthSmallest	16	Nth smallest
crSummaryOperationPercentage	19	Percentage

Member	Value	Description
crSummaryOperationPercentile	14	Percentile
crSummaryOperationPopStandardDeviation	8	Population standard deviation
crSummaryOperationPopVariance	7	Population variance
crSummaryOperationStandardDeviation	3	Standard deviation
crSummaryOperationSum	0	Sum
crSummaryOperationVariance	2	Variance
crSummaryOperationWeightedAvg	12	Weighted average

Formatting Field Data

Most fields that appear on your report will need some type of formatting applied to them. Dates, text, Booleans, and numbers all have their own specific options for formatting. Moreover, all field types use fonts. In the next sections, we'll examine the classes that allow you to apply formatting to your data.

Basic Formatting

The raw data from your data source will not always be in the format you want to display on the report. Dates and numeric values especially almost always need some type of formatting applied. Crystal Reports offers a set of defaults that apply to the various field data types. You can access and change these defaults by selecting File ➤ Options from the main menu and then choosing the Fields tab. Here you can set the default format for string, numeric, date, time, currency, and Boolean values. The Custom Style dialog with the Date tab selected is shown in Figure 8-7.

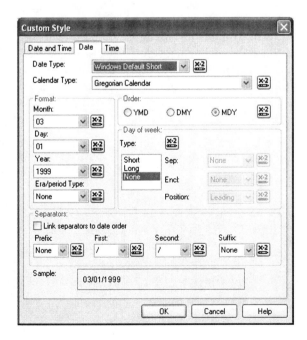

Figure 8-7. *Setting date format defaults*

Though it's certainly helpful to rely on defaults for most of your data formatting, there are times when you need to provide customization for a certain field. The first step in providing this customization is through the FieldFormat class. There are two properties in this class found under the CommonFormat property: EnableSystemDefault and EnableSuppressIfDuplicated. Setting EnableSystemDefault to false will tell the RAS to override any default settings from Crystal Reports and only recognize the formatting settings that are set programmatically. EnableSuppressIfDuplicated will determine whether a column that has successive duplicate values should repeat those duplicate values on each row. The code to set up the FieldFormat object is shown in Listing 8-17.

Listing 8-17. *Preparing Field Formatting*

```
FieldFormat oFieldFormat;

oFieldFormat = new FieldFormatClass();

oFieldFormat.CommonFormat.EnableSystemDefault = false;
oFieldFormat.CommonFormat.EnableSuppressIfDuplicated = false;
```

▓**Note** EnableSystemDefault defaults to True. If you don't set it to False, all the formatting you apply programmatically will be ignored.

Numeric Numeric values can fall into a variety of classifications. They can represent currency, a quantity, or a number that should be treated as if it were text. An order number is an example of this last type. In the Northwind example, the OrderID column is an integer value and the primary key of the Orders table. When it is displayed on the screen, Crystal will likely treat it as a true numeric value and insert a thousands separator and right justify it. Because you won't be performing mathematical functions on it, this default formatting is probably not what you want. To correct this situation, use the code in Listing 8-18 to suppress the thousands separator and display no decimal places.

Listing 8-18. *Formatting the Order Number*

```
FieldFormat oFieldFormat;

oFieldFormat = new FieldFormatClass();

oFieldFormat.CommonFormat.EnableSystemDefault = false;

oFieldFormat.NumericFormat.ThousandsSeparator = false;
oFieldFormat.NumericFormat.RoundingFormat = 0;
oFieldFormat.NumericFormat.NDecimalPlaces = 0;

oFieldObject.FieldFormat = oFieldFormat;
```

Note that the alignment is not a function of the formatting class. There is a property of the FieldObject that will determine how the alignment will display as shown here:

```
oFieldObject.Format.HorizontalAlignment = CrAlignmentEnum.crAlignmentLeft;
```

This property receives a member of the CrAlignmentEnum enumerator. The individual members are shown in Table 8-8.

Table 8-8. *CrAlignmentEnum Enumerator Members*

Name	Value	Description
crAlignmentDecimal	5	Align decimal point to the tab stop.
crAlignmentDefault	0	Default alignment.
crAlignmentHorizontalCenter	2	Center horizontally.
crAlignmentJustified	4	Justify text.
crAlignmentLeft	1	Align left.
crAlignmentRight	3	Align right.

Many RDBMSs have money or currency as a data type. If this is the case, Crystal will apply currency defaults like using a dollar sign, adding a thousands separator, and displaying two digits after the decimal point to represent cents. Again, this may not be what you want. The code shown in Listing 8-19 shows how to format a currency amount as British pounds. To avoid cluttering the page with too many £ symbols, the OneCurrencySymbolPerPage property is set to true.

Listing 8-19. *Formatting a Currency Amount*

```
FieldFormat oFieldFormat;

oFieldFormat = new FieldFormatClass();

oFieldFormat.CommonFormat.EnableSystemDefault = false;

oFieldFormat.NumericFormat.OneCurrencySymbolPerPage = true;
oFieldFormat.NumericFormat.CurrencySymbolFormat =
   CrCurrencySymbolTypeEnum.crCurrencySymbolTypeFixedSymbol;
oFieldFormat.NumericFormat.CurrencyPosition =
   CrCurrencyPositionFormatEnum.
   crCurrencyPositionFormatLeadingCurrencyInsideNegative;
oFieldFormat.NumericFormat.CurrencySymbol = "£";
oFieldFormat.NumericFormat.NDecimalPlaces = 2;
oFieldFormat.NumericFormat.DecimalSymbol = ".";

oFieldObject.FieldFormat = oFieldFormat;
```

Because there are so many currencies throughout the world that display their values in so many ways, the properties of the NumericFormat class allow you customize every aspect of the display. The `CurrencyPosition` property takes as a value a member of the `CrCurrencyPositionFormatEnum` enumerator and determines where the currency symbol will display relative to the value and to the delimiters specified for a negative number. The members of `CrCurrencyPositionFormatEnum` are listed in Table 8-9.

Table 8-9. *CrCurrencyPositionFormatEnum Enumerator Members*

Name	Value	Description
crCurrencyPositionFormatLeadingCurrencyInsideNegative	0	Display as ($100).
crCurrencyPositionFormatLeadingCurrencyOutsideNegative	1	Display as $(100).
crCurrencyPositionFormatTrailingCurrencyInsideNegative	2	Display as (100$).
crCurrencyPositionFormatTrailingCurrencyOutsideNegative	3	Display as (100)$.

The `CurrencySymbolFormat` property allows you to determine the relationship of the currency symbol to the displayed number. This property receives a value of the `CrCurrencySymbolTypeEnum` enumerator, and its members are listed in Table 8-10.

Table 8-10. *CrCurrencySymbolTypeEnum Enumerator Members*

Name	Value	Description
crCurrencySymbolTypeFixedSymbol	1	Display symbol leftmost in the field: $ 100.
crCurrencySymbolTypeFloatingSymbol	2	Display symbol adjacent to number: $100.
crCurrencySymbolTypeNoSymbol	3	Suppress symbol completely.

Date, Time, and DateTime You can format date/time fields as date only, time only, or as a combination of date and time. There are three property collections of the `FieldFormat` class that handle these choices: `DateFormat`, `TimeFormat`, and `DateTimeFormat`. Suppose you have a date/time field that you wish to display in the format 12/05/2006, that is, MM/DD/YYYY. You can accomplish this via the code shown in Listing 8-20.

Listing 8-20. *Preparing Field Formatting*

```
FieldFormat oFieldFormat;

oFieldFormat = new FieldFormatClass();

oFieldFormat.CommonFormat.EnableSystemDefault = false;

oFieldFormat.DateTimeFormat.DateTimeOrder =
   CrDateTimeOrderEnum.crDateTimeOrderDateOnly;

oFieldFormat.DateFormat.DateOrder =
   CrDateOrderEnum.crDateOrderMonthDayYear;
oFieldFormat.DateFormat.DateFirstSeparator = "/";
oFieldFormat.DateFormat.DateSecondSeparator = "/";
```

```
oFieldFormat.DateFormat.MonthFormat =
    CrMonthFormatEnum.crMonthFormatLeadingZeroNumericMonth;
oFieldFormat.DateFormat.DayFormat =
    CrDayFormatEnum.crDayFormatLeadingZeroNumericDay;
oFieldFormat.DateFormat.YearFormat =
    CrYearFormatEnum.crYearFormatLongYear;

oFieldObject.FieldFormat = oFieldFormat;
```

First, specify the DateTimeOrder property with one of the members of the CrDateTimeOrderEnum. This setting will determine whether only the date or time appear or, if both, in what order. The available options are listed in Table 8-11.

Table 8-11. *CrDateTimeOrderEnum Enumerator Members*

Name	Value	Description
crDateTimeOrderDateOnly	2	Show date only.
crDateTimeOrderDateThenTime	0	Show date, then time.
crDateTimeOrderTimeOnly	3	Show time only.
crDateTimeOrderTimeThenDate	1	Show time, then date.

Next, set the DateOrder property as adhering to the MM/DD/YY format. Your other choices are DD/MM/YY or YY/MM/DD. Each will likely depend on the geographic location of your audience. You can also determine the date separators. Here we're using the forward slash, but other regions use dashes and colons. You can format the month, day, and year parts of a date specifically via the MonthFormat, DayFormat, and YearFormat properties, respectively. The enumerators that handle these formatting options are shown in Tables 8-12, 8-13, and 8-14.

Table 8-12. *CrMonthFormatEnum Enumerator Members*

Name	Value	Description
crMonthFormatLeadingZeroNumericMonth	1	Leading zero numeric month
crMonthFormatLongMonth	3	Long month
crMonthFormatNoMonth	4	No month
crMonthFormatNumericMonth	0	Numeric month
crMonthFormatShortMonth	2	Short month

Table 8-13. *CrDayFormatEnum Enumerator Members*

Name	Value	Description
crDayFormatLeadingZeroNumericDay	1	Leading zero numeric day
crDayFormatNoDay	2	No day
crDayFormatNumericDay	0	Numeric day

Table 8-14. *CrYearFormatEnum Enumerator Members*

Name	Value	Description
crYearFormatLongYear	1	Long year
crYearFormatNoYear	2	No year
crYearFormatShortYear	0	Short year

String   Strings may also need some level of formatting. You'll see this primarily when dealing with text that wraps and when attempting to insert RTF or HTML text. The code shown in Listing 8-21 illustrates how to format a string that can wrap to a maximum of two lines.

Listing 8-21. *Formatting a String*

```
FieldFormat oFieldFormat;

oFieldFormat = new FieldFormatClass();

oFieldFormat.StringFormat.TextFormat =
   CrTextFormatEnum.crTextFormatStandardText;
oFieldFormat.StringFormat.EnableWordWrap = true;
oFieldFormat.StringFormat.MaxNumberOfLines = 2;
```

In this example, we used plain text, and so the TextFormat property was set to CrTextFormatEnum.crTextFormatStandardText. The string could also be formatted as either RTF or HTML as illustrated by the enumerator options listed in Table 8-15.

Table 8-15. *CrTextFormatEnum Enumerator Members*

Name	Value	Description
crTextFormatStandardText	0	Display as standard text.
crTextFormatHTMLText	2	Interpret HTML string.
crTextFormatRTFText	1	Interpret RTF string.

Boolean   The Boolean formatting options are rather simple as there is only one property—BooleanFormat.OutputFormat as shown here:

```
oFieldFormat.BooleanFormat.OutputFormat =
   CrBooleanOutputFormatEnum.crBooleanOutputFormatYesOrNo;
```

By assigning this property to one of the enumerated values shown in Table 8-16, you can determine how the underlying Boolean value will be displayed: T or F, Yes or No, etc.

Table 8-16. *CrBooleanOutputFormatEnum Enumerator Members*

Name	Value	Description
crBooleanOutputFormatOneOrZero	4	Display as "1" or "0".
crBooleanOutputFormatTOrF	1	Display as "T" or "F".
crBooleanOutputFormatTrueOrFalse	0	Display as "True" or "False".
crBooleanOutputFormatYesOrNo	2	Display as "Yes" or "No".
crBooleanOutputFormatYOrN	3	Display as "Y" or "N".

Fonts

You can control the appearance of your report by creating Font objects. In the CreateFont() method shown in Listing 8-22, the full namespace of the Font class is used to avoid conflict with the Font class offered by .NET. In an example of less-than-intuitive class naming, the RAS uses a FontColor class, rather than a Font class, as its principal object. The FontColor object has a Font property to which you can set a Font object that specifies the name, size, and other attributes of a font.

Listing 8-22. *Creating Fonts*

```
public FontColor CreateFont(string szFontName,
    decimal iSize,
    bool bBold,
    bool bItalic,
    bool bStrikethrough,
    bool bUnderline,
    Color oColor)
{
    CrystalDecisions.ReportAppServer.ReportDefModel.Font oFont;
    FontColor oFontColor;

    oFont = new FontClass();
    oFont.Name = szFontName;
    oFont.Size = iSize;
    oFont.Bold = bBold;
    oFont.Italic = bItalic;
    oFont.Strikethrough = bStrikethrough;
    oFont.Underline = bUnderline;

    oFontColor = new FontColor();
    oFontColor.Font = oFont;
    oFontColor.Color = uint.Parse(ColorTranslator.ToWin32(oColor).ToString());

    return oFontColor;
}
```

Note It's helpful to declare all the FontColor objects that you will use in a report at the beginning of your report class with class-wide scope. That way they will be visible to the methods that create the individual reports and so ensure a consistent look-and-feel across all your report output.

Listing 8-23 shows how to instantiate a series of FontColor objects that, as suggested by their names, are used for various areas of the report. The invocation of the AddField() method shows the FontColor object being passed to a FieldObject.

Listing 8-23. *Using Fonts*

```
FontColor oCompanyHeaderFieldFont;
FontColor oOrderHeaderTextFont;
FontColor oOrderHeaderFieldFont;
FontColor oDetailHeaderTextFont;
FontColor oDetailHeaderFieldFont;

oCompanyHeaderFieldFont = CreateFont("Arial", 10,
    true, true, false, false, Color.Black);
oOrderHeaderTextFont = CreateFont("Arial", 10,
    true, false, false, false, Color.Black);
oOrderHeaderFieldFont = CreateFont("Arial", 10,
    false, false, false, false, Color.Black);
oDetailHeaderTextFont = CreateFont("Arial", 10,
    false, false, false, false, Color.Black);
oDetailHeaderFieldFont = CreateFont("Arial", 10,
    false, false, false, false, Color.Black);

AddField(oReportClientDocument, oSection, oCompanyHeaderFieldFont,
    CrAlignmentEnum.crAlignmentLeft, "spc_SalesOrders;1",
"CompanyName", 0, 0, 2880, 250);
```

Working with Shapes

You can make a report look very sharp and professional by adding different shapes, particularly lines and boxes, to accentuate important data. The RAS provides the LineObject and BoxObject classes to create these shapes.

Lines

Lines can start and end at almost any point on the page, provided they are either horizontal or vertical. Diagonal lines are not supported. You can determine the type of line—solid, dashed, etc.—the thickness, and the color. The following code displays a dark green line across the page header:

```
oSection = oReportClientDocument.ReportDefinition.PageHeaderArea.Sections[0];

AddLine(oReportClientDocument, oSection, Color.DarkSeaGreen,
    CrLineStyleEnum.crLineStyleSingle, 3, 10, 720, 720, 8000);
```

The AddLine() method is shown in Listing 8-24.

Listing 8-24. *Drawing Lines*

```
public void AddLine(ReportClientDocument oReportClientDocument,
    Section oSection,
    Color oLineColor,
    CrLineStyleEnum sLineStyleEnum,
    int iLineThickness,
    int iLeft,
    int iTop,
    int iBottom,
    int iRight)

{

    LineObject oLineObject;

    oLineObject = new LineObject();

    oLineObject.Top = iTop;
    oLineObject.Bottom = iBottom;
    oLineObject.Left = iLeft;
    oLineObject.Right = iRight;
    oLineObject.LineThickness = iLineThickness;
    oLineObject.LineStyle = sLineStyleEnum;
    oLineObject.EndSectionName = oSection.Name;
    oLineObject.LineColor =
        uint.Parse(ColorTranslator.ToWin32(oLineColor).ToString());

    oReportClientDocument.ReportDefController.
        ReportObjectController.Add(oLineObject, oSection, -1);

}
```

These property settings are all self-explanatory except for EndSectionName. This property stores the name of the section where the line will end.

Boxes

Boxes are another object that can enhance your report display. First, it's important to understand when boxes should and should not be used. If you need to highlight an entire section, you only need to set the background color for that section. Likewise, should you need to highlight a particular field, you can set the border style, border color, and background color for that field. Borders are discussed in the next section. Boxes, like lines, are independent objects on the page not associated with particular fields. The method to add a box to the report is shown in Listing 8-25.

Listing 8-25. *Drawing Boxes*

```
public void AddBox(ReportClientDocument oReportClientDocument,
    Section oSection,
    Color oLineColor,
    Color oFillColor,
    CrLineStyleEnum sLineStyleEnum,
    int iLineThickness,
    int iLeft,
    int iTop,
    int iRight,
    int iBottom)

{
    BoxObject oBoxObject;

    oBoxObject = new BoxObject();

    oBoxObject.Top = iTop;
    oBoxObject.Bottom = iBottom;
    oBoxObject.Left = iLeft;
    oBoxObject.Right = iRight;
    oBoxObject.LineThickness = iLineThickness;
    oBoxObject.LineStyle = sLineStyleEnum;
    oBoxObject.EndSectionName = oSection.Name;
    oBoxObject.LineColor =
        uint.Parse(ColorTranslator.ToWin32(oLineColor).ToString());
    oBoxObject.FillColor =
        uint.Parse(ColorTranslator.ToWin32(oFillColor).ToString());

    oReportClientDocument.ReportDefController.
        ReportObjectController.Add(oBoxObject, oSection, -1);
}
```

As with the LineObject, these property settings are all self-explanatory except for EndSectionName. This property stores the name of the section where the bottom of the box will anchor.

Borders

Border objects define the lines that appear around a field. These lines can be dashed, dotted, double, or single, or you don't need a line at all. The top, bottom, left, and right sides of a field can each have their own line type. You can set the border's color and determine a background color as well. The code in Listing 8-26 shows how to add a rather garish border and color schema to a field.

Listing 8-26. *Defining Borders*

```
Border oBorder;

oBorder = new BorderClass();

oBorder.BorderColor =
   uint.Parse(ColorTranslator.ToWin32(Color.DarkRed).ToString());
oBorder.BackgroundColor =
   uint.Parse(ColorTranslator.ToWin32(Color.LightGreen).ToString());
oBorder.BottomLineStyle = CrLineStyleEnum.crLineStyleDashed;
oBorder.LeftLineStyle = CrLineStyleEnum.crLineStyleDotted;
oBorder.RightLineStyle = CrLineStyleEnum.crLineStyleNoLine;
oBorder.TopLineStyle = CrLineStyleEnum.crLineStyleSingle;

//Assign the border object to the field object
oFieldObject.Border = oBorder;
```

Because borders appear just outside the limits of the field, you need to make sure there is sufficient buffer space between the field and the object around it so the border will display. For example, if you display a field with a Top property set to zero, you will not see the top border line. Change the Top property to 30, and the field will display similar to the image in Figure 8-8.

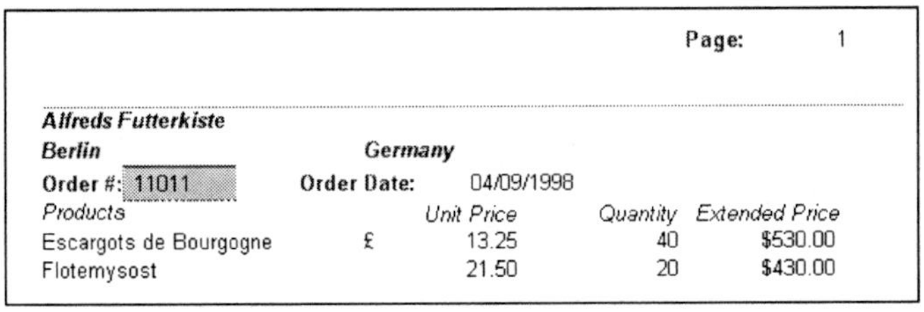

Figure 8-8. *Field border*

Exporting Reports

One area where the RAS can overcome a noticeable limitation in the SDK is in the area of exporting a report instance to a different format. Suppose you have a report that needs to be run to Excel, PDF, and Word to meet the preferences of the individual users who requested it. You could always run the report three times and each time output to a different format. Obviously, this would waste server and database resources, as the same resources are used each time the report is run. Rather, you could run the report just once and save it to a Crystal report format as shown in Listing 8-27.

Listing 8-27. *Scheduling a Report to Run Immediately*

```
szSQL = "SELECT SI_ID " +
   "FROM CI_INFOOBJECTS " +
   "WHERE SI_ID = " + szReportID;
```

```
oReports = oInfoStore.Query(szSQL);

oReport = oReports[1];

oPluginInterface = oReport.GetPluginInterface("");
oReportPlugIn = new Report(oPluginInterface);

oReport.SchedulingInfo.RightNow = true;
oReport.SchedulingInfo.Type = CeScheduleType.ceScheduleTypeOnce;

oReportFormatOpts = oReportPlugIn.ReportFormatOptions;
oReportFormatOpts.Format = CeReportFormat.ceFormatCrystalReport;

oInfoStore.Schedule(oReports);
```

This code runs the selected report immediately. You can keep checking the status of the report job to determine when it is complete before you continue processing. The loop that accomplishes this is shown in Listing 8-28.

Listing 8-28. *Iterating Until a Scheduled Report Is Completed*

```
//This will be the SI_ID value of the report once it is written to the InfoStore
szReportID = oReport.Properties["SI_NEW_JOB_ID"].Value.ToString();

do
{
    szSQL = "SELECT SI_SCHEDULE_STATUS " +
            "FROM CI_INFOOBJECTS " +
            "WHERE SI_ID = " + szReportID;

    oScheduledObjects = oInfoStore.Query(szSQL);

    iStatus = oScheduledObjects[1].SchedulingInfo.Status;

    if (iStatus == CeScheduleStatus.ceStatusFailure)
      break;

    //Wait half a second and try again
    System.Threading.Thread.Sleep(500);

} while (((iStatus != CeScheduleStatus.ceStatusSuccess)));
```

Once the job completes, you can extract the report based on the SI_ID property and, using the RAS's OpenDocument() method, create an object of type ReportClientDocument that encapsulates the report. The PrintOutputController object has a method called Export to which you can pass the format of the destination output—in this example, a PDF file. The report instance will then be converted to a ByteArray that you can send to a file via the FileStream object. This export logic is shown in Listing 8-29.

Listing 8-29. *Outputting Report to PDF*

```
szSQL = "SELECT SI_ID " +
    "FROM CI_INFOOBJECTS " +
    "WHERE SI_ID = " + szReportID;

oReports = oInfoStore.Query(szSQL);

oReport = oReports[1];

oEnterpriseService = oEnterpriseSession.GetService("","RASReportFactory");
oReportAppFactory = ((ReportAppFactory) oEnterpriseService.Interface);
oReportClientDocument = oReportAppFactory.OpenDocument(oReport.ID, 0);

oPrintOutputController = oReportClientDocument.PrintOutputController;

aByteArray = oPrintOutputController.
    Export(CrReportExportFormatEnum.crReportExportFormatPDF, 0);
aByte = aByteArray.ByteArray;

oFileStream = new System.IO.
    FileStream(@"c:\temp\myreport.pdf", System.IO.FileMode.Create);
oFileStream.Write(aByte, 0, aByte.Length - 1);
oFileStream.Close();
```

At this point, you could write the exported file back to the InfoStore or leave it on disk. You don't need to save it to a disk file at all. You could send the ByteArray directly to the browser as shown in Listing 8-30.

Listing 8-30. *Streaming Report to the Browser*

```
Response.Clear();
Response.AddHeader("content-disposition", "inline;filename=untitled.pdf");
Response.ContentType = "application/pdf";
Response.BinaryWrite(aByte);
Response.End();
```

Setting Parameters

Report parameters can either be gateways to filtering data in your stored procedure or externally configurable settings within your report. For example, you could have a parameter that determines whether a certain column is displayed or suppressed depending on the security rights of the user running the report. You can control the parameter settings through the DataDefController.ParameterFieldController class of the ReportClientDocument object. The code to alter report parameters is shown in Listing 8-31.

Listing 8-31. *Setting Parameter Values*

```
oReportClientDocument =
    oReportAppFactory.OpenDocument(int.Parse("1266"), 0);

ParameterFieldController oParameterFieldController;

oParameterFieldController =
    oReportClientDocument.DataDefController.ParameterFieldController;

oParameterFieldController.SetCurrentValue("", "@Country", "UK");
oParameterFieldController.SetCurrentValue("", "@ReportsTo", 2);

crystalReportViewer1.ReportSource = oReportClientDocument;
```

> ■**Note** There is a bug that can cause an "Unknown Database Connector Error" if your data source references a table name that has a space in it. This problem has been resolved by a hot fix, so make sure you have the latest one applied. This error can also be caused if you fail to set the parameter's values before changing the data source location. Type errors can also trigger this problem, for example, passing a numeric value instead of a string.

Filtering Reports

Filters restrict the data that can be seen in a report after the data has been returned from the data source. This is different than passing parameters to the stored procedure and running a new report every time on a data set that is filtered by SQL on the database server. You may apply filters to both the group and record data. Listing 8-32 shows a filter applied to a group. In this example, we're restricting the data to the orders of one company only.

Listing 8-32. *Setting a Group Filter*

```
FilterController oFilterController;
string szFilter;

oFilterController =
    oReportClientDocument.DataDefController.GroupFilterController;

szFilter = "{spc_SalesOrders;1.CompanyName} = 'Around the Horn'";

oFilterController.SetFormulaText(szFilter);
```

Next we'll see how to restrict the report's data to only those records for companies located in the United States. Listing 8-33 shows how this is done.

Listing 8-33. *Setting a Record Filter*

```
oFilterController =
    oReportClientDocument.DataDefController.RecordFilterController;

szFilter = "{spc_SalesOrders;1.Country} = 'USA'";

oFilterController.SetFormulaText(szFilter);
```

Frequently filters are helpful when you wish to do report bursting. If you have a sales report grouped by sales representative, for example, and you wish to send each salesperson a report containing just his data, you could filter this combined report for each individual sales rep. The data source does not need to be hit each time, and management can still see the combined report.

Sorting

The RAS allows you to set or change the sort order of a report without needing to rerun the report entirely with a new ORDER BY designation. This is handled through the SortController class of the DataDefController. You can perform simple sorts via the ModifySortDirection() method. ModifySortDirection() takes two parameters. The first is the index of the object to be sorted—in this example the group index. The second is a member of the CrSortDirectionEnum enumerator that indicates the sort direction. The members of this enumerator are listed in Table 8-17.

Table 8-17. *CrSortDirectionEnum Enumerator Members*

Name	Value	Description
crSortDirectionAscendingOrder	0	Ascending order
crSortDirectionBottomNOrder	5	Bottom n order
crSortDirectionBottomNPercentage	7	Bottom n percentage
crSortDirectionDescendingOrder	1	Descending order
crSortDirectionTopNOrder	4	Top n order
crSortDirectionTopNPercentage	6	Top n percentage

The code shown in Listing 8-34 demonstrates how to set the sort order for the first group—company name—in descending order.

Listing 8-34. *Sorting the First Group in Descending Order*

```
SortController oSortController;

oSortController = oReportClientDocument.DataDefController.SortController;

oSortController.ModifySortDirection(0,
    CrSortDirectionEnum.crSortDirectionDescendingOrder);
```

The first page of the newly sorted report is shown in Figure 8-9.

```
Wolski Zajazd
Warszawa                    Poland
Order #: 10374      Order Date:    12/05/1996
Products                      Unit Price      Quantity   Extended Price
Escargots de Bourgogne      £      10.60           15         $159.00
Gorgonzola Telino                  10.00           30         $300.00


Order #: 10611      Order Date:    07/25/1997
Products                      Unit Price      Quantity   Extended Price
Camembert Pierrot                  34.00           15         $510.00
Chai                               18.00            6         $108.00
Chang                              19.00           10         $190.00


Order #: 10792      Order Date:    12/23/1997
Products                      Unit Price      Quantity   Extended Price
Chang                              19.00           10         $190.00
Scottish Longbreads                12.50           15         $187.50
Tourtière                           7.45            3          $22.35


Order #: 10870      Order Date:    02/04/1998
Products                      Unit Price      Quantity   Extended Price
Manjimup Dried Apples              53.00            2         $106.00
Steeleye Stout                     18.00            3          $54.00


Order #: 10906      Order Date:    02/25/1998
Products                      Unit Price      Quantity   Extended Price
Sirop d'érable                     28.50           15         $427.50


Order #: 10998      Order Date:    04/03/1998
Products                      Unit Price      Quantity   Extended Price
Guaraná Fantástica                  4.50           12          $54.00
Longlife Tofu                      10.00           20         $200.00
Rhönbräu Klosterbier                7.75           30         $232.50
Sirop d'érable                     28.50            7         $199.50


Order #: 11044      Order Date:    04/23/1998
Products                      Unit Price      Quantity   Extended Price
Tarte au sucre                     49.30           12         $591.60

                                                            $3,531.95
Wilman Kala
Helsinki                    Finland
Order #: 10615      Order Date:    07/30/1997
```

Figure 8-9. *Company group sorted in descending order*

The code shown in Listing 8-35 sorts the company name in ascending order and the order numbers within each company in descending order (grouping index 2).

Listing 8-35. *Sorting Both Groups*

```
oSortController.ModifySortDirection(0,
    CrSortDirectionEnum.crSortDirectionAscendingOrder);

oSortController.ModifySortDirection(1,
    CrSortDirectionEnum.crSortDirectionDescendingOrder);
```

This code produces the output displayed in Figure 8-10.

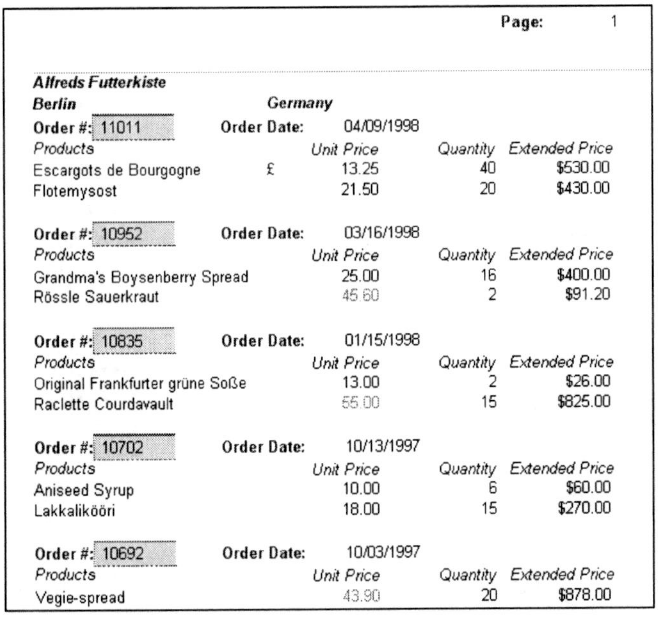

Figure 8-10. *Order group sorted in descending order*

If you want to restrict the report to a certain number or percentage of records based on a summary field, you can do so with the TopNSort class. Suppose you wish to sort the report data based on total sales for each company, and you are only interested in the top three customers. The code in Listing 8-36 will restrict the report output for you.

Listing 8-36. *Applying a Top N Filter*

```
ISCRField oSummaryField;
TopNSort oTopNSort;

oSummaryField =
    oReportClientDocument.DataDefController.DataDefinition.SummaryFields[0];

oTopNSort = new TopNSort();
oTopNSort.Direction = CrSortDirectionEnum.crSortDirectionTopNOrder;
oTopNSort.DiscardOthers = true;
oTopNSort.NIndividualGroups = 3;
oTopNSort.SortField = oSummaryField;

oReportClientDocument.DataDefController.SortController.Add(-1, oTopNSort);
```

In this example, we are assuming that the zero element of the SummaryFields represents the summary field we want to sort by. Then, we need to set the Direction property of the sort to a member of the CrSortDirectionEnum enumerator. This is where the name TopNSort class becomes something of a misnomer. You can also retrieve the bottom numbers as well should you want to display your smallest customers.

The DiscardOthers property will determine whether the customers who don't fit in the specified top (or bottom) number (or percentage) will appear in the report or not. NIndividualGroups
determines how many groupings will actually appear.

Charts

A picture is proverbially worth a thousand words, so there's nothing like graphing business
data to make a report come alive. Fortunately, the RAS provides a programmatic interface to
the Crystal Reports charting features. Suppose you want to graph the sales of your main customers in a bar chart. First, you'll need to define the x and y coordinates. The x coordinate—which
appears across the bottom of the chart—is the names of the customers. The y coordinate,
which appears to the left of the chart, is the total sales amount. The code in Listing 8-37 invokes
the AddChart() method, which receives as parameters the chart captions, an enumerated
value indicating the type of chart, and the location of the chart itself.

Listing 8-37. *Defining a Chart*

```
DataDefinition oDataDefinition;

oDataDefinition =
    oReportClientDocument.DataDefController.DataDefinition;

oSection =
    oReportClientDocument.ReportDefinition.ReportFooterArea.Sections[0];

AddChart(oReportClientDocument, oSection,
    oDataDefinition.Groups[0].ConditionField,
    oDataDefinition.SummaryFields[0],
    CrChartStyleTypeEnum.crChartStyleTypeBar,
    "Sales Report", "(by Customer)",
    "This footnote is cool, isn't it?", 5000, 100);
```

The AddChart() method is shown in Listing 8-38.

Listing 8-38. *AddChart() Method*

```
private void AddChart(ReportClientDocument oReportClientDocument,
    Section oSection,
    ISCRField oConditionField,
    ISCRField oDataField,
    CrChartStyleTypeEnum sChartStyleTypeEnum,
    string szTitle,
    string szSubTitle,
    string szFootnote,
    int iHeight,
    int iTop)
{
    ChartDefinition oChartDefinition;
    ChartObject oChartObject;
```

```
//Define a ChartDefinition class to hold the condition (x axis)
//and data fields (y axis) for the chart.
oChartDefinition = new ChartDefinitionClass();
oChartDefinition.ChartType = CrChartTypeEnum.crChartTypeGroup;
oChartDefinition.ConditionFields.Add(oConditionField);
oChartDefinition.DataFields.Add(oDataField);

//Instantiate the chart object and assign the data definitions established
//in the ChartDefinition class. Indicate the type of chart to display.
oChartObject = new ChartObjectClass();
oChartObject.ChartDefinition = oChartDefinition;
oChartObject.ChartStyle.Type = sChartStyleTypeEnum;
oChartObject.ChartStyle.TextOptions.Title = szTitle;
oChartObject.ChartStyle.TextOptions.Subtitle = szSubTitle;
oChartObject.ChartStyle.TextOptions.Footnote = szFootnote;
oChartObject.Height = iHeight;
oChartObject.Width = oSection.Width;
oChartObject.Top = iTop;

//Add the chart object to the desired section of the report.
//In this case the report footer.
oReportClientDocument.ReportDefController.
   ReportObjectController.Add(oChartObject, oSection, 0);
}
```

The ConditionFields() method of the ChartDefinition class receives the fields that plot the points on the graph. In this case, we're interested in the ConditionField of the first group in the report (the customer level). This field is added to the ConditionFields method of the ChartDefinition class. Next you'll need to define data fields for the y axis. In this case, it is the first summary field in the report, which shows total sales by customer. At this point, you can instantiate a ChartObjectClass object that will receive the ChartDefinition object as well as allow customization of the titles. The ChartStyle.Type property allows you to specify a member of the CrChartStyleTypeEnum enumerator, which determines the type of graph that will be displayed. The members of this class are shown in Table 8-18.

Table 8-18. *CrChartStyleTypeEnum Enumerator Members*

Name	Value	Description
crChartStyleType3DRiser	5	3D riser
crChartStyleType3DSurface	6	3D surface
crChartStyleTypeArea	2	Area
crChartStyleTypeBar	0	Bar
crChartStyleTypeBubble	9	Bubble
crChartStyleTypeDoughnut	4	Doughnut
crChartStyleTypeLine	1	Line
crChartStyleTypePie	3	Pie

Continued

Table 8-18. *Continued*

Name	Value	Description
crChartStyleTypeRadar	8	Radar
crChartStyleTypeStocked	10	Stocked
crChartStyleTypeUnknown	100	Unknown
crChartStyleTypeUserDefined	50	User defined
crChartStyleTypeXYScatter	7	X/Y scatter

This code produces the chart shown in Figure 8-11.

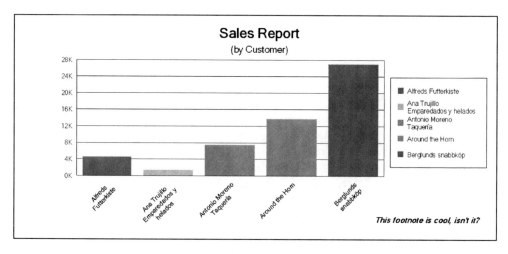

Figure 8-11. *Chart output*

Report Options

Crystal Reports offers an extensive selection of report options that that you can set by selecting File ➤ Options from the main menu. The RAS encapsulates some of these choices in the ReportOptions class. Using ReportOptions, you can specify many of the settings shown on the Crystal Reports options screens in Figures 8-12 and 8-13.

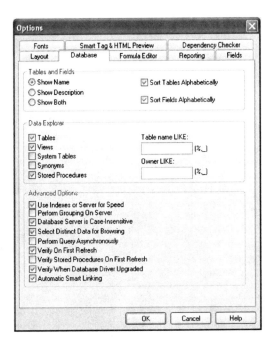

Figure 8-12. *Crystal Reports Database Options screen*

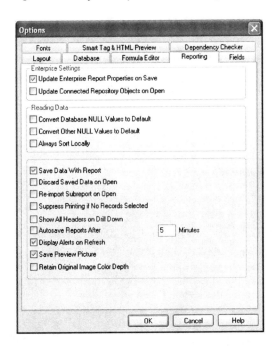

Figure 8-13. *Crystal Reports Reporting Options screen*

The code in Listing 8-39 is not a mirror image of these screens, but you can certainly see the similarities.

Listing 8-39. *Setting Report Options*

```
ReportOptions oReportOptions;

oReportOptions = new ReportOptions();
oReportOptions.DisplayGroupContentView = true;
oReportOptions.EnableAsyncQuery = true;
oReportOptions.EnablePushDownGroupBy = true;
oReportOptions.EnableSaveDataWithReport = true;
oReportOptions.EnableSaveSummariesWithReport = true;
oReportOptions.EnableSelectDistinctRecords = true;
oReportOptions.EnableTranslateDOSMemos = true;
oReportOptions.EnableTranslateDOSStrings = true;
oReportOptions.EnableUseCaseInsensitiveSQLData = true;
oReportOptions.EnableUseDummyData = true;
oReportOptions.EnableUseIndexForSpeed = true;
oReportOptions.EnableVerifyOnEveryPrint = true;
oReportOptions.ErrorOnMaxNumOfRecords = true;
oReportOptions.InitialDataContext;
oReportOptions.MaxNumOfRecords = 10000;
oReportOptions.NumOfBrowsingRecords = 10000;
oReportOptions.NumOfCachedBatches = 10000;
oReportOptions.PreferredView = CrReportDocumentViewEnum.crReportDocumentReportView;
oReportOptions.RefreshCEProperties = true;
oReportOptions.ReportStyle = CrReportStyleEnum.crReportStyleExecutiveLeadingBreak;
oReportOptions.RowsetBatchSize = 10000;
oReportOptions.ConvertDateTimeType =
    CrConvertDateTimeTypeEnum.crConvertDateTimeTypeToDate;

oReportClientDocument.ModifyReportOptions(oReportOptions);
```

Summary Information

Crystal Reports offers a summary information screen for each report. This screen, shown in Figure 8-14, allows you to set descriptive properties for a report like the author's name, the title, keywords, etc.

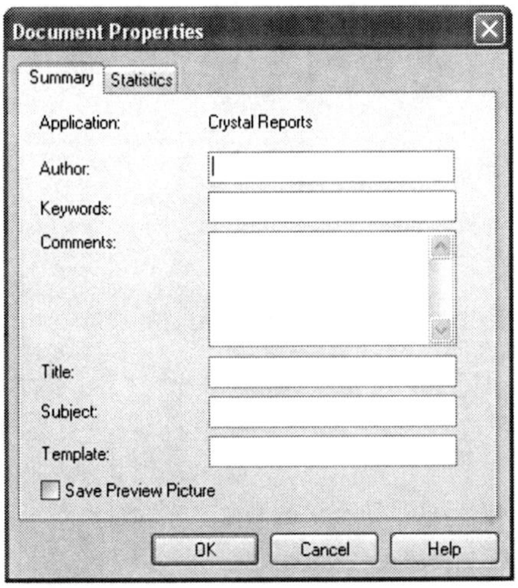

Figure 8-14. *Crystal Reports Summary screen*

Except for the `Template` field, this same information is available to you programmatically through the `SummaryInfo` object. You can instantiate this object, assign the properties, and apply it to the main document via the `ModifySummaryInfo()` method as shown in Listing 8-40.

Listing 8-40. *Assigning Summary Information*

```
SummaryInfo oSummaryInfo;

oSummaryInfo = new SummaryInfo();

oSummaryInfo.Author = "Carl Ganz, Jr.";
oSummaryInfo.Keywords = "Financial;Orders";
oSummaryInfo.Comments = "This is the report which lists " +
   "the order details for each customer";
oSummaryInfo.Title = "Order Details Report";
oSummaryInfo.Subject = "Order Details";
oSummaryInfo.IsSavingWithPreview = true; //save a thumbnail image?

oReportClientDocument.ModifySummaryInfo(oSummaryInfo);
```

Printing Reports

Part and parcel of printing reports is establishing the type of page you'll be working with. In Crystal Reports, the first thing you'll need to do when creating a new report is to determine the margins, paper size, and orientation. This will determine the size and shape of the layout page in the report designer. These settings may be handled programmatically as well via the `PrintOptions` object. The code shown in Listing 8-41 illustrates how to set up a typical letter-size report.

Listing 8-41. *Setting the Print Options*

```
PrintOptions oPrintOptions;

oPrintOptions = new PrintOptionsClass();
oPrintOptions.PaperSize = CrPaperSizeEnum.crPaperSizePaperLetter;
oPrintOptions.PaperSource = CrPaperSourceEnum.crPaperSourceAuto;
oPrintOptions.PrinterDuplex = CrPrinterDuplexEnum.crPrinterDuplexDefault;
```

You have a couple of options when working with the paper orientation. You can set it through the PrintOptions object like this:

```
oPrintOptions.PaperOrientation =
    CrPaperOrientationEnum.crPaperOrientationLandscape;
```

or you can use the ModifyPaperOrientation() method like this:

```
oReportClientDocument.PrintOutputController.
    ModifyPaperOrientation(CrPaperOrientationEnum.crPaperOrientationLandscape);
```

Setting the page margins can also be accomplished through a direct method like this:

```
oReportClientDocument.PrintOutputController.
    ModifyPageMargins(770, 770, 1440, 1440);
```

or you can use a PageMargins object as shown in Listing 8-42. Here you can set the margin properties of the PageMargins object directly and then assign this object to the PageMargins property of the PrintOptions object.

Listing 8-42. *PageMargins Object*

```
PageMargins oPageMargins;

oPageMargins = new PageMarginsClass();
oPageMargins.Left = 770;
oPageMargins.Right = 770;
oPageMargins.Top = 1440;
oPageMargins.Bottom = 1440;
oPrintOptions.PageMargins = oPageMargins;
```

When your page setup is complete, you can commit the PrintOptions object settings to the report via the ModifyPrintOptions() method as shown here:

```
oReportClientDocument.PrintOutputController.ModifyPrintOptions(oPrintOptions);
```

You can obtain a reference to the current report settings before making any modifications by invoking the GetPrintOptions() method as shown in the following code:

```
oPrintOptions = oReportClientDocument.PrintOutputController.GetPrintOptions();
```

Saving Reports

After you've created the report, you'll likely want to save it either to a disk file or to the InfoStore. Before you can save the report to a disk file, you'll need to specify the RAS Report Directory in the Central Configuration Manager. Stop the RAS and select the Parameters tab on the Properties dialog. Select Server in the Option Type combo box, and you'll see a text box called Report Directory as shown in Figure 8-15.

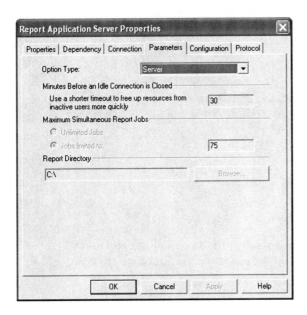

Figure 8-15. *RAS Properties dialog, Parameters tab*

Here you may wish to enter "C:\" to make the entire local drive visible to the RAS. Any subdirectory that you now specify when saving a report will be visible as well. If you try to save a report to a directory that is not visible to the RAS, you'll receive an "access denied" error. Listing 8-43 shows how a report is written to disk.

Listing 8-43. *Saving a Report to Disk*

```
object oTarget;

oTarget = @"c:\temp";

oReportClientDocument.SaveAs("myreport.rpt", ref oTarget,
    ((int) CdReportClientDocumentSaveAsOptionsEnum.
        cdReportClientDocumentSaveAsOverwriteExisting));
```

The Save() method will commit your changes to the InfoStore rather than to a disk file. In the example shown in Listing 8-44, an existing report is opened, a change is made to it, and the modified report is saved back to the InfoStore.

Listing 8-44. *Saving a Report to Disk*

```
oReportClientDocument =
    oReportAppFactory.OpenDocument(int.Parse("1266"), 0);

oSection = oReportClientDocument.ReportDefinition.PageHeaderArea.Sections[0];

AddBox(oReportClientDocument, oSection, Color.Black, Color.Yellow,
    CrLineStyleEnum.crLineStyleSingle, 3, 9000, 720, 9500, 1100);

oReportClientDocument.Save();
```

If you've created a new report using the RAS, you can save it to the InfoStore using an undocumented feature of the SaveAs() method. By creating an object type variable to store the SI_ID of the target folder, you can save your report to that folder as shown in the following code:

```
object oFolderID;

oFolderID = 1233;

oReportClientDocument.SaveAs("Orders Report", ref oFolderID, 0);
```

Though this feature is undocumented, it is supported. Business Objects has not updated the documentation to include this, nor could you infer from the IntelliSense that you can save new reports to a designated folder.

Summary

The RAS is a powerful programming model that gives you almost full control over the structures of your reports. What we covered in this chapter will enable you to perform most of the report creation and modification tasks that you'll likely encounter, but by no means did we cover all the RAS has to offer. To do that subject justice would require a small book. We looked at how to establish a connection to the InfoStore and how to access data sources, whether through stored procedures or as linked tables. Then, we covered the creation of data fields, special fields, formula fields, and summary fields. We examined grouping and even how to create charts.

In the next chapter, we'll look at all the programming concepts covered so far in a broader scope and discuss how to create enterprise solutions.

CHAPTER 9

■ ■ ■

Enterprise Solutions Using the BusinessObjects XI SDK

If you already have experience programming the BusinessObjects XI SDK, this may well be the chapter you turn to first. Here we'll build on what was discussed in the previous chapters to create real-world solutions using the BO XI object model. The material covered in this chapter is adapted from real-world solutions running in production environments. Much of what is described here should be provided by Business Objects as part of an out-of-the-box solution but, unfortunately, is not.

On-Demand Web Service

Possibly the most common tool a developer would need to integrate BusinessObjects XI–hosted reports with their associated applications is an on-demand web service. An on-demand web service offers the best of both worlds for application developers. It is very simple to use and consists of only one method call. If all you need to do is invoke BO XI hosted reports from your application, this web service method will do the trick.

The web service method receives as parameters the name of the main application folder, the name of the report, an enumerated value indicating the format of the report output (PDF, Word, Excel, ASCII, RTF, etc.), a user ID, an optional array of parameters, and another enumerated value indicating the return format of the report. The report is then scheduled to run immediately in BO XI, saved to a disk file of the requested format, and returned to the proxy application either as a Base64-encoded string or a web location reference. Listing 9-1 illustrates the call to the web service from the client application.

Listing 9-1. *Invoking the Web Service*

```
localhost.CEWebService oCEWebService;
localhost.CeReportFormat CeReportFormat;
localhost.CEResponse CEResponse;
DataTable oDT;
string[] aParameters = new string[1];
string szReport;
```

```
string szFileName;
int iUserID;
ListItem oListItem;

//Set report parameter. One parameter for each array element in
//the same ordinal position they are displayed in the parameters tab
aParameters[0] = txtLastName.Text;

oCEWebService = new localhost.CEWebService();
oCEWebService.Credentials = System.Net.CredentialCache.DefaultCredentials;

oListItem = ((ListItem) cmbFormat.SelectedItem);

//Format of report
CeReportFormat = ((localhost.CeReportFormat) Int32.Parse(oListItem.Value));

//What do we want back
CEResponse = localhost.CEResponse.Base64EncodedString;

//Local disk file where report will be created. GetExtension() is a web service
//method that provides the appropriate file extension for the export format
szFileName = @"c:\temp\myreport" +
    oCEWebService.GetExtension(CeReportFormat);

//Some unique ID for the currently logged in user
iUserID = 0;

szReport = oCEWebService.RunReportOnDemand("Dev",
    "Human Resources",
    "Employees",
    CeReportFormat,
    iUserID
    aParameters,
    CEResponse);

//Decode the string to a disk file
Base64Decode(szReport, szFileName);

//Open the file based on the application assigned to its extension
System.Diagnostics.Process.Start(szFileName);
```

On-Demand Web Service Internals

Let's examine how the inner working of the on-demand web service operates. This code touches on several of the most significant areas of the BO XI object model so when you understand how this works, you'll also have a solid understanding of the key features of the object model itself.

Output Options

Web services only transmit ASCII data in an XML wrapper. Therefore, you cannot directly transmit a PDF or an XLS file, for example, as these are both binary objects. You'll need, then, to convert these files into an ASCII format that can receive this XML wrapper—a feat you can achieve with Base64 encoding. Base64 encoding converts binary data into printable characters. The main drawback to this approach is that the resulting encoded data can be between 30 to 50 percent larger than the original file. Fortunately, .NET provides a method of the System namespace that handles Base64 encoding for you. The invocation of this method is shown in Listing 9-2.

Listing 9-2. *Base64Encode() Method*

```
private string Base64Encode(string szFileName)
{
    System.IO.FileStream oFileStream;
    int lBytes;
    string szResult;

    oFileStream = new System.IO.FileStream(szFileName,
        System.IO.FileMode.Open, System.IO.FileAccess.Read);

    byte[] aData = new byte[oFileStream.Length + 1];

    lBytes = oFileStream.Read(aData, 0, ((int) oFileStream.Length + 1));
    oFileStream.Close();

    szResult = System.Convert.ToBase64String(aData, 0, aData.Length);

    return szResult;
}
```

The Base64Encode() method loads the disk file into a FileStream object. Then, the ToBase64String() method receives as parameters an array of integers, an offset, and the length of the integer array. The final output is a text string that looks something like this:

```
JVBERiOxLjINJeLjz9MNCjEzMiAwIG9iagO8PCANLOxpbmVhcml6Z...
```

This string can be decoded client side by the Base64Decode() method shown in Listing 9-3.

Listing 9-3. *Base64Decode() Method*

```
public static void Base64Decode(string szData, string szFileName)
{
    byte[] aData;
    System.IO.FileStream oFileStream;
```

```
    aData = System.Convert.FromBase64String(szData);

    oFileStream = new System.IO.FileStream(szFileName,
        System.IO.FileMode.Create, System.IO.FileAccess.Write);
    oFileStream.Write(aData, 0, aData.Length - 1);
    oFileStream.Close();
}
```

You'll only want to return a Base64-encoded string to a desktop application, as the intent is to create the file on the client machine. You'll need to specify a target directory for this local file. Now whenever users of desktop-based applications run a report, the report file is always available to them on their machines. Many of my clients have used these export files to create rather elaborate archiving schemes showing the snapshots of their data at various points in time.

If your application is web-based, simply pass in the CEResponse.ServerFile enumerator. This will indicate to the web service to return a URL path to the output file's location on the web server, which you can display in a JavaScript window.open method call. After the user's web browser opens the file, he can then save the file locally. On the rare occasion that the file format is not recognized by the user's browser, the user will be prompted to save the file.

Running the Report

After logging on to the InfoStore, the first step the on-demand web service takes is to determine the location of the working directory. Since the web service needs to write a file to disk, the location of the target path needs to be extracted from the XML file depending on whether all the connection information was passed in or a connection indicator only—Dev, Prod, etc.— was passed in. This code is shown in Listing 9-4.

Listing 9-4. *Extracting the Working Directory*

```
if (szServer == null)
    szWorkingDirectory = GetDefaultWorkingDirectory();
else
    szWorkingDirectory = GetCEWorkingDirectory(szServer);
```

The next step is to retrieve an InfoStore object encapsulating the topmost application folder. This web service example uses folder and report names, rather than just a report ID, to locate the desired RPT entry. You may wish to change this when you adapt to your own application. Listing 9-5 shows the code that extracts the folder object from the InfoStore.

Listing 9-5. *Retrieving the Application Folder*

```
szSQL = "SELECT SI_ID,SI_NAME " +
    "FROM CI_INFOOBJECTS " +
    "WHERE SI_KIND = 'Folder' " +
    "AND SI_NAME = '" + szApplication + "'";

oFolders = oInfoStore.Query(szSQL);
oFolder = oFolders[1];
```

We can retrieve the desired report object itself by way of the InfoStore object that encapsulates the application folder. By referring to the SI_ANCESTOR property (see Listing 9-6), we can make sure we get the report regardless of how many folder levels it may be from the top while avoiding the use of recursion. Using SI_ANCESTOR will also ensure we are not confusing it with a report in another application that has the same name.

Listing 9-6. *Retrieving the Report Folder*

```
szSQL = "SELECT SI_ID, SI_NAME, SI_PROCESSINFO.SI_PROMPTS " +
    "FROM CI_INFOOBJECTS " +
    "WHERE SI_KIND = 'Report' " +
    "AND SI_INSTANCE = 0 " +
    "AND SI_ANCESTOR = " + oFolder.Properties["SI_ID"].ToString() +
    "AND SI_NAME = '" + szReportName + "'";

oReports = oInfoStore.Query(szSQL);
oReport = oReports[1];
```

The next step is to assign the parameter values, if any, passed in via the parameters array to the ReportParameters collection of the report. Listing 9-7 illustrates how to walk this array and assign the values by creating individual ReportParameterSingleValue objects.

Listing 9-7. *Assigning the Parameter Values*

```
oPluginInterface = oReport.GetPluginInterface("");
oReportPlugIn = new Report(oPluginInterface);

if (aParams != null)
{
    oReportParameters = oReportPlugIn.ReportParameters;

    iLength = aParams.Length - 1;

    if (oReportParameters.Count > 0)
    {
        for (int i = 0; i <= iLength; i++)
        {
            oReportParameterSingleValue = oReportParameters[i + 1].CreateSingleValue();
            oReportParameterSingleValue.Value = aParams[i];
            oReportParameters[i + 1].CurrentValues.Clear();
            oReportParameters[i + 1].CurrentValues.Add(oReportParameterSingleValue);
        }
    }
}
```

Note Be advised if you have unused parameters set up in your report, regardless of whether they came from the stored procedure or were created in Crystal by the report developer. Strange errors have been know to occur when running the report through the SDK, though the report may execute just fine when run in Crystal Reports or via the CMC. To debug, remove the unused parameters to see if the problem disappears.

At this point, the report is ready to run. You can use the SchedulingInfo object to cause the report to run immediately and specify the destination and output format. Make sure that you have the required destinations enabled on the BusinessObjects server. The user ID that you passed into the RunReport() method is used to facilitate the creation of a unique temporary file name. Though the file names in this example are created by using the system date and time down to the millisecond, it's still theoretically possible on high-concurrency systems to write two reports to the same file name and thus cause an error. The use of the user ID as part of the file name will eliminate this possibility. Listing 9-8 illustrates how this is accomplished.

Listing 9-8. *Scheduling the Report to Run Immediately*

```
//Create an interface to the scheduling options for the report.
oSchedulingInfo = oReport.SchedulingInfo;

//Run the report right now
oSchedulingInfo.RightNow = true;

//Run the report once only
oSchedulingInfo.Type = CeScheduleType.ceScheduleTypeOnce;

//When scheduling to all destinations except the printer,
//you must first retrieve the appropriate destination object.
//Each destination InfoObject is stored in the system
//table (CI_SYSTEMOBJECTS) under the Destination Plugins
//folder. This folder has an ID of 29.
szSQL = "Select Top 1* " +
    "From CI_SYSTEMOBJECTS " +
    "Where SI_PARENTID = 29 " +
    "And SI_NAME = 'DiskUnmanaged'";

oDestinationObjects = oInfoStore.Query(szSQL);

foreach(InfoObject oInfoObject in oDestinationObjects)
{
    oDestinationObject = oInfoObject;
    break;
}

//Create the DestinationPlugin object
oDisk = new DestinationPlugin(oDestinationObject.PluginInterface);
```

```
//Create a diskUnmanagedOptions object and its ScheduleOptions
//from the Destination plug-in
oDiskOpts = new DiskUnmanagedOptions(oDisk.ScheduleOptions);
oDiskOpts.DestinationFiles.Add(szWorkingDirectory + szFileName);

//Copy the properties from the Destination Plugin object into
//the report's scheduling information. This will cause the file
//to be transfered to disk after it has been run.
oDestination = oSchedulingInfo.Destination;
oDestination.SetFromPlugin(oDisk);

oInfoStore.Schedule(oReports);
```

> **Note** The advantage of running reports by scheduling them to run immediately is that an entry will be made in the report history so you'll have an audit trail of all activity.

Of course, you'll need a process to periodically clean out the working directory of the files it creates. The ability to view this directory on the server using Windows Explorer is an easy way to verify older output and perform debugging.

Because the scheduling changes are committed to the BO XI repository, you can use the Central Management Console to view the scheduled instance of the report. If an error occurs, you'll see a more detailed error message.

The code that checks for the completion of the scheduled task is shown in Listing 9-9. This check is accomplished by looping until the Status property of the SchedulingInfo object returns a success flag. Although this web service does not indicate a time-out period, it is a good idea to add one in, perhaps a variable that can be passed in as a parameter by the developer, so as not to get caught in an endless loop if an error occurs and no output file is ever created.

Listing 9-9. *Check for Completion of Report*

```
do
{
    if (!(oScheduledObjects == null))
    {
        oScheduledObjects.Dispose();
        oScheduledObjects = null;
    }

    szSQL = "Select SI_SCHEDULE_STATUS " +
        "From CI_INFOOBJECTS " +
        "Where SI_ID = " + oReports[1].Properties["SI_NEW_JOB_ID"].Value;

    oScheduledObjects = oInfoStore.Query(szSQL);

    foreach(InfoObject oInfoObject in oScheduledObjects)
```

```
        iStatus = oInfoObject.SchedulingInfo.Status;

    if (iStatus == CeScheduleStatus.ceStatusFailure)
        break;

    System.Threading.Thread.Sleep(500);

} while (iStatus != CeScheduleStatus.ceStatusSuccess);
```

The status of a job can be determined by checking the oInfoObject.SchedulingInfo.Status property. This property holds one of the enumerated values listed in Table 9-1.

Table 9-1. *CeScheduleStatus Enumerator Members*

Member	Value	Description
ceStatusFailure	3	The job failed. Check error message or outcome to get more information.
ceStatusPaused	8	The job is paused. Even if all dependencies are satisfied, it will not run.
ceStatusPending	9	The job has not started because dependencies are not satisfied. Dependencies include such things as time constraints and events.
ceStatusRunning	0	The job is currently being processed by the job server.
ceStatusSuccess	1	The job completed successfully.

Similar to the Status property is the Outcome property. Outcome holds the results of the latest job run on the report in the form of a CeScheduleOutcome enumerated value. The list of these enumerated values is shown in Table 9-2.

Table 9-2. *CeScheduleOutcome Enumerator Members*

Member	Value	Description
ceOutcomeFailComponentFailed	8	Object package failed due to a component failure.
ceOutcomeFailEndTime	5	The job's specified end time was exceeded.
ceOutcomeFailJobServer	3	An error occurred while processing a job on a job server.
ceOutcomeFailJobServerChild	7	The Job Server's child process is unresponsive.
ceOutcomeFailJobServerPlugin	2	An error occurred in the Job Server plug-in.
ceOutcomeFailObjectPackageFailed	9	Component failed due to an object package failure.
ceOutcomeFailSchedule	6	The scheduler caused the job to fail.
ceOutcomeFailSecurity	4	The user does not have enough rights to process the job.
ceOutcomePending	0	The job has not yet returned from the Job Server.
ceOutcomeSuccess	1	The job was scheduled successfully.

Finally, the server-based report file is converted to a Base64-encoded string for transmission back to the client application (see Listing 9-10) where it is decoded back into a disk file and opened for the user.

Listing 9-10. *Deliver the Base64-Encoded String*

```
if (sCEResponse == CEResponse.Base64EncodedString)
    szResult = Base64Encode(szWorkingDirectory + szFileName);
else
    szResult = szFileName;
```

Passing Connection Information

This web service did not receive database connection information as parameters because it assumes that this information was already stored in the CMC. Depending on your company's security requirements, this may not be permitted. If you want to apply the connection information programmatically, you can do so and apply it to the object model as shown in Listing 9-11.

Listing 9-11. *Passing Connection Information*

```
ReportLogons oLogons = null;
ReportLogon oLogon = null;

oPluginInterface = oReport.GetPluginInterface("");
oReportPlugIn = new Report(oPluginInterface);

oLogons = oReportPlugIn.ReportLogons;

oLogon = oLogons[1];

oLogon.UseOriginalDataSource = false;

oLogon.CustomDatabaseDLLName = szDatabaseDLLName;
oLogon.CustomServerName = szServerName;
oLogon.CustomDatabaseName = szDatabaseName;
oLogon.CustomUserName = szUserName;
oLogon.CustomPassword = szPassword;
```

An on-demand web service harnesses just part of the power of BO XI. In the next section, you'll learn about what many developers consider to be its most powerful feature—scheduling assemblies.

Scheduling Assemblies

Introduced in Crystal Enterprise 10, the ability to load EXEs (or Java applications or scripts) into the BO XI repository was probably the greatest feature enhancement ever made to the product. Now, rather than scheduling a report only, you can schedule a block of compiled code. This new feature truly opened up the product to the limits of a developer's imagination.

The first solution I developed involved report bursting. Using scheduled assemblies, we programmatically executed reports that went to different users. The report covered daily trading activity, and each user's report was based on the same RPT template but filtered by a different employee code.

Since 30 employees received the reports, we originally had to save 30 copies of the same report template to 30 different folders and set 30 different default parameters to the different employee codes. When the user wanted to make the slightest change to the report template, the RPT had to be saved 30 times and the default employee code parameters reset as well. This caused great anxiety to the system administrator (that was me, in case you were wondering), and so a better solution was obviously needed. After all, what if this same report went to 300 employees?

The solution was to build a front end that allowed the main end user of this report to maintain an Oracle table that stored the names of employees. Then, we built a .NET assembly that read from this table, iterated through the list of employee codes, assigned them individually to different instances of the report, and scheduled them to run immediately. At this point, the end user could add and remove employee designations to his heart's content without involving yours truly.

To install a program in the CMC, select the target folder and click the New Object button. You'll see the screen shown in Figure 9-1.

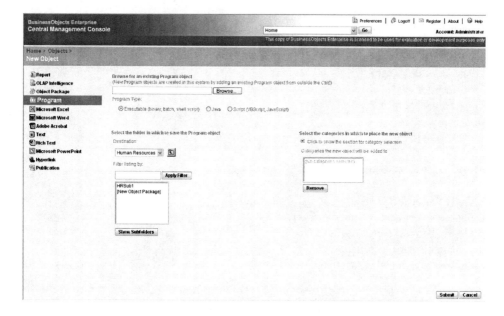

Figure 9-1. *Adding an assembly to the CMC*

Using the Browse button, select your EXE via the file dialog and submit the entry. You may need to add additional DLLs for runtime support or perhaps an XML file for connectivity information. If so, select the Auxiliary Files option under the Process tab and add the required files. This screen is shown in Figure 9-2.

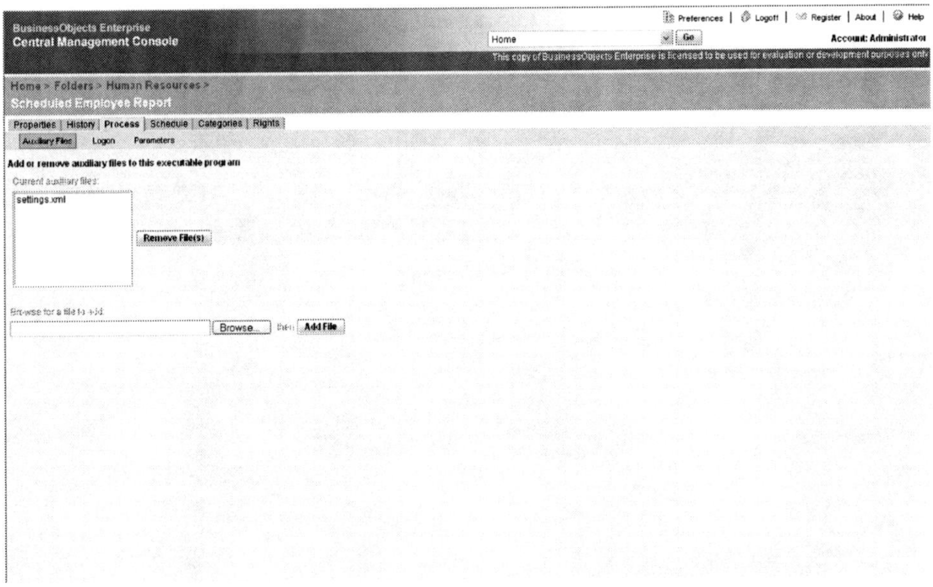

Figure 9-2. *Adding auxiliary files*

You'll need to provide logon credentials in order for the program to execute. You can add your Windows user ID and password through the Logon screen under Process. This screen is shown in Figure 9-3.

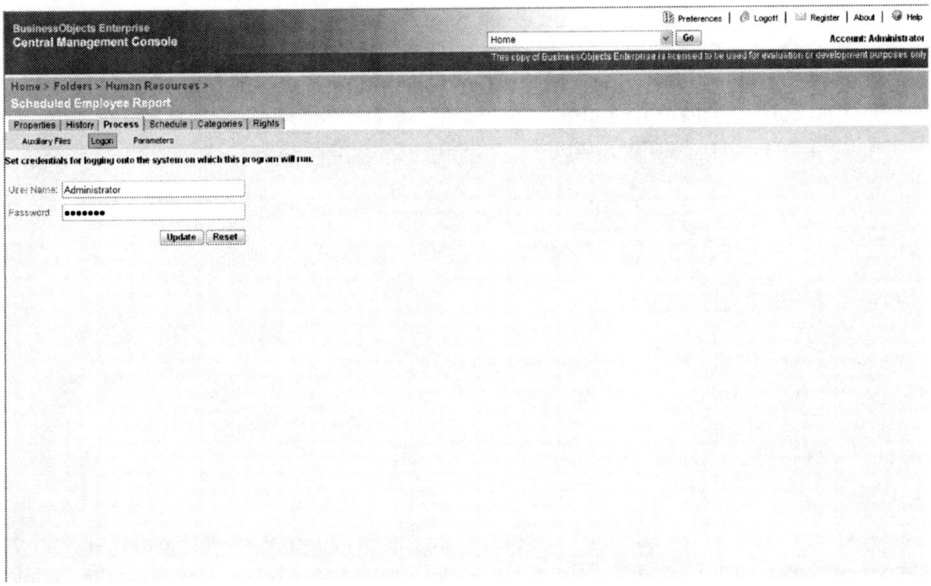

Figure 9-3. *Adding logon credentials*

You may wish to pass some command-line arguments to the EXE. You can establish these, as well as indicate a working directory and any environmental variables, in the Parameters page shown in Figure 9-4.

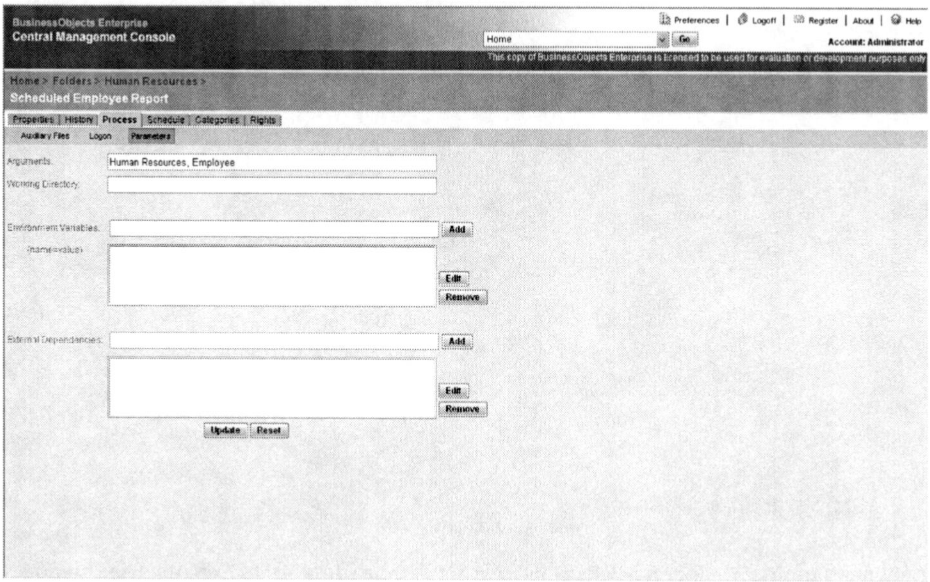

Figure 9-4. *Entering parameters*

External dependencies will permit you to set references to eternal files that the executable code in the InfoStore needs to run.

Your EXE will simply be a Windows application without an interface. This usually consists of a class file that contains an entry point called Main(), which receives any command-line parameters and passes them to the principal reporting method. The Main() method is shown in Listing 9-12.

Listing 9-12. *Main Method Expecting Command-Line Parameters*

```
static void Main(string[] args)
{
    string szFolder = args[0]; //"Human Resources"
    string szReport = args[1]; //"Employee"

    RunReports(szFolder, szReport);
}
```

The key section of the RunReports() method is shown in Listing 9-13. This example, which prints an employee report filtered by a list of countries, extracts the report based on the folder and report names. Then, it iterates through the DataTable containing the country codes and assigns each one to a new report instance, scheduling it to run immediately.

Listing 9-13. *Running Report for Each Employee Code in Table*

```
//Get the folder object
szSQL = "SELECT SI_ID, SI_NAME " +
   "FROM CI_INFOOBJECTS " +
   "WHERE SI_NAME = '" + szFolder + "' " +
   "AND SI_KIND = 'Folder'";

oFolders = oInfoStore.Query(szSQL);
oFolder = oFolders[1];

//Now get the report that beongs to the requested folder
szSQL = "SELECT SI_ID, SI_NAME, SI_PROCESSINFO.SI_PROMPTS " +
   "FROM CI_INFOOBJECTS " +
   "WHERE SI_NAME = '" + szReport + "' " +
   "AND SI_PARENT_FOLDER = " + oFolder.Properties["SI_ID"].ToString() +
   " AND SI_KIND = 'CrystalReport'";

oReports = oInfoStore.Query(szSQL);
oReport = oReports[1];

//Extract the Data and iterate through each row
oDT = GetCountries();

foreach(DataRow oDR in oDT.Rows)
{
   //Get the report plug-in reference
   oPluginInterface = oReport.GetPluginInterface("");
   oReportPlugIn = new Report(oPluginInterface);

   //Retrieve the parameters collection
   oReportParameters = oReportPlugIn.ReportParameters;

   //Create parameter objects and add them to the parameters collection
   oReportParameterSingleValue = oReportParameters[1].CreateSingleValue();
   oReportParameterSingleValue.Value = oDR["Code"].ToString();
   oReportParameters[1].CurrentValues.Clear();
   oReportParameters[1].CurrentValues.Add(oReportParameterSingleValue);

   //Schedule the report to run once and immediately
   oSchedulingInfo = oReport.SchedulingInfo;
   oSchedulingInfo.RightNow = true;
   oSchedulingInfo.Type = CeScheduleType.ceScheduleTypeOnce;

   //Let's send the output to Adobe Acrobat
   oReportFormatOpts = oReportPlugIn.ReportFormatOptions;
   oReportFormatOpts.Format = CeReportFormat.ceFormatPDF;
```

```
    //Then schedule this report and move onto the next parameter
    oInfoStore.Schedule(oReports);
}
```

The result is a report history page that looks like Figure 9-5.

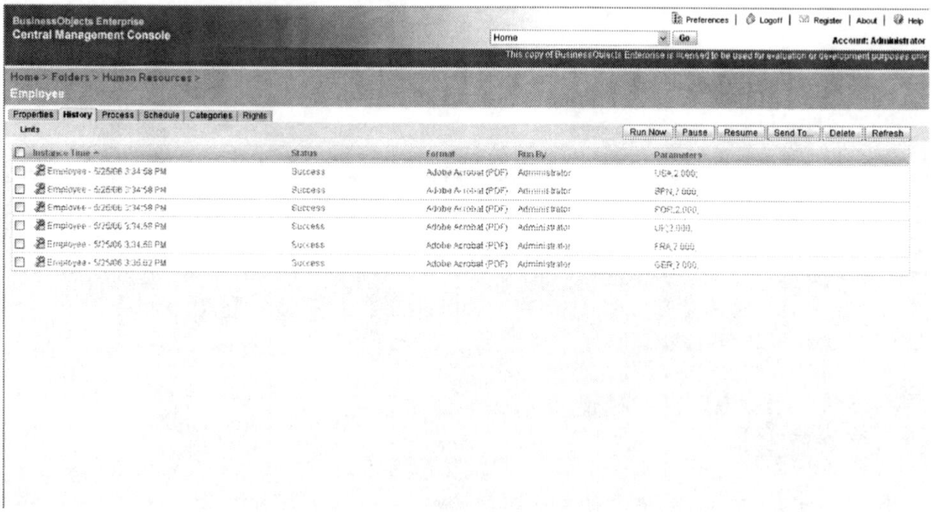

Figure 9-5. *Report history output*

Remember that BO XI is an object scheduler, not just a report scheduler. You don't need to restrict yourself to scheduling EXEs that deal with reports at all. If, say, you wanted to schedule an EXE that cleaned up temporary files on a server directory or sent status e-mails from a nightly database upload, you are free to do so. The tasks you can schedule don't need to be even remotely related to reporting.

Next, we'll take a look at creating data-driven criteria screens.

Creating Criteria Screens

Regardless of the reporting tool you use, you'll generally need to collect criteria data from your users to filter the output. Before building any report, you must first know what criteria the user will require in order to limit the data that will be displayed in the report. Creating criteria screens without the proper tools or methodologies can be a rather time-consuming process and may result in an application that is difficult to maintain.

Whatever style you use for your criteria screens, they should above all be consistent in both appearance and operation. Nothing makes a user more comfortable with an application than consistency. Start by finding out whether the organization for which you're building the application has any user interface (UI) standards in place. If you're lucky enough to be able to create the standard "look and feel" yourself, try to use a set of editing controls in a standard fashion, supported by a common code base.

The controls typically required for criteria screens in any desktop or web applications are text/numeric input boxes, date controls, check boxes, list boxes, and combo boxes. Radio buttons are not necessary, as combo boxes handle these choices just as well. (Radio buttons are also more difficult to work with when using data-driven programming techniques.)

Date criteria should generally be set up in a "from/to" layout and specified by the user as a range. If a user only needs one day's worth of information, the "from/to" dates can be set to the same date. If the particular parameter truly requires only a single date, then certainly offer the user only one date box. Your validation code should preclude the user from entering a "from" date that is later than the "to" date and any other such logical inconsistencies. Optionally, the "to" date can be defaulted to the system date as user needs require. Since there's normally very little free-form data that you would pass to a report engine, most of the error checking can occur before the user selections are submitted to BusinessObjects.

List boxes provide the most flexible criteria control. Use of a list box implies that the user may select more than one option. Each list box should have a button underneath it that allows the user to clear the choices made. This way if a user wishes to run a report for Departments A, D, and G, it is rather easy to do so (see Figure 9-6 in the next section). In those cases where the user is permitted to select only one out of a set of options, use a combo box. In both cases, each control has two columns. The first is invisible to the user and contains the unique ID of the table that contains the filter options. The second column contains the text description that the user would recognize.

Checked list boxes are usually best for making multiple selections on an individual control. Though you can certainly accomplish the same thing with a ListBox control, my experience has been that the user can easily forget to press Ctrl when making multiple selections and then end up deselecting everything he has selected so far. This is not a problem with checked list boxes. ListBox controls are more appropriate in cases where you need mutually exclusive lists—for example, when you want two adjacent list box controls so that when the user double-clicks the first list box, the choice is moved to the second, and vice versa.

Check boxes handle Boolean values. By default, on WinForms applications only, they can be set to the "gray" option, rather than a specific checked or unchecked value. Doing so will indicate that this criteria should be ignored altogether. Finally, text boxes can allow the user to restrict the output based on free-form text—a last name, for example. Often you may wish to treat all entries in the text box as partial search criteria. For example, if in filtering by last name the user enters "Sm", the report could return "Smoot", "Smith", "Smythe", etc. Depending upon the flavor of SQL you are using, this can be accomplished by using the LIKE keyword and appending a percent sign to the end of the search value. For example:

```
SELECT *
FROM Employees
WHERE LastName LIKE 'Sm%'
```

Building the WinForms Interface

Using the classes described in this section, you can dynamically create a WinForms interface for your reports with just a few lines of code. Likewise, you can extract the user selections with a few lines of code also.

Dynamic Criteria Controls

Because criteria screens repeat the same controls and use them in relatively the same fashion, it's possible to build a library that will create them for you dynamically with a few simple method calls. In this section, we'll examine how to dynamically create a list box control, populate it with data, and extract the selections made by the user. The approach for the other types of controls is very similar, and the code for this can be found in the download.

Suppose you want the user to select any number of departments, or none at all, from a list box. You can reduce the creation of the interface to these three lines of code:

```
oDT = GetDepartments();

ShowComboBox(Criteria.Department, oDT, "DictionaryID",
    "Description", 20, 420, 125, 25, "Department:");
```

To accomplish this feat, we'll need to create a report criteria form—and this form should be the only one you'll need to display the criteria for every report. You'll need customized forms only for those reports whose criteria are very unique and/or interact with one another in very specific ways. It's a maintenance nightmare to have one criteria form for every report in your application.

In this new form, you'll need to declare an `ArrayList` with form-wide scope:

```
ArrayList aControlList = new ArrayList();
```

The purpose of this `ArrayList` is to manage the various controls that will be dynamically instantiated. Then, you'll need a class to maintain the collection of controls required to create a list box display. These controls include a CheckedListBox control, a Label control to display the caption above it, and a Button control below to allow the user to clear the selections made. The display will look like the screen shown in Figure 9-6.

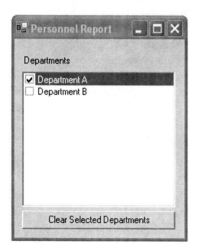

Figure 9-6. *CheckedListBox filter*

The class that maintains this three-control grouping is shown in Listing 9-14. Because every set of controls comes with multiple elements—a text box and a label, a combo box and a label, etc.—they can more easily be managed by storing references to the related component objects in classes designed to hold each set. Since every control has a label and an index, these properties can be stored in a `ControlManager` base class from which the individual control classes inherit.

Listing 9-14. *ControlManager and ListBoxManager Classes*

```
class ControlManager
{
   private Criteria iIndex;
   private Label oLabelControl;

   public Criteria Index
   {
      get { return iIndex; }
      set { iIndex = value; }
   }

   public Label LabelControl
   {
      get { return oLabelControl; }
      set { oLabelControl = value; }
   }
}

class ListBoxManager : ControlManager
{
   private CheckedListBox oListBoxControl;
   private Button oButtonControl;

   public CheckedListBox ListBoxControl
   {
      get { return oListBoxControl; }
      set { oListBoxControl = value; }
   }

   public Button ButtonControl
   {
      get { return oButtonControl; }
      set { oButtonControl = value; }
   }
}
```

You'll need to pass the `Criteria` enumerated value to the `ShowListBox()` method (see Listing 9-15) along with the data source information, the dimensions of the list box, and the caption. `ShowListBox()` instantiates an object of type `ListBoxManager`, which receives the instantiated objects of the Label, CheckListBox, and Button types. These controls are added to the properties of the `ListBoxManager` objects, which in turn are added to the `ArrayList` object that contains all the different criteria collections and allows their form-wide management.

Listing 9-15. *ShowListBox() Method*

```
private void ShowListBox(Criteria iIndex,
    DataTable oDT,
    string szID,
    string szDescription,
    int iLeft,
    int iTop,
    int iWidth,
    int iHeight,
    string szCaption)
{
    ListBoxManager oListBoxManager;

    oListBoxManager = new ListBoxManager();

    oListBoxManager.Index = iIndex;
    oListBoxManager.LabelControl = AddDynamicLabel(iIndex, iLeft, iTop, szCaption);

    iTop = oListBoxManager.LabelControl.Top +
        oListBoxManager.LabelControl.Height + 5;

    oListBoxManager.ListBoxControl =
        AddDynamicListBox(iIndex, iLeft, iTop, iWidth, iHeight);

    iTop = oListBoxManager.ListBoxControl.Top +
        oListBoxManager.ListBoxControl.Height + 5;

    oListBoxManager.ButtonControl =
        AddDynamicListBoxButton(iIndex, iLeft, iTop, iWidth, 23, szCaption);

    LoadCheckedListBox(oListBoxManager.ListBoxControl,
        oDT, "DictionaryID", "Description", false);

    aControlList.Add(oListBoxManager);
}
```

The AddDynamicLabel() method (see Listing 9-16) instantiates a Label object and assigns its location via a Point object. The AutoSize property is set to True so the control sets its width to the size necessary to display the text contained within it. This new Label object is then added to the Controls collection of the owner form. When you display a Label control on a form using the visual designer, the IDE generates code very similar to what you see here.

Listing 9-16. *AddDynamicLabel() Method*

```
private Label AddDynamicLabel(Criteria iIndex,
    int iLeft,
    int iTop,
```

```
    string szCaption)
{
    Label oLabel;

    oLabel = new Label();

    oLabel.AutoSize = true;
    oLabel.Name = "Label" + iIndex.ToString();
    oLabel.Location = new Point(iLeft, iTop);
    oLabel.Text = szCaption;

    this.Controls.Add(oLabel);

    return oLabel;
}
```

Likewise, the CheckedListBox control is displayed in a similar fashion as illustrated in the AddDynamicListBox() method shown in Listing 9-17. Other than the type of control object, the only major difference here is that the size is explicitly set via a Size object.

Listing 9-17. *CheckedListBox() Method*

```
private CheckedListBox AddDynamicListBox(Criteria iIndex,
    int iLeft,
    int iTop,
    int iWidth,
    int iHeight)
{
    CheckedListBox oCheckedListBox;

    oCheckedListBox = new CheckedListBox();

    oCheckedListBox.Name = "ListBox" + iIndex.ToString();
    oCheckedListBox.Size = new Size(iWidth, iHeight);
    oCheckedListBox.Location = new Point(iLeft, iTop);

    this.Controls.Add(oCheckedListBox);

    return oCheckedListBox;
}
```

The Button control is also created and displayed in a similar fashion as the Label and CheckedListBox as shown in Listing 9-18. The Button control triggers an event—that is, when clicked it must clear the selections in the list box to which it is associated. This is accomplished using the System.EventHandler() method, just as it is in the code generated by the IDE.

Listing 9-18. *AddDynamicListBoxButton() Method*

```
private Button AddDynamicListBoxButton(Criteria iIndex,
    int iLeft,
    int iTop,
    int iWidth,
    int iHeight,
    string szCaption)
{
    Button oButton;

    oButton = new Button();

    oButton.Name = "ListBoxButton" + iIndex.ToString();
    oButton.Size = new Size(iWidth, iHeight);
    oButton.Location = new Point(iLeft, iTop);
    oButton.Text = "Clear Selected " + szCaption;

    oButton.Click += new System.EventHandler(this.Button_Click);

    this.Controls.Add(oButton);

    return oButton;
}
```

This event handler, shown in Listing 9-19, needs to identify what button clicked it. It does this by iterating through the aControlList ArrayList object until it finds an entry of type ListBoxCollection. Once it finds one, it extracts a reference to the button associated with it and determines whether that is the button that was clicked. If so, then we've found the right CheckedListBox, and this object can then be referenced and the selections cleared.

Listing 9-19. *Button Event Handler*

```
private void Button_Click(object sender, System.EventArgs e)
{
    ListBoxManager oListBoxManager = null;
    CheckedListBox oListbox;
    int iIndex;

    foreach(object oItem in aControlList)
    {
        if (oItem is ListBoxManager)
        {
            oListBoxManager = oItem as ListBoxManager;

            if (oListBoxManager.ButtonControl == sender)
                break;
        }
```

```
    }

    oListbox = oListBoxManager.ListBoxControl;

    for(iIndex = 0; iIndex <= oListbox.Items.Count - 1; iIndex++)
        oListbox.SetItemChecked(iIndex, false);

}
```

CASCADING PROMPTS

Cascading prompts are those where one control filters the data in another. For example, you may have
a combo box filled with departments and adjacent to it a list box filled with the names of employees who
work in those departments. When you select a department in the combo box, the list box will refresh with the
employees for that department. To accomplish this in the framework of the data-driven controls just examined,
use the SelectedIndexChanged() event handler of the generic combo box control. The code for this is
shown here:

```
ComboBoxManager oComboBoxManager = null;
ListBoxManager oListBoxManager = null;
ComboBox oComboBox;
ListBox oListBox;
DataTable oDT;
ListItem oListItem;
string szData = string.Empty;

//Walk through each control set
foreach(object oSourceItem in aControlList)
{
    //If we find a combo box let's see if
    //it's really the one we want
    if (oSourceItem is ComboBoxManager)
    {
        //Cast to a ComboBoxManager
        oComboBoxManager = ((ComboBoxManager) oSourceItem);

        //Is it the combo box collection we want?
        if (oComboBoxManager.Index == Criteria.Department)
        {
            //If so, extract the combo box control
            oComboBox = ((ComboBox) oComboBoxManager.ComboBoxControl);

            //Get the ListItem object...
            oListItem = ((ListItem) oComboBox.SelectedItem);

            //...and retrieve the unique key for the department
            szData = oListItem.Value;
```

```
            //Loop through the control set again
            foreach(object oTargetItem in aControlList)
            {
                //If this is a list box collection
                if (oTargetItem is ListBoxManager)
                {
                    //Cast to a ListBoxManager
                    oListBoxManager = ((ListBoxManager) oTargetItem);

                    //Is it the list box collection we want?
                    if (oListBoxManager.Index == Criteria.Employee)
                    {
                        //If so, extract the list box control and populate
                        //with the employees belonging to the selected department
                        oListBox = ((ListBox) oListBoxManager.ListBoxControl);

                        oDT = GetDeptEmployees(szData);

                        LoadCheckedListBox(oListBoxManager.ListBoxControl, oDT,
                            "DictionaryID", "Description", false);

                        break;
                    }
                }
            }

            break;
        }
    }
}
```

Extracting the User Selections

Once the user has made his selections, you'll need to extract the information selected and pass it to your data source. Because all the controls are managed via classes, this can be accomplished quite easily and generically using one function call. Just as the list box was displayed with two lines of code, each of the selected values can be retrieved with just one. For example:

```
string szDepartments = GetCriteria(Criteria.Department);
```

will assign a value to the szDepartments variable that looks like this: "(12,45,23)". This is a comma-delimited string that can be used in a SQL IN clause to restrict the departments that are extracted from the database. The GetCriteria() method is partially shown in Listing 9-20. This section shows how the ListBoxManager is handled. Each element in the ArrayList is checked for its class type and then cast to that type. If the Index property, which identifies the control to which it is associated, matches the enumerated value passed to it, then we extract the selected data in a fashion appropriate to the control. All the other control collection types are handled similarly.

Listing 9-20. *GetCriteria() Method*

```
ListBoxManager oListBoxManager = null;
CheckedListBox oListBox = null;
string szData = string.Empty;

foreach(object oItem in aControlList)
{
   if (oItem is ListBoxManager)
   {
      oListBoxManager = ((ListBoxManager) oItem);

      if (oListBoxManager.Index == iIndex)
      {
         oListBoxManager = ((ListBoxManager) oItem);

         oListBox = ((CheckedListBox) oListBoxManager.ListBoxControl);

         szData = ParseIt(oListBox, false, 0, true);
         break;
      }
   }

   ...

}

return szData;
```

The selection extraction approach appropriate to a list box control is the ParseIt() method shown in Listing 9-21. This method receives a CheckedListBox control and a Boolean indicating whether quotes should surround each item, which column (0 = ID or 1 = description) to return, and another Boolean to indicate whether all or only the checked items are returned.

Listing 9-21. *ParseIt() Method*

```
public static string ParseIt(CheckedListBox oList,
   bool bQuotes, int sCol, bool bCheckedOnly)
{
   string szResult = String.Empty;
   string szQuotes = String.Empty;
   string szData = String.Empty;
   System.Text.StringBuilder oResult = new System.Text.StringBuilder();
```

```
//Use quotes or not
szQuotes = (bQuotes) ? "'" : String.Empty;

//Count all or just the checked items
IList oListItems = (bCheckedOnly) ?
   (IList)oList.CheckedItems : (IList)oList.Items;

foreach (object oItem in oListItems)
{
   ListItem oCheckBoxItem = oItem as ListItem;

   if (oCheckBoxItem != null)
   {
      //Depending on the column selected, extract the requested property
      switch (sCol)
      {
         case 0:
            szData = oCheckBoxItem.Value;
            break;

         case 1:
            szData = oCheckBoxItem.Text;
            break;

         case 2:
            szData = oCheckBoxItem.OtherText;
            break;
      }

      if (oResult.Length > 0)
         oResult.Append(",");

      oResult.AppendFormat("{0}{1}{2}", szQuotes, szData, szQuotes);
   }
}

szResult = (oResult.Length == 0) ? string.Empty :
   string.Format("({0})", oResult.ToString());

return szResult;
}
```

To allow the ParseIt() method to handle ListBox, instead of CheckedListBox, controls, simply overload it so that the first parameter receives an object of type ListBox and when iterating through the chosen options, refer to the SelectedItems collection instead of the CheckedItems collection. That's it. That's the only difference.

Once the data as been extracted from the control, you can pass it to a stored procedure. There is a catch here, however. SQL Server, Sybase, and Oracle stored procedures, among others, will not allow you to pass a parameter to an IN clause as shown in Listing 9-22.

Listing 9-22. *Invalid Passing of Parameter to IN Clause*

```
DECLARE @Data Varchar(1000)

SET @Data = '1,2'

SELECT * FROM Employees WHERE EmployeeID IN @Data
```

Therefore you'll need to parse the data using a SQL Server function. Avoid using dynamic SQL if at all possible. It's slow and you're just asking for problems. The way to handle this situation in SQL Server is shown in Listing 9-23.

Listing 9-23. *SQL Server Function to Parse to Virtual Table*

```
DECLARE @Data Varchar(1000)

SET @Data = '1,2'

SELECT *
FROM Employees
WHERE EmployeeID IN
  (SELECT data
   FROM dbo.fnc_NumericCodes(@Data, ','))
```

The function fnc_NumericCodes returns a virtual table containing the parsed values from the delimited string passed into it. You can see this by executing the code in Listing 9-24.

Listing 9-24. *Extracting Virtual Table*

```
DECLARE @Data Varchar(1000)

SET @Data = '1,2'

SELECT data
   FROM dbo.fnc_NumericCodes(@Data, ',')
```

This code will produce the result set shown in Figure 9-7.

	data
1	1
2	2

Figure 9-7. *fnc_NumericCodes result set*

The IN clause is simply performing a subquery on this result set that returns the matching rows in the Employee table just fine. The code for this stored procedure is shown in Listing 9-25.

Listing 9-25. *fnc_NumericCodes Function*

```
CREATE FUNCTION dbo.fnc_NumericCodes

(
@Items varchar(4000),
@Delimiter varchar(1)
)

    RETURNS @DataTable TABLE (data int) AS

BEGIN

    DECLARE @Pos int
    DECLARE @DataPos int
    DECLARE @DataLen smallint
    DECLARE @Temp varchar(4000)
    DECLARE @DataRemain varchar(4000)
    DECLARE @OneItem varchar(4000)

    SET @DataPos = 1
    SET @DataRemain = ''

    WHILE @DataPos <= DATALENGTH(@Items) / 2

        BEGIN

            SET @DataLen = 4000 - DATALENGTH(@DataRemain) / 2
            SET @Temp = @DataRemain + SUBSTRING(@Items, @DataPos, @DataLen)
            SET @DataPos = @DataPos + @DataLen
            SET @Pos = CHARINDEX(@Delimiter, @Temp)

            WHILE @Pos > 0

                BEGIN
                    SET @OneItem = LTRIM(RTRIM(LEFT(@Temp, @Pos - 1)))

                    INSERT @DataTable (data) VALUES(@OneItem)

                    SET @Temp = SUBSTRING(@Temp, @Pos + 1, LEN(@Temp))
                    SET @Pos = CHARINDEX(@Delimiter, @Temp)

                END

        END
```

```
        SET @DataRemain = @Temp

    END

  IF LEN(@Items) = 1
     SET @DataRemain = @Items

  INSERT @DataTable(data) VALUES (LTRIM(RTRIM(@DataRemain)))

  RETURN

END
```

fnc_NumericCodes is a table-valued function that receives a string of delimited values and a delimiter character (usually a comma). By iterating through this string, it breaks off each distinct value and inserts it into a table variable. As the function name suggests, it only returns numeric values because the table variable is defined with a column called data that is of type int. You may wish to perform an IN search on a list of string values also. The code for this is very similar and is included in the downloaded code for this book.

You can also accomplish the same results as an IN clause by using CHARINDEX (or INSTR in Oracle). Both examples are shown in Listing 9-26.

Listing 9-26. *Using CHARINDEX and INSTR*

```
'SQL Server

DECLARE @Data varchar(1000)

SET @Data = ',1,2,3,'

SELECT EmployeeID
FROM Employees
WHERE CHARINDEX(',' + CONVERT(varchar(10), EmployeeID)
   + ',', @Data) <> 0

'Oracle

SELECT EmployeeID
FROM Employees
WHERE INSTR(',1,2,3,',',','||EmployeeID||',') <> 0
```

Each of these SQL statements will return the rows that match on the indicated column value. Since these approaches are using string values and converting numeric table data to strings to perform the match, they won't be as efficient as subquerying numeric values against a numeric column in a temporary table. Test both approaches to see which one works best for you.

Web Interface

Dynamically generating a web interface takes a similar approach to generating the controls for a WinForms interface. Because it's not necessary to persist the code between postbacks, the web implementation is simpler than the WinForms version.

Dynamic Criteria Controls

Suppose you want to display a list box to users that will allow them to select none, one, or multiple items. You can accomplish this with the following three lines of code:

```
oDT = GetDepartments();
ShowListBox(Criteria.Department, oDT, "DictionaryID",
    "Description", 10, 20, 200, 180, "Departments");
```

This code will display the web page shown in Figure 9-8.

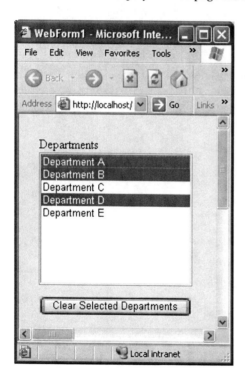

Figure 9-8. *Filtering departments*

In this example, we'll examine the data-driven techniques for creating web ListBox controls on the fly. The reason I'm not using a CheckBoxList control is because the ID values that are assigned to it through the ListItem object do not persist client side and therefore cannot be retrieved through JavaScript. Microsoft KnowledgeBase article Q309338 explains this in more detail.

The goal is to retrieve the user selections client side only because you can always pass the values to the server via hidden controls. Because of the increasing popularity of asynchronous

JavaScript, more and more developers are avoiding postbacks for tasks such as report generation. By retrieving the user selections client side and invoking an on-demand reporting web service asynchronously, you can display the report output with minimal server hits. This approach also simplifies the UI code because we don't need to maintain state between postbacks.

Like its WinForms counterpart, the ShowListBox() method invokes additional methods that display the Label, ListBox, and Button objects that make up the set of controls. These controls are managed in the classes shown in Listing 9-27.

Listing 9-27. *ControlManager and ListBoxManager Classes*

```
class ControlManager
{
   private Criteria iIndex;
   private Label oLabelControl;

   public Criteria Index
   {
      get { return iIndex; }
      set { iIndex = value; }
   }

   public Label LabelControl
   {
      get { return oLabelControl; }
      set { oLabelControl = value; }
   }
}


class ListBoxManager : ControlManager
{
   private System.Web.UI.WebControls.ListBox oListBoxControl;
   private Button oButtonControl;

   public System.Web.UI.WebControls.ListBox ListBoxControl
   {
      get { return oListBoxControl; }
      set { oListBoxControl = value; }
   }

   public Button ButtonControl
   {
      get { return oButtonControl; }
      set { oButtonControl = value; }
   }
}
```

To display the control, you need to pass the Criteria enumerator to the ShowListBox() method (see Listing 9-28) along with the data source information, the dimensions of the list box, and the caption. ShowListBox() instantiates an object of type ListBoxCollection that receives the instantiated objects of the Label, ListBox, and Button types. These controls are then added to the properties of the ListBoxCollection objects.

Listing 9-28. *ShowListBox() Method*

```
private void ShowListBox(Criteria iIndex,
    DataTable oDT,
    string szID,
    string szDescription,
    int iLeft,
    int iTop,
    int iWidth,
    int iHeight,
    string szCaption)
{
    ListBoxManager oListBoxManager;

    oListBoxManager = new ListBoxManager();

    oListBoxManager.Index = iIndex;
    oListBoxManager.LabelControl =
        AddDynamicLabel(iIndex, iLeft, iTop, szCaption);

    oListBoxManager.ListBoxControl =
        AddDynamicListBox(iIndex, iLeft, iTop + 20, iWidth, iHeight);

    oListBoxManager.ButtonControl =
        AddDynamicListBoxButton(iIndex, iLeft,
        iTop + iHeight + 20, iWidth, 23, szCaption);

    LoadListBox(oListBoxManager.ListBoxControl, oDT,
        "DictionaryID", "Description", false);

}
```

The AddDynamicLabel() method (see Listing 9-29) instantiates a Label object and assigns its location via the Style() method. The new control is then added to the Controls collection of the owner Panel object that displays it to the user.

Listing 9-29. *AddDynamicLabel() Method*

```
private Label AddDynamicLabel(Criteria iIndex,
    int iLeft,
    int iTop,
```

```
   string szCaption)
{
   Label oLabel;

   oLabel = new Label();

   oLabel.Style["position"] = "absolute";
   oLabel.Style["left"] = iLeft.ToString() + "px";
   oLabel.Style["top"] = iTop.ToString() + "px";
   oLabel.Text = szCaption;

   Panel1.Controls.Add(oLabel);

   return oLabel;
}
```

Likewise, the ListBox control is displayed in a similar fashion as illustrated in the AddDynamicListBox() method shown in Listing 9-30. The SelectionMode property is always set to multiple selections, otherwise a combo box would suffice.

Listing 9-30. *AddDynamicListBox() Method*

```
private System.Web.UI.WebControls.ListBox AddDynamicListBox(Criteria iIndex,
   int iLeft,
   int iTop,
   int iWidth,
   int iHeight)
{
   System.Web.UI.WebControls.ListBox oListBox;

   oListBox = new System.Web.UI.WebControls.ListBox();

   oListBox.ID = "ListBox" + ((int) iIndex);
   oListBox.Style["position"] = "absolute";
   oListBox.Style["left"] = iLeft.ToString() + "px";
   oListBox.Style["top"] = iTop.ToString() + "px";
   oListBox.Style["height"] = iHeight.ToString() + "px";
   oListBox.Style["width"] = iWidth.ToString() + "px";
   oListBox.BorderStyle = BorderStyle.Solid;
   oListBox.SelectionMode = ListSelectionMode.Multiple;

   Panel1.Controls.Add(oListBox);

   return oListBox;
}
```

The Button control is also created and displayed in a similar fashion as the Label and List-Box as shown in Listing 9-31.

Listing 9-31. *AddDynamicListBoxButton() Method*

```
private Button AddDynamicListBoxButton(Criteria iIndex,
    int iLeft,
    int iTop,
    int iWidth,
    int iHeight,
    string szCaption)
{
    Button oButton;

    oButton = new Button();

    oButton.Style["position"] = "absolute";
    oButton.Style["left"] = iLeft.ToString() + "px";
    oButton.Style["top"] = iTop.ToString() + "px";
    oButton.Style["width"] = iWidth.ToString() + "px";
    oButton.Text = "Clear Selected " + szCaption;

    oButton.Attributes.Add("onclick",
        "return DeselectAll('ListBox" + ((int) iIndex) + "')");

    Panel1.Controls.Add(oButton);

    return oButton;
}
```

The Button control triggers JavaScript code, that is, when clicked it must clear the selections in the list box with which it is associated. The generic JavaScript function that clears the select options in the ListBox is shown in Listing 9-32. The Button's onclick event is wired to this JavaScript function using the `Attributes.Add()` method.

Listing 9-32. *DeselectAll Method*

```
function DeselectAll(szListBox)
{
    var oListBox = document.getElementById(szListBox);

    for (i=0; i < oListBox.options.length; i++)
        oListBox.options[i].selected = false;

    return false;
}
```

Extracting the User Selections

Once the user has completed entering his report criteria, the Get Data button can generically retrieve the information one control at a time. In the code shown in Listing 9-33, the selected departments are retrieved and displayed in an alert box.

Listing 9-33. *Retrieving the User Selections*

```
function GetData()
{
   var szDepartments = "Departments: " + ParseIt("ListBox6", false, true) + "\n";
   alert(szDepartments)
   return false;
}
```

The JavaScript `ParseIt()` function shown in Listing 9-34 performs the same task as its WinForms counterpart.

Listing 9-34. *JavaScript ParseIt Function*

```
function ParseIt(szListBox, bQuotes, bCheckedOnly)
{
   var oListBox = document.getElementById(szListBox);
   var szResult = new String('');
   var szQuotes = '';
   var szValue = '';

   if (bQuotes)
      szQuotes = "'";

   for (i=0; i < oListBox.options.length; i++)
   {
      szValue = oListBox.options[i].value;

      if (bCheckedOnly)
      {
         if (oListBox.options[i].selected)
            szResult += szQuotes + szValue + szQuotes + ",";
      }
      else
            szResult += szQuotes + szValue + szQuotes + ",";

   if (szResult.length > 0)
      szResult = szResult.substring(0, szResult.length - 1);

   return szResult;
}
```

BO XI Windows Service Monitor

Business Objects XI, like its previous incarnations, installs a series of Windows services on the server machine. These services are shown in the Central Configuration Manager depicted in Figure 9-9.

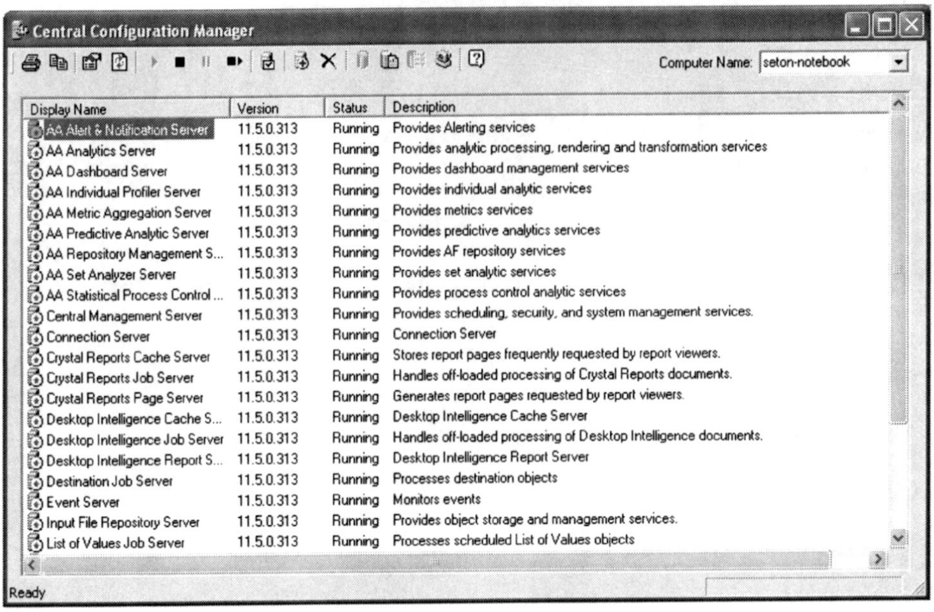

Figure 9-9. *Central Configuration Manager*

Given the mission-critical nature of most reporting servers, it is vital that these services remain up and running around the clock. Unfortunately, experience has proven that they do go down on occasion. Sometimes the production servers are scheduled for periodic reboots, and the BO XI services simply don't restart when the server does.

Regardless of the cause, you'll likely want to know when these services aren't available. One way to monitor this is with a Windows service. This service, called the BO XI Service Monitor, is installed on the server machine and checks periodically, say, every five minutes, to see whether the specified services are up and running. If not, the BO XI service is started, a record of the problem is inserted into the Event Log, and an e-mail sent to the designated individuals informing them of the problem. If a service can't be started in a specified time-out period, the service monitor stops trying, inserts a record of this timeout into the Event log, and sends an e-mail. A time-out error is clearly a much higher priority item, as a service could not be started and BO XI is all or partially unusable.

If you've never developed a Windows service before, the approach is rather simple. Creating a new project as a Windows service will output most of the standard code for you, including OnStart() and OnStop() methods, as well as the Main() method, with code to instantiate and manage what could be multiple service threads running in the same EXE.

The main block of code is created to run in a loop. At the end of the loop, you can place a Thread.Sleep event that pauses the service for the designated interval. The code in Listing 9-35 shows the key part of the Windows service.

Listing 9-35. *BO XI Windows Service Monitor*

```
ServiceController oServiceController;
XmlDocument oXmlDocument;
XmlNode oXmlNode;
```

```csharp
string szService = string.Empty;
string szAppPath = string.Empty;
string szCodeBase = string.Empty;
string szMsg = string.Empty;
string szMachineName = string.Empty;
string szNotifyEmails = string.Empty;
string szSmtpServer = string.Empty;
short sFrequencyInMinutes;
short sMaxWaitInSeconds;
long lStartTicks;
bool bTimeOut = false;

while (true)
{
    //Get the path where the window service is executing
    szCodeBase = System.Reflection.Assembly.
        GetExecutingAssembly().GetName().CodeBase;
    szAppPath = System.IO.Path.GetDirectoryName(szCodeBase);

    //Cut off the first six characters because the directory names
    //returns in this format: @"file:\C:\BOXIServiceMonitor\bin\Debug"
    szAppPath = szAppPath.Substring(6);

    szMachineName = Environment.MachineName;

    //Get the settings from the XML file
    sFrequencyInMinutes = GetFrequencyInMinutes(szAppPath);
    sMaxWaitInSeconds = GetMaxWaitInSeconds(szAppPath);
    szNotifyEmails = GetNotifyEmails(szAppPath);
    szSmtpServer = GetSmtpServer(szAppPath);

    //Open the XML file to obtain a list of BO XI Services
    oXmlDocument = new XmlDocument();
    oXmlDocument.Load(szAppPath + @"\settings.xml");

    oXmlNode = oXmlDocument.SelectSingleNode("/Settings/Services");

    //Iterate through each service
    foreach(XmlNode oChildXmlNode in oXmlNode.ChildNodes)
    {
        szService = oChildXmlNode.ChildNodes[0].InnerText;

        //Obtain an object reference to the service
        oServiceController = new ServiceController(szService);

        //If the service is either stopped or in the process of stopping...
        if (oServiceController.Status == ServiceControllerStatus.Stopped ||
```

```
        oServiceController.Status == ServiceControllerStatus.StopPending)
    {
      szMsg = "The {0} was detected down on {1} at {2}";

      szMsg = string.Format(szMsg, szService, szMachineName,
          DateTime.Now.ToString());

      System.Diagnostics.EventLog.WriteEntry(szService, szMsg);

      SendEmail(szMsg, szNotifyEmails, szSmtpServer);

      lStartTicks = Environment.TickCount;

      //...start it up again
      oServiceController.Start();

      //Keep checking every 1/2 second by refreshing the object
      //reference to see if the service has started again
      do
      {
         oServiceController.Refresh();

         System.Threading.Thread.Sleep(500);

         //If it hasn't started by the before we reach the timeout
         //period then indicate a time-out condition and stop trying
         if ((Environment.TickCount/1000) -
            (lStartTicks/1000)  > sMaxWaitInSeconds)
         {
           bTimeOut = true;
           break;
         }

      }
      while (oServiceController.Status != ServiceControllerStatus.Running);

      //If there was a time-out condition, indicate this in the
      //even log. Otherwise, indicate success.
      if (bTimeOut)
      {
         szMsg = "The {0} could not be restarted on {1} " +
             "in the {2} seconds allotted";

         szMsg = string.Format(szMsg, szService, szMachineName,
             MaxWaitInSeconds.ToString());
         System.Diagnostics.EventLog.WriteEntry(szService, szMsg);

         SendEmail(szMsg, szNotifyEmails, szSmtpServer);
```

```
        }
        else
        {
            szMsg = "The {0} was successfully restarted on {1} at {2}";

            szMsg = string.Format(szMsg, szService, szMachineName,
                DateTime.Now.ToString());
            System.Diagnostics.EventLog.WriteEntry(szService, szMsg);

            SendEmail(szMsg, szNotifyEmails, szSmtpServer);
        }

        bTimeOut = false;
    }

  }
  //Once the services have been checked,
  //sit tight until its time to check again
  System.Threading.Thread.Sleep(sFrequencyInMinutes * 60 * 1000);
}
```

The ServiceController class exists in .NET solely to provide you with programmatic control over the various Windows services. Using this class, you can start them, stop them, and determine what state they're in.

The Windows service XML configuration file is shown in Listing 9-36. The <Services> section lists the name of each BO XI service you wish to check for. The Window service will iterate through each <ServiceName> entry and verify that each one is running.

Listing 9-36. *Windows Service XML File*

```
<Settings>
    <FrequencyInMinutes>5</FrequencyInMinutes>
    <MaxWaitInSeconds>60</MaxWaitInSeconds>
    <NotifyEmails>seton.software@verizon.net</NotifyEmails>
    <SmtpServer>mysmtpserver</SmtpServer>
    <Services>
        <ServiceName>Central Management Server</ServiceName>
        <ServiceName>Crystal Reports Job Server</ServiceName>
        <ServiceName>Crystal Reports Page Server</ServiceName>
    </Services>
</Settings>
```

The entire Windows service project is in the downloadable code. All you need to do is compile and install it. You can install a Windows service using the InstallUtil.exe command-line utility found at C:\WINDOWS\Microsoft.NET\Framework\v1.1.4322. Simply type

```
InstallUtil.exe BOXIServiceMonitor.exe
```

and the Windows service will make its appearance among the list of other installed services as shown in Figure 9-10.

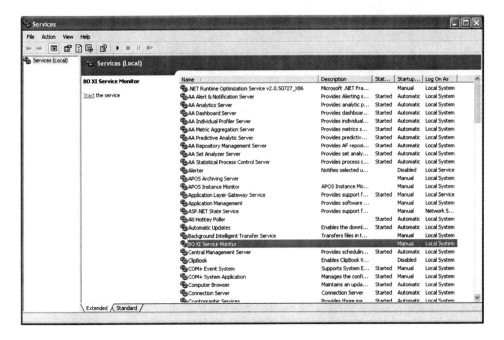

Figure 9-10. *Windows services*

To uninstall the service, simply type

```
InstallUtil.exe /u BOXIServiceMonitor.exe
```

Once it's installed, you don't need to reinstall it every time you make a change to the code. To update a new version of the service, simply stop the existing copy, recompile and copy over the EXE, and then restart the service.

Reporting Against the InfoStore

One major drawback of BO XI is that there is no easy way to extract data from the InfoStore. Sure, you can use the SQL language to extract some basic information, but that has its limits as it's not designed to drill down beyond the first layer in the property bags. Beyond those limits you'll need to write custom code that iterates through many levels of nested property bags just to get your data in a format that can be used in a report. To solve this problem for all time, I use a web service that returns an XML representation of my report information. Because it is XML, it can handle hierarchical relationships like one report–many parameters. The output is essentially what you get when you type the following in the Query Builder:

```
SELECT *
FROM SI_INFOOBJECTS
WHERE SI_KIND = 'CrystalReport'
```

Having your InfoStore data in XML is nice, but now what do you do with it? This is where the XML XPath language comes in. XPath lets you write extraction logic against XML. Suppose you want a list of every report where the EmployeeID parameter is 123 or every report that uses a particular data source, XPath can handle it for you. We'll discuss XPath in more detail in the next section.

GetReportTree Web Service

The GetReportTree() web service method extracts requested data from the InfoStore starting at a specified folder level and returns it in an XML format. You can specify if you want the basic report data, full folder information, prompt information, scheduling information, data source information, or notifications. You can also indicate whether you're interested in report history or just the template instances. The goal is to produce an XML file that looks like Listing 9-37.

Listing 9-37. *XML Output from the GetReportTree() Method*

```xml
<Folder SI_FOLER_NAME="Personnel Reports">
  <SI_CHILDREN>6</SI_CHILDREN>
  <SI_FLAGS>2050</SI_FLAGS>
  <SI_ID>413370</SI_ID>
  <SI_OBTYPE>1</SI_OBTYPE>
  <SI_OWNER>Administrator</SI_OWNER>
  <SI_OWNERID>12</SI_OWNERID>
  <SI_PARENT_FOLDER>413355</SI_PARENT_FOLDER>
  ...
  <Report SI_REPORT_NAME="Direct Reports Summary">
    <SI_CHILDREN>6</SI_CHILDREN>
    <SI_FLAGS>2050</SI_FLAGS>
    <SI_ID>413396</SI_ID>
    <SI_OBTYPE>2</SI_OBTYPE>
    <SI_OWNER>Administrator</SI_OWNER>
    <SI_OWNERID>12</SI_OWNERID>
    <SI_PARENT_FOLDER>413370</SI_PARENT_FOLDER>
    <SI_PROMPTS>
      <SI_VALUE1 SI_NAME="EmployeeId">X647</SI_VALUE1>
      <SI_VALUE2 SI_NAME="ProcessDate">DateTime (2006, 3, 9, 16, 12, 40)
        </SI_VALUE2>
    </SI_PROMPTS>
    <SI_LOGONS>
      <SI_SERVER> Personnel. Personnel</SI_SERVER>
      <SI_USER>
      </SI_USER>
      <SI_SERVER_TYPE>crdb_adoplus</SI_SERVER_TYPE>
    </SI_LOGONS>
    <SI_SCHEDULE>
      <SI_SCHEDULE_TYPE>Calendar</SI_SCHEDULE_TYPE>
      <SI_STARTTIME>2/28/2006 1:00:00 PM</SI_STARTTIME>
      <SI_TEMPLATE_DAY>Monday</SI_TEMPLATE_DAY>
```

```
            <SI_TEMPLATE_DAY>Tuesday</SI_TEMPLATE_DAY>
            ...
        </SI_SCHEDULE>
        <SI_NOTIFICATION>
          <SI_DESTINATION_SUCCESS>
            <SI_PROGID>CrystalEnterprise.Smtp</SI_PROGID>
            <SI_DEST_SCHEDULEOPTIONS>
              <SI_MAIL_MESSAGE>The Direct Reports Summary is ready.
               To view this report please click on the link below:
               www.mylink.com
              </SI_MAIL_MESSAGE>
              <SI_DOMAIN_NAME>
              </SI_DOMAIN_NAME>
              <SI_PORT>25</SI_PORT>
              <SI_SENDER_NAME>snyc11d10041</SI_SENDER_NAME>
              <SI_MAIL_SUBJECT> Direct Reports Summary is ready.</SI_MAIL_SUBJECT>
              <SI_SMTP_ENABLEATTACHMENTS>True</SI_SMTP_ENABLEATTACHMENTS>
              <SI_MAIL_ADDRESSES>
                <SI_MAIL_ADDRESS>ryan.follmer@gmail.com</SI_MAIL_ADDRESS>
                <SI_MAIL_ADDRESS>seton.software@verizon.net</SI_MAIL_ADDRESS>
              </SI_MAIL_ADDRESSES>
              <SI_MAIL_CC>
                <SI_MAIL_CC_ADDRESS>joe.smith@setonsoftware.com</SI_MAIL_CC_ADDRESS>
              </SI_MAIL_CC>
            </SI_DEST_SCHEDULEOPTIONS>
          </SI_DESTINATION_SUCCESS>
          <SI_DESTINATION_FAILURE>
            ...
          </SI_DESTINATION_FAILURE>
        </SI_NOTIFICATION>
      </Report>
...
```

This XML is an abbreviated example of the information that you can extract from the InfoStore. The GetReportTree() web service method iterates through the various properties of the InfoStore to build this XML. Because of the hierarchical nature of the InfoStore, the web service method necessarily uses a lot of recursion. The main method is shown in Listing 9-38.

Listing 9-38. *GetReportTree() Web Service Method*

```
private string GetReportTree(string szUserID,
    string szPassword,
    string szSystem,
    string szAuthentication,
    string szServer,
    string szParentID,
    string szParentName,
```

```
    CEOptions sRecurring,
    CEOptions sTemplateHistory,
    bool bFolderInfo,
    bool bBasicInfo,
    bool bPromptInfo,
    bool bLogonInfo,
    bool bScheduleInfo,
    bool bNotificationInfo)
{
    EnterpriseSession oEnterpriseSession = null;
    EnterpriseService oEnterpriseService = null;
    InfoStore oInfoStore = null;
    XmlDocument oXmlDocument;
    XmlElement oXmlElement;
    string szSQL;

    //Connect to BO XI

    //Remove blank spaces so parent folder name can be used as an XML tag
     szParentName = szParentName.Replace(" ", string.Empty);

    //Get the topmost folders
    szSQL = BuildFolderSQL(szParentID,
       sTemplateHistory,
       bBasicInfo,
       bPromptInfo,
       bLogonInfo,
       bScheduleInfo,
       bNotificationInfo);

    //Instantiate an XMLDocument object that will hold
    //all the InfoStore data
    oXmlDocument = new XmlDocument();
    oXmlElement = oXmlDocument.CreateElement("", szParentName, "");
    oXmlDocument.AppendChild(oXmlElement);

    //Get the data at the levels below the topmost folders
    oXmlDocument = BuildSubTree(oInfoStore,
       oXmlDocument,
       oXmlElement,
       szSQL,
       szParentID,
       sTemplateHistory,
       bFolderInfo,
       bBasicInfo,
       bPromptInfo,
       bLogonInfo,
```

```
        bScheduleInfo,
        bNotificationInfo);

    return oXmlDocument.OuterXml;
}
```

The GetReportTree() method receives as parameters the name and ID of the parent folder plus the options you want to return in the XML file. If all you need is a list of reports, there's no point in asking for all the report and folder properties, database connectivity information, scheduling information, and so on. The BuildFolderSQL() method (see Listing 9-39) creates an SQL string that extracts only the needed data from the InfoStore. Just as in traditional SQL programming against an RDBMS like SQL Server or Oracle, it's good practice to take only what you really need in order to alleviate the burden on the server and network.

Listing 9-39. *Create Folder SQL*

```
private string BuildFolderSQL(string szParentID,
    CEOptions sTemplateHistory,
    bool bBasicInfo,
    bool bPromptInfo,
    bool bLogonInfo,
    bool bScheduleInfo,
    bool bNotificationInfo)
{
    string szSQL = string.Empty;
    string szField = string.Empty;

    szField = "SI_CHILDREN, SI_FLAGS, SI_ID, SI_OBTYPE, SI_OWNER, " +
        "SI_OWNERID, SI_PARENT_FOLDER, SI_PARENTID, SI_INSTANCE, " +
        "SI_UPDATE_TS, SI_OBJECT_IS_CONTAINER, SI_CREATION_TIME, " +
        "SI_HIDDEN_OBJECT, SI_DESCRIPTION, SI_PROGID, SI_KIND, SI_NAME, " +
        "SI_HASTHUMBNAIL, SI_TURNONTHUMBNAIL, SI_TURNONREPOSITORY, " +
        "SI_SYSTEM_OBJECT, SI_RUNNABLE_OBJECT, SI_PLUGIN_OBJECT, " +
        "SI_INSTANCE_OBJECT, SI_GUID, SI_CUID, SI_RUID, " +
        "SI_APPLICATION_OBJECT, SI_TABLE, SI_PARENT_CUID, SI_COMPONENT, " +
        "SI_PARENT_FOLDER_CUID, SI_REFRESH_OPTIONS, SI_RECURRING, ";

    if (bPromptInfo)
        szField += SI_PROCESSINFO.SI_PROMPTS, ";

    if (bLogonInfo)
        szField += "SI_PROCESSINFO.SI_LOGON_INFO, ";

    if (bScheduleInfo)
        szField += "SI_SCHEDULEINFO.SI_SCHEDULE_TYPE, " +
            "SI_SCHEDULEINFO.SI_STARTTIME, " +
            "SI_SCHEDULEINFO.SI_RUN_ON_TEMPLATE, ";
```

```
if (bNotificationInfo)
   szField += "SI_SCHEDULEINFO.SI_NOTIFICATION, ";

szField = szField.Substring(0, szField.Length - 2) + " ";

szSQL ="Select " + szField +
   "From CI_INFOOBJECTS " +
   "Where (SI_KIND = 'Folder' " +
   "Or SI_KIND = 'CrystalReport' " +
   "Or SI_KIND = 'Excel' " +
   "Or SI_KIND = 'Pdf' " +
   "Or SI_KIND = 'Rtf' " +
   "Or SI_KIND = 'Txt' " +
   "Or SI_KIND = 'Word') ";

if (sTemplateHistory == CEOptions.No)
   szSQL += " And SI_INSTANCE = 0 ";

if (sTemplateHistory == CEOptions.Yes)
   szSQL +=  " And SI_INSTANCE = 1 ";

if (szParentID != "0")
   szSQL += "And SI_ANCESTOR = " + szParentID;

return szSQL;
}
```

Once the required data is extracted, the InfoObjects collection can be iterated recursively. If a given object is a folder, the recursion continues as shown in Listing 9-40.

Listing 9-40. *Iterate Through the Properties Recursively*

```
foreach (InfoObject oInfoObject in oInfoObjects)
{
   //If the object is a folder then create a Folder element, optionally
   //add the folder information, and continue with the recursion
   if (oInfoObject.Properties["SI_KIND"].ToString() == "Folder")
   {
      oXmlMainElement = oXmlDocument.CreateElement("Folder");
      oXmlMainElement.SetAttribute("SI_FOLDER_NAME",
         oInfoObject.Properties["SI_NAME"].ToString());

      if (bFolderInfo)
         oXmlMainElement =
            FolderInfo(oInfoObject, oXmlDocument, oXmlMainElement);

      oXmlElement.AppendChild(oXmlMainElement);
```

```
        szParentID = oInfoObject.Properties["SI_ID"].ToString();

        oXmlDocument = BuildSubTree(oInfoStore,
            oXmlDocument,
            oXmlMainElement,
            null,
            szParentID,
            sTemplateHistory,
            bFolderInfo,
            bBasicInfo,
            bPromptInfo,
            bLogonInfo,
            bScheduleInfo,
            bNotificationInfo);
    }
    else
...
```

If it's a report being processed, then determine what report information has been requested and add it as needed. This logic is shown in Listing 9-41.

Listing 9-41. *Addreport Information*

```
...
else
{
    //If this is a report object (or PDF, or Excel, etc.) then
    //create a Report element and add the requested sections of
    //report information. Since there is nothing below
    //a report, no further recursion is necessary.
    oXmlMainElement = oXmlDocument.CreateElement("Report");
    oXmlMainElement.SetAttribute("SI_REPORT_NAME",
        oInfoObject.Properties["SI_NAME"].ToString());

    oXmlMainElement =
        BaseReportInfo(oInfoObject, oXmlDocument, oXmlMainElement, bBasicInfo);

    if (bPromptInfo)
    {
        oXmlSubElement = PromptInfo(oInfoObject, oXmlDocument);

        if (oXmlSubElement != null)
            oXmlMainElement.AppendChild(oXmlSubElement);
    }

    if (bLogonInfo)
    {
        oXmlSubElement = LogonInfo(oInfoObject, oXmlDocument);
```

```
        if (oXmlSubElement != null)
            oXmlMainElement.AppendChild(oXmlSubElement);
    }

    if (bScheduleInfo)
    {
        oXmlSubElement = ScheduleInfo(oInfoObject, oXmlDocument);

        if (oXmlSubElement != null)
            oXmlMainElement.AppendChild(oXmlSubElement);
    }

    if (bNotificationInfo)
    {
        oXmlSubElement = NotificationInfo(oInfoObject, oXmlDocument);

        if (oXmlSubElement != null)
            oXmlMainElement.AppendChild(oXmlSubElement);
    }

    oXmlElement.AppendChild(oXmlMainElement);
}
```

Reporting Against the XML Output

It's great to have the output of the InfoStore in an XML file, but its uses are limited unless you can report against it. One way to work with the XML file is via the XML classes provided by .NET. You can use XPath statements to filter the requested data and then iterate through the results. XPath is to XML data what SQL is to relational databases. A discussion of the .NET XML classes and XPath are beyond the scope of this book, and many excellent tomes have been written about these topics. To get started, examine the code in Listing 9-42, which shows a few examples of filtering the data.

Listing 9-42. *Working with XML Data with XPath*

```
XmlDocument oXmlDocument;
XmlNodeList oNodes;

oXmlDocument = new XmlDocument();
oXmlDocument.Load(@"c:\ganz\ce.xml");

//Get everything under the folder node named 'Human Resources Reports'
oNodes = oXmlDocument.
    SelectNodes("/MyReports//Folder[@SI_NAME='Human Resources Reports']/*");

//Get everything under the report node named 'Hiring Report'
oNodes = oXmlDocument.
    SelectNodes("/MyReports/Folder/Report[@SI_NAME='Hiring Report']/*");
```

```
//Get the report nodes where the SI_OWNERID = 12
oNodes = oXmlDocument.
   SelectNodes("/MyReports/Folder/Report[SI_OWNERID=12]");

//Get the report nodes where the first prompt has a value of 'G320'
oNodes = oXmlDocument.
   SelectNodes("/MyReports/Folder/Report/SI_PROMPTS[SI_VALUE1='G320']");

//Get the SI_ID element where the owner ID is 12
oNodes = oXmlDocument.
   SelectNodes("/MyReports/Folder[SI_OWNERID=12]/SI_ID");

//Get all the folder nodes
oNodes = oXmlDocument.
   SelectNodes("/MyReports/Folder");

//Get the first folder node
oNodes = oXmlDocument.
   SelectNodes("/MyReports/Folder[1]");
```

> ■**Note** If you plan to work with XPath, you may want to download the free XPath Visualizer utility at www.topxml.com/xpathvisualizer/. This utility will allow you to execute XPath expressions interactively and highlight the matching sections of your XML file. This will prove invaluable in debugging.

A more powerful way to report against the XML output is with Crystal Reports itself. You can create a report that uses a data connection type of XML. To do this, you'll first need to generate an XSD schema against your XML file. You can accomplish this using the xsd.exe command-line utility found in either \Program Files\Microsoft Visual Studio .NET 2003\SDK\ v1.1\Bin or \Program Files\Microsoft Visual Studio 8\SDK\v2.0\Bin. Simply type

```
Xsd <XML file name>
```

at the command prompt, and you'll generate an XSD output that looks something like Listing 9-43.

Listing 9-43. *XSD Output*

```
<?xml version="1.0" encoding="utf-8"?>
<xs:schema id="HumanResources" xmlns=""
xmlns:xs="http://www.w3.org/2001/XMLSchema" xmlns:msdata=
"urn:schemas-microsoft-com:xml-msdata">
 <xs:element name="HumanResources" msdata:IsDataSet="true">
    <xs:complexType>
      <xs:choice maxOccurs="unbounded">
        <xs:element name="Report">
```

```
        <xs:complexType>
          <xs:sequence>
            <xs:element name="SI_CHILDREN" type="xs:string"
minOccurs="0" msdata:Ordinal="0" />
            <xs:element name="SI_FLAGS" type="xs:string"
minOccurs="0" msdata:Ordinal="1" />
            <xs:element name="SI_ID" type="xs:string"
minOccurs="0" msdata:Ordinal="2" />
...
```

Crystal will prompt you for the names of both the XML and XSD files. Should you want the data filtered by some criteria, you can do so by choosing Report ➤ Selection Formulas ➤ Record and entering a formula like this:

```
{HumanResources/Report/SI_PROMPTS/SI_VALUE1.body_field} = "GER"
```

This shows only those reports where the first prompt value is set to "GER". The final screen design will look something like Figure 9-11.

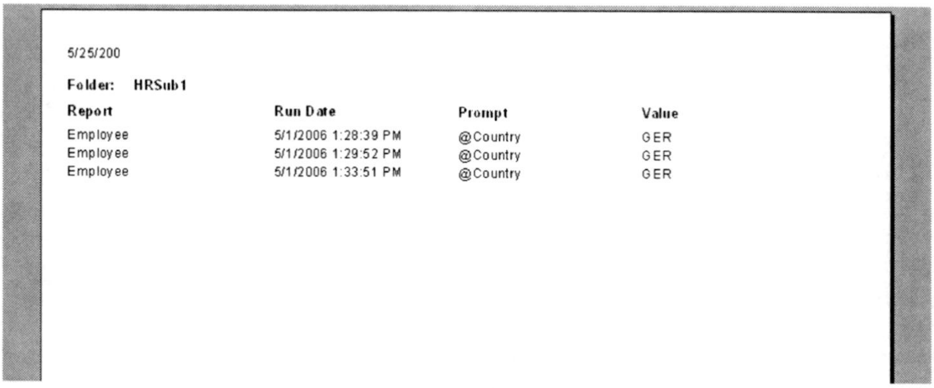

Figure 9-11. *Reporting against an XML output in Crystal Reports*

Building Dynamic Menus

One of the many useful tasks you can perform with an InfoStore data extraction is the creation of dynamic menus. Generally you'll create your BO XI folder structure to match a hierarchical pattern. By extracting only the basic information from the InfoStore you can retrieve an XML dump that looks like the sample in Listing 9-44.

Listing 9-44. *Folder XML Output*

```
<AccountingReports>
  <Folder SI_NAME="Accounts Receivable">
    <Report SI_NAME="Ageing Schedule">
```

```
    <SI_ID>13611</SI_ID>
    <SI_NAME>Ageing Schedule</SI_NAME>
  </Report>
</Folder>
<Folder SI_NAME="Payroll">
  <Report SI_NAME="Paycheck Summary">
    <SI_ID>11969</SI_ID>
    <SI_NAME>Paycheck Summary</SI_NAME>
  </Report>
  <Report SI_NAME="Payroll Taxes Remitted">
    <SI_ID>21287</SI_ID>
    <SI_NAME>Payroll Taxes Remitted</SI_NAME>
  </Report>
  <Folder SI_NAME="Personnel">
    <Report SI_NAME="Employee Listing">
      <SI_ID>87422</SI_ID>
      <SI_NAME>Employee Listing</SI_NAME>
    </Report>
  </Folder>
  <Report SI_NAME="Bonus Schedule">
    <SI_ID>87422</SI_ID>
    <SI_NAME>Bonus Schedule</SI_NAME>
  </Report>
  <Report SI_NAME="Adjustments">
    <SI_ID>87842</SI_ID>
    <SI_NAME>Adjustments</SI_NAME>
  </Report>
</Folder>
</AccountingReports>
```

Since this is XML, the hierarchical relationship is preserved by the nesting of the various elements. Using the LoadMenus() method shown in Listing 9-45, you can convert this XML to a WinForms menu.

Listing 9-45. *LoadMenus() Method*

```
private void LoadMenus(XmlDocument oXmlDocument)
{
    MenuItem oMenuItem;
    XmlNodeList oXmlNodeList;

    //We're not interested in the topmost node
    //so get the child nodes of that immediately
    oXmlNodeList = oXmlDocument.ChildNodes.Item(0).ChildNodes;

    //Create a main menu entry labeled Reports. All other
    //report menu entries will fall under this one
```

```
oMenuItem = new MenuItem();
oMenuItem.Text = "Reports";

//Begin loading the child menus
LoadChildMenus(oXmlNodeList, oMenuItem);

this.Menu.MenuItems.Add(oMenuItem);
}
```

The recursive nature of the code keeps drilling down through the various nodes until they have all been converted into menu item entries. LoadMenus() recursively invokes the LoadChildMenus() method shown in Listing 9-46.

Listing 9-46. *LoadChildMenus() Method*

```
private void LoadChildMenus(XmlNodeList oXmlNodeList, MenuItem oOwnerMenuItem)
{
    MenuItem oMenuItem = null;
    string szDescription;

    //Iterate through the nodes
    foreach (XmlNode oXmlNode in oXmlNodeList)
    {
        //Extract the name of the folder or report...
        szDescription = oXmlNode.Attributes.Item(0).Value;

        //...and add it to the menu with a default event handler
        oMenuItem = new MenuItem();
        oMenuItem.Text = szDescription;
        oMenuItem.Click += new System.EventHandler(this.oMainMenu_Click);

        //If we're dealing with a folder entry see if there are
        //any child nodes and continue the recursion. Reports
        //won't have child entries
        if (oXmlNode.LocalName == "Folder")
        {
            oXmlNodeList = oXmlNode.ChildNodes;

            if (oXmlNodeList.Count != 0)
                LoadChildMenus(oXmlNodeList, oMenuItem);
        }

        //Add the menu item to the main menu
        oOwnerMenuItem.MenuItems.Add(oMenuItem);
    }
}
```

Using this approach, whenever you add or remove a report from BO XI, the main menu in your application will automatically change to reflect it. The final output is shown in Figure 9-12.

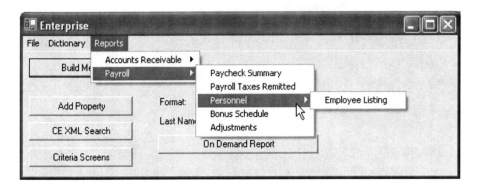

Figure 9-12. *Dynamic menu*

The LoadChildMenus() method attaches a common event handler to each menu item called oMainMenu_Click(). The code for this event handler is shown in Listing 9-47.

Listing 9-47. *oMainMenu_Click() Event Handler*

```
private void oMainMenu_Click(object sender, System.EventArgs e)
{
    MenuItem oMenuItem;

    oMenuItem = ((MenuItem) sender);

    MessageBox.Show(oMenuItem.Text);
}
```

Here the common event handler shows how the Text property is extracted from the MenuItem object that triggered it. This is one way you can identify the report in question. Another way is to create a class that is a subclass of the MenuItem object, which has an ID property that holds the unique SI_ID value of each menu item. Then, you pass this ID value to a web service or as a URL parameter to display your report.

Storing Custom Metadata

Sometimes you'll want to store information about your reports for which there is no matching property in the InfoStore. There are two ways you can do this, one quite painful and one quite easy. We'll look at the painful way first.

Using Your RDBMS

You could store additional information about your BO XI objects in related database tables. Creating a separate set of tables in your RDBMS is an ambitious project, and you'll find it fraught with peril, and, yes, I am writing from experience. Because you are essentially extending the InfoStore database, all the requirements for proper database management become incumbent upon the developer.

You'll first need to create a transaction manager class to keep both data stores in sync so that when a report is deleted from or added to the InfoStore, the associated entry is deleted from or added to the RDBMS. We needed a Windows service that periodically pulled report instance entries from the InfoStore and inserted them into our RDBMS. Likewise, when you perform backups or archiving, you'll need to make sure all are done in sync as well. This approach is certainly possible, but you need to exercise great care when managing your objects. It's best to avoid using an external RDBMS unless your system requirements are such that you have exhausted all other possible alternatives like custom properties.

The metadata approach does have the advantage of unlimited scalability. Because you are using an RDBMS, you can optimize the database for fast searches. Should your InfoStore grow to hundreds of thousands of records, using an RDBMS will prove beneficial when performing queries. Since custom properties are stored in binary columns in the InfoStore and are not indexed, you could take a speed hit when querying very large installations.

Custom Properties

Another possibility for storing metadata is through the creation of custom properties. The collection of "SI_" prefixed properties that store so much information in the InfoStore may be supplemented by the addition of your own properties. (I'd recommend prefixing them with something other that "SI_" to avoid confusion.) The code in Listing 9-48 shows how to add a new property called MY_CRITERIA_PAGE and assign the value "EmployeeRpt.aspx" to it.

Listing 9-48. *Adding a Custom Property*

```
szSQL = "SELECT SI_ID " +
    "FROM CI_INFOOBJECTS " +
    "WHERE SI_ID = " + szID;

oInfoObjects = oInfoStore.Query(szSQL);

//If property of this name already exists the value will be updated
oInfoObjects[1].Properties.Add("MY_CRITERIA_PAGE",
    "GoHere.aspx");

oInfoStore.Commit(oInfoObjects);
```

If the MY_CRITERIA_PAGE property already existed, its value would be updated. Once this new property has been added, you can use the Query Builder to view it as shown in Figure 9-13.

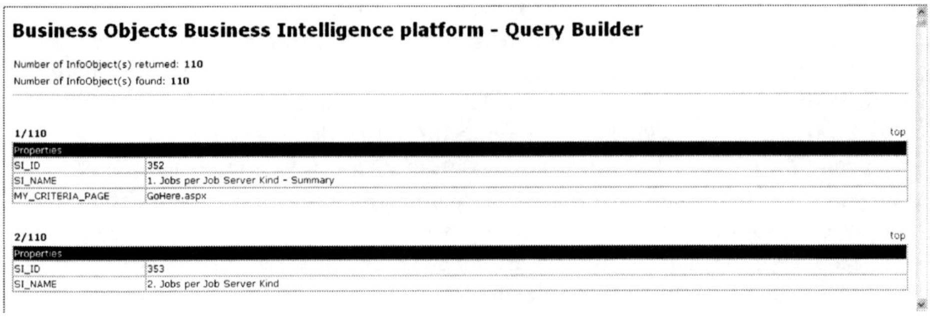

Figure 9-13. *Extracting custom properties*

You can delete the new property like this:

```
oInfoObjects[1].Properties.Delete(MY_CRITERIA_PAGE");
```

BO XI does prevent you from making ordinarily devastating mistakes. Should you try to delete one of the BO-supplied properties like SI_CHILDREN or SI_ID, the delete command will be ignored without generating an error.

Since BO XI works with property bags, you can create nested properties several levels deep. The code shown in Listing 9-49 demonstrates how to create a property and assign it to a Property object. Then, by using the Add() method of the Properties collection of the new Property object, you can add additional properties and values nested underneath. The enumerator CePropFlags.cePropFlagBag indicates the property is really a property bag.

Listing 9-49. *Creating Nested Properties*

```
Property oProperty = oInfoObjects[1].Properties.Add("MY_CUSTOM_HEADER",
    String.Empty, CePropFlags.cePropFlagBag);
oProperty.Properties.Add("MY_LEFT_SIDE", "Seton Software Development, Inc.");
oProperty.Properties.Add("MY_RIGHT_SIDE", "Personal and Confidential");
```

This code will produce the output shown in Figure 9-14.

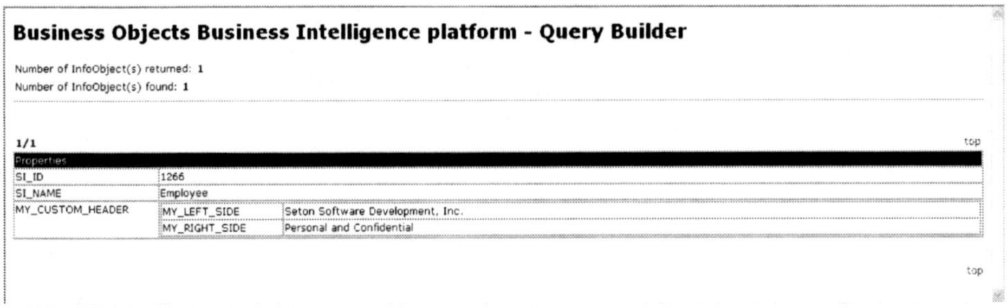

Figure 9-14. *Nested properties*

If you find that you need to associate objects such as Word documents, spreadsheets, or images with InfoStore objects, you can create custom properties that store the Base64-encoded string representations of these objects. Base64 encoding is discussed earlier in the chapter.

Note If you need to store truly complex hierarchical data, you can avoid nested properties altogether, create only one property, and store XML text in it. XML can easily be manipulated with an XMLDocument object.

Adding custom properties is akin to adding columns to a database table. Each object type in the InfoStore—Report, User, UserGroup, etc.—is similar to working with a database table. A Report object has its collection of properties just as a Report table would have its collection of columns. These definitions are stored in the plug-in DLLs that are encapsulated by the PluginManager class as shown in Listing 9-50.

Listing 9-50. *Creating a New Object*

```
oInfoObjects = oInfoStore.NewInfoObjectCollection();

oPluginManager = oInfoStore.PluginManager;
oPluginInfo = oPluginManager.GetPluginInfo("Report");
oInfoObject = oInfoObjects.Add(oPluginInfo);
```

Unfortunately, BO XI does not support the creation of new SI_KIND entries that constitute the BO XI equivalent of creating new tables. If you wanted to create an SI_KIND of "System-Settings", for example, to which you could add custom properties that store such things as URL pointers or screen preferences, you would need to resort to an XML file external to the InfoStore, as such a task is impossible in BO XI. To do this you would need an extension of the SDK that allows creation of plug-in DLLs, a feature that is not yet supported.

As a speed test, I created a property called MY_COMMENTS in an InfoStore that held over 1200 reports. Each instance received almost 10K of XML data. Extracting all of this data into a StringBuilder object using the code shown in Listing 9-51 took only five seconds.

Listing 9-51. *Extracting XML Data*

```
szSQL = "SELECT TOP 10000 SI_ID, MY_COMMENTS " +
    "FROM CI_INFOOBJECTS " +
    "WHERE SI_KIND = 'CrystalReport'";

oInfoObjects = oInfoStore.Query(szSQL);

oStringBuilder = new System.Text.StringBuilder();

oStringBuilder.Append("<MyData>");
```

```
foreach (InfoObject oInfoObject in oInfoObjects)
{
    string szData = "<Report SI_ID='{0}'>{2}</Report>";

    oStringBuilder.AppendFormat(szData,
        oInfoObject.Properties["SI_ID"],
        oInfoObject.Properties["MY_COMMENTS"]);
}

oStringBuilder.Append("</MyData>");

return oStringBuilder.ToString();
```

The amount of data that you can store in your properties is virtually unlimited. Nonindexed properties are stored in a general binary column in the RDBMS back end. The capacity of the binary data type varies from database vendor to database vendor, but it is usually measured in the gigabytes. I've had no problems storing several hundred thousand bytes of data in custom properties. Therefore it's an excellent place to store metadata.

The Limits of Crystal

If you've worked with Crystal Reports long enough, you've probably hit a few road blocks along the way. After ten plus years of working with Crystal, I've found only three things it either can't do without performing unnatural acts or can't do at all.

One drawback is its inability to print a single report to multiple paper bins. I have a client who prints commission checks along with the details of how their earnings were derived. The first page is always a special paper that consists of a check covering the first third of the page with the rest of the page being white. This paper stock is stored in the first paper bin. Any additional pages of the commission report are printed on white paper, which is stored in the second paper bin. The ability to switch between paper bins is impossible for Crystal. The only workaround is to create two reports, the first of which pulls enough records to do the first pages, and the second of which then pulls any additional records to print subsequent pages.

The second area that Crystal can't handle is the creation of reports that have user-selectable columns. Suppose you have a personnel report that could potentially display the employee name and up to a dozen of over a hundred columns of additional data in the personnel table. The user could choose home address, cell number, and university degree; or, department, manager, and base salary. Crystal Reports requires you to connect to a data source and lay out columns in advance. Here, this is a problem because you don't know the columns in advance. One way to handle this is to build your RPT file programmatically using the RAS SDK. Chapter 8 is devoted to this topic.

The third area where Crystal falls short is in the creation of "what-if" reports. Many of my financial and investment banking clients want their reports exported to Excel and rather than just precalculated numbers displaying in sum and average columns, they want formulas instead. The goal is to allow the user to change detail-level numbers to determine the effect on the final and subtotal amounts. Crystal has some functionality to do this via the Excel (Data Only) export, but the functionality is limited to database and group-level summaries. You can, however, skip Crystal completely and create the Excel files directly using one of the Excel creation tools described in Chapter 12.

Summary

This chapter shows how to create enterprise reporting solutions by bringing together all the technology covered in this book so far. We looked at a web service for running reports on demand as well as several techniques for dynamically generating criteria screens to collect data for report parameters. In addition, we examined how to create a Windows service that would make sure all the BO XI services were running. We also looked at how to mine data from the InfoStore and return it in XML format.

Most of what you learned here can be used directly in your own applications. The combination of scheduled EXEs and custom properties especially will open up BusinessObjects XI in ways you can only imagine.

■ ■ ■

CHAPTER 10

Security

BusinessObjects XI offers a built-in security model to enable you to control access to its features and individual objects. You can use the security classes to

- Create users.

- Assign access privileges to those users.

- Assign users to groups.

- Create subgroups within groups.

- Determine what users and groups can access individual objects.

- Determine how many instances or for how long a given report history will be maintained.

In this chapter we'll look at BO XI security through both the CMC and the object model.

Security Considerations

The majority of business reports are tied to specific applications, and these applications normally have their own security features built in that restrict users to specific features. If this is the case, your report security problems are probably solved, since you can then list your reports among the application features and restrict them as you would any other feature of the application. However, not all reports work like this. If your reports are separate from any application and are directly accessible, say, from the company intranet, other approaches to security must be taken.

While a comprehensive discussion of computer security is beyond the scope of this book, a brief mention of report and document-related security issues is appropriate. There are different levels of security related to report information. It could be simply that the ability to print certain reports is available only to specified users. This ability is abused, of course, when one of these users sends a report to a shared printer to which anyone on the floor has access. I once had a user print a list of salary and bonus information that was fortunately found by the human resources director before any damage was done. It is difficult to employ any kind of security measures on a computer system without incurring significant expense. All it takes is one user to write his password on his keyboard and the most elaborate security system is immediately compromised.

One way to track who is being careless is to create a log entry in an audit trail table every time a report is run. You can record what report was run, the criteria used, the date and time it was run, by whom, and on what computer. You could also print the ID of the user who ran the report on all output so that the next time the salary report is carelessly left on a table in the lunchroom you'll know who to blame.

Another form of data access restriction is to allow multiple users permission to run the same report but restrict the set of criteria. Thus, one user could run a compensation report for Department A, B, or C, whereas another user might only be able to run it for Department B. Optionally, any user could be allowed to run the report, but the Compensation column could be suppressed for those users who don't have authorization to view this information.

Some of the technology for securing documents lies in the forms upon which they are printed. Checks are a common example. Most checks have numerous security devices to deter fraud. First, they can be printed on paper that has various color tones throughout the document as well as a distinctive watermark to prevent photocopying. Then, the check amount is printed in several locations on the check itself. I've even seen checks that have heat-sensitive logos on the reverse side that will disappear for a few seconds when heat, say, from your thumb, is applied to them. Taken together, these security devices may not completely prevent fraud, but they'll at least make it very difficult for the culprits and show that you've done due diligence.

Magnetic ink character recognition (MICR) allows you to print the entire check—logo, check and account numbers, signature, etc.—directly on blank paper rather than maintain preprinted check stock, which is easier to steal. In this way, there is no need to constantly void preprinted checks that are destroyed in printing.

Security threads are polyester or plastic bands embedded into paper just beneath the surface. The new U.S. currency employs this device as an anticounterfeiting measure. Security threads restrict visibility in reflected light while permitting visibility in transmitted light. They offer protection against photocopying, as copiers see documents only in reflected light. Also, the presence of threads in a document will provide for easy authentication. You can obtain more information on the different products and techniques for document security from your stationery supplier.

Managing Security Through the CMC

The first thing you'll need to do when approaching BO XI security is to decide whether you'll create a list of named users or have all users connect using the same administrator user ID and password. This decision is akin to deciding whether you'll create a list of users in your RDBMS. Most applications, certainly all the ones I've created, don't allow the user direct access to the RDBMS through tools like SQL Server Enterprise Manager or Oracle's SQL Plus.

Since the database exists only to expose database services to the front-end application, all users of the application connect to the RDBMS through the same user ID/password combination, and the front end handles any entitlements. The application itself will usually offer a security tool for user management that will allow the assigning of rights very specific to that application. Thus, the ability to delete or add rows to the database tables is granted through a separate security interface, hopefully some corporate standard that can be used from application to application.

You probably don't want to maintain two sets of users, one in BO XI and one in your application security interface. If you decide to isolate BO XI on a server, reserving the CMC only for the BO XI administrators, you can expose its functionality as web services for consumption by proxy applications. These web services would connect to BO XI through the same user ID/password combination.

The one drawback to this is that BO XI writes information to the data store as to who performed certain actions, say, running reports. If the same user ID is used for everyone, there will be no way to distinguish, in a way that's easily viewable in the CMC, who has done what. You can still pass a user ID to the web service and have it write the date and time to a custom property in the InfoStore. This will maintain your user-specific audit trail. Custom properties are discussed in Chapter 9.

Creating Users

Users can be created by selecting the Users link from the main menu. This link will take you to the page shown in Figure 10-1.

Figure 10-1. *User management screen*

Every user of the CMC will be listed on this page. To add a new user, click the New User button in the upper right, which will take you to the page shown in Figure 10-2.

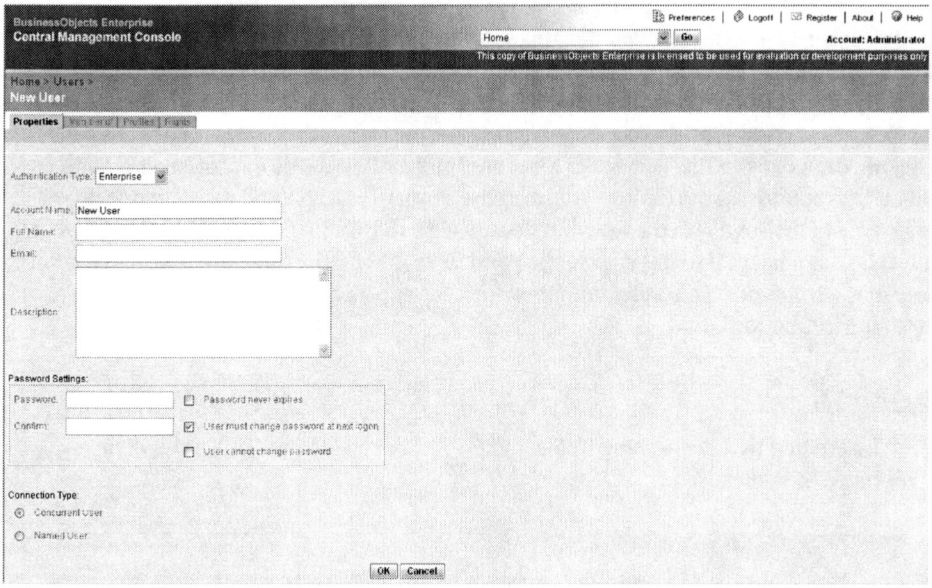

Figure 10-2. *Adding a new user*

Here you can enter the basic information such as name and e-mail, the authentication type, and the password. You can assign a password that either does not change or one that the user must change at the next login. Choosing the password setting—"User must change password at next logon"—allows you to set a temporary password for a user. Then, when the user is first authenticated, he is forced to change the password immediately.

Most corporate security policies do not allow anyone, even the security administrator, to know or have the ability to find out a user's password. I have several clients where sharing a password, with anyone or for any reason, is a termination offense. If a user forgets a password, then it can only be reset and never decrypted.

The connection types—concurrent or named—refer to your BO XI license. Concurrent users belong to license agreements that restrict the number of simultaneous users, whereas named users belong to license agreements that associate a specific user with a specific license.

There are four authentication types available for use in the CMC—Enterprise, Windows NT, Lightweight Directory Access Protocol (LDAP), and Windows Active Directory (AD). Enterprise authentication means that you plan to set up your users in BO XI and use BO XI to authenticate the login attempts. The other three mean that you plan to use Windows security user accounts—NT, Lightweight Directory Access Protocol, or Active Directory.

You can create a user programmatically in a fashion that is structurally similar to creating a folder. User objects have more properties to assign such as title, name, e-mail, and password options. The code to accomplish this is shown in Listing 10-1.

Listing 10-1. *Creating a User*

```
//Connect to BO

oInfoObjects = oInfoStore.NewInfoObjectCollection();
```

```
oPluginManager = oInfoStore.PluginManager;
oPluginInfo = oPluginManager.GetPluginInfo("CrystalEnterprise.User");
oInfoObject = oInfoObjects.Add(oPluginInfo);
oUser = ((User) oInfoObject);

oUser.Title = szAccountName;
oUser.Description = szDescription;
oUser.FullName = szFullName;
oUser.EmailAddress = szEmailAddress;
oUser.PasswordExpires = bPasswordExpires;
oUser.AllowChangePassword = bAllowChangePassword;
oUser.NewPassword = szUserPassword;
oUser.ChangePasswordAtNextLogon = bChangePasswordAtNextLogon;

oInfoStore.Commit(oInfoObjects);
```

Creating Groups

Groups are essentially collections of rights to which users can be assigned. There are two key
default groups called Administrators and Everyone, neither of which can be deleted. The
Administrators group, as the name would suggest, contains the users who have administrative
privileges on the system. The Everyone group is a catch-all that all users belong to. The main
Groups page is accessible from the main menu and shown in Figure 10-3.

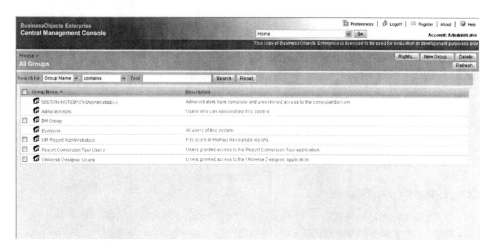

Figure 10-3. *Groups page*

To add a group, click the New Group button, and you'll be presented with the page shown
in Figure 10-4. A group needs nothing more than a name and an optional description.

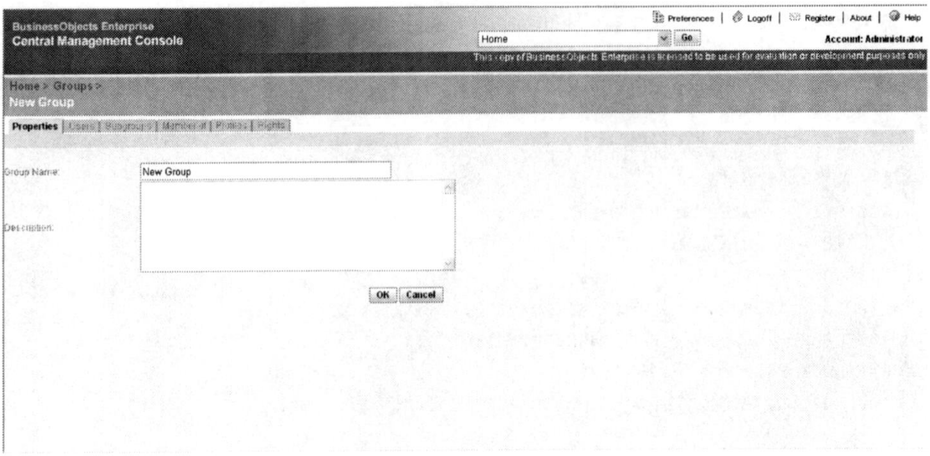

Figure 10-4. *Adding a group*

Groups can easily be created programmatically as the code in Listing 10-2 illustrates.

Listing 10-2. *Creating a New Group*

```
//Connect to BO XI
oInfoObjects = oInfoStore.NewInfoObjectCollection();

oPluginManager = oInfoStore.PluginManager;
oPluginInfo = oPluginManager.GetPluginInfo("CrystalEnterprise.UserGroup");
oInfoObject = oInfoObjects.Add(oPluginInfo);
oUserGroup = ((UserGroup) oInfoObject);

oUserGroup.Title = szName;
oUserGroup.Description = szDescription;

oInfoStore.Commit(oInfoObjects);
```

Adding Users to Groups

The entire purpose of creating groups is to add users to them so that these users may inherit the rights belonging to the group. Users and groups work together in a many-to-many relationship. One group can have many users, and one user can be a member of many groups. Using the CMC, you can add users to groups or add groups to users, depending on how you wish to approach the task.

To add a user to a group, select the Groups option on the main menu. This will take you to a list of the groups entered in the CMC as shown previously in Figure 10-3. By clicking the hyperlink name of the group, you'll be presented with a tab form. One of these tabs is named Users. Select this tab, and you'll see a list of the users already associated with the current group. Click the Add Users button, and you'll be presented with the screen shown in Figure 10-5.

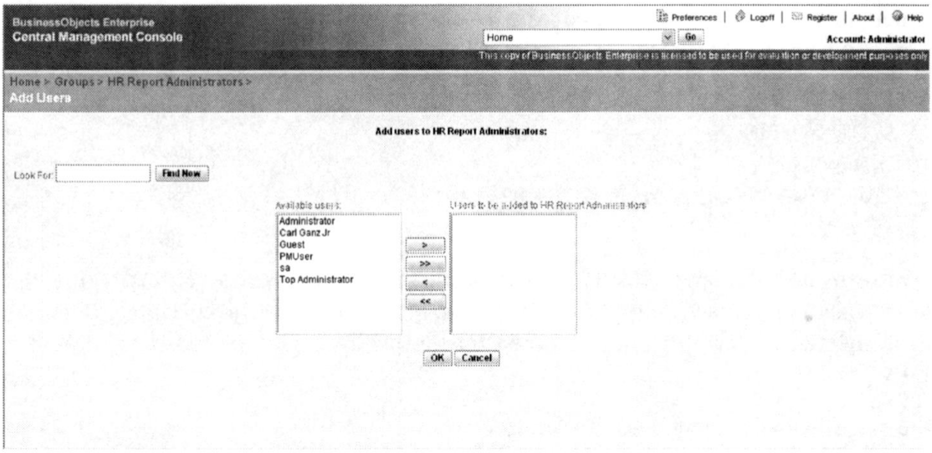

Figure 10-5. *Adding users to a group*

Here you can select all the desired users and move them to the membership side of the mutually exclusive list boxes using the arrow keys. Double-clicking is not supported here. Then, click OK to make these users members of the chosen group.

You can also accomplish the same task programmatically using the code shown in Listing 10-3.

Listing 10-3. *Adding a User to a Group*

```
szSQL = "SELECT SI_ID " +
    "FROM CI_SYSTEMOBJECTS " +
    "WHERE SI_ID = " + szUserCodeID;

oInfoObjects = oInfoStore.Query(szSQL);
oInfoObject = oInfoObjects[1];

oUser = ((User) oInfoObject);

oUser.Groups.Add(int.Parse(szGroupID));

oInfoStore.Commit(oInfoObjects);
```

In this example, we're extracting an InfoObject that is cast to an object of type User. User objects have a Groups collection that contains references to the groups to which the user belongs. By using the Add() method of the Groups collection, you can pass in the integer value representing the ID of the group to which you wish to assign this user. Then, use the Commit() method to save the changes to the InfoStore.

Extracting the Users in a Group

Now that you've created a user, created a group, and assigned a user to a group, you may find that you need to extract a group's membership list. In Chapter 5, we looked at an example of a SQL query that uses an undocumented feature—the SELECTUSINGPROPERTY command—to which you can pass the ID of the group to return a list of users. This SQL statement is shown here:

```
Select SI_ID, SI_NAME, SI_DESCRIPTION, SI_USERFULLNAME
From CI_SYSTEMOBJECTS
Where SI_KIND='User'
And SELECTUSINGPROPERTY(101,SI_ID,SI_GROUP_MEMBERS,SI_ID)
Order By SI_NAME
```

As with any undocumented feature, you must use this at your own risk, as these things tend to get "fixed" in future versions. The safer way to extract a user list given a group ID is to iterate through the property bags that comprise the group object. This approach is shown in Listing 10-4.

Listing 10-4. *Extracting the Members of a Group*

```
//Extract a group object
szSQL = "SELECT SI_GROUP_MEMBERS " +
    "FROM CI_SYSTEMOBJECTS " +
    "WHERE SI_ID = " + szUserGroup;

oInfoObjects = oInfoStore.Query(szSQL);

oDT = new DataTable();

oDT.Columns.Add(new DataColumn("ID"));
oDT.Columns.Add(new DataColumn("Name"));
oDT.Columns.Add(new DataColumn("Description"));

//HasMember() can be found in the code download
if (HasMember(oInfoObjects[1].Properties, "SI_GROUP_MEMBERS"))
{
    //Set a property bag reference so the code's not so long
    oProperty = oInfoObjects[1].Properties["SI_GROUP_MEMBERS"];

    //How many members does the group have?
    iCnt = ((int) oProperty.Properties["SI_TOTAL"].Value);

    //The name starts with the second property
    for (int x = 2; x <= iCnt + 1; x++)
    {
        oDR = oDT.NewRow();

        //Get the user ID of the member
        iUserID = ((int) oProperty.Properties[x].Value);

        //Get a user object for that user...
        szSQL = "SELECT SI_ID, SI_DESCRIPTION, SI_NAME " +
            "FROM CI_SYSTEMOBJECTS " +
            "WHERE SI_ID = " + iUserID.ToString();
```

```
    oUserObjects = oInfoStore.Query(szSQL);

    //...and assign the user's information to the DataTable
    oDR["ID"] = oUserObjects[1].Properties["SI_ID"].Value;
    oDR["Name"] = oUserObjects[1].Properties["SI_NAME"].Value;
    oDR["Description"] =
        oUserObjects[1].Properties["SI_DESCRIPTION"].Value;

    oDT.Rows.Add(oDR);
  }
}
```

Here we're extracting the specified group's SI_GROUP_MEMBERS property from the InfoStore. The results of this query are shown in Figure 10-6.

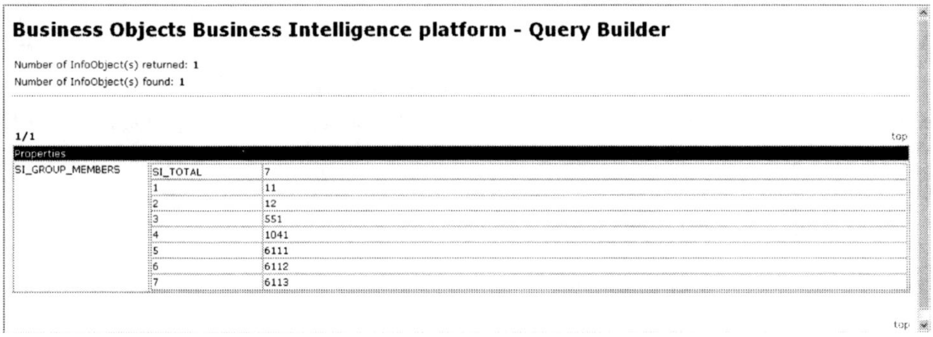

Business Objects Business Intelligence platform - Query Builder

Number of InfoObject(s) returned: 1
Number of InfoObject(s) found: 1

1/1   top

Properties		
SI_GROUP_MEMBERS	SI_TOTAL	7
	1	11
	2	12
	3	551
	4	1041
	5	6111
	6	6112
	7	6113

top ▾

Figure 10-6. *SI_GROUP_MEMBERS data*

SI_TOTAL tells us how many members the group contains so you can use that value to guide your for loop. For each user ID found, you'll need to execute another query to extract the name and other attributes of the user. This is where a JOIN would certainly come in handy, but JOINs are not supported in the InfoStore SQL language.

Subgroups

Subgroups are groups which belong to other groups. You can nest groups several generations deep if you wish. When you come across situations where users need rights that are slightly different than a rights set belonging to one of the existing groups, you can create a subgroup with the slightly altered right and assign those users to it. The code to assign one group as a subgroup of another is shown in Listing 10-5.

Listing 10-5. *Assigning Subgroups*

```
//Get group reference
szSQL = "SELECT SI_ID " +
    "FROM CI_SYSTEMOBJECTS " +
    "WHERE SI_ID = " + szGroupID;
```

```
oInfoObjects = oInfoStore.Query(szSQL);
oInfoObject = oInfoObjects[1];

oUserGroup = ((UserGroup) oInfoObject);

//Give the group a parent group
oUserGroup.ParentGroups.Add(iParentGroupID);

oInfoStore.Commit(oInfoObjects);
```

If a group already inherits from the group you are trying to make it a subgroup of (for example, if B is a subgroup of A and you then try to make A a subgroup of B), you'll receive an error similar to the following:

```
The update to the relationship named UserGroup-User with id number 128 is not
allowed because the object with id number 1050 will be part of a cycle.
```

These relationships are established in the InfoStore like a constraint rule in an RDBMS. In this case, the relationship entry has an SI_ID value of 128. Executing the following SQL statement:

```
SELECT *
FROM CI_SYSTEMOBJECTS
WHERE SI_ID = 128
```

will return the result set shown in Figure 10-7, which shows all the attributes of the relationship.

Business Objects Business Intelligence platform - Query Builder

Number of InfoObject(s) returned: 1
Number of InfoObject(s) found: 1

1/1   top

Properties	
SI_ID	128
SI_NAME	UserGroup-User
SI_TABLE	2
SI_HIDDEN_OBJECT	False
SI_FLAGS	2066
SI_OBTYPE	46
SI_SYSTEM_OBJECT	True
SI_OBJECT_IS_CONTAINER	False
SI_RUID	ASJpG6iXBQRFr_pxli7ML_o
SI_CHILDREN	0
SI_OWNER	System Account
SI_RUNNABLE_OBJECT	False
SI_PARENT_FOLDER	46
SI_COMPONENT	False
SI_APPLICATION_OBJECT	False
SI_INSTANCE_OBJECT	False
SI_GUID	ASJpG6iXBQRFr_pxli7ML_o
SI_INSTANCE	False
SI_CUID	AQBeaSifq3pJqyiBHv560cU
SI_PARENTID	46
SI_PLUGIN_OBJECT	False
SI_OWNERID	10
SI_UPDATE_TS	4/5/2006 11:59:08 AM
SI_CREATION_TIME	4/5/2006 11:59:08 AM
SI_PARENT_CUID	AYYjM86wh3BFpIxkt4m0XBc
SI_PARENT_FOLDER_CUID	AYYjM86wh3BFpIxkt4m0XBc
SI_PATH	C:\Program Files\Business Objects\BusinessObjects Enterprise 11.5\Packages\BusinessObjects_Relation_UserGroups_User_dfo.xml
SI_RELATION_LINK_TYPE	Soft
SI_RELATION_RELATION_IS_A_DAG	True

Figure 10-7. *UserGroup-User relationship*

Access Levels and Security Rights

When users are assigned to a group, they are given access levels, also known as roles, and security rights within that group. There are five options for access rights: Inherited, No Access, Full Control, View, and Advanced (more on which in the "Rights" section later). You can set these rights by selecting a user from the user list and clicking the Rights tab. Doing so will present you with the page shown in Figure 10-8.

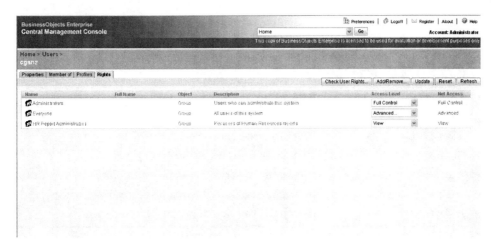

Figure 10-8. *Assigning access levels and rights*

Should you select the Rights tab from a report, you'll navigate to a similar page with two more access-level options—Schedule and View on Demand. Most of these access-level options mean what their names imply:

- No Access means that the user cannot even see the object when he's logged into the CMC.

- View allows the user to see the object settings and view scheduled instances, but prevents him from making any changes, including scheduling.

- The Schedule level permits the user to schedule the object and determine its destination and format in addition to all the View privileges.

- View on Demand offers all the Schedule-level rights plus the ability to refresh the report against the data source.

- Finally, Full Control gives the user complete administrative access to the object.

It's the Inherited options that you'll probably use most often. This means that the rights will be inherited from the owner groups rather than set on an individual basis.

Individual rights are normally not given out on a user-by-user basis, as this presents an internal control problem. Conceivably, if there are 100 users, there could also be 100 permutations of rights that need to be managed. You'll probably want to create groups that contain sets of rights and add users to these groups whose rights they'll inherit. It's much easier this way and adheres to most corporate security policies.

The key class to understand when extracting security information is the ObjectPrincipals collection of the SecurityInfo class. ObjectPrincipals allows you to retrieve and set the rights and roles to objects for specified groups and individual users. The detailed information about these rights—both inherited and explicitly granted—that the user has on the object can be accessed through the InheritedRights and Rights collections of ObjectPrincipals.

Roles

You can assign roles programmatically. The CeRole enumerator, listed in Table 10-1, shows the values used to specify the different roles/access levels available.

Table 10-1. *CeRole Enumerator Members*

Member	Value	Description
ceRoleAdvanced	0	User/group has a list of specific rights on the object.
ceRoleFullControl	5	User/group has complete rights over the object.
ceRoleNoAccess	1	User/group has no access to the object.
ceRoleSchedule	3	User/group can schedule and view the object.
ceRoleView	2	User/group can view this object's processed instances.
ceRoleViewOnDemand	4	User/group can view this object or its instances.

The code in Listing 10-6 shows how to add a user to the ObjectPrincipals collection for an object and then assign that user a role from the CeRole enumerator. This collection name contains the generic term "Principals" because it could refer to either a user or a group.

Listing 10-6. *Assigning Roles*

```
// Connect to BO XI

//Get report reference
szSQL = "SELECT SI_ID " +
   "FROM CI_INFOOBJECTS " +
   "WHERE SI_ID = " + szReportID;

oInfoObjects = oInfoStore.Query(szSQL);
oInfoObject = oInfoObjects[1];

oReport = ((Report) oInfoObject);

oObjectPrincipal = oReport.SecurityInfo.ObjectPrincipals.Add(iUserID);

//Assign the member of the CeRole enumerator
oObjectPrincipal.Role = sRole;

oInfoStore.Commit(oInfoObjects);
```

Rights

Rights may be either inherited or given out on an individual basis. The Advanced option allows you to customize a user's access to an object. Selecting the Advanced option will display the page shown in Figure 10-9. Here you can be very granular in determining what a user can and cannot do.

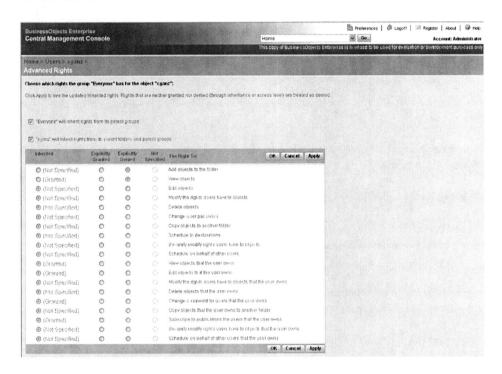

Figure 10-9. *Advanced access level page*

Assigning Rights

You may find that you wish to assign rights to an object for a particular user or group. One way to accomplish this is to create an array of rights you wish explicitly granted and then pass this to a web service method that will assign them. This process is shown in Listing 10-7.

Listing 10-7. *Specifying Explicitly Granted Rights*

```
localhost.BOXIWebService oBOXIWebService;
localhost.CeSystemRights[] aRights = new localhost.CeSystemRights[3];

oBOXIWebService = new localhost.BOXIWebService();
oBOXIWebService.Credentials = System.Net.CredentialCache.DefaultCredentials;

aRights[0] = localhost.CeSystemRights.ceRightAdd;
```

```
aRights[1] = localhost.CeSystemRights.ceRightEdit;
aRights[2] = localhost.CeSystemRights.ceRightScheduleOnBehalfOf;

oBOXIWebService.AssignSecurityRights("Dev", "1266", "1050", aRights);
```

This web service invocation is assigning the array of rights for report 1266 to user 1050. The code that applies these rights is shown in Listing 10-8.

Listing 10-8. *Specifically Granting Rights*

```
//Get report reference
szSQL = "SELECT SI_ID " +
   "FROM CI_INFOOBJECTS " +
   "WHERE SI_ID = " + szReportID;

oInfoObjects = oInfoStore.Query(szSQL);
oInfoObject = oInfoObjects[1];

oReport = ((Report) oInfoObject);

//Retrieve ObjectPrincipals collection and security rights collection
oObjectPrincipals = oReport.SecurityInfo.ObjectPrincipals;

//The "#" is used to tell the collection indexer that
//szUserCode is an ID and not an array index
oSecurityRights = oObjectPrincipals["#" + szUserCode].Rights;

//Deny all rights
foreach(SecurityRight oSecurityRight in oSecurityRights)
   oSecurityRight.Granted = false;

//Iterate through rights array and
//assign only those rights specified
iCnt = aRights.Length;

for (int x=0; x < iCnt; x++)
{
   oNewRight = oSecurityRights.Add((int) aRights[x]);

   if (! oNewRight.Inherited)
      oNewRight.Granted = true;
}

oInfoStore.Commit(oInfoObjects);
```

The ObjectPrincipals collection holds each user's rights to the specified report object. The Rights property will return a SecurityRights object that will contain all of that one user's rights to the object. By iterating through this collection, you can deny the existing rights and start anew by using the Add() method to enable the rights that are passed via the array.

Checking Rights

Suppose you wish to determine what the rights are for a given object. You can use the GetRightsForObject() web method, described later, to extract an XML file listing this information. The XML output will look something like Listing 10-9, which shows the group rights for the Employee report. In this example, the Administrators possess inherited rights while the Employee Report Administrators have explicitly granted rights.

Listing 10-9. *XML Security Rights Output*

```
<Employee SI_KIND="CrystalReport">
  <ObjectPrincipal SI_NAME="Administrators">
    <InheritedRights>
      <ID InheritedRights="Add objects to the folder">1</ID>
      <ID InheritedRights="View objects">3</ID>
      <ID InheritedRights="Edit objects">6</ID>
      <ID InheritedRights="Modify the rights users have to objects">8</ID>
      <ID InheritedRights="Schedule the document to run">21</ID>
      <ID InheritedRights="Delete objects">22</ID>
      <ID InheritedRights="Define server groups to process jobs">23</ID>
      <ID InheritedRights="Delete instances">38</ID>
      <ID InheritedRights="Copy objects to another folder">61</ID>
...
  <ObjectPrincipal SI_NAME="Employee Report Administrators">
    <Rights>
      <ID Rights="Add objects to the folder">1</ID>
      <ID Rights="View objects">3</ID>
      <ID Rights="Edit objects">6</ID>
      <ID Rights="Modify the rights users have to objects">8</ID>
      <ID Rights="Schedule the document to run">21</ID>
    </Rights>
```

The first step in building this XML output is to extract the basic information about the object—ID, name, and type—represented by the SI_ID, SI_NAME, and SI_KIND properties. This information will be added to the main XML element. The code to accomplish this is shown in Listing 10-10.

Listing 10-10. *Extracting Object Information*

```
//Connect to BO XI
szSQL = "SELECT SI_ID, SI_NAME, SI_KIND " +
  "FROM CI_INFOOBJECTS " +
  "WHERE SI_ID = " + szObjectID;

oInfoObjects = oInfoStore.Query(szSQL);
oInfoObject = oInfoObjects[1];

oObjectPrincipals = oInfoObject.SecurityInfo.ObjectPrincipals;
```

```
oXmlDocument = new XmlDocument();

oXmlElement = oXmlDocument.CreateElement("",
   oInfoObject.Properties["SI_NAME"].ToString(), "");

oXmlElement.SetAttribute("SI_KIND",
   oInfoObject.Properties["SI_KIND"].ToString());

oXmlDocument.AppendChild(oXmlElement);
```

Listing 10-11 shows how to iterate through these collections and retrieve the data.

Listing 10-11. *Extracting Inherited and Specifically Granted Rights*

```
foreach (ObjectPrincipal oObjectPrincipal in oObjectPrincipals)
{
   oXmlSubElement = oXmlDocument.CreateElement("", "ObjectPrincipal", "");
   oXmlSubElement.SetAttribute("SI_NAME", oObjectPrincipal.Name);

   oXmlElement.AppendChild(oXmlSubElement);

   if (oObjectPrincipal.Rights.Count > 0)
   {
      oXmlRightsElement = oXmlDocument.CreateElement("", "Rights", "");

      foreach(SecurityRight oSecurityRight in oObjectPrincipal.Rights)
         oXmlRightsElement = AddElement(oXmlDocument, oXmlRightsElement,
            "ID", oSecurityRight.ID.ToString(), "Rights",
            oSecurityRight.Description);

      oXmlSubElement.AppendChild(oXmlRightsElement);

   }

   if (oObjectPrincipal.InheritedRights.Count > 0)
   {
      oXmlRightsElement = oXmlDocument.CreateElement("", "InheritedRights", "");

      foreach(SecurityRight oSecurityRight in oObjectPrincipal.InheritedRights)
         oXmlRightsElement = AddElement(oXmlDocument, oXmlRightsElement,
            "ID", oSecurityRight.ID.ToString(), "InheritedRights",
            oSecurityRight.Description);

      oXmlSubElement.AppendChild(oXmlRightsElement);
   }
}
```

Each right is encapsulated in a SecurityRight object. The Rights and InheritedRights properties both hold collections of type SecurityRights. Though you can't edit inherited rights—this wouldn't make sense anyway since they are inherited from another object—you can explicitly grant and revoke noninherited rights. The rights available on the Advanced rights access page shown in Figure 10-9 are assignable through the Rights collection of ObjectPrincipals. Each right is referenced by one of the enumerated values shown in Table 10-2.

Table 10-2. *CeSystemRights Enumerator Members*

Member	Value	Description
ceRightAdd	1	Add objects to the folder.
ceRightCopy	61	Copy objects to another folder.
ceRightDelete	22	Delete objects.
ceRightDeleteInstance	38	Delete instances.
ceRightEdit	6	Edit objects.
ceRightModifyRights	8	Modify the rights users have to objects.
ceRightOwnerDelete	536870934	Delete objects that the user owns.
ceRightOwnerDeleteInstance	536870950	Delete report instances that the user owns.
ceRightOwnerEdit	536870918	Edit objects that the user owns.
ceRightOwnerModifyRights	536870920	Modify objects that the user owns.
ceRightOwnerPauseResumeSchedule	536870978	Pause and resume scheduled report instances that the user owns.
ceRightOwnerReschedule	536870987	Owner has the right to reschedule.
ceRightOwnerSecuredModifyRights	536870985	Owner has the right to modify security rights.
ceRightOwnerView	536870915	View objects that the user owns.
ceRightOwnerViewInstance	536870977	View instances that the user owns.
ceRightPauseResumeSchedule	66	Pause and resume scheduled report instances.
ceRightPickMachines	23	Specify server groups to process jobs.
ceRightReschedule	75	The right to reschedule a report.
ceRightSchedule	21	Schedule the report to run.
ceRightScheduleOnBehalfOf	76	Schedule on behalf of another user
ceRightSecuredModifyRights	73	The right to modify secured rights.
ceRightSetDestination	62	Schedule to destinations.
ceRightView	3	View (analyze) objects.
ceRightViewInstance	65	View report instances.

You can also determine what rights the current user has on an object by passing a series of rights to the CheckRights() method (or the CheckRight() method if you're only checking one right). The code to accomplish this is shown in Listing 10-12.

Listing 10-12. *Checking Rights on an Object*

```
localhost.BOXIWebService oBOXIWebService;
int[] aRights = new int[10];
object aRightsStatus;
object[] aRightsStatusData;

aRights[0] = ((int) CeSystemRights.ceRightAdd);
aRights[1] = ((int) CeSystemRights.ceRightCopy);
aRights[2] = ((int) CeSystemRights.ceRightDelete);
aRights[3] = ((int) CeSystemRights.ceRightDeleteInstance);
aRights[4] = ((int) CeSystemRights.ceRightEdit);
aRights[5] = ((int) CeSystemRights.ceRightModifyRights);
aRights[6] = ((int) CeSystemRights.ceRightPauseResumeSchedule);
aRights[7] = ((int) CeSystemRights.ceRightPickMachines);
aRights[8] = ((int) CeSystemRights.ceRightReschedule);
aRights[9] = ((int) CeSystemRights.ceRightSchedule);

oBOXIWebService = new localhost.BOXIWebService();
oBOXIWebService.Credentials = System.Net.CredentialCache.DefaultCredentials;

aRightsStatus = oBOXIWebService.CheckRights("Dev", "1266", aRights);
```

This code passes an array of rights to a web service method that in turn hands the array off to the CheckRights() method. This method will return an object array containing Boolean values indicating whether the right in the original array was granted or not. The code that obtains this data and returns it to the proxy application is shown in Listing 10-13.

Listing 10-13. *Returning Array Indicating Rights Availability*

```
//Connect to BO XI

//Get report reference
szSQL = "SELECT SI_ID " +
    "FROM CI_INFOOBJECTS " +
    "WHERE SI_ID = " + szReportID;

oInfoObjects = oInfoStore.Query(szSQL);
oInfoObject = oInfoObjects[1];

oReport = ((Report) oInfoObject);

aRightData = oReport.SecurityInfo.CheckRights(aRights);

aRightDataArray = ((object[]) aRightData);

return aRightDataArray;
```

Limits

Report limits allow you to determine how many instances of a given report are to be kept in the report history or how long they can stay there. BO XI can act as an archiving system for your reports as long as you have disk space, but you may not want to keep your report history around forever. Using the limits settings, you can instruct BO XI to delete more than a specified number of report instances or any instances older than a specified numbers of days. Of course, you may not want any reports deleted at all, since this would eliminate your audit trail. In this case, just don't set any limits and the report history will build indefinitely.

Note Many companies retain reports for a number of years based on their retention policies. Often, these reports will be stored in archiving software. One of my clients uses a tool that employs an Oracle back end and stores the files on a UNIX box. To automate the archiving process, we've set up our BO XI install to send all reports to an FTP client destination where the archiving software picks up the reports and imports them. In this way, all reports are archived as soon as they are run. The reports are also saved in the BO XI report history so the users have immediate access to them through our custom front end. Since our front end extracts the report histories from both BO XI and the archiving tool, they are presented to the user as a seamless garment and the report viewer functions no differently when displaying reports from either location.

Examine the limits page shown in Figure 10-10. Here you can assign limits based on the number of instances to keep or the number of days to keep them. These limits can be assigned on a per-user basis. The check box in the upper left of the page labeled "Delete excess instances when there are more than N instances of an object:" is assigned to the Everyone group.

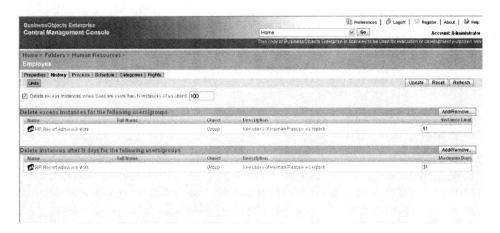

Figure 10-10. *Limits page*

The CeSystemLimits enumeration, shown in Table 10-3, identifies the types of limits. You'll need CeSystemLimits when you set limits programmatically.

Table 10-3. *CeSystemLimits Enumerator Members*

Member	Value	Description
ceLimitMaxInstanceAge	1359	Maximum instance age
ceLimitMaxInstanceCount	1360	Maximum number of instances per object
ceLimitMaxInstanceCountPerUser	1361	Maximum number of instances per object, per user
ceLimitMaxObjectLevelSecurityLimit	1555	Maximum object-level security, per user

Suppose you want to indicate the limits settings for a specific user or group. You can set up the group limits settings in an array of type int, as well as a numeric value for the Everyone setting that sets a maximum value on the number of all instances. The code to invoke this web service method is shown in Listing 10-14.

Listing 10-14. *Assigning Limits*

```
localhost.BOXIWebService oBOXIWebService;
int[][] aLimits = new int[2][];

oBOXIWebService = new localhost.BOXIWebService();
oBOXIWebService.Credentials = System.Net.CredentialCache.DefaultCredentials;

//Using jagged arrays here as multidimensional
//arrays cannot be passed to web services
aLimits[0] = new int[2];
aLimits[1] = new int[2];

aLimits[0][0] = ((int) CeSystemLimits.ceLimitMaxInstanceAge);
aLimits[0][1] = 30;

aLimits[1][0] = ((int) CeSystemLimits.ceLimitMaxInstanceCountPerUser);
aLimits[1][1] = 50;

oBOXIWebService.AssignSecurityLimits("Dev",
    "1266", "1050", aLimits, 100);
```

The AssignSecurityLimits() web method is shown in Listing 10-15. In order to apply the overall maximum instances setting, stored in the iMaxInstances parameter, we must iterate through the ObjectPrincipals collection of the report until we find the Everyone setting. Once this is located, we can then iterate through the SecurityLimits collection of the Everyone entry until we find the one with the description "Maximum instance count per object". This represents the check box setting in the upper left of the page.

Listing 10-15. *AssignSecurityLimits Web Method*

```
//Connect to BO XI

//Get report reference
```

```
szSQL = "SELECT SI_ID " +
   "FROM CI_INFOOBJECTS " +
   "WHERE SI_ID = " + szReportID;

oInfoObjects = oInfoStore.Query(szSQL);
oInfoObject = oInfoObjects[1];

oReport = ((Report) oInfoObject);

//Get ObjectPrincipals reference for the entire report
oObjectPrincipals = oReport.SecurityInfo.ObjectPrincipals;

//Iterate until we find the Everyone entry
foreach(ObjectPrincipal oObjectPrincipal in oObjectPrincipals)
{
   if (oObjectPrincipal.Name == "Everyone")
   {
      //Get the limits for the Everyone entry...
      oSecurityLimits = oObjectPrincipal.Limits;

      //...and iterate until the "Maximum instance
      //count per object" is located
      foreach(SecurityLimit oSecurityLimit in oSecurityLimits)
      {
         if (oSecurityLimit.Description == "Maximum instance count per object")
         {
            //when found assign the limit value
            oSecurityLimits.Add(((int) CeSystemLimits.ceLimitMaxInstanceCount),
               iMaxInstances);
            oInfoStore.Commit(oInfoObjects);
            break;
         }
      }

      break;
   }
}
```

Finally, the code in Listing 10-16 applies the settings passed in the array to the user/report combination specified using the Add() method of the SecurityLimits collection. Limits manipulation operates in a mirror image of the way rights are handled.

Listing 10-16. *Applying User/Group Settings*

```
//Get ObjectPrincipals reference for the specified user
//The "#" is used to tell the collection indexer that
//szUserCode is an ID and not an array index
oSecurityLimits = oObjectPrincipals["#" + szUserCode].Limits;
```

```
//Iterate through rights array and
//assign only those rights specified
iCnt = aLimits.Length;

for (int x=0; x < iCnt; x++)
    oSecurityLimits.Add(aLimits[x][0], aLimits[x][1]);

oInfoStore.Commit(oInfoObjects);
```

If you want to extract the limits set for each object, you can add the code shown in Listing 10-17 to the output loop found in Listing 10-11, which writes the security data for an object to XML.

Listing 10-17. *Extracting Limits*

```
if (oObjectPrincipal.Limits.Count > 0)
{
    oXmlRightsElement = oXmlDocument.CreateElement("", "Limits", "");

    foreach(SecurityLimit oSecurityLimit in oObjectPrincipal.Limits)
        oXmlRightsElement = AddElement(oXmlDocument, oXmlRightsElement,
            "Value", oSecurityLimit.Value.ToString(), "Limits",
            oSecurityLimit.Description);

    oXmlSubElement.AppendChild(oXmlRightsElement);
}
```

The output of the limits XML would look something like Listing 10-18.

Listing 10-18. *Limits XML Output*

```
<ObjectPrincipal SI_NAME="Everyone">
  <InheritedRights>
  ...
  </InheritedRights>
  <Limits>
    <ID Limits="Maximum instance count per object">1360</ID>
    <ID Limits="Maximum instance count per object, per user">1361</ID>
  </Limits>
</ObjectPrincipal>
<ObjectPrincipal SI_NAME="Employee Report Administrators">
  <Rights>
  ...
  </Rights>
  <Limits>
    <Value Limits="Maximum instance age in days">31</Value>
    <Value Limits="Maximum instance count per object">100</Value>
```

```
   <Value Limits="Maximum instance count per object, per user">51</Value>
  </Limits>
</ObjectPrincipal>
```

Non-Enterprise Security Management

Though BO XI provides a powerful and versatile security model, you may still choose to manage your users in NT groups or LDAP or Active Directory. Choose the Authentication options from the main menu, and you'll be presented with a tab page that allows you to establish settings for the four types of security BO XI offers.

The NT, AD, and LDAP authentication options allow you to map users and groups from your NT, AD, and LDAP databases to BO XI. You can then use these Windows databases to verify logins. You can even implement single sign-on where the credentials of the currently logged in user will be used without needing to explicitly log in again.

As an example, let's look at setting up Windows NT authentication. Select Authentication from the main menu and choose the Windows NT tab. You should see the page shown in Figure 10-11.

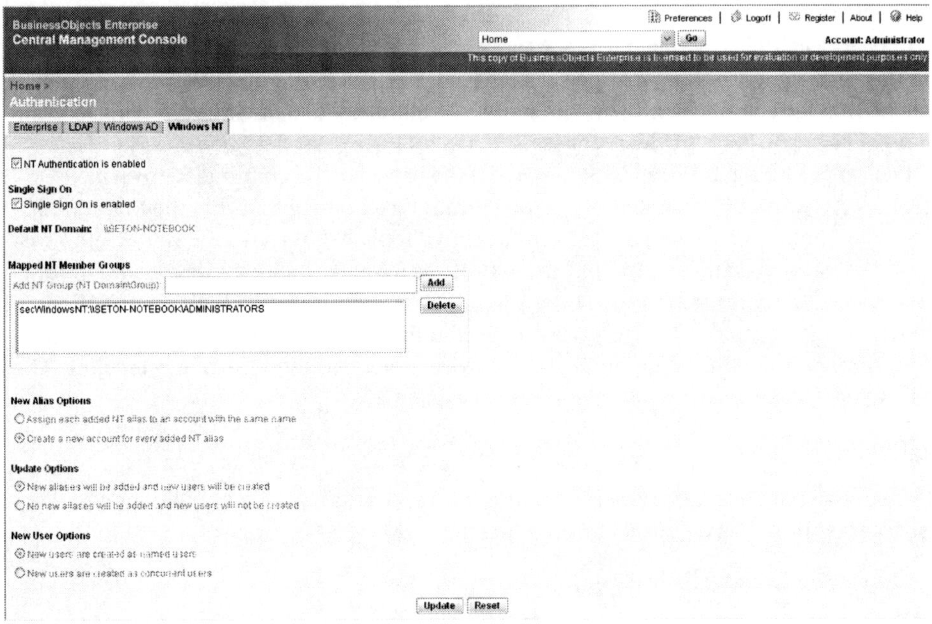

Figure 10-11. *Windows NT authentication*

Here you can enable NT authentication and determine whether single sign-on should be enabled as well. By entering the names of the NT groups that comprise the valid users of BO XI, you can indicate that user logins be validated against these groups.

Should you wish to view the status of any of the four security types available to you, execute the following SQL statement in the Query Builder:

```
SELECT *
FROM CI_SYSTEMOBJECTS
WHERE SI_NAME IN ('secEnterprise', 'secLDAP',
'secWinAD', 'secWindowsNT')
```

Validating NT Group Users

Regardless of the form of authentication you use, BusinessObjects XI itself allows you to create and manage user lists as well as import them from NT, AD, and LDAP security groups. These users can then be assigned rights to various reports or collections of reports. A major drawback of the way BO XI implements this feature is that although its management tools allow you to assign a Windows security group to a report, only those names who are members of this group at the time of the assignment are imported as named users. Any subsequent changes in membership of the group are not recognized, as BO XI does not maintain a dynamic link to Windows security.

To overcome this limitation and enjoy the benefits of having a dynamic link, you'll need to go through the operating system to determine what Windows groups a given user belongs to and whether or not the report that user wishes to access is open to that group.

There are a few issues that must be overcome when determining just who the currently logged in user is, especially when dealing with a web application. Since the Windows user ID is needed to match against the security permissions of the report, obtaining that ID is best picked up directly from the environment. This eliminates the annoyance to the user of having to log in again and of having to encrypt/decrypt passwords as they are passed to the server.

If the user is running Internet Explorer, and if the users can be guaranteed to all have Active Directory accounts, you can restrict the permissions to the folder that the front end is running from. Choose Control Panel ➤ Administrative Tools ➤ Internet Information Services and set the Directory Security properties for that site or folder to include Integrated Windows authentication. This permission restriction will cause the web server to challenge the client for credentials when attempting to load a page. IE will automatically supply your current Active Directory credentials in the background, and the web server will send the requested data. The Active Directory account name can then be retrieved like this:

```
szUserID = Request.ServerVariables("LOGON_USER");
```

If you're accessing BO XI service from a desktop application, you can obtain the domain and user names from the Environment object like this:

```
Console.Write(Environment.UserName);
"Carl Ganz Jr"
```

```
Console.Write(Environment.UserDomainName);
"SETON-NOTEBOOK"
```

To determine whether a user can access a report or not, we'll create a web service that returns a Boolean value indicating whether access is allowed. The invocation of this web service is shown in Listing 10-19.

Listing 10-19. *Invoking the Report Authorization Web Service*

```
localhost.BOXIWebService oBOXIWebService;

oBOXIWebService = new localhost.BOXIWebService();
oBOXIWebService.Credentials = System.Net.CredentialCache.DefaultCredentials;

if (oBOXIWebService.IsAuthorizedForReport("Dev", "1266", @"DOMAIN\GANZC"));
   MessageBox.Show ("Hooray! You're in!");
else
   MessageBox.Show ("Sorry, you're out of luck.");
```

The web service accesses the security object for the requested report and determines whether the indicated user is a member of one of the NT groups that is assigned to the report. The meat of the web service is shown in Listing 10-20.

Listing 10-20. *Determining Group Membership*

```
//Get an ArrayList containing all the NT groups this users belongs to
aUsersGroupMembership = new ArrayList();
aUsersGroupMembership = LoadNTGroups(aUsersGroupMembership, szNTUserID);

if (aUsersGroupMembership.ToArray().Length != 0)
{
   //Get a list of all users and NT Groups authorized for this report
   objObjectPrincipals = objReport.SecurityInfo.ObjectPrincipals;

   //See if there is a match
   foreach (ObjectPrincipal objObjectPrincipal in objObjectPrincipals)
   {
      szGroup = objObjectPrincipal.Name.Replace(szDomain + @"\", string.Empty);

      bResult = (aUsersGroupMembership.IndexOf(szGroup) > -1);

      if (bResult)
         break;
   }
}

return bResult;
```

After logging on to BO XI, create an ArrayList that contains all the groups the specified user belongs to. Then, an ObjectPrincipals collection is retrieved from the report object that contains references to all the groups and individual users that have access to this report as registered in the BO XI InfoStore. By iterating through the ObjectPrincipals collection, you can determine whether any of the groups belonging to the user match any of the groups associated with the report. If one is found, we can set the return value to True and exit the loop.

In order to retrieve a given user's list of Windows group memberships, the web.config file must be set with the proper authentication settings.

```
<authentication mode="Windows" />
  <identity impersonate="true" userName="domain\userid" password="mypass"/>
```

Ideally, you want to get your corporate security people to create an account with a nonexpiring password that only has the minimal rights needed to extract the group information.

At this point, the LoadNTGroups() function shown in Listing 10-21 will respond with a list of group memberships for the specified user. The IADsMembers and IADsGroup objects are obtained by setting a reference to the ActiveDs.Dll found in the \Windows\System32 directory.

Listing 10-21. *LoadNTGroups Function*

```
private ArrayList LoadNTGroups(ArrayList aUsersGroupMembership, string szNTUserID)
{
    IADsMembers oIADsMembers = null;
    DirectoryEntry oDirectoryEntry = null;

    //Passing a name that doesn't exist at all causes an error
    try
    {
        oDirectoryEntry = new DirectoryEntry("WinNT://" + szNTUserID + ",user");
        oIADsMembers = oDirectoryEntry.Invoke("Groups") as IADsMembers;
    }
    catch (Exception ex)
    {
        return aUsersGroupMembership;
    }

    foreach (IADsGroup oIADsGroup in oIADsMembers)
        aUsersGroupMembership.Add(oIADsGroup.Name);

    return aUsersGroupMembership;
}
```

License Keys

The License Keys option off the main menu allows you to monitor your BO XI licenses and all the limitations that may pertain to them. The License page is shown in Figure 10-12. You can have concurrent, named, and processor licenses depending on your key.

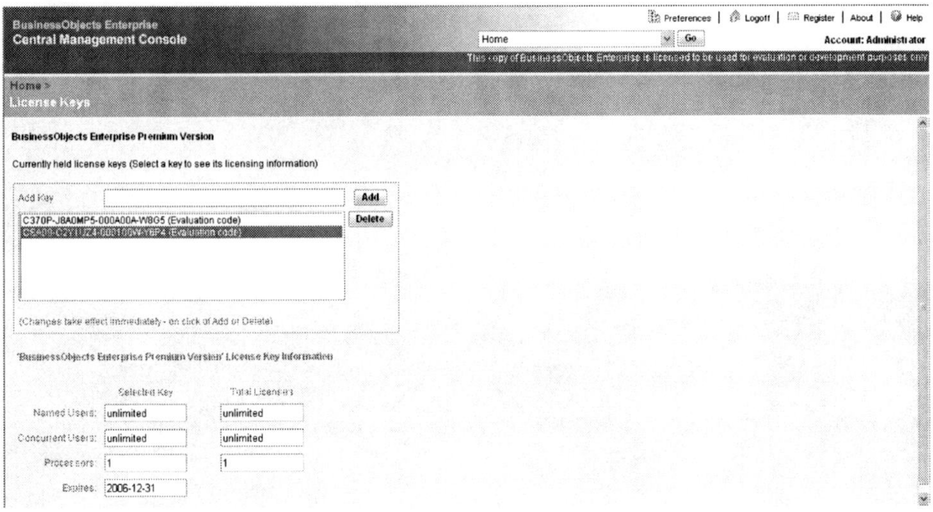

Figure 10-12. *License keys*

To determine the limits your license places on the numbers of users, as well as the number of users logged on at one time, select Settings ➤ Metrics from the main menu, and you'll see the page shown in Figure 10-13.

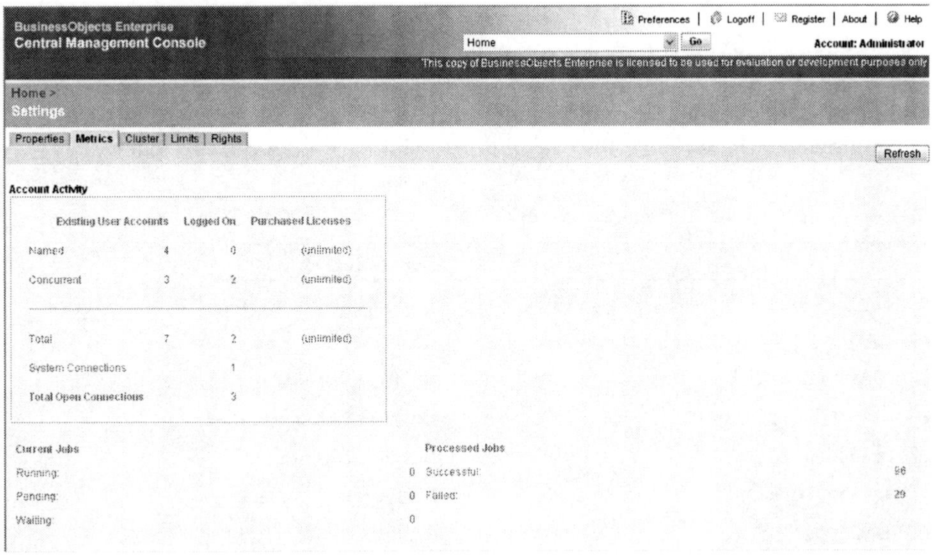

Figure 10-13. *Metrics page*

You can extract license information from the InfoStore by querying where SI_KIND = 'LicenseKey'. Execute the following SQL statement, and you'll see a result set similar to the one shown in Figure 10-14:

```
SELECT SI_ID, SI_LICENSE_KEY, SI_PRODUCT_VERSION, SI_EXPIRY_DATE,
SI_PRODUCT_LEVEL, SI_PRODUCT_NAME, SI_LICENSE_TYPE
FROM CI_SYSTEMOBJECTS
WHERE SI_KIND ='LicenseKey'
```

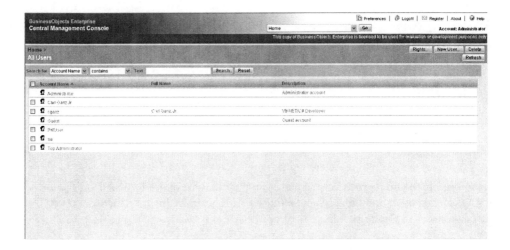

Figure 10-14. *License information*

The numeric designations for product name, product level, and license type all correspond to enumerated values. Table 10-4 shows the possible values for product name.

Table 10-4. *kcProductName Enumerator Members*

Name	Value	Description
kcNameAnalyticsApps	40	Analytic Applications
kcNameBaanPack	16	Baan Kit
kcNameBalanceScorecard	18	Balance Scorecard
kcNameBorlandCSharpBuilder	33	Borland CSharpBuilder
kcNameBorlandJBuilder	34	Borland JBuilder
kcNameBudgetingForecast	20	Budgeting/Forecasting
kcNameCADeveloper	8	CA Developer
kcNameCAProfessional	7	CA Professional
kcNameCAStandard	2	CA Standard
kcNameCEAdvanced	11	CE Advanced
kcNameCEBusinessViews	37	BusinessViews
kcNameCEPremium	35	CE Premium
kcNameCEProfessional	1	CE Professional

Name	Value	Description
kcNameCERASModify	30	CE RAS Modify
kcNameCEReportApplicationServer	26	CE Report Application Server
kcNameCEReportModification	36	CE Report Modification
kcNameCERepositoryOnly	32	CE Repository Only
kcNameCEStandard	3	CE Standard
kcNameCRDeveloper	6	CR Developer
kcNameCREnterprise	27	CR Enterprise
kcNameCRForTheNetPlatform	10	CR for the .NET Platform
kcNameCRProfessional	5	CR Professional
kcNameCRServer	39	CR Server
kcNameCRStandard	0	CR Standard
kcNameCustomerProfiling	19	Customer Profiling
kcNameEDesigner	9	DHTML Designer
kcNameEnterpriseBroadcastLicense	22	Enterprise Broadcast License
kcNameEServerSoftware	21	e-Server Software
kcNameETelecom	17	e-Telecom
kcNameHolosAnalyticClient	13	Holos Analytic Client
kcNameHolosAnalyticServer	12	Holos Analytic Server
kcNameKnowledgeAccelerator	38	Knowledge Accelerator
kcNameMicrosoftCRM	31	Microsoft CRM
kcNameOEMRestricted	25	OEM Restricted
kcNameRCAPI	4	RC API
kcNameReportApplicationServer	24	Report Application Server
kcNameReportServerDeveloper	28	Report Server Developer
kcNameReportServerProfessional	29	Report Server Professional
kcNameSAPPack	15	SAP Pack
kcNameSiebelKit	14	Siebel Kit
kcNameUnixInfoServer	23	Unix Info Server

Product level refers to the type of installation, be it a fully licensed version, an evaluation copy, or something in between. The possible values for the kcProductLevel enumeration are shown in Table 10-5.

Table 10-5. *kcProductLevel Enumerator Members*

Name	Value	Description
kcLevelEvaluation	4	Evaluation
kcLevelFull	0	Full
kcLevelFullPlusSubscription	1	Full and subscription
kcLevelNotForResale	6	Not for resale
kcLevelStandAloneSubscription	5	Stand-alone subscription
kcLevelSummarySI7	16	Summary S17 (return only)
kcLevelUBatchKeycode	7	U-batch keycode
kcLevelUpgrade	2	Upgrade
kcLevelUpgradePlusSubscription	3	Upgrade + Subscription

SI_LICENSE_TYPE equates to a kcUserLicenseType enumeration that indicates the type of license governing the current BO XI installation. The possible values for this property are listed in Table 10-6.

Table 10-6. *kcUserLicenseType Enumerator Members*

Name	Value	Description
kcLicenseConcurrent	1	Concurrent
kcLicenseCrystalCare	5	Crystal Care
kcLicenseDesigner	2	Designer
kcLicenseNamed	0	Named
kcLicenseNotApplicable	−1	Not applicable
kcLicensePerProcessor	3	Per processor
kcLicensePerServer	4	Per server
kcLicenseTypes	8	Types

Summary

As you have learned, the BusinessObjects XI security model can fit most of your security needs. Additional metadata can always be added to the existing security model through the creation of custom properties, which are covered in Chapter 9. If your security needs are so complex that the BO XI security model is not sufficient, you can create your own tables to manage users, groups, and rights separate from the BO XI implementation. Caveats to doing so are also discussed in Chapter 9. In the next chapter, we'll look at the newly introduced BusinessObjects XI Web Services SDK.

BusinessObjects Unified Web Services SDK

The BusinessObjects Unified Web Services SDK allows you to accomplish most of what you can with the .NET SDK. What it doesn't do is allow you to create and modify reports as you can with the RAS. As you would expect, both object models are structurally similar, but they are certainly not syntactical mirror images of one another. Still, knowledge of one certainly expedites the learning path for the other. This SDK is a new developer feature that was only released with BusinessObjects XI Release 2. The intention is to allow developers to implement a service-oriented architecture for their BO XI deployments that will allow applications throughout the enterprise to consume reporting services. In this chapter, we'll look at how to connect to the InfoStore; the new "path" format of the query language; how to extract, view, and add reports; and how to manage servers and security.

Configuring the Unified Web Services SDK

The Unified Web Services SDK is written in Java and based on the J2EE Framework. Though the latest version of the J2EE Framework is 1.5, the Unified Web Services SDK requires version 1.4.2. If you have 1.5 installed on your machine, you must uninstall it and apply version 1.4.2. It runs under the Tomcat server that is optionally installed along with BO XI. If you're not sure whether Tomcat was installed, check for the presence of the \Program Files\Business Objects\Tomcat directory. To install the web services themselves, you'll need to download the install set from the new BusinessObjects developer site at http://devlibrary.businessobjects.com/ BusinessObjectsXIR2/en/en/ws_sdk/wssdk_server/data/wssdkProviders_115.zip. While you're online, search for the file wssdk_admin_doc.pdf—the web services administrator's guide—which offers instructions on how to install Tomcat and the new SDK.

Note In July 2006, Business Objects went live with its new developer site at http://diamond.businessobjects. com. Here you can find all the service packs and documentation for the various SDKs in one place. In addition, the site offers news updates, sample code, and discussion forums.

To install the Unified Web Services SDK, unzip the wssdkProviders_115.zip file that you down-loaded into the \Program Files\Business Objects\BusinessObjects Enterprise 11.5\Assemble directory. Run the batch file dswsBobjeAssemblyEn.bat and pass to it the server name, port, and domain like this:

```
dswsBobjeAssemblyEn SETON-NOTEBOOK 8080 SETON-NOTEBOOK
```

The server name is the web server name or IP address, the port number refers to the port on which the server is listening, and the domain is the name of the BusinessObjects XI CMS server. In this example, the web server name and CMS name are the same. This batch file will create a WAR file in the same directory as the batch file. Copy this WAR file to the \webapps directory under your Tomcat installation on your application server. Shut down and restart Tomcat by using the \Tomcat\Bin\Shutdown.bat and \Tomcat\bin\Restart.bat batch files, and your web services will be available to you. You can also control Tomcat by selecting Tomcat ➤ Tomcat Configuration from the Start menu. This will provide you with a visual interface as an alternative to the batch files.

Once you've installed Tomcat, you'll need to test the deployment and verify that you have the latest version of the web services available. To check this, visit the following URL: http://localhost:8080/dswsbobje/services. If you see a web page that looks like Figure 11-1, then you have the latest version.

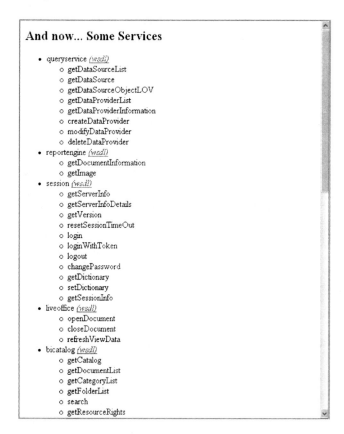

Figure 11-1. *Web service and methods listing*

The biplatform and reportengine services are new and are not included in the original web services installation. If you do not see these, you will not be able to run the code discussed in this section. Also, make sure that you download the latest documentation, as the help file that installs with BusinessObjects XI Release 2 does not cover the biplatform and reportengine services.

Web services are executable code that may be invoked from consumer applications, also known as proxies, utilizing the Simple Object Access Protocol (SOAP). SOAP is an XML-based protocol that primarily uses HTTP as its communication foundation. The point in using the ASCII-based XML is to allow for interoperability of software components. It doesn't matter what language the proxy application is written in or even what operating system it is running on. Any application that recognizes ASCII can use a web service. Each web service exposes its public web methods via the Web Services Description Language (WSDL). WSDL is an XML format that describes the web service and its location as well as each exposed method and all the individual parameters. You can view the WSDL of any web service by typing "?WSDL" after the asmx file name in the web service's URL. A very abbreviated example of WSDL, in this case for the reportengine web service, is shown in Listing 11-1.

Listing 11-1. *WSDL Sample*

```
<definitions targetNamespace="reportengine.dsws.businessobjects.com"
 xmlns="http://schemas.xmlsoap.org/wsdl/" xmlns:http=
   "http://schemas.xmlsoap.org/wsdl/http/"
xmlns:mime="http://schemas.xmlsoap.org/wsdl/mime/"
xmlns:s="http://www.w3.org/2001/XMLSchema"
xmlns:s0="reportengine.dsws.businessobjects.com"
xmlns:soap="http://schemas.xmlsoap.org/wsdl/soap/"
xmlns:tns1="dsws.businessobjects.com">
...
 <!--    ReportEngine Type    -->
...
 <types>
 <s:schema elementFormDefault="qualified"
targetNamespace="reportengine.dsws.businessobjects.com">
  <s:import namespace="dsws.businessobjects.com" />
 <s:complexType name="DocumentInformation">
 <s:sequence>
  <s:element maxOccurs="1" minOccurs="0" name="CurrentReportState"
nillable="true" type="s0:ReportState" />
  <s:element maxOccurs="unbounded" minOccurs="0" name="Reports" nillable="true"
 type="s0:Report" />
  <s:element maxOccurs="1" minOccurs="0" name="View" nillable="true"
 type="s0:View" />
 ...
  <s:any maxOccurs="unbounded" minOccurs="0" namespace="##other"
processContents="lax" />
  </s:sequence>
  <s:attribute form="unqualified" name="DocumentReference" type="s:string" />
  <s:attribute form="unqualified" name="Name" type="s:string" />
```

```
<s:attribute form="unqualified" name="FileType" type="s:string" />
...
<s:anyAttribute namespace="##other" />
</s:complexType>
```

Why Use the Web Services SDK?

You can accomplish most of same tasks using both the Unified Web Services and the .NET SDKs (the one feature not available in the Web Service SDK is RAS support for creating and modifying reports). Of course, you can even wrap the .NET SDK in a web service wrapper as suggested in Chapter 5. The key advantage the Web Services SDK has is that it is already a web service and, unlike the .NET SDK, it allows you to work with BusinessObjects Web Intelligence reports in addition to Crystal reports. Which one you use is simply a matter of preference. The .NET SDK is not being deprecated and it is the intention of BusinessObjects to continue to offer and continue to support both object models.

Programming Web Services

The Unified Web Services SDK has its own object model that is unique, to a greater or lesser degree, from that of the .NET SDK. If you know one, it will certainly give you an advantage in learning the other, but the code is not at all interchangeable. In this section, we'll examine the different web services that comprise the SDK, learn how to connect to the InfoStore, and then cover programming examples for report and folder manipulation, scheduling, servers, and security.

Services

The Unified Web Services SDK is actually a series of services that offer different functionality. These services are listed and explained in Table 11-1.

Table 11-1. *Web Service SDK Servers*

Service	Description
Session	Handles session information, login, user rights, resource, and dictionary information.
BIPlatform	Primary access object to the BO server. Allows you to extract InfoObjects via queries.
BICatalog	Allows you to search for documents, folders, and categories. Business Objects recommends that you use the BIPlatform service instead, which allows you to perform the same tasks.
ReportEngine	Allows access to report documents. You can drill data, access login information, set parameters, and open, navigate, and display documents.
QueryService	Allows creation, modification, and deletion of queries and access to universes.
Publish	Allows you to add, modify, and delete objects on the BO Server. Business Objects recommends that you use the BIPlatform service instead, which allows you perform the same tasks.

Creating a Connection

The first step you'll need to take in working with any of the web services is to establish a connection to the BO XI server. To do this, you'll need the URL of the web services and all the connection information such as user ID, password, domain name, and authorization type. This information is shown in Listing 11-2.

Listing 11-2. *Setting the Connection Information*

```
string szServicesURL = "http://localhost:8080/dswsbobje/services/";
string szAuthType = "secEnterprise";
string szDomain = "SETON-NOTEBOOK";
string szUser = "Administrator";
string szPassword = "";
```

The goal of the connection process is to instantiate a BIPlatform object through which you can perform most of the interaction you'll need with BO XI. BIPlatform is the Unified Web Service SDK's equivalent of the .NET InfoStore object. The GetBIPlatform() method shown in Listing 11-3 illustrates how to create a BIPlatform object.

Listing 11-3. *Building a BIPlatform Object*

```
private BIPlatform GetBIPlatform(string szServicesURL,
    string szAuthType,
    string szDomain,
    string szUser,
    string szPassword)
{
    SessionInfo oSessionInfo;
    Session oSession;
    BusinessObjects.DSWS.Connection oConnection;
    BusinessObjects.DSWS.ConnectionState oConnectionState;
    EnterpriseCredential oEnterpriseCredential;
    BIPlatform oBIPlatform;

    //Create an EnterpriseCredential object using
    //the user's BO XI logon information
    oEnterpriseCredential = new EnterpriseCredential();

    oEnterpriseCredential.AuthType = szAuthType;
    oEnterpriseCredential.Domain = szDomain;
    oEnterpriseCredential.Login = szUser;
    oEnterpriseCredential.Password = szPassword;

    //Create a connection object by referencing the session URL
    oConnection = new BusinessObjects.DSWS.
        Connection(szServicesURL + "session");
```

```
//Instantiate a Session object using the Connection object
oSession = new Session(oConnection);

//Create a SessionInfo object by logging in using the credential's object
oSessionInfo = oSession.Login(oEnterpriseCredential);

//Create a connection state object
oConnectionState = new BusinessObjects.DSWS.
   ConnectionState(oSessionInfo.SessionID);

//Set the Connection object's URL to the biplatform service
oConnection.URL = szServicesURL + "biplatform";

//Finally, create a BIPlatform object using
//a Connection and ConnectionState object
oBIPlatform = new BIPlatform(oConnection, oConnectionState);

return oBIPlatform;
}
```

First, you'll need to create an EnterpriseCredential object to hold the logon information. Next, instantiate a Connection object by referencing the URL of the Session web service. Then, create a Session object by passing the Connection object as a constructor parameter. The Session object's Login() method accepts the EnterpriseCredential object and returns a SessionInfo object that you can use to create a ConnectionState object. Finally, the Connection and ConnectionState objects are used through the BIPlatform web service to create a BIPlatform object.

I'm sure you'll agree that this code is not very intuitive, and much of the rest of the Unified Web Services SDK code is like it. Personally, I find the .NET SDK to be much easier to work with.

Once you have a BIPlatform object, you can examine the system properties. The code shown in Listing 11-4 lists the names and values of the various system properties by retrieving a SystemProperty array from the GetSystemInfoProperties() method of BIPlatform.

Listing 11-4. *Extracting System Information*

```
SystemProperty[] aSystemProperty;

aSystemProperty = oBIPlatform.GetSystemInfoProperties();

for(int y=0; y < aSystemProperty.Length; y++)
   Response.Write(string.Format("Name = {0} Value = {1} <BR>",
      aSystemProperty[y].Name, aSystemProperty[y].Value));
```

This code produces the web page shown in Figure 11-2.

```
Name = SI_CAN_SET_LIMITS Value = false
Name = SI_CAN_USE_THIRD_PARTY_AUTHEN Value = false
Name = SI_CAN_USE_SERVER_GROUPS Value = false
Name = SI_ENABLE_WEBI Value = false
Name = SI_ENABLE_INTERACTIVE_REPORTING Value = false
Name = SI_CAN_USE_METADATA Value = false
Name = SI_CAN_CREATE_GROUPS Value = false
Name = SI_ENABLE_DASHBOARD_MANAGER Value = false
Name = SI_ENABLE_SPC Value = false
Name = SI_ENABLE_MYINFOVIEW_DASHBOARD Value = false
Name = SI_ENABLE_PUBLISH_CA Value = false
Name = SI_ENABLE_PIKS Value = false
Name = SI_RAS_KEYCODE_PRESENT Value = false
Name = SI_CAN_CREATE_USERS Value = false
Name = SI_CAN_USE_PROGRAM_OBJECTS Value = false
Name = SI_ENABLE_SCHEDULE Value = false
Name = SI_IS_EVAL_PRODUCT Value = false
Name = SI_ENABLE_PORTAL Value = false
Name = SI_CAN_USE_CLUSTERING Value = false
Name = SI_OEM_KEYCODE_PRESENT Value = false
Name = SI_CAN_PRINT_REPORTS Value = false
Name = SI_PRO_KEYCODE_PRESENT Value = false
Name = SI_CAN_SCHEDULE_TO_DEST Value = false
Name = SI_PRODUCT_DESCRIPTION Value = 0
Name = SI_ENABLE_PERFORMANCE_MANAGER Value = false
Name = SI_ENABLE_SETS Value = false
Name = SI_CAN_USE_PROCESSING_EXT Value = false
Name = SI_ENABLE_LIVEOFFICE Value = false
Name = SI_PREMIUM_KEYCODE_PRESENT Value = false
Name = SI_ENABLE_BCAP Value = false
Name = SI_CAN_USE_FULLCLIENT Value = false
Name = SI_CAN_CREATE_NEWUSERS Value = false
Name = SI_ENABLE_PREDICTION Value = false
Name = SI_CAN_USE_EVENTS Value = false
Name = SI_CAN_USE_NOTIFICATION Value = false
Name = SI_ENABLE_PUBLISH_CR Value = false
```

Figure 11-2. *System property output*

Queries

Before you can work with the InfoStore objects, you'll need a way of specifying what objects you want to extract. There are four ways you can reference objects in the InfoStore. You can specify the CUID of one or more objects, you can use a SQL SELECT statement as discussed in Chapter 5, you can use the new path statement, or you can use a search statement. Which approach you are taking is indicated to the Unified Web Services SDK by prefixing the query with "cuid://", "query://", "path://", or "search://".

CUID

The CUID is the simplest approach, as you need only specify the unique CUID value of the desired object. The following example uses the "cuid://" prefix and passes an object's CUID.

```
cuid://<AfVEcjaDxd5Is.02mRzz3bI>;
```

Note the angle brackets that surround the CUID. Should you need to extract multiple CUIDs, you can separate them with a comma and enclose the entire series in angle brackets like this:

```
cuid://<AfVEcjaDxd5Is.O2mRzz3bI,AdGpAJuZVl1Bj3b7lyExTos>;
```

Query

If you are more comfortable with the SQL language approach, you may use the "query://" prefix and then surround the SQL statement with braces as shown here:

```
query://{SELECT * FROM CI_INFOOBJECTS WHERE SI_ID = 1566};
```

The syntax of the SQL language is explained in Chapter 5.

Path

BusinessObjects XI Release 2 introduced a new path language, which is prefixed by "path://". Though the documentation may suggest that path queries are replacing SQL queries, Business Objects has confirmed that this is definitely not the case. Path references are being introduced only as a new search option and not as a replacement for anything.

The path approach is similar to the XML XPath syntax. Each query specifies a root table and a base folder. For example, Crystal Reports are stored in the InfoObjects root table, whereas events and calendars are stored in SystemObjects. The base folders differ as well. Crystal Reports uses the root folder, events use Events, and calendars use Calendars. Therefore, a search for a report would begin like this:

```
path://InfoObjects/Root Folder/
```

whereas a search for a calendar would begin like this:

```
path://SystemObjects/Calendars/
```

Let's examine a few examples of how path searches work. To extract an individual report in a folder, specify the full folder path and name of the report as shown here:

```
path://InfoObjects/Root Folder/Human Resources/Employee Report;
```

To retrieve a reference to the folder itself, specify only the name of the folder. This statement returns a reference to the Human Resources folder:

```
path://InfoObjects/Root Folder/Human Resources;
```

Adding a slash at the end will return a collection of all objects within the folder, including subfolders:

```
path://InfoObjects/Root Folder/Human Resources/;
```

The plus sign indicates that the query should return a report and all the instances of that report. The following query will return the Employee Report template entry (SI_INSTANCE = 0) and all the instances (SI_INSTANCE = 1) that have the Employee Report as its parent:

```
path://InfoObjects/Root Folder/Human Resources/Employee Report+/;
```

Should you only need, for example, the scheduling information for a report, you can specify just that data by using the @ sign as shown here:

```
path://InfoObjects/Root Folder/Human Resources/Employee Report@SI_SCHEDULEINFO;
```

Multiple properties can be specified via a comma-separated list like this:

```
path://InfoObjects/Root Folder/Human Resources/Employee Report
@SI_SCHEDULEINFO, SI_PROCESSINFO;
```

The @ sign is the attribute indicator. Failure to use it when extracting an object's information is equivalent to executing SELECT * for the object. Just as with a SQL statement, it is proper form to extract only the information you really need to perform an operation, so be sure to use attributes to restrict searches.

Should you wish to filter your results (akin to a SQL WHERE clause), you can specify a conditional operator using brackets as shown here:

```
path://InfoObjects/Root Folder/Human Resources/[SI_KIND='CrystalReport'];
```

In this example, only Crystal reports are extracted from the Human Resources folder. Still, you have full use of all logical operators as shown by this query, which returns all folders and reports:

```
path://InfoObjects/Root Folder/Human Resources/[SI_KIND='CrystalReport'
OR SI_KIND = 'Folder'];
```

The question mark serves as the parameter operator, that is, you're indicating that data that follows will be passed to the web service. In this example, we're using it to set an ORDER BY field or specify search options. In the following example, all the Crystal report entries in the InfoStore are returned and displayed in name order:

```
path://InfoObjects/Root Folder/**/*?OrderBy=SI_NAME[SI_KIND='CrystalReport'];
```

The ASC clause to indicate an ascending sort is assumed, but if you wish to use DESC to indicate a descending sort, that functionality is also supported.

■**Note** The Unified Web Services SDK does not support the SI_ID and SI_PARENTID properties. Use SI_CUID and SI_PARENTCUID instead. By default, all objects returned are ordered by the SI_ID value. You cannot use the SI_CUID property in an ORDER BY.

Search

The "search://" option allows you to specify a combination of criteria and search options to filter InfoStore objects. For example, the following query will return all objects that have a name or keywords containing the word *Employee*. All instances that match this criteria will be returned as well.

```
search://{Employee}?IncludeInstances=true&SearchKeywords=true;
```

Table 11-2 lists the options available when using the search method.

Table 11-2. *Search Keywords*

Keyword	Default	Description
SearchName	True	Searches for text in the SI_NAME property
SearchKeywords	False	Searches for text in the SI_KEYWORDS property
SearchCaseSensitive	False	Forces a case-sensitive search
SearchAllWords	False	Indicates whether all search terms must match
SearchWithoutWords	False	Searches for objects that do not contain the specified string, like a NOT IN clause in SQL
SearchExact	False	Ignores partial matches and searches only for a matching string
IncludeInstances	False	Indicates whether report instances will be returned

Extracting Data

Once you've settled on your query preferences and determined what data you wish to extract, you can retrieve data in the form of InfoObjects. Listing 11-5 shows what it takes to retrieve a single report object from the InfoStore.

Listing 11-5. *Connecting to the InfoStore and Retrieving an InfoObject*

```
BIPlatform oBIPlatform;
ResponseHolder oResponseHolder;
InfoObjects oInfoObjects;
GetOptions oGetOptions;
CrystalReport oCrystalReport;
string szQuery;

oBIPlatform = GetBIPlatform(szServicesURL,
    szAuthType, szDomain, szUser, szPassword);

oGetOptions = new GetOptions();
oGetOptions.IncludeSecurity = true;

szQuery = "query://{SELECT * FROM CI_INFOOBJECTS WHERE SI_ID = 1566}";

oResponseHolder = new ResponseHolder();
oResponseHolder = oBIPlatform.Get(szQuery, oGetOptions);

oInfoObjects = oResponseHolder.InfoObjects;

oCrystalReport = ((CrystalReport) oInfoObjects.InfoObject[0]);
```

The first task is to connect to the InfoStore and return a BIPlatform object. Next we can optionally create a GetOptions object through which we will indicate what attributes we wish to return with the object collection we are seeking. In this example, it indicates that the security information should be returned.

GETOPTIONS

The GetOptions class is used to set certain properties. The class exposes three main properties: ExportDependencies, IncludeSecurity, and PageSize. By setting these properties, you can pass an object of the GetOptions class to another method, usually the BIPlatform.Get() method, which will apply the values set. We just saw an example of this in the previous section, and coming up we'll see how to use GetOptions to specify a custom page size. Use of these properties can be misleading. For example, it would seem like the way to set the page size would be like this:

```
oResponseHolder.PagingDetails.PageSize = 20
```

Using this code will not cause an error. However, it will have no effect on your application. Rather, you'll need to set the page size like this:

```
oGetOptions.PageSize = 20;
oGetOptions.PageSizeSpecified = true;

oResponseHolder = oBIPlatform.Get("path://InfoObjects/Root Folder/**/*",
    oGetOptions);
```

The Get() method of the BIPlatform object, the counterpart to the InfoStore.Query() method, takes the query string and the optional GetOptions object and returns the matching records to a ResponseHolder collection. The InfoObjects property of the ResponseHolder object contains a collection of objects that match the query. In this example, we know that only one object of type CrystalReport was returned, and so it is type cast into a CrystalReport object. At this point, you can operate on the report as you would expect by assigning parameters, creating schedules, assigning security privileges, and so on.

Paging

In order to facilitate efficient querying in web-based applications, the Unified Web Services SDK implements paging. In order for this to happen, your ORDER BY statement may only contain indexed columns. Paging allows you to return and process query results in sets. Listing 11-6 shows how paging is implemented.

Listing 11-6. *Paging InfoObjects Collection*

```
BIPlatform oBIPlatform;
ResponseHolder oResponseHolder;
ResponseHolder oPageResponseHolder;
GetOptions oGetOptions;
InfoObjects oInfoObjects;
PageInfo[] aPageInfo;
string szData;
int y = 0;
```

```
oBIPlatform = GetBIPlatform(szServicesURL, szAuthType,
    szDomain, szUser, szPassword);

//By default, the page size is set to 100. Here, we're changing it to 20
oGetOptions = new GetOptions();

oGetOptions.PageSize = 20;
oGetOptions.PageSizeSpecified = true;

//Pull everything to get a large result set
oResponseHolder = oBIPlatform.Get("path://InfoObjects/Root Folder/**/*",
    oGetOptions);

oInfoObjects = oResponseHolder.InfoObjects;

aPageInfo = oResponseHolder.PagingDetails.PageInfo;

for(int x=0; x < aPageInfo.Length; x++)
{
    oPageResponseHolder = oBIPlatform.Get(aPageInfo[x].PageURI, null);
    oInfoObjects = oPageResponseHolder.InfoObjects;
    y = 0;

    foreach(InfoObject oInfoObject in oInfoObjects.InfoObject)
    {
        y++;

        szData = string.Format("{0} - SI_ID = {1}  SI_NAME = {2}  SI_KIND = {3} <BR>",
                    y.ToString(),
                    oInfoObject.ID.ToString(),
                    oInfoObject.Name,
                    oInfoObject.Kind);

        Response.Write(szData);
    }

}
```

After executing the query, you can create an array of PageInfo objects to hold references to each page of information. By iterating through this array, you can use the PageURI property of the individual PageInfo object to retrieve the next page of information from the InfoStore, which you can then process. In this example, processing means iterating through each object in the page and writing its ID, Name, and Kind properties to the browser. Then, you can move on to the next page of information and so on until the result set is exhausted. The output of this code is shown in Figure 11-3.

```
1 - SI_ID = 122 SI_NAME = Report Conversion Tool Temporary Documents SI_KIND = Folder
2 - SI_ID = 123 SI_NAME = Report Conversion Tool SI_KIND = Folder
3 - SI_ID = 125 SI_NAME = Report Conversion Tool Audit Documents SI_KIND = Folder
4 - SI_ID = 136 SI_NAME = Report Conversion Tool Documents SI_KIND = Folder
5 - SI_ID = 331 SI_NAME = Report Samples SI_KIND = Folder
6 - SI_ID = 332 SI_NAME = Feature Samples SI_KIND = Folder
7 - SI_ID = 333 SI_NAME = Feature Examples SI_KIND = Folder
8 - SI_ID = 334 SI_NAME = Accessibility SI_KIND = CrystalReport
9 - SI_ID = 342 SI_NAME = Alerting Report SI_KIND = CrystalReport
10 - SI_ID = 348 SI_NAME = Charting SI_KIND = CrystalReport
11 - SI_ID = 354 SI_NAME = Add new formatting features to your cross-tab SI_KIND = CrystalReport
12 - SI_ID = 360 SI_NAME = Custom Functions Demo SI_KIND = CrystalReport
13 - SI_ID = 366 SI_NAME = How to group data in intervals SI_KIND = CrystalReport
14 - SI_ID = 372 SI_NAME = How to create group selection based on countries with sales based on the
parameter values SI_KIND = CrystalReport
15 - SI_ID = 378 SI_NAME = How to group data SI_KIND = CrystalReport
16 - SI_ID = 384 SI_NAME = Hierarchical Grouping SI_KIND = CrystalReport
17 - SI_ID = 390 SI_NAME = How To Use Dynamic Cascading Prompting SI_KIND = CrystalReport
18 - SI_ID = 555 SI_NAME = Record Selection on Date Range SI_KIND = CrystalReport
19 - SI_ID = 561 SI_NAME = How to maintain running totals for a group SI_KIND = CrystalReport
20 - SI_ID = 567 SI_NAME = Universe Report SI_KIND = CrystalReport
1 - SI_ID = 575 SI_NAME = General Business SI_KIND = Folder
2 - SI_ID = 576 SI_NAME = Employee Profile (Alphabetical with Employee Picture) SI_KIND =
CrystalReport
3 - SI_ID = 582 SI_NAME = Employee Sales (Quarterly Report) SI_KIND = CrystalReport
4 - SI_ID = 650 SI_NAME = Inventory Cross-Tab Report by Product Type & Supplier SI_KIND =
CrystalReport
5 - SI_ID = 656 SI_NAME = Mail Labels SI_KIND = CrystalReport
6 - SI_ID = 662 SI_NAME = Order Packing List SI_KIND = CrystalReport
7 - SI_ID = 668 SI_NAME = Order Processing Efficiency Dashboard SI_KIND = CrystalReport
8 - SI_ID = 715 SI_NAME = Product Catalog SI_KIND = CrystalReport
9 - SI_ID = 721 SI_NAME = Geographic Sales Report SI_KIND = CrystalReport
10 - SI_ID = 727 SI_NAME = World Sales Report SI_KIND = CrystalReport
11 - SI_ID = 733 SI_NAME = Navigation Package SI_KIND = ObjectPackage
12 - SI_ID = 734 SI_NAME = Managed Navigation Detail SI_KIND = CrystalReport
13 - SI_ID = 740 SI_NAME = Managed Navigation SI_KIND = CrystalReport
```

Figure 11-3. *Paging data*

"SPECIFIED" PROPERTIES

You may have noticed that many of the properties across the different web services objects have a companion Boolean "Specified" version. For example, the SchedulingInfo object has both a ScheduleType and a ScheduleTypeSpecified property. This "specified" property tells the web service that the data property has been set. Therefore if you set the ScheduleType property and do not set the ScheduleTypeSpecified to True, the web service will not recognize the value you placed in the ScheduleType property. To make sure the value is recognized, you'll need to do this:

```
oSchedulingInfo = new SchedulingInfo();
oSchedulingInfo.ScheduleType = ScheduleTypeEnum.CALENDAR;
oSchedulingInfo.ScheduleTypeSpecified = true;
```

The "Specified" properties exist to increase performance. Their use will inform the web services not to return some of the object information unless it is specifically requested or specifically set. Note that this is a limitation for .NET but not for Java.

Working with Reports

The most fundamental tasks you'll need to perform with BusinessObjects likely involve working with reports. In the next sections, we'll examine the code needed to extract reports and view them, add new reports to the InfoStore, set parameters, and schedule existing reports.

Viewing Reports

Viewing reports is one of the most common tasks in any reporting system. Listing 11-7 shows how to specify a report and display it as a PDF file. The code to accomplish this is quite different from the .NET and RAS SDKs, so we'll examine it in detail.

Listing 11-7. *Viewing a Report*

```
BIPlatform oBIPlatform;
BusinessObjects.DSWS.Connection oConnection;
BusinessObjects.DSWS.ConnectionState oConnectionState;
ResponseHolder oResponseHolder;
ReportEngine oReportEngine;
RetrieveData oRetrieveData;
RetrieveBinaryView oRetrieveBinaryView;
ViewSupport oViewSupport;
DocumentInformation oDocumentInformation;
BinaryView oBinaryView;
Action[] oActions;
string szCUID;

oBIPlatform = GetBIPlatform(szServicesURL, szAuthType,
    szDomain, szUser, szPassword);

oResponseHolder = oBIPlatform.Get(szPath + szReportName, null);

szCUID = oResponseHolder.InfoObjects.InfoObject[0].CUID;

//Since we'll need the Connection and ConnectionState properties to
//create the ReportEngine class, let's extract them from BIPlatform
oConnection = oBIPlatform.Connection;
oConnectionState = oBIPlatform.ConnectionState;

//ReportEngine provides a gateway to the report document
oConnection.URL = szServicesURL + "reportengine";
oReportEngine = new ReportEngine(oConnection, oConnectionState);

//The ViewSupport class maps the viewing preferences
oViewSupport = new ViewSupport();
oViewSupport.OutputFormat = sOutputFormatType;
oViewSupport.ViewType = ViewType.BINARY;
oViewSupport.ViewMode = ViewModeType.DOCUMENT;

//RetrieveBinaryView indicates that a binary document,
//as opposed to a character or XML document, should be retrieved
```

```
oRetrieveBinaryView = new RetrieveBinaryView();
oRetrieveBinaryView.ViewSupport = oViewSupport;

//RetrieveData indicates what report data will be returned
oRetrieveData = new RetrieveData();
oRetrieveData.RetrieveView = oRetrieveBinaryView;

//Indicate that when the report is extracted it should be refreshed
oActions = new Action[1];
oActions[0] = new Refresh();

//Extract the report
oDocumentInformation = oReportEngine.
   GetDocumentInformation(szCUID, null, oActions, null, oRetrieveData);

//Retrieve binary view of report
oBinaryView = ((BinaryView) oDocumentInformation.View);

//Output report to browser
Response.Clear();
Response.AddHeader("Content-Length", oBinaryView.ContentLength.ToString());
Response.AddHeader("Content-Disposition",
   String.Format("inline; filename={0};", szReportName +
   GetExtension(sOutputFormatType)));
Response.ContentType = oBinaryView.MimeType;
Response.BinaryWrite(oBinaryView.Content);
Response.Flush();
Response.End();
```

You can see here that we need to work through a number of objects to reach our goal. After creating the BIPlatform object and obtaining the CUID of the desired report, you'll need to extract both the Connection and ConnectionState objects from BIPlatform object. Set the URL property of the Connection object to the reportengine web service location. From these objects, you can create a ReportEngine object that will encapsulate the report document itself. The requested report format is indicated by a member of the OutputFormatType enumerator. The available options are listed in Table 11-3.

Table 11-3. *OutputFormat Enumerator Members*

Enumerator	Value	Description
BINARY_CONTENT	0	Binary
EXCEL	3	Microsoft Excel
HTML	1	HTML
PDF	2	Adobe Acrobat
RTF	5	Rich Text Format
WORD	4	Microsoft Word
XML	6	XML

The output type is set to the OutputFormat property of the ViewSupport class along with the ViewType and ViewMode settings, which are set to the enumerator values Binary and Document, respectively. The members of the ViewType and ViewMode enumerators are listed in Tables 11-4 and 11-5, respectively.

Table 11-4. *ViewType Enumerator Members*

Enumerator	Value
BINARY	2
CHARACTER	0
XML	1

Table 11-5. *ViewMode Enumerator Members*

Enumerator	Value
ALL_DATA_PROVIDERS	3
DATA_PROVIDER	4
DOCUMENT	0
REPORT	1
REPORT_PAGE	2

Next, you'll instantiate a RetrieveBinaryView object that indicates a binary document, as opposed to a character or XML document, should be retrieved. This object is then packaged in a RetrieveData object by setting the RetrieveView property to the RetrieveBinaryView object.

Next you can determine what the report will do when it is extracted. This is set by the Action class, and in this example a Refresh object will tell it to refresh the report data at this time. The GetDocumentInformation() method will extract the report from the ReportEngine object. This method takes several parameters, which are listed here:

- documentReference: String value that holds the document's unique ID (we use a CUID in this example) or a document reference taken from a DocumentInformation object.

- retrieveMustFillInfo: Expects a RetrieveMustFillInfo object that indicates what information the method will return in DocumentInformation to resolve the MustFillXXX report state in the next roundtrip to the server. Your options are RetrieveQueryContext, which corresponds to MustFillQueryContexts and returns a QueryContext class; RetrievePromptInfo, which corresponds to MustFillPrompts and returns a PromptInfo class; and RetrieveDBLogon, which corresponds to MustFillDBLogon and returns a DBLogoninfo class.

- actions: Expects an array of Action objects. If null is passed, no action takes place. In this example, we're refreshing the report data with a Refresh object, but other options include FillContexts, FillPrompts, FillDBLogons, Drill, and FillPassword.

- navigate: Expects a Navigation object that indicates how to navigate in the document. Navigation objects include NavigateToFirstPage, NavigateToLastPage, NavigateToPath, NavigateToPage, and NavigateToDataProvider. If null is passed, no navigation takes place.

- retrieveData: Accepts an object that indicates how to retrieve other document information. We're using a RetrieveBinaryView object, but you could also use an object of type RetrieveCharacterView. These objects are set to the RetrieveView property of the RetrieveData class, and it is this RetrieveData class that is passed to the GetDocumentInformation() method.

Finally, the contents of the GetDocumentInformation() method's View property are cast to a BinaryView object. It is this BinaryView object that can be streamed to the browser to display the report.

Adding Reports

Uploading reports from a disk file to the InfoStore is also very different from the approach taken with the .NET SDK. The RPT file needs to be encapsulated into a FileStream object where it is moved in chunks into the InfoStore. In this example, I've chosen to use 16-kilobyte chunks. Then, the refresh options are set and a CrystalReport object is created to hold such properties as the report name, description, and the generated CUID. Finally, the FinishUploadWithObject() method of the BIPlatform object completes the upload and finalizes everything by assigning the properties to the new report. Listing 11-8 shows how this file upload is accomplished.

Listing 11-8. *Adding a Report*

```
BIPlatform oBIPlatform;
FileStream oFileStream;
ResponseHolder oResponseHolder;
InfoObject oInfoObject;
InfoObjects oInfoObjects;
CheckSumInfo oCheckSumInfo;
UploadStatus oUploadStatus;
CrystalReport oCrystalReport;
InfoObject[] aInfoObject;
Byte[] aBuffer;
string[] aCUID;
string szFolderCUID;
RefreshOptionsEnum[] aRefreshOptionsEnum;
int iBufferSize = 16384;
int iByteCount = 0;
int iBytesRead;

oBIPlatform = GetBIPlatform(szServicesURL, szAuthType,
    szDomain, szUser, szPassword);
```

```
//Retrieve folder
oResponseHolder = new ResponseHolder();
oResponseHolder = oBIPlatform.Get(szFolder, null);
oInfoObject = oResponseHolder.InfoObjects.InfoObject[0];
szFolderCUID = oInfoObject.CUID;

//Checksum object preserves integrity when uploading RPT file
oCheckSumInfo = new CheckSumInfo();
oCheckSumInfo.CheckSumMethod = CheckSumMethodEnum.NONE;
oCheckSumInfo.CheckSumValue = new Byte[1];

//Begin upload
oUploadStatus = new UploadStatus();
oUploadStatus.UploadID = oBIPlatform.StartUpload();

//Send report to file stream
oFileStream = new FileStream(szReportPath + szReportFileName,
   FileMode.Open, FileAccess.Read);

//Create an array of bytes with a length of the specified buffer size
aBuffer = new byte[iBufferSize];

//Upload the file in 16K chunks
while (oFileStream.Length - iByteCount > iBufferSize)
{
   iBytesRead = oFileStream.Read(aBuffer, 0, iBufferSize);
   oUploadStatus = oBIPlatform.UploadFile(oUploadStatus.UploadID,
      oCheckSumInfo, aBuffer);
   iByteCount += iBytesRead;
}

 aBuffer = new byte[oFileStream.Length - iByteCount];
 iBytesRead = oFileStream.Read(aBuffer, 0,
    ((int) oFileStream.Length) - iByteCount);
 oUploadStatus = oBIPlatform.UploadFile(oUploadStatus.UploadID,
    oCheckSumInfo, aBuffer);
 oFileStream.Close();

 //Obtain a CUID for the new report
 aCUID = oBIPlatform.GenerateCuids(1);

//Set the report refresh properties
aRefreshOptionsEnum = new RefreshOptionsEnum[3];
aRefreshOptionsEnum[0] = RefreshOptionsEnum.DEFAULT_LOGON_INFO_VALUES;
aRefreshOptionsEnum[1] = RefreshOptionsEnum.PRINTER_OPTIONS;
aRefreshOptionsEnum[2] = RefreshOptionsEnum.PROMPT_VALUES;
```

```
//Assign the attributes of the new report
oCrystalReport = new CrystalReport();
oCrystalReport.Name = szReportName;
oCrystalReport.Description = szDescription;
oCrystalReport.ParentCUID = szFolderCUID;
oCrystalReport.CUID = aCUID[0];
oCrystalReport.ReportRefreshOptions = aRefreshOptionsEnum;

//Create a new InfoObjects collection and add the
//Crystalreport object to the collection
oInfoObjects = new InfoObjects();
aInfoObject = new InfoObject[1];

aInfoObject[0] = oCrystalReport;
oInfoObjects.InfoObject = aInfoObject;

//Complete upload process
oUploadStatus = oBIPlatform.FinishUploadWithObject(oUploadStatus.UploadID,
    szReportFileName, oInfoObjects, null);
```

Setting Parameters

Suppose you wish to set the default parameters of an existing report. You can use the
PluginProcessingInterface() method of the CrystalReport class to accomplish this.
Setting parameters is an example of a task that is quite similar to the approach taken by
the .NET SDK. Listing 11-9 shows how to set the default parameters.

Listing 11-9. *Setting Report Parameters*

```
BIPlatform oBIPlatform;
ResponseHolder oResponseHolder;
InfoObjects oInfoObjects;
InfoObject oInfoObject;
ReportProcessingInfo oReportProcessingInfo;
ReportParameter[] aReportParameters;
CrystalReport oCrystalReport;
BusinessObjects.DSWS.BIPlatform.Desktop.PromptValue[] aPromptValue;
BusinessObjects.DSWS.BIPlatform.Desktop.PromptValue oPromptValue;

oBIPlatform = GetBIPlatform(szServicesURL, szAuthType,
    szDomain, szUser, szPassword);

oResponseHolder = new ResponseHolder();
oResponseHolder = oBIPlatform.Get(szReportPath + szReportName +
    "@SI_PROCESSINFO", null);
```

```
oInfoObjects = oResponseHolder.InfoObjects;
oInfoObject = oInfoObjects.InfoObject[0];

oCrystalReport = new CrystalReport();
oCrystalReport = ((CrystalReport) oInfoObject);
oCrystalReport.Name = szReportName;

oReportProcessingInfo = oCrystalReport.PluginProcessingInterface;

aReportParameters = oReportProcessingInfo.ReportParameters;

aPromptValue = new BusinessObjects.DSWS.BIPlatform.Desktop.PromptValue[1];
oPromptValue = new BusinessObjects.DSWS.BIPlatform.Desktop.PromptValue();
oPromptValue.Data = "USA";
aPromptValue[0] = oPromptValue;
aReportParameters[0].CurrentValues = aPromptValue;

aPromptValue = new BusinessObjects.DSWS.BIPlatform.Desktop.PromptValue[2];
oPromptValue = new BusinessObjects.DSWS.BIPlatform.Desktop.PromptValue();
oPromptValue.Data = "1";
aPromptValue[0] = oPromptValue;
aReportParameters[1].CurrentValues = aPromptValue;

oCrystalReport.PluginProcessingInterface = oReportProcessingInfo;

oBIPlatform.Update(oInfoObjects);
```

The parameters collection is found in the `ReportProcessingInfo` object. For each parameter, you can instantiate a `PromptValue` object that will hold the parameter value. This object is then set to the `CurrentValues` property of its matching entry in the `ReportParameters` array. The `Update()` method of the `BIPlatform` object, akin to the `Commit()` method of `InfoStore` object, saves the modified parameters to the server.

Scheduling Reports

Probably the main purpose of having a report server is to schedule reports to run at specified intervals. Listing 11-10 shows how to retrieve a report and set the scheduling properties to run for a list of calendar days. If you've done this in the Enterprise SDK, you'll see that the code to set the `SchedulingInfo` properties is almost identical.

Listing 11-10. *Scheduling a Report*

```
oBIPlatform = GetBIPlatform(szServicesURL, szAuthType,
    szDomain, szUser, szPassword);

//Retrieve the report
oResponseHolder = new ResponseHolder();
oResponseHolder = oBIPlatform.Get(szPath + szReportName + "@SI_SCHEDULEINFO", null);
```

```
//Get the first InfoObject in the collection returned
//to the ResponseHolder by the query
oInfoObjects = oResponseHolder.InfoObjects;
oInfoObject = oInfoObjects.InfoObject[0];

//Set the SchedulingInfo options
oSchedulingInfo = new SchedulingInfo();
oSchedulingInfo.ScheduleType = ScheduleTypeEnum.CALENDAR;
oSchedulingInfo.ScheduleTypeSpecified = true;

//dStartDate should contain both the start date and
//the time of day to run the report
oSchedulingInfo.BeginDate = dStartDate;
oSchedulingInfo.BeginDateSpecified = true;

oSchedulingInfo.EndDate = dEndDate;
oSchedulingInfo.EndDateSpecified = true;

oSchedulingInfo.RightNow = false;
oSchedulingInfo.RightNowSpecified = true;
```

Here we're indicating that the report is a Calendar type. This means that the actual days of the week will be specified individually across date ranges. The ScheduleTypeEnum enumerator options are listed in Table 11-6.

Table 11-6. *ScheduleTypeEnum Enumerator Members*

Enumerator	Value
CALENDAR	8
CALENDAR_TEMPLATE	9
DAILY	2
FIRST_MONDAY	6
HOURLY	1
LAST_DAY	7
MONTHLY	4
NTH_DAY	5
ONCE	0
WEEKLY	3

Listing 11-11 is where things get a little strange. We'll need to create a CalendarDay object to hold the day-of-the-week enumerators that indicate what days the report should run. Set the WeekNumber property of this object to the enumerator member WeekNumberEnum.ALL to indicate all the days of the month. (Your other options are First, Second, Third, Fourth, Fifth, and Last weeks.) Then, using the .NET DayOfWeek enumerator, indicate the day of the week on which you wish to schedule the report. You'll need to increment the value of this enumerator by one to set the correct day of week.

In this example, I'm scheduling the report for Tuesday (DayOfWeek.Monday + 1). The reason for this is that the .NET enumerator is one day off from the values recognized by BO XI. This issue is discussed in Chapter 5, and the enumerator differences are shown in Tables 5-6 and 5-7. Unfortunately, the Web Services SDK does not offer its own day-of-week enumerator with the correct values settings.

Listing 11-11. *Scheduling a Report to Run on Tuesdays*

```
//Create a CalendarDays array
BusinessObjects.DSWS.BIPlatform.Desktop.CalendarDay oCalendarDay;
BusinessObjects.DSWS.BIPlatform.Desktop.CalendarDay[] aCalendarDays;

oCalendarDay = new BusinessObjects.DSWS.BIPlatform.Desktop.CalendarDay();

oCalendarDay.WeekNumber = WeekNumberEnum.ALL;
oCalendarDay.WeekNumberSpecified = true;

oCalendarDay.DayOfWeek = ((int) DayOfWeek.Monday) + 1;
oCalendarDay.DayOfWeekSpecified = true;

oCalendarDay.StartMonth = dStartDate.Month;
oCalendarDay.StartMonthSpecified = true;

oCalendarDay.StartDay = dStartDate.Day;
oCalendarDay.StartDaySpecified = true;

oCalendarDay.StartYear = dStartDate.Year;
oCalendarDay.StartYearSpecified = true;

oCalendarDay.EndMonth = dEndDate.Month;
oCalendarDay.EndMonthSpecified = true;

oCalendarDay.EndDay = dEndDate.Day;
oCalendarDay.EndDaySpecified = true;

oCalendarDay.EndYear = dEndDate.Year;
oCalendarDay.EndYearSpecified = true;

aCalendarDays = new BusinessObjects.DSWS.BIPlatform.Desktop.CalendarDay[1];

aCalendarDays[0] = oCalendarDay;

oSchedulingInfo.CalendarRunDays = aCalendarDays;


//Cast the InfoObject to a CrystalReport object
oCrystalReport = new CrystalReport();
oCrystalReport = ((CrystalReport) oInfoObject);
```

```
oCrystalReport.Name = szReportName;
oCrystalReport.SchedulingInfo = oSchedulingInfo;

oBIPlatform.Schedule(oInfoObjects);
```

Working with Folders

Listing 11-12 shows how to create a new folder. After connecting to BO XI, you'll need to generate a CUID for the folder and assign that value along with the folder name to a new Folder object. The structure represented by FixedCUIDs.RootFolder.FOLDERS will return the CUID of the parent folder to which the new folder will belong. In this case, it is the root folder itself, so our new folder will be top-level. Next, create an InfoObject collection and add the Folder object to it. To avoid an error arising from a naming conflict should another folder with the same name already exist, setting the MatchingNameRename property to True will create another folder with a numerically incremented name. For example, if My Folder already exists and you try to add My Folder again, My Folder (1) will be created.

Listing 11-12. *Creating a New Folder*

```
BIPlatform oBIPlatform;
Folder oFolder;
InfoObjects oInfoObjects;
InfoObject[] aInfoObject;
CreateOptions oCreateOptions;
string[] aCUID;

oBIPlatform = GetBIPlatform(szServicesURL, szAuthType,
    szDomain, szUser, szPassword);

//Generate a new CUID for the new folder
aCUID = oBIPlatform.GenerateCuids(1);

//Create a Folder object and set the name, CUID, and parent CUID
oFolder= new Folder();
oFolder.Name = szFolderName;
oFolder.CUID = aCUID[0];
oFolder.ParentCUID = FixedCUIDs.RootFolder.FOLDERS;

//Create an InfoObject collection and add the Folder object to it
oInfoObjects = new InfoObjects();
aInfoObject = new InfoObject[1];
aInfoObject[0] = oFolder;
oInfoObjects.InfoObject = aInfoObject;

//In case a folder with the same name is already specified,
//another folder with a numerically incremented name will be
//created and no error will occur
oCreateOptions = new CreateOptions();
```

```
oCreateOptions.MatchingNameRename = true;
oCreateOptions.MatchingNameRenameSpecified = true;

//Execute creation process of new folder
oBIPlatform.Create(oInfoObjects, oCreateOptions);
```

If you want to pull a list of the topmost folders in BO XI, you can use the GetTopFolders() method of the BIPlatform object. The code shown in Listing 11-13 extracts these properties and displays them on the web page.

Listing 11-13. *Extracting Top Folders*

```
oResponseHolder = oBIPlatform.GetTopFolders(null);

oInfoObjects = oResponseHolder.InfoObjects;

foreach(InfoObject oInfoObject in oInfoObjects.InfoObject)
{
    y++;

    szData = string.Format("{0} - SI_ID = {1}  SI_NAME = {2}  SI_KIND = {3} BR>",
        y.ToString(),
        oInfoObject.ID.ToString(),
        oInfoObject.Name,
        oInfoObject.Kind);

    Response.Write(szData);
}
```

Managing Servers

You can extract the metrics of any server in your BO XI deployment by using the GetServerMetrics() method of the BIPlatform object. This method receives as a parameter a search string (and in the example in Listing 11-14 a SQL statement is used) that specifies an individual server. Then the values of some selected properties are output to the web page.

Listing 11-14. *Extracting Server Metrics*

```
ServerMetrics oServerMetrics;
string szQuery;

szQuery = "query://{SELECT * " +
    "FROM CI_SYSTEMOBJECTS " +
    "WHERE SI_FRIENDLY_NAME = 'seton-notebook.cms'}";

oServerMetrics = oBIPlatform.GetServerMetrics(szQuery);
```

```
Response.Write("CPU = " + oServerMetrics.CPU + "<BR>");
Response.Write("CPUCount = " +
    oServerMetrics.CPUCount.ToString()  + "<BR>");
Response.Write("DiskSpaceAvailable = " +
    oServerMetrics.DiskSpaceAvailable.ToString() + "<BR>");
Response.Write("DiskSpaceTotal = " +
    oServerMetrics.DiskSpaceTotal.ToString() + "<BR>");
Response.Write("Memory = " + oServerMetrics.Memory.ToString() + "<BR>");
Response.Write("OperatingSystem = " +
    oServerMetrics.OperatingSystem + "<BR>");
Response.Write("ServerCUID = " + oServerMetrics.ServerCUID + "<BR>");
Response.Write("ServerIsAlive = " +
    oServerMetrics.ServerIsAlive.ToString() + "<BR>");
Response.Write("ServerIsEnabled = " +
    oServerMetrics.ServerIsEnabled.ToString() + "<BR>");
Response.Write("StartTime = " +
    oServerMetrics.StartTime.ToString() + "<BR>");
Response.Write("Version = " + oServerMetrics.Version + "<BR>");
```

This code will produce output similar to that shown in Figure 11-4.

```
CPU = Pentium
CPUCount = 2
DiskSpaceAvailable = 10224635904
DiskSpaceTotal = 59954065408
Memory = 1047764
OperatingSystem = Windows .NET 5.1
ServerCUID = ARkANnJGkqtBjGQqESBafew
ServerIsAlive = True
ServerIsEnabled = True
StartTime = 1156197374609
Version = 11.5.0.313
```

Figure 11-4. *Server metrics*

Similarly, you can extract a server's information using the same query string and casting the resulting InfoObject to an object of type Server. The Server class contains summary information showing the ID, names, description, and other such attributes of a server. Listing 11-15 shows a subset of the available properties.

Listing 11-15. *Extracting Server Metrics*

```
Server oServer;

oResponseHolder = oBIPlatform.Get(szQuery, null);

oInfoObjects = oResponseHolder.InfoObjects;

oServer = ((Server) oInfoObjects.InfoObject[0]);
```

```
Response.Write("Description = " + oServer.Description + "<BR>");
Response.Write("FriendlyName = " + oServer.FriendlyName + "<BR>");
Response.Write("Kind = " + oServer.Kind + "<BR>");
Response.Write("Name = " + oServer.Name + "<BR>");
Response.Write("OSServiceName = " + oServer.OSServiceName + "<BR>");
Response.Write("ServerDescriptor = " + oServer.ServerDescriptor + "<BR>");
Response.Write("ServerID = " + oServer.ServerID + "<BR>");
Response.Write("ServerKind = " + oServer.ServerKind  + "<BR>");
Response.Write("ServerName = " + oServer.ServerName  + "<BR>");
```

Managing Security

The Unified Web Services SDK also exposes object security. You can extract the rights to an
individual object by passing the CUID of that object to the BIPlatform.GetKnownRights()
method, you can check a user's rights for a particular InfoObject via the CheckRights() method,
and you can check the limits of an InfoObject via the CheckLimits() method. Listing 11-16
shows how to extract the security rights for a given object.

Listing 11-16. *Extracting Security Rights*

```
RightInfo[] aRightInfo;

aRightInfo = oBIPlatform.GetKnownRights("AWO8OjsfXx9LgQeYdykOzkA");

Response.Write("<TABLE>");

Response.Write("<TR>");
Response.Write("<TD>Object</TD><TD>Right</TD><TD>Denied</TD>");
Response.Write("</TR>");

for(int y=0; y < aRightInfo.Length; y++)
   Response.Write("<TR><TD>" + aRightInfo[y].ObjectKind + "</TD>" +
      "<TD>" + aRightInfo[y].Description + "</TD>" +
      "<TD>" + aRightInfo[y].Denied + "</TD></TR>");

Response.Write("</TABLE>");
```

This code will display the pages shown in Figure 11-5.

Object	Right	Denied
FullClient	View SQL	False
	Schedule to destinations	False
CrystalReport	Refresh the report's data	False
	Reschedule instances that the user owns	False
	Modify the rights users have to objects	False
	Define server groups to process jobs	False
Webi	Edit Query	False
FullClient	Export the report's data	False
	View objects that the user owns	False
	Pause and Resume document instances that the user owns	False
CrystalReport	Export the report's data	False
	Delete objects	False
Note	Allow discussion threads	False
FullClient	Refresh List of Values	False
Webi	Refresh List of Values	False
	Securely modify rights users have to objects.	False
	View document instances	False
	Delete instances that the user owns	False
	Schedule the document to run	False
	Edit objects	False
	Copy objects to another folder	False
	Add objects to the folder	False
FullClientTemplate	Download files associated with the object	False
Webi	Refresh the report's data	False
FullClient	Refresh the report's data	False
Webi	View SQL	False
	Reschedule instances	False
	Modify the rights users have to objects that the user owns	False
CrystalReport	Download files associated with the report	False

Figure 11-5. *Extracting known rights for an object*

Summary

As you can see, the Unified Web Services SDK offers most of the same features as the .NET
SDK but already comes prepackaged as a web service. We saw how the tool can handle report
viewing, scheduling, folder creation, and object querying. This SDK even introduced a new
"path" query syntax for object extraction. Still, it is a new feature that has not yet had a chance
to be widely accepted by the developer community.

CHAPTER 12

■■■

Third-Party Solutions

BusinessObjects XI is a multifaceted product that has become entrenched in the market-place over the years. During this time, a plethora of third-party tools that enhance BO XI's functionality have evolved in a thriving third-party market. In this chapter, we'll examine some of these products. This is not intended to be a series of product reviews; I will not compare one product to another nor will I offer pricing information or my own personal opinion on their individual merits. Personally, I have never used most of the tools described here. The goal of this chapter is to make you aware of the existence of these tools and to examine their features to see whether they may be of some help to you in your BusinessObjects XI deployments.

APOS Systems Inc.

APOS Systems Inc. has been around almost as long as Crystal Reports has been on the market. They are a software development, consulting, custom development firm and Business Objects Technology Partner located in Ontario, Canada. APOS Systems offers a suite of products for BusinessObjects XI and every version of Crystal Enterprise starting with the version 8 initial release and its predecessor, Seagate Info. Check out their Web site at www.apos.com where you can request evaluation licenses and see web demos that offer overviews of most of their tools. These tools are either server components that control aspects of your BO XI installation or desktop-based applications that allow an administrator more flexibility in managing BO XI objects than is offered through the CMC.

In the next sections, we'll examine the products offered by APOS Systems and see how they might be of use in managing your BO XI installation.

AddressBook Gateway

Currently, when BO XI prompts you to enter an e-mail, it provides only a text box on its web interface. You need to enter the e-mail addresses manually or copy and paste them from another source. The AddressBook Gateway allows you to integrate your e-mail address list in the report scheduling page of InfoView. You can access e-mail address sources from BusinessObjects XI, Outlook, or Lotus Notes. AddressBook Gateway offers a familiar Outlook-like interface for selecting e-mail addresses.

The e-mail integration works by adding a search button to the Links toolbar of Internet Explorer. Click this button, and the address book dialog will open, which will then allow you to select e-mails just as you would in Outlook.

Archive Manager

Archive Manager handles archiving—either online or offline—of your report instances. An *online archive* is one where archived report instances are stored in a designated BO XI folder. *Offline archives* are disk directories that hold the same information.

Archive Manager replaces the report limits rules of native BO XI and allows you to specify the maximum number of report instances to retain or the maximum number of days to retain them. You can set these limits by user or group or report folder or individual report. You can select a folder or report and set the parameters for both online and offline archiving as shown on Figure 12-1.

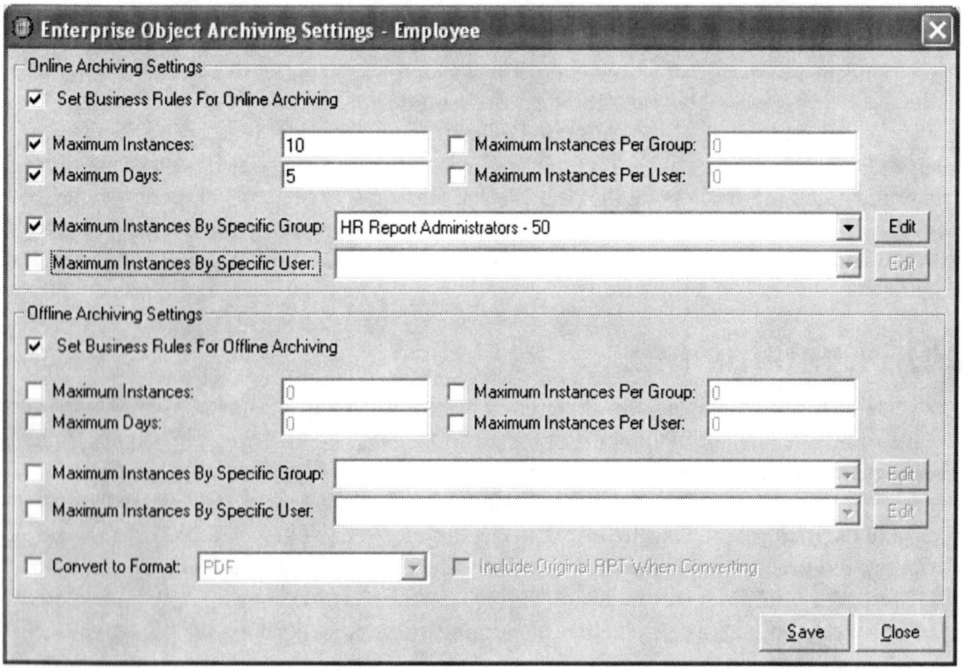

Figure 12-1. *Setting archive parameters for a folder*

To enforce the rules you set, Archive Manager has a Windows service component. This component will execute based on the frequency you determine at the starting time you determine. It will scan your BO XI InfoStore folders and archive your reports as you choose. You can specify the rules as shown in Figure 12-2.

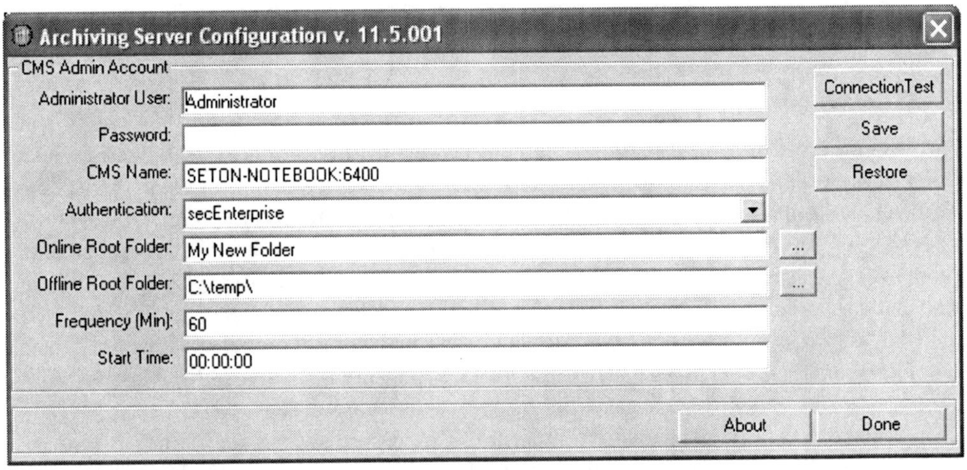

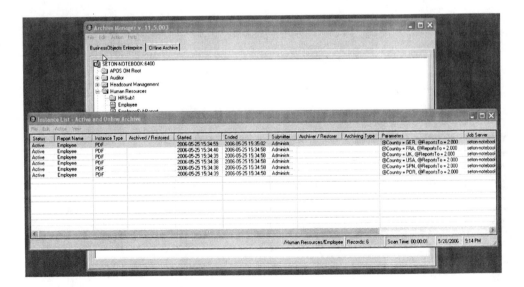

Figure 12-2. *Configuring the Archive Manager Windows service component*

As the tool monitors your BO XI installation and performs its scheduled tasks, it will write its progress to the event log.

Archive Manager also allows you to select individual instances of a report and archive them manually as shown in Figure 12-3. You can send the reports to either the online or offline locations specified in the setup. You can also restore archived files back to their active status in the InfoStore.

Figure 12-3. *Working with individual report instances*

If you wish, Archive Manager converts all RPT instances to another format during archiving—PDF, RTF, DOC, XLS, etc., in addition to archiving the original RPT instance. Archive Manager automatically mimics XI/CE's folder structure for archived instances and automatically deletes successfully archived report instances. Archived report instances are dynamically renamed to reflect report content.

Bursting Manager

Report bursting is the process of sending different views of the same report to multiple users, without necessarily hitting the database every time. Suppose you have a sales commission report that is organized by employee. Every Monday morning, each employee receives a report of their previous week's sales. Each report is generated from the same report template, and the only difference is the employee filter. You could run the report multiple times with a different employee code being passed to the stored procedure as is done in the "Scheduling Assemblies" section in Chapter 9. This approach is known as *multipass bursting*. Or, you could run the report once, extracting the data for all employees, and then specify a different filter for each individual employee. This is known as *single-pass bursting*. Bursting Manager supports both of these approaches.

Single-pass bursting opens an existing report instance and slices it up for distribution of its individual parts. Most likely, you'll find yourself bursting a report to individual instances. Either way, you still have all the features of BO XI's scheduler, whereby you can send your reports to such destinations as e-mail, disk file, or FTP server; choose the export format for the report such as PDF, Excel, Word, ASCII, etc., and, when bursting a report to several instances, you can set up success and failure notification e-mails. You can even set business rules for printing so that individual burst reports can be automatically printed on different printers.

The bursting rules are stored in an external database, and an Access database ships with the product to facilitate this. SQL scripts for creation of the same tables for SQL Server and Oracle come with the product. You can set up bursting definitions by selecting a report and using the screen shown in Figure 12-4.

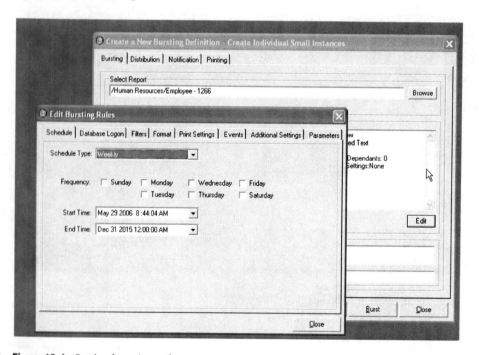

Figure 12-4. *Setting bursting rules*

In this example, an instance of the Employee report is selected. You can set up the report distribution via the Distribution tab shown in Figure 12-5. Once you create a bursting definition, you can schedule it like any other report in BO XI.

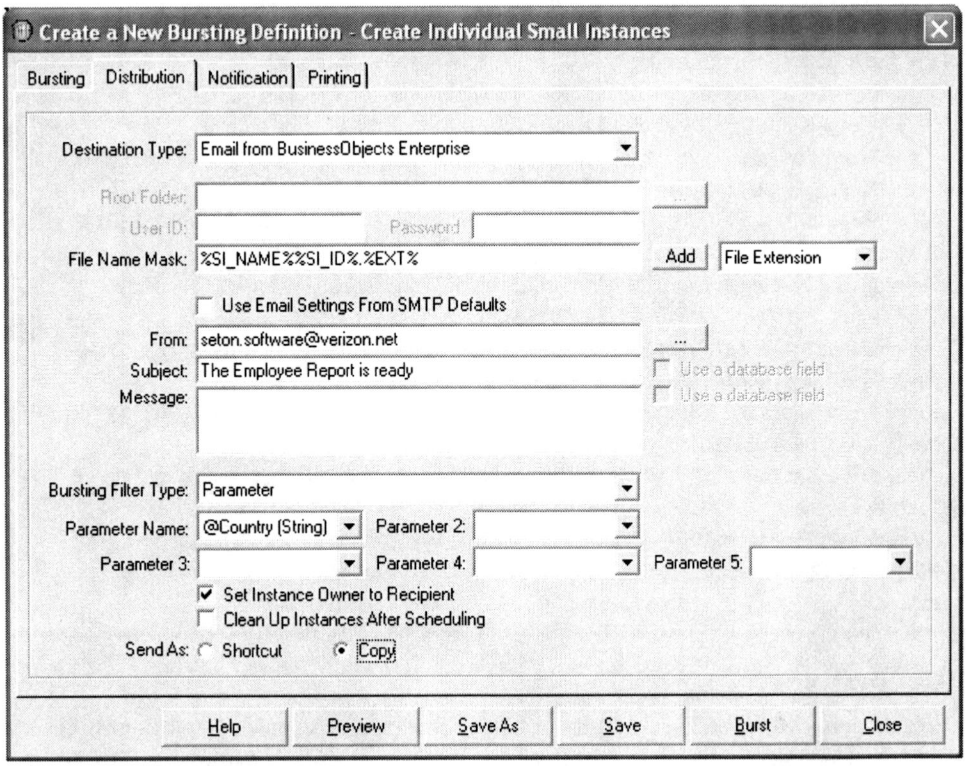

Figure 12-5. *Distribution tab*

Prior to executing a burst, you can view the bursting rules that will be applied in the Preview screen as shown in Figure 12-6.

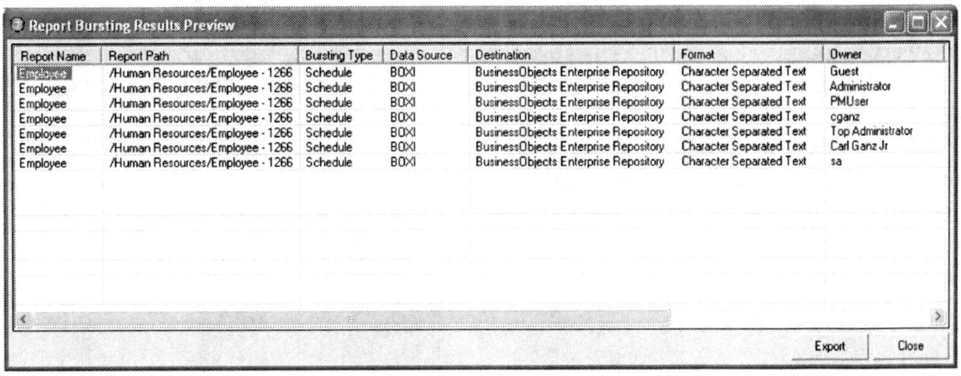

Figure 12-6. *Preview screen*

Bursting Manager also writes an optional audit log of all activity. The audit entry for the Employee Report bursting job is shown here:

```
Bursting Started - 2006-05-29 08:57:38
Bursting Definition:  -  - 2006-05-29 08:57:38
Loading Data source Information: BOXI -  - 2006-05-29 08:57:38
Bursting Reports - 2006-05-29 08:57:38
0000001) User: Guest    - 2006-05-29 08:57:38
    Scheduled Instance ID: 10158 Notification Type: None - 2006-05-29 08:57:38
0000002) User: Administrator   - 2006-05-29 08:57:38
    Scheduled Instance ID: 10159 Notification Type: None - 2006-05-29 08:57:38
0000003) User: PMUser   - 2006-05-29 08:57:38
    Scheduled Instance ID: 10160 Notification Type: None - 2006-05-29 08:57:38
0000004) User: cganz   - 2006-05-29 08:57:38
    Scheduled Instance ID: 10161 Notification Type: None - 2006-05-29 08:57:38
0000005) User: Top Administrator   - 2006-05-29 08:57:38
    Scheduled Instance ID: 10162 Notification Type: None - 2006-05-29 08:57:38
0000006) User: Carl Ganz Jr   - 2006-05-29 08:57:38
    Scheduled Instance ID: 10163 Notification Type: None - 2006-05-29 08:57:38
0000007) User: sa   - 2006-05-29 08:57:38
    Scheduled Instance ID: 10164 Notification Type: None - 2006-05-29 08:57:38
Burst Records Generated:7, Processing Time: 0:0:0 - 2006-05-29 08:57:38
Bursting Ended - 2006-05-29 08:57:38
```

InfoScheduler

InfoScheduler is a Microsoft Excel add-in for batch scheduling that allows you to control access to the BO XI scheduler from within a spreadsheet. You can select reports from the CMC using the object search as shown in Figure 12-7.

Selecting this option will populate the spreadsheet as shown in Figure 12-8. Here you can manage all the scheduling features BO XI has to offer. By entering your choices in the spreadsheet cells, you can set the frequency of the report, determine the output format, the destination, the database logon information, printer information, notifications, and parameters. You may also name and set the values for up to 50 prompts. In addition, you can name and set values for up to 10 custom properties. Any custom properties that already exist for the selected reports will automatically appear in the spreadsheet. This information is then committed to the InfoStore by selecting an Excel APOS menu that calls the macros of the spreadsheet.

Because this product is Excel-based, you can manage multiple spreadsheets containing different report definitions. InfoScheduler can be used as a bridge between BO XI functionality and your legacy systems. If your legacy system can generate ASCII data, it can be imported into InfoScheduler for subsequent editing and batch scheduling, either manually or by automatic scheduling.

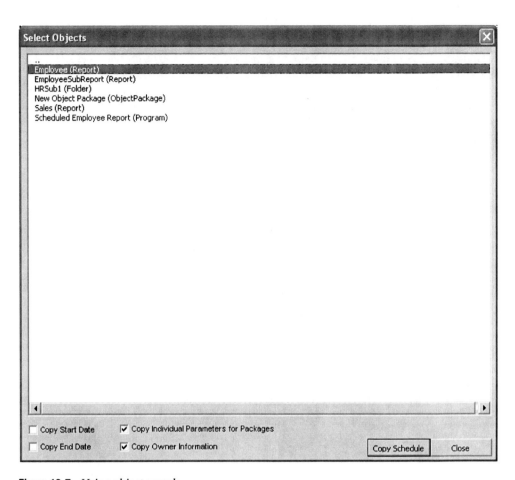

Figure 12-7. *Using object search*

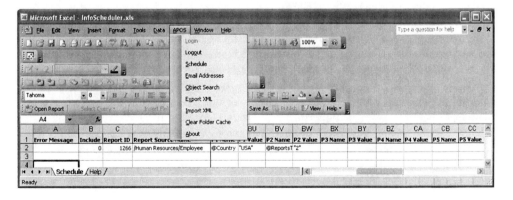

Figure 12-8. *Managing the Employee Report*

InfoScheduler is intended as an end-user tool so that users who need to manage a number of reports don't need to work with them individually using InfoView. It essentially incorporates the settings interface of InfoView into a spreadsheet where each report's properties are displayed one row at a time. As such, you can use it for report bursting by copying one report row, say, ten times and then changing the parameter of each row. You could also change the individual output formats and destinations as well. Then, choose Schedule off the APOS menu in Excel, and your reports will be scheduled in the InfoStore.

InfoScheduler allows you to export your scheduling data to XML and to import XML data from other sources. It also reads from your Outlook e-mail lists so that you may select e-mail addresses when setting the notifications.

Instance Manager

The Instance Manager tool offers you access to all of your report instances at once without needing to drill into the individual folders. You can find instances by status and/or report name and/or by date run, as shown in Figure 12-9.

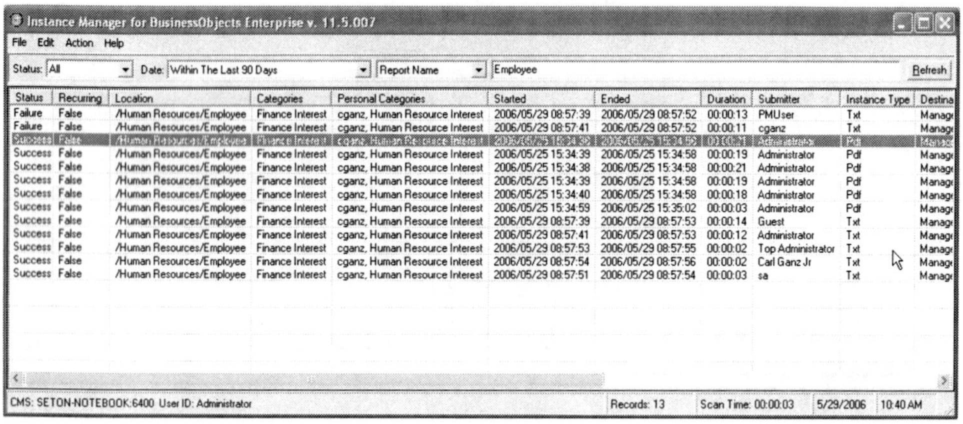

Figure 12-9. *Instance Manager search screen*

If you wanted to see every report that failed in the last 24 hours, you can easily do so. Likewise, you can show all reports that were exported to PDF in the past week across all folders. Because a filtered list of report instances is presented to you at once, you can perform actions on them en masse. You may choose to delete them, export the list to CSV or XML file, print them, stop all those currently processing, change their schedules, or copy them to a file folder, or view an individual instance's properties as shown in Figure 12-10.

Instance Manager allows you to reschedule each report instance and even modify the scheduling properties before doing so. For example, should you wish to change some parameter values before rescheduling, you may do so, as illustrated in Figure 12-11.

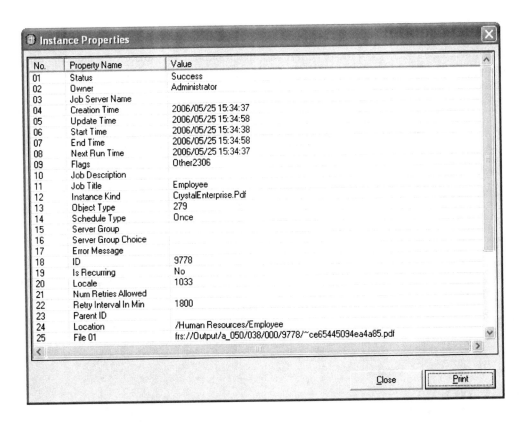

Figure 12-10. *Instance properties*

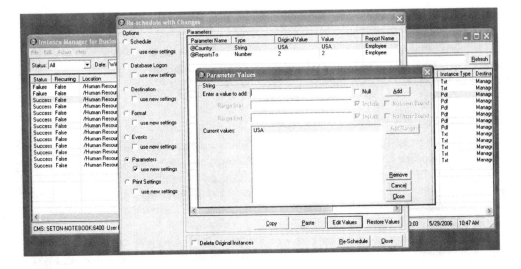

Figure 12-11. *Changing parameters' values*

Instance Monitor

The Instance Monitor tool is a server component that monitors the InfoStore for failed report instances. When failed reports are discovered, Instance Monitor will send e-mail notifications to the destination of your choosing or to initiate a pager call. It can optionally make an entry to the Event Log. The only interface to this tool is the configuration screen shown in Figure 12-12.

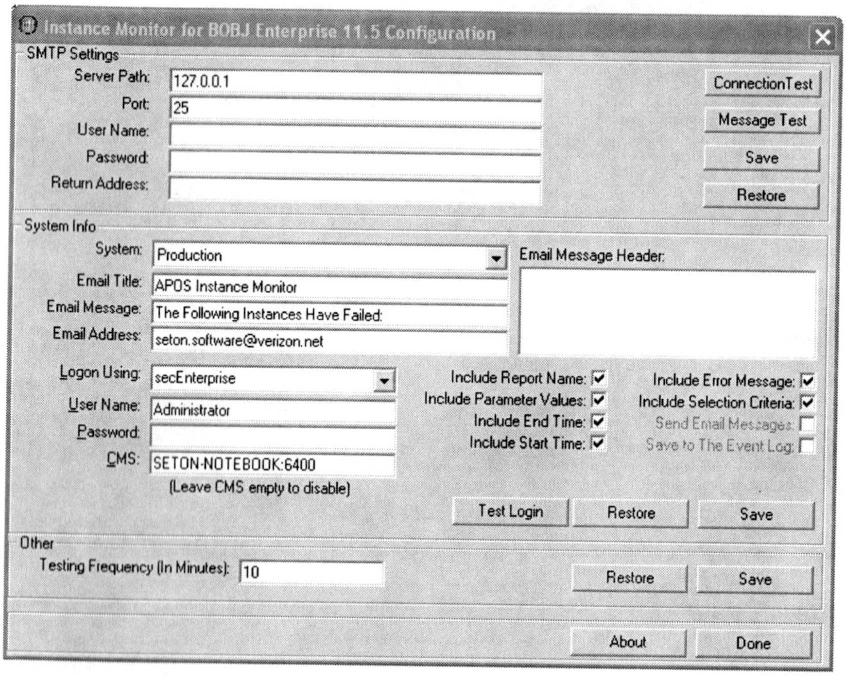

Figure 12-12. *Instance Monitor configuration screen*

Here you can establish the frequency of the failed instance check, the recipients of the notification e-mail, and what information the e-mail will contain. You can also store your SMTP mail and BO XI logon settings here.

Key Performance Indicator

The Key Performance Indicator (KPI) tool collects statistical information about your BO XI installation and posts it as metadata to a database where you can report on it. KPI serves as an audit trail of the system state of all components, who ran what report and when, changes to security settings, success and failure rates of reports along with their processing efficiency, and license usage. KPI ships with a default Access database but includes scripts to create MySQL, SQL Server, or Oracle databases.

APOS KPI also captures and stores information about Business Views and Business Views object relationships. It also captures and stores Business Views links between repository objects and reports, in addition to the links between Business Views and reports. Discussions object information and content is captured and stored. APOS KPI includes a BusinessObjects Universe for the APOS KPI database to facilitate your own report development. APOS KPI includes some Web Intelligence reports that utilize this universe. Also included are some Business Views for the APOS KPI database to facilitate your own report development.

Because some metrics are more appropriate to once-a-day capture than to second-by-second monitoring, two configuration screens are available. The hourly screen is shown in Figure 12-13.

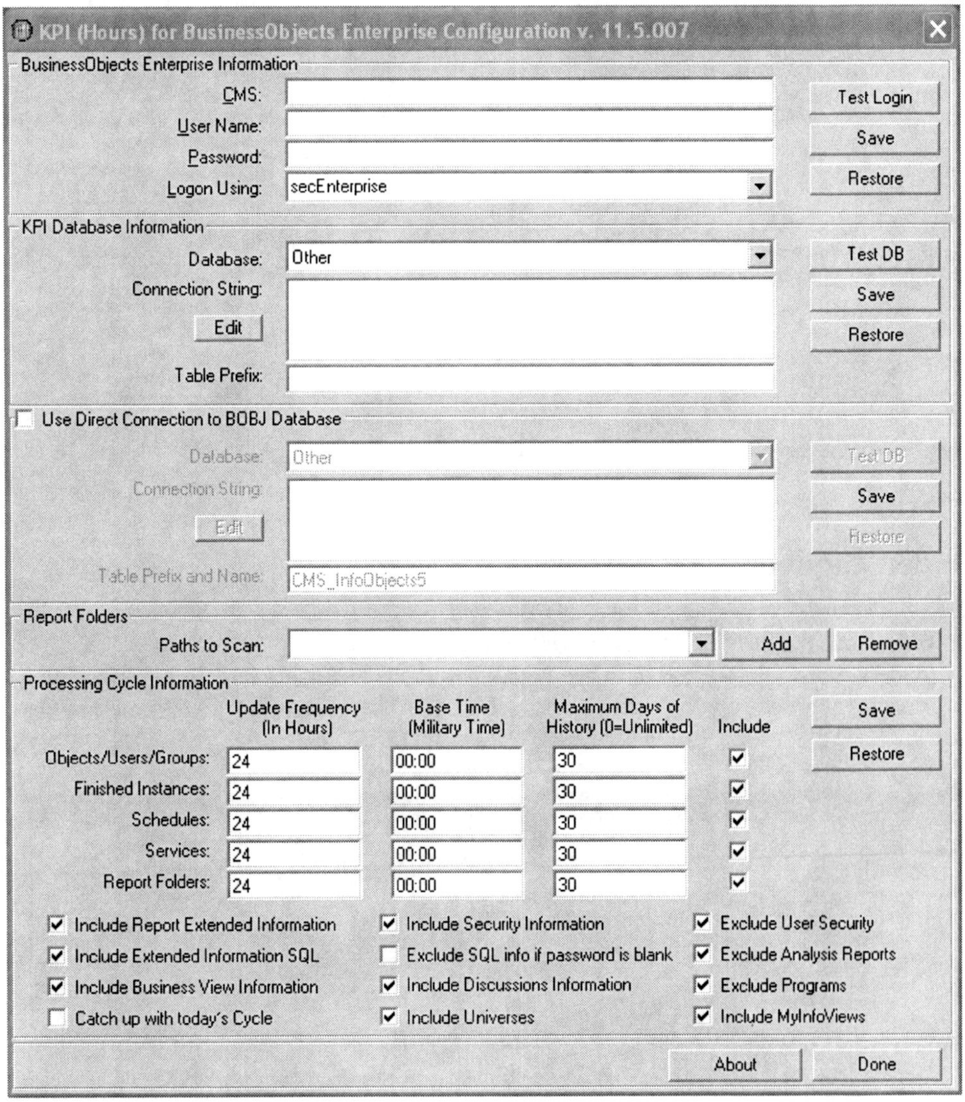

Figure 12-13. *KPI (Hours) configuration screen*

The configuration for the second-by-second capture is shown in Figure 12-14.

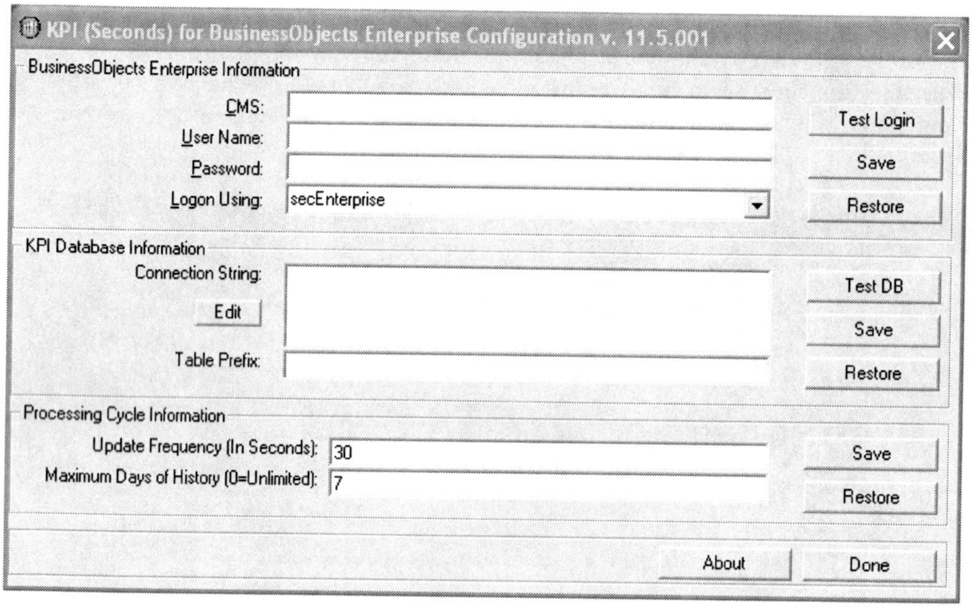

Figure 12-14. *KPI (Seconds) configuration screen*

Object Manager

Object Manager provides a single console from which you can manage all the objects in your BO XI deployment. The main screen allows you to filter on the type of object you wish to work with (folders, reports, PDF, Excel files, hyperlinks, etc.). You can further filter by name, location, and existence of processing extensions, create or modify date, and categories. The main screen is shown in Figure 12-15.

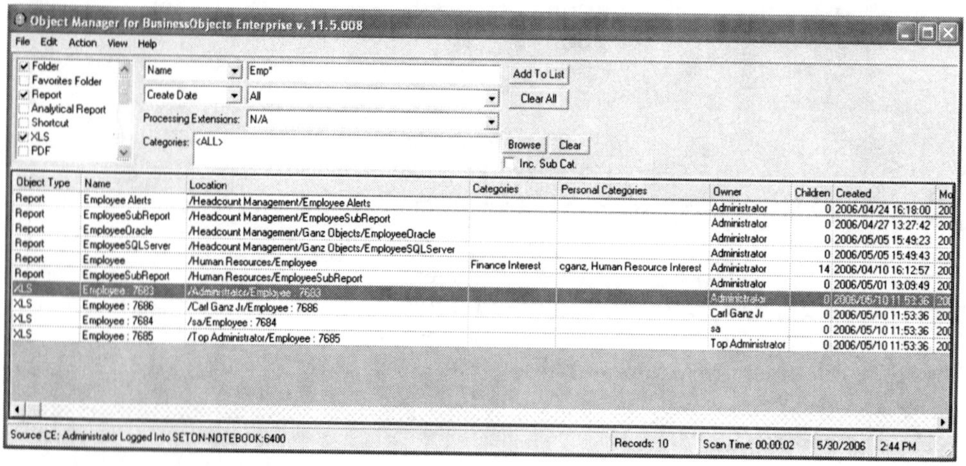

Figure 12-15. *Object Manager search screen*

Through this screen you can handle almost all the object settings that you can apply using the CMC. In Figure 12-16, a report is highlighted, and you can see the menu options that are available for it. Except for the ability to schedule reports, they largely match the options available in the CMC.

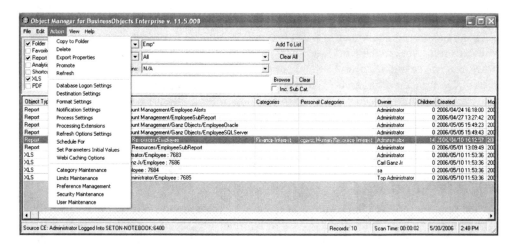

Figure 12-16. *Action options*

Suppose, for example, you'd like to modify one of the default parameter settings. The screen in Figure 12-17 enables you to do this.

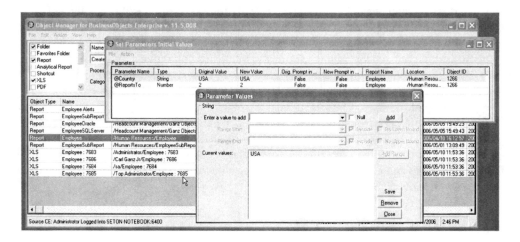

Figure 12-17. *Editing report parameters*

These changes do not need to be performed individually. You can select multiple objects in the grid and make changes en masse. If you wanted to alter the default output format for all the reports in a given folder to Adobe Acrobat, select the reports in that folder and choose Action ➤ Format Settings. This will present you with a screen that contains a combo box listing all the destination formats for a report. Selecting Adobe Acrobat and pressing Save will change the destinations for all the selected reports to Adobe Acrobat. You can also make mass edits of parameter initial values, destination, format, refresh from repository, notification, audit, refresh options, or server preferences.

User maintenance can also be performed in bulk. You can add, edit, and delete users, add and remove users to and from groups, export users to either a CSV or XML file for backup, and import users from either a CSV or XML file or from a database.

Object security and limits settings can be made in bulk, plus you can view these settings in a matrix-style view, making it easier to visualize or change all your security and limits settings. You can create, store, and assign complex user security definitions, sort of a "roles" approach. User preferences can be managed in bulk by user group or user.

Report promotion goes beyond the standard Report Promotion Wizard by allowing you to publish changes but preserve schedules, history, parameter initial values, and destination settings. Promoting to various folders simultaneously is supported, and you can more easily promote from QA to production if separated by a firewall.

RealTime Monitor

RealTime Monitor runs as a background process and allows you to create system alerts as well as generate Simple Network Management Protocol (SNMP) traps and manage your BO XI servers. SNMP is a layer protocol that is part of the TCP/IP protocol suite and enables the exchange of management information between network devices. Using SNMP, you can track network performance and perform troubleshooting.

An SNMP-managed device is a network node—like routers, access servers, switches, bridges, hubs, computer hosts, and printers—that contains an SNMP agent and that resides on a managed network. These managed devices collect and store management information and make this information available using the SNMP protocol. RealTime Monitor allows you to generate an SNMP alert when certain specific conditions exist; this SNMP alert can then be detected by operations management solutions like Microsoft MOM, IBM Tivoli, or CA Unicenter.

Some examples of an alert might include the following: you request an e-mail if the time to view reports on the system deteriorates; if any of the server components go offline; if your Job Server, Page Server, or Cache Server queues exceed a threshold; or if system login time exceeds a threshold.

RealTime Monitor consists of a system agent and a management console. The system agent runs in the background, scans your full BO XI installation regularly, and generates an alert when specific conditions exist. This background service also logs to the database a history of CMS connections and activity on the BusinessObjects servers, and creates SNMP traps. The configuration screen is shown in Figure 12-18.

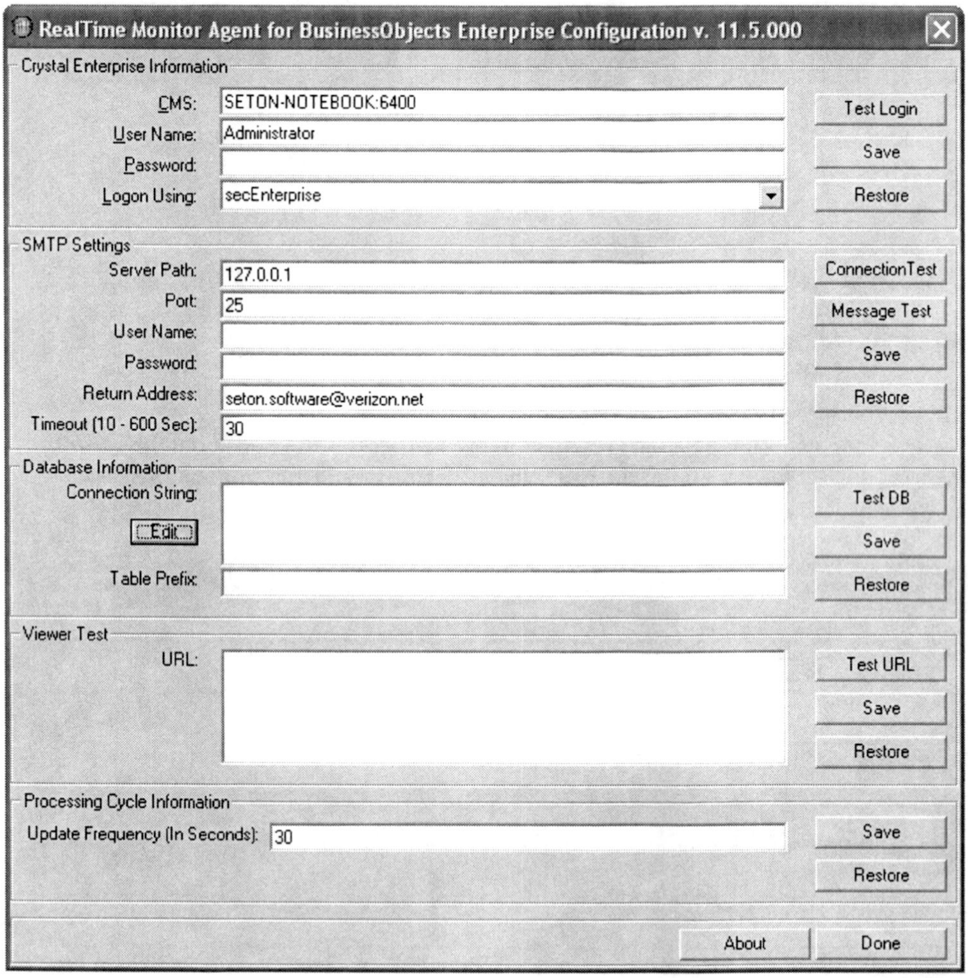

Figure 12-18. *RealTime Monitor agent configuration*

The console application allows you to view the current status of your installation. The Connections option allows you to view the current connections to BO XI as shown in Figure 12-19.

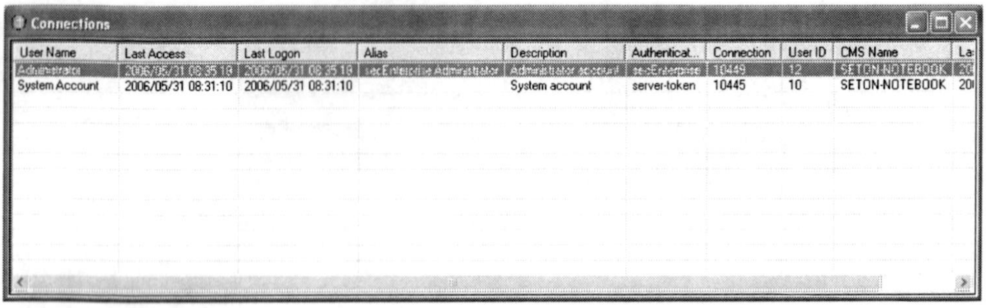

Figure 12-19. *Connections screen*

From this screen you can delete individual connections.

The Server Status option allows you to view the metrics information about the various servers in your BO XI installation. You can select which servers to monitor and then see a management screen like the one shown in Figure 12-20.

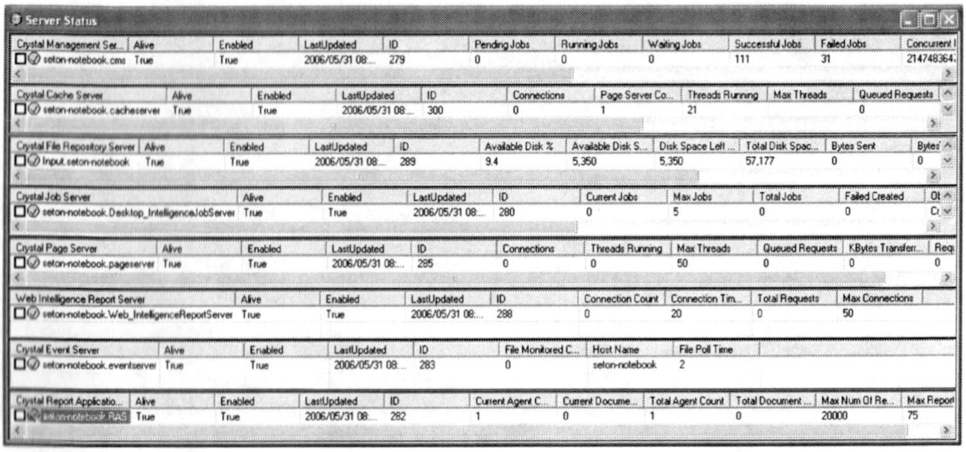

Figure 12-20. *Server management screen*

Here you can manage servers just as you would in the CMC. By selecting one or more servers, you can start, restart, stop, enable, disable, or delete them.

If you need to graph the activity of your BO XI servers, there is a graphing option that allows you to do so. For each server, you can select what attributes you wish to track. Selecting

CMS monitoring allows you to graphically visualize failed, pending, running, waiting, and successful jobs. You can also track the concurrently connected users and those connected via tokens or as named users. By comparison, selecting Cache Server monitoring allows you to visualize bytes transferred, connections, drive space used, hit rate, Page Server connection count, queued requests, threads, and total requests. Each server has its own unique set of attributes, and you can select multiple graphing points to plot as shown in Figure 12-21.

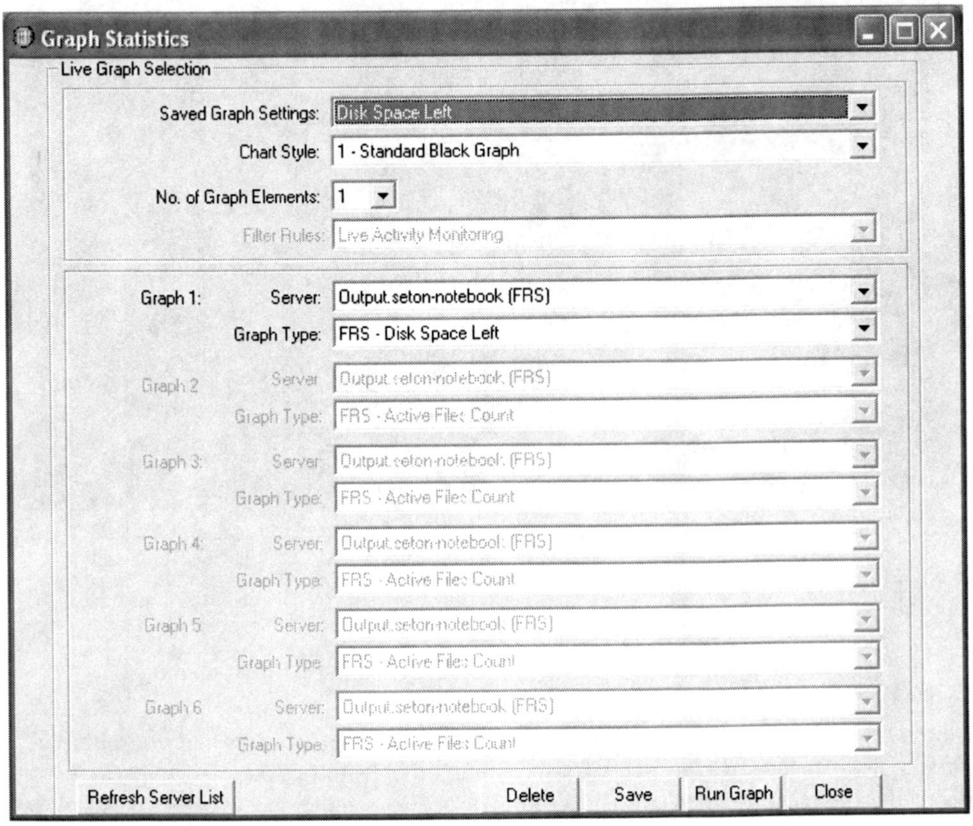

Figure 12-21. *Graph Statistics screen*

This graph setting produces the output shown in Figure 12-22, which plots the available disk space over time.

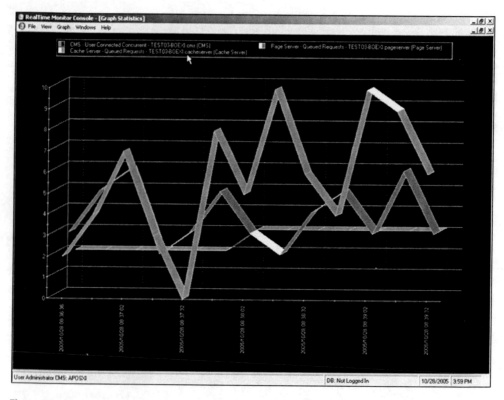

Figure 12-22. *Graph of CMS, Page Server, and Cache Server Activity*

Report Package Booster

BusinessObjects XI allows you to create object packages that can schedule and run multiple reports as a batch. Because these reports are bound up in an object package, they can be scheduled en masse through BO XI. The Report Package Booster enhances object packages by allowing you to consolidate the output from the different reports in an object package into one consolidated file.

Should you choose to consolidate the object package's report output to one consolidated file, you have a few options. You could send it to an RTF or text file, or to a Word document with optional password protection. The Excel export option also provides optional password protection, but you can also specify whether you want all reports consolidated into one worksheet or one worksheet for each report. A PDF output option is the most powerful in that it handles automatic page numbering, bookmarks, table of contents, and printing to multiple printers as well as assigning user and/or owner passwords using 128-bit encryption. Consolidated PDF files can also include "header" and "footer" pages that might be document files stored outside of the BO XI environment, resulting in a form of document generation.

Report Package Booster also allows you to send individual reports in the package via SMTP mail to their own destinations. Likewise, notification e-mails can be sent indicating the success or failure of the consolidating of the object package as a whole.

RunTime Manager

The RunTime Manager tool maintains schedules for all the server components in your BO XI installation except for the CMS. Using this tool, you can set up schedules for each server component to determine when they will be available. You may want to do this during certain hours when there is a nightly database task scheduled during which no reports should be run or during the nightly backup procedure. You may also want to add additional Job Servers during peak periods when large numbers of reports are being processed or to add additional Page Servers during periods when large numbers of reports are being viewed. The scheduling screen for the RunTime Manager is shown in Figure 12-23.

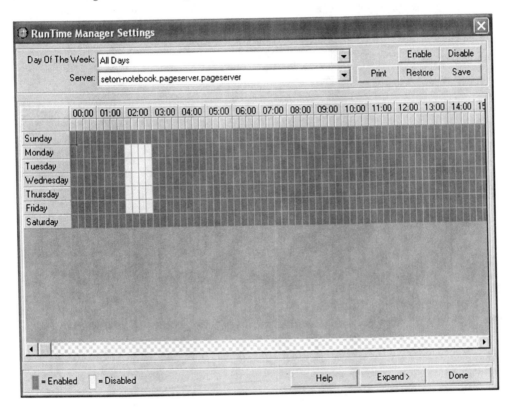

Figure 12-23. *RunTime Manager*

Here, the Page Server is set to be disabled on the morning of every business day from 2 to 3 a.m. RunTime Manager has a server component that runs in the background to enforce these rules.

Solutions Kit for ESRI GIS

The Solutions Kit for ESRI GIS allows you to bidirectionally integrate BO XI with the ESRI ArcIMS GIS solution. ESRI is a developer of geographic information system (GIS) technology located in Redlands, California. Their ArcIMS product is a web-based tool that delivers GIS data, dynamic and interactive maps, and metadata catalogs.

For BO XI users, the Solutions Kit for ESRI GIS allows you to embed dynamically generated maps as images in your reports as well as embedding hyperlinks to load the ArcIMS viewer. A sample Crystal Report with embedded image and a hyperlink to ESRI ArcIMS is shown in Figure 12-24.

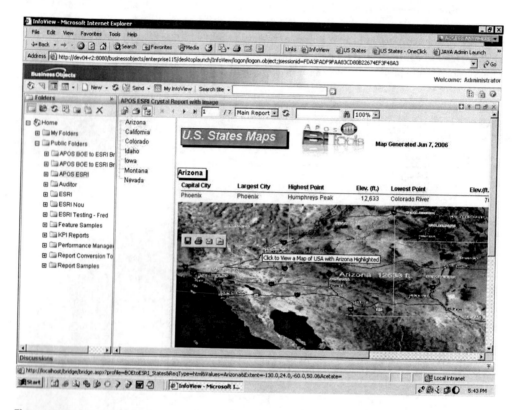

Figure 12-24. *BO XI Crystal Report with embedded, hyperlinked ESRI GIS map image*

ArcIMS users can request that currently selected elements on the map be passed to specific BO XI reports. The available report list screen is shown in Figure 12-25.

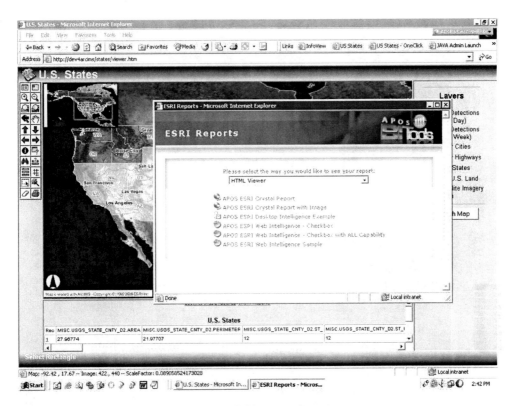

Figure 12-25. *ESRI ArcIMS with BO XI available report list*

ArcIMS users can pick a report, and BO XI will run and display that report using selection criteria based on currently selected map elements. A sample Crystal Report run using selected ArcIMS map elements is shown in Figure 12-26.

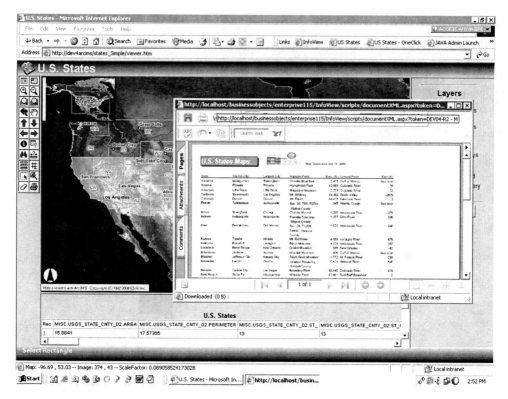

Figure 12-26. *ESRI ArcIMS with BO XI sample report*

An administration tool is included to create and maintain bridge business rules such as which reports to list from a specific map layer, security to BO XI from an ESRI map, parameter matching between a BO XI report and an ESRI ArcIMS map layer, etc. You can create a bidirectional bridge that utilizes any of three BO XI report types—Crystal Reports, Web Intelligence, and Desktop Intelligence. These business rule profiles are stored in the BO XI repository, eliminating the need for an external database.

View Time Security

The View Time Security tool allows you to apply row-level security to your reports. It accomplishes this by providing a series of processing extensions shipped as compiled DLLs that access business rules stored in a database. This database ships as an Access MDB, but scripts are provided to create the same structures in both SQL Server and Oracle.

Processing extensions allow you to create compiled code that can apply custom business logic against the data being processed in your report. The extension manager offers a handle that enables developers to intercept requests before they are processed by the Job Server. View Time Security installs a number of processing extensions for you that enforce this row-level security. To apply one, open the VTS Manager application and filter on a report. You should see a screen that looks like Figure 12-27.

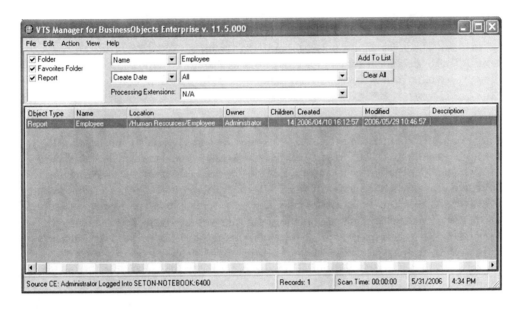

Figure 12-27. *VTS Manager*

Depending on the type of security you are trying to enforce, you can select one of the processing extension DLLs installed in \Program Files\Business Objects\BusinessObjects Enterprise 11.5\win32_x86\ProcessExt. These DLLs are listed in Table 12-1.

Table 12-1. *Processing Extensions*

Processing Extension	Security Type
APOSVTS.DLL	Filters by report ID and user
APOSVTSG.DLL	Filters by report ID and group
APOSVTSG.DLL	Filters by report name and group
APOSVTSG.DLL	Filters by report path and group
APOSVTSG.DLL	Filters by dynamic path and group
APOSVTSN.DLL	Filters by report name and user
APOSVTSP.DLL	Filters by path and user
APOSVTSW.DLL	Filters by dynamic path and user

All of these options show how you could create a report that restricted the data certain users could see when logging in to the CMC. If you build a salary report and User A could see salaries for those employees in Departments 1, 2, and 3, whereas User B could only see employees in Departments 4, 5, and 6, you could accomplish this filtering by using the processing extensions supplied by View Time Security.

Software Forces

Software Forces, LLC (www.softwareforces.com), is a vendor of Crystal Reports and Crystal Enterprise/BusinessObjects XI tools and consulting services located in Forest Hills, New York. In the next sections, we'll examine one of their tools—.rpt Inspector Enterprise Suite.

.rpt Inspector Enterprise Suite

The .rpt Inspector Enterprise Suite is a collection of utilities (19 to be exact) that allows you to manage and monitor the schedules and report instances in BO XI and make mass changes to your Crystal reports, whether located on disk or hosted in BusinessObjects. This mass change ability cuts across almost all features of Crystal Reports. The Enterprise Suite has an undo feature that stores up to the last 99 changes in memory. Most of the changes you make using this tool are made in memory and not committed until the end of your editing session. Each area of Crystal Reports is handled by its own editor or wizard, and these are covered in the sections that follow.

One common feature across most of these utilities is the ability to analyze data. For example, suppose you wish to perform an analysis of the report instances. You can use the drag and group feature shown in Figure 12-28 to accomplish this.

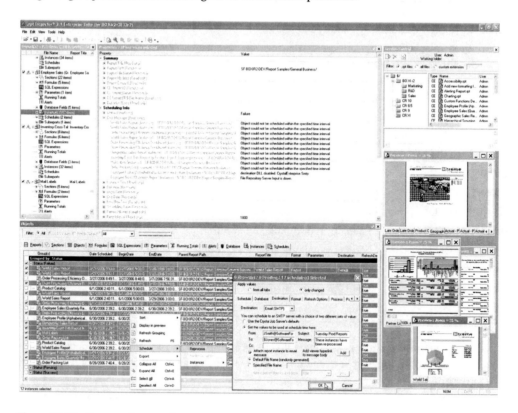

Figure 12-28. *Drag and group feature*

Here, if you wish to look at, say, the instances for a given report, and you wish to group by report status to see all your failed reports together, you can do so by dragging the status field into the group section, and the grid will organize your data accordingly.

The property editors work in a fashion similar to that of the Visual Studio IDE, especially when selecting multiple objects. In this case, those properties that the selected objects have in common will be presented in the property editor and the changes applied to all the selected objects.

Instances

The Enterprise Suite offers both an Instance Monitor and Instance Manager. The Instance Monitor will locate report instances based on their status, who ran them, when they were run, etc. If you wanted, say, to return a list of all reports run by a specified user that failed in the last 24 hours, you could easily do so. This tool is proactive on your part. You'll need to request the failed instances, as it is not a Windows service that continuously checks for failed instances and e-mails you notifications. This feature is slated for a future version of the SmartObjects Admin Desktop, a separate software product from SoftwareForces.

The Instance Manager also lets you extract reports by status, but in addition it allows you to modify the schedules. You can also create and modify reports on behalf of another user. The BusinessObject's XI CMC is limited in that once you create a schedule, you cannot edit it. You need to delete it and create a new one. Instance Manager also permits you to rerun report instances regardless of their status, another feature that BusinessObjects XI does not offer.

Databases

All reports access some kind of data source, and these data sources are often beyond the control of the developers and business units. Sometimes they get moved or structures renamed. If you wanted to repoint every report to a different database, change drivers, or remap fields to reflect structural changes to the underlying tables, you can do this with the Change Data Source and Database Conversion and Migration Wizards. You can also determine which fields are or are not being used across reports and what databases or schemas are being used in order to perform an impact analysis. This utility allows you to analyze reports by field name, definition name, table alias, value type, number of bytes, connection buffer string, database type, and descriptive name.

Text Management and Printing

The Enterprise Suite allows you to manage your text objects and perform spell checking. For example, if your reports all have a Company Name text object and the company name changes, this utility can move through every report in your deployment and change each name. You can use both wildcards and regular expressions in performing your searches. You can also make wholesale changes to text objects by changing their fonts, attributes, and colors as well as their size and position and paragraph properties. This can be very helpful when you need to standardize fonts for a consistent look and feel across reports. In addition, there is a spell checker that is available in the Text, Formula, and Parameter editors.

The Printer Change Wizard allows you to make changes to the default printer.

Version Control

The Enterprise Suite integrates with Microsoft Visual SourceSafe to allow you to maintain version control over your reports. You check reports in and out, view their history, and see whether they are in use by another developer, all within the same interface. The synchronization of reports stored in Enterprise and VSS is automatically handled. Enterprise Suite names the report using the friendly name stored in the CMC rather than the cryptic name used in the FileStore disk version of the RPT.

Formulas and Running Totals

The Formula Editor allows you to search for common patterns across formulas and make common changes across formulas. The editor supports both the VB and Crystal syntax and does validation checking, field completion, syntax highlighting, as well as spell checking. You can also search and modify running totals by searching according to name, value type, field name, and hierarchical summary type. You can also determine which formulas use the VB or Crystal syntax.

Parameters

The Parameters editor allows you to work with parameters and their default values. Commonly, you want to copy parameters from one report to a number of others, or at least standardize their names, ordinal positions, and default values. In two clicks you can copy a whole set of default values from one parameter to any number of destination parameters.

Sections

The Section editor allows you to work with report sections. It lets you edit any of the items offered on the Crystal Reports Section editor shown in Figure 12-29.

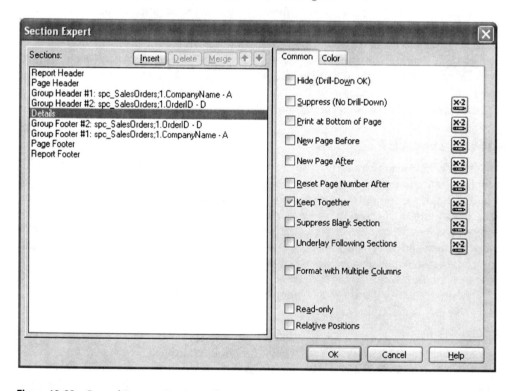

Figure 12-29. *Crystal Reports Section editor*

This editing feature also includes the ability to work with conditional formulas for any of these properties and then standardize them across reports.

Alerts

The Alerts editor allows you to work with alerts by definition name, condition formula, default message, and message formula. Alert formulas are editable by the same editor that the Formula utility provides.

Teleran Technologies

Teleran Technologies (www.teleran.com), based in Roseland, NJ, is a Business Objects Technology Partner and a provider of software products that audit, secure, and manage enterprise applications like BusinessObjects XI, among many others. In addition to their auditing tools, they offer two applications that can be used to track and safeguard your BusinessObjects XI deployments— iGuard and iSight.

iGuard

Tools like BusinessObjects XI often fall victim to users who execute reports that strain the entire system or perform data joins that are syntactically correct but return invalid results. To remedy this, a solution is often necessary to prevent these resource wasting, productivity degrading problems from happening, and guide users to more effectively interact with the application. iGuard accomplishes this task by enforcing policies that prevent the user from making such mistakes as executing runaway queries or accessing secure data. It also delivers a real-time messaging facility, independent of the application, to inform and guide the users. iGuard user messaging serves to reduce help desk calls, improving DBA and IT staff efficiency while increasing user productivity.

iGuard is essentially a "before" solution. The tool positions itself between BusinessObjects and your RDBMS, evaluating queries in real time as they travel across the network. The iGuard policy engine validates these queries against the business rules that you set up to make sure that users have the right to execute them, or that they have not made a logical error, or that they won't return an inordinate number of records. All this will happen "before" the reporting system and the database are affected.

Due to the size and complexity of many databases, it is certainly possible for a user to build a query that simply asks for too much. You can prevent this by creating customized rules as to what the user can and cannot do. For example, you could prohibit a user from executing SELECT * without a WHERE clause, or by preventing any query that doesn't use at least one indexed column. Likewise, you can prohibit access to certain data sources at specified times of the day when resource-intensive processes like data imports are executing.

iGuard is continually aware of the entire BusinessObjects XI environment, including users, applications, query content, and back-end data structures. Using the iGuard Policy Wizard (see Figure 12-30), you can point, click, and enforce policies that can be applied to any BO XI users, groups, Universes, reports, and database objects to prevent user errors, enhance system performance, and increase data-level security. For example, if a user requests a large amount of information, iGuard can intercept the query, determine how long it will take to run based on past experience, and inform the user that he's asked for too many system resources, suggesting he narrow down the scope of what he's looking for.

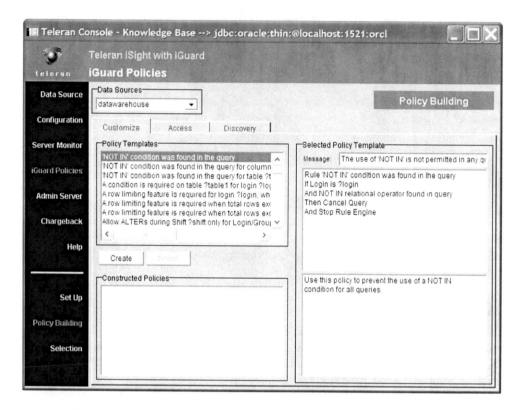

Figure 12-30. *iGuard Policy Wizard*

All iGuard policies can be placed in Test, Advise, or Active modes. In Test mode, policies do not block queries, but the system records and reports on which queries would have been acted upon, and how in-test policies could improve performance, accuracy, or data security. Active mode allows policies to block queries when violated and simultaneously send a real-time message back to the user. Using the Advise mode, queries are not blocked, but users receive e-mail messages associated with specific policies that will guide them in best query practices or remind them of the application, data usage, or privacy policies in place.

iSight

iSight is an SQL auditing facility that allows you to implement application performance tuning, data security compliance auditing, problem query analysis, and system resource management as well as facilitate database conversions and capacity planning. iSight picks up activity from all SQL applications, not just BO XI, which is important for ensuring data compliance with SOX and other regulatory and governance policies. In comparison to iGuard, iSight is an "after" solution as it tracks the results of what happened after the application and database event occurs. Users of business intelligence tools like BO XI often consume resources at varying levels throughout the business day. These varying usage patterns require constant monitoring to ascertain that the tool is performing optimally to the needs of the enterprise over time. iSight automatically compiles such metrics as which BO XI or other application users are straining the system and when; what BO XI reports or queries are being repeated over and over again—information that can help determine whether some reports should simply be cached; and how many reports are running simultaneously—information that can help you determine whether you really need that rather expensive additional BO XI server license. Moreover, you can determine what the system slow times are so as to schedule maintenance during this time.

iSight offers user-defined reports that provide usage profiles to ensure the system is used effectively and user-error reports to identify where user training may be required, or to pinpoint design problems. DBAs and system staff use iSight reports and analyses, such as the All Column Usage Summary, BO XI Queries Detail Report (see Figure 12-31), BO XI User Activity, Group by Clause Analysis, and the Users and Tables Detail Report, that focus on potential performance and user problems. These reports give DBAs the information they need to maintain application efficiency.

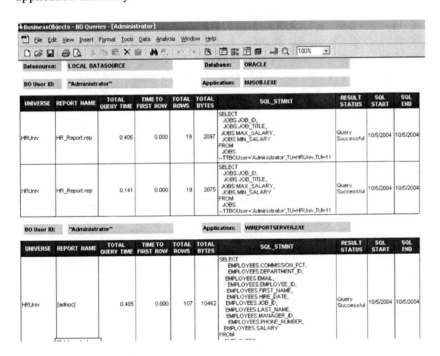

Figure 12-31. *iSight report for BO XI queries*

Management would be interested in iSight's compliance audit reports identifying which users accessed what information and high-level usage reports that illustrate how analytical applications are being used across the enterprise. Data warehouse managers receive summarized performance, resource use, and exception reports that assist them in allocating and efficiently managing system and staff resources as well as in budgeting and capacity planning.

CRD

Christian Steven Software, Ltd. (www.christiansteven.com) publishes CRD, a report distribution product that sits on top of your Crystal Reports installation. Its purpose is to completely replace, not complement, BO XI's offerings in the area of report scheduling and distribution while offering a number of additional features. You do not need a BO XI license to run CRD, only a developer's license for Crystal Reports. CRD uses its own scheduling technology and instantiates the Crystal Reports objects (as described in Chapter 7) to run reports. The ability of Christian Steven Software Ltd., or any third-party vendor, to create software that rests on top of the Crystal Reports runtime, is the result of BusinessObjects loosening the stringent licensing restrictions placed on Crystal Reports by CrystalDecisions. These licensing issues are covered in greater detail in Chapter 1.

CRD is a multithreaded tool that can run up to four reports simultaneously and is a scalable solution that can be set up on a master machine that controls additional slave machines. It doesn't require a powerful server to run, and for a smaller organization it can sit on a desktop machine where it checks the scheduling database for tasks.

CRD allows you to sends e-mails via SMTP mail, but unlike BO XI, it also integrates with MAPI to support Outlook, Outlook Express, Pegasus Mail, and Lotus Notes. It also allows you to specify the data source location of your e-mail addresses. One of the most important features CRD offers is integration with your RDBMS to extract data for report bursting. Report packages are supported, whereby you can schedule a series of reports to run as a batch. CRD allows you to run a report at one time and then deliver it at a future time. You can even ZIP compress the output files before delivery. If you are scheduling a report package, you can choose to place all the reports in one document or maintain them as individual documents. CRD allows you to send them all in the same e-mail or as individual e-mails.

CRD has a more advanced event system than BO XI. Like BO XI, it can check for the existence of a file before running a report. Moreover, it can make report execution contingent on the modification of a file, if a database record changes or is inserted in a table, and it can even use unread POP e-mails as a trigger.

If a report returns no data, you can instruct CRD to send an e-mail indicating this to the report recipient or another named recipient. You can choose to attach the blank report to this e-mail to confirm the recipients are aware that there was no data for the report and to distinguish between a failure and a blank report. Of course, you can tell CRD to ignore the report altogether.

CRD offers several features that BO XI doesn't support. One set of features is additional export options. CRD permits you to export your reports to DBF, TIFF, XML, and Lotus worksheets. You can also specify as destinations printer/fax, SMTP mail, FTP, or disk file. CRD also supports SMS (cell phone text) and ODBC data sources. You can customize some of these options also. The PDF export for example allows you to set a password or determine whether the user can print. You can also indicate whether the group headers of the report should be used as bookmarks as well as set file summary information like author or document description. If you wish, you can even export specified sections of the report.

CRD stores report instances for later retrieval, and like the limits settings in BO XI, you can specify how long they should be retained. Files can be automatically compressed using the ZIP format to conserve disk space and protected with PGP encryption. There is a backup and restore option for archiving your data and handling disaster recovery.

Though CRD does replace most of the functionality offered by BO XI, it does not expose an object model to enable custom development. This is not a developer's tool, and it is intended to be run solely through its user interface. However, you can integrate with existing systems using the command-line interface.

Excel Solutions

One of the most frequent requests I've received over the years from clients is to create report output in Microsoft Excel. Commonly, the users *only* want their reports in Excel, as no other format matters to them. With its row and column architecture and data analysis functionality, it is a natural venue for report delivery. BO XI allows you to export your reports to the Excel format, but with certain limitations. If your report displays a column of numbers and you've created a summary value to show, say, the total of that column, you may optionally export that summary value as an @SUM function in Excel rather than as a precalculated total. This feature will allow your users to perform the "what-if" analysis for which they normally need Excel, whereby they can change detail values in the spreadsheet and examine its effects on the rest of the report. There is, unfortunately, a catch here. Only database field summaries, not formula summaries, may be exported as functions. Moreover, only group-level summaries are available for export as Excel functions regardless of whether they are database or formula summaries. Therefore, you could not export a grand total.

Still another reason you may wish to consider Excel is to handle reports where the users select the columns they wish to see. Since report writers by their nature are intended for design-time report creation, you cannot possibly anticipate all the permutations a user may desire. In such situations you could use the RAS, to which Chapter 8 is dedicated, to create the report at runtime, adding only the desired columns. You would still be constrained by the formula export restrictions that exist for any other Crystal report. To avoid this, you could bypass Crystal Reports entirely and use one of the Excel solutions discussed in the upcoming text to output a spreadsheet containing only the columns that you need. Moreover, because you have full control over what's going into each cell, you can specify what will appear as formulas and what will appear as raw data. Using Excel will allow you to provide your users with the most powerful "what-if" spreadsheets.

If you want to create a server-based reporting solution, the creation of XLS files with Microsoft Excel itself is not a viable solution. The Excel object model has a large memory footprint and was intended to be instantiated individually on desktop machines, not potentially hundred of times simultaneously on servers. Though there are no technical barriers that would preclude you from doing this, the solution will not be scalable, and you'll soon eat up your server's memory. Simply put, Excel was never intended to be used this way. Moreover, if you are not careful about cleaning up and destroying your objects when done, stray Excel instantiations will remain in memory, and you'll need to destroy them through Task Manager or with a reboot. Still, a number of people are taking this approach. At the June 2005 Microsoft TechEd conference, one of the speakers asked how many people were instantiating Excel directly on a server, and at least two dozen of the 80 people in the room raised their hands.

CASE STUDY

A prime example of where visual report writing tools were simply not an appropriate solution occurred on a consulting project I was on a few years ago. The client had a series of 20 reports that consisted of marketing data. The user could select individual marketing demographics to display. So, for a given date range, the user could select any combination of Children, Pre-Teens, Teenagers, Young Adults, etc., and display sales to these groups over a period of time along with estimates of competitor sales over the same time period. The user could also determine whether he wanted these columns summed, averaged, or both, how the columns should be aligned, whether the headers should be bolded, and other such formatting options. All the report output was to be produced in Excel.

A project with this level of visual complexity is not appropriate for any report writer. I suggested that the requested data be created by a stored procedure and the output sent to a spreadsheet using one of the Excel replacement tools described in this chapter. I even created a working prototype of a report as a proof of concept. This prototype consisted of a front end that invoked a web service method that extracted the requested detail data and used the Excel creation tool to build and format the report. Because the web service method would be entering the data into the cells individually from the data source, I always knew exactly where I was in the report creation process and could format accordingly. The advantage of this approach was that the user could now get sums and averages exported as formulas instead of just raw numbers to allow for "what-if" analysis. In addition, as a web service, it was very scalable to new users throughout the enterprise.

Before the consultants on this project were ever, well, consulted, management made a decision to use BusinessObjects 6.5 and licensed the product specifically for this project. Because we couldn't set user-selectable columns at runtime in this design-time tool, all the possible marketing demographic columns were dumped by BO to a spreadsheet. Then, this output was opened by an Excel macro that then removed the undesired columns. The macro to handle these 20 reports eventually consumed 12,000 lines of VBA code. Moreover, the entire process became so fragile that when the slightest change was made to a report, every possible combination of report criteria had to be retested to make sure some subtle bug did not enter the processing logic. The main problem was that much of the macro logic, which manipulated the report data after it was rendered to a spreadsheet, had to be circumstantial. That is, I could only know, for example, that the end of the report detail section was reached when the word *Summary* appeared in a given column. If this word changed or appeared elsewhere in the column, the formatting logic would collapse. Moreover, because BusinessObjects had to be instantiated by the criteria selection tool (a .NET front end), a copy of BusinessObjects had to be installed on the machines of all 30 users of the system. When we found out that this conflicted with an earlier version of BO that already existed on these machines, each user was given an additional machine with BO 6.5 installed on it solely to run the reports for this project—a requirement that would have been eliminated with a server-based solution.

This was by far the worst project I've ever worked on in 15 years as a software developer—I'm the guy who had to write the macros—and it was the only time I ever said to a client: "I beg you not to go down this road." The failure here cannot be blamed on BusinessObjects at all. This situation stands as a powerful example of what happens when a great tool is used the wrong way.

Fortunately, there are two third-party solutions designed specifically as scalable, server-based replacements for Excel—Essential XlsIO from Syncfusion and OfficeWriter for Excel from SoftArtisans. Both have object models similar to that of Excel, so if you know VBA programming, you'll pick up either of these tools very quickly. They are also dramatically faster than Microsoft Excel; both products created sample spreadsheets over 100 times faster than Microsoft Excel. I'll cover these tools in the next sections.

Syncfusion's Essential XlsIO

Syncfusion's (www.syncfusion.com) Essential XlsIO is written completely in .NET code (C#) and optionally comes with the source code. Essential XlsIO offers PageSetup objects, row height settings, page breaks, document property settings, data validation, conditional formatting, comments, rich text, autofilters, charts, hyperlinks, and images. Essential XlsIO does not support PivotTable and Macro objects but preserves them if they are present in template spreadsheets. Essential XlsIO is a fast product. In a test that wrote the same data to 1000 rows across three columns, Essential XlsIO completed the task in one-tenth of a second, whereas Microsoft Excel required almost nine seconds.

Essential XlsIO has an object model similar to that of Excel and allows you to perform most of the data manipulation and formatting tasks that Excel offers. Listing 12-1 shows how to create a spreadsheet.

Listing 12-1. *Setting Up Syncfusion Essential XlsIO Code*

```
//Instantiate the spreadsheet creation engine
oExcelEngine = new ExcelEngine();

//Create a workbook
oWorkBook = oExcelEngine.Excel.Workbooks.Create();

//Reference the first worksheet
oWS = oWorkBook.Worksheets[0];

//Set orientation and paper size
oWS.PageSetup.Orientation = ExcelPageOrientation.Portrait;
oWS.PageSetup.PaperSize = ExcelPaperSize.PaperLetter;

//Set margins
oWS.PageSetup.LeftMargin = 0.25;
oWS.PageSetup.RightMargin = 0.25;
oWS.PageSetup.TopMargin = 1.25;
oWS.PageSetup.BottomMargin = 1.0;

//Set the first row to print at the top of every page
oWS.PageSetup.PrintTitleRows = "$A$1:$IV$1";

//Set header and footer text
oWS.PageSetup.LeftFooter = "Page &P of &N\n&D &T";
oWS.PageSetup.CenterHeader = "Sample Report";

//Set column widths
oWS.SetColumnWidth(1, 20);
oWS.SetColumnWidth(2, 10);

//Set workbook's summary and custom document properties
oWorkBook.BuiltInDocumentProperties.Author = "Essential Essential XlsIO";
oWorkBook.CustomDocumentProperties["Today"].DateTime = DateTime.Today;
```

You need to instantiate the spreadsheet creation engine first and then reference the exist-ing workbook and worksheet as you would in Excel. The PageSetup object encapsulates the same settings as its Excel counterpart, and Essential XlsIO provides its own enumerated values to refer to such properties as Orientation and PaperSize. Headers and footers are set as you would expect them. Finally, the workbook's summary and custom document properties are set.

Listing 12-2 shows how the cells are filled with data from the data source.

Listing 12-2. *Populating the Cells*

```
//Set column headers
oWS.Range[sRow, 1].Text = "Product";
oWS.Range[sRow, 2].Text = "Sales";

//Display headers in bold, centered, with a yellow background
oWS.Range[sRow, 1, sRow, 2].CellStyle.Color =
    Color.Yellow;
oWS.Range[sRow, 1, sRow, 2].CellStyle.HorizontalAlignment =
    ExcelHAlign.HAlignCenter;
oWS.Range[sRow, 1, sRow, 2].CellStyle.Font.Bold = true;
sRow++;

//Get sample data, move through the results, and write data to cells
oDT = GetData();

foreach(DataRow oDR in oDT.Rows)
{
    oWS.Range[sRow, 1].Text = oDR["Product"].ToString();
    oWS.Range[sRow, 2].Value = oDR["Sales"].ToString();

    sRow++;
}

sRow++;

//Display total line via formula in bold
oWS.Range[sRow, 1].Text = "Grand Total";
oWS.Range[sRow, 2].Formula = "SUM(B2:B" + (sRow - 1).ToString() + ")";
oWS.Range[sRow, 1, sRow, 2].CellStyle.Font.Bold = true;

//Format Sales column
oWS.Range[2, 2, sRow, 2].NumberFormat = "0.00";

oWorkBook.SaveAs(@"c:\temp\sample.xls");

oWorkBook.Close();
```

Rather than refer to individual cells, Essential XlsIO refers to ranges. Like Excel, you can use range references to apply data formats and cell attributes like color and font. You can even use ranges to assign values. The last printed page of this spreadsheet produced by this code is shown in Figure 12-32.

	Sample Report
Product	**Sales**
Product1	101.00
Product56	156.00
Product57	157.00
Product58	158.00
Product59	159.00
Product60	160.00
Product61	161.00
Product62	162.00
Product63	163.00
Product64	164.00
Product65	165.00
Product66	166.00
Product67	167.00
Product68	168.00
Product69	169.00
Product70	170.00
Product71	171.00
Product72	172.00
Product73	173.00
Product74	174.00
Product75	175.00
Product76	176.00
Product77	177.00
Product78	178.00
Product79	179.00
Product80	180.00
Product81	181.00
Product82	182.00
Product83	183.00
Product84	184.00
Product85	185.00
Product86	186.00
Product87	187.00
Product88	188.00
Product89	189.00
Product90	190.00
Product91	191.00
Product92	192.00
Product93	193.00
Product94	194.00
Product95	195.00
Product96	196.00
Product97	197.00
Product98	198.00
Product99	199.00
Product100	200.00
Grand Total	15050.00

Page 2 of 2
6/2/2006 3:16 PM

Figure 12-32. *Spreadsheet output from Essential XlsIO*

You can also use several helper methods like the worksheet object's `ImportDataTable` method that make importing ADO.NET data sources like Array, DataTable, DataColumn, and DataView easier than enumerating through the data source.

You can also add data visualization to your Excel report through the use of autofilters, comments, and charts. Listing 12-3 shows how autofilters, comments, and charts are added to the report.

Listing 12-3. *Autofilters, Comments, and Charts*

```
//Insert Autofilter
oFilter = oWS.AutoFilters;

//Set filter range
oFilter.FilterRange = oWS.Range[1, 1, sRow, 2];

//Insert comments
oComment = oWS.Range[sRow, 1].AddComment();
oComment.Text = "Total Sales";

//Insert chart
//Adding a New(Embedded chart) to the Worksheet
oChartShape = oWS.Charts.Add();

//Set chart type
oChartShape.ChartType = ExcelChartType.Column_Clustered;

//Set if series is in rows
oChartShape.IsSeriesInRows = false;

//Set the chart's DataRange and X-axis labels range
oChartShape.DataRange = oWS.Range[2, 2, sRow-1, 2];
oChartShape.PrimaryCategoryAxis.CategoryLabels = oWS.Range[2, 1, sRow-2, 1];

//Set chart titles
oChartShape.PrimaryCategoryAxis.Title = "Products";
oChartShape.PrimaryValueAxis.Title = "Sales";
oChartShape.ChartTitle = "Product Sales";

//Position the chart in the worksheet
oChartShape.BottomRow = 40;
oChartShape.TopRow = 10;
oChartShape.LeftColumn = 3;
oChartShape.RightColumn = 15;
```

In addition to creating Excel reports purely using code, it is also possible to use existing spreadsheets as templates for report generation. Often it is easier to design the look and feel of the report using the Excel GUI and then use Essential XlsIO to dynamically fill data during runtime. Using this approach, it is also possible to have elements like PivotTables and macros in your report that Essential XlsIO does not directly support but retains on resaving if they are present in the template spreadsheet. Listing 12-4 shows how to generate a report based on a template spreadsheet.

Listing 12-4. *Using Templates*

```
//Instantiate the spreadsheet creation engine
oExcelEngine = new ExcelEngine();

//Create a workbook
oWorkBook = oExcelEngine.Excel.Workbooks.Open(@"..\..\Data\Template.xls");

//Reference the first worksheet
oWS = oWorkBook.Worksheets[0];

//Get sample data
oDT = GetTable();

//Import DataTable into worksheet
oWS.ImportDataTable(oDT,false,2,1,-1,-1,false);

//Display total line via formula in bold
oWS.Range[oDT.Rows.Count+1, 1].Text = "Grand Total";
oWS.Range[oDT.Rows.Count+1, 2].Formula =
    "SUM(B2:B" + (oDT.Rows.Count - 1).ToString() + ")";
oWS.Range[oDT.Rows.Count+1, 1,
    oDT.Rows.Count+1, 2].CellStyle.Font.Bold = true;
```

Once the workbook is loaded into memory using the Open method, all the elements in the workbook become accessible through the Essential XlsIO API. This makes it possible to read data from existing spreadsheets that users may upload back to the server after making modifications on their local machines. It is also possible to read and write the spreadsheets to streams, which can be convenient at times. There are no temporary files generated on the server when saving to stream.

Essential XlsIO also has support for another variant of the template-based approach for report generation, whereby the end user can design the template and place special markers in it that will be replaced by data dynamically during runtime. This opens up the possibility of the end users designing the template and placing markers at the positions where they require the data to be filled inside the report.

Essential XlsIO can also read and write SpreadsheetML files, which are Excel-compatible XML files and CSV files in addition to the default binary format. There is also an option to serialize to an XML format that Syncfusion internally uses to add interoperability between their products.

SoftArtisans's OfficeWriter

SoftArtisans's (www.softartisans.com) OfficeWriter tool produces both native Excel and Word files (Office 97, 2000, XP, and 2003) without instantiating Excel or Word. For use on high-request web server environments, OfficeWriter is a lean tool designed specifically to generate Excel and Word documents on a server. There are two versions of this product—the Enterprise Edition and the Standard Edition.

The powerful Application Object in the Enterprise product offers an unlimited number of spreadsheets with full programmatic functionality, including PivotTables, VBA, charts, and macros. The programmatic control allows you to add flexibility to your applications by instantly modifying reports based on runtime data or your users' requests.

This is a great benefit to both the developer and the end user. You can use one standard report and then change logos, charts, graphs, number of sheets, formatting, etc., based on the data being returned when the report is generated on the server. With other reporting solutions you need to create a different template for every single report that you run.

The speedy Standard Edition preserves all of the Excel features in a template or existing spreadsheet. With limited exposure to the OfficeWriter Application Object in the Standard Edition, features such as cell merging and column and row auto fitting are not available at runtime. Many OfficeWriter customers actually combine the quick-and-easy Template Object with the powerful Application Object for ultimate performance and control.

Listing 12-5 shows how to create a spreadsheet using SoftArtisans's OfficeWriter. The output is the same as shown in Figure 12-32. If you've ever created a spreadsheet with VBA code, this should all be familiar territory.

Listing 12-5. *Creating a Spreadsheet Using SoftArtisans's OfficeWriter for Excel*

```
ExcelApplication oExcelApplication;
Workbook oWB;
Worksheet oWS;
GlobalStyle oGlobalStyle;
Area oArea;
DataTable oDT;
int sRow = 0;

//Create a workbook
oExcelApplication = new ExcelApplication();
oWB = oExcelApplication.Create();

//Reference the first worksheet
oWS = oWB.Worksheets[0];

//Set orientation and paper size
oWS.PageSetup.Orientation = PageSetup.PageOrientation.Portrait;
oWS.PageSetup.PaperSize = PageSetup.PagePaperSize.Letter;

//Set margins
oWS.PageSetup.LeftMargin = 0.25;
oWS.PageSetup.RightMargin = 0.25;
oWS.PageSetup.TopMargin = 1.25;
oWS.PageSetup.BottomMargin = 1.0;

oWS.PageSetup.Zoom = 100;

//Set the first row to print at the top of every page
oWS.PageSetup.SetPrintTitleRows(0, 2);
```

```
//Set header and footer text
oWS.PageSetup.LeftFooter = "Page &P of &N\n&D &T";
oWS.PageSetup.CenterHeader = "Sample Report";

//Set column widths
oWS.GetColumnProperties(0).Width = 100;
oWS.GetColumnProperties(1).Width = 50;
```

OfficeWriter instantiates an object of type `ExcelApplication` that is the equivalent of `Excel.Application`. Then, you can create a new workbook and refer to the first worksheet in that workbook. The `PageSetup` interface mirrors Excel's closely.

Populating the cells is accomplished by setting the properties of the `Cells` objects as shown in Listing 12-6.

Listing 12-6. *Populating the Cells*

```
//Set column headers
oWS.Cells[sRow, 0].Value = "Product";
oWS.Cells[sRow, 1].Value = "Sales";

//Display headers in bold, centered, with a yellow background
oWS.Cells[sRow, 0].Style.BackgroundColor = Color.SystemColor.Yellow;
oWS.Cells[sRow, 0].Style.HorizontalAlignment = Style.HAlign.Center;
oWS.Cells[sRow, 0].Style.Font.Bold = true;

oWS.Cells[sRow, 1].Style.BackgroundColor = Color.SystemColor.Yellow;
oWS.Cells[sRow, 1].Style.HorizontalAlignment = Style.HAlign.Center;
oWS.Cells[sRow, 1].Style.Font.Bold = true;
sRow++;

//Get sample data, move through the results, and write data to cells
oDT = GetData();

foreach(DataRow oDR in oDT.Rows)
{
   oWS.Cells[sRow, 0].Value = oDR["Product"].ToString();
   oWS.Cells[sRow, 1].Value = int.Parse(oDR["Sales"].ToString());

   sRow++;
}

sRow++;

//Display total line via formula in bold
oWS.Cells[sRow, 0].Value = "Grand Total";
oWS.Cells[sRow, 1].Formula = "=SUM(B2:B" + (sRow - 1).ToString() + ")";
oWS.Cells[sRow, 0].Style.Font.Bold = true;
oWS.Cells[sRow, 1].Style.Font.Bold = true;
```

```
//Format Sales column
oGlobalStyle = oWB.CreateStyle();
oGlobalStyle.NumberFormat = "0.00";

oArea = oWS.CreateArea(1, 1, sRow, 1);
oArea.SetStyle(oGlobalStyle);

oExcelApplication.Save(oWB, @"c:\temp\sample.xls");

oDT.Dispose();
```

Formatting is performed by creating a GlobalStyle object and determining what the style attributes are. In this example, it sets the NumberFormat to 0.00 but could also set fonts and colors as well. Then, an Area object, which is similar to a Range object in Excel, uses the SetStyle method to apply the new style to the designated area.

In addition to creating and formatting spreadsheets, SoftArtisans offers their exclusive Hot-Cell Technology within Excel. This feature allows you to specify dynamic cells that are linked to and update data sources on the server. Just by modifying a report on a client machine, users can use Excel as a rich front end. With the ability to retrieve or update data on a web server, all end users can now access the same centralized location for up-to-date business information.

Word Solutions

The problems that arise with instantiating Excel on a server machine also manifest themselves when instantiating Word objects. The large, memory-hogging Word object model is too unwieldy to load into memory on a web server where many other users are likely doing the same. If you need a customized solution that outputs Word documents, SoftArtisans has a tool that can help you.

OfficeWriter for Word outputs native Word documents using an object model that is syntactically similar to Word VBA. If you understand Word VBA, then you are that much further ahead in learning the OfficeWriter tool. OfficeWriter allows you to design complex Word documents with watermarks, bulleted and numbered lists, as well as runtime-editable tables. In fact, the newest version of OfficeWriter for Word offers an enhanced Table API so you can add, insert, and delete rows and columns in existing Word tables. You can also merge documents and copy/paste individual elements between files.

The code shown in Listing 12-7 creates a Word document containing a table that lists the same data as shown in Figure 12-32.

Listing 12-7. *Using SoftArtisans's OfficeWriter for Word*

```
WordApplication oWordApplication;
Document oDocument;
Table oTable;
TableCell oTableCell;
Font oTotalFont;
DataTable oDT;
int sRow = 0;
int iTotal = 0;
```

```
oWordApplication = new WordApplication();

oDocument = oWordApplication.Create();

oDocument.InsertTextBefore("This is the payment report\n", true);

oDT = GetData();

oTable = oDocument.InsertTableAfter(oDT.Rows.Count + 1, 2);

foreach(DataRow oDR in oDT.Rows)
{
    oTableCell = oTable[sRow, 0];
    oTableCell.InsertTextAfter(oDR["Product"].ToString(), true);

    oTableCell = oTable[sRow, 1];
    oTableCell.InsertTextAfter(oDR["Sales"].ToString(), true);

    iTotal += int.Parse(oDR["Sales"].ToString());

    sRow++;
}

oTotalFont = oDocument.CreateFont();
oTotalFont.Bold = true;

oTableCell = oTable[sRow, 0];
oTableCell.InsertTextAfter("Grand Total", oTotalFont);

oTableCell = oTable[sRow, 1];
oTableCell.InsertTextAfter(iTotal.ToString(), oTotalFont);

oWordApplication.Save(oDocument, @"c:\temp\myreport.doc");
```

Both editions of OfficeWriter are integrated with SQL Server Reporting Services, allowing users to design and deliver their reports without ever leaving Microsoft Office. SoftArtisans provides a freely distributed add-in toolbar to Excel and Word so SQL Server Reporting Services users can design their reports in environments that are familiar to them. In addition, OfficeWriter adds native Word and Excel to the rendering options within SQL Server Reporting Services.

Summary

No solution could possibly anticipate and meet every possible need, and BusinessObjects XI is no exception. No matter what you're trying to accomplish with BusinessObjects XI, there is a third-party tool that will facilitate your development efforts.

Index

Special Characters

%SI_EMAIL_ADDRESS% variable, 168
%SI_ID% variable, 168
%SI_NAME% variable, 168
%SI_OWNER% variable, 168
%SI_STARTTIME% variable, 168
%SI_USERFULLNAME% variable, 168
%SI_VIEWER_URL% variable, 167–168

Numbers

4_InfoObjects5 table, 13
4Name property, 109

A

a PluginInfo object, 130
absolute links, 78
access levels and security rights
    overview, 347–348
    rights
        assigning, 349–350
        checking, 351–354
        overview, 349
    roles, 348
aControlList ArrayList object, 300
Acrobat, 407
Actions collection, 128
actions method, 382
Active Directory (AD), 340, 360
Active mode, iGuard, 422
AD (Active Directory), 340, 360
Add( ) method, 174, 332, 343, 350, 357
Add Users button, 342
AddChart( ) method, 272
AddDynamicLabel( ) method, 298, 310
AddDynamicListBox( ) method, 299, 311
AddField( ) method, 246, 262
AddGroup( ) method, 237
AddLine( ) method, 263
AddressBook Gateway tool, 395
AddTable( ) method, 232, 234–235
Administration Launchpad
    Administration Tool Console
        Instance Manager, 64
        Manage Groups and User Accounts, 66
        Object Repository Helper, 68
        overview, 62

Query Builder, 68
        Report Datasources, 67
        Schedule Manager, 62–64
        Shortcut Manager, 66–67
        View Server Summary, 64–65
    Central Management Console (CMC), 61
    InfoView, 62
    overview, 61
Administration Tool Console
    Instance Manager, 64
    Manage Groups and User Accounts, 66
    Object Repository Helper, 68
    overview, 62
    Query Builder, 68
    Report Datasources, 67
    Schedule Manager, 62–64
    Shortcut Manager, 66–67
    View Server Summary, 64–65
administration tools
    Administration Launchpad
        Administration Tool Console, 62–68
        Central Management Console (CMC), 61
        InfoView, 62
        overview, 61
    Business View manager, 68
    Central Configuration Manager (CCM)
        Configuration tab, 50–52
        Connection tab, 50
        Dependency tab, 49–50
        overview, 47–48
        Properties tab, 48–49
        Protocol tab, 53
    Crystal Reports Explorer, 69–70, 72
    Import Wizard, 53–57
    overview, 47
    Publishing Wizard, 57–61
Administrators group, 341
Adobe Acrobat, 407
Advanced option, 349
Advise mode, iGuard, 422
aggregates, 116–117
Alert Notification option, 154
Alert Notification page, 89
alerts, 152, 154–156
Alerts editor utility, .rpt Inspector Enterprise
        Suite tool, 421
All Column Usage Summary, 423

ALL keyword, 117
APOS Systems Inc
    AddressBook Gateway tool, 395
    Archive Manager tool, 396–398
    Bursting Manager tool, 398–400
    InfoScheduler tool, 400, 402
    Instance Manager tool, 402
    Instance Monitor tool, 404
    Key Performance Indicator (KPI) tool,
        404–405
    Object Manager tool, 406–408
    overview, 395
    RealTime Monitor tool, 408–411
    Report Package Booster tool, 412
    RunTime Manager tool, 413
    Solutions Kit for ESRI GIS (geographic
        information system) tool, 413–416
    View Time Security tool, 416–417
APOSVTS.DLL extension, 417
APOSVTSG.DLL extension, 417
APOSVTSN.DLL extension, 417
APOSVTSP.DLL extension, 417
APOSVTSW.DLL extension, 417
Application Object, Enterprise, 431–432
applicationName attribute, 194
APSName property, 109
APSVersion property, 109
Archive Manager tool, 396–398
ArcIMS users, 414
Area object, 434
AreaSectionKind enumerator, 217
ArrayList, 361
AS clause and aliasing, 116
ASC clause, 375
ASMX file, 225
Assign Categories button, 94
AssignSecurityLimits( ) web method, 356
attribute indicator, 375
Attributes.Add( ) method, 312
audit notifications, 88, 152
Authentication options, 359
AutoGenerateColumns property, 196
Automatic option, Startup Type property, 49
AutoSize property, 298
Auxiliary Files option, 290

■B

backups and disaster recovery, 44–45
banded report writer, 2
Base64Decode( ) method, 283
batch-management features, 61
BeginDate property, 142
BIAR (Business Intelligence Archive
    Resource), 54
.biar extension, 54

BICatalog server, Web Service SDK, 370
billing software, 7
BIPlatform object, 371, 376, 381, 383, 390
biplatform service, 369
BO XI. *See* BusinessObjects XI (BO XI)
BOEDataSource data control, 192
BOEDataSource object, 195
BOEHierarchicalDataSource data control, 192
BOEHierarchicalDataSourceView class, 195
BOEMembershipProvider class, 193
Boolean formatting, 260
Boolean values, 114–115
Borders object, 264–265
Boxes object, 263–264
BoxObject class, 262
breadcrumbs, 73, 190
broadcast license, 5
Browse button, 76, 290
BuildFolderSQL( ) method, 322
bulk mailing, 7
Bursting Manager tool, 398–400
business intelligence, 2–3
Business Intelligence Archive Resource
    (BIAR), 54
Business Objects Technology Partner, 395
Business View manager, 68
Business Views object, 69, 404
BusinessObjects Enterprise Applications,
    69, 74
BusinessObjects reports, 1, 16
BusinessObjects servers, 408
BusinessObjects Universe, 404
BusinessObjects XI (BO XI). *See also* Crystal
    Reports
    history, 1–2
    overview, 1
    Release 2
        licensing, 4–5
        overview, 3
        service-oriented architecture (SOA), 5–6
    from report writing to business
        intelligence, 2–3
    reporting considerations
        availability and distribution, 8–9
        high-volume printing, 7–8
        legal issues, 8
        overview, 6–7
        preprinted forms, 7
    vs. SQL Server Reporting Services (SSRS)
        feature differences, 11–12
        market considerations, 9–10
        overview, 9
BusinessObjects XI environment, 421
ByteArray array, 267
ByteStream array, 191

C

Cache File Location, 35
Cache Server, 34–36, 64, 411
CacheServerAdmin class, 35
Calendar object, 175
Calendar option, 87
CalendarDay object, 387
CalendarRunDays property, SchedulingInfo
    object, 142
Can Grow option, 165
Categories tab, reports, 94–95
CCM. *See* Central Configuration Manager
    (CCM)
CCM (Configuration tab, Central
    Configuration Manager), 50–52
CCM (Connection tab, Central Configuration
    Manager), 50
ceCustomSettings member, CeReportLayout
    enumerator, 170
CeDayOfWeek enumerator, 141
ceDefaultPrinterSettings member,
    CeReportLayout enumerator, 170
ceFormatCrystalReport member,
    CeReportFormat enumerator, 157
ceFormatExcel member, CeReportFormat
    enumerator, 157
ceFormatExcelDataOnly member,
    CeReportFormat enumerator, 157
ceFormatPDF member, CeReportFormat
    enumerator, 157
ceFormatRTF member, CeReportFormat
    enumerator, 157
ceFormatRTFEditable member,
    CeReportFormat enumerator, 157
ceFormatTextCharacterSeparated member,
    CeReportFormat enumerator, 157
ceFormatTextPaginated member,
    CeReportFormat enumerator, 157
ceFormatTextPlain member,
    CeReportFormat enumerator, 157
ceFormatTextTabSeparated member,
    CeReportFormat enumerator, 157
ceFormatTextTabSeparatedText member,
    CeReportFormat enumerator, 157
ceFormatUserDefined member,
    CeReportFormat enumerator, 157
ceFormatWord member, CeReportFormat
    enumerator, 157
ceLimitMaxInstanceAge member,
    CeSystemLimits Enumerator, 356
ceLimitMaxInstanceCount member,
    CeSystemLimits Enumerator, 356
ceLimitMaxInstanceCountPerUser member,
    CeSystemLimits Enumerator, 356

ceLimitMaxObjectLevelSecurityLimit
    member, CeSystemLimits
    Enumerator, 356
ceNoPrinterSettings member,
    CeReportLayout enumerator, 170
Central Configuration Manager, 64
Central Configuration Manager (CCM)
    Configuration tab, 50–52
    Connection tab, 50
    Dependency tab, 49–50
    overview, 47–48
    Properties tab, 48–49
    Protocol tab, 53
Central Management Console (CMC), 61, 64
    calendars, 97–98
    events
        custom, 101–102
        file and schedule events, 99–101
        overview, 98
    folders, 74–75
    managing security through
        adding users to groups, 342–343
        creating groups, 341–342
        creating users, 339–340
        extracting users in group, 343–345
        overview, 338–339
        subgroups, 345–346
    objects, 96–97
    overview, 73
    reports
        Categories tab, 94–95
        History page, 78–81
        overview, 75–76
        Process tab, 81–87
        Properties tab, 76–78
        Rights tab, 96
        Schedule tab, 87–94
Central Management Server (CMS), 17, 22–24
Central Management Server Properties
    dialog, 48
ceOutcomeFailComponentFailed member,
    CeScheduleOutcome enumerator,
    288
ceOutcomeFailEndTime member,
    CeScheduleOutcome enumerator,
    288
ceOutcomeFailJobServer member,
    CeScheduleOutcome enumerator,
    288
ceOutcomeFailJobServerChild member,
    CeScheduleOutcome enumerator,
    288
ceOutcomeFailJobServerPlugin member,
    CeScheduleOutcome enumerator,
    288

ceOutcomeFailObjectPackageFailed member, CeScheduleOutcome enumerator, 288
ceOutcomeFailSchedule member, CeScheduleOutcome enumerator, 288
ceOutcomeFailSecurity member, CeScheduleOutcome enumerator, 288
ceOutcomePending member, CeScheduleOutcome enumerator, 288
ceOutcomeSuccess member, CeScheduleOutcome enumerator, 288
CeProgramType enumerator, 144
CePropFlags.cePropFlagBag enumerator, 332
ceReportFileSettings member, CeReportLayout enumerator, 170
CeReportRefreshOption enumerator, methods of, 131
ceReportSectionsExportIsolated option, 161
CEResponse.ServerFile enumerator, 284
ceRightAdd member, CeSystemRights enumerator, 353
ceRightCopy member, CeSystemRights enumerator, 353
ceRightDelete member, CeSystemRights enumerator, 353
ceRightDeleteInstance member, CeSystemRights enumerator, 353
ceRightEdit member, CeSystemRights enumerator, 353
ceRightModifyRights member, CeSystemRights enumerator, 353
ceRightOwnerDelete member, CeSystemRights enumerator, 353
ceRightOwnerDeleteInstance member, CeSystemRights enumerator, 353
ceRightOwnerEdit member, CeSystemRights enumerator, 353
ceRightOwnerModifyRights member, CeSystemRights enumerator, 353
ceRightOwnerPauseResumeSchedule member, CeSystemRights enumerator, 353
ceRightOwnerReschedule member, CeSystemRights enumerator, 353
ceRightOwnerSecuredModifyRights member, CeSystemRights enumerator, 353
ceRightOwnerView member, CeSystemRights enumerator, 353
ceRightOwnerViewInstance member, CeSystemRights enumerator, 353
ceRightPauseResumeSchedule member, CeSystemRights enumerator, 353

ceRightPickMachines member, CeSystemRights enumerator, 353
ceRightReschedule member, CeSystemRights enumerator, 353
ceRightSchedule member, CeSystemRights enumerator, 353
ceRightScheduleOnBehalfOf member, CeSystemRights enumerator, 353
ceRightSecuredModifyRights member, CeSystemRights enumerator, 353
ceRightSetDestination member, CeSystemRights enumerator, 353
ceRightView member, CeSystemRights enumerator, 353
ceRightViewInstance member, CeSystemRights enumerator, 353
CeRole enumerator, 348
ceRoleAdvanced member, CeRole enumerator, 348
ceRoleFullControl member, CeRole enumerator, 348
ceRoleNoAccess member, CeRole enumerator, 348
ceRoleSchedule member, CeRole enumerator, 348
ceRoleView member, CeRole enumerator, 348
ceRoleViewOnDemand member, CeRole enumerator, 348
CeScheduleOutcome enumerator, 288
ceSpecifiedPrinterSettings member, CeReportLayout enumerator, 170
ceStatusFailure member, CeScheduleStatus enumerator, 288
ceStatusPaused member, CeScheduleStatus enumerator, 288
ceStatusPending member, CeScheduleStatus enumerator, 288
ceStatusRunning member, CeScheduleStatus enumerator, 288
ceStatusSuccess member, CeScheduleStatus enumerator, 288
CeSystemLimits enumeration, 355
Change button, 63
ChangePassword control, 181
CharactersPerInch property, 159, 163
ChartDefinition class, 273
ChartObjectClass object, 273
ChartStyle.Type property, 273
checked list boxes, 295
CheckedItems collection, 304
CheckedListBox control, 303
CheckLimits( ) method, 392
CheckRights( ) method, 353, 392
Christian Steven Software, Ltd., 5, 424
CI_APPOBJECTS table, 121
CI_INFOOBJECTS table, 121
CI_SYSTEMOBJECTS category, 19

CI_SYSTEMOBJECTS table, 121
Clear( ) method, Cookies collection, 106
clusters, 22, CMS
CMC. *See* Central Management Console (CMC)
CMS. *See* Central Management Server (CMS)
CmsAdmin class, 23
Columns property, 183
Command property, Central Management
    Server, 49
Commit( ) method, 41, 343, 386
CommonFormat property, 256
communication layers, 6
Company Name text object, 419
Compensation column, 338
Condition button, 153
condition formulas, 242–245
ConditionField property, 237
ConditionFields( ) method, 273
ConditionFormulas( ) method, 243, 245
Configuration tab, Central Configuration
    Manager (CCM), 50–52
Connection object, 372, 381
Connection tab, Central Configuration
    Manager (CCM), 50
ConnectionInfo object, 207
Connections option, 409
ConnectionState object, 372, 381
connectionString tag, 194
connectionStringName attribute, 194
connectionStrings element, 194
consulting, 8
ControlManager base class, 296
copyrights, 8
COUNT function, 116
crAlignmentDecimal member,
    CrAlignmentEnum enumerator, 257
crAlignmentDefault member,
    CrAlignmentEnum enumerator, 257
CrAlignmentEnum enumerator, 257
crAlignmentHorizontalCenter member,
    CrAlignmentEnum enumerator, 257
crAlignmentJustified member,
    CrAlignmentEnum enumerator, 257
crAlignmentLeft member,
    CrAlignmentEnum enumerator, 257
crAlignmentRight member,
    CrAlignmentEnum enumerator, 257
CrBooleanFieldFormatConditionFormula
    TypeEnum enumerator, 243
CrBooleanOutputFormatEnum
    enumerator, 261
crBooleanOutputFormatOneOrZero
    member, CrBooleanOutputFormat
    Enum enumerator, 261
crBooleanOutputFormatTOrF member,
    CrBooleanOutputFormatEnum
    enumerator, 261

crBooleanOutputFormatTrueOrFalse
    member,
    CrBooleanOutputFormatEnum
    enumerator, 261
crBooleanOutputFormatYesOrNo member,
    CrBooleanOutputFormatEnum
    enumerator, 261
crBooleanOutputFormatYOrN member,
    CrBooleanOutputFormatEnum
    enumerator, 261
CrBorderConditionFormulaTypeEnum
    enumerator, 243
crChartStyleType3DRiser member,
    CrChartStyleTypeEnum enumerator,
    273
crChartStyleType3DSurface member,
    CrChartStyleTypeEnum enumerator,
    273
crChartStyleTypeArea member,
    CrChartStyleTypeEnum enumerator,
    273
crChartStyleTypeBar member,
    CrChartStyleTypeEnum enumerator,
    273
crChartStyleTypeBubble member,
    CrChartStyleTypeEnum enumerator,
    273
crChartStyleTypeDoughnut member,
    CrChartStyleTypeEnum enumerator,
    273
CrChartStyleTypeEnum enumerator, 273
crChartStyleTypeLine member,
    CrChartStyleTypeEnum enumerator,
    273
crChartStyleTypePie member,
    CrChartStyleTypeEnum enumerator,
    273
crChartStyleTypeRadar member,
    CrChartStyleTypeEnum enumerator,
    274
crChartStyleTypeStocked member,
    CrChartStyleTypeEnum enumerator,
    274
crChartStyleTypeUnknown member,
    CrChartStyleTypeEnum enumerator,
    274
crChartStyleTypeUserDefined member,
    CrChartStyleTypeEnum enumerator,
    274
crChartStyleTypeXYScatter member,
    CrChartStyleTypeEnum enumerator,
    274
CrCommonFieldFormatConditionFormula
    TypeEnum enumerator, 243
CrCurrencyPositionFormatEnum
    enumerator, 258

crCurrencyPositionFormatLeadingCurrency-
    InsideNegative member,
    CrCurrencyPositionFormatEnum
    enumerator, 258
crCurrencyPositionFormatLeadingCurrency-
    OutsideNegative member,
    CrCurrencyPositionFormatEnum
    enumerator, 258
crCurrencyPositionFormatTrailingCurrency-
    InsideNegative member,
    CrCurrencyPositionFormatEnum
    enumerator, 258
crCurrencyPositionFormatTrailingCurrency-
    OutsideNegative member, CrCurrency-
    PositionFormatEnum enumerator,
    258
CrCurrencySymbolTypeEnum enumerator, 258
crCurrencySymbolTypeFixedSymbol
    member, CrCurrencySymbol-
    TypeEnum enumerator, 258
crCurrencySymbolTypeFloatingSymbol
    member, CrCurrencySymbol-
    TypeEnum enumerator, 258
crCurrencySymbolTypeNoSymbol member,
    CrCurrencySymbolTypeEnum
    enumerator, 258
CRD, 424–425
CrDateFieldFormatConditionFormulaType-
    Enum enumerator, 243
CrDateTimeFieldFormatConditionFormula-
    TypeEnum enumerator, 243
crDateTimeOrderDateOnly, 259
crDateTimeOrderDateThenTime, 259
CrDateTimeOrderEnum enumerator, 259
crDateTimeOrderTimeOnly, 259
crDateTimeOrderTimeThenDate, 259
crDayFormatLeadingZeroNumericDay
    member, CrDayFormatEnum
    enumerator, 259
crDayFormatNoDay member, CrDayFormat-
    Enum enumerator, 259
crDayFormatNumericDay member,
    CrDayFormatEnum enumerator, 259
Create Alerts dialog, 152
CreateBookmarksFromGroupTree( ) method,
    164
CreateFont( ) method, 261
CreateWCATokenEx( ) method, 107
crFieldValueTypeBitmapField member,
    CrFieldValueTypeEnum enumerator,
    248
crFieldValueTypeBlobField member,
    CrFieldValueTypeEnum enumerator,
    248
crFieldValueTypeBooleanField member,
    CrFieldValueTypeEnum enumerator,
    248

crFieldValueTypeChartField member,
    CrFieldValueTypeEnum enumerator,
    248
crFieldValueTypeCurrencyField member,
    CrFieldValueTypeEnum enumerator,
    248
crFieldValueTypeDateField member,
    CrFieldValueTypeEnum enumerator,
    248
crFieldValueTypeDateTimeField member,
    CrFieldValueTypeEnum enumerator,
    248
crFieldValueTypeDecimalField member,
    CrFieldValueTypeEnum enumerator,
    248
CrFieldValueTypeEnum enumerator, 247
crFieldValueTypeIconField member, CrField-
    ValueTypeEnum enumerator, 248
crFieldValueTypeInt16sField member,
    CrFieldValueTypeEnum enumerator,
    248
crFieldValueTypeInt16uField member,
    CrFieldValueTypeEnum enumerator,
    248
crFieldValueTypeInt32sField member,
    CrFieldValueTypeEnum enumerator,
    248
crFieldValueTypeInt32uField member,
    CrFieldValueTypeEnum enumerator,
    248
crFieldValueTypeInt64sField member,
    CrFieldValueTypeEnum enumerator,
    248
crFieldValueTypeInt64uField member,
    CrFieldValueTypeEnum enumerator,
    248
crFieldValueTypeInt8sField member,
    CrFieldValueTypeEnum enumerator,
    248
crFieldValueTypeInt8uField member,
    CrFieldValueTypeEnum enumerator,
    248
crFieldValueTypeInterfacePointerField
    member, CrFieldValueTypeEnum
    enumerator, 248
crFieldValueTypeNumberField member,
    CrFieldValueTypeEnum enumerator,
    248
crFieldValueTypeOleField member,
    CrFieldValueTypeEnum enumerator,
    248
crFieldValueTypePersistentMemoField
    member, CrFieldValueTypeEnum
    enumerator, 248
crFieldValueTypePictureField member,
    CrFieldValueTypeEnum enumerator,
    248

crFieldValueTypePointerField member,
CrFieldValueTypeEnum enumerator,
248
crFieldValueTypeSameAsInputField member,
CrFieldValueTypeEnum enumerator,
248
crFieldValueTypeStringField member,
CrFieldValueTypeEnum enumerator,
248
crFieldValueTypeTimeField member,
CrFieldValueTypeEnum enumerator,
248
crFieldValueTypeTransientMemoField
member, CrFieldValueTypeEnum
enumerator, 248
crFieldValueTypeUnknownField member,
CrFieldValueTypeEnum enumerator,
248
CrFontColorConditionFormulaTypeEnum
enumerator, 243
Criteria enumerator, 310
CrMonthFormatEnum enumerator, 259
crMonthFormatLeadingZeroNumericMonth
member, CrMonthFormatEnum
enumerator, 259
crMonthFormatLongMonth member,
CrMonthFormatEnum enumerator,
259
crMonthFormatNoMonth member,
CrMonthFormatEnum enumerator,
259
crMonthFormatNumericMonth member,
CrMonthFormatEnum enumerator,
259
crMonthFormatShortMonth member,
CrMonthFormatEnum enumerator,
259
CrNumericFieldFormatConditionFormula-
TypeEnum enumerator, 243
CrObjectFormatConditionFormulaType-
Enum enumerator, 243
CRPE (Crystal Reports Print Engine), 29
crReportObjectKindBlobField member,
CrReportObjectKindEnum
enumerator, 247
crReportObjectKindBox member,
CrReportObjectKindEnum
enumerator, 247
crReportObjectKindChart member,
CrReportObjectKindEnum
enumerator, 247
crReportObjectKindCrosstab member,
CrReportObjectKindEnum
enumerator, 247
CrReportObjectKindEnum enumerator,
247

crReportObjectKindField member,
CrReportObjectKindEnum
enumerator, 247
crReportObjectKindFieldHeading member,
CrReportObjectKindEnum
enumerator, 247
crReportObjectKindInvalid member,
CrReportObjectKindEnum
enumerator, 247
crReportObjectKindLine member,
CrReportObjectKindEnum
enumerator, 247
crReportObjectKindMap member,
CrReportObjectKindEnum
enumerator, 247
crReportObjectKindOlapGrid member,
CrReportObjectKindEnum
enumerator, 247
crReportObjectKindPicture member,
CrReportObjectKindEnum
enumerator, 247
crReportObjectKindSubreport member,
CrReportObjectKindEnum
enumerator, 247
crReportObjectKindText member,
CrReportObjectKindEnum
enumerator, 247
crSectionAreaConditionFormulaTypeEnable-
HideForDrillDown, 244
crSectionAreaConditionFormulaTypeEnable-
KeepTogether, 244
crSectionAreaConditionFormulaTypeEnable-
NewPageAfter, 244
crSectionAreaConditionFormulaTypeEnable-
NewPageBefore, 244
crSectionAreaConditionFormulaTypeEnable-
PrintAtBottomOfPage, 244
crSectionAreaConditionFormulaTypeEnable-
ResetPageNumberAfter, 244
crSectionAreaConditionFormulaTypeEnable-
Suppress, 244
crSectionAreaConditionFormulaTypeEnable-
SuppressIfBlank, 244
crSectionAreaConditionFormulaTypeEnable-
UnderlaySection, 244
CrSectionAreaFormatConditionFormula-
TypeEnum enumerator, 243–244
crSortDirectionAscendingOrder member,
CrSortDirectionEnum enumerator,
269
crSortDirectionBottomNOrder, 269
crSortDirectionBottomNPercentage, 269
crSortDirectionDescendingOrder, 269
CrSortDirectionEnum enumerator, 269, 271
crSortDirectionTopNOrder, 269
crSortDirectionTopNPercentage, 269

crSpecialFieldTypeDataDate member,
CrSpecialFieldTypeEnum
enumerator, 251
crSpecialFieldTypeDataTime member,
CrSpecialFieldTypeEnum
enumerator, 251
CrSpecialFieldTypeEnum enumerator, 251
crSpecialFieldTypeFileAuthor member,
CrSpecialFieldTypeEnum
enumerator, 251
crSpecialFieldTypeFileCreationDate
member, CrSpecialFieldTypeEnum
enumerator, 251
crSpecialFieldTypeFileName member,
CrSpecialFieldTypeEnum
enumerator, 251
crSpecialFieldTypeGroupNumber member,
CrSpecialFieldTypeEnum
enumerator, 251
crSpecialFieldTypeGroupSelection member,
CrSpecialFieldTypeEnum
enumerator, 251
crSpecialFieldTypeModificationDate
member, CrSpecialFieldTypeEnum
enumerator, 251
crSpecialFieldTypeModificationTime
member, CrSpecialFieldTypeEnum
enumerator, 251
crSpecialFieldTypePageNOfM member,
CrSpecialFieldTypeEnum
enumerator, 251
crSpecialFieldTypePageNumber member,
CrSpecialFieldTypeEnum
enumerator, 251
crSpecialFieldTypePrintDate member,
CrSpecialFieldTypeEnum
enumerator, 251
crSpecialFieldTypePrintTime member,
CrSpecialFieldTypeEnum
enumerator, 251
crSpecialFieldTypeRecordGroupNamePath
member, CrSpecialFieldTypeEnum
enumerator, 251
crSpecialFieldTypeRecordGroupPath
member, CrSpecialFieldTypeEnum
enumerator, 251
crSpecialFieldTypeRecordKey member,
CrSpecialFieldTypeEnum
enumerator, 251
crSpecialFieldTypeRecordNumber member,
CrSpecialFieldTypeEnum
enumerator, 251
crSpecialFieldTypeRecordSelection member,
CrSpecialFieldTypeEnum
enumerator, 251

crSpecialFieldTypeReportComments
member, CrSpecialFieldTypeEnum
enumerator, 251
crSpecialFieldTypeReportPath member,
CrSpecialFieldTypeEnum
enumerator, 251
crSpecialFieldTypeReportTitle member,
CrSpecialFieldTypeEnum
enumerator, 251
crSpecialFieldTypeTotalPageCount member,
CrSpecialFieldTypeEnum
enumerator, 251
crSummaryOperationAverage member,
CrSummaryOperationEnum
enumerator, 254
crSummaryOperationCorrelation member,
CrSummaryOperationEnum
enumerator, 254
crSummaryOperationCount member,
CrSummaryOperationEnum
enumerator, 254
crSummaryOperationCovariance member,
CrSummaryOperationEnum
enumerator, 254
crSummaryOperationDistinctCount
member,
CrSummaryOperationEnum
enumerator, 254
CrSummaryOperationEnum enumerator,
254
crSummaryOperationMaximum member,
CrSummaryOperationEnum
enumerator, 254
crSummaryOperationMedian member,
CrSummaryOperationEnum
enumerator, 254
crSummaryOperationMinimum member,
CrSummaryOperationEnum
enumerator, 254
crSummaryOperationMode member,
CrSummaryOperationEnum
enumerator, 254
crSummaryOperationNthLargest member,
CrSummaryOperationEnum
enumerator, 254
crSummaryOperationNthMostFrequent
member,
CrSummaryOperationEnum
enumerator, 254
crSummaryOperationNthSmallest member,
CrSummaryOperationEnum
enumerator, 254
crSummaryOperationPercentage member,
CrSummaryOperationEnum
enumerator, 254

crSummaryOperationPercentile member,
CrSummaryOperationEnum
enumerator, 255
crSummaryOperationPopStandardDeviation
member,
CrSummaryOperationEnum
enumerator, 255
crSummaryOperationPopVariance member,
CrSummaryOperationEnum
enumerator, 255
crSummaryOperationStandardDeviation
member,
CrSummaryOperationEnum
enumerator, 255
crSummaryOperationSum member,
CrSummaryOperationEnum
enumerator, 255
crSummaryOperationVariance member,
CrSummaryOperationEnum
enumerator, 255
crSummaryOperationWeightedAvg member,
CrSummaryOperationEnum
enumerator, 255
crTableJoinTypeAdvance member,
CrTableJoinTypeEnum enumerator,
235
CrTableJoinTypeEnum enumerator, 235
crTableJoinTypeEqualJoin member,
CrTableJoinTypeEnum enumerator,
235
crTableJoinTypeGreaterOrEqualJoin
member, CrTableJoinTypeEnum
enumerator, 235
crTableJoinTypeGreaterThanJoin member,
CrTableJoinTypeEnum enumerator,
235
crTableJoinTypeLeftOuterJoin member,
CrTableJoinTypeEnum enumerator,
235
crTableJoinTypeLessOrEqualJoin member,
CrTableJoinTypeEnum enumerator,
235
crTableJoinTypeLessThanJoin member,
CrTableJoinTypeEnum enumerator,
235
crTableJoinTypeNotEqualJoin member,
CrTableJoinTypeEnum enumerator,
235
crTableJoinTypeOuterJoin member,
CrTableJoinTypeEnum enumerator,
235
crTableJoinTypeRightOuterJoin member,
CrTableJoinTypeEnum enumerator,
235

CrTextFormatEnum.crTextFormatStandard-
Text enumerator, 260
crTextFormatHTMLText member,
CrTextFormatEnum enumerator, 260
crTextFormatRTFText member,
CrTextFormatEnum enumerator, 260
crTextFormatStandardText member,
CrTextFormatEnum enumerator, 260
CrTimeFieldFormatConditionFormulaType-
Enum enumerator, 243
crYearFormatLongYear member,
CrYearFormatEnum enumerator, 260
crYearFormatNoYear member,
CrYearFormatEnum enumerator, 260
crYearFormatShortYear member,
CrYearFormatEnum enumerator, 260
Crystal Analysis, 3
Crystal Decisions, 2
Crystal Enterprise, 52
Crystal Reports
embedded vs. nonembedded reports
Database connectivity, 220
exporting reports, 213–215
field structure, 216–217
filtering, 215–216
overview, 209–213
printer options, 220
sections, 217–219
summary information, 220
overview, 199
passing data sources, 222–223
unmanaged Report Application Server
(RAS), 221
viewer control
communicating with BO XI server,
204–205
overview, 199
passing entire SQL statement to Crystal
Reports, 208–209
passing parameters, 207–208
running report on disk, 205–207
setting up control, 199, 201–203
web services, 224–227
Crystal Reports Developer Edition, 5
Crystal Reports Explorer utility, 69–70
Crystal Reports Print Engine (CRPE), 29
Crystal Reports Server, 4
Crystal syntax, 420
CrystalDecisions.CrystalReports.Engine
namespace, 212
CrystalReport class, 385
CrystalReport object, 383
CSV file, 408
CUID, 373–374

CurrencyPosition property, 258
CurrencySymbolFormat property, 258
Current Metrics tab, 64
CurrentValues property, 386
Custom Style dialog, 255

▉D

data access techniques, 177–179
data fields, 246–247
Data Source, 69, 419
Database Conversion, 419
Database DLL property, 233
database dumps, 54
Database link, Process tab, reports, 81–82
Database Logon control, 187
Database property, 231
Database Records to Read When Previewing
        Or Refreshing a Report option, 30
DatabaseController object, 232
DatabaseFieldDefinition object, 217
databases utility, .rpt Inspector Enterprise
        Suite tool, 419
DataDefController.ParameterFieldController
        class, ReportClientDocument object,
        267
data-exchange format, 6
DataFields collection, 237
DataPath property, 195
DataSource property, FieldObject, 253
DataSourceID property, 194
Date format, 258–259
date parameters, 83
DateOrder property, 259
dates, 119–120
DateTime format, 258–259
DayOfWeek enumerator, 387
DayOfWeek enumerator, System, 142
debugging, 287
decision support systems, 3
DECODE function, 138
decryption key, 208
default parameters, 60, 83
DefaultWorkingDirectory element, 105
Define Report Data Source option,
        69–70
DeleteNow( ) method, 131
Delimiter property, 161
DepartmentID parameter, 208
Dependencies collections, 174
Dependency tab, Central Configuration
        Manager (CCM), 49–50
deprecated properties, InfoStore SQL
        language, 124–125
DESC clause, 375
Description field, 77
Design tab, 72
Destination control, 187

Destination Job Server, 32
destination options, 166–169
Destination page, Schedule tab
        E-mail option, 91–92
        FTP option, 91
        Inbox, 92–93
        overview, 89
        Unmanaged Disk option, 90
Destination tab, 64
DestinationPlugin object, 152, 167
Destinations property, 33
DestinationsOnFailure property, 152
DestinationsOnSuccess property, 152
Dice, 10
Direction property, 271
Directory Security properties, 360
disabling servers, 17
DiscardOthers property, 272
disk file, 82
DiskFileDestinationOptions class, 215
DISTINCT keyword, 117–118
Distribution tab, 399
DLL modules, 68
Dock in Parent Container option, 201
documentReference method, 382
DrillDownSubreport events, 203
DrillEventArgs object, 203
DrillSubreportEventArgs object, 203

▉E

Edit Alerts dialog, 152
e-mail notifications, 88, 149–152
E-mail option, Destination page, Schedule
        tab, 91–92
embedded vs. nonembedded reports
        database connectivity, 220
        exporting reports, 213–215
        field structure, 216–217
        filtering, 215–216
        overview, 209–213
        printer options, 220
        sections, 217–219
        summary information, 220
Employee Report, 400
Employee Report Administrators, 351
EmployeeID parameter, 318
EmptyText property, 186
enableCookies attribute, 194
EnableSuppressIfDuplicated property,
        256
EnableSystemDefault property, 256
Encapsulated Page Format (EPF) pages, 29
EndSectionName property, 263
Enter BO XI button, 181
Enterprise, 3
Enterprise option, 77
enterprise server licenses, 4

enterprise solutions using BO XI SDK
  BusinessObjects XI (BO XI) Windows
    Service Monitor, 313–318
  creating criteria screens
    overview, 294–295
    web interface, 308–313
    WinForms interface, 295–307
  limits of Crystal Reports, 334
  on-demand web service
    output options, 283–284
    overview, 281–282
    passing connection information, 289
    running report, 284–289
  overview, 281
  reporting against InfoStore
    building dynamic menus, 327–330
    GetReportTree web service, 319–324
    overview, 318–319
    reporting against XML output, 325–327
  scheduling assemblies, 289–294
  storing custom metadata
    custom properties, 331–334
    overview, 330
    using your RDBMS, 330–331
EnterpriseCredential object, 372
EnterpriseItems control, 182–184
EnterpriseItems.Fields collection, 183
EnterpriseLogon property, 205
EnterpriseService object, 231
EnterpriseSession object, 104, 106, 109, 205, 231
EPF (Encapsulated Page Format) pages, 29
Essential XlsIO tool, 427–431
Event creation page, 101
Event Log, 49, 404
Event Server, 26–29
EventHandler( ) method, System class, 299
EventServerAdmin class, 27
Everyone group, 341, 355
Excel APOS menu, 400
Excel creation tool, 426
Excel export option, 412
Excel functions, 425
Excel macro, 426
Excel options, 60
Excel replacement tools, 426
Excel solutions
  overview, 425–426
  SoftArtisans's OfficeWriter tool, 431–434
  Syncfusion's Essential XlsIO tool, 427–431
ExcelApplication object, 432
ExcelDataOnly format, 165–166
ExcelDataOnlyFormatOptions class, 213
ExcelFormat, 164–165
executive support systems, 3
EXEs, 1
ExportDestinationType property, 215

ExportFormatType enumerator, 213
ExportOptions object, 215
ExportReport( ) method, 202
ExportToDisk( ) method, 213
extension manager, 85, 416
ExtractIDFromViewPath( ) method, 195
extracting data
  overview, 376–377
  paging, 377–379

F

FieldFormat class, 256, 258
FieldObject class, 253
FieldObjectClass object, 247
fields
  data fields, 246–247
  formatting field data
    Boolean formatting, 260
    Date, Time, and DateTime format, 258–259
    fonts, 261–262
    formatting string, 260
    numeric format, 256–258
    overview, 255–256
  formula fields, 251–252
  overview, 245
  special fields, 250–251
  summary fields, 253–254
  text fields, 248–250
file event, 26
File Name entry, 76
File Repository servers (FRSs), 24–26, 44
FileServerAdmin class, 25
FileStore, 14–16, 24, 81
FileStream object, 383
FileSystemWatcher class, .NET, 99
Filters control, 187–188
Filters page, Process tab, reports, 84–85
FindByAlias( ) method, 246
FinishUploadWithObject( ) method, 383
Fit Section option, 165
fnc_NumericCodes function, 305, 307
Folder object, 130–131, 389
folders, 389–390
  Central Management Console (CMC), 74–75
  creating, 129–130
  deleting, 130–131
  extracting folder information, 126–128
Font class, 261
FontColor class, 261
fonts, 261–262
for loop, 345
Form_Load event, 184
Format control, 188–189
Format page, Schedule tab, reports, 93–94
Format property, 156
Format text option, 165

FormatInfoStoreDate( ) method, 147
Formats property, 188
formatting string, 260
formula fields, 251–252
FormulaField object, 252
formulas
  condition formulas, 242–245
  creating, 241
formulas and running totals utility, .rpt
    Inspector Enterprise Suite tool, 420
FRSs (File Repository servers), 24–26, 44
FTP option, Destination page, Schedule tab,
    91

▓G
geographic information system (GIS), 413
Get( ) method, BIPlatform class, 377
GetApplications( ) method, 104
GetBIPlatform( ) method, 371
GetCriteria( ) method, 302
GetCurrentPageNumber( ) method, 201
GetData( ) method, 222
GetDocumentInformation( ) method,
    382–383
GetFormatType( ) method, 134
GetIdentity( ) method, 126
GetKnownRights( ) method, BIPlatform
    class, 392
GetOptions object, 376
GetPrintOptions( ) method, 278
GetPropertyValue( ) method, 147
GetRightsForObject( ) method, 351
GetServerMetrics( ) method, 390
GetService( ) method, 231
GetSession( ) method, SessionMgr class, 197
GetSystemInfoProperties( ) method, 372
GetTopFolders( ) method, 390
GIS (geographic information system), 413
GlobalStyle object, 434
Group by Clause Analysis, 423
Group object, 237
groups, 236–237
Groups collection, 343
Groups option, 342
GroupSectionsOption property, 161

▓H
Handled property, 203
HasMember( ) method, 147
high-volume printing, 7–8
history of BO XI, 1–2
History page, 78–81
HotCell Technology, 434
hyperlink menu, 73
hyperlinks, 78

▓I
IADsGroup object, 362
IADsMembers object, 362
ID property, 128
Identity control, 180, 182
Identity property, 183
iGuard tool, 421–422
iMaxInstances parameter, 356
Import Wizard, 52–57
ImportDataTable method, 429
IN clause, 305
Inbox, Destination page, Schedule tab, 92–93
IncludeInstances keyword, 376
Index property, 302
IndexOf( ) method, String class, 209
InfoObject collection, 343, 389
InfoObject property, 184, 191
InfoObjects collection, 41, 113, 126–128, 130,
    138, 148, 182, 323
InfoObjects property, 377
InfoScheduler tool, 400, 402
InfoStore, 13–14, 50, 68, 103, 284, 327, 371
  creating folders, 129–130
  deleting folders, 130–131
  extracting folder information, 126–128
  overview, 125
InfoStore SQL language
  overview, 113
  properties, 121–125
  property storage, 118–119
  SQL basics
    aggregates, 116–117
    Boolean values, 114–115
    AS clause and aliasing, 116
    DISTINCT keyword, 117–118
    overview, 113–114
    Subqueries, 115–116
    Top n, 118
  working with dates, 119–120
InfoStoreDefaultTopNValue, 118
InfoView, 61–62, 402
Inherited options, 347
InheritedRights property, 353
ink cartridges, 7
ink-jet printers, 7
Input directory, 14
Input File Repository Server, 24
INSERT stored procedure, 130
Instance Manager tool, 64, 402, 419
Instance Monitor tool, 404
instances utility, .rpt Inspector Enterprise
    Suite tool, 419
intelligence tier, 17
invocation mechanism, 6
ISCRReportSource object, 197

iSight tool, 422–423

IsSameDate property, ReportFormatOptions object, 159

IsSameNumber property, ReportFormatOptions object, 159

ItemClicked event, 183

ItemEventArgs parameter, 184

ItemID property, 184

ItemsGrid control, 182–184

ItemSource property, ItemsGrid, 183

ItemType property, 184

ItemTypes collection property, 182

▉ J

J2EE Framework, 367

job servers, 32–34, 413

JobServerAdmin class, 32

JOIN command, 235

JoinType property, 235

▉ K

kcLevelEvaluation member, kcProductLevel enumeration, 366

kcLevelFull member, kcProductLevel enumeration, 366

kcLevelFullPlusSubscription member, kcProductLevel enumeration, 366

kcLevelNotForResale member, kcProductLevel enumeration, 366

kcLevelStandAloneSubscription member, kcProductLevel enumeration, 366

kcLevelSummarySI7 member, kcProductLevel enumeration, 366

kcLevelUBatchKeycode member, kcProductLevel enumeration, 366

kcLevelUpgrade member, kcProductLevel enumeration, 366

kcLevelUpgradePlusSubscription member, kcProductLevel enumeration, 366

kcLicenseConcurrent member, kcUserLicenseType enumerator, 366

kcLicenseCrystalCare member, kcUserLicenseType enumerator, 366

kcLicenseDesigner member, kcUserLicenseType enumerator, 366

kcLicenseNamed member, kcUserLicenseType enumerator, 366

kcLicenseNotApplicable member, kcUserLicenseType enumerator, 366

kcLicensePerProcessor member, kcUserLicenseType enumerator, 366

kcLicensePerServer member, kcUserLicenseType enumerator, 366

kcLicenseTypes member, kcUserLicenseType enumerator, 366

kcNameAnalyticsApps member, kcProductName enumerator, 364

kcNameBaanPack member, kcProductName enumerator, 364

kcNameBalanceScorecard member, kcProductName enumerator, 364

kcNameBorlandCSharpBuilder member, kcProductName enumerator, 364

kcNameBorlandJBuilder member, kcProductName enumerator, 364

kcNameBudgetingForecast member, kcProductName enumerator, 364

kcNameCADeveloper member, kcProductName enumerator, 364

kcNameCAProfessional member, kcProductName enumerator, 364

kcNameCAStandard member, kcProductName enumerator, 364

kcNameCEAdvanced member, kcProductName enumerator, 364

kcNameCEBusinessViews member, kcProductName enumerator, 364

kcNameCEPremium member, kcProductName enumerator, 364

kcNameCEProfessional member, kcProductName enumerator, 364

kcNameCERASModify member, kcProductName enumerator, 365

kcNameCEReportApplicationServer member, kcProductName enumerator, 365

kcNameCEReportModification member, kcProductName enumerator, 365

kcNameCERepositoryOnly member, kcProductName enumerator, 365

kcNameCEStandard member, kcProductName enumerator, 365

kcNameCRDeveloper member, kcProductName enumerator, 365

kcNameCREnterprise member, kcProductName enumerator, 365

kcNameCRForTheNetPlatform member, kcProductName enumerator, 365

kcNameCRProfessional member, kcProductName enumerator, 365

kcNameCRServer member, kcProductName enumerator, 365

kcNameCRStandard member, kcProductName enumerator, 365

kcNameCustomerProfiling member, kcProductName enumerator, 365

kcNameEDesigner member, kcProductName enumerator, 365

kcNameEnterpriseBroadcastLicense member, kcProductName enumerator, 365

kcNameEServerSoftware member, kcProductName enumerator, 365
kcNameETelecom member, kcProductName enumerator, 365
kcNameHolosAnalyticClient member, kcProductName enumerator, 365
kcNameHolosAnalyticServer member, kcProductName enumerator, 365
kcNameKnowledgeAccelerator member, kcProductName enumerator, 365
kcNameMicrosoftCRM member, kcProductName enumerator, 365
kcNameOEMRestricted member, kcProductName enumerator, 365
kcNameRCAPI member, kcProductName enumerator, 365
kcNameReportApplicationServer member, kcProductName enumerator, 365
kcNameReportServerDeveloper member, kcProductName enumerator, 365
kcNameReportServerProfessional member, kcProductName enumerator, 365
kcNameSAPPack member, kcProductName enumerator, 365
kcNameSiebelKit member, kcProductName enumerator, 365
kcNameUnixInfoServer member, kcProductName enumerator, 365
kcProductLevel enumeration, 365
key class, 348
Key Performance Indicator (KPI) tool, 3, 404–405
Kind property, 216
Knowledgebase, Crystal, 11
KPI (Key Performance Indicator) tool, 3, 404–405

L

Label object, 298
LDAP (Lightweight Directory Access Protocol), 340
legal issues, 8
Length property, String, 209
Liautaud, Bernard, 2
License Keys option, 362–366
licensing, Release 2 of BusinessObjects XI (BO XI), 4–5
Lightweight Directory Access Protocol (LDAP), 340
LIKE keyword, 295
LIKE statement, 114
LineObject class, 262, 264
Lines object, 262–263
Link Tables option, 71
list boxes, 295
ListActiveFiles property, 26

ListBox control, 295
ListBoxCollection objects, 310
ListBoxManager object, 297
ListItem object, 308
LoadChildMenus( ) method, 329
LoadMenus( ) method, 328
LoadNTGroups( ) function, 362
Log On As property, Central Management Server, 49
LoggedOffText property, 186
LoggedOn event, 181
loggingPath switch, 18
Login( ) method, 372
LogOff( ) method, 106
Logon( ) method, 104, 231
Logon methods, 197
Logon visual interface component, 180
LogonFailed event, 181
LogonTokenMgr.DefaultToken property, 107
Lotus, 10

M

Macro objects, 427
magnetic ink character recognition (MICR), 338
Main( ) method, 292, 314
MakeDateParameter( ) method, 83
Manage Groups and User Accounts, 66
MatchingNameRename property, 389
Maximum Idle Time setting, 25
Maximum Jobs Allowed setting, 32
Maximum Simultaneous Report Jobs setting, 30
Membership provider, 193–194
MembershipProvider abstract base class, 194
MenuItem object, 330
MessageName method, 104
MICR (magnetic ink character recognition), 338
Migration Wizards, 419
Minutes Before an Idle Connection is Closed setting, 30
Minutes Before an Idle Report Job is Closed setting, 30
ModifyPrintOptions( ) method, 278
ModifySortDirection( ) method, 269
ModifySummaryInfo( ) method, 277
modules.zip, 68
Monster, 10
MSSQLSERVER service, 49
multicore processors, 4
multipass bursting, 398
multithreaded tool, 424
MY_COMMENTS property, 333
MY_CRITERIA_PAGE property, 331

N

navigate method, 383
NavigateEventArgs object, 203
.NET assembly, 82
.NET Providers
  Membership provider, 193–194
  overview, 192–193
  using, 194–197
.NET Server Controls, 193
.NET XML class, 325
Netscape, 10
New Calendar button, 97
New Event button, 99
New Folder button, 74
New Group button, 341
New Object button, 75, 97, 290
New Server Group button, 39
New User button, 339
NewInfoObjectCollection( ) method, 41, 130, 138, 174
non-enterprise security management, 359–362
Northwind database, 222, 231, 236
Notification option, 43
notifications
  audit notifications, 152
  e-mail notifications, 149–152
  overview, 149
  Schedule tab, reports
    audit notifications, 88
    e-mail notifications, 88
    overview, 87
Notifications tab, 152
Novell, 10
NT authentication, 359
NT group users, validating, 360–362
NT LM Security Support Provider service, 49
numeric format, 256–258
NumericFormat class, 257

O

Object Manager tool, 406–408
object package, 78, 96
Object Repository, 59
Object Repository Helper, 68
ObjectPrincipals collection, 348, 350, 356, 361
OfficeWriter Application Object, 431–432
OfficeWriter tool, 431–434
offline archives, 396
oInfoObject.SchedulingInfo.Status property, 288
OLAP (On Line Analytical Processing) tool, 3
Oldest On-Demand Data Given To a Client setting, 30, 37, 39
oMainMenu_Click( ) method, 330

On Line Analytical Processing (OLAP) tool, 3
on-demand web service
  output options, 283–284
  overview, 281–282
  passing connection information, 289
  running report, 284–289
OneCurrencySymbolPerPage property, 257
online archive, 396
OnStart( ) method, 314
OnStop( ) method, 314
Open( ) method, 231
Open method, 431
OpenDocument( ) method, 231, 266
oPluginInfo.Category property, 130
oPluginInfo.IsFunctional property, 130
ORDER BY statement, 269, 377
OrderID column, 256
Orders object, 212
Orientation property, 428
Outcome property, 288
Outlook, 395
Output directory, 14
Output File Repository Server, 24
OutputFormat property, BooleanFormat, 260
OutputFormat property, ViewSupport class, 382
OutputFormatType enumerator, 381

P

page layout parameters, 87
Page Server, 29–31, 411, 413
Page_Load event, 180, 194
PageBreakAfterEachReportPage property, 163
PageInfo objects, 378
PageLayout property, 170
PageMargins settings, 220
PageServerAdmin class, 31
PageServerConnection property, 36
PageSetup interface, 432
PageSetup object, 427–428
PageURI property, 378
paging, 377–379
PaperSize property, 428
ParagraphElements collection object, 248
ParagraphElements property, Paragraph object, 248
ParagraphTextElement object, 248
ParameterDiscreteValue class, 206
ParameterFieldInfo property, 206
ParameterFields object, 206
Parameters control, 189
Parameters link, Process tab, reports, 83–84
parameters utility, .rpt Inspector Enterprise Suite tool, 420
ParseIt( ) method, 303, 313

PasswordExpired event, 181
path, 374–375
Path control, 190
PDAs (Personal Data Assistants), 9
PDF output option, 412
PDFFormat, 163–164
personal categories, 95
Personal Data Assistants (PDAs), 9
Pitney Bowes machine, 7
PivotTable, 427
placeholder variables, 90
PlainTextFormat, 163
plug-in objects, 130
PluginManager class, 130, 138, 333
PluginProcessingInterface( ) method,
    CrystalReport class, 385
Policy Wizard, iGuard, 421
preprinted forms, 7
Print control, 189–190
Print Setup page, Process tab, reports
    custom settings, 86–87
    overview, 85
    specified printer settings, 85–86
Printer Change Wizard, 419
printer options, 170
PrintFormats property, 189
PrintOptions object, 277–278
PrintOutputController object, 266
PrintReport( ) method, 203
Process tab, reports
    Database link, 81–82
    Filters page, 84–85
    overview, 81
    Parameters link, 83–84
    Print Setup page
        custom settings, 86–87
        overview, 85
        specified printer settings, 85–86
processing tier, 17
ProcessingInfo plug-in, 136
Program class, 144
Program Job Server, 32, 89
Program option, 76
programming calendars, 175–176
programming categories, 171–173
programming events, 173–174
PromptValue object, 386
properties, InfoStore SQL language, 121–125
properties, of PDF files, 59
Properties collection, 332
Properties option, 18
Properties tab
    CCM, 48–49
    reports, 76–78
property editors, 419
Property object, 137, 332
PropertyBag objects, 233

Protocol tab, Central Configuration Manager
    (CCM), 53
PSReportFactory service, 197
Publish as Web Service option, 224
Publish server, Web Service SDK, 370
Publishing Wizard, 57–61
push vs. pull approach, 9

■Q
QE_SQLDB element, 233
queries
    CUID, 373–374
    overview, 373
    path, 374–375
    query, 374
    search, 375–376
Queries Detail Report, 423
Query( ) method, 112, 377
Query Analyzer, 68
Query Builder tool, 68, 112, 359
QueryService server, Web Service SDK, 370

■R
radio button, 82, 87
Range object, 434
RAS. See Report Application Server (RAS)
RASReportFactory object, 231
RDBMS (Relational Database Management
    System), 331
RDL (Report Definition Language) format, 10
RealTime Monitor, 408
RealTime Monitor tool, 408–411
RecordSelectionFormula property, 215
Refresh Options link, Properties tab, reports,
    77–78
Refresh Options tab, 68
Refreshing reports, 25
Relational Database Management System
    (RDBMS), 331
relative links, 78
Release 2 of BusinessObjects XI (BO XI)
    licensing, 4–5
    overview, 3
    service-oriented architecture (SOA), 5–6
Remote Procedure Call (RPC) service, 49
Remove( ) method, 176
Render( ) method, ReportExecutionService
    web service, 12
Report Application Server (RAS), 11, 34,
    37–39, 79, 221, 229
Report Application Server (RAS),
        programming
    building body of report
        condition formulas, 242–245
        creating formulas, 241
        fields, 245–254
        formatting field data, 255–262

groups, 236–237
overview, 236
sections, 237–240
shapes, 262–265
charts, 272–274
connecting to data source
linking tables, 234–235
overview, 231
using stored procedures, 235–236
using tables, 231–234
exporting reports, 265–267
filtering reports, 268–269
overview, 229–231
printing reports, 277–278
report options, 274, 276
saving reports, 279–280
setting parameters, 267–268
sorting, 269–272
summary information, 276–277
report bursting, 84
Report class, 170
Report Datasources, 67
Report Definition Language (RDL) format, 10
report distribution, 6
report format options
ExcelDataOnly, 165–166
ExcelFormat, 164–165
overview, 156–157, 159
PDFFormat, 163–164
PlainTextFormat, 163
RichTextEditableFormat, 163
RichTextFormat, 162
TextFormatCharacterSeparated, 160–161
TextFormatPaginated, 159–160
TextFormatTabSeparated, 159
Report Job Database Connection option, 31, 38
Report Job Database Connection Page Server setting, 37
Report Job Server, 32
report layout screen, 72
Report object, 156, 205
report output, 281
Report Package Booster tool, 412
Report Properties page, 14
report writing, 2
Report2Browser( ) method, 191
ReportAppFactory object, 231
ReportAppServerAdmin class, 38
ReportClientDocument class, 221, 230–231, 241
ReportDefinition class, 216, 237
ReportEngine object, 381–382
ReportEngine server, Web Service SDK, 370
reportengine service, 369
ReportExecutionService web service, 12
Report.Files collection, 139

ReportFormatOptions class, 156
ReportFormatOptions object, 158
reporting considerations, BO XI
availability and distribution, 8–9
high-volume printing, 7–8
legal issues, 8
overview, 6–7
preprinted forms, 7
Report.Instance property, 139
ReportObjectKind enumerator, 216
ReportObjects collection, 219
ReportObjects property, 240
ReportOptions class, 274
ReportParameters array, 386
ReportParameters collection, 205, 285
ReportParameterSingleValue object, 285
ReportPrinterOptions method, 170
ReportPrintType enumerator, 190
ReportProcessingInfo object, 386
ReportRefreshOptions( ) method, Report object, 131
reports
adding, 383–385
Categories tab, 94–95
History page, 78–81
overview, 75–76, 380
Process tab
Database link, 81–82
Filters page, 84–85
overview, 81
Parameters link, 83–84
Print Setup page, 85–87
Properties tab, 76–78
Rights tab, 96
Schedule tab
Alert Notification page, 89
Destination page, 89–93
Format page, 93–94
notifications, 87–88
overview, 87
Schedule For page, 94
scheduling, 386–388
adding executable code, 144–145
adding new reports, 138–139
building own report history, 133–138
handling report parameters generically, 145–148
overview, 131
report history in CMC, 132
retrieving and saving schedules, 140–144
RunNow( ) method, 139
setting parameters, 385–386
viewing, 380–383
ReportSectionController class, 240
ReportSectionsOption property, 161
ReportServiceBase, 224

ReportSource property, 205, 231
ResponseHolder object, 377
RetrieveBinaryView object, 382
retrieveData method, 383
retrieveMustFillInfo method, 382
RetrieveView property, 382
RichTextEditableFormat, 163
RichTextFormat, 162
rights
    assigning, 349–350
    checking, 351–354
    overview, 349
Rights tab, 96, 347
roles, 348
RPC (Remote Procedure Call) service, 49
RPT file, 15, 222
.rpt Inspector Enterprise Suite tool
    Alerts editor utility, 421
    databases utility, 419
    formulas and running totals utility, 420
    instances utility, 419
    overview, 418–419
    parameters utility, 420
    sections utility, 420–421
    text management and printing utility, 419
    version control utility, 419–420
RPT instances, 397
Run Now button, 79
RunNow( ) method, 139
RunReport( ) method, 286
RunReports( ) method, 292
RunTime Manager tool, 413

■S

Save( ) method, 279
Save Preview Picture check box, 76
SaveAs( ) method, 280
SaveSchedule( ) method, 143
scalability, server architecture, BO XI, 43–44
Schedule control, 184–186
Schedule For page, Schedule tab, reports, 94
Schedule Manager, 62–64
Schedule tab, reports
    Alert Notification page, 89
    Destination page
        E-mail option, 91–92
        FTP option, 91
        Inbox, 92–93
        overview, 89
        Unmanaged Disk option, 90
    Format page, 93–94
    notifications
        audit notifications, 88
        e-mail notifications, 88
        overview, 87
    overview, 87
    Schedule For page, 94

ScheduleType property, 379
ScheduleTypeEnum enumerator, 387
ScheduleTypeSpecified property, 379
scheduling
    alerts, 152, 154–156
    assemblies, 289–294
    notifications
        audit notifications, 152
        e-mail notifications, 149–152
        overview, 149
    overview, 149
    reports, 386–388
        adding executable code, 144–145
        adding new reports, 138–139
        building own report history, 133–138
        handling report parameters generically,
            145–148
        overview, 131
        report history in CMC, 132
        retrieving and saving schedules,
            140–144
        RunNow( ) method, 139
SchedulingInfo object, 142, 174, 286–287, 386
SDK programming. *See also* enterprise
        solutions using BO XI SDK
    BO XI web controls
        connecting to BO XI, 180–182
        CrystalReportViewer control, 190–191
        Database Logon control, 187
        Destination control, 187
        EnterpriseItems and ItemsGrid
            controls, 182–184
        Filters control, 187–188
        Format control, 188–189
        overview, 179–180, 187
        Parameters control, 189
        Path control, 190
        Print control, 189–190
        using Schedule control, 184–186
    connecting to BO XI
        examining connection objects, 109–112
        overview, 103–104
        with tokens, 106–108
        with trusted connections, 108–109
        with user IDs, 104–106
    data access techniques, 177–179
    destination options, 166–169
    InfoStore SQL language
        overview, 113
        properties, 121–125
        property storage, 118–119
        SQL basics, 113–118
        working with dates, 119–120
    .NET Providers
        Membership provider, 193–194
        overview, 192–193
        using, 194–197

overview, 103, 149
printer options, 170
programming calendars, 175–176
programming categories, 171–173
programming events, 173–174
report format options
    ExcelDataOnly format, 165–166
    ExcelFormat, 164–165
    overview, 156–159
    PDFFormat, 163–164
    PlainTextFormat, 163
    RichTextEditableFormat, 163
    RichTextFormat, 162
    TextFormatCharacterSeparated format,
        160–161
    TextFormatPaginated format, 159–160
    TextFormatTabSeparated format, 159
Report Refresh Options, 131
scheduling
    alerts, 152–156
    notifications, 149–152
    overview, 149
scheduling reports
    adding executable code, 144–145
    adding new reports, 138–139
    building own report history, 133–138
    handling report parameters generically,
        145–148
    overview, 131
    report history in CMC, 132
    retrieving and saving schedules,
        140–144
    RunNow( ) method, 139
working with InfoStore
    creating folders, 129–130
    deleting folders, 130–131
    extracting folder information, 126–128
    overview, 125
Seagate Info, 395
Seagate Technology, 2
search, 375–376
SearchAllWords keyword, 376
SearchCaseSensitive keyword, 376
SearchExact keyword, 376
SearchForText( ) method, 201
SearchKeywords keyword, 376
SearchName keyword, 376
SearchWithoutWords keyword, 376
Section editor, Crystal Reports, 420
SectionFormat class, 239
SectionFormat object, 217
sections, 237–240
Sections collection, 219
sections utility, .rpt Inspector Enterprise
    Suite tool, 420–421
SectionSettings( ) method, 218
Secure Sockets Layer (SSL), 53

security
    access levels and security rights
        overview, 347–348
        rights, 349–354
        roles, 348
    License Keys option, 362–366
    limits, 355–358
    managing, 392–393
    managing through CMC
        adding users to groups, 342–343
        creating groups, 341–342
        creating users, 339–340
        extracting users in group, 343–345
        overview, 338–339
        subgroups, 345–346
    non-enterprise security management
        overview, 359
        validating NT group users, 360–362
    overview, 337–338
SecurityLimits collection, 356
SecurityRight object, 353
SecurityRights object, 350
SELECT statement, 373
SelectCommand property, 195–196
SelectedIndexChanged( ) event handler, 301
SelectedItems collection, 304
SelectedNodeChanged event, 195
SelectedPrintFormat property, 189
SelectedType property, 189
SelectionFormula property, 202
SelectionMode property, 311
SELECTUSINGPROPERTY command, 118,
    344
self-descriptive component (WSDL), 6
Send To button, 80
Separator property, 161
server architecture, BO XI
    auditing database, 42–43
    backups and disaster recovery, 44–45
    FileStore, 14–16
    InfoStore, 13–14
    overview, 13
    scalability, 43–44
    server groups
        adding servers to, 41–42
        creating, 41
        extracting servers in, 42
        overview, 39–40
    servers
        Cache Server, 34–36
        Central Management Server (CMS),
            22–24
        Event Server, 26–29
        File Repository servers (FRSs), 24–26
        job servers, 32–34
        overview, 16–19
        Page Server, 29–31

programmatic access, 19–22
Report Application Server (RAS), 37–39
Server class, 391
Server license, 9, SQL
Server object, 21
Server Status option, 410
ServerAdmin property, 23
ServerGeneralAdmin property, 21
ServerGeneralMetrics object, 21
ServerKind property, 22
servers, managing, 390–391
service packs, 57
ServiceController class, 317
service-oriented architecture (SOA), 5–6
Session server, Web Service SDK, 370
Session.Abandon( ) method, 106
SessionInfo object, 372
SessionMgr class, 104, 106, 197, 231
Set as Data Sources Folder option, 69
SetDataSource( ) method, 222
SetProperty( ) method, 240
SetStyle method, 434
sFieldValueTypeEnum parameter, 252
shapes
    Borders object, 264–265
    Boxes object, 263–264
    Lines object, 262–263
    overview, 262
Shortcut Manager, 66–67
Show report thumbnail check box, 76
ShowListBox( ) method, 297, 309
ShowNthPage( ) method, 201
SI_AGGREGATE_COUNT property, 117
SI_ANCESTOR property, 123, 285
SI_CHILDREN property, 124
SI_CREATION_TIME property, 119
SI_CUID property, 55
SI_DATA property, 148
SI_DAYLIGHT property, 125
SI_DESCRIPTION property, 122
SI_ERROR_MESSAGE property, 125
SI_GROUP_MEMBERS property, 42, 345
SI_GUID property, 121
SI_ID property, 121, 195, 266
SI_ID value, 14, 55, 76, 346
SI_INSTANCE property, 122, 132–133
SI_INTERVAL_TYPE property, 125
SI_ISMACHINE property, 125
SI_KIND property, 122, 132, 134, 184
SI_KIND value, 19
SI_NAME property, 122, 133, 195
SI_NUM_PROMPTS property, 136, 147
SI_NUM_TEMPLATE_DAYS property, 141
SI_OBJECT_IS_CONTAINER property, 125
SI_OBTYPE property, 125
SI_PARENTID property, 123, 126, 139
SI_PLUGIN_CAT property, 125

SI_PLUGIN_NAME property, 125
SI_PLUGIN_OBJECTTYPENAME property, 125
SI_PLUGIN_PROGID property, 125
SI_PLUGIN_SETUPCMD property, 125
SI_PLUGIN_SETUPFILE property, 125
SI_PLUGIN_SETUPPROGRAM property, 125
SI_PLUGIN_UNINSTALLCOMMAND property, 125
SI_PLUGIN_UNINSTALLFILE property, 125
SI_PROCESSINFO.SI_PROMPTS property, 135
SI_PROGID property, 122
SI_PROMPT_TYPE property, 145–146
SI_PROMPTS property, 136
SI_RECURRING property, 124, 132
SI_RUN_NOW property, 125
SI_SCHEDULEINFO property, 124
SI_SCHEDULEINFO.SI_OUTCOME property, 125
SI_SCHEDULEINFO.STATUSINFO property, 125
SI_TARGETID property, 125
SI_TIMEZONE property, 125
SI_TOTAL property, 345
SI_UISTATUS property, 125
SI_VERSIONS property, 125
Simple Network Management Protocol (SNMP), 408
Simple Object Access Protocol (SOAP), 369
single-pass bursting, 398
Smart Tag, 200
SmartObjects Admin Desktop, 419
SmtpOptions object, 150, 155, 167
SNMP (Simple Network Management Protocol), 408
SOA (service-oriented architecture), 5–6
SOAP (Simple Object Access Protocol), 369
SOCKS proxy servers, 50
SoftArtisans, 434–435
SoftArtisans's OfficeWriter tool, 431–434
Software Forces, LLC
    overview, 418
    .rpt Inspector Enterprise Suite tool
        Alerts editor utility, 421
        databases utility, 419
        formulas and running totals utility, 420
        instances utility, 419
        overview, 418–419
        parameters utility, 420
        sections utility, 420–421
        text management and printing utility, 419
        version control utility, 419–420
Solutions Kit for ESRI GIS (geographic information system) tool, 413–414, 416

sp_makewebtask stored procedure, 209, SQL
    Server
special fields, 250–251
SpecialType property, 251
Specify button, 51
SpreadsheetML files, 431
SQL basics
    aggregates, 116–117
    Boolean values, 114–115
    AS clause and aliasing, 116
    DISTINCT keyword, 117–118
    overview, 113–114
    Subqueries, 115–116
    Top n, 118
SQL Plus, Oracle, 68
SQL Server, 398
SQL Server Reporting Services (SSRS), 9, 435
    vs. BusinessObjects XI (BO XI)
        feature differences, 11–12
        market considerations, 9–10
        overview, 9
SQL statements, 68
SSL (Secure Sockets Layer), 53
SSRS. See SQL Server Reporting Services
    (SSRS)
Startup Type property, Central Management
    Server, 49
Status hyperlink, 79
Status page, 64
Status property, 287–288
stopping servers, 17
stored procedures, 235–236
StringBuilder object, 333
Submit( ) method, 185
Submit button, 76
SubmitClicked event, 185
Subqueries, 115–116
subscriptions, 11
SummarizedField property, 253
summary fields, 253–254
SummaryField object, 253
SummaryFields property, 271
SummaryInfo object, 220, 277
Syncfusion, 431
Syncfusion's Essential XlsIO tool, 427–431
Syntax property, 241
System namespace, 283
SystemInfoProperty class, 109
SystemProperty array, 372
szFolderName variable, 129
szReportID variable, 128

T

Table Linking dialog, 71
TableClass object, 234
tables, and Report Application Server (RAS),
    231–235

tabular format option, 64
Task Manager, 425
Teleran Technologies
    iGuard tool, 421–422
    iSight tool, 422–423
    overview, 421
Temp Files option, 29
Template field, 220, 277
Template Object, 431
Test mode, iGuard, 422
text fields, 248–250
text management and printing utility, .rpt
    Inspector Enterprise Suite tool, 419
Text property, 330
TextFormat property, 260
TextFormatCharacterSeparated format,
    160–161
TextFormatPaginated format, 159–160
TextFormatTabSeparated format, 159
third-party solutions
    APOS Systems Inc
        AddressBook Gateway tool, 395
        Archive Manager tool, 396–398
        Bursting Manager tool, 398–400
        InfoScheduler tool, 400–402
        Instance Manager tool, 402
        Instance Monitor tool, 404
        Key Performance Indicator (KPI) tool,
            404–405
        Object Manager tool, 406–408
        overview, 395
        RealTime Monitor tool, 408–411
        Report Package Booster tool, 412
        RunTime Manager tool, 413
        Solutions Kit for ESRI GIS (geographic
            information system) tool, 413–416
        View Time Security tool, 416–417
    CRD, 424–425
    Excel solutions
        overview, 425–426
        SoftArtisans's OfficeWriter tool, 431–434
        Syncfusion's Essential XlsIO tool,
            427–431
    overview, 395
    Software Forces, LLC, 418–421
    Teleran Technologies
        iGuard tool, 421–422
        iSight tool, 422–423
        overview, 421
    Word solutions, 434–435
Thread.Sleep event, 314
Time format, 258–259
Time Security, 416
Title property, 130
tokenExpiry attribute, 194
tokens, connecting to BO XI with, 106–108
Tomcat, 368

toolbox tab, 179
Top n, 118
TOP n statement, 118
Top property, 265
TopNSort class, 271
Total Metrics tab, 65
trace switch, 19, 49
transaction manager class, 331
Trigger( ) method, 174
trusted connections, connecting to BO XI
    with, 108–109
TrustedPrincipal.conf file, 108
Type property, Field object, 247

▮U

UAT (user-acceptance-testing) database
    password, 82
Unified Web Services SDK
    configuring, 367–370
    overview, 367
    programming web services
        creating connection, 371–372
        extracting data, 376–379
        folders, 389–390
        managing security, 392–393
        managing servers, 390–391
        overview, 370
        queries, 373–376
        reports, 380–388
        services, 370
Unmanaged Disk option, Destination page,
    Schedule tab, 90
unmanaged Report Application Server (RAS),
    229
Update( ) method, 386
UseOptionsInReportFile property,
    ReportFormatOptions object, 158
User Activity, BO XI, 423
user IDs, connecting to BO XI with, 104–106
user licenses, 4
User objects, 343
user-acceptance-testing (UAT) database
    password, 82
userIsOnlineTimeWindow tag, 194
Users and Tables Detail Report, 423
Users link, 339
UseWorksheetFunc property, 166
UTCConverter class, 119

▮V

ValidateUser( ) method, 193
validating NT group users, 360–362
version control utility, .rpt Inspector
    Enterprise Suite tool, 419–420
View property, 383
View Server Summary, 64–65
View Time Security tool, 416–417

Viewer Hyperlink, 91
Viewer Refresh Always Yields Current Data
    check box, 31
ViewMode enumerator, 382
ViewSupport class, 382
ViewType enumerator, 382
VisibleFormats property, 188
VisiblePrintFormats property, 189
Visual Basic syntax, 420
Visual SourceSafe, Microsoft, 419
VTS Manager, 416

▮W

web controls, BO XI
    connecting to BO XI, 180–182
    CrystalReportViewer control, 190–191
    Database Logon control, 187
    Destination control, 187
    EnterpriseItems and ItemsGrid controls,
        182–184
    Filters control, 187–188
    Format control, 188–189
    overview, 179–180
    Parameters control, 189
    Path control, 190
    Print control, 189–190
    using Schedule control, 184–186
web interface
    dynamic criteria controls, 308–312
    extracting user selections, 312–313
    overview, 308
web services, Crystal Reports, 224–227
web services, programming
    creating connection, 371–372
    extracting data
        overview, 376–377
        paging, 377–379
    folders, 389–390
    managing security, 392–393
    managing servers, 390–391
    overview, 370
    queries
        CUID, 373–374
        overview, 373
        path, 374–375
        query, 374
        search, 375–376
    reports
        adding, 383–385
        overview, 380
        scheduling, 386–388
        setting parameters, 385–386
        viewing, 380–383
    services, 370
web.config file, 193
WeekNumber property, 387
WHERE clause, 14, 421

window.open method, 284
Windows service, 48
WinForms interface
 dynamic criteria controls, 295–302
 extracting user selections, 302–307
 overview, 295
wireless LAN cards, 9
Word object model, 434
Word solutions, 434–435
WordPerfect, 10
WorkingDirectory element, 105
WSDL (self-descriptive component), 6

X

XI Technical Papers, BusinessObjects, 58
XML file, 408
XmlWriter object, 11

Z

ZIP format, 424
Zoom( ) method, 202
ZoomEventArgs object, 203

Printed in the United States
136347LV00002B/1/P